VOLUME ONE

ECONOMY AND SOCIETY

Translators: EPHRAIM FISCHOFF

HANS GERTH

A. M. HENDERSON

FERDINAND KOLEGAR

C. WRIGHT MILLS

TALCOTT PARSONS

MAX RHEINSTEIN

GUENTHER ROTH

EDWARD SHILS

CLAUS WITTICH

Max Weber

ECONOMY
AND
SOCIETY

AN OUTLINE OF INTERPRETIVE SOCIOLOGY

Edited by Guenther Roth
and Claus Wittich

B
P

BEDMINSTER PRESS, *New York, 1968*

Bedminster Press International AB, Stockholm, Sweden

Library of Congress Catalog Card Number: 68–27095

First Printing

Economy and Society is a translation of Max Weber, *Wirtschaft und Gesellschaft. Grundriss der verstehenden Soziologie,* based on the 4th German edition, Johannes Winckelmann (ed.), Tübingen: J. C. B. Mohr (Paul Siebeck), 1956, pp. 1–550, 559–822, as revised in the 1964 paperback edition (Köln-Berlin: Kiepenheuer & Witsch), with appendices from Max Weber, *Gesammelte Aufsätze zur Wissenschaftslehre,* 2nd rev. edition, Johannes Winckelmann (ed.), Tübingen: J. C. B. Mohr (Paul Siebeck), 1951, pp. 441–467 (selected passages), and Max Weber, *Gesammelte politische Schriften,* 2nd expanded edition, Johannes Winckelmann (ed.), Tübingen: J. C. B. Mohr (Paul Siebeck), 1958, pp. 294–394.

The exclusive license to make this English edition has been granted to Bedminster Press by the German holder of rights, J. C. B. Mohr (Paul Siebeck), Tübingen.

The English text includes (with revisions and with addition of notes) material previously published and copyrighted by these publishers:

Beacon Press:
Ephraim Fischoff, trans., *The Sociology of Religion* (Boston: Beacon Press, 1963), pp. 1–274. Copyright © 1963 by Beacon Press. Reprinted by arrangement with Beacon Press.

Oxford University Press:
Hans Gerth and C. Wright Mills, trans. and eds., *From Max Weber: Essays in Sociology* (New York: Oxford University Press, 1946), pp. 159–244, 253–262. Copyright 1946 by Oxford University Press, Inc. British Commonwealth rights by Routledge and Kegan Paul Ltd. Reprinted by permission.

The Free Press of Glencoe:
Ferdinand Kolegar, trans., "The Household Community" and "Ethnic Groups," in Talcott Parsons *et al.,* eds., *Theories of Society* (New York: The Free Press of Glencoe, 1961), vol. 1, pp. 296–298, 302–309. Copyright © 1961 by The Free Press of Glencoe. Reprinted by permission.

Talcott Parsons, ed. (A. M. Henderson and T. Parsons, trans.), *The Theory of Social and Economic Organization* (New York: The Free Press of Glencoe, 1964; originally published by Oxford University Press, 1947), pp. 87–423. Copyright 1947 by The Free Press of Glencoe. Reprinted by permission.

Harvard University Press:
Max Rheinstein, ed. (Edward Shils and Max Rheinstein, trans.), *Max Weber on Law in Economy and Society* (20th Century Legal Philosophy Series, Vol. VI; Cambridge, Mass.: Harvard University Press, 1954), pp. 11–348. Copyright, 1954 by the President and Fellows of Harvard College. Reprinted by permission.

Correspondence about these sections of the English translation should be directed to the above publishers. See editors' preface for details about their location in this edition.

SUMMARY CONTENTS

VOLUME 3

APPENDICES

INDEX*

* The index for the entire work is bound with each volume.

ANALYTICAL CONTENTS

VOLUME I

Part One: CONCEPTUAL EXPOSITION

Chapter III

THE TYPES OF LEGITIMATE DOMINATION   212

Chapter IV

STATUS GROUPS AND CLASSES   302

VOLUME 2

Chapter VI

* *The index for the entire work is bound with each volume.*

VOLUME 3

The index for the entire work is bound with each volume.

Chapter XI

BUREAUCRACY 956

Appendices

Preface

This is the first complete English edition of *Economy and Society*. All hitherto unavailable chapters and sections have been translated and the annotation has been considerably expanded. The Appendix contains a brief terminological supplement and one of Weber's major political essays. All previously translated parts used here have been thoroughly revised and many passages have been rewritten. The original translators of these chapters are absolved from all responsibility for the present version of their work. We would like to thank Ephraim Fischoff for going over our revision of his translation of the "Sociology of Religion" (Part Two, ch. VI) and for making further suggestions and offering other help. However, he too should not be held responsible for the final version.

A number of extant translations were completely replaced: in Part One, ch. IV, "Status Groups and Classes"; in Part Two, ch. III:3, "The Regulation of Sexual Relations in the Household," ch. IV:3, "The Oikos," ch. XIV:*i–ii*, "Charisma and Its Transformations," and ch. XVI, "The City." This last book-length chapter was newly translated by Wittich; all other new translations were first done by Roth. Our strategy of translation is explained in the Introduction.

The following earlier translations of sections of *Wirtschaft und Gesellschaft* have been used and revised with the permission of the publishers, which is gratefully acknowledged.

Ephraim Fischoff, trans., *The Sociology of Religion* (Boston: Beacon Press, 1963), pp. 1–274; now Part Two, ch. VI;

Hans Gerth and C. Wright Mills, trans. and eds., *From Max Weber: Essays in Sociology* (New York: Oxford University Press, 1946), pp. 159–244, 253–262; now Part Two, chs. IX:3–6, XI, and XIV:*iii;*

Ferdinand Kolegar, trans., "The Household Community" and "Ethnic

Groups," in Talcott Parsons *et al.*, eds., *Theories of Society* (New York: The Free Press of Glencoe, 1961), vol. I, pp. 296–298, 302–309; now Part Two, ch. III:1, ch. IV:2, and ch. V:2;

Talcott Parsons, ed. (A. M. Henderson and T. Parsons, trans.), *The Theory of Social and Economic Organization* (New York: The Free Press of Glencoe, 1964; originally published by Oxford University Press, 1947), pp. 87–423; now Part One, chs. I–III;

Max Rheinstein, ed. (Edward Shils and Max Rheinstein, trans.), *Max Weber on Law in Economy and Society* (Cambridge, Mass.: Harvard University Press, 1954), pp. 11–348; now Part Two, ch. I, chs. VII–VIII, ch. IX:1–2, and ch. X.

Without the dedication and hard labor of the previous translators the present edition might never have been undertaken. Hans Gerth, who spent a singular amount of time on the translation of Weber's works, deserves special recognition. The broadest contribution to the reception of Weber's thought has clearly been made by Talcott Parsons' translations and writings.

Our special gratitude goes to Prof. Johannes Winckelmann, the German editor of Weber's works and head of the Max Weber Institute at the University of Munich, who gave us access to his text revisions for the forthcoming 5th edition of *Wirtschaft und Gesellschaft* and always freely shared his thoughts on textual and other problems.

Finally, we want to thank Hans L. Zetterberg, who combines scholarship and entrepreneurship; he held out the challenge, patiently waited for the manuscript, and then saw it through to its publication. We are also grateful to Mr. Robert Palmer for preparing the index and to Mr. Sidney Solomon of the Free Press for supervising the technical preparation of the work and for designing the volumes.

BERLIN AND NEW YORK   *Guenther Roth*

March 1968   *Claus Wittich*

INTRODUCTION
by Guenther Roth

We know of no scientifically ascertainable ideals. To be sure, that makes our efforts more arduous than those of the past, since we are expected to create our ideals from within our breast in the very age of subjectivist culture; but we must not and cannot promise a fool's paradise and an easy road to it, neither in thought nor in action. It is the stigma of our human dignity that the peace of our souls cannot be as great as the peace of one who dreams of such a paradise.

Weber in 1909

1. A Claim

This work is the sum of Max Weber's scholarly vision of society. It has become a constitutive part of the sociological imagination as it is understood today. *Economy and Society* was the first strictly empirical comparison of social structure and normative order in world-historical depth. In this manner it transcended the plenitude of "systems" that remained speculative even as they claimed to establish a science of society.

Decades have passed since the manuscript was begun and left unfinished, yet few works in the realm of social science have aged so little. Its impact has been considerable over the years, although in a fragmented and erratic fashion as the various parts became available only piecemeal to the English reader or remained altogether out of reach. Weber's ideas on social action and sociological typology, on instrumental and substantive rationality, on formal and material justice, on bureaucracy and charisma, on religious beliefs and economic conduct, have been gradually assimilated by social scientists—by way of accurate reception, imaginative adaptation and, not too infrequently, inventive misinterpretation.

The renaissance of comparative study in the nineteen-sixties has restored some of the original intellectual setting of *Economy and Society*.

This has given a new pertinency to the work and is one reason for the complete English edition; another is the hoped-for correction of the uneven influence exerted by the isolated parts. Now the work has a fair chance to be understood as a whole, and its readers have a better opportunity to comprehend it—this will be a test for both.

Economy and Society is Weber's only major didactic treatise. It was meant to be merely an introduction, but in its own way it is the most demanding "text" yet written by a sociologist. The precision of its definitions, the complexity of its typologies and the wealth of its historical content make the work, as it were, a continuous challenge at several levels of comprehension: for the advanced undergraduate who gropes for his sense of society, for the graduate student who must develop his own analytical skills, and for the scholar who must match wits with Weber.

Economy and Society is part of the body of knowledge on which Weber drew in his unwitting testament, his speeches on "Science as a Vocation" and "Politics as a Vocation," which he delivered shortly after the end of the first World War before a small number of politically bewildered students. By now thousands of students have read these two rhetorical masterpieces with their poignant synopsis of his philosophical and political outlook as well as of his scholarly animus. Yet the very compactness of the two speeches impedes easy comprehension. *Economy and Society* elaborates much that is barely visible in them. However, it minimizes the propagation of Weber's own philosophical and political views, since it wants to establish a common ground for empirical investigation on which men of different persuasions can stand; in contrast to some of the methodological polemics, *Economy and Society* is meant to set a positive example. Yet there is more to it than is readily apparent. The work contains a theory of the possibilities and limitations of political democracy in an industrialized and bureaucratized society, a theory that Weber considered not only empirically valid but politically realistic as against a host of political isms: romanticist nationalism, agrarianism, corporate statism, syndicalism, anarchism, and the Marxism of the time. Hence, there is in the work an irreducible element of what Weber considered political common sense, but this does not vitiate the relative value-neutrality of the conceptual structure. Moreover, the work is full of irony, sarcasm and the love of paradox; a dead-pan expression may imply a swipe at the *Kaiser,* status-conscious professors or pretentious *littérateurs.*[1] And finally, with all its seemingly static typologies, the

1. Ironic formulations and wordplays are hard to render in translation, and it would have been self-defeating pedantry to explain more than a fraction in the editorial notes.

work is a sociologist's world history, his way of reconstructing the paths of major civilizations.

2. *Sociological Theory, Comparative Study and Historical Explanation*

Economy and Society builds a sociological scaffolding for raising some of the big questions about the origins and the possible directions of the modern world. Weber set out to find more specific and empirically tenable answers to those questions than had been given previously. He belonged to the small number of concerned men who shared neither the wide-spread belief in Progress, which was about to be shattered by the first World War, nor the new philosophical irrationalism, which had begun to appeal to many younger men.

Weber's image of "economy and society" is so widely shared today among research-oriented students of society that in its *most general* formulation it no longer appears exceptional, unless we remember that it drew the lines against Social Darwinism, Marxism and other isms of the time. Weber rejected the prevalent evolutionary and mono-causal theories, whether idealist or materialist, mechanistic or organicist; he fought both the reductionism of social scientists and the surface approach of historians, both the persistent search for hidden "deeper" causes and the ingrained aversion against historically transcendent concepts. He took it for granted that the economic structure of a group was one of its major if variable determinants and that society was an arena for group conflicts. He did not believe, however, in the laws of class struggle, jungle or race; rather, he saw men struggle most of the time under created laws and within established organizations. Given the incomplete reception of his work, the roles he attributed to force and legitimacy have been overemphasized in isolation. *Economy and Society* clearly states that men act as they do because of belief in authority, enforcement by staffs, a calculus of self-interest, and a good dose of habit. However, Weber was not much interested in master-key statements on the nature of Society and was set against the "need for world-formulae" (*Weltformelbedürfnis*). Unlike Engels, he saw no grounds for assuming an "ultimately determining element in history." *Economy and Society* demonstrates the rather concrete level on which he wanted to approach sociological theory and historical generalization.

After 1903 Weber clarified his methodological position toward the cultural and social sciences in half a dozen essays.[2] But in *Economy and*

2. Cf. 1. *Roscher und Knies und die logischen Probleme der historischen Nationalökonomie* (1903/6), 145 pp.; 2. *Die "Objektivität" sozialwissenschaft-*

Society he focussed on those concepts and typologies that would directly aid the researcher. He developed his sociological theory—his *Kategorien-lehre,* as he sometimes called it—as an open-ended, yet logically consistent formulation of fundamental aspects of social action, on the one hand, and of historical types of concerted action ("general ideal types") on the other. The construction of such trans-epochal and trans-cultural types as, for example, enterprise and *oikos* or bureaucracy and hierocracy, makes sociological theory historically comparative. In this way sociological theory provides the researcher with the dimensional concepts and empirical types that are prerequisites for the kind of comparative mental experiment and imaginative extrapolation without which causal explanation is impossible in history.

Weber's sociological theory, then, grew out of wide-ranging historical research and was meant to be applied again to history, past and in the making. In addition to theory in this generically historical sense, he employed substantive theories of differing degrees of historical specificity:

1. Theories explaining a relatively homogeneous historical configuration ("individual ideal type"), such as the spirit of capitalism;

2. Theories about relatively heterogeneous, but historically interrelated configurations, such as the "economic theory of the ancient states of the Mediterranean";

3. Theories ("rules of experience") that amount to a summary of a number of historical constellations, without being testable propositions in the strict sense: for example, the observation that foreign conquerors and native priests have formed alliances, or that reform-minded monks and secular rulers have at times cooperated in spite of their ineradicable antagonism. The occurrence of the former kind of collaboration, as in ancient Judaism, or its failure to come about in Hellas, due to the battle at Marathon,[3] may have far-reaching historical consequences—one reason for the scholar's interest in such historical "summaries."

---

licher und sozialpolitischer Erkenntnis (1904), 68 pp.; 3. *Kritische Studien auf dem Gebiet der kulturwissenschaftlichen Logik* (1905), 75 pp.; 4. *Stammlers "Überwindung" der materialistischen Geschichtsauffassung* (1907), 68 pp., with a posthumously published postscript (20 pp.); 5. *Die Grenznutzlehre und das "psychophysische Grundgesetz"* (1908), 15 pp.; 6. *"Energetische" Kulturtheorien* (1909), 26 pp.; 7. *Über den Sinn der "Wertfreiheit" der soziologischen und ökonomischen Wissenschaften* (1917/18), prepared as a memorandum for a meeting of the *Verein für Sozialpolitik* in 1913. All are reprinted in *GAzW* (for this and other abbreviations used for Weber's works, see the list following this Introduction). For English versions of essays 2, 3, and 7, see Max Weber, *The Methodology of the Social Sciences* (Edward A. Shils and Henry A. Finch, trans. and eds.; Glencoe, Ill.: The Free Press, 1949).

3. On the battle of Marathon and the category of objective possibility, cf. Weber in Shils and Finch (eds.), *Methodology . . . , 174.*

Of course, the explanation of any specific historical event also remains "theoretical" in that it subsumes many discrete actions and is merely plausible, because unverifiable in the manner of the experimental sciences. Weber was acutely aware of this difficulty, which was exacerbated by the scarcity and unreliability of the sources in most areas of his investigations, ancient and modern.

Sociologists live, and suffer, from their dual task: to develop generalizations and to explain particular cases. This is the *raison d'être* of sociology as well as its inherent tension. It would be incompatible with the spirit of Weber's approach to value the transhistorical ("functionalist") generalizations of any formal sociological theory more highly than the competent analysis of a major historical phenomenon with the help of a fitting typology. The sociology of *Economy and Society* is "Clio's handmaiden"; the purpose of comparative study is the explanation of a given historical problem. Analogies and parallels, which at the time tended to be used for evolutionary and morphological constructions and spurious causal interpretations, had for Weber merely instrumental purpose:

> Whoever does not see the *exclusive* task of "history" in making itself superfluous through the demonstration that "everything has happened before" and that all, or almost all, differences are matters of *degree*—an obvious truth—will put the stress on the *changes* (*Verschiebungen*) that emerge in spite of all parallels, and will use the similarities only to establish the *distinctiveness* (*Eigenart*) vis-à-vis each other of the two orbits [i.e., the ancient and the medieval]. . . . A genuinely critical *comparison* of the developmental stages of the ancient polis and the medieval city . . . would be rewarding and fruitful—but only if such a comparison does *not* chase after "analogies" and "parallels" in the manner of the presently fashionable general schemes of development; in other words, it should be concerned with the *distinctiveness* of each of the two developments that were finally so different, and the purpose of the comparison must be the causal *explanation* of the difference. It remains true, of course, that this causal explanation requires as an indispensable preparation the isolation (that means, abstraction) of the individual components of the course of events, and for each component the orientation toward rules of experience and the formulation of *clear concepts* without which causal attribution is nowhere possible. This should be taken into account especially in the economic field in which inadequate conceptual precision can produce the most distorted evaluations.[4]

Weber had in mind men like Wilhelm Roscher, Ranke's pupil, for whom

4. "Agrarverhältnisse im Altertum," in *GAzSW*, 257, 288. (Cf. below, n. 27.)

peoples are "generic biological entities"—as Hintze put it quite adequately. Roscher has explicitly stated that for science the development of peoples is in principle *always the same,* and in spite of appearances to the contrary, in truth nothing new happens under the sun, but always the old with "random" and hence scientifically irrelevant admixtures. This obviously is a specifically "scientific" (*naturwissenschaftliche*) perspective.[5]

Weber's comparative approach was directed against theories of historical sameness as well as theories of universal stages. He opposed in particular the interpretation of Antiquity, including ancient capitalism, as a "modern" phenomenon; this interpretation was advanced by "realistic" historians reacting against the humanist tradition with its idealization of classic Greece and Rome. Weber equally rejected the contemporary stage theories of rural and urban economic development. He, too, believed in a "general cultural development," but he focussed on the dynamics of specific historical phenomena, their development as well as their decline. For this purpose he employed several comparative devices (which will be illustrated below, p. xliii): (a) the identification of similarities as a first step in causal explanation; (b) the negative comparison; (c) the illustrative analogy; (d) the metaphorical analogy.

The ideal type too has a comparative purpose. It was Weber's solution to the old issue of conceptual realism versus nominalism, but in the context of the time it was his primary answer to the scientific notion of law and to the evolutionary stage theories. Weber wrote much more on the logical status of the ideal type than on his comparative strategy. This imbalance is reflected in the literature; a great deal has been written about the ideal type, but very little that is pertinent to the art of comparative study. As historical "summaries" of varying degrees of specificity, ideal types are compared with slices of historical reality.[6] For the researcher the issue is not whether the ideal type is less "real" than other historical concepts; rather, his task consists in choosing the level of conceptual specificity appropriate for the problem at hand. Weber's ideal types, as the reader can himself see, involve a theory about the dynamics and alternative courses of the phenomena involved. They are not meant

5. "Roscher und Knies . . . ," in *GAzW,* 23.
6. "All expositions for example of the 'essence' of Christianity are ideal types enjoying only a necessarily very relative and problematic validity when they are intended . . . as the historical portrayal of facts. On the other hand, such presentations are of great value for research and of high systematic value for expository purposes when they are used as conceptual instruments for *comparison* and the *measurement* of reality. They are indispensable for this purpose." Weber in Shils and Finch (eds.), *Methodology . . . ,* 97.

to fit an evolutionary scheme, but they do have a developmental dimension.

Ideal types are constructed with the help of historical rules of experience, which are used as heuristic propositions. For example, Weber's theory of monarchy includes the observation that monarchs throughout the ages, from ancient Mesopotamia up to Imperial Germany, have been welfare-minded because they needed the support of the lower strata against the higher; however, these higher strata, nobility and priesthood, usually remain important to the maintenance of monarchic power and legitimacy. Hence, the stability of monarchy rests in part on the ruler's ability to balance the two groups. It is from such observations, which permit the necessary specification, that the ideal type of patrimonialism (Part Two, ch. XII below) emerges.

Weber's comparative strategy was directed toward establishing, with the aid of his typologies, (1) the *differences* between modern and older conditions, and (2) the *causes* of the differences. This involved the exploration of secular phenomena that had "dropped out" of history (for example, ancient capitalism) but that were culturally important in themselves or useful for identifying modernity; it also involved the search for the "causal chains" of history.

In the absence of a reductionist one-factor scheme and of historical "one-way streets," the relationship of economy, society and polity became for Weber a multi-faceted set of problems encompassing the interplay of organization and technique of production, social stratification, civil and military administration, and religious and secular ideology. Apart from the issue of the uniqueness of Western civilization, this perspective too led Weber to a comparative interest in the workings of civilizations.

Such a comprehensive program of research required broad knowledge and expertise in several fields. The historical content of *Economy and Society* rests on a large body of scholarly literature, but also on Weber's previous research. In drawing on historical sources and secondary literature, Weber had an advantage over those historians whose training had been mainly philosophical and philological, partly because he was a trained jurist and economist, partly because he had developed a sociological framework within which he could address precise questions to the secondary literature.

An adequate understanding of *Economy and Society* should encompass Weber's previous research and writings and perceive the close links. Since Weber rendered no systematic account of his strategy of comparative study or of the intellectual development that led him to the writing of *Economy and Society*, it appears worthwhile to trace here the methodological and substantive lines of reasoning that converge in the later work; since almost all of the earlier writings are untranslated, they will be quoted more extensively than would otherwise be desirable.[7]

3. The Legal Forms of Medieval Trading Enterprises

Even for a man of Weber's generation it was rare to gain competence as historian of both Antiquity and the Middle Ages, and then to combine this with the study of contemporary concerns—industrialization, bureaucratization, democratization. Weber began his career in legal and economic history as both a "Romanist" and "Germanist"; he transcended the ideological antagonism of the two schools that so sharply divided German jurisprudence in the 19th century. Weber wanted, first of all, a good grasp of the varieties of legal and economic arrangements; hence he emulated the tremendous learning of an Otto Gierke, but he was out of sympathy with the persistent inclination of the Germanists to reduce European history to the dichotomy of Romanized authoritarian organization (*Herrschaftsverband*) and Germanic egalitarian association (*Genossenschaft*).

From the beginning of his academic career Weber addressed himself to two broad historical questions: The origins and nature of (1) capitalism in Antiquity, the Middle Ages and modern times, (2) political domination and social stratification in the three ages. His dissertation of 1889 dealt with legal institutions of medieval capitalism, his *Habilitation* of 1891 (that is, the second doctorate required for academic teaching) with the relationship between Roman politics and capitalism.

The dissertation was a "Germanist" study, *On the History of the Medieval Trading Companies*, written under Levin Goldschmidt.[8] Based largely on printed Italian and Spanish sources, it dealt with various forms of limited and unlimited partnership that emerged with the revival of maritime and inland trade and urban craft production.

---

7. In the following, attention will be given particularly to those studies that were omitted in Reinhard Bendix, *Max Weber: An Intellectual Portrait* (New York: Doubleday, 1960), Anchor edition, xxiii; see chs. I and II on Weber's early activities, his scholarly and political response to the problems of industrialization in Germany, especially the agrarian issue in Prussia east of the Elbe river (East Elbia). The present introduction is an effort to supplement Bendix' work and the introduction by Hans Gerth and C. Wright Mills in *From Max Weber: Essays in Sociology* (New York: Oxford University Press, 1946).

8. *Zur Geschichte der Handelsgesellschaften im Mittelalter (Nach südeuropäischen Quellen)* (Stuttgart: Enke, 1889), reprinted in *GAzSW*, 312–443.

Medieval capitalism required legal institutions for implementing the sharing of risk and profit and defining the liabilities and responsibilities of the parties to a joint venture. Weber investigated the differences between the partnership forms originating from the institutions of overseas trade in cities like Genoa and Pisa and those that emerged from the family craft enterprises of inland cities like Florence. The former were typically *ad hoc* associations for trading ventures, the latter more commonly continuous households, with family and other members, often surviving several generations. The partnership forms of overseas trade (*commenda, societas maris*) were only concerned with delimiting responsibilities and benefits, but the household enterprises long combined capitalist and communist modes of operation, before internal closure set in and they disintegrated as units of commercial enterprise.

A few Weberian guidelines can already be perceived in this highly technical analysis. Economic and legal development are intertwined, yet "law follows criteria that are, from the economic viewpoint, frequently extraneous";[9] it may regulate economic conditions far removed from its own dogmatic and social origins—this was a critique of correspondence theories, especially of the economically determinist variety. The insistence on the importance of the legal order for economic action is also the starting point of the first chapter of *Economy and Society* (Ch. I:1 of the older Part Two). Here the consistency of Weber's basic perspectives over time is indicated. But the strength of the dissertation lay less in such a general position than in the vivid and detailed treatment and the ability to argue firmly with the historical opinions of renowned scholars such as Gierke and Rudolf Sohm. Yet Weber conceded his inability to arrive at novel overall conclusions. Already in the preparatory stage of the dissertation he commented in his ironic fashion:

> I had to learn Italian and Spanish well enough to work myself through books and to read hundreds of statutes . . . worst of all, statutes written in such ancient dreadful dialects that one can only be astonished by the ability of men at the time to understand such jargon. Well, I was kept busy, and if not much has come out of it, it is less my fault than that of the Italian and Spanish magistrates who failed to include in the statutes the very things I sought.[10]

Weber felt that he had not been able to answer a controversial question of the time: To what extent were the early forms of the capitalist partnership and firm shaped by Roman and Germanic legal influ-

9. *GAzSW*, 322.
10. Max Weber, *Jugendbriefe*, ed. Marianne Weber (Tübingen: Mohr, n.d.), 274.

ences? Conclusive answers to Gierke and Sohm appeared possible to him only after further comparative study, including also Germany. As it was, the dissertation limited itself to the differences among various forms of commercial institutions, in order to lay the groundwork for later research.

The dissertation shows that the exposition in *Economy and Society* of the open and closed relationships of household, family, kin-group and enterprise (esp. chs. II:2, III:1, and IV:2 of Part Two) rests on long-standing knowledge of historical specifics and early familiarity with the literature. The later treatment of the associations is a mere summary with a systematic place in a wider context, yet the illustrations, which at first sight seem to fill the "empty boxes" somewhat arbitrarily, are often based on careful consideration in those earlier studies.

Two years after the dissertation Weber completed a "Romanist" *Habilitation* on *The Roman Agrarian History in Its Bearing on Public and Private Law,*[11] which qualified him to read Roman, Germanic and commercial law. He became a law professor in Berlin in 1893 and almost immediately took over for the ailing Goldschmidt.

4. *Economic and Political Power in Ancient Germanic History*

Weber wrote his *Roman Agrarian History* with the encouragement of August Meitzen, who was then working on his monumental comparative study, *The Settlement and Agrarian Structure of the Western and Eastern Germanic Tribes, Celts, Romans, Finns and Slaves* (3 vols., 1895). For his analysis of property forms and social structure Meitzen ingeniously used the ancient survey maps of the villages. Weber proceeded from Meitzen's chapter on the Roman land surveys. This undertaking was far more difficult than the study of the medieval trading companies; the findings were bound to be much more hypothetical because of the paucity and ambiguity of the sources. Weber believed he had shown that Roman agriculture could be analyzed adequately with concepts derived from other Indo-Germanic agrarian structures. However, seventeen years later, in his second major work on Antiquity, he wrote that he was still defending the work, but that it had indeed been full of "youthful sins" and particularly mistaken in its attempt "to apply Meitzen's categories to heterogeneous conditions."[12] Thus, in his early years Weber too had been influenced by evolutionary analogues, but by

---

11. *Die römische Agrargeschichte in ihrer Bedeutung für das Staats- und Privatrecht* (Stuttgart: Enke, 1891).

12. Cf. *Agrargeschichte,* 2, and "Agrarverhältnisse . . . ," *GAzSW,* 287.

1904, when he intervened in the dispute about ancient Germanic social structure,[13] he combatted them energetically. Together with the critique of his contemporaries' methodology, Weber elaborated his view of the historic relationship between political and economic power, a view that became important for the typology of domination in *Economy and Society*. At issue was the origin of manorial domination (*Grundherrschaft*), for decades the center of scholarly debate. There was a tendency to explain the whole political and economic history of Germany in terms of the *Grundherrschaft* and its variants.

The thesis of the predominance of manorial domination as early as the period of Caesar and Tacitus was upheld by Georg Friedrich Knapp and his school, especially by Werner Wittich; they rejected the older view according to which manorial domination resulted from the transformation of the Frankish levy into a cavalry of feudal vassals. As against the thesis of the Knapp school, Meitzen asserted the free status of the Germanic peasantry of late Antiquity and pointed to the equal parcelling of land in the communes. Meitzen did leave an opening to his adversaries by acknowledging the nomadic way of life of Germanic tribes in Caesar's time, but he interpreted the transition from nomadic stockbreeding to husbandry as an emancipation of "labor from property," a phrase reminiscent of Karl Rodbertus' views. For Meitzen the Germanic settlement was the creation of the drive for economic independence inherent in the equalitarian spirit of the people. Knapp's school, however, insisted that the free Germanic man of Caesar's day had been a cattle-owner who despised agriculture and those who tilled the soil. The origin of *Grundherrschaft* was seen then to lie in the rule of cattle-owners over peasants. Wittich, for one, buttressed his view with Richard Hildebrand's scheme of cultural and legal development. "This theory," Weber commented, "is one of the attempts, recently so numerous, to comprehend cultural development in the manner of biological processes as a lawful sequence of universal stages."[14] Hence the assertion of a universal nomadic stage, at least in the Occident. The theory worked with analogies from the contemporary nomadic life of Bedouins and

13. "Der Streit um den Charakter der altgermanischen Sozialverfassung in der deutschen Literatur des letzten Jahrzehnts," in *GAzSW*, 508–556; first published in *Jahrbücher für Nationalökonomie und Statistik*, 3d series, vol. 28 (1904).

14. *GAzSW*, 513. Cf. Richard Hildebrand, *Recht und Sitte auf den primitiveren wirtschaftlichen Kulturstufen* (Jena: Fischer, 1896); for Hildebrand's counterattack, which rejects Weber's interpretation of Germanic agriculture in Caesar's time, see the second edition of 1907, pp. 55f., 64f.; see also Werner Wittich's review essay on Hildebrand, "Die wirtschaftliche Kultur der Deutschen zur Zeit Caesar's," *Historische Zeitschrift*, vol. 79, 1897, 45–67.

Kirghiz, applying them to elucidate Germanic prehistory. If these nomads scorned agricultural labor, by inference the Germanic nomads must
have done likewise. Weber objected:

> This procedure of a scholar whom I too hold in high esteem is a
> good example of the manner in which the concept of "cultural stages"
> should not be applied scientifically. Concepts such as "nomadic," "semi-
> nomadic," etc., are indispensable for descriptive purposes. For research,
> the continuous comparison of the developmental stages of peoples and
> the search for analogies are a heuristic means well suited, if cautiously
> used, to explain the causes of distinctiveness of each individual develop-
> ment. But it is a serious misunderstanding of the rationale of cultural
> history to consider the construction of stages as *more* than such a
> heuristic means, and the subsumption of historical events under such
> abstractions as the *purpose* of scholarly work—as Hildebrand does—;
> it is a violation of proper methodology to view a "cultural stage" as
> anything but a concept, to treat it as an entity in the manner of bio-
> logical organisms, or an Hegelian "idea," from which the individual
> components "emanate," and hence to use the "stage" for arriving at
> *conclusions* by analogy: If the historic phenomenon y usually follows
> x, or if both tend to be co-existent, y_1 must follow x_1, or be co-existent,
> since x and x_1 are conceptual components of "analogous" stages of
> culture.
>
> The mental construct of a cultural stage merely means, analyti-
> cally speaking, that the individual phenomena of which it is composed
> are "adequate" to one another, that they have—as we could say—a
> certain measure of inner "affinity," but not that they are related in any
> determinate way (*Gesetzmässigkeit*). . . .
>
> The belief in a universal "stage" of nomadic existence, through
> which all tribes passed and from which the settlement developed, can
> no longer be retained in view of our knowledge of the development of
> Asiatic peoples and after Hahn's investigations [*Die Haustiere,* 1896].
> At any rate, the knowledge of a by no means primitive form of agri-
> culture among the Indo-Germanic peoples goes back into the darkest
> past.[15]

In Weber's view the Germanic tribes of Caesar's day were not nomadic nor were the freemen a stratum of landlords (*Grundherren*) who
left most work to slaves and women; slaves were not a substantial part
of the workforce and the status differentiation between warrior and
peasant did not exist at the beginning of recorded history; rather, the
Germanic freemen were transformed very gradually into the politically
disenfranchised and economically harassed peasants of the Middle Ages.

Weber accepted Meitzen's view that the German village with its land
distribution was a product of legal autonomy, a monopolistic association
of relative equals, not a product of manorial decree. However, in contrast

15. *GAzSW,* 517, 524.

to Meitzen's assumption of an equalitarian folk spirit, Weber took an economically more realistic line and reasoned persuasively that the equal parcelling out of land by a closed association pointed to the narrowing of economic opportunities (land shortage), similar to the monopolistic policies of medieval guilds.[16]

In examining the Roman sources, Weber pointed out that Caesar's report about the Suevi was no proof for a nomadic way of life of the Germanic tribes. The Suevi, a frontier people, had developed into a group of professional warriors, engaging in periodic raids on adjacent areas and neglecting agriculture. This brought Weber to the phenomenon of warrior communism and his most general point: the historical primacy of political over economic factors:

> If one wants at all to search for distant analogies such as might be offered by the Kirghiz and Bedouins, the traits of an "autarkous state" [an allusion to Fichte's collectivist utopia] found among the Suevi will remind one much more of the robber communism that existed in Antiquity on the Liparian islands or—if the expression be permitted— the "officers' mess communism" of the ancient Spartans, or of the grandiose booty communism of a Caliph Omar. In one phrase, these traits are the outcome of "warrior communism." They can easily be explained as a result of purely military interests. . . . They would scarcely be in tune with the living conditions of a tribe stagnant at the nomadic stage and ruled by great cattle-owners in a patriarchal manner. . . .
>
> The oldest social differentiation of Germanic and Mediterranean prehistory is, as far as we can see, determined primarily politically, in part religiously, *not,* however, primarily economically. Economic differentiation must be considered more as a consequence and epiphenomenon or, if you want it in the most fashionable terms, as a "function" of the former, rather than vice versa. . . .
>
> If the term may be applied to prehistory at all, a "knightly" life style . . . often goes together with a manorial position; in fact, this is the rule once private hereditary landownership has fully developed. . . . However, it is by no means generally true that this life style leads to, or is related to, manorial superordination over other freemen—in the age of Homer and Hesiod as little as in that of the Germanic epics. It means a reversal of the usual causal relationship to view the later manorial constitution not as a consequence but as the original basis of the privileged position of the high-ranking families. The historical primacy of manorial domination appears highly unlikely, first of all, because in an age of land surplus mere land ownership could not very well be the basis of economic power.[17]

16. This is again the phenomenon of closed economic relationships treated in Part Two, ch. II:2 below.

17. *GAzSW,* 523, 554f.

Weber concluded his essay with a reminder about the triviality inherent in correct scholarly results and anticipated that the older view would probably survive the recent challenges: "This may appear trivial. But unfortunately, trivial results, by their very quality, are often the correct ones."

It is from concrete historical issues such as these that Weber fashioned, in *Economy and Society,* his contrast between patrimonial domination and charismatic rule. The joining of these military with religious phenomena established the category of charismatic domination.[18]

5. *The Roman Empire and Imperial Germany*

Weber had an early interest in the comparison and comparability of Imperial Germany and Imperial Rome. On this score he was close to Theodor Mommsen, who described the Roman Republic in the terms of liberal political theory and polemicized against Imperial Germany with analogies from Antiquity. In the academic public Weber's comparative interest was at first not widely noticed. The *Roman Agrarian History* proved technically too difficult to be understood by more than a very small group of scholars. Alfred Heuss, today counted among the foremost Roman historians, has pointed out that Weber

> was the first to take the Roman agrarian writers (Cato, Varro, Columella) seriously, examining them in a matter-of-fact way . . . and uncovering the crass principles of Roman agrarian capitalism in its technical details. In this respect, the book, although generally neglected by the historians, became path-breaking, and subsequent research had to continue along its line of inquiry. . . . Who else among the historians of the time was capable of handling the legal sources and the technical language of land surveyors, both of which Weber combined in a virtuoso fashion? The book, hard to understand because of its dry and remote subject matter, is an ingenious work.[19]

Among the historians of the time the aged Mommsen was best qualified to judge Weber's work. He hailed its publication and welcomed its author onto his previously exclusive ground: the borderlines of Roman private and public law. As early as the occasion of Weber's doctoral defense Mommsen had said: "When the time comes for me to descend into the grave, there is no one to whom I would rather say: 'Son, here is my spear, it has become too heavy for my arm,' than Max

18. Specifically, booty and military communism is treated in Part Two, ch. XIV:6.

19. Alfred Heuss, "Max Webers Bedeutung für die Geschichte des griechisch-römischen Altertums," *Historische Zeitschrift,* vol. 201, 1965, 535.

Weber."[20] However, Weber did not become his successor and quickly moved beyond the confines of ancient history. In the early nineties he involved himself in a questionnaire study of the conditions of rural laborers conducted under the auspices of the *Verein für Sozialpolitik,* the most important association of professors, politicians and higher civil servants for the study of the Social Question in Imperial Germany. Between 1892 and 1894 Weber published extensively on farm labor, and, in contrast to the *Roman Agrarian History,* his new writings did attract considerable attention. Weber's turn of interest was acknowledged with the offer of an economics chair at the University of Freiburg, which he accepted in 1894; this was an extraordinary offer for a jurist—not even the usual "rehabilitation" (that is, the writing of a second *Habilitation* to qualify in a different academic field) was required.

In Freiburg Weber delivered a popular lecture on "The Social Causes of the Decay of Ancient Civilization" (1896).[21] The major political link between his studies of Antiquity and of East Elbia was the problem of the "rise and fall of empire." The common theme was the self-destruction of empire through the cleavage between the rich and the poor. In the *Roman Agrarian History* Weber had searched for the "social strata and economic interest groups" behind the expansionism of the Empire and the unparalleled capitalist exploitation: "It is likely that the political domination of a large polity has never been so lucrative."[22] The Roman state suffered from a "convulsive sickness of its social body." Weber freely stated his value judgment. The transition from the condition of the barrack slaves to that of hereditarily attached peasants, who were permitted families of their own and conditional land use, appeared to him a decisive change for the better:

> The moral significance of this development need scarcely be emphasized. One must remember that at the beginning of the Empire Bebel's ideal of legal marriage [i.e., freely contracted and dissoluble marriage] was realized *de facto* among the upper strata, *de jure* for citizens in general. The consequences are known. In this study it has not been possible to show the connection between the influence of the Christian ideal of marriage and this economic development, but it should be obvious that the separation of the slaves from the manorial household was an element of profound internal recovery (*Gesundung*), which

20. Marianne Weber, *Max Weber. Ein Lebensbild* (Tübingen: Mohr, 1926), 121—(henceforth cited as *Lebensbild*).

21. "Die sozialen Gründe des Untergangs der antiken Kultur," in *GAzSW*, 289–311; a translation by Christian Mackauer in *Journal of General Education,* V, 1950–51, 75–88.

22. *Agrargeschichte*, 6.

was by no means bought too dearly with the relapse of the "upper ten thousand" into centuries of barbarism.[23]

Weber saw the social developments in East Elbia against the background of Roman history. He observed with apprehension the proletarization of the peasants in the second half of the 19th century. The manorial *Junkers* gradually turned into capitalist entrepreneurs; they preferred cheap seasonal labor—little more than barrack slaves—from beyond the Russian frontier to a permanent and landowning German workforce. Weber foresaw grave dangers in the *Junkers'* labor and tariff policies and rejected their hollow claim to be the military pillars of the Empire even as they undermined it socially and economically. He warned his elders in the *Verein für Sozialpolitik* in 1893 that "the most horrible of all horrors is a landowning proletariat for whom the inherited land has become a curse."[24]

In his 1896 Freiburg address Weber repeated his judgments and cautioned his classically educated audience against its ready belief that the decline of the Roman Empire could provide lessons for the solution of modern social problems. He even went so far as to label the topic as "merely of historic interest." But this was primarily a didactic stricture. He did mean to teach his listeners something about the *relative* importance of the economic factor and of social changes in the lower strata. An intellectual and political culture should not be viewed in isolation from the economic and social structure, as the Humanists had done up to Jakob Burckhardt, and as the classical schools were still doing; basic shifts in the mode and division of labor, and especially economic and cultural changes within the lower strata, could be historically as significant as changes in the ruling groups and their culture. Imperial Germany faced such shifts with the growth of its industrial

---

23. *Ibid.*, 274f. Weber's view was later detailed by Marianne Weber, *Ehefrau und Mutter in der Rechtsentwicklung* (Tübingen: Mohr, 1907); on marriage in the Roman upper classes, 168–173, on slavery, marriage and Christianity, 177–187, on Bebel, 80. This voluminous comparative study, which Weber suggested to his wife and in which he took a hand, should be seen as the background for the cursory treatment of marriage and property rights in chs. III and IV of Part Two below.

The sudden ironic reference to August Bebel, after many highly technical pages, is to the most popular socialist book of the time, *Woman and Socialism* (1879), esp. ch. 28. In the 9th edition of 1891, Bebel popularized Friedrich Engels' *The Origin of the Family, Private Property and the State* (1884), the Marxist sequel to Lewis H. Morgan's *Ancient Society* (1877). Throughout his career Weber gave attention to the socialist theory of marriage and property. For the last statement (1919/20), see *Economic History*, 20.

24. "Die ländliche Arbeitsverfassung," *GAzSW*, 462.

and agrarian proletariat, although her specific troubles were largely the opposite of those that had brought down the Roman Empire.

Weber presented a simplified version of his explanation for the decline of the Roman Empire—later part of his economic theory of the ancient states: With the stabilization of the Empire the flow of new slaves, the chief capital good of ancient capitalism, began to dwindle. Commerce waned. Administering the vast conquered inland areas with the means of a maritime city state proved increasingly difficult. The latifundia established themselves as administrative units independent of the cities. Local troops replaced the standing army that had been largely self-perpetuating, up to one half of the recruits being the sons of soldiers. As economy and culture became rural, cosmopolitanism vanished. Thus the economic development of Antiquity, which had started out as a localized subsistence economy, came full circle. However, for Weber this circularity (*Kreislauf*) did not involve morphological assumptions in the mode of Oswald Spengler.

The disintegration of the Empire was a problem of super- and sub-structure: "In essence, the decline meant merely that the urban ad-ministrative apparatus disappeared, and with it the political superstruc-ture dependent upon a money economy, since it was no longer adapted to the economic substructure with its natural economy."[25] What had been an urban substructure, the money economy and commerce, became a superstructure without sustaining basis as the shift occurred from a maritime to an inland economy. Thus Weber handled the relationship of super- and substructure in terms of geographical shift as well as time sequence.

Throughout the address, Weber used various comparative devices. He began with the similarities of the ancient and the medieval city in order to identify the causes for their difference; the more similarities he found, the more he could narrow down the area of crucial difference. In order to clarify the dissolution of the ancient municipalities, he resorted to a negative contemporary analogy, the resistance of the Prussian *Junkers* to the administrative incorporation of their estates into the rural "communes" (*Landgemeinden*),[26] and he contrasted the familiar me-dieval and modern flight from the land with the late Roman flight from the cities. He made the military discipline of the Roman slaves more understandable to his listeners by comparing it illustratively to an ex-perience they knew: military service with is regimented barrack life

---

25. "Die sozialen Gründe . . . ," *GAzSW*, 308.
26. On the Prussian *Gutsbezirke*, the *Junker*-ruled "estate-districts," see be-low, ch. XVI:*v*, n. 9 (p. 1369).

for the unmarried recruits ("slaves"), who were drilled by married non-commissioned officers ("*villici*"). Comparing the slaves on the Roman latifundia with those on the Carolingian estates, Weber pointed to the decisive difference: the latter were permitted a family and the use of land upon their separation from the lord's *oikos*.

6. *The Economic Theory of Antiquity*

Weber's most comprehensive work on Antiquity was written shortly before *Economy and Society*. Behind the title "Agrarian Conditions in Antiquity"[27] was hidden nothing less than a comparative social and economic study of Mesopotamia, Egypt, Israel, Greece, the Hellenist realm, and Republican and Imperial Rome. Alfred Heuss called it "the most original, daring and persuasive analysis ever made of the economic and social development of Antiquity . . . the area in which Weber's judgment, especially in the details, was most sovereign and surefooted, . . . a claim that stands although he was even more 'original' in the sociology of religion."[28]

In contrast to *Economy and Society*, the study focussed on an economic and politico-military typology and did not yet include the categories of legitimate domination. It should be noted that in Weber's thinking the category of appropriation, both of economic and military resources, is older than that of legitimacy; furthermore, that differences in the mode of appropriation in both areas remained equally important to him:

> Whether a military constitution rests on the principle of self-equipment or that of provisioning by the warlord who supplies horses, arms and food, is as fundamental a distinction for social history as is

27. "Agrarverhältnisse im Altertum," *GAzSW*, 1–288; originally published in the *Handwörterbuch der Staatswissenschaften*, third ed. (1909), vol. I, 52–188. The restricted title was determined by the division of the handbook. The ten-page annotated bibliography should be consulted for *Economy and Society*. The book-length study was dashed off in four months in 1908, a feat made possible by the fact that Weber had done his thinking ahead of the period of writing and was thoroughly familiar with the literature.

Weber seems to have divided some of the subject matter with Rostovzeff, who contributed the handbook article on *coloni*. Rostovzeff, who in the United States became much better known than Weber as an ancient economic historian, was one of the few to utilize Weber's analysis. Other historians rediscovered some of Weber's results after the First World War—another instance of the discontinuity that plagues most scholarly disciplines. By and large, it still appears that Weber's ancient studies have not yet been followed through sufficiently.

28. Heuss, *loc. cit.*, 538.

another: whether the means of production are owned by the workers or appropriated by a capitalist entrepreneur.[29]

Given this perspective Weber set himself the task of relating the ancient economy to the major political structures. Almost incidentally, he further clarified his comparative approach. Two issues stood out: (1) If there are no universal evolutionary stages, at any rate, if they cannot be identified historically, what kind of typology is suitable for analysis? (2) If the categories of economic history appropriate for medieval and modern conditions are not applicable to Antiquity, which conceptual alternatives should be used?

As against evolutionary conceptions, Weber advanced a limited developmental scheme that left the actual historical sequences open and put in their stead logical "states" or "conditions"—a model-building device that became basic for *Economy and Society*. This was a "static" approach only in comparison with evolutionary sequences. Weber argued that ancient social history had no visible starting point, since most historical phenomena appeared to be secondary, militarily determined, developments, such as the phratries, phylae and *tribus*. Nothing reliable was known about the primeval rural structure. For Weber even the "plausible hypothesis" that the ruling families at least originated as nomadic conquerors was not generally acceptable, since the aristocratic polity developed at the Mediterranean coast and could be proven to have other origins; the starting points were lost in the darkness of prehistory. All that could be historically reconstructed were "certain organizational states, which apparently repeated themselves to some extent in all those ancient peoples, from the Seine to the Euphrates, that had at least some urban development."[30]

Weber began his analysis with a series of brief comparisons that linked up with his reasoning in "The Controversy About Ancient Germanic Social Structure." European and Asian agrarian history differed in a crucial category: land appropriation. Comparing the course of early settlement in Europe and Asia, Weber saw the former proceeding from initial nomadic livestock raising to mixed crop and livestock agriculture, the latter from nomadic crop raising to intensive agriculture of a gardening type. Hence the development in Europe, but relative absence in Asia, of communal property in grazing grounds.

Next, Weber compared ancient and medieval agriculture in the Occident. In both cases agriculture intensified with the narrowing of economic opportunities. Agricultural preoccupation made the majority

29. Cf. *Economic History*, 237, for a slightly different wording.
30. "Agrarverhältnisse . . . ," *GAzSW*, 35.

of men economically unavailable for military service. Thus arose the professional warriors who exploited the masses. Weber defined feudalism in a manner transcending the medieval case. This enabled him to point to the decisive difference between the ancient and the medieval conditions. Medieval feudalism dispersed the warriors over the countryside as manorial lords (*Grundherren*); ancient feudalism was urban: the warriors lived together in the polis.

In this development military technology was partly cause, partly epiphenomenon. Weber emphasized that in Antiquity, in contrast to the Middle Ages, both the diffusion of superior military techniques and the spread of commerce occurred by sea. Whereas central and western Europe became manorial and feudal at a time when trade by land had declined, "feudal" development in Antiquity led to the creation of the city state. This centralization had the consequence that citizenship was a much firmer bond than were the ties of personal loyalty typical of decentralized medieval feudalism.

At this point Weber cautioned again not to mistake analogy for identity:

> The relationship of ancient urban feudalism to the exchange economy is reminiscent of the rise of the free crafts in our medieval cities, the decline of patrician rule, the latent struggle between urban and manorial economy, and the distintegration of the feudal polity under the impact of the money economy. . . . But these ever present analogies with medieval and modern phenomena are frequently most unreliable and often outright detrimental to unbiassed comprehension. . . . Ancient civilization has specific characteristics that distinguish it sharply from the medieval and the modern.[31]

Weber listed a series of features: Ancient civilization centered on the coasts and the rivers; trade was widespread and highly profitable, but lacked the volume it had in the late Middle Ages; the great ancient empires were more mercantilist than the modern Mercantilist states; private trade was insufficiently developed to guarantee the politically crucial grain supply of the urban centers, which maintained a consumer proletariat of declassed citizens, not a working class; slavery was more important than in the Middle Ages.[32]

These comparisons led Weber to the issue, heatedly debated for many decades, whether the categories of modern and medieval economic history were appropriate for Antiquity. In the eighteen sixties

31. *Ibid.*, 4.
32. Weber conceded that in earlier writings he had overestimated the importance of slavery relative to free labor, but insisted that in the classic period of the "free" polities slavery was especially important. Cf. *GAzSW*, 7–11, as against his older view, *ibid.*, 293.

Karl Rodbertus, himself a country squire, had investigated the master's extended household (the *oikos*) as the dominant unit of ancient economy; he also gave much attention to ancient capitalism. As a scholar of Antiquity, the conservative socialist Rodbertus surpassed Marx, who had labelled the agrarian developments the "secret history of the Romans." Karl Bücher, whose work proceeded from Rodbertus, Marx, Engels and Schmoller, accepted the *oikos* as one stage within his influential scheme of economic development—household, urban and national economy.[33] Bücher, who believed in the "lawful course of economic development" (Preface, *iii*), was criticized by Eduard Meyer, who denied the need for particular economic concepts in the study of Antiquity. Weber, in turn, warned of the futility of Meyer's approach: "Nothing could be more dangerous than to conceive of ancient conditions as 'modern.' Whoever does it underestimates, as so often happens, the structural differences. . . ."[34]

Weber recognized the importance of the *oikos,* but viewed it, within the Roman context, as the "developmental product" of the Imperial period and as the transition to medieval feudalism; by contrast, the Oriental *oikos* had existed from the beginning of history. As against Rodbertus, who saw the *oikos* developing directly out of the self-sufficient household, Weber pointed for the Orient to its origins in the irrigation economy and trade profit: The early military chieftains were also merchants.

Weber affirmed that Antiquity had a capitalist economy "to a degree relevant for cultural history." He opposed the view that there had been no capitalism because the large-scale enterprise with free and differentiated labor was absent. Such an approach focussed too narrowly, he thought, on the social problems of modern capitalism. Instead, he insisted on a purely economic concept of capitalism: "If the terminology is to have any classificatory value at all," capital must mean private acquisitive capital (*Erwerbskapital*) used for profit in an exchange economy.[35] In this sense the "greatest" periods of Antiquity did have capitalism. The ancient polis began with ground rents and tributes collected by the ruler and the patriciate; its economic prosperity was

33. Cf. Karl Rodbertus, "Zur Geschichte der römischen Tributsteuern seit Augustus," *Jahrbücher für Nationalökonomie und Statistik,* V, 1865, 241–315; "Zur Frage des Sachwerts des Geldes im Altertum," *loc. cit.,* XIV, 1870, 341– 420; Karl Marx, *Das Kapital,* in *Werke,* vol. 23 (Berlin: Dietz, 1962), 96; Karl Bücher, *Die Entstehung der Volkswirtschaft* (14th ed.; Tübingen: Laupp, 1920), 83–160—first published in 1893 as a collection of older articles; an English edition s.t. *Industrial Evolution* (New York: Holt, 1901).

34. *GAzSW,* 10.

35. *Ibid.,* 13.

politically determined. However, the mere rendering of tributes to personal rulers lay outside the realm of capitalism and the exchange economy. In this case neither the rent-yielding land nor the retainers could be considered "capital," since domination had a traditional, not a market basis: it was manorial domination (*Grundherrschaft*). When the landowners leased land in an exchange economy, ownership became a capitalist rent fund. But the capitalist enterprise proper came into existence only when both land and slaves became transferrable on the market. The classic cities did not have large-scale private enterprise for any length of time. There was no qualitative division of labor; instead of machinery, debt serfs and purchased slaves were used; the crafts played a secondary role, and the guilds remained unimportant. Much of the ancient economy, then, was a "mixed economy," partly manorial, partly capitalist.

Weber considered the political and administrative structure of the ancient states decisive for the fate of capitalism. The state administration, especially public finance, constituted the biggest enterprise. Only in the city state, which lacked a bureaucratic apparatus for the administration of its territories, could public finances act as a pacemaker for private capital formation—because the polity was for its financing dependent upon the private tax farmer. Weber pointed to a major difference between monarchic and republican states: Ancient capitalism culminated in the Roman Republic, where the public lands became the object of the crassest form of private exploitation. The monarchies constricted capitalism; in the interest of dynastic continuity they were concerned with the subjects' loyalty. In the city republic the primary goal was capitalist exploitation, in the monarchy it was political stability. "In republics tax-farming is always at the ready to turn the state into an enterprise of the state creditors and tax-farmers in the manner of medieval Genoa." Whereas the city state allowed private capital accumulation of a highly unstable kind, the bureaucratic order of the monarchic state economy gradually destroyed the opportunities for private gain. "The monarchic order, so beneficial for the masses of the subjects, was the death of capitalist development and of everything dependent on it."[36]

7. *A Political Typology of Antiquity*

Beyond the contrast between republics and monarchies, well-known from ancient political theory, Weber elaborated a developmental scheme

36. *Ibid.,* 29 and 31.

with open historical direction. Apart from its classificatory uses, he hoped that it would remind the reader of the very different stages of development at which the polities entered the light of history—depending on the "accidental" availability of the sources. In contrast to Greece, Mesopotamia and Egypt had had some kind of urban culture many centuries before the first records were made.

Weber based his typology on the "military constitution" and distinguished:

i. the merely fortified location; ii. the petty "castle kings"; iii. the clan polity; iv. the bureaucratic urban principality; v. the liturgic monarchy; vi. the polis of privileged citizens; vii. the democratic polis; and outside the scheme, viii. the military peasant confraternity.

i. The distant forerunner of the city is the walled settlement. Household and village constitute the organizational environment of the individual. Associations for blood revenge, cultic activities, and defense provide police, sacral and political protection, but nothing historically certain can be established about the functional division or overlap of these early associations which come out of prehistory. Free members share in the landed property; the extent of slavery seems to be moderate. Political chieftains, if they exist at all, have mainly arbitrational functions. "It depends on the political situation whether there are any joint political affairs."[37]

ii. A closer forerunner of the city is the castle controlled by an owner of land, slaves, cattle and precious metals, that is, a ruler with a personal following. Almost nothing is known about the state of the countryside. The exploitation of the subjects seems to have varied greatly. Fertile land and trade profits led to the rise of these "castle kings"; their law was set against popular law. The separation of the followers from the rural population was important; according to tradition and fact, the following often consisted of bands of aliens and adventurers ("robber bands"). The ancient states originated in the victory of one "castle king" over others.

iii. Another approximation to the classic polis is the clan polity (*Adelsstaat*). The nobility is made up of creditors who develop into a stratum of landed *rentiers*. The peasants become first debt serfs and then hereditary dependents. A group of noble families that have accumulated enough land and retainers to equip and train themselves as professional warriors rules the countryside from an acropolis. The "king" loses influence and becomes *primus inter pares* in a militarily organized urban community (in contrast to the feudal-manorial development of the

37. *Ibid.*, 36. Weber deals here with the relatively "universal groups" to which he returned again below, in Part Two, chs. III–VI and VIII.

continental Middle Ages). There is no bureaucracy; at most there are elected officials. The peasants may be legally separate from the status group of free men, but ancient trial and debt procedures as well as the manipulation of the courts by the ruling class are sufficient to maintain the social distance without formal barriers.

IV. From state II (the "castle kingship") development may proceed in a direction contrary to state III: The king may succeed in effectively subordinating his following and in establishing an officialdom through which he governs the "subjects." In this case the city is not autonomous (witness Egypt, Assur and Babylon). The economy may approach "state socialism" or an exchange economy, depending on the mode of want satisfaction of the royal household. Under condition III and IV the extent of the direct utilization of the labor force by the rulers is inversely correlated with the development of the private exchange economy. Insofar as domination rests on taxation, free transfer of real estate may be tolerated. However, the bureaucratic king tends to oppose land accumulation by the aristocracy, whereas he may permit land fragmentation. Witness the Greek tyrants—and Napoleon I.

V. With the rationalization of royal want satisfaction the bureaucratic city or river kingdom may develop into the authoritarian liturgy state, which meets its demands through "an artful system of compulsory services and treats the subjects as mere objects."[38] Even in such a state there may be free trade and geographical mobility, as long as they produce revenue. In fact, the state may favor both, in the manner of the "enlightened despotism" of the 17th and 18th century—another illustrative analogy.

VI. This type emerges from state III, but not without the most heterogeneous transitions. It is the "polis of hoplites," in which the citizens form a heavily armed infantry. The rule of the noble kinship groups over the city and of the city over the countryside is broken. The citizens' army of hoplites comprises all owners of land; hence military service is relatively democratized.

VII. The democratic polis proper is a further development of condition VI. Military service and even citizenship are emancipated from the requirement of landownership, and there is an inconsistent trend to formally qualify for office-holding everyone who has served in the navy, a military branch not requiring self-equipment.

VIII. A major case outside this typology is the association of peasants organized as hoplites, which in some instances made history, from ancient Israel to the medieval Swiss confederation.

38. *Ibid.*, 40.

One important dimension cuts across this typology of military-political organization: "the manifest and latent struggle of the secular-political and the theocratic powers, a struggle that affects the whole structure of social life."[39] Functional specialization separated the primeval linkage of princely and priestly power. The priests became powerful through their control of economic resources, their hold over the religious anxieties of the masses, their possession of early "science" and, especially, their control of education in the bureaucratized states. This struggle led to the historical ups and downs of secularization and restoration in the "substantive development of culture," with usurpers ultimately striving for legitimacy and hence restoration.

Thus did Weber assemble the elements that went into the making of his Sociology of Domination in *Economy and Society:* patrimonialism, feudalism, charisma (as military communism), the city and hierocracy. In sum, Weber's ancient and medieval studies contain not only much of the historical substance of the later work, but also its gradual conceptualization.

8. *Weber's Vision of the Future and His Academic Politics*

Weber did not hesitate to draw political lessons from academic studies, but the relationship must be properly understood. He believed that scholars should unflinchingly face the arduous work of fact-finding and only then express political views. He insisted on detachment in order to gain a hearing for his views—the basic strategy in his academic politics. Sociology became for him a weapon in the struggle against the predominant views in the *Verein für Sozialpolitik* and the founding of the German Sociological Association a vehicle for the same purpose. The two great issues, closely related, were the social dynamics and future of German society and the feasibility and desirability of value-neutrality in social science.[40]

In warning of the political dangers he foresaw, Weber used historical parallels, although he rejected the use of analogies for historical explanation. Thus he appended one page of warnings to his 1908 study of Antiquity in order to impress his readers with vivid parallels. Without

39. *Ibid.,* 44.

40. On the tensions between politics and scholarship in the men of the *Verein für Sozialpolitik,* see Dieter Lindenlaub, *Richtungskämpfe im Verein für Sozialpolitik. Wissenschaft und Sozialpolitik im Kaiserreich* (Wiesbaden: Steiner, 1967). This massive study will be the standard work on the politics of German academic men during the period; the present introduction was still written independently of it.

implying any historical inevitability he upheld—at least didactically—the maxim: "If it has happened before, it may happen again." At issue were the effects of bureaucratization:

The paralysis of private economic initiative through bureaucracy is not limited to Antiquity. Every bureaucracy, including ours, has the same tendency by virtue of its expansionism. In Antiquity the policies of the city state paved the way for capitalism; today capitalism is the pacemaker for the bureaucratization of the economy. Let us imagine coal, iron and mining products, metallurgy, distilleries, sugar, tobacco, matches —in short, all mass products that are already highly cartellized—taken over by state-owned or state-controlled enterprises; let the crown domains, entailed estates, and state-controlled resettlement holdings (Rentengüter) proliferate and let the "Kanitz motion" be passed and executed with all its consequences;[41] let all military and civilian needs of the state administration be met by state-operated workshops and cooperatives; let shipping operations on inland waterways be compelled to use state tugs [as partly realized in 1913], put the merchant marine under state supervision, have all railroads etc. nationalized, and perhaps subject cotton imports to international agreements; let all these enterprises be managed in bureaucratic "order," introduce state-supervised syndicates, and let the rest of the economy be regulated on the guild principle with innumerable certificates of competency, academic and otherwise; let the citizenry in general be of the rentier paisible type—then, under a militarist-dynastic regime, the condition of the late Roman Empire will have been reached, albeit on a technologically more elaborate basis. After all, the German burgher of today has retained scarcely more of his ancestors' qualities from the medieval Town Leagues than the Athenean in Caesar's time had preserved those of the fighters at Marathon. "Order" is the motto of the German burgher—even, in most cases, if he calls himself a Social Democrat. It is very likely that the bureaucratization of society will one day subdue capitalism just as it did in Antiquity. Then the "anarchy of production" will be replaced by that "order" which, in a very similar way, characterized the late Roman Empire and, even more, the New Kingdom and the rule of the Ptolemies in Egypt. Let no one believe that the citizens' service in a barracked army, bureaucratically equipped, clothed, fed, drilled and commanded, can provide a countervailing force to such bureaucratization or, more generally, that

41. Rentengüter were small holdings, indivisible and inalienable except with government permission, created for the "inner colonization" (Germanisation) of the eastern part of the Reich, first under the Prussian resettlement act of 1886.— Count Kanitz, a Conservative Reichstag deputy, in 1894 demanded the institution of a state monopoly for grain imports in the interest of price supports for the output of the grain-producing Junker estates of eastern Germany. The so-called "Kanitz motion" failed, but was thereafter resubmitted year after year by the agrarian groups.

modern conscription in dynastic states has any inner affinity with the spirit of the citizenry-in-arms of the distant past. However, these perspectives do not belong here.[42]

It is, of course, significant that Weber added these perspectives in spite of his disclaimer. In the fall of 1909 the Weber brothers, Max and Alfred, clashed with an older generation of scholars at the Vienna meeting of the *Verein für Sozialpolitik*. Some younger members were critical of the state metaphysics of men like Gustav von Schmoller and were ready to go beyond their elders in matters of social reform, against them with regard to democratization. The two Webers attacked the belief of the older reform generation that strengthening the power of the state and extending the economic functions of its bureaucracy would lead to greater social harmony. Opposing the conservative State Socialism of the aged Adolf Wagner, they pointed to the dangers of bureaucratization. *Economy and Society* later demonstrated how the bureaucratic phenomenon could be studied comparatively in a non-ideological way. But at Vienna Weber expressed his sentiments and convictions, which should be seen not only as the counterpoint, but as one of the motives, for the Sociology of Domination. Weber granted to the older view of bureaucracy—perhaps in part as a tactical concession—that

> no machinery in the world functions so precisely as this apparatus of men and, moreover, so cheaply. . . . When the *Verein für Sozialpolitik* was founded [in 1872], the generation of Privy Councillor. Wagner called for more than purely technical yardsticks in economic affairs; at the time this group was just as small as we who think differently are today in relation to you. Gentlemen, you then had to fight the salvo of applause for the purely technological accomplishments of industrial mechanization emanating from the laissez-faire doctrine. It appears to me that today you are in danger of providing such cheap applause to mechanical efficiency as an administrative and political criterion. . . . Rational calculation . . . reduces every worker to a cog in this [bureaucratic] machine and, seeing himself in this light, he will merely ask how to transform himself from a little into a somewhat bigger cog, . . . an attitude you find, just as in the Egyptian *papyri*, increasingly among our civil servants and especially their successors, our students. The passion for bureaucratization at this meeting drives us to despair.[43]

Weber was not opposed to the *Verein für Sozialpolitik* as a propaganda association, as he called it, but its academic activities were unduly handicapped, he felt, by its ideological preoccupations. Hence, after the

42. *GAzSW*, 277f.
43. *GAzSS*, 413f.

Vienna meeting, he proposed the founding of the German Sociological Association—to be an instrument of collective empirical research and "purely scientific discussions." In the winter of 1909/10 he suggested team projects on the press, voluntary associations, and the relationship of technology and culture. Weber apparently sustained most of the organizing effort. It was soon clear that his colleagues resisted project cooperation and only hesitantly accepted organizational responsibilities. And some men whose academic careers had suffered because of their novel sociological interests, Weber noted with chagrin, viewed the association as compensation for status deprivation—he spoke of a *salon des refusés.* The Sociological Association first met in the fall of 1910. Weber summarized the intent of the statutes: "The association rejects, in principle and definitely, all propaganda for action-oriented ideas from its midst." He immediately added that this had nothing to do with general non-partisanship or the "popular middle-of-the-road line"; rather, it meant studying "what is, why something is the way it is, for what historical and social reasons."[44] Secondly, the association should not be an assembly of notables for whom membership in one or another committee was a matter of honor. Thirdly, the association should not engage in "empire-building" and arrogate to itself tasks better left to decentralized study.

Sociology, then, was to be disciplined discourse and information gathering, but sociologists should be politically articulate. Weber wanted to separate the organizational setting for research from political action. In the fall of 1912 he attempted to organize men from the left wing of the *Verein für Sozialpolitik;* a few met in Leipzig to arrange periodic meetings on the failures and the future of welfare legislation and social reform. Differences of opinion, however, proved too great and no further meetings took place.[45]

At the second annual gathering of the German Sociological Association Weber pleaded once more for the *raison d'être* of the association,

44. *Verhandlungen des Ersten Deutschen Soziologentages,* Frankfurt, 19.– 22. Okt. 1910 (Tübingen: Mohr, 1911), 39f. On the contrast between scientific assessment and ideological judgment and the need for a technical terminology, see also Friedrich von Gottl-Ottlilienfeld, *Die Herrschaft des Wortes* (Jena: Fischer, 1901). Weber esteemed this neglected work and acknowledged it in the prefatory note to *Economy and Society.* Gottl was one of the first expositors and defenders of "jargon" in social science, that means, of terms removed from both common sense meanings and ideological preference. On the definition of value-neutrality (*Werturteilsfreiheit*) see Johannes Winckelmann's article in *Historisches Wörterbuch der Philosophie* (forthcoming).

45. See Weber's *post mortem* circular to the participants dated Nov. 15, 1912, in Bernhard Schäfer, ed., "Ein Rundschreiben Max Webers zur Sozialpolitik," *Soziale Welt,* XVIII, 1967, 261–271.

"somber discussion" and the study of "questions of fact," since the habit of value judgment persisted. As he later said: "Will the gentlemen, none of whom can manage to hold back his subjective 'valuations,' all infinitely uninteresting to me, please stay with their kind. I am absolutely tired of appearing time and again as the Don Quixote of an allegedly unworkable approach and of provoking embarrassing scenes."[46]

This aggressive stand for detachment must be seen in the institutional context of the time. Weber especially abhorred the misuse of the rostrum for the indoctrination of the students, who could neither answer nor argue. "The least tolerable of all prophecies is surely the professor's with its highly personal tinge."[47] However, many students indulged in "zoological nationalism." In that case Weber's postulate involved the attempt to face them with inconvenient facts. Weber also continued Mommsen's struggle for a "science without presuppositions"—Mommsen's war-cry against the repeated intrusion of religious criteria in academic appointments.

Weber's advocacy of field and survey research, a crucial part of his notion of "value-neutral" fact-finding,[48] put him ahead of most of his colleagues, but here he was also his own worst enemy. He was quite successful at raising funds and opening channels for the large-scale projects of the Sociological Association, yet he was not well-suited for the role of project or institute director who furthers research by diplomatically avoiding controversy with clients and colleagues. The press study did not materialize when Weber withdrew as director to avoid biassing the project: Early in 1911 he had begun a lawsuit to force a newspaper to reveal a slanderous source, a move that made him controversial in some press circles.[49] Weber was never content to be a mere student of law; in the nineties he had practiced law along with his teaching and writing. He considered the suit an honorable and pragmatic form of normatively controlled struggle—one of his major scholarly concerns.

46. Marianne Weber, *Lebensbild,* 430.

47. *Ibid.,* 335.

48. On the pioneering efforts of Weber and Tönnies, see Anthony R. Oberschall, *Empirical Social Research in Germany, 1848–1914* (The Hague: Mouton, 1965). Weber and Tönnies stood firmly together in their advocacy of field and survey research. Tönnies strongly backed Weber's notion of value-neutral sociology against Troeltsch. See Ferdinand Tönnies, "Troeltsch und die Philosophie der Geschichte," in his *Soziologische Studien und Kritiken* (Jena: Fischer, 1926), 419f.

49. For Weber's explanation see *Verhandlungen des Zweiten Deutschen Soziologentages,* Berlin, 20.–22. Okt. 1912 (Tübingen: Mohr, 1913), 75ff. On the background of the suit, see below, p. 354, n. 6.

His willingness to fight openly, and to sue if necessary, in academic and personal affairs made him a highly inconvenient man and tended to impair his effectiveness as an organizer of academic enterprises. Weber persistently criticized the corporate failings of the professorial estate. His articles and statements on academic improprieties, the general state of the universities and the need for university reform elicited the public counter-attack, at one time or another, of groups of professors and officials of the ministries of education.[50] In general, his intellectual, political and moral demands were beyond the capabilities of most of his colleagues.

At any rate, in 1912 Weber withdrew completely from his executive duties in the Sociological Association: "I must return now to my scientific work. Things can't go on this way; I am the only one to sacrifice personal scholarly interests, yet I have achieved no more than the bare running of a coasting machine."[51] The work to which he returned was *Economy and Society*.

9. *The Planning of* Economy and Society

Marianne Weber reminisced in her husband's biography that *Economy and Society* "unintendedly grew into the major work of his life."[52] The impetus came from Paul Siebeck, publisher of the famed *Archiv für Sozialwissenschaft und Sozialpolitik,* which Weber, Werner Sombart and Edgar Jaffé had taken over in 1904. In 1909 Siebeck proposed to replace the outdated *Handbuch der politischen Oekonomie* edited by Gustav Schönberg in the eighteen-eighties,[53] which among two dozen contributions contained Schönberg's theory of economic stages (2nd ed., I, 25–45; criticized below on p. 117) and August Meitzen's rationale for agrarian research from a liberal point of view (2nd ed., II, 149–224). Weber agreed to edit an entirely new series. However, the fact that this was a new venture did not prevent an acrimonious academic row, when a young professor who had failed to find contributors for a revised edition of the old handbook accused the publisher and, by implication, Weber of slighting the financial interests of Schönberg's impoverished heirs. Weber came to Siebeck's defense; the young man, in turn, mobilized a group of older professors and threatened a public

50. For an account, see Marianne Weber, *Lebensbild,* 413–17, 430–56.
51. *Ibid.,* 429.
52. *Ibid.,* 425.
53. Gustav Schönberg (ed.), *Handbuch der Politischen Oekonomie* (2 vols.; Tübingen: Laupp, 1882; 2nd revised and enlarged ed. in 3 vols., 1885–86).

scandal. In the ensuing morality play Weber's acute sense of honor and propriety was once again engaged.[54]

The old handbook was limited to the traditional topics of political economy. Weber titled his series *Outline of Social Economics* (*Grundriss der Sozialökonomik*); the term, wider than "institutional economics" and less inclusive than "sociology," enabled him to encompass all relationships of economy and society. He asked a number of men for contributions to be completed within two years. However, some failed in their promises, others produced disappointing manuscripts, still others were dismayed as their contributions were outdated by the resulting delays. The first volumes did not appear until 1914; then the war interrupted the venture. The series closed in 1930 with more than a dozen volumes published. Among contributors well-known in the United States were Robert Michels, Werner Sombart, Joseph Schumpeter, Emil Lederer, Karl Bücher and Alfred Weber. Some titles in the series were: *The Economy and the Science of Economics; Economic Theory; Economy and Nature; Modern Capitalist Economy; Social Stratification Under Capitalism; Welfare Politics Under Capitalism; Foreign Trade and Trade Policies;* there were also several volumes on primary, secondary and tertiary industries.

As the coordination troubles of the projected series mounted, Weber expanded his own contribution. Without this exigency, he might never have attempted a *summa* of his sociology, given his absorption in other interests and his conviction of the "futility of the idea . . . that it could be the goal of the cultural sciences, no matter how distant, to construct a closed system of concepts which can encompass and classify reality in some definitive manner and from which it can be deduced again."[55] Now, however, he was motivated to attempt his own historically open systematization: "Since it was impossible to find a substitute for some [promised but unwritten] contributions, I concluded that I should write a rather comprehensive sociological treatise for the section on *Economy and Society,* to provide an equivalent presentation and to improve the quality of the series. I had to sacrifice other projects much more important to me; in other circumstances I would never have taken on such a task." His wife saw through these complaints: "At last he was under the spell of a great unified task."[56]

In his 1914 introduction to the series Weber spelled out the rationale

54. Marianne Weber, *Lebensbild,* 446–453.
55. GAzW, 184; cf. Shils and Finch (eds.), *Methodology* . . . , 84.
56. Marianne Weber, *Lebensbild,* 424.

of the project: "The basic idea was to study economic development particularly as part of the general rationalization of life. In view of the systematic character of the work the addition of a general economic history has not been planned for the time being."[57]

Tracing the historical lines of rationalization was certainly one of Weber's intentions in *Economy and Society,* as is also indicated by scattered remarks in the text (for example, below, 333). However, the work is not primarily a study in the rationalization and the "disenchantment" of the world.[58] In a letter of June 21, 1914, Weber explained to the redoubtable medievalist Georg von Below his specifically sociological intention:

> This winter I will probably begin with the printing of a fairly voluminous contribution to the *Outline of Social Economics.* I am dealing with the structure of the political organizations in a comparative and systematic manner, at the risk of falling under the anathema: "dilettantes compare." We are absolutely in accord that history should establish what is specific to, say, the medieval city; but this is possible only if we first find what is missing in other cities (ancient, Chinese, Islamic). And so it is with everything else. It is the subsequent task of history to find a causal explanation for these specific traits. I cannot believe that ultimately you think otherwise; some of your remarks speak more for than against my assumption. Sociology, as I understand it, can perform this very modest preparatory work. In this endeavor it is unfortunately almost inevitable to give offense to the researcher who *completely* masters *one* broad field, since it is, after all, impossible to be a specialist in *all* areas. But this does not convince me of the scientific futility of such work. Even my hastily written essay on ancient agrarian history (in the *Handwörterbuch der Staatswissenschaften*) has been useful, including those findings that have been superseded. This seems to me proven

57. In Karl Bücher *et al., Wirtschaft und Wirtschaftswissenschaft,* Section I, Vol. 1 of *Grundriss der Sozialökonomik* (2nd ed.; Tübingen: Mohr, 1924), vii. Upon the urging of students, Weber turned to the task of a general economic history in the winter of 1919/20. This was his last completed lecture course. After his death the lectures were reconstructed from student notes and published as *Wirtschaftsgeschichte. Abriss der universalen Sozial- und Wirtschaftsgeschichte* (3rd ed.; Berlin: Duncker & Humblot, 1958), translated by Frank H. Knight as *General Economic History* (New York: Greenberg, 1927). The *Economic History* suffers from various gaps; the English edition also omits the terminological introduction. The work makes easier reading than *Economy and Society* insofar as it treats phenomena such as the household, neighborhood, kin-group, village, and manor in greater historical continuity; it is inferior in terminological and systematic respects.

58. For an interpretation merely along this line, see Günter Abramowski, *Das Geschichtsbild Max Webers. Universalgeschichte am Leitfaden des okzidentalen Rationalisierungsprozesses* (Stuttgart: Klett, 1966).

by the dissertations of Wilcken's pupils in Leipzig. But the essay was certainly no masterpiece.[59]

In the same year—1914—Weber published a projected table of contents for the *Outline of Social Economics,* including a detailed plan for the manuscript (Part Two) he had written between 1910 and 1914 —Part One was written years later. The table of contents shows that Section III of the *Outline* was titled "Economy and Society" and was to contain two parts, "The Evolution of Systems and Ideals in Economic Policy and Social Reform" by Eugen von Philippovich[60] and "The Economy and the Normative and De Facto Powers" (*Die Wirtschaft und die gesellschaftlichen Ordnungen und Mächte*) by Weber. *Economy and Society* is not, then, the original title of Weber's work. The title now used for Part Two of the work is the "true" one, if more cumbersome in English. However, its meaning is not obvious. Weber does not proceed from the national economy and its relation to society; rather he begins with social action, of which economic action is that rational case concerned with want-satisfaction under conditions of resource scarcity and a limited number of possible actions. The basic "economy" is the "household" in the archaic English sense; in common German parlance *Wirtschaft* may refer to a farm or an inn as well as to the national economy.

The "normative and de facto powers" are the laws and conventions, on the one hand, and the groups that sustain them on the other. The relationship between the normative and the merely coercive, between legitimacy and force, is ever varying in the flux of ideal and material interests and the vicissitudes of power struggle. There are no historically effective ideas and ideals without social interests backing them, and force is rarely used without at least the semblance of a rationale before the staff and the subjects. The formulation of the title expresses these dual forces that impinge on the individual's social action.

Weber's projected table of contents (of Part Two) compares with the chapters of the English edition (in parentheses) as follows:[61]

---

59. The letter is reprinted in the second edition of Georg von Below, *Der deutsche Staat des Mittelalters* (Leipzig: Quelle und Meyer, 1925), xxiv. The dictum "dilettantes compare" was coined by Goethe and hurled by Heinrich Brunner against representatives of the comparative method (cf. *ibid.,* 333).— Weber certainly addressed himself *ad hominem,* but more in emphasis than content.

60. Published in Karl Bücher *et al., op. cit.,* 126–183.

61. The table of contents, which was included in the early volumes of the *Grundriss der Sozialökonomik,* is reprinted in Johannes Winckelmann, "Max Webers Opus Posthumum," *Zeitschrift für die gesamten Staatswissenschaften,* vol. 105, 1949, 370f. In this essay Winckelmann first proposed his reorganization

1. Categories of the Various forms of Social Order (*partly contained in ch. I:1–2, but mostly in "On Some Categories of Interpretive Sociology"; cf. Appendix I, below*)
The Most General Relationships Between Economy and Law (*ch. I:4*)
The Economic Relationships of Organized Groups (*ch. II*)
2. Household, Oikos and Enterprise (*ch. IV*)
3. Neighborhood, Kin Group and Local Community (*ch. III*)
4. Ethnic Group Relationships (*ch. V*)
5. Religious Groups
The Class Basis of the Religions; Complex Religions and Economic Orientation (*ch. VI*)
6. The Market (*ch. VII*)
7. The Political Association (*ch. IX*)
The Social Determinants of Legal Development (*ch. VIII*)
Status Groups, Classes, Parties (*ch. IX:6*)
The Nation (*ch. IX:5*)
8. Domination
   a) The Three Types of Legitimate Domination (*ch. X–XIV*)
   b) Political and Hierocratic Domination (*ch. XV*)
   c) Non-Legitimate Domination. The Typology of Cities (*ch. XVI*)
   d) The Development of the Modern State
   e) The Modern Political Parties

Weber died in 1920 before finishing either Part Two or the later Part One. The last two sections on the modern state and the modern political parties remained unwritten. Weber's table of contents of Part Two was not followed in the two editions undertaken by Marianne Weber and Melchior Palyi (1922 and 1925) and the reprint of 1947 (third ed.). It was not until Johannes Winckelmann's edition of 1956 (fourth ed.) that the intended structure of the manuscript was largely restored.

10. *The Structure of* Economy and Society

The following remarks are not intended to summarize *Economy and Society*, but to elucidate some of Weber's underlying reasoning as well as

of *Wirtschaft und Gesellschaft*. See also his introduction to the 1956 edition (*WuG*, xi–xvii); the preface for the 1964 paperback edition (*WuG*-Studienausgabe, xv–xvi) indicates some further changes.

some of the systematic connections among the chapters, irrespective of their length. Particular attention will be given to the previously untranslated chapters and sections and their relationship with the other parts.

I. PART TWO: THE EARLIER PART

CH. I. THE ECONOMY AND SOCIAL NORMS: ON STAMMLER

Most books have a foil as well as a model. They are written to criticize some books and emulate others. One visible starting point of *Economy and Society* is the attempt at a positive statement of what Rudolf Stammler "should have meant," as Weber put it in the prefatory note to his essay "On Some Categories of Interpretive Sociology" (1913).[62] This essay was part of a longer methodological introduction to the work and corresponds to the first section in the 1914 outline, "Categories of the Various Forms of Social Order."

Like his friends Jellinek, Simmel and Sombart, Weber wrote a critique of Stammler's *Economy and Law According to the Materialist Interpretation of History*.[63] Weber bluntly denied its "right to scientific existence,"[64] but his critique was not identical with his objections to historical materialism. Stammler, a neo-Kantian philosopher, claimed to have systematically deduced the feasibility of objectively correct social action and laid a new epistemological foundation for social science by demonstrating the identity of social ideal and social law. He discussed at great length the relations between legal and economic order and denied their causal relationship in favor of their correspondence as form and content, a position diametrically opposed to Weber's, who repeated in *Economy and Society* (below, 325ff. and 32f.) that his critique was directed against (a) the confusion of the normative with the empirical validity of an order, (b) the confusion of regularities of action due to normative orientation with merely factual regularities, (c) the contrast between convention and law in terms of free will—as if conventions

62. "Über einige Kategorien der verstehenden Soziologie," *Logos*, IV, 1913, reprinted in *GAzW*, 427. See also below, p. 4.

63. Cf. Rudolf Stammler, *Wirtschaft und Recht nach der materialistischen Geschichtsauffassung. Eine sozialphilosophische Untersuchung* (2nd improved ed.; Leipzig: Veit, 1906). For Stammler's definition of the task of the social sciences and a summary of his theory, see 574ff. Weber spoke on the difference between Marx and Stammler at the 1910 meeting of the Sociological Association; cf. *Verhandlungen des Ersten Deutschen Soziologentages*, 96.

64. "R. Stammler's 'Überwindung' der materialistischen Geschichtsauffassung" (1907), reprinted in *GAzW*, 291.

were not coercive—, and (d) the identification of law and convention as the "forms" of conduct as against its "substance."

As a trained jurist and economist Weber was faced with both the normative orientation of jurisprudence and the ethical components of laissez-faire and state-socialist economics. He could develop a sociological approach only by insisting on the separation of the normative and the empirical, a separation accomplished with his theory of social action. In the essay on interpretive sociology and in Part Two of *Economy and Society* he defined social action just as he did later in Part One: subjectively meaningful action oriented to the behavior of others—it is called *Gemeinschaftshandeln* in the older part and *soziales Handeln* in the newer. Normatively regulated action is only one variant of social action. "Sociology, insofar as it is concerned with law, deals not with the logically correct 'objective' content of legal norms but with action for which, *among other considerations,* the ideas of men about the meaning and validity of certain regulations may play a significant role as both determinants and resultants."[65]

Weber elaborated a continuous typology of social action along the line of increasing rational control, persistence and legal compulsion. This typology—partly presented in Appendix I—ranges from mere consensual action (*Einverständnishandeln*) and *ad hoc* agreement (*Gelegenheitsvergesellschaftung*), through various kinds of regulated action and enduring association (*Vergesellschaftung*), to the organization (*Verband*) and compulsory institution (*Anstalt*). These kinds of action differ from behavior that is not social or borderline: *Massenhandeln,* which may be rendered "mass action," "statistically frequent action" or "collective behavior."

In this scheme only men act, neither society nor individual groups. However, men acting in concert form groups (*Gemeinschaften*), and these persist only if they have a "constitution" in the sociological sense, that is, if their order is consensually accepted by members (or outsiders) for whatever reasons. Belief in legitimacy need not be the primary reason. Therefore, Weber deals in the first chapter with the consequences of the factual impact of law on economic conduct.

The economic order is made up of the actual control over goods and services insofar as it is consensually recognized. Sociological economics, then, deals with the actions of men insofar as they are conditioned "by the necessity to take into account the facts of economic life." However, instrumentally rational action must also take into account the fact of law, defined empirically as "guaranteed law": A legal order exists whenever an association is ready to enforce it. Weber makes it immediately

65. *GAzW,* 440. Emphasis added.

clear that law is by no means in all cases "guaranteed" by violence (*Gewalt*), and he rejects the view that "a state exists only if the coercive means of the political community are superior to all other communities" (below, 316).

The two basic categories of an order—convention and law—Weber defines in close proximity to Sumner and in contrast to Stammler. Although conventions are not safeguarded by men (a staff or apparatus) specifically associated to uphold them, they can be enforced just as effectively as law by psychological, and even physical, coercion on the part of the group members. Compliance with a conventional or legal order is frequently determined by a person's self-interest in the continuation of consensual action. Unreflecting habit is another universal reason for regular and regulated behavior. The beginnings of convention and law in habit, usage and custom lie in the realm of inaccessible prehistory. Yet, in view of these powers of persistence, the historian must be able to account for the innovating capacity of men. Rejecting older views of imitation, Weber prefers Hellpach's theory of innovation through inspiration and empathy—an anticipation of the theory of charisma in chs. VI and XIV.

Throughout his analysis, Weber combines his effort at terminological precision with an insistently realistic approach to human affairs: Men are creatures of habit, but they are also strongly motivated by their material and ideal interests to circumvent conventional and legal rules; in all societies the economically powerful tend to have a strong influence on the enactment and interpretation of the law. However, the presence of law, with its various forms of coercion, makes a great deal of difference for social action. On a general level more cannot be said. Here as elsewhere Weber carefully points out the limits of generalization: "The extent of the law's factual impact on economic conduct cannot be determined generally, but must be calculated for each particular case."

CH. II: ON MARX, MICHELS AND SOMBART

Weber's emphasis on the limits of generalization has here a critical thrust directed against historical materialism and economic functionalism (below, 341). A work on economy and society must sooner or later take a stand on historical materialism—Weber took his stand at the first appropriate moment. It would be wrong, however, to say that the critique of historical materialism occupies the dominant place in the work, above and beyond Weber's other polemical and positive interests. What may appear at first sight as "reaction" to, or "reflection" of, historical materialism—such as Weber's interest in ancient capitalism—more often stands in a tradition of economic and legal history of which Marxism was an extreme offshoot. Weber recognized historical materialism as a political force but did not take its ultimate claims seriously. About the time this chapter was written, he told his peers at the first meeting of the Sociological Association:

> I would like to protest the statement by one of the speakers that some one factor, be it technology or economy, can be the "ultimate" or "true" cause of another. If we look at the causal lines, we see them run, at one time, from technical to economic and political matters, at another from political to religious and economic ones, etc. There is no resting point. In my opinion, the view of historical materialism, frequently espoused, that the economic is in some sense the ultimate point in the chain of causes is completely finished as a scientific proposition.[66]

Weber also rejects economic functionalism insofar as it postulated an unambiguous interdependence of economic and non-economic elements. Not all social action is economically influenced, and not all groups are economically relevant. Culturally important groups, however, have some kind of relationship with economic elements; all persistent groups must in some way meet their wants. Weber presents a simple typology of economically active groups, ranging from economic groups proper, through various economically active groups and those merely influenced by economic factors, to regulatory groups of a political, religious or other nature.[67] (In line with the reasoning in ch. I, regulatory groups belong into an economic typology of groups.)

Although Weber gave attention to the technological factor in history, he related want satisfaction primarily to modes of appropriation and expropriation, not to modes of production. The crucial importance of appropriation appears at first sight as a "quasi-Marxist" position, but in fact is another difference from Marx. Weber saw the Marxist concept of the mode of production blurring the technological and economic aspects. He explained before the Sociological Association:

> To my knowledge, Marx has not defined technology. There are many things in Marx that not only appear contradictory but actually are found contrary to fact if we undertake a thorough and pedantic analysis, as indeed we must. Among other things, there is an oft-quoted passage: The hand-mill results in feudalism, the steam-mill in capitalism. That is a technological, not an economic construction, and as an assertion it is simply false, as we can clearly prove. For the age of the hand-mill, which extended up to modern times, had cultural "super-structures" of all conceivable kinds in all fields.[68]

66. *Verhandlungen des Ersten Deutschen Soziologentages*, 101.

67. In Part Two the economically active groups are called *Gemeinschaften*, in Part One *Verbände* (organizations).

68. *Verhandlungen, op. cit.*, 95f. The point is repeated below, 1091.

Such superstructures are related to modes of appropriation, which emerge from the competition for livelihood but also depend on the nature of an object, material or immaterial. Weber does accept the historical generalization that free property and acquired rights grew out of the gradual appropriation by group members of their shares in the group's holdings. Private property became important with the disintegration of the old monopolist associations. It is a recurrent process in history that decreasing opportunities lead to monopolization; then legally privileged groups with privileged members (*Rechtsgenossen*) and organs come into being. Weber lists the stages of the appropriation of opportunities through external and internal closure. With fine nominalist irony he mixes contemporary examples from Imperial Germany with historically early illustrations (below, 342).

Once an organization has been established, the vested interests of the organs (functionaries, officials) tend to perpetuate or transform it beyond the original purpose. This phenomenon of institutionalization was a controversial point between Weber and his friend Robert Michels, who was just completing his *Political Parties* (1911).[69] Whereas Michels reified his observations into the "iron law of oligarchy" and thus stressed the sameness of the phenomena at issue, Weber pointed to the multiple, and often contradictory, consequences of institutionalization, which might lead to monopolization *or* expansionism (ch. II:3). For Weber the greatest historical example for the expansionist tendency was the age-old connection of capitalist interests with imperialism. The expansionist tendencies of an organization could, however, be restrained by monopolist interests. In voluntary organizations the rational primary purpose might be overshadowed by "communal" goals if social action involved personal elements (below, 346), thus promoting closure and establishing social legitimacy.

Irrespective of this dualism, most rationally organized groups must satisfy their wants in one or more of the following ways: (1) the *oikos*; (2) market-oriented assessments; (3) production for the market; (4) maecenatic support; (5) contributions and services linked to positive and negative privileges (ch. II:4).

With this typology Weber completes the economic framework for the substantive theme that runs through all of *Economy and Society*: the preconditions and the rise of modern capitalism. Subsequently, this

69. On the close intellectual relationship between Michels and Weber, see my *The Social Democrats in Imperial Germany* (Totowa, N.J.: Bedminster Press, 1963), 249–257; cf. also Juan Linz, "Michels e il suo contributo alla sociologia politica," introduction to Roberto Michels, *La Sociologia del Partito politico nella Democrazia moderna* (Bologna: Il Mulino, 1966), 7–119.

problem is treated from several vantage points: the household and other relatively universal groups (chs. III–V), religion (ch. VI), law (ch. VIII), political community (ch. IX), and the various kinds of rulership (chs. X–XVI). This underlying theme, however, does not determine the typological structure of the chapters; moreover, it is paralleled by the themes of rationalization in religion, law and politics. In view of the importance that Weber attributed to the political factor in his previous work, it is no surprise that his first historical explanation (ch. II:5) concerns the way in which the fiscal and monetary policies of the modern states made possible the rise and persistence of capitalism.

The issue of the origins of capitalism puts *Economy and Society* besides the work that apparently was both inspiration and foil: Werner Sombart's *Modern Capitalism*.[70] Its two massive volumes were published in 1902, shortly before Weber began writing "The Protestant Ethic and the Spirit of Capitalism." Sombart and Weber had been close allies since the mid-nineties. Weber unsuccessfully tried to have Sombart succeed him in Freiburg when he left for Heidelberg in 1897; in the reactionary nineties—the so-called Era Stumm—official resistance to Sombart was too strong. Both men shared a wide interest in the capitalist enterprise, the spirit of capitalism, social reform and the labor movement, and together they advocated the value-neutral approach in the *Archiv für Sozialwissenschaft*. Sombart was the more flamboyant of the two and proved to be more mercurial. On the one hand, he demanded "facts, facts, facts—this admonition rang in my ears all the time I was writing the book." On the other, he also tried to explain them from ultimate causes: "What separates me from Schmoller and his school is the constructive element in the ordering of the material, the radical postulate of a uniform explanation from last causes, the reconstruction of all historical phenomena as a social system, in short, what I call the specifically theoretical. I also might say: Karl Marx."[71]

This was not much more than a rhetorical declaration exaggerating the difference from his former teacher Schmoller. The work failed to link the many facts with its postulate and showed that Sombart was

70. Werner Sombart, *Der moderne Kapitalismus,* vol. I: *Die Genesis des Kapitalismus,* vol. II: *Die Theorie der kapitalistischen Entwicklung* (Leipzig: Duncker & Humblot, 1902). Vol. III appeared much later as *Das Wirtschaftsleben im Zeitalter des Hochkapitalismus* (Munich: Duncker & Humblot, 1927). For Talcott Parsons' interpretation of Sombart's relation to Marx, on the one hand, and to Weber on the other, see his *Structure of Social Action* (Glencoe, Ill.: The Free Press, 1949), 495–499, and "Capitalism in Recent German Literature: Sombart and Weber," *Journal of Political Economy,* vol. 36, 1928, 641–661, and vol. 37, 1929, 31–51. Parsons, however, does not deal with the question of the extent to which Weber's writings were a direct response to Sombart.

71. Sombart, *op. cit.,* I, xii and xxix.

already far removed from Marxism, if he ever was an orthodox Marxist. At any rate, Weber did not consider the postulate feasible, but he was interested in Sombart's facts and decided to approach them through systematic comparative study. Since this involved a methodological difference, it was more than a mere sensible division of labor.[72] Sombart contrasted the traditionalist orientation of craft production with the spirit of capitalism, which to both men appeared very different from the universal desire for wealth. This spirit was a peculiarly European phenomenon, but Sombart barely hinted at the comparative perspective: "A glance at other major civilizations, such as the Chinese, Indian, or ancient American, is enough to prove, in this regard too, the insufficiency of the view that the genesis of modern capitalism can be explained from a 'general law of development' of the human economy."[73] Where Sombart merely glanced, Weber proceeded to the comparisons of *Economy and Society* and, immediately afterwards, the studies of China, India and ancient Judaism.

CHS. III–V: THE RELATIVELY UNIVERSAL GROUPS

At the beginning of ch. III Weber limits his use of the term "society" to "the general kinds of human groups." He intends to deal with economy and society in this sense, not with economy and *Kultur*—literature, art, science. The first groups to be treated are relatively universal—household, neighborhood, kin group, ethnic group, religious group, political community—; in other words, they are found at various levels of historical development. The "developmental forms" of these groups are taken up in the Sociology of Domination. The treatment of the more basic forms is intentionally brief, in part because Weber is primarily interested in the more differentiated associations and their relationship to religion, law and politics, in part, presumably, because Marianne Weber had dealt with some of the subject matter at length in her work on *Wife and Mother in Legal Development* (1907). Weber limits himself to a series of points that either have polemical value or prepare the later exposition. His critical targets are evolutionary conceptions, especially the theory of matriarchy and the related socialist theory of family, property and the state (Engels and Bebel); the neighborhood sentimentalism of agrarian romantics; Gierke's notion of the kin group as the first political association; and racist and nationalist ideas. Against the Romanticist notions of those mourning the passing of Community, but also against the apostles of Progress, Weber endeavors to show that

72. Cf. Parsons, "Capitalism . . . ," *loc. cit.*, 31, 50.
73. Sombart, *op. cit.*, I, 379.

"communal" and rationalist, capitalist and communist, traditionalist and modernist elements appear in ever new combinations—in short, that history is not the progression from *Gemeinschaft* to *Gesellschaft*.

Positively, Weber points out: The household is the original locus of patriarchal rulership and the capitalist enterprise; the neighborhood is an unsentimental economic brotherhood; the kin group is the protective counter-force to the authoritarian household; ethnic groups are not groups, strictly speaking, but propensities for, or residues of, group formation. Weber particularly stresses the pluralism of group affiliation in relatively undeveloped societies before the emerging political community gradually monopolizes the use of force—contrary to the view that modern society is more pluralist than traditionalist society in this respect.

Weber sees no evidence for a universal stage of matriarchy. He explains maternal groupings as a result of military separation of the males from the household. This separation produces the men's house, which nowadays appears in residual form in army barracks and student dormitories—Weber likes to move back and forth, often with ironic undertones, between the ancient origin of a phenomenon and its survival into modern times. The patriarchal household emerges with the military dispersion of warriors in the countryside. In dealing with polygamy and monogamy Weber provides a specifically economic, non-romantic explanation. Monogamy suited the household of the emergent urban patriciate; only later did Christianity raise it to an ethical level. With the dowry the calculative spirit entered the domestic communism of the family. This spirit reached a high point with the rise of the capitalist family enterprise. The legal forms of early modern capitalism originated in part in the communistic household, as Weber had already shown in his dissertation. The enterprise was eventually separated from the household, but Weber points to an historical twist: a "later" economic stage, such as capitalism, may perpetuate or recreate an "earlier" (communistic) family structure in which the extended family remains a unit: "Beyond the balance sheet, those lucky enough to participate enter the realm of equality and brotherhood" (below, 360)—a reference to the communist slogan. Here Weber takes obvious pleasure in outdoing the dialectic of historical materialism. His general point is that the household and domestic authority are relatively independent of economic conditions; in fact, they often shape economic relationships because of their historically developed structure. Weber believed that the contractual regulation of household relations was a peculiarly Occidental phenomenon. Only in Europe did the household create out of itself the capitalist enterprise; elsewhere it developed into the *oikos,* the economic basis of patrimonial domination.

Households are related to one another through neighborliness in an unpathetic, economic sense. The neighbor is the typical helper in need. Thus, neighborliness is not restricted to social equals, but customary help rendered by social inferiors may gradually turn into manorial service. The neighborhood may become an economic group proper or an economically regulatory group, but even in the self-sufficient economy of early times there is no necessary identity between neighborhood and other associations. Only in the case of joint political action can the neighborhood develop into a local community.

The kin group is usually not an extension of the household but a protective group guaranteeing the security and legal protection of the individual. Collective self-help is the most typical means for the defense of its interests. The oldest trial procedures originate in compulsory arbitration within, and between, kin groups. Insofar as kin groups do not have a head with powers of command and a staff, they are not organizations in Weber's sense. Through their regulation of marriage and lineage relations kin groups may effectively curb domestic authority. Similarly, the property laws of the great empires steadily weaken unlimited patriarchal power, but because of the very predominance of patriarchalism—another dialectical feature of historical development. Kin groups may oppose political associations and cross the boundaries of political communities. They tend to become associations only when economic conditions make it desirable to erect monopolies against outsiders.

Race and ethnicity are familiar devices for the monopolist protection of interests. Weber doubts the sociological utility of both concepts if understood in a naturalistic way. He insists that, regardless of the outcome of genetic research, social behavior must be interpreted primarily in social terms. Ethnic membership derives from some consciousness of kind due to common customs, common language and common historical experiences. It may be the product of political association and may remain after the group has dissolved politically. The cultural and political importance of ethnicity rests on the fact that the sense of ethnic honor is a specific honor of the masses and, in the extreme, leads to the notion of the chosen people.

Weber's sketch of nationality and cultural prestige (ch. V:4) illuminates the political situation of Central Europe before the first World War. The section is closely linked to the chapter on the political communities (ch. IX). However, Weber had one more major universal group to deal with: the religious *Gemeinschaft*. In theoretical complexity, originality and sheer size the chapter on religious groups was bound to transcend the preceding chapters.

CH. VI: THE SOCIOLOGY OF RELIGION

In 1902 Sombart touched on the impact of Calvinism and Quakerism on capitalist development and noted that it was "too well-known a fact to require detailed explanation."[74] Weber, far from being deterred by this dismissal, proceeded to state more fully the case for the Protestant ethic's impact on the spirit of capitalism.[75] He may also have been prompted by Schmoller, who in a masterful review of Sombart, his most exasperating pupil, observed:

> Whatever Marx and the Social Democrats have against the capitalist—the "hunger for profit" and the untrammeled ruthlessness toward the worker's welfare—concerns primarily the manner in which the individualist drive for acquisition developed between 1500 and 1900 and cut itself loose from most earlier moral and social restraints. These phenomena must be investigated if one wants to understand today's economy.[76]

If it is unclear whether Schmoller's suggestion really was a major factor in Weber's decision to write the "Protestant Ethic and the Spirit of Capitalism," it can be stated affirmatively that the relationship between Calvinism and capitalism had been an "internal" academic issue for some time and that Weber wrote in response to other studies, and

74. Sombart, *op. cit.*, I, 381.

75. Weber stated the major differences between Sombart's approach and his own in the 1920 re-issue of "Die Protestantische Ethik und der Geist des Kapitalismus," GAzRS, I (1920), 34; for other references to Sombart see *ibid.*, 5, 21, 33, 38 *et passim;* these include his replies to Sombart's later critiques. Weber explained: "Although the essays go back, in all important respects, to much earlier studies of mine, I need scarcely emphasize how much their presentation owes to the mere existence of Sombart's substantial works, with their pointed formulations, even—and especially—where they diverge from them" (*ibid.*, 42). In his last anti-critique Weber mentioned that he had presented some of his ideas on the Protestant ethic in his courses at the University of Heidelberg in 1897/98. See "Antikritisches zum 'Geist' des Kapitalismus," AfS, XXX, 1910, 177.

76. Gustav Schmoller on Sombart in his *Jahrbuch für Gesetzgebung, Verwaltung und Volkswirtschaft,* vol. 27, 1903, 298; cf. Lindenlaub, *Richtungskämpfe . . . , op. cit.,* 287. It is true that Weber did not recognize Schmoller, the most powerful figure in the *Verein für Sozialpolitik,* as one of his teachers and openly disagreed with him in political matters, but this may have been more of an additional incentive than a hindrance to prove to him what could be done in this regard. In fact, Schmoller later worked Weber's findings into his *Grundriss der allgemeinen Volkswirtschaftslehre* (Leipzig: Duncker & Humblot, 1908). Marianne Weber believed that Weber had started the first essay on the Protestant ethic ". . . in 1903, probably in the second half, just after finishing the first part of his treatise on Roscher and Knies" (*Lebensbild,* 340). Schmoller published Weber's treatise on "Roscher and Knies and the Logical Problems of Historical Economics" in his *Jahrbuch* in the fourth issue of the 1903 volume, having reviewed Sombart in the first issue.

not just against historical materialism as has sometimes been suggested in spite of his own denial at the end of the work.[77] Weber acknowledged particularly the earlier work of three colleagues: Eberhard Gothein's monumental study modestly entitled *Economic History of the Black Forest,* Werner Wittich's "tremendously perceptive remarks" on religious differences between France and Germany, and Georg Jellinek's "proof of religious traces in the genesis of the Rights of Man . . . which gave me a crucial stimulus . . . to investigate the impact of religion in areas where one might not otherwise look."[78]

The publication of the two essays on the Protestant ethic in the *Archiv für Sozialwissenschaft* in 1904/5 was an instantaneous literary success and almost immediately led to the controversy that has since continued unabated. The exchange of critiques and anti-critiques between Weber and his adversaries lasted until 1910.[79] Weber considered the exchanges "pretty unrewarding" and decided on another positive statement, which became the present chapter. He left the historical treatment of Protestantism to his friend Ernst Troeltsch, who was then working on *The Social Teachings of the Christian Churches and Sects,*[80] and instead put the theme in a comparative perspective. Yet neither the "underlying" issue of the rise of capitalism nor that of rationalization and secularization over the ages determines the structure of the Sociology of Religion; it is built, rather, around the relation of *religions* to

77. For example, Parsons has written that "the essay was intended to be a refutation of the Marxian thesis in a particular historical case." However, Weber's general theoretical interest in the critique of historical materialism should not be equated with his reasons for writing the essays at that time. Cf. Parsons, "Capitalism . . . ," *loc. cit.,* 40.

78. Cf. Eberhard Gothein, *Wirtschaftsgeschichte des Schwarzwaldes* (Strassburg: Trübner, 1892), 674; Werner Wittich, *Deutsche und französische Kultur im Elsass* (Strassburg: Schlesier & Schweikhardt, 1900), 18–32 (the quote is from GAzRS, I, 25; cf. below, 396); Georg Jellinek, *Die Erklärung der Menschen- und Bürgerrechte* (Leipzig: Duncker & Humblot, 1895; 2nd ed., 1904), *passim* (cf. below, 1209)—the quote is from Weber's memorial address on Jellinek (René König and Johannes Winckelmann, eds., *Max Weber zum Gedächtnis* [Köln: Westdeutscher Verlag, 1963], 15).—On the general familiarity of the 18th and 19th-century literature with the relationship between religious dissent and economic motivation, Protestantism and capitalism, see Reinhard Bendix, "The Protestant Ethic—Revisited," in *Comparative Studies in Society and History,* IX:3, 1967, 266–273.

79. For an account, see Ephraim Fischoff, "The Protestant Ethic and the Spirit of Capitalism: The History of a Controversy," *Social Research,* XI, 1944, 52–77.

80. Ernst Troeltsch, *Die Soziallehren der christlichen Kirchen und Gruppen* (Tübingen: Mohr, 1912), in part published earlier in the form of articles in *AfS,* 1908–10; trsl. by O. Wyon (London: Allen & Unwin, 1931).

their organizational carriers (functionaries), to the status groups and classes supporting them, and to their inherent theological elaboration. Weber took the general functions of religion, whether in a Durkheimian or a Marxist sense, for granted. With his customary realism, he stressed the compensatory functions of religion and, even more, the political uses of religion for legitimation and pacification. In a limited way, it is possible to see his sociology of religion as a vast paraphrase of Marx's dictum that "religion is the sigh of a creature in distress, the heart of a heartless world, the spirit of times without spirit. It is the opiate of the people."[81] But there is an important difference: Weber had a much more profound sense than Marx for the meaning of ethical conduct. The religious polemics of Engels, August Bebel and Karl Kautsky appeared to him as shallow rationalism. Possibly, Weber was familiar with Engels' fleeting remarks on Calvinism: "Where Luther failed, Calvin triumphed. His dogma was adapted to the most daring of the bourgeois. His doctrine of predestination was the religious expression of the fact that in the commercial world of competition success or bankruptcy depend not on the enterprise or skill of the individual but on circumstances independent of him."[82] At any rate, the "Protestant Ethic and the Spirit of Capitalism" reversed this materialist interpretation without substituting a mere spiritualist one. Behind the divergent perspectives of Weber and the Marxists was a personal difference: The Marxists were psychologically unable to take religion seriously enough to undertake his kind of study. Weber called himself "unmusical" in matters religious—this gave him the necessary analytical distance—, but he lived in an extended family in which the women were devout and articulate believers. With his strong family sense, Weber could have disdained religion only at the price of offending those closest to him—this gave him the requisite empathy for the study of religion.[83]

For systematic reasons, ch. VI begins with a brief treatment of primitive religion and the original this-worldly orientation of magical and religious action (secs. i–ii).[84] Weber quickly sketches the rise of functional, local and, finally, universalist and monotheist conceptions of deity. As in the preceding chapters, his ethnographic examples are occasionally doubtful or erroneous, or a statement may suffer from the telescoping of historical events over millennia, or the love of paradox

81. Karl Marx, "Zur Kritik der Hegelschen Rechtsphilosophie," in Die Frühschriften (Stuttgart: Kröner, 1953), 208.

82. Friedrich Engels, English introduction to Socialism Utopian and Scientific (London 1892), published in German in Neue Zeit, XI:1–2, 1892/93; Marx/Engels, Werke (Berlin: Dietz, 1963), vol. 22, 300.

83. Cf. Marianne Weber, Lebensbild, 27, 84, 88, 91f, 351f.

84. For an explanation of Weber's intention, see below, 421, n. 1.

carries him to an extreme. When he comes to the rationalization of conduct through ethical and exemplary prophecy (secs. *iii–iv*), Weber strikes out on his own. Building on Harnack's typology, he isolates the features peculiar to the prophet through a comparison with magicians, lawgivers, teachers of ethics and mystagogues. Prophets and priests organize the permanent association of laymen: the congregation. Prophets develop preaching and pastoral care, priests the dogmata and the canonical writings.

After thus dealing with the religious leaders and the associations created by them Weber turns to an examination of all major social strata and their affinity to religion (secs. *v–vi*). This provides a comparative frame for assessing the Puritan bourgeoisie, but in the context of the present work it also prepares the treatment of aristocratic and bureaucratic rulership, the role of the intelligentsia, and the themes of bureaucratization and democratization. Aristocrats tend toward irreligion, unless they are warriors for the faith, an historically important, but transitional phenomenon. Bureaucrats are inclined toward a formalistic religion or philosophy, while permitting less complex magical beliefs among the masses for the sake of "mass domestication." The urban bourgeois, even though concerned with economic rationality, tends to be more religious than the aristocrat and bureaucrat. In fact, the rationalist piety of bourgeois believers is a step on the road that ultimately led to the Protestant ethic. Non-privileged strata have powerful needs for salvation, but they may find primarily passive or purely affective expression. Weber goes down the social ladder from the craftsmen's piety, so important in early Christianity, to the religious disinclinations of slaves, day laborers and the modern proletariat. Peasants are traditionally concerned not with salvation but with the practical, magical effects of religion, even though in modern times the rural population is a mainstay of Christian conservatism. Salvation religions, usually the creation of intellectuals of higher social rank, can devolve into the creed of non-privileged strata, changing their function from legitimation to compensation. Pariah peoples tend to develop an intense religious attachment —Judaism being the historically decisive case.

After this tour de force in the sociology of knowledge Weber balances his analysis of status tendencies with an investigation of religious intellectualism (secs. *vii–xi*). Intellectuals of *diverse* status elaborate religions on logical and theological grounds. Status differences may recede in the face of changing political fortunes; an important case is the escapism of intellectuals of politically declining strata or defeated communities. Conversely, nativist lower-class intellectuals may turn against the intellectualism of higher strata, as it happened in Judaism and early

Christianity vis-à-vis Hellenized intellectuals. Weber carries his analysis up to his own time, ending with secular salvation ideologies and some biting remarks on café-house intellectuals (sec. *vii*:8).

The last part (secs. *xii–xv*) examines the influence of religious ethics on the "world": the sphere of the economic, political, artistic, and sexual. The last extant section breaks off with yet another attempt to contrast Jewish rationalism, Puritan asceticism, Islamic this-worldliness, Buddhist other-worldliness and Jesus' indifference to the world—all with a look back toward "The Protestant Ethic," but also in anticipation of the subsequent large-scale studies of the great world religions, to which Weber turned without completing Part Two of *Economy and Society*.

CH. VII. THE MARKET: ITS IMPERSONALITY AND ETHIC

The chapter on the market—another group (*Gemeinschaft*) in Weber's terminology—logically follows the treatment of religion. The economically rationalized, hence ethically irrational, character of pure market relationships is basically irreconcilable with ethical religion— with the historic exception of Calvinism. Whereas Weber gave much attention to the chapter on religion, his market chapter is only a brief sketch. Unlike the sociology of religion, the market was a topic that could be handled by many other men. Perhaps Weber postponed writing the chapter because he waited for other contributions to the series, the better to coordinate the various expositions. In any case, the fragment he did write was sufficient to distinguish the market (*Marktgemeinschaft* or *Marktvergemeinschaftung*) from the more "natural" groups and the political community. The market is the *Gemeinschaft* based on the most rational kind of social action: association (*Vergesellschaftung*) through exchange. The association may last only for the duration of the exchange, or it may develop into a continuous relationship.

In early history the market was the only peaceful relationship of men who were not linked through household, kinship or tribal ties. The participants were strangers, "enemies" who did not expect action in accordance with an ethic of brotherhood. The "community" of the market is the most impersonal group, but not because it involves struggle (*Kampf*) between opposed interests—there is struggle also in the most intimate relationships; rather, the market is the more impersonal, the more the struggle of the participants is oriented merely to actual or potential exchanges. In this manner the market is the exact opposite of any association (*Vergesellschaftung*) based on a formal order, voluntary or imposed. Even so, neither the use of money nor the impersonality of exchange prevent the eventual rise of a market ethic binding on those who continually trade. Such exchange partners develop expectations of reciprocity which make them abide by the rules. Occasional traders are most likely to ignore the maxim that "honesty is the best policy"; Weber sarcastically cites aristocratic cavalry officers trading horses—a familiar current example is the private sale of automobiles. One aspect of the market ethic is the fixed price, a peculiarly European phenomenon that became one of the preconditions of modern capitalism.

The market proved destructive to many status monopolies of the past. Yet the very success of capitalist interests on the free market led to new monopolies based either on political alliances or sheer superiority over competitors. As markets increased in importance, religious and political associations moved to protect them for reasons of their own. This brings Weber to the organizations concerned with legal regulation.

CH. VIII. THE SOCIOLOGY OF LAW

The Sociology of Law gives historical depth to the introductory statement on convention and law (ch. I).[85] After the earlier methodological critique of Stammler's approach Weber now demonstrates what a sociology of law should be, in contrast to legal philosophy, jurisprudence, and mere legal history. The chapter provides a typological setting within which a given legal phenomenon can be located, not with regard to any systematically or dogmatically proper placement but for the sake of historical explanation. The impact of Roman law and common law on the rise of capitalism constitutes one link with the overall theme of *Economy and Society;* another is the varieties of rationalization, which may be mutually incompatible. The chapter is also constructed with a view to the frequently mentioned Sociology of Domination: Here Weber treats the creation and administration of law by political and other associations,

85. Chs. I and VIII are the only sections of *Wirtschaft und Gesellschaft* that could be compared with the original manuscript. Marianne Weber put these chapters in an envelope marked "Sociology of Law"—ch. VIII had no manuscript title—and presented them as a gift to Karl Loewenstein, whom they accompanied into exile, thus escaping the fate of the rest of the manuscript. On the basis of this original, now at the Max Weber Institute in Munich, Johannes Winckelmann prepared a definitive edition—although Weber's almost illegible handwriting leaves some passages doubtful—of the two chapters; see *Rechtssoziologie* (2nd ed.; Neuwied: Luchterhand, 1967). The text now differs considerably from that in the 1925 edition of *Wirtschaft und Gesellschaft,* on which the Rheinstein-Shils translation of the Sociology of Law was based. The changes involve not merely many printing errors, but also the sequence of sections and terminological clarifications. For example, the category of the "coercive contract" (*Zwangskontrakt*) turned out to be a misreading of *Zweckkontrakt,* which (in sec. *ii*) contrasts with *Statuskontrakt,* a distinction related to Henry Sumner Maine's *Ancient Law* (1861).

there the ruler's legitimation, organizational power and motives for im-posing law.

If Weber was a self-made scholar in affairs religious, he was on academic homeground in the Sociology of Law. Not only do legal topics of his dissertation and *Habilitation* of two decades before appear, but so does much of the later literature. Even as Weber broadened his intellec-tual concerns, he retained an active interest in legal studies. His ability to write the Sociology of Law as a legal historian makes this the most difficult chapter for the legal layman and mere sociologist, for whom it may be helpful to perceive the broad structural parallels with the So-ciology of Religion.[86] The substitution of legal for religious topics yields the following rough outline: the basic categories of public and private law; the development of contracts and of juristic personality; early forms of law administered by non-political associations; an occupational typol-ogy of "specialists," ranging from charismatic law prophets to legal *honoratiores* and university-trained judges; a typology of various forms of legal training; the historical systems of theocratic and secular law; a comparison of Indian, Islamic, Persian, Jewish, Canon and Roman law; the great codifications; the revolutionary power of natural law; formal and substantive rationalization and the ineradicable tension between formal and substantive justice; finally, the irrationalist trends at the eve of the first World War, with their "characteristic reaction" to formal ra-tionality and the dominance of legal experts—paralleling the fashion of surrogate religions in intellectual circles and the "romantic game of syndicalism." Here Weber continues the sociology of intellectuals with an examination of their propensity for substantive justice, on the one hand, and skepticism on the other; he points to another historical dialectic: 19th-century socialist intellectuals first advanced substantive natural law against the formalist natural law of the bourgeoisie and then undermined their own position through positivistic relativism and Marxist evolutionism.

The gradual ascendancy of state law over the law of the other groups is part of the larger theme of the rise of the political community. Weber follows juridical usage when he makes the existence of a legal order dependent on a staff ready to resort to physical or psychic coercion, and when he defines the *modern* political community—the state—in terms of its monopoly on the legal use of force. As a sociologist, however, he is

---

86. For interpretations of the Sociology of Law by jurists, see the introduc-tions by Rheinstein (*Max Weber on Law in Economy and Society*, 1954, xxv–lxxi) and Winckelmann (*Rechtssoziologie*, 1967, 15–49); also Karl Engisch, "Max Weber als Rechtsphilosoph und als Rechtssoziologe," in K. Engisch, B. Pfister and J. Winckelmann, eds., *Max Weber: Gedächtnisschrift der Ludwig-Maximilians-Universität München* (Berlin: Duncker & Humblot, 1966), 67–88.

equally concerned with the extent to which this claim is *de facto* limited in the modern state, where conventional and religious sanctions continue to be powerful. Weber remembered as one of his youthful lessons the inability of the mighty Prussian state to triumph over the Catholic church in the *Kulturkampf* of the eighteen-seventies and again over the Social Democrats in the eighties, the period of the anti-socialist laws.

The chapter on political communities links the chapters on the more "universal" groups and the Sociology of Law with the Sociology of Domination; it describes the development of political community from rudimentary beginnings to complex differentiation.[87] For many centuries the political community differed only quantitatively from the other relatively "universal" groups that gradually lost their protective and coercive functions as the old political pluralism declined. Eventually a qualitative difference developed: a belief in the right of the state to define the legal order and the use of legitimate force. This belief in legitimacy resulted from gradual usurpation. Previously, the notion of legitimate force was part of the *consensual* action of kin members engaging in blood revenge; now it became part of the *organized* action (*Verbandshandeln*) of community members. In the modern state, the exercise of political powers (*Gewalt*) is a part of *institutional* action (*anstaltsmaessiges Handeln*).[88]

87. Until the fourth (1956) edition of *Wirtschaft und Gesellschaft,* the *Gemeinschaften* ranging from the household to the religious and legal associations and even the city were arranged into a separate part (Part Two, "Typen der Vergemeinschaftung und Vergesellschaftung") set off against the types of domination (Part Three, "Typen der Herrschaft") which included the political community. There is no warrant for this division in Weber's 1914 outline or in the logic of his exposition. The categories of social action and group formation (*Vergemeinschaftung, Vergesellschaftung, Herrschaft*) encompass all of the present Part Two, although the detailed treatment of *Herrschaft* is reserved for the last chapters. The definition of *Herrschaft* appears first, together with the other basic concepts, in "The Categories of Interpretive Sociology" (App. I, 1378 below) and in the first chapter of Part One.

88. In English, the use of "political power" for *politische Gewalt* can easily be misleading. Therefore the plural "powers" or the singular "authority" has been used. Linguistic habit and stylistic convenience make it difficult to render Weber's social action terms always in such ways as to avoid the impression that it is groups, rather than individuals, which act. "Organized action" is *organization-oriented* action and "institutional action" *institution-oriented* action; likewise, "class action" (below, 929) is *class-oriented* action and "party action" (below, 938) *party-oriented* action—four varieties of social action that contrast with "mass action." The juxtaposition of social and mass action was obscured in the Gerth and Mills translation of ch. IX:6, which interpolated the terminology of Part One (ch. I:9) into the text of Part Two (cf. Gerth and Mills, *From Max Weber* . . . , 183). In the different terminology of Part Two, *Gemeinschaftshandeln* means "social action," not "communal action," and *Vergesellschaftung* means

CH. IX. POLITICAL COMMUNITY AND STATE

The political community is a group ready to defend a given territory with force against outsiders. This minimum definition is designed to encompass all historical communities and thus does not even include the guarantee of internal security. Many communities actually did limit themselves to nothing more than the maintenance of territorial control. The Pennsylvanian commonwealth of the Quakers was exceptional in that it refused for a time to use external force. Between these two extremes social action may be oriented to any number of goals, and therefore a community may be robber state, welfare state, constitutional state or *Kulturstaat*. Communities united merely for defense may in peacetime relapse into a state of anarchy (in the strict sense)—the mere consensual recognition among the members of the given economic order. And external peacetime may also be a period of internal war. Thus the ascendancy of the political community over other groups becomes the history of internal pacification: of the peace edicts of kings, bishops and cities during their struggles with the feuding nobility. Old and new groups whose ideal and material interests were not adequately protected by the traditional arrangements demanded pacification and the "nationalization" of legal norms (treated in the Sociology of Law).

Weber clearly distinguishes between patriarchal powers, "nonauthoritarian" consensual and arbitral powers, and political powers proper—autonomous military and judicial authority. The prototype for political powers is the *imperium* of the legitimate Roman officials (ch. VIII:*vi*), which later was usurped by military leaders who received *ex post facto* confirmation by the Senate. Political authority (*Gewalt*) involves the power over life and death which gives the political community its specific pathos. As the community develops, political coercion frequently becomes internal, since many demands of the political order are accepted by the members only under pressure. However, a political community is held together not only through coercion but also through common historical experiences: it is a "community of shared memory" (*Erinnerungsgemeinschaft*). Yet both the pathos of the supreme sacrifice and the shared memory of dangers persist also in other groups ranging from those practicing violence—the Camorra, nowadays the Mafia—to those suffering it, as in persecuted sects.

After an historical sketch of the development of political community

---

"association," not "societal action"—i.e., it is not a contrast in Toennies' sense (cf. below, 60, n. 24). Hence, terminological adjustments had to be made. For example, the seemingly illogical passage, "The communal actions of parties always mean a societalization" (Gerth and Mills, *op. cit.*, 194) now reads "party-oriented social action always involves association" (below, 938).

(sec. 2) Weber again takes up the European state of affairs on the eve of the first World War (cf. ch. V:4), comparing it with the capitalism and imperialism of Antiquity. The dynamics of international and national stratification is his dual theme: the relations of prestige and power among and within political communities. Here again was an issue previously raised by Sombart. His *Socialism and Social Movement in the 19th Century* (1896) opened with the dictum of the *Communist Manifesto* that "the history of all hitherto existing society has been a history of class struggles." Sombart considered this

> one of the greatest truths of the century . . . , but not the whole truth. For it is incorrect to say that all history of society is merely a history of class struggles. If it be worthwhile at all to subsume world history under one formula, we will have to say that social history has moved between two poles . . . which I will call the social and [inter-] national antagonisms (*Gegensätze*). . . . We find the same striving for wealth, power and prestige among communities as among individuals. . . . Today we are at the end of an historical epoch of national exaltation and in the midst of a period of great social cleavage; it seems to me that all the antagonistic viewpoints of the various groups can be reduced to the alternative: national or social.[89]

Sombart did not further pursue the topic of international stratification and instead focussed on the Marxist concept of class. Weber, however, carried the juxtaposition of the external and internal realm of honor to its logical conclusion and elaborated a scheme that also incorporated the Marxist approach as one segment. In the external sphere, he was concerned with power prestige, not just with national pride, which can also be found in non-expansionist Switzerland or Norway. Since power prestige derives from power over other political communities, it promotes expansionism and is thus a major component cause of war. The prestige pretensions of one country escalate those of others—Weber points to the deteriorating relations between France and Germany in the first decade of the century when, in contrast to the eighteen-nineties that Sombart had in mind, nationalist antagonisms prevailed again over internal cleavage. The carriers of power prestige are the "Great Powers," yet their ruling groups, fearing the seizure of power by their own victorious generals, are not always expansionist—witness ancient Rome and early 19th-century England. In both cases, however, capitalist interests enforced the resumption of political expansion.

Weber's theory of imperialism adds the economic element to the prestige factor. Building on his earlier writings, Weber constructs his

89. Werner Sombart, *Socialismus und sociale Bewegung im 19. Jahrhundert* (Jena: Fischer, 1896), 1f.

notion of imperialist capitalism from the first great historical case: ancient Rome with its tax-farmers and state purveyors. In modern times, as in Antiquity, it is the general structure of the economy, rather than trade interests, which is crucial for political expansionism. Imperialist capitalism may be restrained by the profitableness of "pacifist" capitalism, but for his own time Weber foresees the former's ascendancy, largely because of the state's role as the biggest customer of the defense contractors and similar enterprises. The economic-pacifist interests of the petty-bourgeois and proletarian strata are easily reduced by appeals to the emotive idea of "the nation."

Weber reviews the diverse cultural and social characteristics of individuals that may define membership in a nation. He emphasizes three elements: (1) the speed with which certain historical experiences can create the sense of nationhood, (2) the different meanings of the term from one country, and one stratum, to another, (3) the intellectuals' role in fashioning a sense of national identity. His unfinished analysis of the intellectuals—"those who usurp leadership in a *Kulturgemeinschaft*"—breaks off with a hint at the affinity of cultural prestige and power prestige, but not without the skeptical reminder that "art and literature of a specifically German character did *not* develop in the political center of Germany" (below, 926).

Weber's improvement on the Marxian class analysis lies in the detailed typology of the three phenomena of power distribution within the political community: class, status group, and party. Those powerful in the economic order need have neither political power nor social honor, but they often do have both. Apart from the economic order, the distribution of political power is codetermined by the legal order and the social or status order. Weber proposes to consider classes not as communities but as propensities for social action, similar to ethnic groups. Therefore, he speaks of "class situation," which is defined by market situation and has two basic categories: property and the lack of property. Property, in turn, differs according to whether it is used for rent income or profit-making. Although it does make a difference whether communities are based on labor, as in soil-tilling villages, or merely on property, as among cattle-breeders, the historical origin of class struggles lies not in the countryside but within the city: in the clash between creditors and debtors. At a later economic stage the class struggle was transformed into the struggle on the commodity market; in modern times it has come to center in wage disputes on the labor market. The contemporary bitterness of wage-earners is primarily directed against the entrepreneurs and managers, who are more visible than the "real" capitalists, the shareholders and bankers. This opaqueness is only one of the many social and cultural factors that influence the way in which class situation may (or may not) become the basis for class-oriented or party-oriented action.

The major polemical target of this exposition on class and class situation was "that kind of pseudo-scientific operation with the concepts of class and class interests which is so frequent these days and which has found its most classic expression in the assertion (*Behauptung*) of a talented author that the individual may be in error about his interests, but that the class is infallible" (below, 930)—a reference, it seems, to none other than the young Georg Lukács.[90] As against this class reification by a new breed of Marxian metaphysicians Weber insisted on his own empirical dialectic of class and status. Status groups are real, if often amorphous, groups limiting the sheer market principle with its opposition of class interests. Positive or negative social honor is the basis of status groups. Status differences express themselves in the style of life: a phenomenon extensively treated in the Sociology of Domination. In the extreme, status differentiation leads to caste formation: a link with the earlier exposition of ethnic and religious groups. Status groups are the bearers of all conventions: a structural explanation for the coercive character of conventions that Weber upheld against Stammler. In sum, classes are part of the economic order, status groups, of the social order; put in another way, classes are rooted in the sphere of production and acquisition, status groups in the realm of consumption.

Class interests as well as status interests may be represented by parties. In contrast to classes and status groups, parties are always purpose-rational associations, since their goal is the acquisition of power in larger associations. Thus parties are frequently authoritarian organizations—an issue of paramount concern for the sociology of political parties in modern democracy. However, adequately to understand the structure

90. When Weber wrote this passage, Georg Lukács was one of his close young friends. He had attracted public attention through his first German book, *Die Seele und die Formen* (1911). At the time he was preparing himself for an academic career, a plan destroyed by the onset of the war. In Weber's Heidelberg circle Lukács and Ernst Bloch represented a new generation of Marxians who were highly critical of "vulgar" Marxism. If the identification is correct, Weber refers to conversations rather than publications, as he also does elsewhere in the text. An early formulation of Lukács' theory that the proletariat as a whole is infallible about its interests is found in an Hungarian essay of 1919, "Tactics and Ethics"; see his *Schriften zur Ideologie und Politik*, ed. Peter Ludz (Neuwied: Luchterhand, 1967), esp. 9, 18f., 31. Lukács later adapted Weber's class terminology in his famous work on *History and Class Consciousness* (1923). On the relation of Weber and Lukács, see Marianne Weber, *Lebensbild*, 473–76, and Paul Honigsheim, "Erinnerungen an Max Weber," in R. König and J. Winckelmann, eds., *Max Weber zum Gedächtnis*, 184–88.

of parties one must first examine the larger associations within which they operate.

Herewith Weber has reached the Sociology of Domination. Parties vary not only according to class and status structure but also according to the larger group's structure of domination. In line with his comparative interests in earlier studies, Weber now proceeds to a broad typology comprising parties and polities of Antiquity as well as of the Middle Ages and of some non-European areas.

CHS. X–XVI. THE SOCIOLOGY OF DOMINATION

The Sociology of Domination is the core of *Economy and Society*.[91] The major purpose of the work was the construction of a typology of associations, with most prominence given to the types of domination and their relation to want-satisfaction through appropriation. To be sure, religion and law were constituent parts of the work, irrespective of whether Weber planned the chapters to be as comprehensive as they finally came to be, but the 1914 outline and the proportions of the manuscript show the Sociology of Domination to be the central theme. In the reception of the piecemeal translation of *Economy and Society,* the Sociology of Domination has been obscured as a whole. Until now, nearly half of it was untranslated; the other half was divided among three different translations.[92] In the theoretical discussions the three types of legitimate domination have usually been treated in isolation, and in research the complex typology of domination has all too frequently been reduced to the simple dichotomy of charisma and bureaucracy, if not just to the so-called Weberian "formal model of bureaucracy." Too

91. Weber was in the habit of speaking, respectively, of his Sociology of Law, Religion, Domination, and State, and he employed these terms in cross-references. However, since the 1914 outline does not contain the terms and the manuscript of ch. VIII was untitled, it appears likely that he did not want to use the phrase "sociology of" in a chapter title. At any rate, in view of the great overall length of chs. X–XVI, no summary title was chosen in the text for the Sociology of Domination. Even in its incomplete state this section is twice as long as the chapters on religion and law—a quantitative indicator of their importance for the work as a whole.

92. If ch. III of Part One is included, there are four different translations. The incomplete terminological summary of Part One further telescopes the historical dimension. It does not parallel the structure of the Sociology of Domination in Part Two, especially in the chapters on secular and hierocratic rulership and the city; the contrast of secular and hierocratic domination appears in Part One in ch. I:17, and the forms of legitimate rulership peculiar to the city are found mostly under rule by notables (ch. III:15–20). Moreover, feudalism is in Part Two a variant of patrimonialism, in Part One a variant of charisma— equally feasible classifications.

often a rulership has been measured only against the formal features of bureaucracy or of charismatic domination. In this manner the technical sense of the typology (see below, 263) has been disregarded: More than one type should be compared to any given case, rather than just one "ideal type" with one "natural system."

The Sociology of Domination is the mold in which some of Weber's most substantive interests, and the influences arousing them, were fused into a conceptual unity. As a basic influence Weber acknowledged the work of his friend Georg Jellinek: "From his great studies I received decisive impulses for whatever fate has permitted me to accomplish. . . . [Among these was] his coinage of the concept of the 'social theory of the state,' clarifying the blurred tasks of sociology."[93] In his *Allgemeine Staatslehre* Jellinek defined as the ultimate objective elements of the state the social relations of men, as against metaphysical notions of its corporeality:

> More precisely, the state exists in relations of will among a plurality of persons. Men who command and others who obey form the basis of the state. . . . In the state the relations of will, concentrated in an organizational unit, are essentially relations of domination. The quality of domination does not exhaust the essence of the state. But relations of domination are so necessary to the state that it cannot be conceived without them. The state has the powers of rulership (*Herrschergewalt*). To rule (*herrschen*) means the ability to impose one's own will upon others unconditionally. . . . Only the state has this power to enforce its will unconditionally against other wills. It is the only organization that rules by virtue of its inherently autonomous powers. . . . The state, then, is that organizational unit equipped with underived powers of command.[94]

Weber differentiated Jellinek's notion of rule. What Jellinek called *Herrschen,* he called "power" (*Macht*); this left the term *Herrschaft* (domination) free for an adaptation of the Kantian categorical imperative: "The situation in which the manifested will (command) of the ruler or rulers is meant to influence the conduct of one or more others (the ruled) and actually does influence it in such a way that their conduct, to a socially relevant degree, occurs as if the ruled had made the content of the command the maxim of their conduct for its very own sake" (below, 946). Domination transforms amorphous and intermittent social action into persistent association. Weber exemplifies the difference of domination from mere power with the case of monopolistic control in the market. In their own rational interest, the unorganized

93. R. König and J. Winckelmann, eds., *Max Weber zum Gedächtnis*, 15.
94. Georg Jellinek, *Allgemeine Staatslehre*, 2nd ed. (Berlin: Häring, 1905; 1st ed., 1900), 169, 172.

customers of a monopolistic enterprise may comply with its market dictate: this is domination by virtue of interest constellation. Through many gradual transitions, this relationship may be transformed into domination proper, that means, by virtue of the authoritarian power of command, as it prevails in the large-scale industrial enterprise and on the manor—the two most important economic structures of domination. Domination exists insofar as there is obedience to a command; in general, obedience is due to a mixture of habit, expediency and belief in legitimacy. The subjects' willingness to comply with a command is enhanced by the existence of a staff, which again acts on the basis of habit, legitimacy and self-interest. Sociologically, then, a *Herrschaft* is a structure of superordination and subordination sustained by a variety of motives and means of enforcement.[95] For the historical persistence of structures of domination, staff enforcement on whatever grounds is no less important than belief in legitimacy. In fact, explains Weber, he is "primarily interested in domination insofar as it is administration" (below, 948). Only after defining domination in terms of rule by a master and his apparatus does Weber add the ultimate grounds for its validity. He turns to legitimacy because of its inherent historical importance—the need of those who have power, wealth and honor to justify their good fortune.

The resulting typology of domination goes far beyond the three familiar types of authority. The substance of the Sociology of Domination consists in the general historical models of rulership. Weber does not wish to work out a "political system" applicable to all political groups irrespective of time and place; rather, he aims at a "systems analysis" of these models. Here he takes up the postulate of a "social theory of the state," but whereas Jellinek's typology of states remains largely on the level of constitutional theory and political philosophy, Weber "descends" to a level of greater historical descriptiveness. With the nature of the modern state and of industrial capitalism as underlying themes, Weber puts together a comparative scheme within which he integrates the major topics and results of his earlier studies:

i. the ancient and medieval city state as an autonomous polity, ranging from the patrimonial-bureaucratic kingdom to the confraternity of equals (cf. above, secs. 6 and 7);

ii. manorial domination (*Grundherrschaft*) in Germanic Antiquity and the Middle Ages, involving the issues of patriarchalism, feudalism, and military communism (cf. above, sec. 4);

95. For the terminological resolution of the translation of *Herrschaft* as domination or authority, see below, 61, n. 31.

III. the rise of modern public and private bureaucracy and the organizational realities of modern democracy (cf. above, sec. 8);

IV. the perennial tension between usurpation and legitimation (cf. above, sec. 7, p. li).

In the Sociology of Domination, theme I is treated mostly under patrimonialism (ch. XII) and the city (ch. XVI); theme II under feudalism (ch. XIII) and charismatic rulership (ch. XIV); theme III under bureaucracy (ch. XI) and again under charisma (ch. XIV); theme IV under caesaropapism and hierocracy (ch. XV) and under the special aspect of non-legitimate domination (again ch. XVI). However, Weber puts at the beginning of the Sociology of Domination (ch. X) what was politically most important to him: the meaning of democracy in an industrialized and bureaucratized society.

(A) THE THEORY OF MODERN DEMOCRACY. Since domination and administration are interdependent, domination is an irreducible component of democratic administration. So-called direct democracy is nothing primeval, but a product of historical development. Its aim is the minimization of domination; its precondition is the relative equality of the participants. Here is another historical twist: Direct democracy is most feasible in an aristocracy, whether it be Venetian noblemen or the vaunted German "aristocracy of the spirit"—the university professors. Direct democracy, however, is inherently unstable, and wherever there is economic differentiation in the group, domination tends to fall into the hands of those who have the economic requisites for performing administrative and political tasks. This is, first of all, a matter of "economic availability," not necessarily of high status; thus, managers of large-scale enterprises, teachers and medical doctors are less available than lawyers, country squires and urban *rentiers*. In general, the available groups also have social honor, and then they are *honoratiores* (notables). If direct democracy turns into rule by *honoratiores*, the demand for democracy easily becomes the battle cry of those lacking in wealth or honor. In that case both sides may form parties, which tend to be tightly organized because their object is, after all, the struggle for power. If this happens, and if the community grows beyond a certain size, "the meaning of democracy changes so radically that it no longer makes sense for the sociologist to ascribe to the term the same meaning as in the case discussed so far" (below, 951).

Weber's own theory of modern democracy was directed against the many intellectuals ("*literati*") to his right and left who failed to understand the *facts* of parliamentary government and democratic party organization and were thus unable to weigh them against the prevalent monarchic constitutionalism or against panaceas such as the "corporate" state, just as they failed to comprehend the *technical* imperatives of a private capitalist economy in contrast to state socialism and capitalism. Weber stressed the formal similarity of the democratic party and the capitalist enterprise: If parties are legal and party affiliation is voluntary, the business of politics is the pursuit of ideal and material interests, which is as inevitable as the activism of the few against the passivity of the many. Under the conditions of mass suffrage, the leadership of the few rests on mass mobilization, and this in turn requires an effective party apparatus. The party bureaucracies parallel those of state and economy. However, the bureaucratization of the parties does not necessarily spell the end of meaningful political democratization or of charismatic leadership. Here Weber's disagreements with Robert Michels reappear.[96] Michels' "iron law of oligarchy" became for a time very influential in the American literature on democracy and party organization, but eventually Weber's conception gained ground through its popularization in Joseph Schumpeter's *Capitalism, Socialism and Democracy*.[97]

The chapter on bureaucracy (ch. XI) elaborates the partly supportive and partly antagonistic relations between bureaucracy and modern democracy, and between passive and active democratization. The chapter on charisma (ch. XIV) adds the transition to democratic suffrage and the selection of democratic leadership. It contains the important recogni-

96. Traces of Weber's objections to Michels' arguments are found in chs. XI and XIV (cf. below, 991 and 1003, n. 8), apart from ch. II. Weber did not publicly state his disagreement with Michels, whose academic career in Germany had been forestalled by official disapproval of his political activities and in whose behalf he had protested vociferously in an article on "The So-Called Freedom of Teaching" (*Frankfurter Zeitung*, Sept. 20, 1908; cf. Marianne Weber, *Lebensbild*, 361). In 1913 Michels became co-editor of the *Archiv für Sozialwissenschaft und Sozialpolitik*. The two men corresponded extensively; Michels mentioned in the second edition of his *Political Parties* that he took into consideration a lengthy critique by Weber, to whom he had dedicated the first edition. The difficulties of reconstructing Weber's critical thrusts are similar in the case of Georg Simmel, whose career he tried to further against strong (in part anti-Semitic) resistance. In order to protect him, Weber terminated a projected severe critique after writing a few pages of personal testimonial to Simmel and a bitter denunciation of his academic and bureaucratic detractors.

97. Schumpeter, *Capitalism, Socialism, and Democracy* (3rd ed.; New York: Harper & Brothers, 1950), ch. XXII. Schumpeter, one of the earliest contributors to the *Outline of Social Economics* (1914), did not here mention Weber's name, but there is a point-by-point correspondence of his description with passages in both parts of *Economy and Society*. For Schumpeter's account of his relationship to Weber, see his *History of Economic Analysis*, ed. Elizabeth Boody Schumpeter (New York: Oxford University Press, 1954), 815–820, and his 1920 necrologue on Weber, reprinted in R. König and J. Winckelmann, eds., *Max Weber zum Gedächtnis*, 64–71.

tion that, far from being irreconcilable, charisma and bureaucracy may be interdependent. The adjustment of the Catholic church to bourgeois democracy, especially in the United States, appears in the chapter on political and hierocratic domination (ch. XV). The chapter on the city (ch. XVI) deals with the theory of ancient and medieval democracy, providing the historical contrast to modern democracy.[98]

(B) THE DIMENSIONS OF RULERSHIP. From the beginning, Weber deals with bureaucracy not only in its formal aspects but as a status group with vested interests. At the core of his approach to rulership is the three-way struggle between ruler, staff, and subjects. The types of rulership are distinguished by differing forms of appropriation—Weber speaks of appropriation because the legal concept of property is too narrow for many historical cases. Appropriation involves the means and positions of administration, ranging from economic resources and weaponry to managerial and political functions. The seizure of goods and the extraction of services often originate in usurpation. Normally, appropriation is carried through by a group rather than individuals. Legitimacy is used to defend appropriation. Weber suggests, for example, that European feudalism, although in many ways an "impossible" structure of domination, survived as long as it did because the vassals needed the shield of legitimacy. This "functional" emphasis on legitimacy pervades the whole exposition.

From the viewpoint of legitimation, the structure of the Sociology of Domination is the following:

(1) The historical models of bureaucracy, patriarchalism, patrimonialism, feudalism, *Ständestaat,* and military (and monastic) communism are subsumed under the three types of legitimate domination (chs. XI–XIV);

(2) As the greatest force of legitimation in history, the priesthood is ceaselessly struggling for power with secular rulership (ch. XV); their relationship is one of mutual antagonism as well as dependence;

(3) The city is the locus of specifically non-legitimate domination in history (ch. XVI).

However, the bulk of each chapter is concerned not with legitimacy, but with the various strategies and resources of domination on the part of ruler and staff. In each chapter, the military constituency, which was basic to the analysis of the ancient states in the "Agrarian Conditions of Antiquity," is treated next to the civilian administration. Each chapter also contains a section on the ethos and education of the status groups.

98. In Part One, the theory of democracy is treated especially in ch. III:*vii* and *x.*

Finally, the relation between each form of domination and economic development is examined. Weber finds that it is easier to state the impact of domination on the economy than vice versa. There are, for instance, striking similarities between the class struggle in the Italian cities of the Middle Ages and in the Roman Republic, although the economic conditions were quite different. The reason lies in the limited number of administrative techniques available for effecting compromises among the status groups of a polity. Therefore, similarities of political administration must not be interpreted as identical superstructures rising over identical economic foundations: "These things obey their own law" (below, 1309).

(c) THE TERMINOLOGY OF DOMINATION. The terminological integration of the Sociology of Domination was a remarkable achievement. By drawing on concepts from ancient, medieval and modern history Weber succeeded in fashioning a terminology applicable to all three eras. It should be remembered that this did not involve any assumptions about historical sameness, but an insistence on typological gradation. Weber addressed his comparative terminology to medievalists like Below and Gierke, who wrote on both manorial domination (*Grundherrschaft*) and the city, to ancient historians like Eduard Meyer, and to church and legal historians like Rudolf Sohm. He demonstrated some of the typological implications of their terminology.

The term *Herrschaft* has a very concrete and a very abstract meaning. In historiography a *Herrschaft* is a noble estate, corresponding to the French *seigneurie* and the English manor. In the philosophy of history, *Herrschaft* is the basic category of superordination, and in this sense it loomed large in the work of the young Marx. Weber uses the term frequently in the historical sense and occasionally in the philosophical meaning. Sometimes he refers to the "domination of man over man." However, this is not technically relevant to his typology. The *Herrschaftsverband* (authoritarian association)[99] was a term widely used after the late eighteen-sixties when Gierke made it the standard contrast to the *Genossenschaft* (equalitarian association). The term "patrimonial state" was older still; it was introduced early in the nineteenth century by Carl Ludwig von Haller.[100] Haller fought against the liberal doctrines

99. Since Weber did not use the term *Herrschaftsverband* as a contrast to *Genossenschaft*, the translation "ruling organization" was chosen for the most general formulation in the basic definitions (cf. below, 53) in order to exclude the colloquial connotations of "authoritarianism." In Weber's terminology even the most democratic organization is a *Herrschaftsverband*.

100. Carl Ludwig von Haller, *Restauration der Staats-Wissenschaft, oder Theorie des natürlich-geselligen Zustands der Chimäre des künstlich-bürgerlichen entgegengesetzt* (Winterthur: Steiner, 1817/18), vols. II and III.

of the social contract and for the thesis that all governmental authority was the private property of the ruler. He also elaborated the early ideal type of patrimonial bureaucracy. Whereas Haller equated patriarchalism and patrimonialism, Weber contrasted the two concepts and defined the latter as the *political* domination of a ruler with the help of his *personal* apparatus (consisting of slaves, retainers, *ministeriales*). This change reflected the controversy over the importance of *Grundherrschaft* (manorial domination) in Germanic history, which Weber downgraded in favor of the charismatic origin of political rulership. His 1914 letter to Georg von Below stressed the distinction between patriarchal and patrimonial domination:

> Although I have good reason to think very modestly of my own expertise, I have no doubt that you are right [about the existence of genuine political authority, not just private powers, in European feudalism]. It is astonishing that the old contrary theory—to which, admittedly, I too once adhered—is still so persistently defended. . . . Terminologically, I must limit the concept of patrimonialism to certain kinds of *political* domination. I hope you will find that I have sufficiently emphasized the absolute distinction between domestic, personal and manorial authority, on the one hand, and political *Herrschaft* on the other, which is none of these but rather military and judicial authority. This main thesis of your book will find no objection from my side. I will only show that this difference is as old as history.[101]

Weber demonstrated his point by drawing on examples from Antiquity and the Chinese empire. Patrimonialism was the most important kind of administration before the emergence of modern bureaucracy. In the most centralized case, it constituted a patrimonial-bureaucratic administration with a "state-socialist" *oikos* economy—Rodbertus' concept—; European feudalism was its most fragmented case, with its sole and limited analogy in Japan. Only European feudalism developed the *Ständestaat*, the consociation of ruler, nobility and *honoratiores* under a quasi-constitutional division of powers. Feudalism was for Weber a marginal case of patrimonialism, because the feudal vassal was a patrimonial lord in relation to his own retainers and because the feudal principle did not completely replace the patrimonial administration of the realm. Feudalism had charismatic features as well; the status group of warriors was first distinguished by personal military prowess and later by "noble" descent.

Precisely because feudalism was a unique medieval phenomenon, Weber's distinction between feudalism and patrimonialism has consider-

101. Weber's letter of June 21, 1914, printed in G. von Below, *Der deutsche Staat des Mittelalters,* 2nd ed. (1925), xxiv f.

able terminological utility today when "feudalism" is all too often an indiscriminate pejorative term referring to sundry situations in all countries where large-scale landownership and political power are still closely related. The concepts of patrimonialism and personal rulership—divested of traditionalist legitimation—are frequently more applicable to the New States than feudalism, bureaucracy or charismatic rulership.[102]

If patrimonialism has been conceptually underemployed, charisma has been used indiscriminately to label almost all non-bureaucratic forms of leadership.[103] Weber chose the term to characterize, first of all, the relationship between the military chieftain and his free following, the subject of his 1905 essay (sec. 4 above). He secularized Rudolf Sohm's notion of the charisma of the Christian church. In his major work on *Church Law* (1892), Sohm, a devout believer and conservative columnist, had described the church not as a "legal" but a "charismatic" organization—i.e., an organization established by virtue of divine inspiration, not man-made law. After using the concept of charisma in its religious connotations in the Sociology of Religion, Weber apparently decided that it could also denote the self-legitimation of political leadership, a usurpatory challenge from the viewpoint of patriarchal, patrimonial and bureaucratic legitimacy.

Throughout history political and religious charisma have warred and cooperated with one another. The secular rulers had to face, in one way or another, the institutionalized charisma of the priesthood—theocracy. Since Weber concerned himself with the charisma of both powers, he differentiated the traditional notion of theocracy—still his terminology in the "Agrarian Conditions in Antiquity"—into a typology of hierocracy contrasting with caesaropapism.[104] The latter term denoted the complete control of the secular ruler over the church, and since this was true of both the Anglican and Lutheran rulers, the phrase also suited Weber's penchant for nominalist irony.[105] Successful political usurpers or their successors often endeavored to fortify their rule through religious

102. For a proposal along these lines, see my "Personal Rulership, Patrimonialism and Empire-Building in the New States," *World Politics*, XX, 1968, 194–206.

103. On the indiscriminate application of the concept of charisma, cf. Reinhard Bendix, "Reflections on Charismatic Leadership," *Asian Survey*, VII, 1967, 341–352.

104. In this he followed the terminology of Byzantine studies; cf. *Religion in Geschichte und Gegenwart*, I (Tübingen: Mohr, 1909), cols. 1527–31.

105. The analytical advance made by Weber can be seen by comparing, for example, Wilhelm Roscher's treatment of "priestly aristocracy" in his *Politik: Geschichtliche Naturlehre der Monarchie, Aristokratie und Demokratie* (Stuttgart: Cotta, 1892), 87–117.

legitimation: the foremost European examples were Charlemagne and Napoleon I. Whereas these two rulers controlled the church, others were more dependent. European history was profoundly influenced by the great clash and subsequent stalemate between emperor and pope—a subject about which Weber wrote his first major essay at the age of thirteen.[106] This gave the Italian cities their historic opportunity to gain autonomy for a time from the patrimonial and hierocratic powers and to usher in the Renaissance with its unbridled individualism: an age of illegitimacy.

(D) THE CITY: USURPATION AND REVOLUTION.[107] It has been asserted occasionally that the Sociology of Domination, with its "static" ideal types, cannot explain revolutionary change. Were this true, Marxism as well could not have advanced a theory of revolution, since its "laws" and developmental constructs are nothing if not ideal types—as Weber pointed out in 1904.[108] The fact is that his own theory of revolution appears in the guise of usurpation and non-legitimate domination because of its attention to administration and legitimacy, marginal concerns to Marxism. Weber looked more closely at the consequences of the seizure of power than did Marx in spite of the "dictatorship of the proletariat"; he saw that revolutionary domination can survive only when an efficient administration suppresses the expropriated former holders of legitimate power.

The city as an autonomous, oath-bound commune of armed men existed only in the Occident, and then only in Antiquity and the Middle Ages. It was the specific locus of revolutionary domination in two respects: It was a "state within a state" erected by the patricians against the patrimonial rulerships with their traditionalist legitimation; it also was the scene of the uprising of the "people" against the patricians who had in turn assumed the mantle of legitimacy. The people's leaders created another "state within a state." Weber maintained that the oldest

106. In the same year, 1877, Weber wrote an essay on "The Roman Empire from Constantine to the Teutonic Migrations"; at the age of fifteen he wrote "Reflections on the Character, Development and History of the Indo-Germanic Peoples." These were standard topics in the classical schools, but the essays also indicate the early origins and the continuity of some of Weber's basic interests.

107. The chapter on the city was the fulfilment of a project that Weber had declared to be worthwhile in 1908/9 (cf. above, p. xxxi); he took himself by his own words and demonstrated how the ancient polis and medieval city could be compared to explain their differences and how an indirect contribution could be made to the study of modern democracy.

108. Cf. Shils and Finch, eds., *Methodology . . . ,* 103. For a comparison of the ideal-typical constructs of Marx and Weber, see Judith Janoska-Bendl, *Methodologische Aspekte des Idealtypus. Max Weber und die Soziologie der Geschichte* (Berlin: Duncker & Humblot, 1965), 89–114.

historical records of the city as a commune proved its revolutionary character, but that this was often obscured in documents which purposively hid usurpations of political power.[109]

The first great usurpation of the early Middle Ages was the "revolutionary movement of 726 that led to the defection of Italy from Byzantine domination and centered around Venice. It was called forth especially by opposition to the icon destruction ordered by the emperor who was under the pressure of [the Islamic sympathies of] his own army. Thus the religious element, although not the only factor, triggered the revolution."[110] After a period of patrician rule, the Italian *popolo* rose under its leaders and established "the first deliberately nonlegitimate and revolutionary political association" (below, 1302).

Weber contrasted the patrician city with the plebeian city of the Middle Ages and of Antiquity, exploring the different forms of class struggle in each type and era. He stressed the remarkable parallels between the Italian *popolo* with its *capitano* and the ancient Roman plebs with its tribune. In the absence of traditional legitimation, the tribune was sustained by armed popular support. He checked the power of the senate and instigated the *plebiscita*.

Democratization means the political expropriation of the upper strata, which in these historical cases were as "closely policed, disenfranchized and outlawed as is the Russian bourgeoisie by Lenin. The basis of democratization is everywhere of a military nature; it lies in the emergence of a disciplined infantry. . . . Military discipline signified the victory of democracy, for the wish and the need to call on the non-knightly masses gave them arms and thereby political power. The parallels to the German revolution of 1918 are obvious."[111] However, democratization by no means leads to the waning of domination. Ancient and medieval democracy passed through the state of the *tyrannis* and the *signoria* before the city state disappeared, reverting to patrimonial rulership through internal transformation or external defeat. But this his-

109. Weber rejected Sombart's theory that "ground rent is the mother of the city" (cf. *Economic History*, 239). The two men differed in their interest and interpretation of the city. Sombart was primarily concerned with the economic aspects; cf. *Der moderne Kapitalismus*, II, 176–249, and his "Der Begriff der Stadt und das Wesen der Städtebildung," *AfS*, XXV, 1907, 1–9. In dealing with the city as a political phenomenon, Weber followed the tradition of ancient and medieval history. However, he reversed the standard political definition of the German medieval city as a self-governing body with a town council subject to confirmation by the legitimate overlord, and instead emphasized the aspect of usurpation. For the older definition, see Freiherr Roth von Schreckenstein, *Das Patriziat in den deutschen Städten* (Tübingen: Mohr, 1856), 28.

110. *Wirtschaftsgeschichte*, 274; cf. *Economic History*, 236.

111. *Wirtschaftsgeschichte*, 278f.; cf. *Economic History*, 240.

torical "cycle" had very different results in the two eras: In Antiquity a universal empire came into being, suppressing private capitalism; at the beginning of modern history, the competing patrimonial-bureaucratic states created the European balance of power, one of the preconditions of modern capitalism. They further developed the rational administration first promoted by the non-legitimate dictatorship of the Italian *signoria*. Thus the modern state and modern democracy were not the direct successors of the medieval city. Their rise was prepared by the struggle for representation in the *Ständestaat* and the absolutist state, which preceded their violent establishment in the American and French revolutions.

From the viewpoint of legitimacy and administrative control there is no basic difference between *coups d'état* and mass uprisings. Weber's reference to the Russian and German "revolutions" was more than a mere illustrative analogy. Structurally, the modern state, whether parliamentary, plebiscitary or a "people's democracy," is one city. Non-legitimate domination is at the root of modern democracies, whether they are more libertarian or more authoritarian. The United States, the "first new nation" in Seymour Martin Lipset's phrase, came into being in rejection of monarchic legitimacy and instead created a polity that, in analogous terms, resembles the Roman Republic: its President (tribune) and the plebeian House of Representatives contrast with the Senate, an imitation of the House of Lords, as the most traditionalist and aristocratic element.

It is a moot point which contemporary state should be considered less similar to a city and closer to patrimonial rulership. Hierocracy and caesaropapism continue to exist in some of their traditional ways, but more frequently in a new secularized form. Secular intellectuals have replaced priests as the new legitimizers, especially in the New States. Weber did not foresee how quickly and terribly totalitarianism would seize and exercise power, although he described it as an "objective possibility" (below, 644, 661, n.4). Toward the end of his life he considered it more likely that a Bonapartist *coup d'état* might occur in Bolshevist Russia or in Weimar Germany, a reasonable guess on the basis of historical precedent. But Weber had no deterministic view of history: "The continuum of cultural development in the Mediterranean-European realm has up to now shown neither completed 'cycles' nor an unambiguous unilinear development."[112] Despite his fulminations, he did not consider the oppressive dominance of bureaucracy politically inescapable (cf. below, 991). In his showdown with Oswald Spengler in

112. "Agrarverhältnisse . . . ," *GAzSW*, 278.

February of 1920, Weber extracted the admission from the author of the *Decline of the West* that his morphology was historical poetry. Domination in large-scale communities was for Weber the only historic inevitability—a point directed at the same occasion against a young communist who was dreaming of the perfect commune of intellectuals and proletarians in Siberia.[113]

If the course of history is not predetermined but domination inescapable at the same time that its forms are limited, a historically saturated typology is the best analytical tool for the researcher. This is the ultimate rationale for the typologies of *Economy and Society*.

II. PART ONE: THE LATER PART

Between 1918 and 1920, during and after the Empire's collapse, Weber turned to the terminological summary. In contrast to Part Two, where after 1918 he revised only the chapter on bureaucracy, he rewrote the definitions many times. Weber spent so much energy on the categories because he recognized that the discursive exposition of his complex and novel terminology made retention difficult. Several colleagues, among them the philosopher Heinrich Rickert, had told him that the Stammler critique and the essay on "Some Categories of Interpretive Sociology" were excessively hard to read. Weber heeded their advice and simplified the terminology. He divided the text into numbered main definitions and small-print comments, a device frequently employed in the older literature, as in Schönberg's *Handbook of Political Economy*.

In the first edition of *Wirtschaft und Gesellschaft*, Part One was published under the title now carried by Part Two, but Weber liked to call it his *Kategorienlehre* or casuistry. In those last months of his life he seems to have expressed some satisfaction with his progress—with the feeling, however: "People will shake their heads." He expected resistance to his redefining of well-known historical, economic, legal and theological terms for his sociological purposes. Thus, he wanted it clearly understood that his definitions were nothing more than a clarification of his own terms to be tested by their scholarly yield; they were not an attempt to impose a new terminology on his colleagues. Hundreds of students attended his courses at this time—in Vienna in 1918 and in Munich in 1919/20—but the course on the categories drove them away *en masse*.[114] Upon their urging, Weber compensated the students for

113. Cf. Marianne Weber, *Lebensbild*, 685ff., and Eduard Baumgarten, ed., *Max Weber: Werk und Person* (Tübingen: Mohr, 1964), 554f.

114. In a period when political agitation is again an issue at American universities, it may be worthwhile to recount that Weber opened the course on the most general categories of sociology with a statement showing that he was for

his definitions with his lectures on economic history. It is certainly true that the definitions are not "readable." Part One is really a reference text, and it would indeed have greatly facilitated the reading of Part Two had Weber lived to revise the old terminology in the light of the new. The discrepancy as it now exists makes additional demands upon the reader of both parts, but it also offers researchers the opportunity to work with Weber's alternative terminology.

When Schmoller wrote his critique of Sombart's *Modern Capitalism* he advanced a complaint that might have applied also to Weber: "Every few pages we find the sentence: 'I call this such and such,' and the reader is overwhelmed by a flood of new names, new etiquettes and pigeon-holes."[115] Sombart considered his own terminological introduction a "considerable esthetic impairment" but an inevitable nuisance since he wanted to introduce a personal terminology; similarly, Weber acknowledged the stylistic awkwardness of his precise definitions. Sombart called for an esthetic science: "The guilt toward all living things that every science brings upon itself [by its deadening generalities] can be expiated only if scholarship produces new life through its creations, shaping them into works of art . . . It seems to me that we should strive to make a scientific scheme *beautiful* in itself."[116] Weber never advanced such an exuberant demand, but the casuistry of Part One, which is so much indebted to his legal training, does indeed have an esthetic quality, which will be revealed especially to the reader who works his way first through Part Two with its descriptive richness.

Weber finished three chapters of Part One and the beginning of chapter IV. These are the only chapters he could rework in the proofs.[117] Both parts of the work begin with basic definitions of social action and then take up economic action. In Part One, however, the typology of

"profession" even as he was against "indoctrination." In Marianne Weber's phrasing (*Lebensbild*, 673f.), he wanted to say a "first and last word on politics, which has no place in the lecture hall and in science, but rather belongs in an arena where the free airing of opposing judgements is possible. . . . We can have only *one* common goal: To turn the Versailles treaty into a scrap of paper. At the moment this is not possible, but the right of rebellion against foreign domination cannot be foresworn. Now we must practice the art of silence and return to the sober tasks of everyday life." Cf. Baumgarten, ed., *op. cit.*, 553, 716.

115. Schmoller, *loc. cit.*, 297.

116. Sombart, *op. cit.*, I, xxx.

117. The translation of chs. I–II of Part One was drafted by Henderson and reworked by Parsons, who did the subsequent chapters on his own. Terminologically, the original translation diverged from the German text by using "type" and "system" much more freely than did Weber, who in general spoke of "type" only when he really meant "ideal type" and for the rest employed terms such as "kind" or "phenomenon"; the term "system" was rarely used by Weber.

domination appears already in ch. III; classes and status groups (ch. IV) follow rather than precede it. Notes found with the manuscript indicate that Weber intended to go on to status groups of warriors. At least two chapters anticipated in the text of Part One are missing altogether: One on the more "universal" groups (household, kin group, etc.) treated early in Part Two, and another one on the theory of revolution (cf. the anticipatory reference below, 266), corresponding in Part Two to the chapter on the city as non-legitimate domination (ch. XVI). This chapter would have dealt with the German and Russian revolutions within a typology designed to give a more precise description than that afforded by the mere label "revolution."

Almost half of the first chapter of Part One is given over to a simplified presentation of the meaning of "interpretive sociology" and the concept of "social action."[118] This is Weber's easiest methodological statement, but because of its very conciseness the reader cannot afford to disregard the other methodological writings. In the second half of the chapter, the basic definitions of social action and association, Weber abandoned the older, more differentiated typology of Part Two (cf. below, Appendix I). He changed *Gemeinschaftshandeln* into *soziales Handeln* (social action) and *Gemeinschaft* mostly into *Verband* (organization). This made it possible to contrast *Vergemeinschaftung* and *Vergesellschaftung* (communal and associative relationships) in sec. 9 and to come closer to Tönnies' terminology without accepting his basic dichotomy. Tönnies' distinction had gained wide currency after the turn of the century, especially after the second edition of his work (1912). Apparently Weber felt that he should not insist on a quite different terminology. Weber treated Tönnies considerately as a comrade-in-arms in the struggle for social research and expressed himself with somewhat distant politeness about *Gemeinschaft und Gesellschaft* (1887), but there is no indication that the work was a major influence on his intellectual development, and *Economy and Society* appears partly conceived in opposition to it.[119]

118. For recent additions to the large literature on social action, see Helmut Girndt, *Das soziale Handeln als Grundkategorie erfahrungswissenschaftlicher Soziologie* ("Veröffentlichungen des Max Weber Instituts der Universität München"; Tübingen: Mohr, 1967); on the origin of the terminology of social action, see Johannes Winckelmann's introduction to Girndt, *ibid.*, 1–20; for an interpretation of Weber's theory of science in the light of subsequent developments in the natural and social sciences, see Winckelmann, "Max Webers Verständnis von Mensch und Gesellschaft," in K. Engisch *et al.*, eds., *Max Weber: Gedächtnisschrift der Ludwig-Maximilians-Universität München*, 195–243.

119. On the theoretical differences between Tönnies and Weber, see the definitive critique of Tönnies by René König, "Die Begriffe Gemeinschaft und

In communal as well as associative relationships conflict is normal (sec. 8). As in the case of power and domination, the definition of conflict has been wrenched out of context in discussions of Weber's orientation to power. He certainly was a political realist, but the purpose of the section is the definition of peaceful and regulated conflict ("competition") as against social selection and the free-for-all. The target of the section is Social Darwinism. Unrestrained struggle and social selection are marginal to Weber's analytical interest. Up to now the reversal of a key sentence has confused both German and English readers. Instead of the sentence: "The treatment of conflict involving the use of physical violence as a separate type is justified by the special characteristics of the employment of this means and the corresponding peculiarities of the sociological consequences of its use" (Parsons, ed., *Theory*, 133), it must read: "The conceptual separation (*Absonderung*) of peaceful [from violent] conflict is justified by the quality of the means normal to it and the peculiar sociological consequences of its occurrence" (below, 38). Weber goes on to emphasize the importance of the rules of the game as against inherent personal qualities (whether social or biological) and states that "we want to speak of conflict only when there really is competition" (cf. below, 39). He refers ahead to ch. II, where economic action is defined "as a peaceful use of the actor's control over resources" (below, 63).

The chapter on the sociological categories of economic action is remarkable for its length, the same as chs. I and III together. It is likely that Weber wanted to compensate for the relatively brief economic casuistry of Part Two. However, the many pages of seemingly dry definitions and comments owe some of their length—and hidden fervor—to Weber's political involvement with the problems of postwar economic and political reconstruction in the wake of the Empire's collapse and in the face of the victor's harsh demands at Versailles. The chapter also reflects the phenomenon of the wartime "state-socialist" economy and the syndicalist and socialist proposals for economic reconstruction. Some of Weber's comments on the much-debated question of the economic feasibility of socialism are definitely time-bound; other passages in this

---

Gesellschaft bei Ferdinand Tönnies," *Kölner Zeitschrift für Soziologie*, VII, 1955, 348–420. In the American literature the relationship apparently was misperceived for two reasons: (1) the early date (1887) of Tönnies work, which for a long time received little attention, and the fact that the *Gemeinschaft—Gesellschaft* dichotomy became well-known so much earlier than *Economy and Society*. For illustrations, see Robert Nisbet, *The Sociological Tradition* (New York: Basic Books, 1966), 79 and 326; Robert Presthus, *Men at the Top. A Study in Community Power* (New York: Oxford University Press, 1964), 9.

chapter show him years ahead of the critique that welfare economists later were to direct against classical economics, even though he did not use their technical apparatus.

While he was working intermittently on the economic categories, Weber in speeches and statements strenuously opposed the nationalization of the major industries. He considered neither the remaining state bureaucracy nor the inexperienced functionaries of the socialist labor movement capable of running the economy. In April, 1920, when the Democratic Party he had helped to establish in November, 1918, asked him to serve on the Nationalization Commission, he resigned, explaining that "the politician *must* make compromises—the scholar must not whitewash them."[120] A few weeks later he died.

11. Political Writings

"Parliament and Government in a Reconstructed Germany" (Appendix II) is offered for three reasons: (1) to compensate for the unwritten part on the sociology of the state; (2) to provide a corrective to the one-sided reception of the chapter on bureaucracy (ch. XI)—as if Weber had somehow missed the facts of bureaucracy as a vested interest group or a network of informal cliques; (3) to introduce to the English reader one of his major political writings, almost all of which are untranslated.[121]

The essay is a revision of newspaper articles originally written for

120. E. Baumgarten, ed., *Max Weber: Werk und Person*, 530; cf. also *ibid.*, 608 and Wolfgang Mommsen, *Max Weber und die deutsche Politik 1890–1920* (Tübingen: Mohr, 1959), 303f.

121. In the fourth edition of *Wirtschaft und Gesellschaft*, as a substitute for the chapters on the modern state and its parties that Weber did not live to write, Johannes Winckelmann provides a Sociology of the State constructed out of passages from *Economic History*, "Politics as a Vocation," and "Parliament and Government" with the omission of the more polemical and time-bound sections (for a separate edition, see Max Weber, *Staatssoziologie*, ed. Johannes Winckelmann; 2nd rev. ed., Berlin: Duncker & Humblot, 1966). In the English edition this imaginative didactic effort has been replaced by a continuous translation of the last essay. This appeared desirable because of the English reader's lack of familiarity with the political writings; by contrast, the *Economic History* was the first Weber translation (1927) and "Politics as a Vocation," a philosophical statement rather than a polemical article, is already well-known in the Gerth and Mills translation (*From Max Weber* . . . , 77–128). The list of Weber's political newspaper articles and journal essays is lengthy; it includes two essays on the 1905 Russian revolution, "On the Conditions of Bourgeois Democracy in Russia" and "Russia's Transition to Pseudo-Constitutionalism" (both 1906). The *Gesammelte Politische Schriften* comprise only part of the political writings. The Gerth and Mills volume contains somewhat more than one quarter of

the leftwing-liberal *Frankfurter Zeitung,* one of the best-known European newspapers until its suppression by the Nazis. The articles appeared in the summer of 1917, after Woodrow Wilson entered the war. They launched a sensational attack on the political incompetency of the Imperial and Prussian bureaucracy; the paper was subsequently put under pre-publication censorship, but the very publication of the articles is enough to show that even in wartime Imperial Germany was far less oppressive than Nazi Germany.

Weber made his impassioned plea for political democratization at a time when reform seemed highly uncertain and revolution only a slight possibility. His siding with parliamentarism was by no means a sudden conversion under the shadow of military disaster, as it was for Ludendorff and the general staff in September 1918. Weber had for many years advocated parliamentary government. He considered himself part of a vigorous but loyal opposition to the monarchy. He argued from premises of national interest, partly out of deep conviction, partly for tactical reasons, hoping that parliamentary government would make possible a more rational politics in the international no less than the national interest. He wanted Germany to play a major part in the rather discordant concert of European powers, but he never advocated her hegemony over Europe. In domestic politics he wanted to be recognized as a "class-conscious bourgeois" who opposed the entrenched Junkers and the rightwing romantics no less than the petty-bourgeois labor movement and the utopian leftwing intellectuals. He positively scorned the *litterateurs* of the right and left—witness his outbursts in "Parliament and Government." Weber took a humanitarian commitment for granted but was convinced that it would suffer from noisy display and moralistic sermonizing. He saluted pacifists as well as revolutionaries with a pure "ethic of ultimate ends" (*Gesinnungsethik*). But he believed in politics as the art of the possible—the morally imperative compromise in a world of irreconcilable ideologies and raw interests.

These few remarks cannot do justice to Weber's politics or to his political critics.[122] The reader of "Parliament and Government" should bear in mind that it represents only one phase of Weber's politics, neither the early period when the very young professor intentionally shocked his father's liberal generation with tough nationalist rhetoric in his Frei-

---

"Suffrage and Democracy in Germany" (1917) under the heading "National Character and the Junkers" (*op. cit.,* 386–95). Weber's political writings are, of course, partly dated; however, in part they can also be read as discussions of democratization, especially the issue of political development in "new" states.

122. For a review of the critics, see my "Political Critiques of Max Weber: Some Implications for Political Sociology," *American Sociological Review,* vol. 30, 1965, 213–23.

burg inaugural address of 1895—only to regret it later—, nor the last phase when the despairing democrat returned from the Versailles treaty meetings with grave forbodings, just like John Maynard Keynes. Weber foresaw Wilson's failure at Versailles. In an unsigned editorial statement in the *Frankfurter Zeitung* (October 27, 1918) he lectured his colleague-in-politics on the hard facts of the power balance and the art of peace-making:

> Men of good will and understanding do not question President Wilson's sincerity. However, it appears that he does not sufficiently grasp the following: If the German government accepts his armistice conditions, which make any further military resistance impossible, not only Germany *but he too* would be eliminated as a major factor in the peace settlement. His own position as arbiter for the world rests on the fact that the German army is at least strong enough to avoid defeat without the help of American troops on the Allied side. Were this to become different, the absolutely intransigent elements, which no doubt exist in other enemy countries, would gain the upper hand and simply push the President aside with polite thanks for his previous support. *His role would be over,* unless he went to war against his present allies. The German government, too, should have considered this state of affairs. Even though an armistice is desirable to avoid unnecessary bloodshed, it would certainly have been better not to focus deliberations so exclusively on the armistice offer as has been done. Peace negotiations could take place without an armistice if the enemies insist on continuation of the slaughter.[123]

In extremis, Weber was not averse to a *levée en masse* and guerrilla warfare ("national wars of liberation"), as he demonstrated in his speech at an anti-Versailles meeting of the University of Heidelberg in March, 1919; he protested against what appeared to him a flagrant violation of Wilson's promise of self-determination for all peoples. Such national pride, however, did not prevent rightwing students from picketing his house and disrupting his lectures. Emotional appeals aside, he devoted much constructive energy to the drafting of the Weimar constitution, through his writings and as member of the revolutionary government's planning committee.[124]

123. *GPS,* 435.

124. In the past, Weber's contribution to the presidential features of the Weimar constitution was exaggerated by friend and foe. For a correction, see Gerhard Schulz, *Zwischen Demokratie und Diktatur: Verfassungspolitik und Reichsreform in der Weimarer Republik* (Berlin: de Gruyter, 1963), I, 114–42. Schulz points out that far from taking a blunt position in favor of a "Caesarist" leader, Weber gradually shifted his opinions in response to the changing political situation and the diversity of opinion in committee meetings. Eventually he came to favor a popularly elected President as a mediator between the *Reichstag* and the States. Cf. also Weber, *GPS,* 394–471, 486–89.

In essence, Weber stood for the rational support of a political order that can be affirmed in most essentials. His sociology can serve the self-clarification of critical-minded organization men in industrialized and democratized society. This was the ultimate dialectic in Weber's position: He was a sharp critic of human and institutional failures, but basically a moralist with reformist convictions, not a revolutionary temper.[125]

12. *On Editing and Translating* Economy and Society

There are some misunderstandings abroad about the readability of *Economy and Society*. They relate in part to the original, in part to the translations. To begin with, it must be pointed out that Weber wrote lucidly and subtly. He wrote more clearly than did most of his colleagues, including Sombart, Tönnies, Troeltsch and his own brother Alfred, not to mention the legion of "ordinary" professors of his time. Weber does not stand in the tradition of German philosophical prose with its murky profundity that has usually suggested dangerous obscurantism to Anglo-Saxon readers. Considering that most of *Economy and Society* is a first draft, Weber's power of formulation proves extraordinary. Yet there are difficulties:

(1) Since Part Two was written with great speed, stylistic editing and judicious cutting would have been helpful to the reader, but this would also have been incompatible with the requirements of a complete edition.

(2) Weber never wrote a well-wrought book. His larger works are longish problem-centered research papers. *Economy and Society* is the only work conceived for a wider audience, but it never reached the stage of final literary form; moreover, it was simply not meant as a trot for introductory courses, or as the kind of polished study in cultural pessimism so popular in the nineteen-twenties.

(3) Weber uses a profusion of quotation marks as an alienating device to indicate that he employs familiar terms with reservations, with a new meaning, or in an ironic sense. This habit was the counterpoint to his concern with terminological precision and at times is a drawback. In the translation, the quotation marks were used more sparingly.

(4) Weber tended to overqualify his sentences, using terms such as

125. For a sketch of this dialectic, see Guenther Roth and Bennett M. Berger, "Max Weber and the Organized Society," *New York Times Book Review*, April 3, 1966, 6 and 44f.

"perhaps," "more or less," "in general," "as a rule," "frequently but not always," etc. This reflected the difficulty both of formulating historical generalizations and of identifying a specific cause. Weber's sense of caution became a stylistic mannerism.

Similar to the second and third volume of *Das Kapital*, Weber's work was edited from literary remains written in a scarcely legible handwriting. The early editions of *Wirtschaft und Gesellschaft* contained hundreds of reading and identification errors. For thirty-five years this distorted, or outright destroyed, the meaning of many passages and obviously affected the translations. In 1956, after many years of painstaking labor, Johannes Winckelmann published his critically revised (fourth) edition. In close cooperation, Winckelmann and the English editors have decided on a large number of further changes in wording, clauses, names and dates; some of these have been incorporated in the 1964 German paperback edition. The projected fifth edition will identify all these changes; listing them in the English edition would have been too cumbersome. The definitive German edition will be almost identical with the present English text, with the exception of Winckelmann's compilation of the Sociology of the State.[126] However, the German and English edition differ in the subheadings of the chapters. The manuscript had no subheadings, it seems, excepting the Sociology of Law, which in turn had no title. The early editions summarized the chapter contents, often inadequately, below the chapter headings. Winckelmann extensively revised them. The English editors proceeded at their own discretion and used subheadings in the text to improve its readability.

The systematic checking of the text required considerable library research, invisible where there are no corrections and annotations. The revision of the extant translations proved almost as time-consuming and difficult as the new translation since every sentence had to be compared to the German text and changed if it appeared necessary for textual, terminological and, more rarely, stylistic reasons. Weber's skilful use of German syntax permits more complex construction than is feasible in English. Thus, Weber is not really improved by "streamlining," by breaking up his carefully balanced and qualified sentences into a series of linear constructs. A more linear rendering was inevitable in the English version, but our inclination was to retain, and in some cases to restore, Weber's architecture. However, in most cases pragmatic pre-

126. Like the German paperback edition of 1964, the English edition omits Weber's essay on "The Rational and Social Foundations of Music," which was not part of the original but was appended to the second German edition. For an English version, see the translation by Don Martindale, Johannes Riedel and Gertrude Neuwirth (Carbondale: Southern Illinois University Press, 1958).

vailed over stylistic considerations, whether the revision of previous translations or our own formulations were involved.

In most academic translations, the task involves prosaic accuracy, not an esthetic recreation. Academic translation should properly be teamwork. Individual "heroism" is bound to be affected by the limitations of any single translator, as was proven by Parsons, Fischoff and Kolegar. Some of the English translations have been undertaken by two men, one familiar with each language. This arrangement could not, however, lighten the burden of the primary translator. Our translation was aided by two-fold familiarity with the original language, which permitted collateral reading and prevented premature closure by either one of us. Our revision of the extant translations has also been in the nature of collateral reading, backed by the wisdom of hindsight. The ideal translation, however, requires a third man: the stylist in the language of translation. Our third man was missing.

Everett C. Hughes once remarked that, as a matter of principle, a work should only be translated as a whole. Each piecemeal translation tends to reduce the incentive for publishing the whole. This leads to unanticipated and fortuitous intellectual consequences. Theoretical developments in American sociology have been considerably influenced by the vagaries of the Weber translations. Thus, the Gerth and Mills edition created the impression that the Sociology of Domination centers about the contrast of bureaucracy and charisma. Parsons' translation of only Part One perforce attenuated the historical dimension of the work and led some writers to believe that Weber did not follow up on his categories.[127] Weber's case is far from exceptional. In recent years it has become clear that the translations of Durkheim and Nietzsche have had similar distorting consequences.

Without sustained support by foundations and institutes the desiderata of academic translation cannot be fulfilled in most cases. This support has been lacking largely because translation and editing are the most underestimated kind of work in the social sciences. But as long as sociologists continue to lean on the Sociological Tradition, the need for translation will persist. Moreover, in an era of world-wide comparative research the linguistic problem will be perpetual without adequate translation facilities and better linguistic training for social scientists.

127. Since David Easton explicitly aimed at a forceful and incisive improvement of Weber, it appears legitimate to observe that his *A Systems Analysis of Political Life* (New York: Wiley, 1965) is a major example for some unintended consequences of the partial translations by Gerth and Mills and by Parsons. The Rheinstein-Shils translation, which would have corrected part of his interpretation, was not consulted. This may be indicative of the difficulty to see partial translations as part of a whole. (See Easton, *op. cit.,* 183, 281, 283, 301 ff.)

13. Acknowledgements

I owe thanks to many persons, foremost to the following:

Reinhard Bendix, who has carried on the tradition of comparative study in creative adaptation to the American setting. In the late nineteen-fifties he gave me an opportunity, without insistence, to feel my way into Weber's work, to overcome some early preconceptions, and to watch the writing of his *Max Weber: An Intellectual Portrait* (1960);

Juan Linz, a scholar of Weberian breadth, who insisted for a long time on the necessity of a complete edition and kept wondering skeptically who would take on the task;

Benjamin Nelson, a critic with a Weberian temper, who suggested "rulership" as one translation of *Herrschaft* and insisted on standards to which mortals have difficulty measuring up;

My wife, who accommodated my abstract preoccupation with the "oct-opus" in her sensuous household of flora and fauna and took out time to improve the style of the introduction.

I greatly appreciate the support of the Research Foundation of the State University of New York (Stony Brook), which granted me fellowships in the summers of 1963 and 1964; the assistance of the Department of Sociology, University of California at Davis; the typing of Jeannette Freeman, who claims that she gained an education through it.

It was a great pleasure to share the task with Claus Wittich, native of my hometown and fellow graduate of its classical school where we learned our basic linguistic and historical skills.

List of Abbreviations

Some of the extant translations were extensively annotated by the original translators. This annotation was to the largest part retained, and in some cases complemented by the editors; we also used some of the annotation provided for the 4th German edition of *Wirtschaft und Gesellschaft* by Johannes Winckelmann. The unsigned notes in Part One, chs. I–III are by Talcott Parsons, in Part Two, chs. VII–VIII by Max Rheinstein, and elsewhere by one of the editors as identified at the head of each section of notes. The following abbreviations were used to identify the authors of other notes:

(GM):	Hans Gerth and C. Wright Mills
(R):	Guenther Roth
(Rh):	Max Rheinstein
(W):	Johannes Winckelmann
(Wi):	Claus Wittich

In the editorial notes, a number of abbreviations were used for works (or translations of works) by Max Weber; these are listed below. A group of further bibliographical abbreviations used only in Max Rheinstein's annotation to the "Sociology of Law" is given in Part Two, ch. VIII:*i*, n. 1 (pp. 658–661 below).

AfS or *Archiv*
Archiv für Sozialwissenschaft und Sozialpolitik. Tübingen: J. C. B. Mohr (Paul Siebeck). (A scholarly periodical edited by Max Weber, Edgar Jaffé and Werner Sombart from 1904 on.)

Agrargeschichte
Die römische Agrargeschichte in ihrer Bedeutung für das Staats- und Privatrecht. Stuttgart: Ferdinand Enke, 1891. (Weber's second dissertation.)

"Agrarverhältnisse"
"Agrarverhältnisse im Altertum," in *Handwörterbuch der Staats-*

wissenschaften, 3rd ed., I (1909), 52–188. Reprinted in *GAzSW,* 1–288. (Page references are to this reprint.)

Ancient Judaism or *AJ*
Ancient Judaism. Translated and edited by Hans H. Gerth and Don Martindale. Glencoe, Ill.: The Free Press, 1952. (A translation of "Das antike Judentum," Part III of "Die Wirtschaftsethik der Welt-religionen," first published in *AfS,* 1917–19, and of a posthumously published study, "Die Pharisäer," both in *GAzRS,* III.)

Economic History
General Economic History. Translated by Frank H. Knight. London and New York: Allen & Unwin, 1927; paperback re-issue, New York: Collier Books, 1961. (A translation of *Wirtschaftsgeschichte.* Page references in ch. VIII are to the 1927 edition, elsewhere to the 1961 paperback.)

Fischoff
The Sociology of Religion. Translated by Ephraim Fischoff, with an introduction by Talcott Parsons. Boston: Beacon Press, 1963.

GAzRS
Gesammelte Aufsätze zur Religionssoziologie. 3 vols. Tübingen: J. C. B. Mohr (Paul Siebeck), 1920–21; unchanged re-issue 1922–23.

GAzSS
Gesammelte Aufsätze zur Soziologie und Sozialpolitik. Tübingen: J. C. B. Mohr (Paul Siebeck), 1924.

GAzSW
Gesammelte Aufsätze zur Sozial- und Wirtschaftsgeschichte. Tübingen: J. C. B. Mohr (Paul Siebeck), 1924.

GAzW
Gesammelte Aufsätze zur Wissenschaftslehre. 2nd ed. revised and expanded by Johannes Winckelmann. Tübingen: J. C. B. Mohr (Paul Siebeck), 1951. (1st ed. 1922.)

Gerth and Mills
From Max Weber: Essays in Sociology. Translated and edited by Hans H. Gerth and C. Wright Mills. New York: Oxford University Press, 1946.

GPS
Gesammelte Politische Schriften. 2nd ed. revised and expanded by Johannes Winckelmann, with an introduction by Theodor Heuss. Tübingen: J. C. B. Mohr (Paul Siebeck), 1958. (1st ed. München: Drei Masken Verlag, 1921.)

Handelsgesellschaften
Zur Geschichte der Handelsgesellschaften in Mittelalter. (Nach

südeuropäischen Quellen). Stuttgart: Ferdinand Enke, 1889. Reprinted in *GAzSW*, 312–443. (Page references are to the reprint. This was Weber's first dissertation.)

Protestant Ethic
The Protestant Ethic and the Spirit of Capitalism. Translated by Talcott Parsons, with a foreword by R. H. Tawney. New York: Charles Scribner's Sons, 1958 (first publ. London, 1930). (A translation of "Die protestantische Ethik und der Geist des Kapitalismus," *GAzRS*, I, 1–206; first published in *AfS*, 1904–05.)

Rechtssoziologie
Rechtssoziologie. Newly edited from the manuscript with an introduction by Johannes Winckelmann. ("Soziologische Texte," vol. 2.) Neuwied: Hermann Luchterhand Verlag, 1960 (2nd rev. ed. 1967). (This is the German edition of the "Sociology of Law" underlying the revised translation in Part Two, ch. VIII, below.)

Religion of China
The Religion of China. Confucianism and Taoism. Translated and edited by Hans H. Gerth. New edition, with an introduction by C. K. Yang. New York: Macmillan, 1964 (1st ed. Free Press, 1951). (A translation of "Konfuzianismus und Taoismus," Part I of "Die Wirtschaftsethik der Weltreligionen," first published in *AfS*, 1916, reprinted in *GAzRS*, I, 276–536.)

Religion of India
The Religion of India. The Sociology of Hinduism and Buddhism. Translated and edited by Hans H. Gerth and Don Martindale. Glencoe, Ill.: The Free Press, 1958. (A translation of "Hinduismus und Buddhismus," Part II of "Die Wirtschaftsethik der Weltreligionen," first published in *AfS*, 1916–17, reprinted in *GAzRS*, II.)

Rheinstein and Shils
Max Weber on Law in Economy and Society. Translated by Edward Shils and Max Rheinstein, edited and annotated by Rheinstein. Cambridge, Mass.: Harvard University Press, 1954.

Shils and Finch
The Methodology of the Social Sciences. Translated and edited by Edward A. Shils and Henry A. Finch. Glencoe, Ill.: The Free Press, 1949. (A translation of three methodological essays, "Die 'Objektivität' sozialwissenschaftlicher und sozialpolitischer Erkenntnis," *AfS*, 1904; "Kritische Studien auf dem Gebiet kulturwissenschaftlicher Logik," *AfS*, 1906; "Der Sinn der 'Wertfreiheit' der soziologischen und ökonomischen Wissenschaften," *Logos*, 1917/18; reprinted in *GAzW*, 146–214, 215–290, 475–526.)

Theory

    The Theory of Social and Economic Organization. Translated by A. M. Henderson and Talcott Parsons, edited with an introduction by Parsons. New York: The Free Press, 1964 (first publ. New York: Oxford University Press, 1947).

Wirtschaftsgeschichte or *Universalgeschichte*

    Wirtschaftsgeschichte. Abriss der universalen Sozial- und Wirtschaftsgeschichte. Edited from lecture scripts by Siegmund Hellmann and Melchior Palyi. München: Duncker & Humblot, 1923. (2nd ed. 1924; 3rd rev. ed. by Johannes Winckelmann, 1958.)

WuG and *WuG*-Studienausgabe

    Wirtschaft und Gesellschaft. Grundriss der verstehenden Soziologie. 4th edition, revised and arranged by Johannes Winckelmann. 2 vols. Tübingen: J. C. B. Mohr (Paul Siebeck), 1956. *WuG*-Studienausgabe refers to the licensed paperback edition (2 vols.; Köln-Berlin: Kiepenheuer & Witsch, 1964) which already incorporates some of Winckelmann's further revisions for the forthcoming definitive 5th German edition.

VOLUME ONE

ECONOMY
AND
SOCIETY

Part One and Part Two, chapters I to V

PART ONE

Conceptual Exposition

CHAPTER I

BASIC SOCIOLOGICAL TERMS

Prefatory Note

An introductory discussion of concepts can hardly be dispensed with, in spite of the fact that it is unavoidably abstract and hence gives the impression of remoteness from reality. The method employed makes no claim to any kind of novelty. On the contrary it attempts only to formulate what all empirical sociology really means when it deals with the same problems, in what it is hoped is a more convenient and somewhat more exact terminology, even though on that account it may seem pedantic. This is true even where terms are used which are apparently new or unfamiliar. As compared to the author's essay in *Logos*,[1] the terminology has been simplified as far as possible and hence considerably changed in order to render it more easily understandable. The most precise formulation cannot always be reconciled with a form which can readily be popularized. In such cases the latter aim has had to be sacrificed.

On the concept of "understanding"[2] compare the *Allgemeine Psychopathologie* of Karl Jaspers, also a few observations by Heinrich Rickert in the second edition of the *Grenzen der naturwissenschaftlichen Begriffsbildung* and particularly some of Simmel's discussions in the *Probleme der Geschichtsphilosophie*. For certain methodological considerations the reader may here be referred, as often before in the author's writings, to the procedure of Friedrich Gottl in his work *Die Herrschaft des Wortes*; this book, to be sure, is written in a somewhat difficult style and its argument does not appear everywhere to have been thoroughly thought through. As regards content, reference may be made especially to the fine work of Ferdinand Tönnies, *Gemeinschaft und Gesellschaft,* and also to the gravely misleading book of Rudolf Stammler, *Wirtschaft und Recht nach der materialistischen Geschichtsauffassung,* which may be compared with my criticism in the *Archiv für Sozialwissenschaft* (vol. 14, 1907, [GAzW, 291-359]). This critical essay contains many of the fundamental ideas of the following exposition. The present work departs from Simmel's method (in his *Soziologie* and his *Philosophie des Geldes*) in drawing a sharp distinction between subjectively intended and objectively valid "meanings"; two different things which Simmel not only fails to distinguish but often deliberately treats as belonging together.

1. *The Definition of Sociology and of Social Action*

Sociology (in the sense in which this highly ambiguous word is used here) is a science concerning itself with the interpretive understanding of social action and thereby with a causal explanation of its course and consequences. We shall speak of "action" insofar as the acting individual attaches a subjective meaning to his behavior—be it overt or covert, omission or acquiescence. Action is "social"insofar as its subjective meaning takes account of the behavior of others and is thereby oriented in its course.[3]

A. METHODOLOGICAL FOUNDATIONS[4]

1. "Meaning" may be of two kinds. The term may refer first to the actual existing meaning in the given concrete case of a particular actor, or to the average or approximate meaning attributable to a given plurality of actors; or secondly to the theoretically conceived *pure type*[5] of subjective meaning attributed to the hypothetical actor or actors in a given type of action. In no case does it refer to an objectively "correct" meaning or one which is "true" in some metaphysical sense. It is this which distinguishes the empirical sciences of action, such as sociology and history, from the dogmatic disciplines in that area, such as jurisprudence, logic, ethics, and esthetics, which seek to asceratin the "true" and "valid" meanings associated with the objects of their investigation.

2. The line between meaningful action and merely reactive behavior to which no subjective meaning is attached, cannot be sharply drawn empirically. A very considerable part of all sociologically relevant behavior, especially purely traditional behavior, is marginal between the

two. In the case of some psychophysical processes, meaningful, i.e., subjectively understandable, action is not to be found at all; in others it is discernible only by the psychologist. Many mystical experiences which cannot be adequately communicated in words are, for a person who is not susceptible to such experiences, not fully understandable. At the same time the ability to perform a similar action is not a necessary prerequisite to understanding; "one need not have been Caesar in order to understand Caesar." "Recapturing an experience" is important for accurate understanding, but not an absolute precondition for its interpretation. Understandable and non-understandable components of a process are often intermingled and bound up together.

3. All interpretation of meaning, like all scientific observations, strives for clarity and verifiable accuracy of insight and comprehension (*Evidenz*).[6] The basis for certainty in understanding can be either rational, which can be further subdivided into logical and mathematical, or it can be of an emotionally empathic or artistically appreciative quality. Action is rationally evident chiefly when we attain a completely clear intellectual grasp of the action-elements in their intended context of meaning. Empathic or appreciative accuracy is attained when, through sympathetic participation, we can adequately grasp the emotional context in which the action took place. The highest degree of rational understanding is attained in cases involving the meanings of logically or mathematically related propositions; their meaning may be immediately and unambiguously intelligible. We have a perfectly clear understanding of what it means when somebody employs the proposition $2 \times 2 = 4$ or the Pythagorean theorem in reasoning or argument, or when someone correctly carries out a logical train of reasoning according to our accepted modes of thinking. In the same way we also understand what a person is doing when he tries to achieve certain ends by choosing appropriate means on the basis of the facts of the situation, as experience has accustomed us to interpret them. The interpretation of such rationally purposeful action possesses, for the understanding of the choice of means, the highest degree of verifiable certainty. With a lower degree of certainty, which is, however, adequate for most purposes of explanation, we are able to understand errors, including confusion of problems of the sort that we ourselves are liable to, or the origin of which we can detect by sympathetic self-analysis.

On the other hand, many ultimate ends or values toward which experience shows that human action may be oriented, often cannot be understood completely, though sometimes we are able to grasp them intellectually. The more radically they differ from our own ultimate values, however, the more difficult it is for us to understand them empathically. Depending upon the circumstances of the particular case we must be content either with a purely intellectual understanding of such values or when even that fails, sometimes we must simply accept them as given data. Then we can try to understand the action motivated by them on the basis of whatever opportunities for approximate emotional and intellectual interpretation seem to be available at different points in its course. These difficulties confront, for instance, people not susceptible to unusual acts of religious and charitable zeal, or persons who abhor extreme rationalist fanaticism (such as the fanatic advocacy of the "rights of man").

The more we ourselves are susceptible to such emotional reactions as anxiety, anger, ambition, envy, jealousy, love, enthusiasm, pride, vengefulness, loyalty, devotion, and appetites of all sorts, and to the "irrational" conduct which grows out of them, the more readily can we empathize with them. Even when such emotions are found in a degree of intensity of which the observer himself is completely incapable, he can still have a significant degree of emotional understanding of their meaning and can interpret intellectually their influence on the course of action and the selection of means.

For the purposes of a typological scientific analysis it is convenient to treat all irrational, affectually determined elements of behavior as factors of deviation from a conceptually pure type of rational action. For example a panic on the stock exchange can be most conveniently analysed by attempting to determine first what the course of action would have been if it had not been influenced by irrational affects; it is then possible to introduce the irrational components as accounting for the observed deviations from this hypothetical course. Similarly, in analysing a political or military campaign it is convenient to determine in the first place what would have been a rational course, given the ends of the participants and adequate knowledge of all the circumstances. Only in this way is it possible to assess the causal significance of irrational factors as accounting for the deviations from this type. The construction of a purely rational course of action in such cases serves the sociologist as a type (ideal type) which has the merit of clear understandability and lack of ambiguity. By comparison with this it is possible to understand the ways in which actual action is influenced by irrational factors of all sorts, such as affects and errors, in that they account for the deviation from the line of conduct which would be expected on the hypothesis that the action were purely rational.

Only in this respect and for these reasons of methodological convenience is the method of sociology "rationalistic." It is naturally not legitimate to interpret this procedure as involving a rationalistic bias of sociology, but only as a methodological device. It certainly does not involve a belief in the actual predominance of rational elements in human life, for on the question of how far this predominance does or does not exist, nothing whatever has been said. That there is, however, a danger of rationalistic interpretations where they are out of place cannot be denied. All experience unfortunately confirms the existence of this danger.

4. In all the sciences of human action, account must be taken of processes and phenomena which are devoid of subjective meaning, in the role of stimuli, results, favoring or hindering circumstances. To be devoid of meaning is not identical with being lifeless or non-human; every artifact, such as for example a machine, can be understood only in terms of the meaning which its production and use have had or were intended to have; a meaning which may derive from a relation to exceedingly various purposes. Without reference to this meaning such an object remains wholly unintelligible. That which is intelligible or understandable about it is thus its relation to human action in the role either of means or of end; a relation of which the actor or actors can be said to have been aware and to which their action has been oriented. Only in terms of such categories is it possible to "understand" objects of this kind. On the other hand processes or conditions, whether they are animate or inanimate, human or non-human, are in the present sense devoid of meaning in so far as they cannot be related to an intended purpose. That is to say they are devoid of meaning if they cannot be related to action in the role of means or ends but constitute only the stimulus, the favoring or hindering circumstances. It may be that the flooding of the Dollart [at the mouth of the Ems river near the Dutch-German border] in 1277 had historical significance as a stimulus to the beginning of certain migrations of considerable importance. Human mortality, indeed the organic life cycle from the helplessness of infancy to that of old age, is naturally of the very greatest sociological importance through the various ways in which human action has been oriented to these facts. To still another category of facts devoid of meaning belong certain psychic or psychophysical phenomena such as fatigue, habituation, memory, etc.; also certain typical states of euphoria under some conditions of ascetic mortification; finally, typical variations in the reactions of individuals according to reaction-time, precision, and other modes. But in the last analysis the same principle applies to these as to other phenomena which are devoid of meaning. Both the actor and the sociologist must accept them as data to be taken into account.

It is possible that future research may be able to discover non-interpretable uniformities underlying what has appeared to be specifically meaningful action, though little has been accomplished in this direction thus far. Thus, for example, differences in hereditary biological constitution, as of "races," would have to be treated by sociology as given data in the same way as the physiological facts of the need of nutrition or the effect of senescence on action. This would be the case if, and insofar as, we had statistically conclusive proof of their influence on sociologically relevant behavior. The recognition of the causal significance of such factors would not in the least alter the specific task of sociological analysis or of that of the other sciences of action, which is the interpretation of action in terms of its subjective meaning. The effect would be only to introduce certain non-interpretable data of the same order as others which are already present, into the complex of subjectively understandable motivation at certain points. (Thus it may come to be known that there are typical relations between the frequency of certain types of teleological orientation of action or of the degree of certain kinds of rationality and the cephalic index or skin color or any other biologically inherited characteristic.)

5. Understanding may be of two kinds: the first is the direct observational understanding[7] of the subjective meaning of a given act as such, including verbal utterances. We thus understand by direct observation, in this case, the meaning of the proposition $2 \times 2 = 4$ when we hear or read it. This is a case of the direct rational understanding of ideas. We also understand an outbreak of anger as manifested by facial expression, exclamations or irrational movements. This is direct observational understanding of irrational emotional reactions. We can understand in a similar observational way the action of a woodcutter or of somebody who reaches for the knob to shut a door or who aims a gun at an animal. This is rational observational understanding of actions.

Understanding may, however, be of another sort, namely explanatory understanding. Thus we understand in terms of *motive* the meaning an actor attaches to the proposition twice two equals four, when he states it or writes it down, in that we understand what makes him do this at precisely this moment and in these circumstances. Understanding in this sense is attained if we know that he is engaged in balancing a ledger or in making a scientific demonstration, or is engaged in some other task of which this particular act would be an appropriate part. This is rational understanding of motivation, which consists in placing the act in an intelligible and more inclusive context of meaning.[8] Thus we understand the chopping of wood or aiming of a gun in terms of motive in addition to direct observation of we know that the woodchopper is working for a wage or is chopping a supply of firewood for his own use or possibly is doing it for recreation. But he might also be working off a fit of rage, an irrational case. Similarly we understand the motive of a person aiming a gun if we know that he has been commanded to shoot as a member of a firing squad, that he is fighting against an enemy, or that he is doing it for revenge. The last is affectually determined and thus in a certain sense irrational. Finally we have a motivational understanding of the outburst of anger if we know that it has been provoked by jealousy, injured pride, or an insult. The last examples are all affectually determined and hence derived from irrational motives. In all the above cases the particular act has been placed in an understandable sequence of motivation, the understanding of which can be treated as an explanation of the actual course of behavior. Thus for a science which is concerned with the subjective meaning of action, explanation requires a grasp of the complex of meaning in which an actual course of understandable action thus interpreted belongs. In all such cases, even where the processes are largely affectual, the subjective meaning of the action, including that also of the relevant meaning complexes, will be called the intended meaning.[9] (This involves a departure from ordinary usage, which speaks of intention in this sense only in the case of rationally purposive action.)

6. In all these cases understanding involves the interpretive grasp of the meaning present in one of the following contexts: (a) as in the historical approach, the actually intended meaning for concrete individual action; or (b) as in cases of sociological mass phenomena, the average of, or an approximation to, the actually intended meaning; or (c) the meaning appropriate to a scientifically formulated pure type (an ideal type) of a common phenomenon. The concepts and "laws" of pure economic theory are examples of this kind of ideal type. They state what course a given type of human action would take if it were strictly rational, unaffected by errors or emotional factors and if, furthermore, it were completely and unequivocally directed to a single end, the maximization of economic advantage. In reality, action takes exactly this course only in unusual cases, as sometimes on the stock exchange; and even then there is usually only an approximation to the ideal type. (On the purpose of such constructions, see my essay in *AfS*, 19 [cf. n. 5] and point 11 below.)

Every interpretation attempts to attain clarity and certainty, but no matter how clear an interpretation as such appears to be from the point of view of meaning, it cannot on this account claim to be the causally valid interpretation. On this level it must remain only a peculiarly plausible hypothesis. In the first place the "conscious motives" may well, even to the actor himself, conceal the various "motives" and "repressions" which constitute the real driving force of his action. Thus in such cases even subjectively honest self-analysis has only a relative value. Then it is the task of the sociologist to be aware of this motivational situation and to describe and analyse it, even though it has not actually been concretely part of the conscious intention of the actor; possibly not at all, at least not fully. This is a borderline case of the interpretation of meaning. Secondly, processes of action which seem to an observer to be the same or similar may fit into exceedingly various complexes of motive in the case of the actual actor. Then even though the situations appear superficially to be very similar we must actually understand them or interpret them as very different, perhaps, in terms of meaning, directly opposed. (Simmel, in his *Probleme der Geschichtsphilosophie*, gives a number of examples.) Third, the actors in any given situation are often subject to opposing and conflicting impulses, all of which we are able to understand. In a large number of cases we know from experience it is not possible to arrive at even an approximate estimate of the relative strength of conflicting motives and very often we cannot be certain of our interpretation. Only the actual outcome of the conflict gives a solid basis of judgment.

More generally, verification of subjective interpretation by comparison with the concrete course of events is, as in the case of all hypotheses, indispensable. Unfortunately this type of verification is feasible with relative accuracy only in the few very special cases susceptible of psychological experimentation. In very different degrees of approximation, such verification is also feasible in the limited number of cases of mass phenomena which can be statistically described and unambiguously interpreted. For the rest there remains only the possibility of comparing the largest possible number of historical or contemporary processes which, while otherwise similar, differ in the one decisive point of their relation to the particular motive or factor the role of which is being investigated. This is a fundamental task of comparative sociology. Often, unfortunately, there is available only the uncertain procedure of the "imaginary experiment" which consists in thinking away certain elements of a chain of motivation and working out the course of action which would then probably ensue, thus arriving at a causal judgment.[10]

For example, the generalization called Gresham's Law is a rationally clear interpretation of human action under certain conditions and under the assumption that it will follow a purely rational course. How far any actual course of action corresponds to this can be verified only by the available statistical evidence for the actual disappearance of under-valued monetary units from circulation. In this case our information serves to demonstrate a high degree of accuracy. The facts of experience were known before the generalization, which was formulated afterwards; but without this successful interpretation our need for causal understanding would evidently be left unsatisfied. On the other hand, without the demonstration that what can here be assumed to be a theoretically adequate interpretation also is in some degree relevant to an actual course of action, a "law," no matter how fully demonstrated theoretically, would be worthless for the understanding of action in the real world. In this case the correspondence between the theoretical interpretation of motivation and its empirical verification is entirely satisfactory and the cases are numerous enough so that verification can be considered established. But to take another example, Eduard Meyer has advanced an ingenious theory of the causal significance of the battles of Marathon, Salamis, and Platea for the development of the cultural peculiarities of Greek, and hence, more generally, Western, civilization.[11] This is derived from a meaningful interpretation of certain symptomatic facts having to do with the attitudes of the Greek oracles and prophets towards the Persians. It can only be directly verified by reference to the examples of the conduct of the Persians in cases where they were victorious, as in Jerusalem, Egypt, and Asia Minor, and even this verification must necessarily remain unsatisfactory in certain respects. The striking rational plausibility of the hypothesis must here necessarily be relied on as a support. In very many cases of historical interpretation which seem highly plausible, however, there is not even a possibility of the order of verification which was feasible in this case. Where this is true the interpretation must necessarily remain a hypothesis.

7. A motive is a complex of subjective meaning which seems to the actor himself or to the observer an adequate ground for the conduct in question. The interpretation of a coherent course of conduct is "subjectively adequate" (or "adequate on the level of meaning"), insofar as, according to our habitual modes of thought and feeling, its component parts taken in their mutual relation are recognized to constitute a "typical" complex of meaning.[12] It is more common to say "correct." The interpretation of a sequence of events will on the other hand be called *causally* adequate insofar as, according to established generalizations from experience, there is a probability that it will always actually occur in the same way. An example of adequacy on the level of meaning in this sense is what is, according to our current norms of calculation or thinking, the correct solution of an arithmetical problem. On the other hand, a causally adequate interpretation of the same phenomenon would concern the statistical probability that, according to verified generalizations from experience, there would be a correct or an erroneous solution of the same problem. This also refers to currently accepted norms but includes taking account of typical errors or of typical confusions. Thus causal explanation depends on being able to determine that there is a

probability, which in the rare ideal case can be numerically stated, but is always in some sense calculable, that a given observable event (overt or subjective) will be followed or accompanied by another event.

A correct causal interpretation of a concrete course of action is arrived at when the overt action and the motives have both been correctly apprehended and at the same time their relation has become meaningfully comprehensible. A correct causal interpretation of typical action means that the process which is claimed to be typical is shown to be both adequately grasped on the level of meaning and at the same time the interpretation is to some degree causally adequate. If adequacy in respect to meaning is lacking, then no matter how high the degree of uniformity and how precisely its probability can be numerically determined, it is still an incomprehensible statistical probability, whether we deal with overt or subjective processes. On the other hand, even the most perfect adequacy on the level of meaning has causal significance from a sociological point of view only insofar as there is some kind of proof for the existence of a probability[13] that action in fact normally takes the course which has been held to be meaningful. For this there must be some degree of determinable frequency of approximation to an average or a pure type.

Statistical uniformities constitute understandable types of action, and thus constitute sociological generalizations, only when they can be regarded as manifestations of the understandable subjective meaning of a course of social action. Conversely, formulations of a rational course of subjectively understandable action constitute sociological types of empirical process only when they can be empirically observed with a significant degree of approximation. By no means is the actual likelihood of the occurrence of a given course of overt action always directly proportional to the clarity of subjective interpretation. Only actual experience can prove whether this is so in a given case. There are statistics of processes devoid of subjective meaning, such as death rates, phenomena of fatigue, the production rate of machines, the amount of rainfall, in exactly the same sense as there are statistics of meaningful phenomena. But only when the phenomena are meaningful do we speak of sociological statistics. Examples are such cases as crime rates, occupational distributions, price statistics, and statistics of crop acreage. Naturally there are many cases where both components are involved, as in crop statistics.

8. Processes and uniformities which it has here seemed convenient not to designate as sociological phenomena or uniformities because they are not "understandable," are naturally not on that account any the less important. This is true even for sociology in our sense which is restricted

to subjectively understandable phenomena—a usage which there is no intention of attempting to impose on anyone else. Such phenomena, however important, are simply treated by a different method from the others; they become conditions, stimuli, furthering or hindering circumstances of action.

9. Action in the sense of subjectively understandable orientation of behavior exists only as the behavior of one or more *individual* human beings. For other cognitive purposes it may be useful or necessary to consider the individual, for instance, as a collection of cells, as a complex of bio-chemical reactions, or to conceive his psychic life as made up of a variety of different elements, however these may be defined. Undoubtedly such procedures yield valuable knowledge of causal relationships. But the behavior of these elements, as expressed in such uniformities, is not subjectively understandable. This is true even of psychic elements because the more precisely they are formulated from a point of view of natural science, the less they are accessible to subjective understanding. This is never the road to interpretation in terms of subjective meaning. On the contrary, both for sociology in the present sense, and for history, the object of cognition is the subjective meaning-complex of action. The behavior of physiological entities such as cells, or of any sort of psychic elements, may at least in principle be observed and an attempt made to derive uniformities from such observations. It is further possible to attempt, with their help, to obtain a causal explanation of individual phenomena, that is, to subsume them under uniformities. But the subjective understanding of action takes the same account of this type of fact and uniformity as of any others not capable of subjective interpretation. (This is true, for example, of physical, astronomical, geological, meteorological, geographical, botanical, zoological, and anatomical facts, of those aspects of psycho-pathology which are devoid of subjective meaning, or of the natural conditions of technological processes.)

For still other cognitive purposes—for instance, juristic ones—or for practical ends, it may on the other hand be convenient or even indispensable to treat social collectivities, such as states, associations, business corporations, foundations, as if they were individual persons. Thus they may be treated as the subjects of rights and duties or as the performers of legally significant actions. But for the subjective interpretation of action in sociological work these collectivities must be treated as *solely* the resultants and modes of organization of the particular acts of individual persons, since these alone can be treated as agents in a course of subjectively understandable action. Nevertheless, the sociologist cannot for his purposes afford to ignore these collective concepts derived from other disciplines. For the subjective interpretation of action has at least three important relations to these concepts. In the first place it is often necessary to employ very similar collective concepts, indeed often using the same terms, in order to obtain an intelligible terminology. Thus both in legal terminology and in everyday speech the term "state" is used both for the legal concept of the state and for the phenomena of social action to which its legal rules are relevant. For sociological purposes, however, the phenomenon "the state" does not consist necessarily or even primarily of the elements which are relevant to legal analysis; and for sociological purposes there is no such thing as a collective personality which "acts." When reference is made in a sociological context to a state, a nation, a corporation, a family, or an army corps, or to similar collectivities, what is meant is, on the contrary, *only* a certain kind of development of actual or possible social actions of individual persons. Both because of its precision and because it is established in general usage the juristic concept is taken over, but is used in an entirely different meaning.

Secondly, the subjective interpretation of action must take account of a fundamentally important fact. These concepts of collective entities which are found both in common sense and in juristic and other technical forms of thought, have a meaning in the minds of individual persons, partly as of something actually existing, partly as something with normative authority. This is true not only of judges and officials, but of ordinary private individuals as well. Actors thus in part orient their action to them, and in this role such ideas have a powerful, often a decisive, causal influence on the course of action of real individuals. This is above all true where the ideas involve normative prescription or prohibition. Thus, for instance, one of the important aspects of the existence of a modern state, precisely as a complex of social interaction of individual persons, consists in the fact that the action of various individuals is oriented to the belief that it exists or should exist, thus that its acts and laws are valid in the legal sense. This will be further discussed below. Though extremely pedantic and cumbersome, it would be possible, if purposes of sociological terminology alone were involved, to eliminate such terms entirely, and substitute newly-coined words. This would be possible even though the word "state" is used ordinarily not only to designate the legal concept but also the real process of action. But in the above important connexion, at least, this would naturally be impossible.

Thirdly, it is the method of the so-called "organic" school of sociology —classical example: Schäffle's brilliant work, *Bau und Leben des sozialen Körpers*—to attempt to understand social interaction by using as a point of departure the "whole" within which the individual acts. His action and behavior are then interpreted somewhat in the way that a physiologist would treat the role of an organ of the body in the "economy" of the organism, that is from the point of view of the survival of the latter. (Compare the famous dictum of a well-known physiologist: "Sec. 10. The spleen. Of the spleen, gentlemen, we know nothing. So much for the spleen." Actually, of course, he knew a good deal about the spleen—its position, size, shape, etc.; but he could say nothing about its function, and it was his inability to do this that he called "ignorance.") How far in other disciplines this type of functional analysis of the relation of "parts" to a "whole" can be regarded as definitive, cannot be discussed here; but it is well known that the bio-chemical and bio-physical modes of analysis of the organism are on principle opposed to stopping there. For purposes of sociological analysis two things can be said. First this functional frame of reference is convenient for purposes of practical illustration and for provisional orientation. In these respects it is not only useful but indispensable. But at the same time if its cognitive value is overestimated and its concepts illegitimately "reified,"[14] it can be highly dangerous. Secondly, in certain circumstances this is the only available way of determining just what processes of social action it is important to understand in order to explain a given phenomenon. But this is only the beginning of sociological analysis as here understood. In the case of social collectivities, precisely as distinguished from organisms, we are in a position to go beyond merely demonstrating functional relationships and uniformities. We can accomplish something which is never attainable in the natural sciences, namely the subjective understanding of the action of the component individuals. The natural sciences on the other hand cannot do this, being limited to the formulation of causal uniformities in objects and events and the explanation of individual facts by applying them. We do not "understand" the behavior of cells, but can only observe the relevant functional relationships and generalize on the basis of these observations. This additional achievement of explanation by interpretive understanding, as distinguished from external observation, is of course attained only at a price—the more hypothetical and fragmentary character of its results. Nevertheless, subjective understanding is the specific characteristic of sociological knowledge.

It would lead too far afield even to attempt to discuss how far the behavior of animals is subjectively understandable to us and vice versa; in both cases the meaning of the term understanding and its extent of application would be highly problematical. But in so far as such understanding existed it would be theoretically possible to formulate a sociology of the relations of men to animals, both domestic and wild. Thus many animals "understand" commands, anger, love, hostility, and react to them in ways which are evidently often by no means purely instinctive and mechanical and in some sense both consciously meaningful and affected by experience. In a way, our ability to share the feelings of primitive men is not very much greater. We either do not have any reliable means of determining the subjective state of mind of an animal or what we have is at best very unsatisfactory. It is well known that the problems of animal psychology, however interesting, are very thorny ones. There are in particular various forms of social organization among animals: monogamous and polygamous "families," herds, flocks, and finally "states," with a functional division of labour. (The extent of functional differentiation found in these animal societies is by no means, however, entirely a matter of the degree of organic or morphological differentiation of the individual members of the species. Thus, the functional differentiation found among the termites, and in consequence that of the products of their social activities, is much more advanced than in the case of the bees and ants.) In this field it goes without saying that a purely functional point of view is often the best that can, at least for the present, be attained, and the investigator must be content with it. Thus it is possible to study the ways in which the species provides for its survival; that is, for nutrition, defence, reproduction, and reconstruction of the social units. As the principal bearers of these functions, differentiated types of individuals can be identified: "kings," "queens," "workers," "soldiers," "drones," "propagators," "queen's substitutes," and so on. Anything more than that was for a long time merely a matter of speculation or of an attempt to determine the extent to which heredity on the one hand and environment on the other would be involved in the development of these "social" proclivities. This was particularly true of the controversies between Götte and Weismann.[15] The latter's conception in *Die Allmacht der Naturzüchtung* was largely based on wholly non-empirical deductions. But all serious authorities are naturally fully agreed that the limitation of analysis to the functional level is only a necessity imposed by our present ignorance, which it is hoped will only be temporary. (For an account of the state of knowledge of the termites, for example, see the study by Karl Escherich, *Die Termiten oder weissen Ameisen,* 1909.)

The researchers would like to understand not only the relatively obvious survival functions of these various differentiated types, but also the bearing of different variants of the theory of heredity or its reverse on the problem of explaining how these differentiations have come about. Moreover, they would like to know first what factors account for the original differentiation of specialized types from the still neutral undifferentiated species-type. Secondly, it would be important to know what leads the differentiated individual in the typical case to behave in a way which actually serves the survival value of the organized group. Wherever research has made any progress in the solution of these problems it has been through the experimental demonstration of the probability or possibility of the role of chemical stimuli or physiological processes, such as nutritional states, the effects of parasitic castration, etc., in the case of the individual organism. How far there is even a hope that the existence of "subjective" or "meaningful" orientation could be made experimentally probable, even the specialist today would hardly be in a position to say. A verifiable conception of the state of mind of these social animals accessible to meaningful understanding, would seem to be attainable even as an ideal goal only within narrow limits. However that may be, a contribution to the understanding of human social action is hardly to be expected from this quarter. On the contrary, in the field of animal psychology, human analogies are and must be continually employed. The most that can be hoped for is, then, that these biological analogies may some day be useful in suggesting significant problems. For instance they may throw light on the question of the relative role in the early stages of human social differentiation of mechanical and instinctive factors, as compared with that of the factors which are accessible to subjective interpretation generally, and more particularly to the role of consciously rational action. It is necessary for the sociologist to be thoroughly aware of the fact that in the early stages even of human development, the first set of factors is completely predominant. Even in the later stages he must take account of their continual interaction with the others in a role which is often of decisive importance. This is particularly true of all "traditional" action and of many aspects of charisma, which contain the seeds of certain types of psychic "contagion" and thus give rise to new social developments. These types of action are very closely related to phenomena which are understandable either only in biological terms or can be interpreted in terms of subjective motives only in fragments. But all these facts do not discharge sociology from the obligation, in full awareness of the narrow limits to which it is confined, to accomplish what it alone can do.

The various works of Othmar Spann [1878–1950] are often full of suggestive ideas though at the same time he is guilty of occasional misunderstandings and above all of arguing on the basis of pure value judgments which have no place in an empirical investigation. But he is undoubtedly correct in doing something to which, however, no one seriously objects, namely, emphasizing the sociological significance of the functional point of view for preliminary orientation to problems. This is what he calls the "universalistic method." It is true that we must know what kind of action is functionally necessary for "survival," but even more so for the maintenance of a cultural type and the continuity of the corresponding modes of social action, before it is possible even to inquire how this action has come about and what motives determine it. It is necessary to know what a "king," an "official," an "entrepreneur," a "procurer," or a "magician" does, that is, what kind of typical action, which justifies classifying an individual in one of these categories, is important and relevant for an analysis, before it is possible to undertake the analysis itself. (This is what Rickert means by *Wertbezogenheit*.) But it is only this analysis itself which can achieve the sociological understanding of the actions of typically differentiated human (and only human) individuals, and which hence constitutes the specific function of sociology. It is a tremendous misunderstanding to think that an "individualistic" *method* should involve what is in any conceivable sense an individualistic system of *values*. It is as important to avoid this error as the related one which confuses the unavoidable tendency of sociological concepts to assume a rationalistic character with a belief in the predominance of rational motives, or even a positive valuation of rationalism. Even a socialistic economy would have to be understood sociologically in exactly the same kind of "individualistic" terms; that is, in terms of the action of individuals, the types of officials found in it, as would be the case with a system of free exchange analysed in terms of the theory of marginal utility or a "better," but in this respect similar theory). The real empirical sociological investigation begins with the question: What motives determine and lead the individual members and participants in this socialistic community to behave in such a way that the community came into being in the first place and that it continues to exist? Any form of functional analysis which proceeds from the whole to the parts can accomplish only a preliminary preparation for this investigation—a preparation, the utility and indispensability of which, if properly carried out, is naturally beyond question.

10. It is customary to designate various sociological generalizations, as for example "Gresham's Law," as "laws." These are in fact typical probabilities confirmed by observation to the effect that under certain given conditions an expected course of social action will occur, which is understandable in terms of the typical motives and typical subjective intentions of the actors. These generalizations are both understandable and definite in the highest degree insofar as the typically observed course of action can be understood in terms of the purely rational pursuit of an end, or where for reasons of methodological convenience such a theoretical type can be heuristically employed. In such cases the relations of means and end will be clearly understandable on grounds of experience, particularly where the choice of means was "inevitable." In such

cases it is legitimate to assert that insofar as the action was rigorously rational it could not have taken any other course because for technical reasons, given their clearly defined ends, no other means were available to the actors. This very case demonstrates how erroneous it is to regard any kind of psychology as the ultimate foundation of the sociological interpretation of action. The term psychology, to be sure, is today understood in a wide variety of senses. For certain quite specific methodological purposes the type of treatment which attempts to follow the procedures of the natural sciences employs a distinction between "physical" and "psychic" phenomena which is entirely foreign to the disciplines concerned with human action, at least in the present sense. The results of a type of psychological investigation which employs the methods of the natural sciences in any one of various possible ways may naturally, like the results of any other science, have outstanding significance for sociological problems; indeed this has often happened. But this use of the results of psychology is something quite different from the investigation of human behavior in terms of its subjective meaning. Hence sociology has no closer relationship on a general analytical level to this type of psychology than to any other science. The source of error lies in the concept of the "psychic." It is held that everything which is not physical is *ipso facto* psychic. However, the *meaning* of a train of mathematical reasoning which a person carries out is not in the relevant sense "psychic." Similarly the rational deliberation of an actor as to whether the results of a given proposed course of action will or will not promote certain specific interests, and the corresponding decision, do not become one bit more understandable by taking "psychological" considerations into account. But it is precisely on the basis of such rational assumptions that most of the laws of sociology, including those of economics, are built up. On the other hand, in explaining the irrationalities of action sociologically, that form of psychology which employs the method of subjective understanding undoubtedly can make decisively important contributions. But this does not alter the fundamental methodological situation.

11. We have taken for granted that sociology seeks to formulate type concepts and generalized uniformities of empirical process. This distinguishes it from history, which is oriented to the causal analysis and explanation of individual actions, structures, and personalities possessing cultural significance. The empirical material which underlies the concepts of sociology consists to a very large extent, though by no means exclusively, of the same concrete processes of action which are dealt with by historians. An important consideration in the formulation of sociological concepts and generalizations is the contribution that sociology

can make toward the causal explanation of some historically and culturally important phenomenon. As in the case of every generalizing science the abstract character of the concepts of sociology is responsible for the fact that, compared with actual historical reality, they are relatively lacking in fullness of concrete content. To compensate for this disadvantage, sociological analysis can offer a greater precision of concepts. This precision is obtained by striving for the highest possible degree of adequacy on the level of meaning. It has already been repeatedly stressed that this aim can be realized in a particularly high degree in the case of concepts and generalizations which formulate rational processes. But sociological investigation attempts to include in its scope various irrational phenomena, such as prophetic, mystic, and affectual modes of action, formulated in terms of theoretical concepts which are adequate on the level of meaning. In *all* cases, rational or irrational, sociological analysis both abstracts from reality and at the same time helps us to understand it, in that it shows with what degree of approximation a concrete historical phenomenon can be subsumed under one or more of these concepts. For example, the same historical phenomenon may be in one aspect feudal, in another patrimonial, in another bureaucratic, and in still another charismatic. In order to give a precise meaning to these terms, it is necessary for the sociologist to formulate pure ideal types of the corresponding forms of action which in each case involve the highest possible degree of logical integration by virtue of their complete adequacy on the level of meaning. But precisely because this is true, it is probably seldom if ever that a real phenomenon can be found which corresponds exactly to one of these ideally constructed pure types. The case is similar to a physical reaction which has been calculated on the assumption of an absolute vacuum. Theoretical differentiation (*Kasuistik*) is possible in sociology only in terms of ideal or pure types. It goes without saying that in addition it is convenient for the sociologist from time to time to employ average types of an empirical statistical character, concepts which do not require methodological discussion. But when reference is made to "typical" cases, the term should always be understood, unless otherwise stated, as meaning *ideal* types, which may in turn be rational or irrational as the case may be (thus in economic theory they are always rational), but in any case are always constructed with a view to adequacy on the level of meaning.

It is important to realize that in the sociological field as elsewhere, averages, and hence average types, can be formulated with a relative degree of precision only where they are concerned with differences of degree in respect to action which remains qualitatively the same. Such cases do occur, but in the majority of cases of action important to history or sociology the motives which determine it are qualitatively heterogeneous. Then it is quite impossible to speak of an "average" in the true sense. The ideal types of social action which for instance are used in economic theory are thus unrealistic or abstract in that they always ask what course of action would take place if it were purely rational and oriented to economic ends alone. This construction can be used to aid in the understanding of action not purely economically determined but which involves deviations arising from traditional restraints, affects, errors, and the intrusion of other than economic purposes or considerations. This can take place in two ways. First, in analysing the extent to which in the concrete case, or on the average for a class of cases, the action was in part economically determined along with the other factors. Secondly, by throwing the discrepancy between the actual course of events and the ideal type into relief, the analysis of the non-economic motives actually involved is facilitated. The procedure would be very similar in employing an ideal type of mystical orientation, with its appropriate attitude of indifference to worldly things, as a tool for analysing its consequences for the actor's relation to ordinary life—for instance, to political or economic affairs. The more sharply and precisely the ideal type has been constructed, thus the more abstract and unrealistic in this sense it is, the better it is able to perform its functions in formulating terminology, classifications, and hypotheses. In working out a concrete causal explanation of individual events, the procedure of the historian is essentially the same. Thus in attempting to explain the campaign of 1866, it is indispensable both in the case of Moltke and of Benedek to attempt to construct imaginatively how each, given fully adequate knowledge both of his own situation and of that of his opponent, would have acted. Then it is possible to compare with this the actual course of action and to arrive at a causal explanation of the observed deviations, which will be attributed to such factors as misinformation, strategical errors, logical fallacies, personal temperament, or considerations outside the realm of strategy. Here, too, an ideal-typical construction of rational action is actually employed even though it is not made explicit.

The theoretical concepts of sociology are ideal types not only from the objective point of view, but also in their application to subjective processes. In the great majority of cases actual action goes on in a state of inarticulate half-consciousness or actual unconsciousness of its subjective meaning. The actor is more likely to "be aware" of it in a vague sense than he is to "know" what he is doing or be explicitly self-conscious about it. In most cases his action is governed by impulse or habit. Only occasionally and, in the uniform action of large numbers, often only in the case of a few individuals, is the subjective meaning of the action, whether rational or irrational, brought clearly into consciousness. The ideal type of meaningful action where the meaning is fully conscious and explicit is a marginal case. Every sociological or historical investigation, in applying its analysis to the empirical facts, must take this fact into account. But the difficulty need not prevent the sociologist from systematizing his concepts by the classification of possible types of subjective meaning. That is, he may reason as if action actually proceeded on the basis of clearly self-conscious meaning. The resulting deviation from the concrete facts must continually be kept in mind whenever it is a question of this level of concreteness, and must be carefully studied with reference both to degree and kind. It is often necessary to choose between terms which are either clear or unclear. Those which are clear will, to be sure, have the abstractness of ideal types, but they are none the less preferable for scientific purposes. (On all these questions see " 'Objectivity' in Social Science and Social Policy.")

B. SOCIAL ACTION

1. Social action, which includes both failure to act and passive acquiescence, may be oriented to the past, present, or expected future behavior of others. Thus it may be motivated by revenge for a past attack, defence against present, or measures of defence against future aggression. The "others" may be individual persons, and may be known to the actor as such, or may constitute an indefinite plurality and may be entirely unknown as individuals. (Thus, money is a means of exchange which the actor accepts in payment because he orients his action to the expectation that a large but unknown number of individuals he is personally unacquainted with will be ready to accept it in exchange on some future occasion.)

2. Not every kind of action, even of overt action, is "social" in the sense of the present discussion. Overt action is non-social if it is oriented solely to the behavior of inanimate objects. Subjective attitudes constitute social action only so far as they are oriented to the behavior of others. For example, religious behavior is not social if it is simply a matter of contemplation or of solitary prayer. The economic activity of an individual is social only if it takes account of the behavior of someone else. Thus very generally it becomes social insofar as the actor assumes that others will respect his actual control over economic goods. Concretely it is social, for instance, if in relation to the actor's own consumption the future wants of others are taken into account and this becomes one consideration affecting the actor's own saving. Or, in another connexion, production may be oriented to the future wants of other people.

3. Not every type of contact of human beings has a social character; this is rather confined to cases where the actor's behavior is meaningfully oriented to that of others. For example, a mere collision of two cyclists may be compared to a natural event. On the other hand, their attempt to avoid hitting each other, or whatever insults, blows, or friendly discussion might follow the collision, would constitute "social action."

4. Social action is not identical either with the similar actions of many persons or with every action influenced by other persons. Thus, if at the beginning of a shower a number of people on the street put up their umbrellas at the same time, this would not ordinarily be a case of action mutually oriented to that of each other, but rather of all reacting in the same way to the like need of protection from the rain. It is well known that the actions of the individual are strongly influenced by the mere fact that he is a member of a crowd confined within a limited space. Thus, the subject matter of studies of "crowd psychology," such as those of Le Bon, will be called "action conditioned by crowds." It is also possible for large numbers, though dispersed, to be influenced simultaneously or successively by a source of influence operating similarly on all the individuals, as by means of the press. Here also the behavior of an individual is influenced by his membership in a "mass" and by the fact that he is aware of being a member. Some types of reaction are only made possible by the mere fact that the individual acts as part of a crowd. Others become more difficult under these conditions. Hence it is possible that a particular event or mode of human behavior can give rise to the most diverse kinds of feeling—gaiety, anger, enthusiasm, despair, and passions of all sorts—in a crowd situation which would not occur at all or not nearly so readily if the individual were alone. But for this to happen there need not, at least in many cases, be any meaningful relation between the behavior of the individual and the fact that he is a member of a crowd. It is not proposed in the present sense to call action "social" when it is merely a result of the effect on the individual of the existence of a crowd as such and the action is not oriented to that fact on the level of meaning. At the same time the borderline is naturally highly indefinite. In such cases as that of the influence of the demagogue, there may be a wide variation in the extent to which his mass clientele is affected by a meaningful reaction to the fact of its large numbers; and whatever this relation may be, it is open to varying interpretations.

But furthermore, mere "imitation" of the action of others, such as that on which Tarde has rightly laid emphasis, will not be considered a case of specifically social action if it is purely reactive so that there is no meaningful orientation to the actor imitated. The borderline is, however, so indefinite that it is often hardly possible to discriminate. The mere fact that a person is found to employ some apparently useful procedure which he learned from someone else does not, however, constitute, in the present sense, social action. Action such as this is not oriented to the action of the other person, but the actor has, through observing the other, become acquainted with certain objective facts; and it is these to which his action is oriented. His action is then *causally* determined by the action of others, but not meaningfully. On the other hand, if the action of others is imitated because it is fashionable or traditional or exemplary, or lends social distinction, or on similar grounds, it is mean-ingfully oriented either to the behavior of the source of imitation or of third persons or of both. There are of course all manner of transitional cases between the two types of imitation. Both the phenomena discussed above, the behavior of crowds and imitation, stand on the indefinite borderline of social action. The same is true, as will often appear, of traditionalism and charisma. The reason for the indefiniteness of the line in these and other cases lies in the fact that both the orientation to the behavior of others and the meaning which can be imputed by the actor himself, are by no means always capable of clear determination and are often altogether unconscious and seldom fully self-conscious. Mere "influence" and meaningful orientation cannot therefore always be clearly differentiated on the empirical level. But conceptually it is essential to distinguish them, even though merely reactive imitation may well have a degree of sociological importance at least equal to that of the type which can be called social action in the strict sense. Sociology, it goes without saying, is by no means confined to the study of social action; this is only, at least for the kind of sociology being developed here, its central subject matter, that which may be said to be decisive for its status as a science. But this does not imply any judgment on the comparative importance of this and other factors.

2. *Types of Social Action*

Social action, like all action, may be oriented in four ways. It may be:

(1) *instrumentally rational (zweckrational)*, that is, determined by expectations as to the behavior of objects in the environment and of other human beings; these expectations are used as "conditions" or "means" for the attainment of the actor's own rationally pursued and calculated ends;

(2) *value-rational (wertrational)*, that is, determined by a conscious

belief in the value for its own sake of some ethical, aesthetic, religious, or other form of behavior, independently of its prospects of success;
(3) *affectual* (especially emotional), that is, determined by the actor's specific affects and feeling states;
(4) *traditional,* that is, determined by ingrained habituation.

1. Strictly traditional behavior, like the reactive type of imitation discussed above, lies very close to the borderline of what can justifiably be called meaningfully oriented action, and indeed often on the other side. For it is very often a matter of almost automatic reaction to habitual stimuli which guide behavior in a course which has been repeatedly followed. The great bulk of all everyday action to which people have become habitually accustomed approaches this type. Hence, its place in a systematic classification is not merely that of a limiting case because, as will be shown later, attachment to habitual forms can be upheld with varying degrees of self-consciousness and in a variety of senses. In this case the type may shade over into value rationality (*Wertrationalität*).

2. Purely affectual behavior also stands on the borderline of what can be considered "meaningfully" oriented, and often it, too, goes over the line. It may, for instance, consist in an uncontrolled reaction to some exceptional stimulus. It is a case of sublimation when affectually determined action occurs in the form of conscious release of emotional tension. When this happens it is usually well on the road to rationalization in one or the other or both of the above senses.

3. The orientation of value-rational action is distinguished from the affectual type by its clearly self-conscious formulation of the ultimate values governing the action and the consistently planned orientation of its detailed course to these values. At the same time the two types have a common element, namely that the meaning of the action does not lie in the achievement of a result ulterior to it, but in carrying out the specific type of action for its own sake. Action is affectual if it satisfies a need for revenge, sensual gratification, devotion, contemplative bliss, or for working off emotional tensions (irrespective of the level of sublimation).

Examples of pure value-rational orientation would be the actions of persons who, regardless of possible cost to themselves, act to put into practice their convictions of what seems to them to be required by duty, honor, the pursuit of beauty, a religious call, personal loyalty, or the importance of some "cause" no matter in what it consists. In our terminology, value-rational action always involves "commands" or "demands" which, in the actor's opinion, are binding on him. It is only in cases where human action is motivated by the fulfillment of such unconditional demands that it will be called value-rational. This is the case in widely varying degrees, but for the most part only to a relatively slight extent. Nevertheless, it will be shown that the occurrence of this mode of action is important enough to justify its formulation as a distinct type;

though it may be remarked that there is no intention here of attempting to formulate in any sense an exhaustive classification of types of action.

4. Action is instrumentally rational (*zweckrational*) when the end, the means, and the secondary results are all rationally taken into account and weighed. This involves rational consideration of alternative means to the end, of the relations of the end to the secondary consequences, and finally of the relative importance of different possible ends. Determination of action either in affectual or in traditional terms is thus incompatible with this type. Choice between alternative and conflicting ends and results may well be determined in a value-rational manner. In that case, action is instrumentally rational only in respect to the choice of means. On the other hand, the actor may, instead of deciding between alternative and conflicting ends in terms of a rational orientation to a system of values, simply take them as given subjective wants and arrange them in a scale of consciously assessed relative urgency. He may then orient his action to this scale in such a way that they are satisfied as far as possible in order of urgency, as formulated in the principle of "marginal utility." Value-rational action may thus have various different relations to the instrumentally rational action. From the latter point of view, however, value-rationality is always irrational. Indeed, the more the value to which action is oriented is elevated to the status of an absolute value, the more "irrational" in this sense the corresponding action is. For, the more unconditionally the actor devotes himself to this value for its own sake, to pure sentiment or beauty, to absolute goodness or devotion to duty, the less is he influenced by considerations of the consequences of his action. The orientation of action wholly to the rational achievement of ends without relation to fundamental values is, to be sure, essentially only a limiting case.

5. It would be very unusual to find concrete cases of action, especially of social action, which were oriented *only* in one or another of these ways. Furthermore, this classification of the modes of orientation of action is in no sense meant to exhaust the possibilities of the field, but only to formulate in conceptually pure form certain sociologically important types to which actual action is more or less closely approximated or, in much the more common case, which constitute its elements. The usefulness of the classification for the purposes of this investigation can only be judged in terms of its results.

3. *The Concept of Social Relationship*

The term "social relationship" will be used to denote the behavior of a plurality of actors insofar as, in its meaningful content, the action of each takes account of that of the others and is oriented in these terms. The social relationship thus consists entirely and exclusively in the exist-

ence of a probability that there will be a meaningful course of social action
—irrespective, for the time being, of the basis for this probability.

1. Thus, as a defining criterion, it is essential that there should be
at least a minimum of mutual orientation of the action of each to that
of the others. Its content may be of the most varied nature: conflict,
hostility, sexual attraction, friendship, loyalty, or economic exchange. It
may involve the fulfillment, the evasion, or the violation of the terms
of an agreement; economic, erotic, or some other form of "competition";
common membership in status, national or class groups (provided it
leads to social action). Hence, the definition does not specify whether
the relation of the actors is co-operative or the opposite.

2. The "meaning" relevant in this context is always a case of the
meaning imputed to the parties in a given concrete case, on the average,
or in a theoretically formulated pure type—it is never a normatively
"correct" or a metaphysically "true" meaning. Even in cases of such
forms of social organization as a state, church, association, or marriage,
the social relationship consists exclusively in the fact that there has existed, exists, or will exist a probability of action in some definite way
appropriate to this meaning. It is vital to be continually clear about this
in order to avoid the "reification" of those concepts. A "state," for example, ceases to exist in a sociologically relevant sense whenever there
is no longer a probability that certain kinds of meaningfully oriented
social action will take place. This probability may be very high or it may
be negligibly low. But in any case it is only in the sense and degree in
which it does exist that the corresponding social relationship exists. It is
impossible to find any other clear meaning for the statement that, for
instance, a given "state" exists or has ceased to exist.

3. The subjective meaning need not necessarily be the same for all
the parties who are mutually oriented in a given social relationship;
there need not in this sense be "reciprocity." "Friendship," "love,"
"loyalty," "fidelity to contracts," "patriotism," on one side, may well be
faced with an entirely different attitude on the other. In such cases the
parties associate different meanings with their actions, and the social
relationship is insofar objectively "asymmetrical" from the points of view
of the two parties. It may nevertheless be a case of mutual orientation
insofar as, even though partly or wholly erroneously, one party pre-
sumes a particular attitude toward him on the part of the other and
orients his action to this expectation. This can, and usually will, have
consequences for the course of action and the form of the relationship.
A relationship is objectively symmetrical only as, according to the typical expectations of the parties, the meaning for one party is the same as
that for the other. Thus the actual attitude of a child to its father may be
a least approximately that which the father, in the individual case, on
the average or typically, has come to expect. A social relationship in
which the attitudes are completely and fully corresponding is in reality
a limiting case. But the absence of reciprocity will, for terminological

purposes, be held to exclude the existence of a social relationship only if it actually results in the absence of a mutual orientation of the action of the parties. Here as elsewhere all sorts of transitional cases are the rule rather than the exception.

4. A social relationship can be of a very fleeting character or of varying degrees of permanence. In the latter case there is a probability of the repeated recurrence of the behavior which corresponds to its subjective meaning and hence is expected. In order to avoid fallacious impressions, let it be repeated that it is *only* the existence of the probability that, corresponding to a given subjective meaning, a certain type of action will take place which constitutes the "existence" of the social relationship. Thus that a "friendship" or a "state" exists or has existed means this and only this: that we, the observers, judge that there is or has been a probability that on the basis of certain kinds of known subjective attitude of certain individuals there will result in the average sense a certain specific type of action. For the purposes of legal reasoning it is essential to be able to decide whether a rule of law does or does not carry legal authority, hence whether a legal relationship does or does not "exist." This type of question is not, however, relevant to sociological problems.

5. The subjective meaning of a social relationship may change, thus a political relationship once based on solidarity may develop into a conflict of interests. In that case it is only a matter of terminological convenience and of the degree of continuity of the change whether we say that a new relationship has come into existence or that the old one continues but has acquired a new meaning. It is also possible for the meaning to be partly constant, partly changing.

6. The meaningful content which remains relatively constant in a social relationship is capable of formulation in terms of maxims which the parties concerned expect to be adhered to by their partners on the average and approximately. The more rational in relation to values or to given ends the action is, the more is this likely to be the case. There is far less possibility of a rational formulation of subjective meaning in the case of a relation of erotic attraction or of personal loyalty or any other affectual type than, for example, in the case of a business contract.

7. The meaning of a social relationship may be agreed upon by mutual consent. This implies that the parties make promises covering their future behavior, whether toward each other or toward third persons. In such cases each party then normally counts, so far as he acts rationally, in some degree on the fact that the other will orient his action to the meaning of the agreement as he (the first actor) understands it. In part he orients his action rationally (*zweckrational*) to these expectations as given facts with, to be sure, varying degrees of subjectively "loyal" intention of doing his part. But in part also he is motivated value-rationally by a sense of duty, which makes him adhere to the agreement as he understands it. This much may be anticipated. (For a further elaboration, see secs. 9 and 13 below.)

4. *Types of Action Orientation: Usage, Custom, Self-Interest*

Within the realm of social action certain empirical uniformities can be observed, that is, courses of action that are repeated by the actor or (simultaneously) occur among numerous actors since the subjective meaning is meant to be the same. Sociological investigation is concerned with these typical modes of action. Thereby it differs from history, the subject of which is rather the causal explanation of important individual events; important, that is, in having an influence on human destiny.

If an orientation toward social action occurs regularly, it will be called "usage" (*Brauch*) insofar as the probability of its existence within a group is based on nothing but actual practice. A usage will be called a "custom" (*Sitte*) if the practice is based upon long standing. On the other hand, a uniformity of orientation may be said to be "determined by self-interest," if and insofar as the actors' conduct is instrumentally (*zweckrational*) oriented toward identical expectations.[16]

1. Usage also includes "fashion" (*Mode*). As distinguished from custom and in direct contrast to it, usage will be called fashion so far as the mere fact of the *novelty* of the corresponding behavior is the basis of the orientation of action. Its locus is in the neighborhood of "convention,"[17] since both of them usually spring from a desire for social prestige. Fashion, however, will not be further discussed here.

2. As distinguished from both "convention" and "law," "custom" refers to rules devoid of any external sanction. The actor conforms with them of his own free will, whether his motivation lies in the fact that he merely fails to think about it, that it is more comfortable to conform, or whatever else the reason may be. For the same reasons he can consider it likely that other members of the group will adhere to a custom.

Thus custom is not "valid" in anything like the legal sense; conformity with it is not "demanded" by anybody. Naturally, the transition from this to validly enforced convention and to law is gradual. Everywhere what has been traditionally handed down has been an important source of what has come to be enforced. Today it is customary every morning to eat a breakfast which, within limits, conforms to a certain pattern. But there is no obligation to do so, except possibly for hotel guests, and it has not always been customary. On the other hand, the current mode of dress, even though it has partly originated in custom, is today very largely no longer customary alone, but conventional.

(On the concepts of usage and custom, the relevant parts of vol. II of R. von Jhering's *Zweck im Recht* are still worth reading. Compare also, P. Oertmann, *Rechtsordnung und Verkehrssitte* (1914); and more recently E. Weigelin, *Sitte, Recht und Moral* (1919), which agrees with the author's position as opposed to that of Stammler.)

3. Many of the especially notable uniformities in the course of social action are not determined by orientation to any sort of norm which is held to be valid, nor do they rest on custom, but entirely on the fact that the corresponding type of social action is in the nature of the case best adapted to the normal interests of the actors as they themselves are aware of them. This is above all true of economic action, for example, the uniformities of price determination in a "free" market, but is by no means confined to such cases. The dealers in a market thus treat their own actions as means for obtaining the satisfaction of the ends defined by what they realize to be their own typical economic interests, and similarly treat as conditions the corresponding typical expectations as to the prospective behavior of others. The more strictly rational (*zweckrational*) their action is, the more will they tend to react similarly to the same situation. In this way there arise similarities, uniformities, and continuities in their attitudes and actions which are often far more stable than they would be if action were oriented to a system of norms and duties which were considered binding on the members of a group. This phenomenon—the fact that orientation to the situation in terms of the pure self-interest of the individual and of the others to whom he is related can bring about results comparable to those which imposed norms prescribe, very often in vain—has aroused a lively interest, especially in economic affairs. Observation of this has, in fact, been one of the important sources of economics as a science. But it is true in all other spheres of action as well. This type, with its clarity of self-consciousness and freedom from subjective scruples, is the polar antithesis of every sort of unthinking acquiescence in customary ways as well as of devotion to norms consciously accepted as absolute values. One of the most important aspects of the process of "rationalization" of action is the substitution for the unthinking acceptance of ancient custom, of deliberate adaptation to situations in terms of self-interest. To be sure, this process by no means exhausts the concept of rationalization of action. For in addition this can proceed in a variety of other directions; positively in that of a deliberate formulation of ultimate values (*Wertrationalisierung*); or negatively, at the expense not only of custom, but of emotional values; and, finally, in favor of a morally sceptical type of rationality, at the expense of any belief in absolute values. The many possible meanings of the concept of rationalization will often enter into the discussion.[18] (Further remarks on the analytial problem will be found at the end.)[19]

4. The stability of merely customary action rests essentially on the fact that the person who does not adapt himself to it is subjected to both petty and major inconveniences and annoyances as long as the majority of the people he comes in contact with continue to uphold the custom and conform with it.

Similarly, the stability of action in terms of self-interest rests on the fact that the person who does not orient his action to the interests of others, does not "take account" of them, arouses their antagonism or may end up in a situation different from that which he had foreseen or wished to bring about. He thus runs the risk of damaging his own interests.

5. *Legitimate Order*

Action, especially social action which involves a social relationship, may be guided by the belief in the existence of a legitimate order. The probability that action will actually be so governed will be called the "validity" (*Geltung*) of the order in question.

1. Thus, the validity of an order means more than the mere existence of a uniformity of social action determined by custom or self-interest. If furniture movers regularly advertise at the time many leases expire, this uniformity is determined by self-interest. If a salesman visits certain customers on particular days of the month or the week, it is either a case of customary behavior or a product of self-interested orientation. However, when a civil servant appears in his office daily at a fixed time, he does not act only on the basis of custom or self-interest which he could disregard if he wanted to; as a rule, his action is also determined by the validity of an order (viz., the civil service rules), which he fulfills partly because disobedience would be disadvantageous to him but also because its violation would be abhorrent to his sense of duty (of course, in varying degrees).

2. Only then will the content of a social relationship be called an order if the conduct is, approximately or on the average, oriented toward determinable "maxims." Only then will an order be called "valid" if the orientation toward these maxims occurs, among other reasons, also because it is in some appreciable way regarded by the actor as in some way obligatory or exemplary for him. Naturally, in concrete cases, the orientation of action to an order involves a wide variety of motives. But the circumstance that, along with the other sources of conformity, the order is also held by at least part of the actors to define a model or to be binding, naturally increases the probability that action will in fact conform to it, often to a very considerable degree. An order which is adhered to from motives of pure expediency is generally much less stable than one upheld on a purely customary basis through the fact that the corresponding behavior has become habitual. The latter is much the most common type of subjective attitude. But even this type of order is in turn much less stable than an order which enjoys the prestige of being considered binding, or, as it may be expressed, of "legitimacy." The transitions between orientation to an order from motives of tradition or of expediency to the case where a belief in its legitimacy is involved are empirically gradual.

3. It is possible for action to be oriented to an order in other ways than through conformity with its prescriptions, as they are generally understood by the actors. Even in the case of evasion or disobedience, the probability of their being recognized as valid norms may have an effect on action. This may, in the first place, be true from the point of view of sheer expediency. A thief orients his action to the validity of the criminal law in that he acts surreptitiously. The fact that the order is recognized as valid in his society is made evident by the fact that he cannot violate it openly without punishment. But apart from this limiting case, it is very common for violation of an order to be confined to more or less numerous partial deviations from it, or for the attempt to be made, with varying degrees of good faith, to justify the deviation as legitimate. Furthermore, there may exist at the same time different interpretations of the meaning of the order. In such cases, for sociological purposes, each can be said to be valid insofar as it actually determines the course of action. The fact that, in the same social group, a plurality of contradictory systems of order may all be recognized as valid, is not a source of difficulty for the sociological approach. Indeed, it is even possible for the same individual to orient his action to contradictory systems of order. This can take place not only at different times, as is an everyday occurrence, but even in the case of the same concrete act. A person who fights a duel follows the code of honor; but at the same time, insofar as he either keeps it secret or conversely gives himself up to the police, he takes account of the criminal law. To be sure, when evasion or contravention of the generally understood meaning of an order has become the rule, the order can be said to be "valid" only in a limited degree and, in the extreme case, not at all. Thus for sociological purposes there does not exist, as there does for the law, a rigid alternative between the validity and lack of validity of a given order. On the contrary, there is a gradual transition between the two extremes; and also it is possible, as it has been pointed out, for contradictory systems of order to exist at the same time. In that case each is "valid" precisely to the extent that there is a probability that action will in fact be oriented to it.

[Excursus:] Those familiar with the literature of this subject will recall the part played by the concept of "order" in the brilliant book of Rudolf Stammler, which was cited in the prefatory note, a book which, though like all his works it is very able, is nevertheless fundamentally misleading and confuses the issues in a catastrophic fashion. (The reader may compare the author's critical discussion of it, which was also cited in the same place, a discussion which, because of the author's annoyance at Stammler's confusion, was unfortunately written in somewhat too acrimonious a tone.) Stammler fails to distinguish the normative meaning of "validity" from the empirical. He further fails to recognize that social action is oriented to other things beside systems of order. Above all, however, in a way which is wholly indefensible from a logical point of view, he treats order as a "form" of social action and then attempts to bring it into a type of relation to "content," which is analogous to that of form and content in the theory of knowledge. Other errors in his argument will be left aside. But economic action, for instance, is oriented to knowledge of the relative scarcity of certain available means to want satisfaction, in relation to the actor's state of needs and to the present and probable action of others, insofar as the latter affects the same resources. But at the same time, of course, the actor in his choice of economic procedures naturally orients himself *in addition* to the conventional and legal rules which he recognizes as valid, that is, of which he knows that a violation on his part would call forth a given reaction of other persons. Stammler succeeds in introducing a state of hopeless confusion into this very simple empirical situation, particularly in that he maintains that a causal relationship between an order and actual empirical action involves a contradiction in terms. It is true, of course, that there is no causal relationship between the *normative* validity of an order in the legal sense and any empirical process. In that context there is only the question of whether the order as correctly interpreted in the legal sense "applies" to the empirical situation. The question is whether in a *normative* sense it *should* be treated as valid and, if so, what the content of its normative prescriptions for this situation should be. But for sociological purposes, as distinguished from legal, it is only the probability of orientation to the subjective *belief* in the validity of an order which constitutes the valid order itself. It is undeniable that, in the ordinary sense of the word "causal," there is a causal relationship between this probability and the relevant course of economic action.

6. *Types of Legitimate Order: Convention and Law*

The legitimacy of an order may be guaranteed in two principal ways:[20]

I. The guarantee may be purely subjective, being either
  1. affectual: resulting from emotional surrender; or
  2. value-rational: determined by the belief in the absolute validity of the order as the expression of. ultimate values of an ethical, esthetic or of any other type; or
  3. religious: determined by the belief that salvation depends upon obedience to the order.
II. The legitimacy of an order may, however, be guaranteed also (or merely) by the expectation of specific external effects, that is, by interest situations.

An order will be called

(a) *convention* so far as its validity is externally guaranteed by the probability that deviation from it within a given social group will result in a relatively general and practically significant reaction of disapproval;

(b) *law* if it is externally guaranteed by the probability that physical or psychological coercion will be applied by a *staff* of people in order to bring about compliance or avenge violation.

(On the concept of convention see Weigelin, *op. cit.*, and F. Tönnies, *Die Sitte* [1909], besides Jhering, *op. cit.*)

1. The term convention will be employed to designate that part of the custom followed within a given social group which is recognized as "binding" and protected against violation by sanctions of disapproval. As distinguished from "law" in the sense of the present discussion, it is not enforced by a staff. Stammler distinguishes convention from law in terms of the entirely voluntary character of conformity. This is not, however, in accord with everyday usage and does not even fit the examples he gives. Conformity with convention in such matters as the usual forms of greeting, the mode of dress recognized as appropriate or respectable, and various of the rules governing the restrictions on social intercourse, both in form and in content, is very definitely expected of the individual and regarded as binding on him. It is not, as in the case of certain ways of preparing food, a mere usage, which he is free to conform to or not as he sees fit. A violation of conventional rules—such as standards of "respectability" (*Standessitte*)—often leads to the extremely severe and effective sanction of an informal boycott on the part of members of one's status group. This may actually be a more severe punishment than any legal penalty. The only thing lacking is a staff with the specialized function of maintaining enforcement of the order, such as judges, prosecuting attorneys, administrative officials, or sheriffs. The transition, however, is gradual. The case of conventional guarantee of an order which most closely approaches the legal is the application of a formally threatened and organized boycott. For terminological purposes, this is best considered a form of legal coercion. Conventional rules may, in addition to mere disapproval, also be upheld by other means; thus domestic authority may be employed to expel a visitor who defies convention. This fact is not, however, important in the present context. The decisive point is that the individual, by virtue of the existence of conventional disapproval, applies these sanctions, however drastic, on his own authority, not as a member of a staff endowed with a specific authority for this purpose.

2. For the purposes of this discussion the concept "law" will be made to turn on the presence of a staff engaged in enforcement, however useful it might be to define it differently for other purposes. The

character of this agency naturally need not be at all similar to what is at present familiar. In particular it is not necessary that there should be any specifically "judicial" authority. The clan, as an agency of blood revenge and of the prosecution of feuds, is such an enforcing agency if there exist any sort of rules which governs its behavior in such situations. But this is on the extreme borderline of what can be called legal enforcement. As is well known, it has often been denied that international law could be called law, precisely because there is no legal authority above the state capable of enforcing it. In terms of the present terminology this would be correct, for we could not call "law" a system the sanctions of which consisted wholly in expectations of disapproval and of the reprisals of injured parties, which is thus guaranteed entirely by convention and self-interest without the help of a specialized enforcement agency. But for purposes of legal terminology exactly the opposite might well be acceptable.

In any case the means of coercion are irrelevant. Even a "brotherly admonition," such as has been used in various religious sects as the first degree of mild coercion of the sinner, is "law" provided it is regulated by some order and applied by a staff. The same is to be said about the [Roman] censorial reprimand as a means to guarantee the observance of ethical duties and, even more so, about psychological coercion through ecclesiastic discipline. Hence "law" may be guaranteed by hierocratic as well as political authority, by the statutes of a voluntary association or domestic authority or through a sodality or some other association. The rules of [German students' fraternities known as] the *Komment* [and regulating such matters as convivial drinking or singing] are also law in our sense, just as the case of those [legally regulated but unenforceable] duties which are mentioned in Section 888, paragraph 2 of the German Code of Civil Procedure [for instance, the duty arising from an engagement to marry].[21] The *leges imperfectae* and the category of "natural obligations" are forms of legal terminology which express indirectly limits or conditions of the application of compulsion. In the same sense a trade practice which is compulsorily enforced is also law. See secs. 157 and 242 of the German Civil Code. On the concept of "fair practice" (*gute Sitte*), that is, desirable custom which is worthy of legal sanction, see Max Rümelin's essay in the *Schwäbische Heimatgabe für Theodor Häring* (1918).

3. It is not necessary for a valid order to be of a general and abstract character. The distinction between a legal norm and the judicial decision in a concrete case, for instance, has not always and everywhere been as clearly made as we have today come to expect. An "order" may thus occur simply as the order governing a single concrete situation. The details of this subject belong in the Sociology of Law. But for present purposes, unless otherwise specified, the modern distinction between a norm and a specific decision will be taken for granted.

4. A system of order which is guaranteed by external sanctions may at the same time be guaranteed by disinterested subjective attitudes.

The relations of law, convention, and "ethics" do not constitute a problem for sociology. From a sociological point of view an "ethical" standard is one to which men attribute a certain type of value and which, by virtue of this belief, they treat as a valid norm governing their action. In this sense it can be spoken of as defining what is ethically good in the same way that action which is called beautiful is measured by esthetic standards. It is possible for ethically normative beliefs of this kind to have a profound influence on action in the absence of any sort of external guarantee. This is often the case when the interests of others would be little affected by their violation.

Such ethical beliefs are also often guaranteed by religious motives, but they may at the same time, in the present terminology, be upheld to an important extent by disapproval of violations and the consequent boycott, or even legally with the corresponding sanctions of criminal or private law or of police measures. Every system of ethics which has in a sociological sense become validly established is likely to be upheld to a large extent by the probability that disapproval will result from its violation, that is, by convention. On the other hand, it is by no means necessary that all conventionally or legally guaranteed forms of order should claim the authority of ethical norms. Legal rules, much more often than conventional ones, may have been established entirely on grounds of expediency. Whether a belief in the validity of an order as such, which is current in a social group, is to be regarded as belonging to the realm of "ethics" or is a mere convention or a mere legal norm, cannot, for sociological purposes, be decided in general terms. It must be treated as relative to the conception of what values are treated as "ethical" in the social group in question.

7. *Bases of Legitimacy: Tradition, Faith, Enactment*

The actors may ascribe legitimacy to a social order by virtue of:

(a) *tradition:* valid is that which has always been;

(b) *affectual,* especially emotional, *faith:* valid is that which is newly revealed or exemplary;

(c) *value-rational* faith: valid is that which has been deduced as an absolute;

(d) positive enactment which is believed to be *legal.*

Such legality may be treated as legitimate because:

(α) it derives from a voluntary agreement of the interested parties;

(β) it is imposed by an authority which is held to be legitimate and therefore meets with compliance.

All further details, except for a few other concepts to be defined below, belong in the Sociology of Law and the Sociology of Domination. For the present, only a few remarks are necessary.

1. The validity of a social order by virtue of the sacredness of tradition is the oldest and most universal type of legitimacy. The fear of magical evils reinforces the general psychological inhibitions against any sort of change in customary modes of action. At the same time the manifold vested interests which tend to favor conformity with an established order help to perpetuate it. (More in ch. III.)

2. Conscious departures from tradition in the establishment of a new order were originally almost entirely due to prophetic oracles or at least to pronouncements which were sanctioned as prophetic and thus were considered sacred. This was true as late as the statutes of the Greek *aisymnetai*. Conformity thus depended on belief in the legitimacy of the prophet. In times of strict traditionalism a new order—one actually regarded as new—was not possible without revelation unless it was claimed that it had always been valid though not yet rightly known, or that it had been obscured for a time and was now being restored to its rightful place.

3. The purest type of legitimacy based on value-rationality is *natural law*. The influence of its logically deduced propositions upon actual conduct has lagged far behind its ideal claims; that they have had some influence cannot be denied, however. Its propositions must be distinguished from those of revealed, enacted, and traditional law.

4. Today the most common form of legitimacy is the belief in legality, the compliance with enactments which are *formally* correct and which have been made in the accustomed manner. In this respect, the distinction between an order derived from voluntary agreement and one which has been imposed is only relative. For so far as the agreement underlying the order is not unanimous, as in the past has often been held necessary for complete legitimacy, the order is actually imposed upon the minority; in this frequent case the order in a given group depends upon the acquiescence of those who hold different opinions. On the other hand, it is very common for minorities, by force or by the use of more ruthless and far-sighted methods, to impose an order which in the course of time comes to be regarded as legitimate by those who originally resisted it. Insofar as the ballot is used as a legal means of altering an order, it is very common for the will of a minority to attain a formal majority and for the majority to submit. In this case majority rule is a mere illusion. The belief in the legality of an order as established by voluntary agreement is relatively ancient and is occasionally found among so-called primitive people; but in these cases it is almost always supplemented by the authority of oracles.

5. So far as it is not derived merely from fear or from motives of expediency, a willingness to submit to an order imposed by one man or a small group, always implies a belief in the legitimate authority (*Herrschaftsgewalt*) of the source imposing it. This subject will be dealt with separately below: see sections 13 and 16 and ch. III.

6. Submission to an order is almost always determined by a variety of interests and by a mixture of adherence to tradition and belief in

legality, unless it is a case of entirely new regulations. In a very large proportion of cases, the actors subject to the order are of course not even aware how far it is a matter of custom, of convention, or of law. In such cases the sociologist must attempt to formulate the typical basis of validity.

8. *Conflict, Competition, Selection*

A social relationship will be referred to as "conflict" (*Kampf*) insofar as action is oriented intentionally to carrying out the actor's own will against the resistance of the other party or parties. The term "peaceful" conflict will be applied to cases in which actual physical violence is not employed. A peaceful conflict is "competition" insofar as it consists in a formally peaceful attempt to attain control over opportunities and advantages which are also desired by others. A competitive process is "regulated" competition to the extent that its ends and means are oriented to an order. The struggle, often latent, which takes place between human individuals or social types, for advantages and for survival, but without a meaningful mutual orientation in terms of conflict, will be called "selection." Insofar as it is a matter of the relative opportunities of individuals during their own lifetime, it is "social selection"; insofar as it concerns differential chances for the survival of hereditary characteristics, "biological selection."

1. There are all manner of continuous transitions ranging from the bloody type of conflict which, setting aside all rules, aims at the destruction of the adversary, to the case of the battles of medieval chivalry, bound as they were to the strictest conventions, and to the strict regulations imposed on sport by the rules of the game. A classic example of conventional regulation in war is the herald's call before the battle of Fontenoy: "Messieurs les Anglais, tirez les premiers."[22] There are transitions such as that from unregulated competition of, let us say, suitors for the favor of a woman to the competition for economic advantages in exchange relationships, bound as that is by the order governing the market, or to strictly regulated competitions for artistic awards or, finally, to the struggle for victory in election campaigns. The conceptual separation of peaceful [from violent] conflict is justified by the quality of the means normal to it and the peculiar sociological consequences of its occurrence (see ch. II and later).

2. All typical struggles and modes of competition which take place on a large scale will lead, in the long run, despite the decisive importance in many individual cases of accidental factors and luck, to a selection of those who have in the higher degree, on the average, possessed the personal qualities important to success. What qualities are

important depends on the conditions in which the conflict or competition takes place. It may be a matter of physical strength or of unscrupulous cunning, of the level of mental ability or mere lung power and skill in the technique of demagoguery, of loyalty to superiors or of ability to flatter the masses, of creative originality, or of adaptability, of qualities which are unusual, or of those which are possessed by the mediocre majority. *Among* the decisive conditions, it must not be forgotten, belong the systems of order to which the behavior of the parties is oriented, whether traditionally, as a matter of rationally disinterested loyalty (*wertrational*), or of expediency. Each type of order influences opportunities in the process of social selection differently.

Not every process of social selection is, in the present sense, a case of conflict. Social selection, on the contrary, means only in the first instance that certain types of behavior, and possibly of the corresponding personal qualities, lead more easily to success in the role of "lover," "husband," "member of parliament," "official," "contractor," "managing director," "successful business man," and so on. But the concept does not specify whether this differential advantage in selection for social success is brought to bear through conflict or not, neither does it specify whether the biological chances of survival of the type are affected one way or the other.

It is only where there is a genuine competitive process that the term conflict will be used [i.e., where regulation is, in principle, possible].[23] It is only in the sense of "selection" that it seems, according to our experience, that conflict is empirically inevitable, and it is furthermore only in the sense of *biological* selection that it is inevitable in principle. Selection is inevitable because apparently no way can be worked out of eliminating it completely. Even the most strictly pacific order can eliminate means of conflict and the objects of and impulses to conflict only partially. Other modes of conflict would come to the fore, possibly in processes of open competition. But even on the utopian assumption that all competition were completely eliminated, conditions would still lead to a latent process of selection, biological or social, which would favor the types best adapted to the conditions, whether their relevant qualities were mainly determined by heredity or by environment. On an empirical level the elimination of conflict cannot go beyond a point which leaves room for some social selection, and in principle a process of biological selection necessarily remains.

3. From the struggle of individuals for personal advantages and survival, it is naturally necessary to distinguish the "conflict" and the "selection" of social relationships. It is only in a metaphorical sense that these concepts can be applied to the latter. For relationships exist only as individual actions with particular subjective meanings. Thus a process of selection or a conflict between them means only that one type of action has in the course of time been displaced by another, whether it is action by the same persons or by others. This may occur in various ways. Human action may in the first place be consciously aimed to alter cer-

tain social relationships—that is, to alter the corresponding action—or it may be directed to the prevention of their development or continuance. Thus a "state" may be destroyed by war or revolution, or a conspiracy may be broken up by savage suppression; prostitution may be suppressed by police action; "usurious" business practices, by denial of legal protection or by penalties. Furthermore, social relationships may be influenced by the creation of differential advantages which favor one type over another. It is possible either for individuals or for organized groups to pursue such ends. Secondly, it may, in various ways, be an unanticipated consequence of a course of social action and its relevant conditions that certain types of social relationships (meaning, of course, the corresponding actions) will be adversely affected in their opportunities to maintain themselves or to arise. All changes of natural and social conditions have some sort of effect on the differential probabilities of survival of social relationships. Anyone is at liberty to speak in such cases of a process of "selection" of social relationships. For instance, he may say that among several states the "strongest," in the sense of the best "adapted," is victorious. It must, however, be kept in mind that this so-called "selection" has nothing to do with the selection of types of human individuals in either the social or the biological sense. In every case it is necessary to inquire into the reasons which have led to a change in the chances of survival of one or another form of social action or social relationship, which have broken up a social relationship or permitted it to continue at the expense of other competing forms. The explanation of these processes involves so many factors that it does not seem expedient to employ a single term for them. When this is done, there is always a danger of introducing uncritical value-judgments into empirical investigation. There is, above all, a danger of being primarily concerned with justifying the success of an individual case. Since individual cases are often dependent on highly exceptional circumstances, they may be in a certain sense "fortuitous." In recent years there has been more than enough of this kind of argument. The fact that a given specific social relationship has been eliminated for reasons peculiar to a particular situation, proves nothing whatever about its "fitness to survive" in general terms.

9. *Communal and Associative Relationships*

A social relationship will be called "communal" (*Vergemeinschaftung*) if and so far as the orientation of social action—whether in the individual case, on the average, or in the pure type—is based on a subjective feeling of the parties, whether affectual or traditional, that they belong together.

A social relationship will be called "associative" (*Vergesellschaftung*) if and insofar as the orientation of social action within it rests on a rationally motivated adjustment of interests or a similarly motivated agreement, whether the basis of rational judgment be absolute values or reasons of expediency. It is especially common, though by no means inevitable, for the associative type of relationship to rest on a rational agreement by mutual consent. In that case the corresponding action is, at the pole of rationality, oriented either to a value-rational belief in one's own obligation, or to a rational (*zweckrationale*) expectation that the other party will live up to it.

This terminology is similar to the distinction made by Ferdinand Tönnies in his pioneering work, *Gemeinschaft und Gesellschaft*; but for his purposes, Tönnies has given this distinction a rather more specific meaning than would be convenient for purposes of the present discussion.[24] The purest cases of associative relationships are: (a) rational free market exchange, which constitutes a compromise of opposed but complementary interests; (b) the pure voluntary association based on self-interest (*Zweckverein*), a case of agreement as to a long-run course of action oriented purely to the promotion of specific ulterior interests, economic or other, of its members; (c) the voluntary association of individuals motivated by an adherence to a set of common absolute values (*Gesinnungsverein*), for example, the rational sect, insofar as it does not cultivate emotional and affective interests, but seeks only to serve a "cause." This last case, to be sure, seldom occurs in anything approaching the pure type.

2. Communal relationships may rest on various types of affectual, emotional, or traditional bases. Examples are a religious brotherhood, an erotic relationship, a relation of personal loyalty, a national community, the *esprit de corps* of a military unit. The type case is most conveniently illustrated by the family. But the great majority of social relationships has this characteristic to some degree, while being at the same time to some degree determined by associative factors. No matter how calculating and hard-headed the ruling considerations in such a social relationship—as that of a merchant to his customers—may be, it is quite possible for it to involve emotional values which transcend its utilitarian significance. Every social relationship which goes beyond the pursuit of immediate common ends, which hence lasts for long periods, involves relatively permanent social relationships between the same persons, and these cannot be exclusively confined to the technically necessary activities. Hence in such cases as association in the same military unit, in the same school class, in the same workshop or office, there is always some tendency in this direction, although the degree, to be sure, varies enormously. Conversely, a social relationship which is normally considered primarily communal may involve action on the part of some or even all of the participants which is to an important degree oriented to considerations of expediency. There is, for instance, a wide variation in the extent to which the members of a family group feel a genuine community of interests or, on the other hand, exploit the relationship for

their own ends. The concept of communal relationship has been intentionally defined in very general terms and hence includes a very heterogeneous group of phenomena.

3. The communal type of relationship is, according to the usual interpretation of its subjective meaning, the most radical antithesis of conflict. This should not, however, be allowed to obscure the fact that coercion of all sorts is a very common thing in even the most intimate of such communal relationships if one party is weaker in character than the other. Furthermore, a process of the selection of types leading to differences in opportunity and survival, goes on within these relationships just the same as anywhere else. Associative relationships, on the other hand, very often consist only in compromises between rival interests, where only a part of the occasion or means of conflict has been eliminated, or even an attempt has been made to do so. Hence, outside the area of compromise, the conflict of interests, with its attendant competition for supremacy, remains unchanged. Conflict and communal relationships are relative concepts. Conflict varies enormously according to the means employed, especially whether they are violent or peaceful, and to the ruthlessness with which they are used. It has already been pointed out that any type of order governing social action in some way leaves room for a process of selection among various rival human types.

4. It is by no means true that the existence of common qualities, a common situation, or common modes of behavior imply the existence of a communal social relationship. Thus, for instance, the possession of a common biological inheritance by virtue of which persons are classified as belonging to the same "race," naturally implies no sort of communal social relationship between them. By restrictions on social intercourse and on marriage persons may find themselves in a similar situation, a situation of isolation from the environment which imposes these distinctions. But even if they all react to this situation in the same way, this does not constitute a communal relationship. The latter does not even exist if they have a common "feeling" about this situation and its consequences. It is only when this feeling leads to a mutual orientation of their behavior to each other that a social relationship arises between them rather than of each to the environment. Furthermore, it is only so far as this relationship involves feelings of belonging together that it is a "communal" relationship. In the case of the Jews, for instance, except for Zionist circles and the action of certain associations promoting specifically Jewish interests, there thus exist communal relationships only to a relatively small extent; indeed, Jews often repudiate the existence of a Jewish "community."

A common language, which arises from a similarity of tradition through the family and the surrounding social environment, facilitates mutual understanding, and thus the formation of all types of social relationships, in the highest degree. But taken by itself it is not sufficient to constitute a communal relationship, rather, it facilitates intercourse within the groups concerned, hence the development of associate relationships. This takes place between *individuals,* not because they speak the same language, but because they have other types of interests. Orientation to the rules of a common language is thus primarily important as a means of communication, not as the content of a social relationship. It is only with the emergence of a consciousness of difference from third persons who speak a different language that the fact that two persons speak the same language, and in that respect share a common situation, can lead them to a feeling of community and to modes of social organization consciously based on the sharing of the common language.

Participation in a "market" is of still another kind. It encourages association between the exchanging parties and a social relationship, above all that of competition, between the individual participants who must mutually orient their action to each other. But no further modes of association develop except in cases where certain participants enter into agreements in order to better their competitive situations, or where they all agree on rules for the purpose of regulating transactions and of securing favorable general conditions for all. (It may further be remarked that the market and the competitive economy resting on it form the most important type of the reciprocal determination of action in terms of pure self-interest, a type which is characteristic of modern economic life.)

1 0. *Open and Closed Relationships*

A social relationship, regardless of whether it is communal or associative in character, will be spoken of as "open" to outsiders if and insofar as its system of order does not deny participation to anyone who wishes to join and is actually in a position to do so. A relationship will, on the other hand, bes called "closed" against outsiders so far as, according to its subjective meaning and its binding rules, participation of certain persons is excluded, limited, or subjected to conditions. Whether a relationship is open or closed may be determined traditionally, affectually, or rationally in terms of values or of expediency. It is especially likely to be closed, for rational reasons, in the following type of situation: a social relationship may provide the parties to it with opportunities for the satisfaction of spiritual or material interests, whether absolutely or instrumentally, or whether it is achieved through co-operative action or by a compromise of interests. If the participants expect that the admission of others will lead to an improvement of their situation, an improvement in degree, in kind in the security or the value of the satisfaction, their interest will be in keeping the relationship open. If, on the other hand, their expectations are of improving their position by monopolistic tactics, their interest is in a closed relationship.

There are various ways in which it is possible for a closed social relationship to guarantee its monopolized advantages to the parties. (a) Such advantages may be left free to competitive struggle within the group; (b) they may be regulated or rationed in amount and kind, or (c) they may be appropriated by individuals or sub-groups on a permanent basis and become more or less inalienable. The last is a case of closure within, as well as against outsiders. Appropriated advantages will be called "rights." As determined by the relevant order, appropriated may be (1) for the benefit of the members of particular communal or associative groups for instance, household groups), or (2) for the benefit of individuals. In the latter case, the individual may enjoy his rights on a purely personal basis or in such a way that in case of his death one or more other persons related to the holder of the right by birth (kinship), or by some other social relationship, may inherit the rights in question. Or the rights may pass to one or more individuals specifically designated by the holder. These are cases of hereditary appropriation. Finally, (3) it may be that the holder is more or less fully empowered to alienate his rights by voluntary agreement, either to other specific persons or to anyone he chooses. This is alienable appropriation. A party to a closed social relationship will be called a "member"; in case his participation is regulated in such a way as to guarantee him appropriated advantages, a privileged member (*Rechtsgenosse*). Appropriated rights which are enjoyed by individuals through inheritance or by hereditary groups, whether communal or associative, will be called the "property" of the individual or of groups in question; and, insofar as they are alienable, "free" property.

The apparently gratuitous tediousness involved in the elaborate definition of the above concepts is an example of the fact that we often neglect to think out clearly what seems to be obvious, because it is intuitively familiar.

  1. (a) Examples of communal relationships, which tend to be closed on a traditional basis, are those in which membership is determined by family relationship.

  (b) Personal emotional relationships are usually affectually closed. Examples are erotic relationships and, very commonly, relations of personal loyalty.

  (c) Closure on the basis of value-rational commitment to values is usual in groups sharing a common system of explicit religious belief.

  (d) Typical cases of rational closure on grounds of expediency are economic associations of a monopolistic or a plutocratic character.

  A few examples may be taken at random. Whether a group of people engaged in conversation is open or closed depends on its content. General conversation is apt to be open, as contrasted with intimate conversation or the imparting of official information. Market relationships are in most, or at least in many, cases essentially open. In the case of many relationships, both communal and associative, there is a tendency to shift from a phase of expansion to one of exclusiveness. Examples are the guilds and the democratic city-states of Antiquity and the Middle Ages. At times these groups sought to increase their membership in the interest of improving the security of their position of power by adequate numbers. At other times they restricted their membership to protect the value of their monopolistic position. The same phenomenon is not uncommon in monastic orders and religious sects which have passed from a stage of religious proselytizing to one of restriction in the interest of the maintenance of an ethical standard or for the protection of material interests. There is a similar close relationship between the extension of market relationships in the interest of increased turnover on the one hand, their monopolistic restriction on the other. The promotion of linguistic uniformity is today a natural result of the interests of publishers and writers, as opposed to the earlier, not uncommon, tendency for status groups to maintain linguistic peculiarities or even for secret languages to emerge.

2. Both the extent and the methods of regulation and exclusion in relation to outsiders may vary widely, so that the transition from a state of openness to one of regulation and closure is gradual. Various conditions of participation may be laid down; qualifying tests, a period of probation, requirement of possession of a share which can be purchased under certain conditions, election of new members by ballot, membership or eligibility by birth or by virtue of achievements open to anyone. Finally, in case of closure and the appropriation of rights within the group, participation may be dependent on the acquisition of an appropriated right. There is a wide variety of different degrees of closure and of conditions of participation. Thus regulation and closure are relative concepts. There are all manner of gradual shadings as between an exclusive club, a theatrical audience the members of which have purchased tickets, and a party rally to which the largest possible number has been urged to come; similarly, from a church service open to the general public through the rituals of a limited sect to the mysteries of a secret cult.

3. Similarly, closure within the group may also assume the most varied forms. Thus a caste, a guild, or a group of stock exchange brokers, which is closed to outsiders, may allow to its members a perfectly free competition for all the advantages which the group as a whole monopolizes for itself. Or it may assign every member strictly to the enjoyment of certain advantages, such as claims over customers or particular business opportunities, for life or even on a hereditary basis. This is particularly characteristic of India. Similarly, a closed group of settlers (*Markgenossenschaft*) may allow its members free use of the resources of its area or may restrict them rigidly to a plot assigned to each individual household. A closed group of colonists may allow free use of the land or sanction and guarantee permanent appropriation of

separate holdings. In such cases all conceivable transitional and inter-mediate forms can be found. Historically, the closure of eligibility to fiefs, benefices, and offices within the group, and the appropriation on the part of those enjoying them, have occurred in the most varied forms. Similarly, the establishment of rights to and possession of particular jobs on the part of workers may develop all the way from the "closed shop" to a right to a particular job. The first step in this development may be to prohibit the dismissal of a worker without the consent of the workers' representatives. The development of the "works councils" [in Germany after 1918] might be a first step in this direction, though it need not be.[25]

All the details must be reserved for the later analysis. The most extreme form of permanent appropriation is found in cases where par-ticular rights are guaranteed to an individual or to certain groups of them, such as households, clans, families, in such a way that it is speci-fied in the order either that, in case of death, the rights descend to specific heirs, or that the possessor is free to transfer them to any other person at will. Such a person thereby becomes a party to the social relation-ship so that, when appropriation has reached this extreme within the group, it becomes to that extent an open group in relation to outsiders. This is true so long as acquisition of membership is not subject to the ratification of the other, prior members.

4. The principal motives for closure of a relationship are: (a) The maintenance of quality, which is often combined with the interest in prestige and the consequent opportunities to enjoy honor, and even profit; examples are communities of ascetics, monastic orders, especially, for instance, the Indian mendicant orders, religious sects like the Puri-tans, organized groups of warriors, of *ministeriales* and other func-tionaries, organized citizen bodies as in the Greek states, craft guilds; (b) the contraction of advantages in relation to consumption needs (*Nahrungsspielraum*);[26] examples are monopolies of consumption, the most developed form of which is a self-subsistent village community; (c) the growing scarcity of opportunities for acquisition (*Erwerbsspiel-raum*). This is found in trade monopolies such as guilds, the an-cient monopolies of fishing rights, and so on. Usually motive (a) is combined with (b) or (c).

11. *The Imputation of Social Action: Representation and Mutual Responsibility*

Within a social relationship, whether it is traditional or enacted, cer-tain kinds of action of *each* participant may be imputed to *all* others, in which case we speak of "mutually responsible members"; or the action of certain members (the "representatives") may be attributed to the others (the "represented"). In both cases, the members will share the resulting advantages as well as the disadvantages.

In accordance with the prevailing order, the power of representation may be (a) completely appropriated in all its forms—the case of self-appointed authority (*Eigenvollmacht*); (b) conferred in accordance with particular *characteristics,* permanently or for a limited term; (c) conferred by specific *acts* of the members or of outside persons, again permanently or for a limited term—the cases of "derived" or "delegated" powers.

There are many different conditions which determine the ways in which social relationships, communal or associative, develop relations of mutual responsibility or of representation. In general terms, it is possible only to say that one of the most decisive is the extent to which the action of the group is oriented to violent conflict or to peaceful exchange as its end. Besides these, many special circumstances, which can only be discussed in the detailed analysis, may be of crucial importance. It is not surprising that this development is least conspicuous in groups which pursue purely ideal ends by peaceful means. Often the degree of closure against outsiders is closely related to the development of mutual responsibility or of representation. But this is by no means always the case.

1. Imputation may in practice involve both active and passive mutual responsibility. All participants may be held responsible for the action of any one just as he himself is, and similarly may be entitled to enjoy any benefits resulting from this action. This responsibility may be owed to spirits or gods, that is, involve a religious orientation; or it may be responsibility to other human beings, as regulated by convention or by law. Examples of regulation by convention are blood revenge carried out against or with the help of members of the kin group, and reprisals against the inhabitants of the town or the country of the offender; of the legal type, formal punishment of relatives and members of the household or community, and personal liability of members of a household or of a commercial partnership for each other's debts. Mutual responsibility in relation to gods has also had very significant historical results. For instance, in the covenant of Israel with Jahveh, in early Christianity, and in the early Puritan community.

On the other hand, the imputation may mean no more than that the participants in a closed social relationship, by virtue of the traditional or legal order, accept as legally binding a representative's decisions, especially over economic resources. (Examples are the "validity" of decisions by the executive committee of a voluntary association or by the responsible agent of a political or economic organization over resources which, as specified in the statutes, are meant to serve the group's purposes.)

2. Mutual responsibility is typically found in the following cases: (a) In traditional, communal groups based on birth or the sharing of a

common life; for example, the household and the kinship unit; (b) in closed relationships which maintain by force a monopolized position and control over the corresponding benefits; the typical case is the political association, especially in the past, but also today, most strikingly in time of war; (c) in profit-oriented enterprises whose participants personally conduct the business; the type case is the business partnership; (d) in some cases, in labor associations; e.g., the [Russian] *artel.*

Representation is most frequently found in associations devoted to specific purposes and in legally organized groups, especially when funds have been collected and must be administered in the interests of the group. This will be further discussed in the Sociology of Law.

3. The power of representation is conferred according to characteristics when it goes by seniority or some other such rule.

4. It is not possible to carry the analysis of this subject further in general terms; its elaboration must be reserved to the detailed investigation. The most ancient and most universal phenomenon in this field is that of reprisal, meant either as revenge or as a means of gaining control of hostages, or some other kind of security against future injury.

12. *The Organization*

A social relationship which is either closed or limits the admission of outsiders will be called an organization (*Verband*) when its regulations are enforced by specific individuals: a chief and, possibly, an administrative staff, which normally also has representative powers. The incumbency of a policy-making position or participation in the functions of the staff constitute "executive powers" (*Regierungsgewalten*). These may be appropriated, or they may be assigned, in accordance with the regulations of the organization, to specific persons or to individuals selected on the basis of specific characteristics or procedures. "Organized action" is (a) either the staff's action, which is legitimated by its executive or representative powers and oriented to realizing the organization's order, or (b) the members' action as directed by the staff.[27]

1. It is terminologically indifferent whether the relationship is of a communal or associative character. It is sufficient for there to be a person or persons in authority—the head of a family, the executive committee of an association, a managing director, a prince, a president, the head of a church—whose action is concerned with carrying into effect the order governing the organization. This criterion is decisive because it is not merely a matter of action which is *oriented* to an order, but which is specifically directed to its *enforcement*. Sociologically, this adds to the concept of a closed social relationship a further element, which is of far-reaching empirical importance. For by no means every closed communal or associative relationship is an organization. For instance, this is

not true of an erotic relationship or of a kinship group without a head.

2. Whether or not an organization exists is entirely a matter of the presence of a person in authority, with or without an administrative staff. More precisely, it exists so far as there is a probability that certain persons will act in such a way as to carry out the order governing the organization; that is, that persons are present who can be counted on to act in this way whenever the occasion arises. For purposes of definition, it is indifferent what is the basis of the relevant expectation, whether it is a case of traditional, affectual or value-rational devotion (such as feudal fealty, loyalty to an officer or to a service). It may, on the other hand, be a matter of expediency, as, for instance, a pecuniary interest in the attached salary. Thus, for our purposes, the organization does not exist apart from the probability that a course of action oriented in this way will take place. If there is no probability of this type of action on the part of a particular group of persons or of a given individual, there is in these terms only a social relationship. On the other hand, so long as there is a probability of such action, the organization as a sociological phenomenon continues to exist, in spite of the fact that the specific individuals whose action is oriented to the order in question, may have been completely changed. The concept has been defined intentionally to include precisely this phenomenon.

3. It is possible (a) that, in addition to the action of the administrative staff itself or that which takes place under its direction, there may be other cases where action of the participants is intended to uphold the authority of the order; for instance, contributions or "liturgies," that is, certain types of personal services, such as jury service or military service. It is also possible (b) for the order to include norms to which it is expected that the action of the members of an organization will be oriented in respects other than those pertaining to the affairs of the organization as a unit. For instance, the law of the state includes rules governing private economic relations which are not concerned with the enforcement of the state's legal order as such, but with action in the service of private interests. This is true of most of the "civil" law. In the first case (a) one may speak of action oriented to organizational affairs (*verbandsbezogenes Handeln*); in the second (b) of action subject to the organization's regulation (*verbandsgeregeltes Handeln*). It is only in the cases of the action of the administrative staff itself and of that deliberately directed by it that the term "organized action" (*Verbandshandeln*) will be used. Examples of such action would be participation in any capacity in a war fought by a state, or a motion which is passed by the members at the behest of its executive committee, or a contract entered into by the person in authority, the validity of which is imposed on all members and for which they are held responsible (cf. section 11). Further, all administration of justice and administrative procedure belongs in this category (cf. section 14).

An organization may be (a) autonomous or heteronomous, (b) autocephalous or heterocephalous. Autonomy means that the order governing the organization has been established by its own members on their own authority, regardless of how this has taken place in other respects. In the case of heteronomy, it has been imposed by an outside agency. Autocephaly means that the chief and his staff are selected according to the autonomous order of the organization itself, not, as in the case of heterocephaly, that they are appointed by outsiders. Again, this is regardless of any other aspects of the relationship.

A case of heterocephaly is the appointment of the governors of the Canadian provinces by the central government of the Dominion. It is possible for a heterocephalous group to be autonomous and an autocephalous group to be heteronomous. It is also possible in both respects for an organization to have both characters at the same time in different spheres. The member-states of the German Empire, a federal state, were autocephalous. But in spite of this, within the sphere of authority of the Reich, they were heteronomous; whereas, within their own sphere, in such matters as religion and education, they were autonomous. Alsace-Lorraine was, under German jurisdiction, in a limited degree autonomous, but at the same time heterocephalous in that the governor was appointed by the Kaiser. All those elements may be present in the same situation to some degree. An organization which is at the same time completely heteronomous and completely heterocephalous is usually best treated as a "part" of the more extensive group, as would ordinarily be done with a "regiment" as part of an army. But whether this is the case depends on the actual extent of independence in the orientation of action in the particular case. For terminological purposes, it is entirely a question of convenience.

1 3. *Consensual and Imposed Order in Organizations*

An association's enacted order may be established in one of two ways: by voluntary agreement, or by being imposed and acquiesced in. The leadership in an organization may claim a legitimate right to impose new rules. The "constitution" of an organization is the empirically existing porbability, varying in extent, kind and conditions, that rules imposed by the leadership will be acceded to. The existing rules may specify that certain groups or sections of the members must consent, or at least have been heard. Besides this, there may be any number of other conditions.

An organization's order may be imposed not only on its members but also on certain non-members. This is especially true of persons who are linked to a given territorial area by virtue of residence, birth, or the performance of certain actions. In this case the order possesses "territorial validity" (*Gebietsgeltung*). An organization which imposes its order in principle on a territory will be called a "territorial organization" (*Gebiets-*

verband). This usage will be employed regardless of how far the claim to the validity of its order over its own members is also confined to matters pertaining to the area. (Such a limitation is possible[28] and indeed occurs to some extent.)

1. In our terminology, an order is always "imposed" to the extent that it does not originate from a voluntary personal agreement of all the individuals concerned. The concept of imposition hence includes "majority rule," in that the minority must submit. For that reason there have been long periods when the legitimacy of majority rule has either not been recognized at all, or been held doubtful. This was true in the case of the Estates of the Middle Ages, and in very recent times, in the Russian *obshchina*. (This will be further discussed in the Sociology of Law and of Domination.)

2. Even in cases where there is formally voluntary agreement, it is very common, as is generally known, for there to be a large measure of imposition. (This is true of the *obshchina*.) In that case, it is the actual state of affairs which is decisive for sociological purposes.

3. The concept of constitution made use of here is that also used by Lassalle. It is not the same as what is meant by a "written" constitution, or indeed by "constitution" in any sort of legal meaning.[29] The only relevant question for sociological purposes is when, for what purposes, and *within what limits*, or possibly under what special conditions (such as the approval of gods or priests or the consent of electors), the members of the organization will submit to the leadership. Furthermore, under what circumstances the administrative staff and the organized actions of the group will be at the leadership's disposal when it issues orders, in particular, new rules.

4. The major cases of the territorial imposition of an order are criminal law and various other legal rules the applicability of which depends on whether the actor was resident, born, performed or completed the action within the area controlled by a political organization. (Compare the concept of the "territorial corporate organization"— *Gebietskörperschaft*—as used by Gierke and Preuss.)[30]

14. *Administrative and Regulative Order*

Rules which govern organized action constitute an administrative order (*Verwaltungsordnung*). Rules which govern other kinds of social action and thereby protect the actors' enjoyment of the resulting benefits will be called a regulative order (*Regulierungsordnung*). So far as an organization is solely oriented to the first type, it will be called an administrative organization; so far as it is oriented to the second type, a regulative organization.

1. It goes without saying that the majority of actual organizations partake of both characteristics. An example of a merely regulative organization would be a theoretically conceivable state based purely on the upholding of public order (*Rechtsstaat*) and committed to absolute laissez-faire. (This would imply that even the control of the monetary system was left to private enterprise.)

2. On the concept of organized action see above, sec. 12:3. Under the concept of administrative order would be included all the rules which govern not only the action of the administrative staff, but also that of the members in their direct relation to the organization; hence these rules pertain to those goals the pursuit of which the administrative order seeks to facilitate through prescribed and coordinated action on the part of the administrative staff and the members. In a completely communist economy almost all social action would be of this character. In an absolute laissez-faire state (*Rechtsstaat*) only the functions of judges, police authorities, jurors and soldiers, and activity as legislator and voter would be included. The distinction between administrative and regulative order coincides in its broad lines, though not always in detail, with the distinction between public and private law. (All further details are treated in the Sociology of Law.)

15. Enterprise, Formal Organization, Voluntary and Compulsory Association

Continuous rational activity of a specified kind will be called an *enterprise;* an association with a continuously and rationally operating staff will be called a *formal organization.*

An organization which claims authority only over voluntary members will be called a *voluntary association* (*Verein*); an organization which imposes, within a specifiable sphere of operations, its order (with relative success) on all action conforming with certain criteria will be called a *compulsory organization* or *association* (*Anstalt*).

1. The concept of the enterprise covers business conducted by political and ecclesiastic organizations as well as by voluntary associations insofar as it has rational continuity.

2. Voluntary as well as compulsory associations are organizations with rationally established rules. More correctly, insofar as an organization has rationaly established rules, it is either a voluntary or a compulsory association. Compulsory organizations are, above all, the state with its subsidiary heterocephalous organizations, and the church insofar as its order is rationally established. The order governing a compulsory association claims to be binding on all persons to whom the particular relevant criteria apply—such as birth, residence, or the use of certain facilities. It makes no difference whether the individual joined volun-

tarily; nor does it matter whether he has taken any part in establishing the order. It is thus a case of imposed order in the most definite sense. Compulsory associations are frequently territorial organizations.

3. The distinction between voluntary and compulsory associations is relative in its empirical application. The rules of a voluntary association may affect the interests of non-members, and recognition of the validity of these rules may be imposed upon them by usurpation and the exercize of naked power, but also by legal regulation, as in the case of the law governing corporate securities.

4. It is hardly necessary to emphasize that the concepts of voluntary and compulsory associations are by no means exhaustive of all conceivable types of organizations. Furthermore, they are to be thought of as polar types, as are sect and church in the religious sphere.

16. Power and Domination

A. "Power" (*Macht*) is the probability that one actor within a social relationship will be in a position to carry out his own will despite resistance, regardless of the basis on which this probability rests.

B. "Domination" (*Herrschaft*)[31] is the probability that a command with a given specific content will be obeyed by a given group of persons. "Discipline" is the probability that by virtue of habituation a command will receive prompt and automatic obedience in stereotyped forms, on the part of a given group of persons.[32]

1. The concept of power is sociologically amorphous. All conceivable qualities of a person and all conceivable combinations of circumstances may put him in a position to impose his will in a given situation. The sociological concept of domination must hence be more precise and can only mean the probability that a *command* will be obeyed.

2. The concept of discipline includes the habituation characteristic of uncritical and unresisting mass obedience.

C. The existence of domination turns only on the actual presence of one person successfully issuing orders to others; it does not necessarily imply either the existence of an administrative staff or, for that matter, of an organization. It is, however, uncommon to find it unrelated to at least one of these. A "ruling organization" (*Herrschaftsverband*) exists insofar as its members are subject to domination by virtue of the established order.

1. The head of a household rules without an administrative staff. A Bedouin chief, who levies contributions from the caravans, persons and shipments which pass his stronghold, controls this group of changing individuals, who do not belong to the same organization, as soon and as

long as they face the same situation; but to do this, he needs a following which, on the appropriate occasions, serves as his administrative staff
in exercising the necessary compulsion. (However, it is theoretically
conceivable that this type of control is exercised by a single individual.)

2. If it possesses an administrative staff, an organization is always to
some degree based on domination. But the concept is relative. In general, an effectively ruling organization is also an administrative one. The
character of the organization is determined by a variety of factors: the
mode in which the administration is carried out, the character of the
personnel, the objects over which it exercises control, and the extent of
effective jurisdiction. The first two factors in particular are dependent in
the highest degree on the way in which domination is legitimized (see
ch. III).

17. Political and Hierocratic Organizations

A "ruling organization" will be called "political" insofar as its existence and order is continuously safeguarded within a given *territorial* area
by the threat and application of physical force on the part of the administrative staff. A compulsory political organization with continuous operations (*politischer Anstaltsbetrieb*) will be called a "state" insofar as its
administrative staff successfully upholds the claim to the *monopoly* of
the *legitimate* use of physical force in the enforcement of its order. Social
action, especially organized action, will be spoken of as "politically
oriented" if it aims at exerting influence on the government of a political
organization; especially at the appropriation, expropriation, redistribution
or allocation of the powers of government.

A "hierocratic organization" is an organization which enforces its
order through psychic coercion by distributing or denying religious
benefits ("hierocratic coercion"). A compulsory hierocratic organization
will be called a "church" insofar as its administrative staff claims a
monopoly of the legitimate use of hierocratic coercion.

1. It goes without saying that the use of physical force (*Gewaltsam-
keit*) is neither the sole, nor even the most usual, method of administration of political organizations. On the contrary, their heads have employed all conceivable means to bring about their ends. But, at the same
time, the threat of force, and in the case of need its actual use, is the
method which is specific to political organizations and is always the last
resort when others have failed. Conversely, physical force is by no means
limited to political groups even as a legitimate method of enforcement.
It has been freely used by kinship groups, household groups, consociations and, in the Middle Ages, under certain circumstances by all those
entitled to bear arms. In addition to the fact that it uses, among other

means, physical force to enforce its system of order, the political organization is further characterized by the fact that the authority of its administrative staff is claimed as binding within a territorial area and this claim is upheld by force. Whenever organizations which make use of force are also characterized by the claim to territorial jurisdiction, such as village communities or even some household groups, federations of guilds or of workers' associations ("soviets"), they are by definition to that extent political organizations.

2. It is not possible to define a political organization, including the state, in terms of the end to which its action is devoted. All the way from provision for subsistence to the patronage of art, there is no conceivable end which *some* political association has not at some time pursued. And from the protection of personal security to the administration of justice, there is none which *all* have recognized. Thus it is possible to define the "political" character of an organization only in terms of the *means* peculiar to it, the use of force. This means is, however, in the above sense specific, and is indispensable to its character. It is even, under certain circumstances, elevated into an end in itself.

This usage does not exactly conform to everyday speech. But the latter is too inconsistent to be used for technical purposes. We speak of the foreign currency *policy*[33] of a central bank, the financial *policy* of an association, or the educational *policy* of a local authority, and mean the systematic treatment and conduct of particular affairs. It comes considerably closer to the present meaning when we distinguish the "political" aspect or implication of a question. Thus there is the "political" official, the "political" newspaper, the "political" revolution, the "political" club, the "political" party, and the "political" consequences of an action, as distinguished from others such as the economic, cultural, or religious aspect of the persons, affairs or processes in question. In this usage we generally mean by "political," things that have to do with relations of authority within what is, in the present terminology, a political organization, the state. The reference is to things which are likely to uphold, to change or overthrow, to hinder or promote, these authority relations as distinguished from persons, things, and processes which have nothing to do with it. This usage thus seeks to bring out the common features of domination, the way it is exercised by the state, irrespective of the ends involved. Hence it is legitimate to claim that the definition put forward here is only a more precise formulation of what is meant in everyday usage in that it gives sharp emphasis to what is most characteristic of this *means:* the actual or threatened use of force. It is, of course, true that everyday usage applies the term "political," not only to groups which are the direct agents of the legitimate use of force itself, but also to other, often wholly peaceful groups, which attempt to influence the activities of the political organization. It seems best for present purposes to distinguish this type of social action, "politically oriented" action, from political action as such, the actual organized action of political groups.

3. Since the concept of the state has only in modern times reached its full development, it is best to define it in terms appropriate to the modern type of state, but at the same time, in terms which abstract from the values of the present day, since these are particularly subject to change. The primary formal characteristics of the modern state are as follows: It possesses an administrative and legal order subject to change by legislation, to which the organized activities of the administrative staff, which are also controlled by regulations, are oriented. This system of order claims binding authority, not only over the members of the state, the citizens, most of whom have obtained membership by birth, but also to a very large extent over all action taking place in the area of its jurisdiction. It is thus a compulsory organization with a territorial basis. Furthermore, today, the use of force is regarded as legitimate only so far as it is either permitted by the state or prescribed by it. Thus the right of a father to discipline his children is recognized—a survival of the former independent authority of the head of a household, which in the right to use force has sometimes extended to a power of life and death over children and slaves. The claim of the modern state to monopolize the use of force is as essential to it as its character of compulsory jurisdiction and of continuous operation.

4. In formulating the concept of a hierocratic organization, it is not possible to use the character of the religious benefits it offers, whether worldly or other-worldly, material or spiritual, as the decisive criterion. What is important is rather the fact that its control over these values can form the basis of a system of spiritual domination over human beings. What is most characteristic of the church, even in the common usage of the term, is the fact that it is a rational, compulsory association with continuous operation and that it claims a monopolistic authority. It is normal for a church to strive for complete control on a territorial basis and to attempt to set up the corresponding territorial or parochial organization. So far as this takes place, the means by which this claim to monopoly is upheld will vary from case to case. But historically, its control over territorial areas has not been nearly so essential to the church as to political associations; and this is particularly true today. It is its character as a compulsory association, particularly the fact that one beomes a member of the church by birth, which distinguishes the church from a "sect." It is characteristic of the latter that it is a voluntary association and admits only persons with specific religious qualifications. (This subject will be further discussed in the Sociology of Religion.)

NOTES

Unless otherwise noted, all notes in this chapter are by Talcott Parsons. For Parsons' exposition and critique of Weber's methodology, see his introduction to *The Theory of Social and Economic Organization* and his *Structure of Social Action*.

1. "Über einige Kategorien der verstehenden Soziologie," originally in *Logos,* IV, 1913, 253ff; reprinted in *GAzW,* 427–74. However, the reader should be aware from the very beginning that Part Two below, the older and major body of the manuscript, follows the terminology of this essay. For some of the relevant terminology, see Appendix I. (R)

2. It has not seemed advisable to attempt a rigorous use of a single English term whenever Weber employs *Verstehen.* "Understanding" has been most commonly used. Other expressions such as "subjectively understandable," "interpretation in subjective terms," "comprehension," etc., have been used from time to time as the context seemed to demand.

3. In this series of definitions Weber employs several important terms which need dicsussion. In addition to *Verstehen,* which has already been commented upon, there are four important ones: *Deuten, Sinn, Handeln,* and *Verhalten. Deuten* has generally been translated as "interpret." As used by Weber in this context it refers to the interpretation of subjective states of mind and the meanings which can be imputed as intended by an actor. Any other meaning of the word "interpretation" is irrelevant to Weber's discussion. The term *Sinn* has generally been translated as "meaning"; and its variations, particularly the corresponding adjectives, *sinnhaft, sinnvoll, sinnfremd,* have been dealt with by appropriately modifying the term *meaning.* The reference here again is always to features of the content of subjective states of mind or of symbolic systems which are ultimately referable to such states of mind.

The terms *Handeln* and *Verhalten* are directly related. *Verhalten* is the broader term referring to any mode of behavior of human individuals, regardless of the frame of reference in terms of which it is analysed. "Behavior" has seemed to be the most appropriate English equivalent. *Handeln,* on the other hand, refers to the concrete phenomenon of human behavior only insofar as it is capable of "understanding," in Weber's technical sense, in terms of subjective categories. The most appropriate English equivalent has seemed to be "action." This corresponds to [Parson's] usage in *The Structure of Social Action* and would seem to be fairly well established. "Conduct" is also similar and has sometimes been used. *Deuten, Verstehen,* and *Sinn* are thus applicable to human behavior only insofar as it constitutes action or conduct in this specific sense.

4. Weber's text in Part One is organized in a manner frequently found in the German academic literature of his day, in that he first lays down certain fundamental definitions and then proceeds to comment on them. These comments, which apparently were not intended to be "read" in the ordinary sense, but rather serve as reference material for the clarification and systematization of the theoretical concepts and their implications, are in the German edition printed in a smaller type, a convention which we have followed in the rest of Part One. However, while in most cases the comments are relatively brief, under the definitions of "sociology" and "social action" Weber wrote what are essentially methodological essays (sec. 1:A–B), which because of their length we have printed in the ordinary type. (R)

5. Weber means by "pure type" what he himself generally called and what has come to be known in the literature about his methodology as the "ideal type." The reader may be referred for general orientation to Weber's own essay (to which he himself refers below), "Die 'Objektivität' sozialwissenschaftlicher Erkenntnis" (" 'Objectivity' in Social Science and Social Policy," in *Max Weber: The Methodology of the Social Sciences.* Edward Shils and Henry Finch, trans. and eds. (Glencoe: The Free Press, 1949), 50–113; originally published in *AfS,* vol. 19, 1904, reprinted in *GAzW,* 146–214); to two works of Alexander von Schelting, "Die logische Theorie der historischen Kulturwissenschaften von Max

Weber," *AfS*, vol. 49, 1922, 623ff and *Max Webers Wissenschaftslehre*, 1934; Talcott Parsons, *The Structure of Social Action* (New York: McGraw-Hill, 1937), ch. 16; Theodore Abel, *Systematic Sociology in Germany*, (New York: Columbia University Press, 1929). [See now also Raymond Aron, *German Sociology*, trans. by M. and T. Bottomore (New York: The Free Press of Glencoe, 1964), based on 2nd French ed. of 1950.]

6. This is an imperfect rendering of the German term *Evidenz*, for which, unfortunately, there is no good English equivalent. It has hence been rendered in a number of different ways, varying with the particular context in which it occurs. The primary meaning refers to the basis on which a scientist or thinker becomes satisfied of the certainty or acceptability of a proposition. As Weber himself points out, there are two primary aspects of this. On the one hand a conclusion can be "seen" to follow from given premises by virtue of logical, mathematical, or possibly other modes of meaningful relation. In this sense one "sees" the solution of an arithmetical problem or the correctness of the proof of a geometrical theorem. The other aspect is concerned with empirical observation. If an act of observation is competently performed, in a similar sense one "sees" the truth of the relevant descriptive proposition. The term *Evidenz* does not refer to the process of observing, but to the quality of its result, by virtue of which the observer feels justified in affirming a given statement. Hence "certainty" has seemed a suitable translation in some contexts, "clarity" in others, "accuracy" in still others. The term "intuition" is not usable because it refers to the process rather than to he result.

7. Weber here uses the term *aktuelles Verstehen*, which he contrasts with *erklärendes Verstehen*. The latter he also refers to as *motivationsmässig*. "*Aktuell*" in this context has been translated as "observational." It is clear from Weber's discussion that the primary criterion is the possibility of deriving the meaning of an act or symbolic expression from immediate observation without reference to any broader context. In *erklärendes Verstehen*, on the other hand, the particular act must be placed in a broader context of meaning involving facts which cannot be derived from immediate observation of a particular act or expression.

8. The German term is *Sinnzusammenhang*. It refers to a plurality of elements which form a coherent whole on the level of meaning. There are several possible modes of meaningful relation between such elements, such as logical consistency, the esthetic harmony of a style, or the appropriateness of means to an end. In any case, however, a *Sinnzusammenhang* must be distinguished from a system of elements which are causally interdependent. There seems to be no single English term or phrase which is always adequate. According to variations in context, "context of meaning," "complex of meaning," and sometimes "meaningful system" have been employed.

9. The German is *gemeinter Sinn*. Weber departs from ordinary usage not only in broadening the meaning of this conception. As he states at the end of the present methodological discussion, he does not restrict the use of this concept to cases where a clear self-conscious awareness of such meaning can be reasonably attributed to every individual actor. Essentially, what Weber is doing is to formulate an operational concept. The question is not whether in a sense obvious to the ordinary person such an intended meaning "really exists," but whether the concept is capable of providing a logical framework within which scientifically important observations can be made. The test of validity of the observations is not whether their object is immediately clear to common sense, but whether the results of these technical observations can be satisfactorily organized and related to those of others in a systematic body of knowledge.

10. The above passage is an exceedingly compact statement of Weber's theory of the logical conditions of proof of causal relationship. He developed this most fully in his essay on "'Objectivity' in Social Science . . . ," *op. cit.* It is also discussed in other parts of *GAzW*. The best and fullest secondary discussion is to be found in Schelting's book, *Max Webers Wissenschaftslehre.* There is a briefer discussion in Parsons' *Structure of Social Action,* ch. 16.

11. See Eduard Meyer, *Geschichte des Altertums,* 1901, vol. III, 420, 444ff, and Weber's essay on "Critical Studies in the Logic of the Cultural Sciences," in Shils and Finch, eds., *op. cit.,* 113–188; also in *GAzW,* 215–90. (R)

12. The expression *sinnhafte Adäquanz* is one of the most difficult of Weber's technical terms to translate. In most places the cumbrous phrase "adequacy on the level of meaning" has had to be employed. It should be clear from the progress of the discussion that what Weber refers to is a satisfying level of knowledge for the particular purposes of the subjective state of mind of the actor or actors. He is, however, careful to point out that *causal* adequacy involves in addition to this a satisfactory correspondence between the results of observations from the subjective point of view and from the objective; that is, observations of the overt course of action which can be described without reference to the state of mind of the actor. For a discussion of the methodological problem involved here, see *Structure of Social Action,* chaps. II and V.

13. This is the first occurrence in Weber's text of the term *Chance* which he uses very frequently. It is here translated by "probability," because he uses it as interchangeable with *Wahrscheinlichkeit.* As the term "probability" is used in a technical mathematical and statistical sense, however, it implies the possibility of numerical statement. In most of the cases where Weber uses *Chance* this is out of the question. It is, however, possible to speak in terms of higher and lower degrees of probability. To avoid confusion with the technical mathematical concept, the term "likelihood" will often be used in the translation. It is by means of this concept that Weber, in a highly ingenious way, has bridged the gap between the interpretation of meaning and the inevitably more complex facts of overt action.

14. The term "reification" as used by Professor Morris Cohen in his book, *Reason and Nature,* seems to fit Weber's meaning exactly. A concept or system of concepts, which critical analysis can show to be abstract, is "reified" when it is used naively as though it provided an adequate total description of the concrete phenomenon in question. The fallacy of "reification" is virtually another name for what Professor Whitehead has called "the fallacy of misplaced concreteness." See his *Science and the Modern World.*

15. See August Weismann, *Die Allmacht der Naturzüchtung* (Jena: Fischer, 1893); his opponent was probably Alexander Götte (1840–1922), author of *Lehrbuch der Zoologie* (Leipzig: Engelmann, 1902) and of *Tierkunde* (Strasbourg: Trübner, 1904). (R)

16. In the above classification as well as in some of those which follow, the terminology is not standardized either in German or in English. Hence, just as there is a certain arbitrariness in Weber's definitions, the same is true of any corresponding set of definitions in English. It should be kept in mind that all of them are modes of orientation of action to patterns which contain a normative element. "Usage" has seemed to be the most appropriate translation of *Brauch* since, according to Weber's own definition, the principal criterion is that "it is done to conform with the pattern." There would also seem to be good precedent for the translation of *Sitte* by "custom." The contrast with fashion, which Weber takes up in his first comment, is essentially the same in both languages. The term *Interessenlage* presents greater difficulty. It involves

two components: the motivation in terms of self-interest and orientation to the opportunities presented by the situation. It has not seemed possible to use any single term to convey this meaning in English and hence, a more roundabout expression has had to be resorted to.

17. The term "convention" in Weber's usage is narrower than *Brauch*. The difference consists in the fact that a normative pattern to which action is oriented is conventional only insofar as it is regarded as part of a legitimate order, whereas the question of moral obligation to conformity which legitimacy implies is not involved in "usage." The distinction is closely related to that of W. G. Sumner between "mores" and "folkways." It has seemed best to retain the English term closest to Weber's own.

18. It is, in a sense, the empirical reference of this statement which constitutes the central theme of Weber's series of studies in the Sociology of Religion. Insofar as he finds it possible to attribute importance to "ideas" in the determination of action, the most important differences between systems of ideas are not so much those in the degree of rationalization as in the direction which the process of rationalization in each case has taken. This series of studies was left uncompleted at his death, but all the material which was in a condition fit for publication has been assembled in the three volumes of the *Gesammelte Aufsätze zur Religionssoziologie* (*GAzRS*).

19. It has not been possible to identify this reference of Weber's. It refers most probably to a projected conclusion which was never written.

20. The reader may readily become confused as to the basis of the following classification, as compared with that presented in sec. 7. The first classification is one of motives for maintaining a legitimate order in force, whereas the second is one of motives for attributing legitimacy to the order. This explains the inclusion of self-interested motives in the first classification, but not in the second. It is quite possible, for instance, for irreligious persons to support the doctrine of the divine right of kings, because they feel that the breakdown of an order which depends on this would have undesirable consequences. This is not, however, a possible motive on which to base a direct sense of personal moral obligation to conform with the order.

21. Rheinstein's emendation, see his edition, *op. cit.*, 7. (R)

22. In 1745, Maurice de Saxe defeated the British under the Duke of Cumberland even though he sustained heavy losses in the one-sided opening round. (R)

23. A cautionary note is in order here: The definitions of conflict or struggle (*Kampf*) and of power (section 16) have often been wrenched out of context in discussions of Weber as a "power politician." The present section, however, defines the *varieties* of conflict, from the extreme case of violent, unlimited and unregulated struggle to peaceful and regulated competition. In fact, mere conflict and power are not Weber's major concern, which is rather with variously regulated and legitimated actions and their group context. (R)

24. As Weber goes on to explain, he uses *Vergemeinschaftung* and *Vergesellschaftung* in a continuous rather than a dichotomous sense, and thus maintains his critical distance from Tönnies' paired contrast of *Gemeinschaft* and *Gesellschaft*. Similarly, Weber rejected Gierke's invidious contrast between "cold-blooded" Roman law and "communal" Germanic law, even though he started his career as a Germanist rather than a Romanist. (R)

25. This is a reference to the *Betriebsräte* which were formed in German industrial plants during the Revolution of 1918–19 and were recognized in the Weimar Constitution as entitled to representation in the Federal Economic

Council. The standard work in English is W. C. Guillebaud, *The Works Council. A German Experiment in Industrial Democracy* (Cambridge University Press, 1928).

26. Weber's term here is *Nahrungsspielraum*. The concept refers to the scope of economic resources and opportunities on which the standard of living of an individual or a group is dependent. By contrast with this, *Erwerbsspielraum* is a similar scope of resources and economic opportunities seen from the point of view of their possible role as sources of profit. The basic distinction implied in this contrast is of central importance to Weber's analysis later on (see chapter II, sec. 10ff.).

27. The term "corporate group" for *Verband*, as used by Parsons, is open to misunderstandings on both the common-sense and the historical level since Weber's term includes more than either economic groups or self-governing, often professional bodies. Parsons' alternative term, "organized group," has been retained. The term "organization" should be understood literally in the sense of a group with an "organ," but not necessarily of a rationalized kind; the latter would make it an "enterprise" or a "formal organization" (see sec. 15). —For Weber's older definition of *Verband* and *Verbandshandeln* see Appendix I. (R)

28. The concept "objective possibility" (*objektive Möglichkeit*) plays an important technical role in Weber's methodological studies. According to his usage, a thing is "objectively possible" if it "makes sense" to conceive it as an empirically existing entity. It is a question of conforming with the formal, logical conditions. The question whether a phenomenon which is in this sense "objectively possible" will actually be found with any significant degree of probability or approximation, is a logically distinct question.

29. See Ferdinand Lassalle, "Über Verfassungswesen" (1862), in *Gesammelte Reden und Schriften*, Eduard Bernstein, ed. (Berlin: Cassirer, 1919), 7–62. (R)

30. See Otto Gierke, *Geschichte des deutschen Körperschaftsbegriffs* (Berlin: Weidmann, 1873), 829; Hugo Preuss, *Gemeinde, Staat, Reich als Gebietskörperschaft* (1889). Preuss, one of Gierke's pupils, exerted decisive influence on the making of the Weimar constitution, to which Weber also contributed at about the same time that he worked intermittently on these definitions. (W and R)

31. In his translation Parsons pointed out that "the term *Herrschaft* has no satisfactory English equivalent. The term "imperative control," however, as used by N. S. Timasheff in his *Introduction to the Sociology of Law* is close to Weber's meaning" (Parsons, ed., *op. cit.*, 152). Therefore, he borrowed this term "for the most general purposes." At a later time, Parsons indicated that he now preferred the term "leadership." For more specific purposes, however, he used the term "authority." In objecting to "domination" (as used by Bendix and Rheinstein/Shils) Parsons noted: "It is true to be sure that the term *Herrschaft*, which in its most general meaning I should now translate as "leadership," implies that a leader has power *over* his followers. But "domination" suggests that this fact, rather than the integration of the collectivity, in the interest of effective functioning (especially the integration of the crucial *Verband* or corporate group), is the critical factor from Weber's point of view. I do not believe that the former interpretation represents the main trend of Weber's thought, although he was in certain respects a "realist" in the analysis of power. The preferable interpretation, as I see it, is represented especially by his tremendous emphasis on the importance of legitimation. I should therefore wish to stick to my own decision to translate *legitime Herrschaft*, which for Weber was overwhelmingly the most significant case for general structural analysis, as authority." (See T. Parsons' review article

of Reinhard Bendix, *Max Weber: An Intellectual Portrait*, in *American Socio-logical Review*, 25:5, 1960, 752.)

I prefer the term domination in this section because Weber stresses the fact of mere compliance with a command, which may be due to habit, a belief in legitimacy, or to considerations of expediency. However, Weber emphasizes here as later that, in addition to the willingness of subjects to comply with a command, there is usually a staff, which again may act on the basis of habit, legitimacy or self-interest. Sociologically, a *Herrschaft* is a structure of superordination and subordination, of leaders and led, rulers and ruled; it is based on a variety of motives and of means of enforcement. In ch. III, Weber presents a typology of legitimate *Herrschaft* where the term "authority" is indeed feasible. However, in ch. X, he deals extensively with both faces of *Herrschaft*: legitimacy and force. It should be clear to the reader that both "domination" and "authority" are "correct" although each stresses a different component of *Herrschaft*. Moreover, in Part Two a *Herrschaft* is quite specifically the medieval *seigneurie* or manor or similar structures in patrimonial regimes. This is also the historical derivation of the term. For a major, and sociologically valuable, study see Otto Brunner, *Land und Herrschaft: Grundfragen der territorialen Verfassungsgeschichte Österreichs im Mittelalter* (Vienna, 1959). (R)

32. For the earlier discussion of discipline, see Part Two, ch. XIV:*iii*:1, "The Meaning of Discipline."

33. The German is *Devisenpolitik*. Translation in this context is made more difficult by the fact that the German language does not distinguish between "politics" and "policy," *Politik* having both meanings. The remarks which Weber makes about various kinds of policy would have been unnecessary, had he written originally in English.

CHAPTER II

SOCIOLOGICAL CATEGORIES
OF ECONOMIC ACTION

Prefatory Note

What follows is not intended in any sense to be "eonomic theory." Rather, it consists only in an attempt to define certain concepts which are frequently used and to analyze certain of the simplest sociological relationships in the economic sphere. As in the first chapter, the procedure here has been determined entirely by considerations of convenience. It has proved possible entirely to avoid the controversial concept of "value."[1] The usage here, in the relevant sections on the division of labor [see sec. 15ff.], has deviated from the terminology of Karl Bücher only so far as seemed necessary for the purposes of the present undertaking. For the present all questions of dynamic process will be left out of account.

1. The Concept of Economic Action

Action will be said to be "economically oriented" so far as, according to its subjective meaning, it is concerned with the satisfaction of a desire for "utilities" (Nutzleistungen). "Economic action" (Wirtschaften) is a peaceful use of the actor's control over resources, which is rationally oriented, by deliberate planning, to economic ends. An "economy" (Wirtschaft) is autocephalous economic action. An "economic establishment" (Wirtschaftbetrieb) is an organized system of continuous economic action.

    1. It was pointed out above (ch. I, sec. 1:B) that economic action as such need not be social action.

[63]

2. The definition of economic action must be as general as possible and must bring out the fact that all "economic" processes and objects are characterized as such entirely by the *meaning* they have for human action in such roles as ends, means, obstacles, and by-products. It is not, however, permissible to express this by saying, as is sometimes done, that economic action is a "psychic" phenomenon. The production of goods, prices, or even the "subjective valuation" of goods, if they are empirical processes, are far from being merely psychic phenomena. But underlying this misleading phrase is a correct insight. It is a fact that these phenomena have a peculiar type of subjective *meaning*. This alone defines the unity of the corresponding processes, and this alone makes them accessible to subjective interpretation.

The definition of "economic action" must, furthermore, be formulated in such a way as to include the operation of a modern business enterprise run for profit. Hence the definition cannot be based directly on "consumption needs" and the "satisfaction" of these needs, but must, rather, start out on the one hand from the fact that there is a *desire* (demand) for utilities (which is true even in the case of orientation to purely monetary gains), and on the other hand from the fact that *provision* is being made to furnish the supplies to meet this demand (which is true even in the most primitive economy merely "satisfying needs," and regardless of how primitive and frozen in tradition the methods of this provision are).

3. As distinguished from "economic action" as such, the term "economically oriented action" will be applied to two types: (a) every action which, though primarily oriented to other ends, takes account, in the pursuit of them, of economic considerations; that is, of the consciously recognized necessity for economic prudence. Or (b) that which, though primarily oriented to economic ends, makes use of physical force as a means. It thus includes all primarily non-economic action and all non-peaceful action which is influenced by economic considerations. "Economic action" thus is a *conscious, primary* orientation to economic considerations. It must be conscious, for what matters is not the objective necessity of making economic provision, but the belief that is is necessary. Robert Liefmann has rightly laid emphasis on the subjective understandable orientation of action which makes it economic action. He is not, however, correct in attributing the contrary view to all other authors.[2]

4. Every type of action, including the use of violence, may be economically *oriented*. This is true, for instance, of war-like action, such as marauding expeditions and trade wars. Franz Oppenheimer, in particular, has rightly distinguished "economic" means from "political" means.[3] It is essential to distinguish the latter from economic action. The use of force is unquestionably very strongly opposed to the spirit of economic acquisition in the usual sense. Hence the term "economic action" will not be applied to the direct appropriation of goods by force and the direct coercion of the other party by threats of force. It goes without saying, at

the same time, that exchange is not the *only* economic means, though it is one of the most important. Furthermore, the formally peaceful provision for the means and the success of a projected exercise of force, as in the case of armament production and economic organization for war, is just as much economic action as any other.

Every rational course of political action is economically oriented with respect to provision for the necessary means, and it is always possible for political action to serve the interest of economic ends. Similarly, though it is not necessarily true of every economic system, certainly the modern economic order under modern conditions could not continue if its control of resources were not upheld by the legal compulsion of the state; that is, if its formally "legal" rights were not upheld by the threat of force. But the fact that an economic system is thus dependent on protection by force, does not mean that it is itself an example of the use of force.

How entirely untenable it is to maintain that the economy, however defined, is only a *means,* by contrast, for instance, with the state, becomes evident from the fact that it is possible to define the state itself only in terms of the means which it today monopolizes, namely, the use of force. If anything, the most essential aspect of economic action for practical purposes is the prudent choice *between ends.* This choice is, however, oriented to the scarcity of the means which are available or could be procured for these various ends.

5. Not every type of action which is rational in its choice of means will be called "rational economic action," or even "economic action" in any sense; in particular, the term "economy" will be distinguished from that of "technology."[4] The "technique" of an action refers to the means employed as opposed to the meaning or end to which the action is, in the last analysis, oriented. "Rational" technique is a choice of means which is consciously and systematically oriented to the experience and reflection of the actor, which consists, at the highest level of rationality, in scientific knowledge. What is concretely to be treated as a "technique" is thus variable. The ultimate meaning of a concrete act may, seen in the total context of action, be of a "technical" order; that is, it may be significant only as a means in this broader context. Then the "meaning" of the concrete act (viewed from the larger context) lies in its technical function; and, conversely, the means which are applied in order to accomplish this are its "techniques." In this sense there are techniques of every conceivable type of action, techniques of prayer, of asceticism, of thought and research, of memorizing, of education, of exercising political or hierocratic domination, of administration, of making love, of making war, of musical performances, of sculpture and painting, of arriving at legal decisions. All these are capable of the widest variation in degree of rationality. The presence of a "technical question" always means that there is some doubt over the choice of the most rational *means* to an end. Among others, the standard of rationality for a technique may be the famous principle of "least effort," the achievement of

an optimum *in the relation* between the result and the means to be expended on it (and not the attainment of a result with the *absolute* minimum of means). Seemingly the same principle, of course, applies to economic action—or to any type of rational action. But there it has a different *meaning*. As long as the action is purely "technical" in the present sense, it is oriented only to the selection of the means which, with equal quality, certainty, and permanence of the result, are comparatively most "economical" of effort in the attainment of a *given* end; comparatively, that is, insofar as there are at all directly comparable expenditures of means in different methods of achieving the end. The end itself is accepted as beyond question, and a purely technical consideration ignores other wants. Thus, in a question of whether to make a technically necessary part of a machine out of iron or platinum, a decision on technical grounds alone would, so long as the requisite quantities of both metals for their particular purpose were available, consider only which of the two would in this case best bring about the given result and would at the same time minimize the other comparable expenditure of resources, such as labor. But once consideration is extended to take account of the relative scarcity of iron and platinum in relation to their potential uses, as today every technician is accustomed to do even in the chemical laboratory, the action is no longer in the present sense purely technical, but *also* economic. From the economic point of view, "technical" questions always involve the consideration of "costs." This is a question of crucial importance for economic purposes and in this context always takes the form of asking what would be the effect on the satisfaction of other wants if this particular means were not used for satisfaction of one given want. The "other wants" may be qualitatively different present wants or qualitatively identical future wants. (A similar position is taken by Friedrich von Gottl-Ottlilienfeld in *Grundriss der Sozialökonomik*, Part II, 2; an extensive and very good discussion of this issue in R. Liefmann, *Grundsätze der Volkswirtschaftslehre*, vol. I (3rd ed.), p. 322ff. Any attempt to reduce all means to "ultimate expenditures of labor" is erroneous.)

For the answer to the question, what is, in comparative terms, the "cost" of using various means for a given technical end, depends in the last analysis on their potential usefulness as means to other ends. This is particularly true of labor. A *technical* problem in the present sense is, for instance, that of what equipment is necessary in order to move loads of a particular kind or in order to raise mineral products from a given depth in a mine, and which of the alternatives is the most "suited," that is, among other things, which achieves a given degree of success with the least expenditure of effort. It is, on the other hand, an *economic* problem whether, on the assumption of a market economy, these expenditures will pay off in terms of money obtained through the sale of the goods; or, on the assumption of a planned economy, whether the necessary labor and other means of production can be provided without damage to the satisfaction of other wants held to be more urgent. In both cases, it is a problem of the comparison of *ends*. Economic action is primarily oriented to the problem of choosing the *end* to which a thing shall be applied; technology, to the problem, given the end, of choosing the appropriate *means*. For purposes of the theoretical (not, of course, the practical) definition of technical rationality it is wholly indifferent whether the product of a technical process is in any sense useful. In the present terminology we can conceive of a rational technique for achieving ends which no one desires. It would, for instance, be possible, as a kind of technical amusement, to apply all the most modern methods to the production of atmospheric air. And no one could take the slightest exception to the purely technical rationality of the action. Economically, on the other hand, the procedure would under normal circumstances be clearly irrational because there would be no demand for the product. (On all this, compare v. Gottl-Ottlilienfeld, *op. cit.*)

The fact that what is called the technological development of modern times has been so largely oriented economically to profit-making is one of the fundamental facts of the history of technology. But however fundamental it has been, this economic orientation has by no means stood alone in shaping the development of technology. In addition, a part has been played by the games and cogitations of impractical ideologists, a part by other-worldly interests and all sorts of fantasies, a part by preoccupation with artistic problems, and by various other non-economic motives. None the less, the main emphasis at all times, and especially the present, has lain in the economic determination of technological development. Had not rational calculation formed the basis of economic activity, had there not been certain very particular conditions in its economic background, rational technology could never have come into existence.

The fact that the aspects of economic orientation which distinguish it from technology were not explicitly brought into the initial definition, is a consequence of the sociological starting point. From a sociological point of view, the weighing of alternative ends in relation to each other and to costs is a consequence of "continuity." This is true at least so far as costs mean something other than altogether giving up one end in favor of more urgent ones. An economic theory, on the other hand, would do well to emphasize this criterion from the start.

6. It is essential to include the criterion of power of control and disposal (*Verfügungsgewalt*)[5] in the sociological concept of economic action, if for no other reason than that at least a modern market economy (*Erwerbswirtschaft*) essentially consists in a complete network of exchange contracts, that is, in deliberate planned acquisitions of powers of control and disposal. This, in such an economy, is the principal source of the relation of economic action to the law. But any other type of organization of economic activities would involve some kind of *de facto* distribution of powers of control and disposal, however different its underlying principles might be from those of the modern private enterprise economy with its legal protection of such powers held by autonomous and autocephalous economic units. Either the central authority, as in the case of socialism, or the subsidiary parts, as in anarchism, must be able

to count on having some kind of control over the necessary services of labor and of the means of production. It is possible to obscure this fact by verbal devices, but it cannot be interpreted out of existence. For purposes of definition it is a matter of indifference in what way this control is guaranteed; whether by convention or by law, or whether it does not even enjoy the protection of any external sanctions at all, but its security rests only on actual expectations in terms of custom or self-interest. These possibilities must be taken into account, however essential legal compulsion may be for the modern economic order. The indispensability of powers of control for the concept of social action in its economic aspects thus does not imply that *legal* order is part of that concept by definition, however important it may be held to be on empirical grounds.

7. The concept of powers of control and disposal will here be taken to include the possibility of control over the actor's own labor power, whether this is in some way enforced or merely exists in fact. That this is not to be taken for granted is shown by its absence in the case of slaves.

8. It is necessary for the purposes of a sociological theory of economic action to introduce the concept of "goods" at an early stage, as is done in sec. 2. For this theory is concerned with a type of action which is given its specific *meaning* by the *results* of the actors' deliberations, which themselves can be isolated only in theory [but cannot be observed empirically]. Economic theory, the theoretical insights of which provide the basis for the sociology of economic action, might (perhaps) be able to proceed differently; the latter may find it necessary to create its own theoretical constructs.

2. *The Concept of Utility*

By "utilities" (*Nutzleistungen*) will always be meant the specific and concrete, real or imagined, advantages (*Chancen*) of opportunities for present or future use as they are estimated and made an object of specific provision by one or more economically acting individuals. The action of these individuals is oriented to the estimated importance of such utilities as means for the ends of their economic action.

Utilities may be the services of non-human or inanimate objects or of human beings. Non-human objects which are the sources of potential utilities of whatever sort will be called "goods." Utilities derived from a human source, so far as this source consists in active conduct, will be called "services" (*Leistungen*). Social relationships which are valued as a potential source of present or future disposal over utilities are, however, also objects of economic provision. The opportunities of economic advantage, which are made available by custom, by the constellation of interest, or by a conventional or legal order for the purposes of an economic unit, will be called "economic advantages."

On the following comments, compare E. von Böhm-Bawerk, *Rechte und Verhältnisse vom Standpunkt der volkswirtschaftlichen Güterlehre* (Innsbruck 1881).

1. The categories of goods and services do not exhaust those aspects of the environment which may be important to an individual for economic purposes and which may hence be an object of economic concern. Such things as "good will," or the tolerance of economic measures on the part of individuals in a position to interfere with them, and numerous other forms of behavior, may have the same kind of economic importance and may be the object of economic provision and, for instance, of contracts. It would, however, result in a confusion of concepts to try to bring such things under either of these two categories. This choice of concepts is thus entirely determined by consideration of convenience.

2. As Böhm-Bawerk has correctly pointed out, it would be equally imprecise if all *concrete* objects of life and of everyday speech were without distinction designated as "goods," and the concept of a good were then equated to that of a material utility. In the strict sense of utility, it is not a "horse" or a "bar of iron" which is an economic "good," but the specific ways in which they can be put to desirable and practical uses; for instance the power to haul loads or to carry weights, or something of the sort. Nor can we, in the present terminology, call *goods* such potential future advantages (*Chancen*) which appear as objects of exchange in economic transactions, as "good will," "mortgage," "property." Instead, for simplicity's sake, we shall call the services of such potential powers of control and disposal over the utilities of goods and services, promised or guaranteed by the traditional or legal order, "economic advantages" (*Chancen*) or simply "advantages" wherever this is not likely to be misunderstood.

3. The fact that only active conduct, and not mere acquiescence, permission, or omission, are treated as "services" is a matter of convenience. But it must be remembered that it follows from this that goods and services do not constitute an exhaustive classification of all economically significant utilities.

On the concept of "labor," see below, sec. 15.

3. *Modes of the Economic Orientation of Action*

Economic orientation may be a matter of tradition or of goal-oriented rationality. Even in cases where there is a high degree of rationalization of action, the element of traditional orientation remains considerable. For the most part, rational orientation is primarily significant for "managerial" action, no matter under what form of organization. (See below, sec. 15.) The development of rational economic action from the instinctively reactive search for food or traditional acceptance of inherited techniques and customary social relationships has been to a large extent determined by non-economic events and actions, including those outside everyday routine,[6] and also by the pressure of necessity in cases of increasing absolute or relative limitations on subsistence.

1. Naturally there cannot in principle be any scientific standard for any such concept as that of an "original economic state." It would be possible to agree arbitrarily to take the economic state on a given technological level, as, for instance, that characterized by the lowest development of tools and equipment known to us, and to treat it and analyze it as the most primitive. But there is no scientific justification for concluding from observations of living primitive peoples on a low technological level that the economic organization of all peoples of the past with similar technological standing has been the same as, for instance, that of the Vedda or of certain tribes of the Amazon region. For, from a purely economic point of view, this level of technology has been just as compatible with large-scale organization of labor as with extreme dispersal in small groups (see below, sec. 16). It is impossible to infer from the economic aspects of the natural environment alone, which of these would be more nearly approached. Various non-economic factors, for instance, military, could make a substantial difference.

2. War and migration are not in themselves economic processes, though particularly in early times they have been largely oriented to economic considerations. At all times, however, indeed up to the present, they have often been responsible for radical changes in the economic system. In cases where, through such factors as climatic changes, inroads of sand, or deforestation, there has been an absolute decrease in the means of subsistence, human groups have adapted themselves in widely differing ways, depending on the structure of interests and on the manner in which non-economic factors have played a role. The typical reactions, however, have been a fall in the standard of living and an absolute decrease in population. Similarly, in cases of relative impoverishment in means of subsistence, as determined by a given standard of living and of the distribution of chances of acquisition, there have also been wide variations. But on the whole, this type of situation has, more frequently than the other, been met by the increasing rationalization of economic activities. Even in this case, however, it is not possible to make general statements. So far as the "statistical" information can be relied upon, there was a tremendous increase of population in China after the beginning of the eighteenth century, but it had exactly the opposite effect from the similar phenomenon of about the same time in Europe. It is, however, possible to say at least something about the reasons for this (see below, sec. 11.). The chronic scarcity of the means of subsistence in the Arabian desert has only at certain times resulted in a change in the economic and political structure, and these changes have been

most prominent when non-economic (religious) developments have played a part.

3. A high degree of traditionalism in habits of life, such as characterized the laboring classes in early modern times, has not prevented a great increase in the rationalization of economic enterprise under capitalistic direction. But it was also compatible with, for instance, the rationalization of public finances in Egypt on a state-socialistic model. Nevertheless, this traditionalistic attitude had to be at least partly overcome in the Western World before the further development to the specifically modern type of rational capitalistic economy could take place.

4. *Typical Measures of Rational Economic Action*

The following are typical measures of rational economic action:

(1) The systematic allocation as between present and future of utilities, on the control of which the actor for whatever reason feels able to count. (These are the essential features of saving.)

(2) The systematic allocation of available utilities to various potential uses in the order of their estimated relative urgency, ranked according to the principle of marginal utility.

These two cases, the most definitely "static," have been most highly developed in times of peace. Today, for the most part, they take the form of the allocation of money incomes.

(3) The systematic procurement[7] through production or transportation of such utilities for which all the necessary means of production are controlled by the actor himself. Where action is rational, this type of action will take place so far as, according to the actor's estimate, the urgency of his demand for the expected result of the action exceeds the necessary expenditure, which may consist in (a) the irksomeness of the requisite labor services, and (b) the other potential uses to which the requisite goods could be put; including, that is, the utility of the potential alternative products and their uses. This is "production" in the broader sense, which includes transportation.

(4) The systematic acquisition, by agreement (*Vergesellschaftung*) with the present possessors or with competing bidders, of assured powers of control and disposal over utilities. The powers of control may or may not be shared with others. The occasion may lie in the fact that utilities themselves are in the control of others, that their means of procurement are in such control, or that third persons desire to acquire them in such a way as to endanger the actor's own supply.

The relevant rational association (*Vergesellschaftung*) with the present possessor of a power of control or disposal may consist in (a) the establishment of an organization with an order to which the procurement and use of utilities is to be oriented, or (b) in exchange. In the first case the purpose of the organization may be to ration the procurement, use, or consumption, in order to limit competition of procuring actors. Then it is a "regulative organization." Or, secondly, its purpose may be to set up a unified authority for the systematic administration of the utilities which had hitherto been subject to a dispersed control. In this case there is an "administrative organization."

"Exchange" is a compromise of interests on the part of the parties in the course of which goods or other advantages are passed as reciprocal compensation. The exchange may be traditional or conventional,[8] and hence, especially in the latter case, not economically rational. Or, secondly, it may be economically rational both in intention and in result. Every case of a rationally oriented exchange is the resolution of a previously open or latent conflict of interests by means of a compromise. The opposition of interests which is resolved in the compromise involves the actor potentially in two different conflicts. On the one hand, there is the conflict over the price to be agreed upon with the partner in exchange; the typical method is bargaining. On the other hand, there may also be competition with actual or potential rivals, either in the present or in the future, who are competitors in the same market. Here, the typical method is competitive bidding and offering.

1. Utilities, and the goods or labor which are their sources, are under the control (*Eigenverfügung*) of an economically acting individual if he is in a position to be able in fact to make use of them at his convenience (at least, up to a point) without interference from other persons, regardless of whether this ability rests on the legal order, on convention, on custom or on a complex of interests. It is by no means true that only the legal assurance of powers of disposal is decisive, either for the concept or in fact. It is, however, today empirically an indispensable basis for economic activitiy with the *material* means of production.

2. The fact that goods are not as yet consumable may be a result of the fact that while they are, as such, finished, they are not yet in a suitable place for consumption; hence the transportation of goods, which is naturally to be distinguished from trade, a change in the control over the goods, may here be treated as part of the process of production.

3. When there is a lack of control (*Eigenverfügung*) over desired utilities, it is in principle indifferent whether the individual is typically prevented from forcibly interfering with the control of others by a legal order, convention, custom, his own self-interest, or his consciously-held moral standards.

4. Competition in procurement may exist under the most various conditions. It is particularly important when supplies are obtained by seizure, as in hunting, fishing, lumbering, pasturage, and clearing new

land. It may also, and most frequently does, exist within an organization which is closed to outsiders. An order which seeks to restrain such competition then always consists in the rationing of supplies, usually combined with the appropriation of the procurement possibilities thus guaranteed for the benefit of a limited number of individuals or, more often, households. All medieval *Mark-* and fishing associations, the regulation of forest clearing, pasturage and wood gathering rights in the common fields and wastes, the grazing rights on Alpine meadows, and so on, have this character. Various types of hereditary property-rights in land owe their development to this type of regulation.

5. Anything which may in any way be transferred from the control of one person to that of another and for which another is willing to give compensation, may be an object of exchange. It is not restricted to goods and services, but includes all kinds of potential economic advantages; for instance, "good will," which exists only by custom or self-interest and cannot be enforced; in particular, however, it includes all manner of advantages, claims to which are enforceable under some kind of order. Thus objects of exchange are not necessarily presently existing utilities.

For present purposes, by "exchange" in the broadest sense will be meant every case of a formally voluntary agreement involving the offer of any sort of present, continuing, or future utility in exchange for utilities of any sort offered in return. Thus it includes the turning over of the utility of goods or money in exchange for the future return of the same kind of goods. It also includes any sort of permission for, or tolerance of, the use of an object in return for "rent" or "hire," or the hiring of any kind of services for wages or salary. The fact that the last example today involves, from a sociological point of view, the subjection of the "worker," as defined in sec. 15 below, under a form of domination will, for preliminary purposes, be neglected, as will the distinction between loan and purchase.

6. The conditions of exchange may be traditional, partly traditional though enforced by convention, or rational. Examples of conventional exchanges are exchanges of gifts between friends, heroes, chiefs, princes; as, for instance, the exchange of armor between Diomedes and Glaucos. It is not uncommon for these to be rationally oriented and controlled to a high degree, as can be seen in the Tell-el-Amarna documents. Rational exchange is only possible when both parties expect to profit from it, or when one is under compulsion because of his own need or the other's economic power. Exchange may serve either purposes of consumption or of acquisition (see below, sec. 11). It may thus be oriented to provision for the personal use of the actor or to opportunities for profit. In the first case, its conditions are to a large extent differentiated from case to case, and it is in *this* sense irrational. Thus, for instance, household surpluses will be valued according to the individual marginal utilities of the particular household economy and may on occasion be sold very cheaply, and the fortuitous desires of the moment may establish the marginal utility of goods which are sought in ex-

change at a very high level. Thus the exchange ratios, as determined by marginal utility, will fluctuate widely. Rational competition develops only in the case of "marketable goods" (see sec. 8) and, to the highest degree, when goods are used and sold in a profit system (see sec. 11).

7. The modes of intervention of a regulatory system mentioned above under point (4) are not the only possible ones, but merely those which are relevant here because they are the most immediate consequences of a tightening of the supply basis. The regulation of marketing processes will be discussed below.

5. *Types of Economic Organizations*

According to its relation to the economic system, an economically oriented organization may be: (a) an "economically active organization" (*wirtschaftender Verband*) if the primarily non-economic organized action oriented to its order includes economic action; (b) an "economic organization" (*Wirtschaftsverband*) if its organized action, as governed by the order, is *primarily* autocephalous economic action of a given kind; (c) an "economically regulative organization" (*wirtschaftsregulierender Verband*) if the autocephalous economic activity of the members is directly oriented to the order governing the group; that is, if economic action is heteronomous in that respect; (d) an "organization enforcing a formal order" (*Ordnungsverband*)[9] if its order merely guarantees, by means of formal rules, the autocephalous and autonomous economic activities of its members and the corresponding economic advantages thus acquired.

1. The state, except for the socialistic or communist type, and all other organizations like churches and voluntary associations are economically active groups if they manage their own financial affairs. This is also true of educational institutions and all other organizations which are not primarily economic.

2. In the category of "economic organizations" in the present sense are included not only business corporations, co-operative associations, cartels, partnerships, and so on, but all permanent economic establishments (*Betriebe*) which involve the activities of a plurality of persons, all the way from a workshop run by two artisans to a conceivable communistic organization of the whole world.

3. "Economically regulative organizations" are the following: medieval village associations, guilds, trade unions, employers' associations, cartels, and all other groups, the directing authorities of which carry on an "economic policy" which seeks to regulate both the ends and the procedures of economic activity. It thus includes the villages and towns of the Middle Ages, just as much as a modern state which follows such a policy.

4. An example of a group confined to the "enforcement of a formal order" is the pure laissez-faire state, which would leave the economic activity of individual households and enterprises entirely free and confine its regulation to the formal function of settling disputes connected with the fulfillment of free contractual obligations.

5. The existence of organizations "regulating economic activity" or merely "enforcing a formal order" presupposes in principle a certain amount of autonomy in the field of economic activity. Thus there is in principle a sphere of free disposal over economic resources, though it may be limited in varying degrees by means of rules to which the actors are oriented. This implies, further, the (at least relative) appropriation of economic advantages, over which the actors then have autonomous control. The purest type of a group "enforcing a formal order" is thus present when all *human* action is autonomous with respect to content, and oriented to regulation only with respect to form, and when all *non-human* sources of utility are completely appropriated so that individuals can have free disposal of them, in particular by exchange, as is the case in a modern property system. Any other kind of limitation on appropriation and autonomy implies "regulation of economic activity," because it restricts the orientation of human activities.

6. The dividing line between "regulation of economic activity" and mere "enforcement of a formal order" is vague. For, naturally, the type of "formal" order not only may, but must, in some way also exert a material influence on action; in some cases, a fundamental influence. Numerous modern legal ordinances, which claim to do no more than set up formal rules, are so drawn up that they actually exert a material influence (see "Soc. of Law," Part Two, ch. VIII). Indeed, a really strict limitation to purely formal rules is possible only in theory. Many of the recognized "overriding" principles of law, of a kind which cannot be dispensed with, imply to an appreciable degree important limitations on the content of economic activity. Especially "enabling provisions" can under certain circumstances, as in corporation law, involve quite appreciable limitations on economic autonomy.

7. The limits of the material regulation of economic activity may be reached when it results in (a) the abandonment of certain kinds of economic activity, as when a tax on turnover leads to the cultivation of land only for consumption; or (b) in evasion, in such cases as smuggling, bootlegging, etc.

6. *Media of Exchange, Means of Payment, Money*

A material object offered in exchange will be called a "medium of exchange" so far as it is typically accepted primarily by virtue of the fact that the recipients estimate that they will, within the relevant time horizon, be able to utilize it in another exchange to procure other goods at an acceptable exchange ratio, regardless of whether it is exchangable for *all* other goods or only for certain specific goods. The probability that the medium of exchange will be accepted at a given rate for specific other goods will be called its "substantive validity" (*materiale Geltung*) in relation to these. The use itself will be called the "formal validity" (*formale Geltung*).

An object will be called a "means of payment" so far as its acceptance in payment of specific agreed or imposed obligations is *guaranteed* by convention or by law. This is the "formal validity" of the means of payment, which may also signify its formal validity as a means of exchange. Means of exchange or of payment will be called "chartal" (*chartal*)[10] when they are artifacts which, by virtue of their specific form, enjoy a definite quantum, conventional or legal, agreed or imposed, of formal validity within the membership of a group of persons or within a territorial area; and when (b) they are divisible in such a way that they represent a particular unit of nominal value or a multiple or a fraction of it, so that it is possible to use them in arithmetical calculations.

"Money" we call a chartal means of payment which is also a means of exchange.

An organization will be called a "means of exchange," "means of payment," or "money" group insofar as it effectively imposes within the sphere of authority of its orders the conventional or legal (formal) validity of a means of exchange, of payment, or money; these will be termed "internal" means of exchange, etc. Means used in transactions with non-members will be called "external" means of exchange.

Means of exchange or of payment which are not chartal are "natural" means. They may be differentiated (a) in technical terms, according to their physical characteristic—they may be ornaments, clothing, useful objects of various sorts—or according to whether their utilization occurs in terms of weight or not. They may also (b) be distinguished economically according to whether they are used primarily as means of exchange or for purposes of social prestige, the prestige of possession. They may also be distinguished according to whether they are used as means of exchange and payment in internal or in external transactions.

Money, means of exchange or of payment are "tokens" so far as they do not or no longer possess a value independent of their use as means of exchange and of payment. They are, on the other hand, "material" means so far as their value as such is influenced by their possible use for other purposes, or may be so influenced.

Money may consist either of coined or of note (document) money. Notes are usually adapted to a system of coinage or have a name which is historically derived from it.

(1) Coined money will be called "free" money or "market" money so far as the monetary metal will be coined by the mint on the initiative

of any possessor of it without limit of amount. This means that in effect the amount issued is determined by the demand of parties to market transactions.

(2) It will be called "limited" money or "administrative" money if the transformation of the metal into its chartal form (coinage) is subject to the formally quite arbitrary decisions of the governing authority of an organization and is in effect primarily oriented to its fiscal needs.

(3) It will be called "regulated" money if, though its issue is limited, the kind and amount of coinage is effectively subject to rules.

The term "means of circulation" will be applied to a document which functions as "note" money, if it is accepted in normal transactions as "provisional" money with the expectation that it can, at any time, be converted into "definitive" money, that is into coins, or a given weight of monetary metal. It is a "certificate" if this is assured by regulations which require maintenance of stocks providing full coverage in coin or bullion.

We call "conversion scales" the conventional or legally imposed exchange ratios valid within an organization for the different "natural" means of exchange or payment.

"Currency money" is the money which by the effective arrangements within an organization has validity as a means of payment without limitation on the amount that need be accepted. "Monetary material" is the material from which money is made; "monetary metal" is this material in the case of market money. "Monetary value scale" we call the relative valuation of the various subdivisions and denominations, consisting of different material substances, of "note" or "administrative" money; the same ratios in the case of types of market money made of different metals we call "exchange ratios."

"International" means of payment are those means of payment which serve to balance accounts between different monetary systems, that is, so far as payments are not postponed by funding operations.

Every reform of the monetary system by an organization must necessarily take account of the fact that certain means of payment have previously been used for the liquidation of debts. It must either accept as legal their continued use as a means of payment, or impose new ones. In the latter case an exchange ratio must be established between the old units, whether natural, by weight, or chartal, and the new ones. This is the principle of the so-called "historical" definition of money as a means of payment. It is impossible here to discuss how far this reacts upon the exchange relation between money as a means of exchange and goods.

> It should be strongly emphasized that the present discussion is not an essay in monetary theory, but only an attempt to work out the simplest possible formulations of a set of concepts which will have to be

frequently employed later on. In addition, this discussion is concerned primarily with certain very elementary *sociological* consequences of the use of money. The formulation of monetary theory, which has been most acceptable to the author, is that of von Mises.[11] The *Staatliche Theorie des Geldes* by G. F. Knapp[12] is the most imposing work in the field and in its way solves the formal problem brilliantly. It is, however, as will be seen below, incomplete for substantive monetary problems. Its able and valuable attempt to systematize terminology and concepts will be left out of account at this point.

1. Means of exchange and means of payment very often, though by no means always, coincide empirically. They are, however, particularly likely not to do so in primitive conditions. The means of payment for dowries, tribute, obligatory gifts, fines, wergild, etc., are often specified in convention or by law without regard to any relation to the means of exchange actually in circulation. It is only when the economic affairs of the organization are administered in money terms that von Mises' contention that even the state seeks means of payment only as a means of exchange becomes tenable. This has not been true of cases where the possession of certain means of payment has been primarily significant as a mark of social status. (See Heinrich Schurtz, *Grundriss einer Entstehungsgeschichte des Geldes,* 1898). With the introduction of regulation of money by the state, means of payment becomes the legal concept and means of exchange the economic concept.

2. There seems at first sight to be an indistinct line between a "good" which is purchased solely with a view to its future resale and a medium of exchange. In fact, however, even under conditions which are otherwise primitive there is a strong tendency for particular objects to monopolize the function of medium of exchange so completely that there is no doubt about their status. Wheat futures are traded in terms which imply that there will be a final buyer. Therefore they cannot be treated as means of payment or medium of exchange, let alone money.

3. So long as there is no officially sanctioned money, what is used as means of exchange is primarily determined by the customs, interests, and conventions to which the agreements between the parties to transactions are oriented. The reasons why specific things have become accepted as means of exchange cannot be gone into here. They have, however, been exceedingly various and tend to be determined by the type of exchange which has been of the greatest importance. By no means every medium of exchange, even within the social group where it has been employed, has been universally acceptable for every type of exchange. For instance, cowry shells, though used for other things, have not been acceptable in payment for wives or cattle.

4. Sometimes means of payment which were not the usual means of exchange have played an important part in the development of money to its special status. As G. F. Knapp has pointed out, the fact that various types of debt have existed, such as obligations stemming from tributes, dowries, payments for bride purchase, conventional gifts to kings

or by kings to each other, wergild, etc., and the fact that these have often been payable in certain specific media, has created for these media, by convention or by law, a special position. Very often they have been specific types of artifacts.

5. Money in the meaning of the present terminology may have been the one-fifth shekel pieces bearing the stamp of merchant firms which are mentioned in the Babylonian records, on the assumption, that is, that they were actually used as means of exchange. On the other hand, bars of bullion which were not coined, but weighed, will here not be treated as money, but only as means of payment and exchange. The fact, however, that they were weighed has been enormously important for the development of the habit of economic calculations. There are, naturally, many transitional forms, such as the acceptance of coins by weight rather than by denomination.

6. "Chartal" is a term introduced by Knapp in his *Staatliche Theorie des Geldes*. All types of money which have been stamped or coined, endowed with validity by law or by agreement, belong in this category, whether they were metal or not. It does not, however, seem reasonable to confine the concept to regulations by the state and not to include cases where acceptance is made compulsory by convention or by some agreement. There seems, furthermore, to be no reason why actual minting by the state or under the control of the political authorities should be a decisive criterion. For long periods this did not exist in China at all and was very much limited in the European Middle Ages. As Knapp would agree, it is only the existence of norms regulating the monetary form which is decisive. As will be noted below, validity as a means of payment and formal acceptability as means of exchange in private transactions may be made compulsory by law within the jurisdiction of the political authority.

7. Natural means of exchange and of payment may sometimes be used more for internal transactions, sometimes more for external. The details need not be considered here. The question of the substantive validity of money will be taken up later.

8. This is, furthermore, not the place to take up the substantive theory of money in its relation to prices so far as this subject belongs in the field of economic sociology at all. For present purposes it will suffice to state the fact that money, in its most important forms, is used, and then to proceed to develop some of the most general sociological consequences of this fact, which is merely a formal matter when seen from an economic point of view. It must, however, be emphasized that money can *never* be merely a harmless "voucher" or a purely nominal unit of accounting so long as it *is* money. Its valuation is always in very complex ways dependent also on its scarcity or, in case of inflation, on its overabundance. This has been particularly evident in recent times, but is equally true for all times.

A socialistic regime might issue vouchers, in payment for a given quantity of socially useful "labor," valid for the purchase of certain types of goods. These might be saved or used in exchange, but their behavior would follow the rules of barter exchange, not of money, though the exchange might be indirect.

9. Perhaps the most instructive case of the far-reaching economic consequences of the relations between the monetary and non-monetary uses of a monetary metal is that of Chinese monetary history, because copper money, with high costs of production and wide fluctuations in output of the monetary metal, permits an especially clear view of the phenomena involved.

7. *The Primary Consequences of the Use of Money. Credit*

The primary consequences of the widespread use of money are:

(1) The so-called "indirect exchange" as a means of satisfying consumers' wants. The use of money makes it possible to obtain goods which are separated from those offered in exchange for them in space, in time, in respect to the persons involved, and, what is very important, in respect to the quantity on each side of the transaction. This results in a tremendous extension of the area of possible exchange relationships.

(2) The valuation in terms of money of delayed obligations, especially of compensatory obligations arising out of an exchange (that is, debts). This is, of course, closely related to the first point.

(3) The so-called "storage of value"; that is, the accumulation of money in specie or in the form of claims to payment collectable at any time as a means of insuring future control over opportunities of advantageous economic exchange.

(4) The increasing transformation of all economic advantages into the ability to control sums of money.

(5) The qualitative individuation of consumption and, indirectly, its expansion for those who have control of money, of claims to money payment, or of opportunities to acquire money. This means the ability to offer money as a means of obtaining goods and services of all kinds.

(6) The orientation of the procurement of utilities, as it has become widespread today, to their bearing on the marginal utility of the sums of money which the directing authorities of an economic unit expect to be able to control in the relevant future.

(7) With this goes the orientation of acquisitive activities to all the opportunities which are made available by the extension of the area of possible exchanges, in time, in place, and with respect to personal agents, as noted above.

(8) All of these consequences are dependent on what is, in principle, the most important fact of all, the possibility of monetary *calculation;* that is, the possibility of assigning money values to all goods and services which in any way might enter into transactions of purchase and sale.

In substantive as distinguished from formal terms, monetary calculation means that goods are not evaluated merely in terms of their immediate importance as utilities at the given time and place and for the given person only. Rather, goods are more or less systematically compared, whether for consumption or for production, with all potential future opportunities of utilization or of gaining a return, including their possible utility to an indefinite number of other persons who can be brought into the comparison insofar as they are potential buyers of the powers of control and disposal of the present owner. Where money calculations have become typical, this defines the "market situation" of the good in question. (The above statement formulates only the simplest and best-known elements of any discussion of "money" and does not need to be further commented upon. The sociology of the "market" will not yet be developed here. On the formal concepts, see secs. 8 and 10.)

The term "credit" in the most general sense will be used to designate any exchange of goods presently possessed against the promise of a future transfer of disposal over utilities, no matter what they may be. The granting of credit means in the first instance that action is oriented to the probability that this future transfer of disposal will actually take place. In this sense the primary significance of credit lies in the fact that it makes it possible for an economic unit to exchange an expected future surplus of control over goods or money against the present control of some other unit over goods which the latter does not now intend to use. Where the action is rational, both parties expect an improvement in their position, regardless of what it consists in, over what it would be under the present distribution of resources without the exchange.

1. It is by no means necessary for the advantages in question to be economic. Credit may be granted and accepted for all conceivable purposes; for instance, charitable and military.

2. Credit may be granted and accepted in kind or in money, and in both cases the promises may be of concrete goods or services or of money payments. Carrying out credit transactions in terms of money, however, means that they become the subject of monetary calculations with all the attendant consequences, which will be discussed below.

3. This definition (of credit) for the most part corresponds to the usual one. It is clear that credit relationships may exist between organizations or all sorts, especially socialist or communist organizations. If there exist side by side several such groups, which are not economically autarkic, credit relationships are unavoidable. When the use of money

is completely absent,[13] there is a difficult problem of finding a rational basis of calculation. For the mere fact of the possibility of transactions involving compensation in the future does not tell us anything about the degree of rationality with which the parties agree on the conditions, especially in the case of long-term credit. Such parties would be in somewhat the same situation as the household economic units (*oikos*) of ancient times which exchanged their surpluses for things they had need of. But there is this difference, that in the present situation the interests of huge masses on a long-term basis would be at stake; and for the great masses of the low-income groups, the marginal utility of present consumption is particularly high. Thus there would be a probability that goods urgently needed could only be obtained on unfavorable terms.

4. Credit may be obtained and used for the purpose of satisfying present consumption needs which are inadequately provided for. Even in that case it will, so far as the action is economically rational, only be granted in exchange for advantages. This is not, however, historically usual for the earliest type of consumption credit and especially for emergency credit, the motives for which more frequently stemmed from an appeal to ethical obligations. This will be discussed in Part Two, chap. III:2.

5. What is the most common basis of credit, in money or in kind, when it is granted for profit, is very obvious. It is the fact that, because the lender is usually in a better economic situation, the marginal utility of future expectations, as compared with present ones, is higher than it is for the borrower. It should, however, be noted that what constitutes a "better" situation is highly relative.

8. *The Market*

By the "market situation" (*Marktlage*) for any object of exchange is meant all the opportunities of exchanging it for money which are known to the participants in exchange relationships and aid their orientation in the competitive price struggle.

"Marketability" (*Marktgängigkeit*) is the degree of regularity with which an object tends to be an object of exchange on the market.

"Market freedom" is the degree of autonomy enjoyed by the parties to market relationships in the price struggle and in competition.

"Regulation of the market," on the contrary, is the state of affairs where there is a substantive restriction, effectively enforced by the provisions of an order, on the marketability of certain potential objects of exchange or on the market freedom of certain participants. Regulation of the market may be determined (1) traditionally, by the actors' becoming accustomed to traditionally accepted limitations on exchange or to traditional conditions; (2) by convention, through social disapproval of treating certain utilities as marketable or of subjecting certain objects of exchange to free competition and free price determination, in general or when undertaken by certain groups of persons; (3) by law, through legal restrictions on exchange or on the freedom of competition, in general or for particular groups of persons or for particular objects of exchange. Legal regulations may take the form of influencing the market situation of objects of exchange by price regulation, or of limiting the possession, acquisition, or exchange of rights of control and disposal over certain goods to certain specific groups of persons, as in the case of legally guaranteed monopolies or of legal limitations on economic action. (4) By voluntary action arising from the structure of interests. In this case there is substantive regulation of the market, though the market remains formally free. This type of regulation tends to develop when certain participants in the market are, by virtue of their totally or approximately exclusive control of the possession of or opportunities to acquire certain utilities—that is, of their monopolistic powers—in a position to influence the market situation in such a way as actually to abolish the market freedom of others. In particular, they may make agreements with each other and with typical exchange partners for regulating market conditions. Typical examples are market quota agreements and price cartels.

1. It is convenient, though not necessary, to confine the term "market situation" to cases of exchange for money, because it is only then that uniform numerical statements of relationships become possible. Opportunities for exchange *in kind* are best described simply as "exchange opportunities." Different kinds of goods are and have been marketable in widely different and variable degrees, even where a money economy was well developed. The details cannot be gone into here. In general, articles produced in standardized form in large quantities and widely consumed have been the most marketable; unusual goods, only occasionally in demand, the least. Durable consumption goods which can be used up over long periods and means of production with a long or indefinite life, above all, agricultural and forest land, have been marketable to a much less degree than finished goods of everyday use or means of production which are quickly used up, which can be used only once, or which give quick returns.

2. Rationality of the regulation of markets has been historically associated with the growth of formal market freedom and the extension of marketability of goods. The original modes of market regulation have been various, partly traditional and magical, partly dictated by kinship relations, by status privileges, by military needs, by welfare policies, and not least by the interests and requirements of the governing authorities of organizations. But in each of these cases the dominant interests have not been primarily concerned with maximizing the opportunities of acquisition and economic provision of the participants in the market

themselves; have, indeed, often been in conflict with them. (1) Sometimes the effect has been to exclude certain objects from market dealings,
either permanently or for a time. This has happened in the magical
case, by taboo; in that of kinship, by the entailing of landed property;
on the basis of social status, as with knightly fiefs. In times of famine
the sale of grain has been temporarily prohibited. In other cases permission to sell has been made conditional on a prior offer of the good
to certain persons, such as kinsmen, co-members of the status group, of
the guild, or of the town association; or the sale has been limited by
maximum prices, as is common in war time, or by minimum prices.
Thus, in the interests of their status dignity magicians, lawyers, or physicians may not be allowed to accept fees below a certain minimum. (2)
Sometimes certain categories of persons, such as members of the nobility, peasants, or sometimes even artisans, have been excluded from
market trade in general or with respect to certain commodities. (3)
Sometimes the market freedom of consumers has been restricted by regulations, as by the sumptuary laws regulating the consumption of different
status groups, or by rationing in case of war or famine. (4) Another type
is the restriction of the market freedom of potential competitors in the
interest of the market position of certain groups, such as the professions or
the guilds. Finally, (5) certain economic opportunities have been reserved
to the political authorities (royal monopolies) or to those holding a charter
from such authorities. This was typical for the early capitalistic monopolies.

Of all these, the fifth type of market regulation had the highest
"market-rationality," and the first the lowest. By "rationality" we here
mean a force which promotes the orientation of the economic activity
of strata interested in purchase and sale of goods on the market to the
market situations. The other types of regulation fit in between these two
with respect to their rationality-impeding effect. The groups which, relative to these forms of regulation, have been most interested in the freedom of the market, have been those whose interests lay in the greatest
possible extension of the marketability of goods, whether from the point
of view of availability for consumption, or of ready opportunities for
sale. Voluntary market regulation first appeared extensively and permanently only on behalf of highly developed profit-making interests.
With a view to the securing of monopolistic advantages, this could take
several forms: (1) the pure regulation of opportunities for purchase and
sale, which is typical of the widespread phenomena of trading monopolies: (2) the regulation of transportation facilities, as in shipping and
railway monopolies; (3) the monopolization of the production of certain
goods; and (4) that of the extension of credit and of financing. The last
two types generally are accompanied by an increase in the regulation of
economic activity by organizations. But unlike the primitive, irrational
forms of regulation, this is apt to be oriented in a methodical manner to the
market situation. The starting point of voluntary market regulation has in
general been the fact that certain groups with a far-reaching degree of

actual control over economic resources have been in a position to take advantage of the formal freedom of the market to establish monopolies. Voluntary associations of consumers, such as consumers' co-operatives, have, on the other hand, tended to originate among those who were in an economically weak position. They have hence often been able to accomplish savings for their members, but only occasionally and limited to particular localities have they been able to establish an effective system of market regulation.

9. Formal and Substantive Rationality of Economic Action

The term "formal rationality of economic action" will be used to designate the extent of quantitative calculation or accounting which is technically possible and which is actually applied. The "substantive rationality," on the other hand, is the degree to which the provisioning of given groups of persons (no matter how delimited) with goods is shaped by economically oriented social action under some criterion (past, present, or potential) of ultimate values (*wertende Postulate*), regardless of the nature of these ends. These may be of a great variety.

1. The terminology suggested above is thought of merely as a means of securing greater consistency in the use of the word "rational" in this field. It is actually only a more precise form of the meanings which are continually recurring in the discussion of "nationalization" and of the economic calculus in money and in kind.

2. A system of economic activity will be called "formally" rational according to the degree in which the provision for needs, which is essential to every rational economy, is capable of being expressed in numerical, calculable terms, and is so expressed. In the first instance, it is quite independent of the technical form these calculations take, particularly whether estimates are expressed in money or in kind. The concept is thus unambiguous, at least in the sense that expression in money term yields the highest degree of formal calculability. Naturally, even this is true only relatively, so long as other things are equal.

3. The concept of "substantive rationality," on the other hand, is full of ambiguities. It conveys only one element common to all "substantive" analyses: namely, that they do not restrict themselves to note the purely formal and (relatively) unambiguous fact that action is based on "goal-oriented" rational calculation with the technically most adequate available methods, but apply certain criteria of ultimate ends, whether they be ethical, political, utilitarian, hedonistic, feudal (*ständisch*), egalitarian, or whatever, and measure the results of the economic action, however formally "rational" in the sense of correct calculation they may be, against these scales of "value rationality" or "*substantive* goal ration-

ality." There is an infinite number of possible value scales for this type
of rationality, of which the socialist and communist standards constitute only one group. The latter, although by no means unambiguous
in themselves, always involve elements of social justice and equality.
Others are criteria of status distinctions, or of the capacity for power,
especially of the war capacity, of a political unit; all these and many
others are of potential "substantive" significance. These points of view
are, however, significant only as bases from which to judge the *outcome* of economic action. In addition and quite independently, it is
possible to judge from an ethical, ascetic, or esthetic point of view the
spirit of economic activity (*Wirtschaftsgesinnung*) as well as the
instruments of economic activity. All of these approaches may consider
the "purely formal" rationality of calculation in monetary terms as of
quite secondary importance or even as fundamentally inimical to their
respective ultimate ends, even before anything has been said about the
consequences of the specifically modern calculating attitude. There is
no question in this discussion of attempting value judgments in this
field, but only of determining and delimiting what is to be called
"formal." In this context the concept "substantive" is itself in a certain
sense "formal;" that is, it is an abstract, generic concept.

10. *The Rationality of Monetary Accounting. Manage-*
ment and Budgeting

From a purely technical point of view, money is the most "perfect"
means of economic calculation. That is, it is formally the most rational
means of orienting economic activity. Calculation in terms of money,
and not its actual use, is thus the specific means of rational, economic
provision. So far as it is completely rational, money accounting has the
following primary consequences:

(1) The valuation of all the means of achieving a productive purpose
in terms of the present or expected market situation. This includes everything which is needed at present or is expected to be needed in the future; everything actually in the actor's control, which he may come to
control or may acquire by exchange from the control of others; everything
lost, or in danger of damage or destruction; all types of utilities, of means
of production, or any other sort of economic advantage.

(2) The quantitative statement of (a) the expected advantages of
every projected course of economic action and (b) the actual results of
every completed action, in the form of an account comparing money costs
and money returns and the estimated net profit to be gained from alternatives of action.

(3) A periodical comparison of all the goods and other assets con-

trolled by an economic unit at a given time with those controlled at the beginning of a period, both in terms of money.

(4) An *ex-ante* estimate and an *ex-post* verification of receipts and expenditures, either those in money itself, or those which can be valued in money, which the economic unit is likely to have available for its use during a period if it maintains the money value of the means at its disposal intact.

(5) The orientation of consumption to these data by the utilization of the money available (on the basis of point 4) during the accounting period for the acquisition of the requisite utilities in accordance with the principle of marginal utility.

The continual utilization and procurement of goods, whether through production or exchange, by an economic unit for purposes of its own *consumption* or to procure other goods for *consumption* will be called "budgetary management" (*Haushalt*).[14] Where rationality exists, its basis for an individual or for a group economically oriented in this way is the "budget" (*Haushaltsplan*), which states systematically in what way the needs expected for an accounting period—needs for utilities or for means of procurement to obtain them—can be covered by the anticipated income.

The "income" of a "budgetary unit" is the total of goods valued in money, which, as estimated according to the principle stated above in point (4), has been available during a previous period or on the availability of which the unit is likely to be able to count on the basis of a rational estimate for the present or for a future period. The total estimated value of the goods at the disposal of a budgetary unit which are normally utilized over a longer period, either directly or as a source of income, will be called its "wealth" (*Vermögen*).[15] The possibility of complete monetary budgeting for the budgetary unit is dependent on the possibility that its income and wealth consist either in money or in goods which are at any time subject to exchange for money; that is, which are in the highest degree marketable.

A rational type of management and budgeting of a budgetary unit is possible also where calculation is carried out in terms of physical units, as will be further discussed below. It is true that in that case there is no such thing as "wealth" capable of being expressed in a single sum of money, nor is there a single "income" in the same sense. Calculation is in terms of "holdings" of concrete goods and, where acquisition is limited to peaceful means, of concrete "receipts" from the expenditure of available real goods and services, which will be administered with a view to attaining the optimum provision for the satisfaction of wants. If the wants are strictly given, this involves a comparatively simple problem from the technical point of view so long as the situation does not require a very precise estimate of the comparative utility to be gained from the allocation of the available resources to each of a large number of very heterogeneous modes of use. If the situation is markedly different, even the simple self-sufficient household is faced with problems which are only to a very limited degree subject to a formally exact solution by calculation. The actual solution is usually found partly by the application of purely traditional standards, partly by making very rough estimates, which, however, may be quite adequate where both the wants concerned and the conditions of provision for them are well known and readily comparable. When the "holdings" consist in heterogeneous goods, as must be the case in the absence of exchange, a formally exact calculable comparison of the state of holdings at the beginning and the end of a period, or of the comparison of different possible ways of securing receipts, is possible only for categories of goods which are qualitatively identical. The typical result is that all available goods are treated as forming a totality of physical holdings, and certain quantities of goods are treated as available for consumption, so long as it appears that this will not in the long run diminish the available resources. But every change in the conditions of production—as, for instance, through a bad harvest —or any change in wants necessitates a new allocation, since it alters the scale of relative marginal utilities. Under conditions which are simple and adequately understood, this adaptation may be carried out without much difficulty. Otherwise, it is technically more difficult than if money terms could be used, in which case any change in the price situation in principle influences the satisfaction only of the wants which are marginal on the scale of relative urgency and are met with the last increments of money income.

As accounting in kind becomes completely rational and is emancipated from tradition, the estimation of marginal utilities in terms of the relative urgency of wants encounters grave complications; whereas, if it were carried out in terms of monetary wealth and income, it would be relatively simple. In the latter case the question is merely a "marginal" one, namely whether to apply *more* labor or whether to satisfy or sacrifice, as the case may be, one or more wants, rather than others. For when the problems of budgetary management are expressed in money terms, this is the form the "costs" take [opportunity cost]. But if calculations are in physical terms, it becomes necessary to take into account, besides the scale of urgency of the wants, also (1) the alternative modes of utilization of *all* means of production, including the *entire* amount of labor hitherto expended, which means different (according to the mode of utilization) and variable ratios between want satisfaction and the expenditure of resources, and therefore, (2), requires a consideration of the volume and type of *additional* labor which the householder would have to expend to secure additional receipts and, (3), of the mode of utilization of the material expenditures if the goods to be procured can be of various types. It is one of the most important tasks of economic theory to analyse the various possible ways in which these evaluations can be rationally carried out. It is, on the other hand, a task for economic history to pursue the ways in which the budgetary management in physical terms has been actually worked out in the course of various historical epochs. In general, the following may be said: (1) that the degree of formal rationality has, generally speaking, fallen short of the level which was even empirically possible, to say nothing of the theoretical maximum. As a matter of necessity, the calculations of money-less budgetary management have in the great majority of cases remained strongly bound to tradition. (2) In the larger units of this type, precisely because an expansion and refinement of everyday wants has not taken place, there has been a tendency to employ surpluses for uses of a non-routine nature—above all, for artistic purposes. This is an important basis for the artistic, strongly stylized cultures of epochs with a "natural economy."

1. The category of "wealth" includes more than physical goods. Rather, it covers *all* economic advantages over which the budgetary unit has an assured control, whether that control is due to custom, to the play of interests, to convention, or to law. The "good will" of a profit-making organization, whether it be a medical or legal practice, or a retail shop, belongs to the "wealth" of the owner if it is, for whatever reason, relatively stable since, if it is legally appropriated, it can constitute "property" in the terms of the definition in ch. I:10 above.

2. Monetary calculation can be found without the actual use of money or with its use limited to the settlement of balances which cannot be paid in kind in the goods being exchanged on both sides. Evidence of this is common in the Egyptian and Babylonian records. The use of money accounting as a measure for payments in kind is found in the permission in Hammurabi's Code and in provincial Roman and early Medieval law that a debtor may pay an amount due expressed in money "in whatever form he will be able" (*in quo potuerit*). The establishment of equivalents must in such cases have been carried out on the basis of traditional prices or of prices laid down by decree.

3. Apart from this, the above discussion contains only commonplaces, which are introduced to facilitate the formulation of a precise concept of the rational budgetary unit as distinguished from that of a rational profit-making enterprise—the latter will be discussed presently. It is important to state explicitly that both can take rational forms. The satisfaction of needs is not something more "primitive" than profit-seeking; "wealth" is not necessarily a more primitive category

than capital; "income," than profit. It is, however, true that historically the budgetary unit has been prior and has been the dominant form in most periods of the past.

4. It is indifferent what unit is the bearer of a budgetary management economy. Both the budget of a state and the family budget of a worker fall under the same category.

5. Empirically the administration of budgetary units and profit-making are not mutually exclusive alternatives. The business of a consumers' cooperative, for instance, is normally oriented to the economical provision for wants; but in the form of its activity, it is a "profit-making organization" without being oriented to profit as a substantive end. In the action of an individual, the two elements may be so intimately intertwined, and in the past have typically been so, that only the concluding act—namely, the sale or the consumption of the product—can serve as a basis for interpreting the meaning of the action. This has been particularly true of small peasants. Exchange may well be a part of the process of budgetary management where it is a matter of acquiring consumption goods by exchange and of disposing of surpluses. On the other hand, the budgetary economy of a prince or a landed lord may include profit-making enterprises in the sense of the following discussion. This has been true on a large scale in earlier times. Whole industries have developed out of the heterocephalous and heteronomous auxiliary enterprises which seigneurial landowners, monasteries, princes, etc., have established to exploit the products of their lands and forests. All sorts of profit-making enterprises today are part of the economy of such budgetary units as local authorities or even states. In these cases it is legitimate to include in the "income" of the budgetary units, if they are rationally administered, only the net profits of these enterprises. Conversely, it is possible for profit-making enterprises to establish various types of heteronomous budgetary units under their direction for such purposes as providing subsistence for slaves or wage workers—among them are "welfare" organizations, housing and eating facilities. Net profits in the sense of point (2) of this section are money surpluses after the deduction of all money costs.

6. It has been possible here to give only the most elementary starting points for analysing the significance of economic calculations in kind for general social development.

11. *The Concept and Types of Profit-Making. The Role of Capital*

"Profit-making" (*Erwerben*)[16] is activity which is oriented to opportunities for seeking new powers of control over goods on a single occasion, repeatedly, or continuously. "Profit-making activity" is activity which is oriented at least in part to opportunities of profit-making. Profit-making is "economic" if it is oriented to acquisition by peaceful methods. It may be oriented to the exploitation of market situations. "Means of profit-making" (*Erwerbsmittel*) are those goods and other economic advantages which are used in the interests of economic profit-making. "Exchange for profit" is that which is oriented to market situations in order to increase control over goods rather than to secure means for consumption (budgetary exchange). "Business credit" is that credit which is extended or taken up as a means of increasing control over the requisites of profit-making activity.

There is a form of monetary accounting which is peculiar to rational economic profit-making; namely, "capital accounting." Capital accounting is the valuation and verification of opportunities for profit and of the success of profit-making activity by means of a valuation of the total assets (goods and money) of the enterprise at the beginning of a profit-making venture, and the comparison of this with a similar valuation of the assets still present and newly acquired, at the end of the process; in the case of a profit-making organization operating continuously, the same is done for an accounting period. In either case a balance is drawn between the initial and final states of the assets. "Capital" is the money value of the means of profit-making available to the enterprise at the balancing of the books; "profit" and correspondingly "loss," the difference between the initial balance and that drawn at the conclusion of the period. "Capital risk" is the estimated probability of a loss in this balance. An economic "enterprise" (*Unternehmen*) is autonomous action capable of orientation to capital accounting. This orientation takes place by means of "calculation": ex-ante calculation of the probable risks and chances of profit, ex-post calculation for the verification of the actual profit or loss resulting. "Profitability" means, in the rational case, one of two things: (1) the profit estimated as possible by ex-ante calculations, the attainment of which is made an objective of the entrepreneur's activity; or (2) that which the ex-post calculation shows actually to have been earned in a given period, and which is available for the consumption uses of the entrepreneur without prejudice to his chances of future profitability. In both cases it is usually expressed in ratios—today, percentages—in relation to the capital of the initial balance.

Enterprises based on capital accounting may be oriented to the exploitation of opportunities of acquisition afforded by the market, or they may be oriented toward other chances of acquisition, such as those based on power relations, as in the case of tax farming or the sale of offices.

Each individual operation undertaken by a rational profit-making enterprise is oriented to estimated profitability by means of calculation. In the case of profit-making activities on the market, capital accounting requires: (1) that there exist, subject to estimate beforehand, adequately extensive and assured opportunities for sale of the goods which the enterprise procures; that is, normally, a high degree of marketability; (2) that the means of carrying on the enterprise, such as the potential means of production and the services of labor, are also available in the market at costs which can be estimated with an adequate degree of certainty; and finally, (3) that the technical and legal conditions, to which the process from the acquisition of the means of production to final sale, including transport, manufacturing operations, storage, etc., is subjected, give rise to money costs which in principle are calculable.

The extraordinary importance of the highest possible degree of calculability as the basis for efficient capital accounting will be noted time and again throughout the discussion of the sociological conditions of economic activity. It is far from the case that only economic factors are important to it. On the contrary, it will be shown that the most varied sorts of external and subjective barriers account for the fact that capital accounting has arisen as a basic form of economic calculation only in the Western World.

As distinguished from the calculations appropriate to a budgetary unit, the capital accounting and calculations of the market entrepreneur are oriented not to marginal utility, but to profitability. To be sure, the probabilities of profit are in the last analysis dependent on the income of consumption units and, through this, on the marginal utility structure of the disposable money incomes of the final consumers of consumption goods. As it is usually put, it depends on their "purchasing power" for the relevant commodities. But from a technical point of view, the accounting calculations of a profit-making enterprise and of a consumption unit differ as fundamentally as do the ends of want satisfaction and of profit-making which they serve. For purposes of economic theory, it is the marginal *consumer* who determines the direction of production. In actual fact, given the actual distribution of power, this is only true in a limited sense for the modern situation. To a large degree, even though the consumer has to be in a position to buy, his wants are "awakened" and "directed" by the entrepreneur.

In a market economy every form of rational calculation, especially of capital accounting, is oriented to expectations of prices and their changes as they are determined by the conflicts of interests in bargaining and competition and the resolution of these conflicts. In profitability-accounting this is made particularly clear in that system of bookkeeping which is (up to now) the most highly developed one from a technical point of view, in the so-called double-entry bookkeeping. Through a system of individual accounts the fiction is here created that different departments within an enterprise, or individual accounts, conduct exchange operations with each other, thus permitting a check in the technically most perfect manner on the profitability of each individual step or measure.

Capital accounting in its formally most rational shape thus presupposes the *battle of man with man*. And this in turn involves a further very specific condition. No economic system can directly translate subjective "feelings of need" into effective demand, that is, into demand which needs to be taken into account and satisfied through the production of goods. For whether or not a subjective want can be satisfied depends, on the one hand, on its place in the scale of relative urgency; on the other hand, on the goods which are estimated to be actually or potentially available for its satisfaction. Satisfaction does not take place if the utilities needed for it are applied to other more urgent uses, or if they either cannot be procured at all, or only by such sacrifices of labor and goods that future wants, which are still, from a present point of view, adjudged more urgent, could not be satisfied. This is true of consumption in every kind of economic system, including a communist one.

In an economy which makes use of capital accounting and which is thus characterized by the appropriation of the means of production by individual units, that is by "property" (see ch. I, sec. 10), profitability depends on the prices which the "consumers," according to the marginal utility of money in relation to their income, can and will pay. It is possible to produce profitably only for those consumers who, in these terms, have sufficient income. A need may fail to be satisfied not only when an individual's own demand for other goods takes precedence, but also when the greater purchasing power of others for *all* types of goods prevails. Thus the fact that the battle of man against man on the market is an essential condition for the existence of rational money–accounting further implies that the outcome of the economic process is decisively influenced by the ability of persons who are more plentifully supplied with money to outbid the others, and of those more favorably situated for production to underbid their rivals on the selling side. The latter are particularly those well supplied with goods essential to production or with money. In particular, rational money–accounting presupposes the existence of effective prices and not merely of fictitious prices conventionally employed for technical accounting purposes. This, in turn, presupposes money functioning as an effective medium of exchange, which is in demand as such, not mere tokens used as purely technical accounting units.[17] Thus the orientation of action to money prices and to profit has the following consequences: (1) that the differences in the distribution of money or marketable goods between the individual parties in the market is decisive in determining the direction taken by the production of goods, so far as it is carried on by profit-making enterprises, in that it is only demand made effective through the possession of purchasing power which is and can be satisfied. Further, (2) the question, what type of demand is to be satisfied by the production of goods, becomes in turn dependent on the profitability of production itself. Profitability is indeed *formally* a rational category, but for that very reason it is indifferent with respect to *substantive* postulates unless these can make themselves felt in the market in the form of sufficient purchasing power.

"Capital goods," as distinguished from mere possessions or parts of wealth of a budgetary unit, are all such goods as are administered on the basis of capital accounting. "Capital interest," as distinct from various other possible kinds of interest on loans, is: (1) what is estimated to be the minimum normal profitability of the use of material means of profit-making; (2) the rate of interest at which profit-making enterprises can obtain money or capital goods.

This exposition only repeats generally known things in a somewhat more precise form. For the technical aspects of capital accounting, compare the standard textbooks of accountancy, which are, in part, excellent. E.g. those of Leitner, Schär, etc.

1. The concept of capital has been defined strictly with reference to the individual private enterprise and in accordance with private business-accounting practice, which was, indeed, the most convenient method for present purposes. This usage is much less in conflict with everyday speech than with the usage which in the past was frequently found in the social sciences and which has by no means been consistent. In order to test the usefulness of the present business-accounting term, which is now being increasingly employed in scientific writings again, it is necessary only to ask the following questions: (1) What does it mean when we say that a corporation has a "basic capital" (net worth) of one million pounds? And (2), what when we say that capital is "written down"? What, (3), when corporation law prescribes what objects may be "brought in" as capital and in what manner? The first statement means that only that part of a surplus of assets over liabilities, as shown on the balance-sheet after proper inventory control and verification, which *exceeds* one million pounds can be accounted as "profit" and distributed to the share-holders to do with as they please (or, in the case of a one-man enterprise, that only this excess can be consumed in the household). The second statement concerns a situation where there have been heavy business losses, and means that the distribution of profit need not be postponed until perhaps after many years a surplus exceeding one million pounds has again been accumulated, but that the distribution of "profits" may begin at a lower surplus. But in order to do this, it is necessary to "write down" the capital, and this is the purpose of the operation. Finally, the purpose

of prescriptions as to how basic capital (net worth, or ownership) can be "covered" through the bringing into the company of material assets, and how it may be "written up" or "written down," is to give creditors and purchasers of shares the guarantee that the distribution of profits will be carried out "correctly" in accordance with the rules of rational business accounting, i.e., in such a way that (a) long-run profitability is maintained and, (b), that the security of creditors is not impaired. The rules about "bringing in" are all concerned with the admissability and valuation of objects as paid-in capital. (4) What does it mean when we say that as a result of unprofitability capital "seeks different investments"? Either we are talking about "wealth," for "investment" (*Anlegen*) is a category of the administration of wealth, not of profit-making enterprise. Or else, more rarely, it may mean that real capital *goods* on the one hand have ceased to be such by being sold, for instance as scrap or junk, and on the other have regained that quality in other uses. (5) What is meant when we speak of the "power of capital"? We mean that the possessors of control over the means of production and over economic advantages which can be used as capital *goods* in a profit-making enterprise enjoy, by virtue of this control and of the orientation of economic action to the principles of capitalistic business calculation, a specific position of power in relation to others.

In the earliest beginnings of rational profit-making activity capital appears, though not under this name, and only as a sum of money used in accounting. Thus in the *commenda* relationship various types of goods were entrusted to a travelling merchant to sell in a foreign market and at times for the purchase of other goods wanted for sale at home. The profit or loss was then divided in a particular proportion between the travelling merchant and the entrepreneur who had advanced the capital. For for this to take place it was necessary to value the goods in money; that is, to strike balances at the beginning and the conclusion of the venture. The "capital" of the *commenda* or the *societas maris* was simply this money valuation, which served only the purpose of settling accounts between the parties and no other.

What do we mean by the term "capital market"? We mean that certain "goods," including in particular money, are in demand in order to be used as capital goods, and that there exist profit-making enterprises, especially certain types of "banks," which derive their profit from the business of providing these goods. In the case of so-called "loan capital," which consists in handing over money against a promise to return the same amount at a later time with or without the addition of interest, the term "capital" will be used only if lending is the object of a profit-making enterprise. Otherwise, the term "money loans" will be used. Everyday speech tends to talk about "capital" whenever "interest" is paid, because the latter is usually expressed as a percentage of the basic sum; only because of this calculatory function is the amount of a loan or a deposit called a "capital." It is true, of course, that this was the origin of the term: *capitale* was the principal sum of a loan; the term is said, though it cannot be proved, to derive from the heads counted in a loan of cattle. But this is irrelevant. Even in very early times a loan of real goods was reckoned in money terms, on which basic interest was then calculated, so that already here capital goods and capital accounting are typically related, as has been true in later times. In the case of an ordinary loan, which is made simply as a phase in the administration of budgetary wealth and so far as it is employed for the needs of a budgetary unit, the term "loan capital" will not be used. The same, of course, applies to the recipient of the loan.

The concept of an "enterprise" is in accord with the ordinary usage, except for the fact that the orientation to capital accounting, which is usually taken for granted, is made explicit. This is done in order to emphasize that not every case of search for profit as such constitutes an "enterprise," but only when it is capable of orientation to capital accounting, regardless of whether it is on a large or a small scale. At the same time it is indifferent whether this capital accounting is in fact rationally carried out according to rational principles. Similarly the terms "profit" and "loss" will be used only as applying to enterprises oriented to capital accounting. The money earned without the use of capital by such persons as authors, physicians, lawyers, civil servants, professors, clerks, technicians, or workers, naturally is also "acquisition" (*Erwerb*), but shall here not be called "profit." Even everyday usage would not call it profit. "Profitability" is a concept which is applicable to every discrete act which can be individually evaluated in terms of business accounting technique with respect to profit and loss, such as the employment of a particular worker, the purchase of a new machine, the determination of rest periods in the working day, etc.

It is not expedient in defining the concept of interest on capital to start with contracted interest returns on any type of loan. If somebody helps out a peasant by giving him seed and demands an increment on its return, or if the same is done in the case of money loaned to a household to be returned with interest, we would hardly want to call this a "capitalistic" process. It is possible, where action is rational, for the lender to secure an additional amount because his creditor is in a position to expect benefits from the use of the loan greater than the amount of the interest he pays; when, that is, the situation is seen in terms of what it would be if he had to do without the loan. Similarly, the lender, being aware of the situation, is in a position to exploit it, in that for him the marginal utility of his present control over the goods he lends is exceeded by the marginal utility at the relevant future time of the repayment with the addition of the interest. These are essentially categories of the administration of budgetary units and their wealth, not of capital accounting. Even a person who secures an emergency loan for his urgent personal needs from a "Shylock" is not for purposes of the present discussion said to be paying interest on capital, nor does the lender receive such interest. It is rather a case of return for the loan. The person who makes a business of lending charges *himself* interest on

his business capital if he acts rationally, and must consider that he has suffered a "loss" if the returns from loans do not cover this rate of profitability. *This* interest we will consider "interest on capital"; the former is
simply "interest." Thus for the present terminological purposes, interest
on capital is always that which is calculated *on* capital, not that which
is a payment *for* capital. It is always oriented to money valuations, and
thus to the sociological fact that disposal over profit-making means,
whether through the market or not, is in private hands; that is, appropriated. Without this, capital accounting, and thus calculation of interest,
would be unthinkable.

In a rational profit-making enterprise, the interest, which is charged
on the books to a capital sum, is the minimum of profitability. It is in
terms of whether or not this minimum is reached that a judgment of
the advisability of this particular mode of use of capital goods is arrived
at. Advisability in this context is naturally conceived from the point of
view of profitability. The rate for this minimum profitability is, it is well
known, only approximately that which it is possible to obtain by giving
credit on the capital market at the time. But nevertheless, the existence
of the capital market is the reason why calculations are made on this
basis, just as the existence of market exchange is the basis for making
entries against the different accounts. It is one of the fundamental phenomena of a capitalistic economy that entrepreneurs are permanently
willing to pay interest for loan capital. This phenomenon can only be
explained by understanding how it is that the average entrepreneur may
hope in the long run to earn a profit, or that entrepreneurs on the
average in fact do earn it, over and above what they have to pay as
interest on loan capital—that is, under what conditions it is, on the
average, rational to exchange 100 at the present against 100 *plus* X in
the future.

Economic theory approaches this problem in terms of the relative
marginal utilities of goods under present and under future control. So
far, so good. But the sociologist would then like to know in what human
actions this supposed relation is reflected in such a manner that the
actors can take the consequences of this differential valuation [of present and future goods], in the form of an "interest rate," as a criterion
for their own operations. For it is by no means obvious that this should
happen at all times and places. It does indeed happen, as we know, in
profit-making economic units. But here the primary cause is the economic power distribution (*Machtlage*) between profit-making enterprises and budgetary units (households), both those consuming the
goods offered and those offering certain means of production (mainly
labor). Profit-making enterprises will be founded and operated continuously (capitalistically) *only if* it is expected that the minimum rate of
interest on capital can be earned. Economic theory—which could, however, also be developed along very different lines—might then very well
say that this exploitation of the power distribution (which itself is a
consequence of the institution of private property in goods and the

means of production) permits it only to this particular class of economic actors to conduct their operations in accordance with the "interest" criterion.

2. The administration of budgetary "wealth" and profit-making enterprises may be outwardly so similar as to appear identical. They are in fact in the analysis only distinguishable in terms of the difference in *meaningful* orientation of the corresponding economic activities. In the one case, it is oriented to maintaining and improving profitability and the market position of the enterprise; in the other, to the security and increase of wealth and income. It is, however, by no means necessary that this fundamental orientation should always, in a concrete case, be turned exclusively in one direction or the other; sometimes, indeed, this is impossible. In cases where the private wealth of an entrepreneur is identical with this business control over the means of production of his firm and his private income is identical with the profit of the business, the two things seem to go entirely hand in hand. But all manner of personal considerations may in such a case cause the entrepreneur to enter upon business policies which, in terms of the rationality of the conduct of enterprise, are irrational. Yet very generally private wealth and control of the business are not identical. Furthermore, such factors as personal indebtedness of the proprietor, his personal demand for a higher present income, division of an inheritance, and the like, often exert what is, in terms of business considerations, a highly irrational influence on the business. Such situations often lead to measures intended to eliminate these influences altogether, as in the incorporation of family businesses.

The tendency to separate the sphere of private affairs from the business is thus not fortuitous. It is a consequence of the fact that, from the point of view of business interest, the interest in maintaining the private wealth of the owner is often irrational, as is his interest in income receipts at any given time from the point of view of the profitability of the enterprise. Considerations relevant to the profitability of a business are also not identical with those governing the private interests of persons who are related to it as workers or as consumers. Conversely, the interests growing out of the private fortunes and income of persons or organizations having powers of control over an enterprise do not necessarily lie in the same direction as the long-run considerations of optimizing its profitability and its market power position. This is definitely, even especially, also true when a profit-making enterprise is controlled by a producers' co-operative association. The objective interests of rational management of a business enterprise and the personal interest of the individuals who control it are by no means identical and are often opposed. This fact implies the separation as a matter of principle of the budgetary unit and the enterprise, even where both, with respect to powers of control and the objects controlled, are identical.

The sharp distinction between the budgetary unit and the profit-making enterprise should also be clearly brought out in the terminology. The purchase of securities on the part of a private investor who wishes to consume the proceeds is not a "*capital*-investment," but a "*wealth*-investment." A money loan made by a private individual for obtaining the interest is, when regarded from the standpoint of the lender, entirely different from one made by a bank to the same borrower. On the other hand, a loan made to a consumer and one to an entrepreneur for business purposes are quite different from the point of view of the borrower. The bank is investing *capital* and the entrepreneur is borrowing *capital;* but in the first case, it may be for the borrower a matter simply of borrowing for purposes of budgetary management; in the second it may be, for the lender, a case of investment of private *wealth*. This distinction between private wealth and capital, between the budgetary unit and the profit-making enterprise, is of far-reaching importance. In particular, without it it is impossible to understand the economic development of the ancient world and the limitations on the development of the capitalism of those times. (The well-known articles of Rodbertus are, in spite of their errors and incompleteness, still important in this context, but should be supplemented by the excellent discussion of Karl Bücher.)[18]

3. By no means all profit-making enterprises with capital accounting are doubly oriented to the market in that they both purchase means of production on the market and sell their product or final services there. Tax farming and all sorts of financial operations have been carried on with capital accounting, but without selling any products. The very important consequences of this will be discussed later. It is a case of capitalistic profit-making which is not oriented to the market.

4. For reasons of convenience, acquisitive activity (*Erwerbstätigkeit*) and profit-making enterprise (*Erwerbsbetrieb*) have been distinguished. Anyone is engaged in acquisitive activity so far as he seeks, among other things, in given ways to acquire goods—money or others—which he does not yet possess. This includes the civil servant and the worker, no less than the entrepreneur. But the term "profit-making enterprise" will be confined to those types of acquisitive activity which are continually oriented to market advantages, using goods as means to secure profit, either (a) through the production and sale of goods in demand, or (b) through the offer of services in demand in exchange for money, be it through free exchange or through the exploitation of appropriated advantages, as has been pointed out above under (3). The person who is a mere rentier or investor of private wealth is, in the present terminology, not engaged in profit-making, no matter how rationally he administers his resources.

5. It goes without saying that in terms of *economic* theory the direction in which goods can be profitably produced by profit-making enterprises is determined by the marginal utilities for the last consumers in conjunction with the latter's incomes. But from a *sociological* point of view it should not be forgotten that, to a large extent, in a capitalistic economy (a) new wants are created and others allowed to disappear and (b) capitalistic enterprises, through their aggressive advertising policies,

exercise an important influence on the demand functions of consumers. Indeed, these are essential traits of a capitalistic economy. It is true that this applies primarily to wants which are not of the highest degree of necessity, but even types of food provision and housing are importantly determined by the producers in a capitalistic economy.

12. *Calculations in Kind*

Calculations in kind can occur in the most varied form. We speak of a "money economy," meaning an economy where the use of money is typical and where action is typically oriented to market situations in terms of money prices. The term "natural economy" (*Naturalwirtschaft*), on the other hand, means an economy where money is not used. The different economic systems known to history can be classified according to the degree to which they approximate the one or the other.

The concept "natural economy" is not, however, very definite, since it can cover systems with widely varying structures. It may mean (a) an economy where no exchange at all takes place or (b) one where exchange is only by barter, and thus money is not used as a medium of exchange. The first type may be an individual economic unit organized on a completely communistic basis, or with some determinate distribution of rights of participation. In both cases, there would be a complete lack of autonomy or autocephaly of the component parts. This may be called a "closed household economy." Or, secondly, it may be a combination of otherwise autonomous and autocephalous individual units, all of which, however, are obligated to make contributions in kind to a central organization which exists for the exercise of authority or as a communal institution. This is an "economy based on payments in kind" (*oikos* economy, "liturgically" organized political group). In both cases, so far as the pure type is conformed to, there is only calculation in kind.

In the second case, type (b), where exchange is involved, there may be natural economies where exchange is only by barter without either the use of money or calculation in money terms. Or there may be economies where there is exchange in kind, but where calculation is occasionally or even typically carried out in money terms. This was typical of the Orient in ancient times and has been common everywhere.

For the purposes of analysing calculation in kind, it is only the cases of type (a) which are of interest, where the unit is either completely self-sufficient, or the liturgies are produced in rationally organized permanent units, such as would be inevitable in attempting to employ modern technology in a completely "socialized" economy.

Calculation in kind is in its essence oriented to consumption, the satisfaction of wants. It is, of course, quite possible to have something analogous to profit-making on this basis. This may occur (a) in that, without resort to exchange, available material means of production and labor are systematically applied to the production and transportation of goods on the basis of calculations, according to which the state of want satisfaction thus attained is compared with the state which would exist without these measures or if the resources were used in another way, and thus a judgment as to the most advantageous procedure is arrived at. Or (b) in a barter economy, goods may be disposed of and acquired by exchange, perhaps in systematically repeated barters, though strictly without the use of money. Such action would be systematically oriented to securing a supply of goods which, as compared with the state which would exist without these measures, is judged to establish a more adequate provision for the needs of the unit. It is, in such cases, only when quantities of goods which are qualitatively similar are compared that it is possible to use numerical terms unambiguously and without a wholly subjective valuation. It is possible, of course, to set up a system of in-kind wages consisting of typical bundles of consumer goods (*Konsum-Deputate*), such as were the in-kind salaries and benefices particularly of the ancient Orient (where they even became objects of exchange transactions, similar to our government bonds). In the case of certain very homogenous commodities, such as the grain of the Nile valley, a system of storage and trade purely in terms of paper claims to certain quantities of the commodity was of course technically just as possible as it is with silver bars under the conditions of *banco*-currencies.[19] What is more important, it is in that case also possible to express the technical efficiency of a process of production in numerical terms and thereby compare it with other types of technical processes. This may be done, if the final product is the same, by comparing the relative requirements of different processes in both the quantity and the type of means of production. Or, where the means of production are the same, the different products which result from different production processes may be compared. It is often, though by no means always, possible in this way to secure numerical comparisons for the purposes of important, though sectorally restricted, problems. But the more difficult problems of calculation begin when it becomes a question of comparing different *kinds* of means of production, their different possible modes of use, and qualitatively different final products.

Every capitalistic enterprise is, to be sure, continually concerned with calculations in kind. For instance, given a certain type of loom and a certain quality of yarn, it is a question of ascertaining, given certain other relevant data such as the efficiency of machines, the humidity of the air, the rate of consumption of coal, lubricating oil, etc., what will be the product per hour per worker and thus the amount of the product which is attributable to any individual worker for each unit of time. For industries with typical waste products or by-products, this can be determined without any use of money accounting and is in fact so determined. Similarly, under given conditions, it is possible to work out, in technical terms without the use of money, the normally expected annual consumption of raw materials by the enterprise according to its technical production capacity, the depreciation period for buildings and machinery, the typical loss by spoiling or other forms of waste. But the comparison of different kinds of processes of production, with the use of different kinds of raw materials and different ways of treating them, is carried out today by making a calculation of comparative profitability in terms of money costs. For accounting in kind, on the other hand, there are formidable problems involved here which are incapable of objective solution. Though it does not at first sight seem to be necessary, a modern enterprise tends to employ money terms in its capital calculations even where such difficulties do not arise. But this is not entirely fortuitous. In the case of depreciation write-offs, for example, money accounting is used because this is the method of assuring the conditions of future productivity of the business which combines the greatest degree of certainty with the greatest flexibility in relation to changing circumstances; with any storing of real stocks of materials or any other mode of provision in kind such flexibility would be irrationally and severely impeded. It is difficult to see, without money accounting, how "reserves" could be built up without being specified in detail. Further, an enterprise is always faced with the question as to whether any of its parts is operating irrationally: that is, unprofitably, and if so, why. It is a question of determining which components of its real physical expenditures (that is, of the "costs" in terms of capital accounting) could be saved and, above all, could more rationally be used elsewhere. This can be determined with relative ease in an ex-post calculation of the relation between accounting "costs" and "receipts" in money terms, the former including in particular the interest charge allocated to that account. But it is exceedingly difficult to do this entirely in terms of an in-kind calculation, and indeed it can be accomplished at all only in very simple cases. This, one may believe, is not a matter of circumstances which could be overcome by technical improvements in the methods of calculation, but of fundamental limitations, which make really exact accounting in terms of calculations in kind impossible in principle.

It is true this might be disputed, though naturally not with arguments drawn from the Taylor system and from the possibility of achieving improvements in efficiency by employing a system of bonus points without the use of money. The essential question is that of how it is possible to discover *at what point* in the organization it would be profitable to employ such measures because there existed at that point certain elements of irrationality. It is in finding out these points that accounting in kind encounters difficulties which an ex-post calculation in money terms does not have to contend with. The fundamental limitations of accounting in kind as the *basis* of calculation in enterprises—of a type which would include the heterocephalous and heteronomous units of production in a planned economy—are to be found in the problem of imputation, which in such a system cannot take the simple form of an ex-post calculation of profit or loss on the books, but rather that very controversial form which it has in the theory of marginal utility. In order to make possible a rational utilization of the means of production, a system of in-kind accounting would have to determine "value"-indicators of some kind for the individual capital goods which could take over the role of the "prices" used in book valuation in modern business accounting. But it is not at all clear how such indicators could be established and, in particular, verified; whether, for instance, they should vary from one production unit to the next (on the basis of economic location), or whether they should be uniform for the entire economy, on the basis of "social utility," that is, of (present *and future*) consumption requirements?

Nothing is gained by assuming that, if only the problem of a non-monetary economy were seriously enough attacked, a suitable accounting method would be discovered or invented. The problem is fundamental to any kind of complete socialization. We cannot speak of a *rational* "planned economy" so long as in this decisive respect we have no instrument for elaborating a rational "plan."

The difficulties of accounting in kind become more marked when the question is considered of whether, from the point of view of efficiently satisfying the wants of a given group of persons, it is rational to locate a certain enterprise with a given productive function at one or an alternative site. The same difficulties arise if we want to determine whether a given economic unit, from the point of view of the most rational use of the labor and raw materials available to it, would do better to obtain certain products by exchange with other units or by producing them itself. It is true that the criteria for the location of industries consist of "natural" considerations and its simplest data are capable of formulation in non-monetary terms. (On this point, see Alfred Weber in the *Grundriss der Sozialökonomik*, Part IV [English ed.: *The Theory of Location*, trsl. C. J. Friedrich, Chicago 1929]). Nevertheless, the concrete determination of whether, according to the relevant circumstances of its particular location, a production unit with a given set of output possibilities or one with a different set would be rational, is in terms of calculation in kind capable of solution only in terms of very crude estimates, apart from the few cases where the solution is given by some natural peculiarity, such as a unique source of a raw material. But in spite of the numerous unknowns which may be present, the problem in money terms is always capable of a determinate solution in principle.

Finally, there is the independent problem of the comparative importance of the satisfaction of different wants, provision for which is, under the given conditions, equally feasible. In the last analysis, this problem is, in at least some of its implications, involved in every particular case of the calculations of a productive unit. Under conditions of money accounting, it has a decisive influence on profitability and thereby on the direction of production of profit-making enterprises. But where calculation is only in kind, it is in principle soluble only in one of two ways: by adherence to tradition or by an arbitary dictatorial regulation which, on whatever basis, lays down the pattern of consumption *and* enforces obedience. Even when that is resorted to, it still remains a fact that the problem of imputation of the part contributed to the total output of an economic unit by the different factors of production and by different executive decisions is not capable of the kind of solution which is at present attained by calculations of profitability in terms of money. It is precisely the process of provision for mass demand by mass production so typical of the present day which would encounter the greatest difficulties.

1. The problems of accounting in kind have been raised in a particularly penetrating form by Dr. Otto Neurath in his numerous works[20] apropos of the tendencies to "socialization" in recent years. The problem is a central one in any discussion of *complete* socialization; that is, that which would lead to the disappearance of effective prices. It may, however, be explicitly noted that the fact that it is incapable of rational solution serves only to point out some of the "costs," including economic ones, which would have to be incurred for the sake of enacting this type of socialism; however, this does not touch the question of the justification of such a program, so far as it does not rest on *technical* considerations, but, like most such movements, on *ethical* postulates or other forms of absolute value. A "refutation" of these is beyond the scope of any science. From a purely technical point of view, however, the possibility must be considered that the maintenance of a certain density of population within a given area may be possible only on the basis of accurate calculation. Insofar as this is true, a limit to the possible degree of socialization would be set by the necessity of maintaining a system of effective prices. That cannot, however, be considered here. It may be

noted, though, that the distinction between "socialism" and "social reform," if there is any such, should be made in these terms.

2. It is naturally entirely correct that mere money accounts, whether
they refer to single enterprises, to any number of them, or to all enterprises—indeed, even the most complete statistical information about the
movement of goods in money terms—tell us nothing whatever about the
nature of the real provision of a given group with what it needs;
namely, real articles of consumption. Furthermore, the much discussed
estimates of "national wealth" in money terms are only to be taken seriously so far as they serve fiscal ends; that is, as they determine taxable
wealth. This stricture does not apply, of course, in any similar degree
to income statistics in money terms, provided the prices of goods in
money are known. But even then there is no possibility of checking real
welfare in terms of substantive rationality. It is further true, as has been
convincingly shown for the case of extensive farming in the Roman
campagna by Sismondi and Sombart,[21] that satisfactory profitability,
which in the *campagna* existed for all participants, in numerous cases
has nothing to do with an optimum use of the available productive resources for the provision of consumers' goods for a given population.
The mode of appropriation, especially that of land (this much must be
conceded to Franz Oppenheimer),[22] leads to a system of claims to rent
and earnings of various kinds which may well obstruct permanently the
development of a technical optimum in the exploitation of productive
resources. This is, however, very far from being a peculiarity of capitalistic economies. In particular, the much-discussed limitation of production in the interest of profitability was very highly developed in the
economy of the Middle Ages, and the modern labor movement is acquiring a position of power which may lead to similar consequences. But
there is no doubt that this phenomenon exists in the modern capitalistic
economy.

The existence of statistics (or estimates) of money flows has not, as
some writers have tended to give the impression, hindered the development of statistics of physical quantities. This is true, however much fault
we may find with the available statistics when measured by ideal standards. Probably more than nine-tenths of economic statistics are not in
terms of money, but of physical quantities.

The work of a whole generation of economists has been concentrated
almost entirely on a critique of the orientation of economic action to
profitability with respect to its effects on the provision of the population
with real goods. All the work of the so-called "socialists of the lectern"
(*Kathedersozialisten*) was, in the last analysis, quite consciously concerned with this. They have, however, employed as a standard of judgment a mode of social reform oriented to social welfare, implying (in
contrast to a moneyless economy) the continued existence of effective
prices, rather than full socialization, as the only solution possible either
at the present or at any time in an economy at the stage of mass production. It is, of course, quite possible to consider this merely a half-
measure, but it is not in itself a nonsensical attitude. It is true that the
problems of a non-monetary economy, and especially of the possibility

of rational action in terms of calculations in kind, have not received much attention. Indeed most of the attention they have received has been historical and not concerned with present problems. But the World War, like every war in history, has brought these problems emphatically to the fore in the form of the problems of war economy and the post-war adjustment. It is, indeed, one of the merits of Otto Neurath to have produced an analysis of just these problems, which, however much it is open to criticism both in principle and in detail, was one of the first and was very penetrating. That "the profession" has taken little notice of his work is not surprising because until now he has given us only stimulating suggestions, which are, however, so very broad that it is difficult to use them as a basis of intensive analysis. The problem only begins at the point where his public pronouncements up to date have left off.

3. It is only with the greatest caution that the results and methods of war economy can be used as a basis for criticizing the substantive rationality of forms of economic organization. In wartime the whole economy is oriented to what is in principle a single clear goal, and the authorities are in a position to make use of powers which would generally not be tolerated in peace except in cases where the subjects are "slaves" of an authoritarian state. Furthermore, it is an economy with an inherent attitude of "going for broke": the overwhelming urgency of the immediate end overshadows almost all concern for the post-war economy. Only on the engineering level does preciseness of calculations exist, but economic constraints on the consumption, especially of labor and of all materials not directly threatened with exhaustion, are only of the roughest nature. Hence calculation has predominantly, though not exclusively, a technical character. So far as it has a genuinely economic character—that is, so far as it takes account of alternative ends and not only of means for a given end—it is restricted to what is, from the standpoint of careful monetary calculation, a relatively primitive level of calculation on the marginal utility principle. In type this belongs to the class of budgetary calculations, and it is not meant to guarantee long-run rationality for the chosen allocation of labor and the means of production. Hence, however illuminating the experience of war-time and post-war adjustments is for the analysis of the possible range of variation of economic forms, it is unwise to draw conclusions from the type of in-kind accounting associated with it for its suitability in a peacetime economy with its long-run concerns.

It may be freely conceded: (1) That it is necessary also in money accounting to make arbitrary assumptions in connection with means of production which have no market price. This is particularly common in the case of agricultural accounting; (2) that to a less extent something similar is true of the allocation of overhead costs among the different branches of a complicated enterprise; (3) that the formation of cartel agreements, no matter how rational their basis in relation to the market situation may be, immediately diminishes the stimulus to accurate calculation on the basis of capital accounting, because calculation declines in the absence of an enforced objective need for it. If calculation were in kind, however, the situation described under (1) would be universal;

any type of accurate allocation of overhead costs, which, however roughly, is now somehow achieved in money terms, would become impossible; and, finally, every stimulus to exact calculation would be eliminated and would have to be created anew by artificial means, the effectiveness of which would be questionable.

It has been suggested that the huge clerical staff of the private sector of the economy, which is actually to a large extent concerned with calculations, should be turned into a universal Statistical Office which would have the function of replacing the monetary business accounting of the present system with a statistical accounting in kind. This idea not only fails to take account of the fundamentally different motives underlying "statistics" and "business accounting," it also fails to distinguish their fundamentally different functions. They differ just like the bureaucrat differs from the entrepreneur.

4. Both calculation in kind and in money are rational techniques. They do not, however, by any means exhaust the totality of economic action. There also exist types of action which, though actually oriented to economic considerations, do not know calculation. Economic action may be traditionally oriented or may be affectually determined. In its more primitive aspects, the search for food on the part of human beings is closely related to that of animals, dominated as the latter is by instinct. Economically oriented action dominated by a religious faith, by war-like passions, or by attitudes of personal loyalty and similar modes of orientation, is likely to have a very low level of rational calculation, even though the motives are fully self-conscious. Haggling is excluded "between brothers," whether they be brothers in kinship, in a guild, or in a religious group. It is not usual to be calculating within a family, a group of comrades, or of disciples. At most, in cases of necessity, a rough sort of rationing is resorted to, which is a very modest beginning of calculation. In Part Two, ch. IV, the process by which calculation gradually penetrates into the earlier form of family communism will be taken up. Everywhere it has been money which was the propagator of calculation. This explains the fact that calculation in kind has remained on an even lower technical level than the actual nature of its problems might have necessitated; hence in this respect Otto Neurath appears to be right.

During the printing of this work an essay by Ludwig von Mises dealing with these problems came out. See his "Die Wirtschaftsrechnung im sozialistischen Gemeinwesen," *Archiv für Sozialwissenschaft,* vol. 47 (1920).[23]

13. *Substantive Conditions of Formal Rationality in a Money Economy*

It is thus clear that the formal rationality of money calculation is dependent on certain quite specific substantive conditions. Those which are of a particular sociological importance for present purposes are the

following: (1) Market struggle of economic units which are at least relatively autonomous. Money prices are the product of conflicts of interest
and of compromises; they thus result from power constellations. Money
is not a mere "voucher for unspecified utilities," which could be altered
at will without any fundamental effect on the character of the price system as a struggle of man against man. "Money" is, rather, primarily a
weapon in this struggle, and prices are expressions of the struggle; they
are instruments of calculation only as estimated quantifications of relative
chances in this struggle of interests. (2) Money accounting attains the
highest level of rationality, as an instrument of calculatory orientation of
economic action, when it is applied in the form of capital accounting.
The substantive precondition here is a thorough market freedom, that is,
the absence of monopolies, both of the imposed and economically irrational and of the voluntary and economically rational (i.e., market-
oriented) varieties. The competitive struggle for customers, which is
associated with this state, gives rise to a great volume of expenditures,
especially with regard to the organization of sales and advertising, which
in the absence of competition—in a planned economy or under complete
monopolization—would not have to be incurred. Strict capital accounting is further associated with the social phenomena of "shop discipline"
and appropriation of the means of production, and that means: with the
existence of a "system of domination" (*Herrschaftsverhältniss*). (3) It is
not "demand" (wants) as such, but "effective demand" for utilities which,
in a substantive respect, regulates the production of goods by profit-
making enterprises through the intermediary of capital accounting.
What is to be produced is thus determined, given the distribution of
wealth, by the structure of marginal utilities in the income group which
has both the inclination and the resources to purchase a given utility.
In combination with the complete indifference of even the formally
most perfect rationality of capital accounting towards all substantive
postulates, an indifference which is absolute if the market is perfectly
free, the above statement permits us to see the ultimate limitation, inherent in its very structure, of the rationality of monetary economic
calculation. It is, after all, of a purely formal character. Formal and
substantive rationality, no matter by what standard the latter is measured,
are always in principle separate things, no matter that in many (and
under certain very artificial assumptions even in all) cases they may
coincide empirically. For the formal rationality of money accounting does
not reveal anything about the actual distribution of goods. This must
always be considered separately. Yet, if the standard used is that of the
provision of a certain minimum of subsistence for the maximum size of
population, the experience of the last few decades would seem to show

that formal and substantive rationality coincide to a relatively high degree. The reasons lie in the nature of the incentives which are set into motion by the type of economically oriented social action which alone is adequate to money calculations. But it nevertheless holds true under all circumstances that formal rationality itself does not tell us anything about real want satisfaction unless it is combined with an analysis of the distribution of income.[24]

14. *Market Economies and Planned Economies*

Want satisfaction will be said to take place through a "market economy" so far as it results from action oriented to advantages in exchange on the basis of self-interest and where co-operation takes place only through the exchange process. It results, on the other hand, from a "planned economy" so far as economic action is oriented systematically to an established substantive order, whether agreed or imposed, which is valid within an organization.

Want satisfaction through a market economy normally, and in proportion to the degree of rationality, presupposes money calculation. Where capital accounting is used it presupposes the economic separation of the budgetary unit (household) and the enterprise. Want satisfaction by means of a planned economy is dependent, in ways which vary in kind and degree according to its extensiveness, on calculation in kind as the ultimate basis of the *substantive* orientation of economic action. Formally, however, the action of the producing individual is oriented to the instructions of an administrative staff, the existence of which is indispensable. In a market economy the individual units are autocephalous and their action is autonomously oriented. In the administration of budgetary units (households), the basis of orientation is the marginal utility of money holdings and of anticipated money income; in the case of intermittent entrepreneurship (*Gelegenheitserwerben*), the probabilities of market gain, and in the case of profit-making enterprises, capital accounting are the basis of orientation. In a planned economy, all economic action, so far as "planning" is really carried through, is oriented heteronomously and in a strictly "budgetary" manner, to rules which enjoin certain modes of action and forbid others, and which establish a system of rewards and punishments. When, in a planned economy, the prospect of additional individual income is used as a means of stimulating self-interest, the type and direction of the action thus rewarded is substantively heteronomously determined. It is possible for the same thing to be true of a market economy, though in a formally voluntary way. This is true wherever the unequal distribution of wealth, and particularly of capital goods, forces the non-owning group to comply with the authority of others in order to obtain any return at all for the utilities they can offer on the market—either with the authority of a wealthy householder, or with the decisions, oriented to capital accounting, of the owners of capital or of their agents. In a purely capitalistic organization of production, this is the fate of the entire working class.

The following are decisive as elements of the motivation of economic activity under the conditions of a market economy: (1) For those without substantial property: (a) the fact that they run the risk of going entirely without provisions, both for themselves and for those personal dependents, such as children, wives, sometimes parents, whom the individual typically maintains on his own account; (b) that, in varying degrees subjectively they value economically productive work as a mode of life. (2) For those who enjoy a privileged position by virtue of wealth or the education which is usually in turn dependent on wealth: (a) opportunities for large income from profitable undertakings; (b) ambition; (c) the valuation as a "calling" of types of work enjoying high prestige, such as intellectual work, artistic performance, and work involving high technical competence. (3) For those sharing in the fortunes of profit-making enterprises: (a) the risk to the individual's own capital, and his own opportunities for profit, combined with (b) the valuation of rational acquisitive activity as a "calling." The latter may be significant as a proof of the individual's own achievement or as a symbol and a means of autonomous control over the individuals subject to his authority, or of control over economic advantages which are culturally or materially important to an indefinite plurality of persons—in a word, power.

A planned economy oriented to want satisfaction must, in proportion as it is radically carried through, weaken the incentive to labor so far as the risk of lack of support is involved. For it would, at least so far as there is a rational system of provision for wants, be impossible to allow a worker's dependents to suffer the full consequences of his lack of efficiency in production. Furthermore, autonomy in the direction of organized productive units would have to be greatly reduced or, in the extreme case, eliminated. Hence it would be impossible to retain capital risk and proof of merit by a formally autonomous achievement. The same would be true of autonomous power over other individuals and important features of their economic situation. Along with opportunities for special material rewards, a planned economy may have command over certain ideal motives of what is in the broadest sense an altruistic type, which can be used to stimulate a level of achievement in economic production comparable to that which autonomous orientation to opportunities for profit, by producing for the satisfaction of effective demand, has empirically been able to achieve in a market economy. Where a planned economy is radically carried out, it must further accept the inevitable reduction in formal, calculatory rationality which would result from the elimination of money and capital accounting. Substantive and formal (in the sense of exact *calculation*) rationality are, it should be stated again, after all largely distinct problems. This fundamental and, in the last analysis, unavoidable element of irrationality in economic systems is one of the important sources of all "social" problems, and above all, of the problems of socialism.

The following remarks apply to both secs. 13 and 14.

1. The above exposition obviously formulates only things which are generally known, in a somewhat more precise form. The market economy is by far the most important case of typical widespread social action predominantly oriented to "self-interest." The process by which this type of action results in the satisfaction of wants is the subject matter of economic theory, knowledge of which in general terms is here presupposed. The use of the term "planned economy" (*Planwirtschaft*) naturally does not imply acceptance of the well-known proposals of the former German Minister of Economic Affairs.[25] The term has been chosen because, while it does not do violence to general usage, it has, since it was used officially, been widely accepted. This fact makes it preferable to the term used by Otto Neurath, "administered economy" (*Verwaltungswirtschaft*), which would otherwise be suitable.

2. So far as it is oriented to profit-making, the economic activity of organizations, or that regulated by organizations, is not included in the concept of "planned economy," whether the organization be a guild, a cartel, or a trust. "Planned economy" includes the economic activity of organizations only so far as it is oriented to the provision for needs. Any system of economic activity oriented to profit-making, no matter how strictly it is regulated or how stringently controlled by an administrative staff, presupposes effective prices, and thus capital accounting as a basis of action; this includes the limiting case of total cartellization, in which prices would be determined by negotiation between the cartel groups and by negotiated wage agreements with labor organizations. In spite of the identity of their objectives, *complete* socialization in the sense of a planned economy administered purely as a budgetary unit and *partial* socialization of various branches of production with the retention of capital accounting are technically examples of quite different types. A preliminary step in the direction of the budgetary planned economy is to be found wherever consumption is rationed or wherever measures are taken to effect the direct "in-kind" distribution of goods. A planned direction of *production*, whether it is undertaken by voluntary or authoritatively imposed cartels, or by agencies of the government, is primarily concerned with a rational organization of the use of means of production and labor resources and cannot, on its own terms, do without prices—

or at least, not yet. It is thus by no means fortuitous that the "rationing-type" of socialism gets along quite well with the "works councils" (*Betriebsräte*) type of socialism which, against the will of its leading personalities (who are in favor of a rationalistic solution), must pursue the income interests of the workers.

3. It will not be possible to enter at this point into a detailed discussion of the formation of such economic organizations as cartels, corporations or guilds. Their general tendency is orientation to the regulation or monopolistic exploitation of opportunities for profit. They may arise by voluntary agreement, but are more generally imposed even where formally voluntary. Compare in the most general terms, chap. I, sec. 10, and also the discussion of the appropriation of economic advantages, sec. 19ff. of the present chapter.

The conflict between two rival forms of socialism has not died down since the publication of Marx's *Misère de la Philosophie.* On the one hand, there is the type, which includes especially the Marxists, which is evolutionary and oriented to the problem of production; on the other, the type which takes the problem of distribution as its starting point and advocates a rational planned economy. The latter is again today coming to be called "communism." The conflict within the Russian socialist movement, especially as exemplified in the passionate disputes between Plekhanov and Lenin, was, after all, also concerned with this issue. While the internal divisions of present-day socialism are very largely concerned with competition for leadership and for "benefices," along with these issues goes the same set of problems. In particular, the economic experience of the War has given impetus to the idea of a planned economy, but at the same time to the development of interests in appropriation.

The question of whether a planned economy, in whatever meaning or extent, *should* be introduced, is naturally not in this form a scientific problem. On scientific grounds it is possible only to inquire, what would be the probable results of any given specific proposal, and thus what consequences would have to be accepted if the attempt were made. Honesty requires that all parties should admit that, while some of the factors are known, many of those which would be important are only very partially understood. In the present discussion, it is not possible to enter into the details of the problem in such a way as to arrive at concretely conclusive results. The points which will be taken up can be dealt with only in a fragmentary way in connection with forms of organizations, particularly the state. It was possible above only to introduce an unavoidably brief discussion of the most elementary aspects of the technical problem. The phenomenon of a *regulated* market economy has, for the reasons noted above, not yet been taken up.

4. The organization of economic activity on the basis of a market economy presupposes the appropriation of the material sources of utilities on the one hand, and market freedom on the other. The effectiveness of market freedom increases with the degree to which these sources of utility, particularly the means of transport and production, are ap-

propriated. For, the higher the degree of marketability, the more will economic action be oriented to market situations. But the effectiveness of market freedom also increases with the degree to which appropriation is limited to *material* sources of utility. Every case of the appropriation of human beings through slavery or serfdom, or of economic advantages through market monopolies, restricts the range of human action which can be market-oriented. Fichte, in his *Der geschlossene Handelsstaat* (Tübingen, 1800), was right in treating this limitation of the concept of "property" to material goods, along with the increased autonomy of control over the objects which do fall under this concept, as characteristic of the modern market-oriented system. All parties to market relations have had an interest in this expansion of property rights because it increased the area within which they could orient their action to the opportunities of profit offered by the market situation. The development of this type of property is hence attributable to their influence.

5. For reasons of accuracy of expression, we have avoided the term "communal economy" (*Gemeinwirtschaft*), which others have frequently used [in the German discussions of 1918–1920], because it pretends the existence of a "common interest" or of a "feeling of community" (*Gemeinschaftsgefühl*) as the normal thing, which conceptually is not required: the economic organization of a feudal lord exacting *corvée* labor or that of rulers like the Pharaohs of the New Kingdom belongs to the same category as a family household. Both are equally to be distinguished from a market economy.

6. For the purposes of the definition of a "market economy," it is indifferent whether or to what extent economic action is "capitalistic," that is, is oriented to capital accounting. This applies also to the normal case of a market economy, that in which the satisfaction of wants is effected in a monetary economy. It would be a mistake to assume that the development of capitalistic enterprises must occur proportionally to the growth of want satisfaction in the monetary economy, and an even larger mistake to believe that this development must take the form it has assumed in the Western world. In fact, the contrary is true. The extension of money economy might well go hand in hand with the increasing monopolization of the larger sources of profit by the *oikos* economy of a prince. Ptolemaic Egypt is an outstanding example. According to the evidence of the accounts which have survived, it was a highly developed money economy, but its accounting remained budgetary accounting and did not develop into capital accounting. It is also possible that with the extension of a money economy could go a process of "feudalization" (*Verpfründung*) of fiscal advantages resulting in a traditionalistic stabilization of the economic system. This happened in China, as will have to be shown elsewhere. Finally, the capitalistic utilization of money resources could take place through investment in sources of potential profit which were not oriented to opportunities of exchange in a free commodity market and thus not to the production of goods. For reasons which will be discussed below, this has been almost universally true outside the area of the modern Western economic order.

15. *Types of Economic Division of Labor*

Every type of social action in a group which is oriented to economic considerations and every associative relationship of economic significance involves to some degree a particular mode of division and organization of human services in the interest of production. A mere glance at the facts of economic action reveals that different persons perform different types of work and that these are combined in the service of common ends, with each other and with the non-human means of production, in the most varied ways. The complexity of these phenomena is extreme, but yet it is possible to distinguish a few types.

Human services for economic purposes may be distinguished as (a) "managerial," or (b) oriented to the instructions of a managerial agency. The latter type will be called "labor" for purposes of the following discussion.

> It goes without saying that managerial activity constitutes "labor" in the most definite sense if labor is taken to mean the expenditure of time and effort as such. The use of the term "labor" in the sense defined above, as something distinct from managerial activity, has, however, come to be generally accepted for social reasons, and this usage will be followed in the present discussion. For more general purposes, the terms "services" or "work" (*Leistungen*) will be used.

Within a social group the ways in which labor or other work may be carried on may be classified in the following way: (1) *technically,* according to the way in which the services of a plurality of co-operating individuals are divided up and combined, with each other and with the non-human means of production, to carry out the technical procedures of production; (2) *socially.* In the first place, classification may be according to whether particular services do or do not fall within the jurisdiction of autocephalous and autonomous economic units, and according to the economic character of these units. Closely connected with this is classification according to the modes and extent to which the various services, the material means of production, and the opportunities for economic profit used as sources of profit or as means of acquisition, are or are not appropriated. These factors determine the mode of occupational differentiation, a social phenomenon, and the organization of the market, an economic phenomenon; (3) finally, an *economic* criterion: for every case of combination of services with each other and with material means of production, of division among different types of economic units, and of mode of appropriation, one must ask separately whether they are used in a context of budgetary administration or of profit-making enterprise.

> For this and the following section, compare the authoritative discussion by Karl Bücher in his article "Gewerbe" in the *Handwörterbuch*

der Staatwissenschaften and in his book, *Die Entstehung der Volkswirt-schaft.*[26] These are fundamentally important works. Both the terminol-ogy and the classification here presented have departed from Bücher's only where it seemed necessary for reasons of convenience. There is little reason to cite other references, for the following exposition does not pretend to achieve new results, but only to provide a scheme of analysis useful for the purposes of this work.

1. It should be emphatically stated that the present discussion is concerned only with a brief summary of the *sociological* aspects of these phenomena, so far as they are relevant to its context. The *economic* aspect is included only insofar as it is expressed in what are formally sociological categories. The presentation would be economic in the *sub-stantive* sense only if the price and market conditions, which so far have been dealt with only on the theoretical level, were brought in. But these substantive aspects of the general problem could be worked into such a summary introduction only in the form of terse theses, which would involve some very dubious distortions. The explanatory methods of *pure* economics are as tempting as they are misleading. To take an example: It might be argued that for the development of medieval, corporately regulated, but "free" labor the decisive period should be seen in the "dark" ages from the tenth to the twelfth century, and in particular in the situation during that period of the skilled (peasant, mining, and artisan) labor force whose production activity was oriented to the reve-nue chances of the feudal lords with rights over the land, the persons, and the courts—powers which were fighting for their separate interests and competing for these revenue sources. The decisive period for the development of capitalism could be claimed to be the great chronic price revolution of the sixteenth century. The argument would be that this led both to an absolute and a relative increase in the prices of almost all products of the soil in the West, and hence—on the basis of well-known principles of agricultural economics—provided both incentives and pos-sibilities for market production and thus for production on a large scale; in part, as in England, this took the form of capitalistic enterprise, and in part, as in the lands between the Elbe river and Russia, that of *corvée*-labor estates. For non-agricultural products, this inflation signified in most cases a rise in absolute prices, but, it would be argued, rarely one in relative prices; typically, relative prices for industrial goods would fall, thus stimulating, so far as the necessary organizational and other external and subjective preconditions were given, attempts to create market enterprises able to stand up under competitive conditions. The claim that these preconditions were not given in Germany would be adduced to account for the economic decline which started there about that time. The later consequence of all this, the argument would run, was the development of capitalist industrial entrepreneurship. A neces-sary prerequisite for this would be the development of mass markets. An indication that this was actually happening could be seen in certain changes of English commercial policy, to say nothing of other phenom-ena.

In order to verify *theoretical* reasoning about the *substantive* economic conditions of the development of economic structure, theses such as these and similar ones would have to be utilized. But this is simply not admissible. These and numerous other equally controversial theories, even so far as they could be proved not to be wholly erroneous, cannot be incorporated into the present scheme which is intentionally limited to sociological *concepts*. In renouncing any attempt of this sort, however, the following exposition in this chapter explicitly repudiates any claim to concrete "explanation" and restricts itself to working out a sociological typology. The same is true of the previous discussion in that it consciously omitted to develop a theory of money and price determination. This must be strongly emphasized. For only the facts of the economic situation provide the flesh and blood for a genuine explanation of also that process of development relevant for sociological theory. What can be done here is only to supply a scaffolding adequate to provide the analysis with relatively unambiguous and definite concepts.

It is obvious not only that no attempt is made here to do justice to the historical aspect of economic development, but also that the typology of the genetic sequence of possible forms is neglected. The present aim is only to develop a schematic system of classification.

2. A common and justified objection to the usual terminology of economics is that it frequently fails to make a distinction between the business "establishment" (*Betrieb*) and the "firm" (*Unternehmung*).[27] In the area of economically oriented action, "establishment" is a *technical* category which designates the continuity of the combination of certain types of services with each other and with material means of production. The antithesis of this category is either intermittent action, or action which is constitutionally discontinuous (such as is found in every household). By contrast, the antithesis to "firm," which is a category of *economic* orientation (to profit), is the "budgetary unit" (*Haushalt*), which is economically oriented to provision for needs. But the classification in terms of "firm" and "budgetary unit" is not exhaustive, for there exist actions oriented to acquisition which cannot be subsumed under the category "firm." All activity in which earnings are due purely to "work," such as the activity of the writer, the artist, the civil servant, is neither the one nor the other. The drawing and consumption of rents and annuities, however, obviously belong into the category of "budgetary administration."

In spite of this distinction [between the "establishment" and the "firm"], we have in the earlier discussion used the term "profit-making establishment" (*Erwerbsbetrieb*) wherever continuously coordinated, uninterrupted entrepreneurial activity was meant;[28] such activity is in fact unthinkable without the constitution of an "establishment," if only one consisting of nothing but the entrepreneur's own activity without the aid of a staff. Our concern so far was mainly to stress the separation of the household (budgetary unit) and the continuously organized business establishment. It should now be noted that use of the term "profit-making establishment" as a substitute for "continuously organized business firm" is fitting and unambiguous only in the simplest case where the technical unit, the "establishment," coincides with the economic unit, the "firm."

In the market economy this need not be the case, for several technically separate "establishments" can be combined into a single "firm." The latter is not, of course, constituted through the mere relationship of the various technical units to the same entrepreneur, but through the fact that in their exploitation for profit these units are oriented to a coordinated plan; hence transitional forms are possible. When the term "establishment" or "enterprise" (*Betrieb*) is used by itself, it will always refer to such *technical* units consisting of buildings, equipment, labor, and a *technical* management, the latter possibly heterocephalous and heteronomous—units such as exist even in the communist economy (as the terminology presently in use also recognizes). The term "profit-making establishment or enterprise" will henceforth be used only in cases where the technical and the economic unit (the "firm") are identical.

The relation between "establishment" and "firm" raises particularly difficult terminological questions in the analysis of such categories as "factory" and "putting-out enterprise." The latter is quite clearly a type of "firm." In terms of "establishments," it consists of two types of units: a commercial establishment, and establishments which are component parts of the workers' households (in the absence of larger workshops such as might be organized by master craftsmen as intermediaries under a "hiring-boss" system); the household establishments perform certain specified functions for the commercial establishment, and vice versa. Viewed only from the point of view of "establishments," the process as a whole cannot be understood at all; for this it is necessary to employ additional categories, such as: market, firm, household (of the individual workers), commercial exploitation of purchased services.

The concept of "factory" could, as has been proposed, be defined in entirely non-economic terms as a mode of technical organization, leaving aside consideration of the status of the workers, whether free or unfree, the mode of division of labor, involving the extent of internal technical specialization, and the type of means of production, whether machines or tools. That is, it would be defined simply as an organized workshop. However, it would seem necessary in addition to include in the definition the mode of appropriation of premises and means of production—namely: to *one* owner—, for otherwise the concept would become as vague as that of the *ergasterion*.[29] But once this is done, it would as a matter of principle seem more expedient to classify "factory" and "putting-out enterprise" as two strictly *economic* categories of the "firm" conducted on the basis of capital accounting. In a fully socialist order the category "factory" could then occur as little as that of "putting-out enterprise," but only such categories as: workshops, buildings, tools, shop labor services and domestic labor services of all kinds.

3. The question of stages of economic development will be considered only insofar as it is absolutely necessary, and then only incidentally. The following points will suffice for the present.

It has fortunately become more common lately to distinguish types of economic system from types of economic policy.[30] The stages which Schönberg first suggested and which, in a somewhat altered form, have become identified with Schmoller's name, "domestic economy," "village economy," with the further stages of "seigneurial and princely patrimonial household economy," "town economy," "territorial economy," and "national economy,"[31] were in his terminology defined by the type of organization regulating economic activity. But it is not claimed that even the *types* of regulation, to which economic activity has been subjected by the different organizations thus classified in terms of the extent of their jurisdiction, were at all different. Thus the so-called territorial economic policies in Germany consisted to a large extent simply of an adoption of the measures developed in the town economy. Furthermore, such innovations as did occur were not greatly different from the "mercantilist" policies of those of the patrimonial states which had already achieved a relatively high level of rationality; they were thus to that extent "national economic policies," to use the common term, which, however, is not very appropriate. This classification, further, clearly does not claim that the inner structure of the economic system, the modes in which work roles were assigned, differentiated, and combined, the ways in which these different functions were divided between independent economic units, and the modes of appropriation of control over labor, means of production, and opportunities for profit, in any way were correlated with the dimensions of the organizations which were (potential) agents of an economic policy; above all this classification does not claim that they always changed in the same direction with changes in these dimensions. A comparison of the Western World with Asia, and of the modern West with that of Antiquity, would show the untenability of such an assumption. At the same time, in considering economic structure, it is by no means legitimate to ignore the existence or absence of organizations with substantive powers of regulation of economic activity, nor to ignore essential purposes of their regulation. The modes of profit-making activity are strongly influenced by such regulation, but it is by no means only political organizations which are important in this respect.

4. In this connection, as well as others, the purpose of the discussion has been to determine the optimum conditions for the *formal* rationality of economic activity and its relation to the various types of *substantive* demands which may be made on the economic system.

16. *Types of the Technical Division of Labor*

From a *technical* point of view the division of labor may be classified as follows: (1) In the first place, it may vary according to modes of differentiation and combination of work services as such: (a) They may vary according to the type of functions (*Leistungen*) undertaken by the same person. He may combine managerial functions with those of carrying out specifications; or his work may be specialized in terms of one or the other.

The distinction is naturally relative. It is common for an individual who normally supervises to take a hand in the work from time to time, as in the case of the peasants with larger holdings. The type cases of combination of the two functions are: The small peasant, the independent artisan, or the small boatman.

Further, a given individual may (b) perform functions which are *technically* different and contribute to different results, or he may perform only technically specialized functions. In the first case, the lack of specialization may be due to the technical level of work which does not permit further dividing up, to seasonal variation, or to the exploitation of labor services as a side line at times when they are not taken up by their primary occupation. In the second case, the function may be specialized in terms of the product in such a way that the same worker carries out all the processes necessary for this product, though they differ technically from each other. In a sense, this involves a combination of different functions and will be called the "specification of function." On the other hand, the functions may be differentiated according to the type of work, so that the product is brought to completion only by combining, simultaneously or successively, the work of a number of persons. This is the "specialization of function." The distinction is to a large extent relative, but it exists in principle and is historically important.

The case where there is little division of labor because of the low technical level is typical of primitive household economies. There, with the exception of the differentiation of sex roles (of which more in Part Two, ch. III) every individual performs every function as the occasion arises. Seasonal variation has been common in the alternation of agricultural work in the summer with the crafts in the winter. An example of side lines is the tendency for urban workers to take up agricultural work at certain times, such as the harvest, and also the various cases of secondary functions undertaken in otherwise free time, which is common even in modern offices.

The case of specification of function is typical of the occupational structure of the Middle Ages: a large number of crafts, each of which specialized in the production of a single article, completely unperturbed by the technical heterogeneity of the functions involved. There was thus a combination of functions. The specialization of functions, on the other hand, is crucial to the modern development of the organization of labor. There are, however, important physiological and psychological reasons why it has virtually never been pushed to the absolute extreme of isolation, even on the highest levels of specialization. There is almost always an element of specification of function involved. It is not, however, as in the Middle Ages, oriented to the final product.

(2) The differentiation and combination of different functions may further vary according to the modes in which the services of a plurality of persons are combined to achieve a co-ordinated result. There are two

main possibilities: (a) the "accumulation" of functions; that is the employment of a number of persons all performing the same function to achieve a result. This may take the form either of identical, but technically independent efforts co-ordinated in parallel, or of identical efforts organized technically into a single collective effort.

> Examples of the first case are the functions performed by mowers or road pavers, several of whom work in parallel. The second type was exemplified on a grand scale in ancient Egypt in such cases as the transportation of huge stones by thousands of workers, large numbers of them performing the same acts, such as pulling on ropes, on the same object.

The second type, (b) is the "combination" of functions—that is, of efforts which are qualitatively different, and thus specialized—in order to achieve a result. These efforts may be technically independent and either simultaneous or successive; or they may involve technically organized co-operation in the simultaneous performance of technically complementary efforts.

> 1. A particularly simple example of simultaneous, technically independent functions is furnished by the parallel spinning of the warp and the woof for a given cloth. In the same class are to be placed a very large number of processes which are, from a technical point of view, undertaken independently, but are all designed as part of the production of the same final product.
> 2. An example of the successive type of technically independent processes is furnished by the relation of spinning, weaving, fulling, dyeing, and finishing. Similar examples are to be found in every industry.
> 3. The combination of specialized functions is found all the way from the case of an assistant holding a piece of iron while a blacksmith forges it, a case which is repeated in every modern foundry, to the complicated situations, which, though not specific to modern factories, are an important characteristic of them. One of the most highly developed types outside the factory is the organization of a symphony orchestra or of the cast of a theatrical production.

17. *Types of the Technical Division of Labor—* *(Continued)*

The division of labor efforts varies also, from a technical point of view, in terms of the extent and nature of combinations with complementary material means of production.

1. Forms may vary according to whether they consist purely in personal services, as in the case of wash-women, barbers, the performance of

actors, or whether they produce or transform goods by "working up" or transporting raw materials. The latter may consist in construction work, as that of plasterers, decorators, and stucco workers, in production of commodities and in transport of commodities. There are many transitional forms between them.

2. They may be further distinguished according to the stage at which they stand in the progression from original raw material to consumption: thus, from the original products of agriculture and mining to goods which are not only ready to be consumed, but available at the desired place for consumption.

3. The forms may further vary according to the ways in which they use: (a) Fixed plant and facilities (*Anlagen*). These may consist in sources of power; that is, means of harnessing energy, either that of natural forces, such as the power of water, wind, or heat from fire, or that which is produced mechanically, especially steam and electrical power, or in special premises for work, or they may use (b) implements of work (*Arbeitsmittel*), which include tools, apparatus, and machines. In some cases only one or another of these means of production may be used, or none. "Tools" are those aids to labor, the design of which is adapted to the physiological and psychological conditions of manual labor. "Apparatus" is something which is "tended" by the worker. "Machines" are mechanized apparatus. These rather vague distinctions have a certain significance for characterizing epochs in the development of industrial technology.

The use of mechanized sources of power and of machinery, characteristic of modern industry, is from a *technical* point of view due to their specific productivity and the resulting saving of human labor, and also to the uniformity and calculability of performance, both in quality and quantity. It is thus rational only where there exists a sufficiently wide demand for the particular types of products. In the case of a market economy, this means adequate purchasing power for the relevant goods; and this in turn depends on a certain type of income distribution.

It is quite out of the question here to undertake to develop even the most modest outline of a theory of the evolution of the technology and economics of tools and machinery. The concept of "apparatus" refers to such things as the type of loom which was operated by a foot-pedal and to numerous other similar devices. These already involve a certain relative independence on the part of the mechanical process, as distinguished from the functioning of the human or, in some cases, the animal organism. Without such apparatus—which included in particular various devices for moving materials in mines—machines, with their importance in modern technology, would never have come into existence. Leonardo's famous inventions were types of apparatus.

18. Social Aspects of the Division of Labor

From the social point of view, types of the division of labor may be classified in the following way: In the first place, according to the ways in which qualitatively different, especially complementary functions, are distributed among more or less autocephalous and autonomous economic units, which may further be distinguished economically according to whether these are budgetary units or profit-making enterprises. There are two polar possibilities:

(1) A "unitary" economy (*Einheitswirtschaft*) where the specialization (or specification) of functions is wholly internal, completely heterocephalous and heteronomous and determined on a purely technical basis. The same would be true of the co-ordination of functions. A unitary economy may, from an economic point of view, be either a budgetary unit or a profit-making enterprise.

> On the largest possible scale, a communist national economy would be a unitary budgetary economy; on the smallest scale it was the primitive family unit, which included all or the great majority of production functions in a "closed household economy." The type case of a "unitary" profit-making enterprise with purely internal specialization and co-ordination of functions is naturally the great vertical combination[32] which treats with outsiders only as an integrated unit. These two distinctions will suffice for the moment as a treatment of the development of autonomous unitary economy.

(2) The distribution of functions may, on the other hand, take place between autocephalous economic units. (a) It may consist in the specialization or specification of functions between heteronomous, but autocephalous units which are oriented to an order established by agreement or imposed. The order, in turn, may be substantively oriented in a variety of ways. Its main concern may be to provide for the needs of a superior economic unit, which may be the budgetary unit (household) of a lord, an *oikos,* or it may be oriented to profit-making for an economic unit controlled by a political body or lord. The order may, on the other hand, be concerned with providing for the needs of the members of some closed group (*genossenschaftlicher Verband*). From an economic point of view, this may be accomplished either in the "budgetary" (household) or in the "profit-making" mode. The organization in all these cases may either be confined to the mere regulation of economic activity or it may, at the same time, be engaged in economic action on its own account. (b) The other main type is the specialization of autocephalous and autonomous units in a market economy, which are oriented on the one hand substantively only to their own self-interest, formally only to the

order of an organization such as the laissez-faire state, which enforces only formal, rather than substantive rules (See above, chap. II, sec. 5:d).

1. A typical example of the organization which, limiting its function to the regulation of economic activity, takes the form of a budgetary unit administered by an association of the members under case 2(a), is the organization of village handicrafts in India ("establishment"). An organization with autocephalous but heteronomous units oriented in their economic activity to the household of a lord, as under 2(a), may be illustrated by structures which provide for the household wants of princes or landlords (in the case of princes, also for the political wants) by means of contributions from the individual holdings of subjects, dependents, serfs, slaves, cottars, or sometimes "demiurgic" (see below) village artisans, such are found everywhere in the world. The exactions of services or products for a landlord or a town corporation should usually be classified as "mere regulation of economic activity," insofar as they usually served only fiscal, not substantive ends. A case of market order with units oriented to profit-making for the lord exists where putting-out type production tasks contracted for are reallocated to the individual households.

The types where there is specialization and specification of function between heteronomous units under the aegis of a co-operative organization can be illustrated by the specialization common in many very old small-scale industries. The Solingen metal trades were originally organized in terms of a voluntary association determining the division of labor by agreement. It was only later that they became organized in terms of domination, namely as a "putting-out industry." The type where the autocephalous economic units are subject only to regulation by an organization is illustrated by innumerable cases of the rules established by village communities and town corporations for the regulation of trade, so far at least as these have a substantive influence on the processes of production.

The case of specialization as between autonomous and autocephalous units in a market economy is best illustrated by the modern economic order.

2. A few further details may be added. The order of the organizations which attempt to provide for the wants of their members on a budgetary basis is "budgetary" in a particular way—that is, it is oriented to the prospective needs of the individual members, not of the organized group, such as a village itself. Specified service obligations of this kind will be called "demiurgic liturgies,"[33] and this type of provision for needs, correspondingly, "demiurgic provision." It always is a question of corporate regulation governing the division of labor and, in some cases, the mode of combination of labor services.

This term will not, on the other hand, be applied to an organization, whether it is based on domination or on voluntary co-operation, if it carries on economic activity on its own account, contributions to which are sub-allocated on a specialized basis. The type cases of this category are the specialized and specified contributions in kind of *corvée* estates (*Fronhöfe*), seigneurial estates, and other types of large household units. But sub-allocated obligations are also common in various types of organizations which are not primarily oriented to economic ends, such as the households of princes, political groups and the budgetary administration of local communities. These contributions are generally for the benefit of the budgetary needs of the governing authority or for corporate purposes. These in-kind obligations of services and products imposed on peasants, artisans, and tradesmen will be called "*oikos* liturgies in kind" when they are owed to the household establishment of an individual, and "corporate liturgies in kind" when they are payable to the budgetary unit of an organization as such. The principle governing this mode of provision for the budgetary needs of an organization engaged in economic action, is called "liturgical provision." This mode of organization has played an exceedingly important historical role and will have to be discussed frequently. In political organizations, it held the place of modern "public finances," and in economic groups it made possible a decentralization of the main household by providing for its needs through actors who were no longer maintained and utilized in it. Each sub-unit managed its own affairs, but assumed the obligation to fulfill certain functions for the central unit and to that extent was dependent on it. Examples are peasants and serfs subject to various kinds of labor services and payments in kind; craftsmen attached to an estate; and a large number of other types. Rodbertus[34] was the first to apply the term "*oikos*" to the large-scale household economies of Antiquity. He accepted as the principal criterion the essential autarky of want satisfaction through utilization of the services of household members or of dependent labor, material means of production being made available on a non-exchange basis. It is a fact that the landed estates, and still more the royal households, of Antiquity, especially of the New Kingdom in Egypt, were cases where the greater part of the needs of the unit were provided by services and payments in kind, which were obligations of dependent household units, although the degree of approach to the pure type varies widely. The same phenomena are to be found at times in China and India, and to a less extent in our own Middle Ages, beginning with the *capitulare de villis*.[35] It is true that exchange with the outside was generally not entirely lacking, but it tended to have the character of budgetary exchange. Obligations to money payment have also not been uncommon, but have generally played a subsidiary part in the main provision for needs and have tended to be traditionally fixed. For the economic units subject to liturgical obligations it also has not been uncommon to be involved in exchange relations. But the decisive point is that the bulk of the subsistence of these units was covered by the in-kind benefits—either in the form of certain quotas of products, or in that of the use of pieces of land—which they received in compensation for the liturgical deliveries imposed on them. There are, of course, many transitional forms. But in each case there is some kind of regulation of functions by an organization which is concerned with the mode of division of labor and of its co-ordination.

3. The cases where an organization regulating economic activity is oriented to considerations of economic profit are well illustrated by those economic regulations of the communes of medieval Europe, and by the guilds and castes of China and India, which restricted the number of master craftsmen and their functions and also the techniques of the crafts, that is, the way in which labor was oriented in the handicrafts. They belonged to this type so far as the rules were intended not primarily to secure provision of the consumer with the products of the craftsmen, but, as was often though not always the case, to secure the market position of the artisans by maintaining the quality of performance and by dividing up the market. Like every other type of economic regulation, this type also involved limitations on market freedom and hence on the fully autonomous business orientation of the craftsmen. It was unquestionably intended to maintain the "livings" for the existing craft shops, and to that extent, in spite of its apparent "business" character, it was more closely related to the budgetary mode of orientation.

4. The case of an organization itself engaged in economic activity with an orientation to profit-making can be illustrated, apart from the pure type of putting-out industry already discussed, by the agricultural estates of the German East with a labor force holding small plots of estate land on a service tenure and entirely oriented to the order of the estate (*Instleute*), or by those of the German North-West with similar types of tenant labor (*Heuerlinge*) who, however, hold their plots on a rental basis. The agricultural estates, just like the putting-out industries, are profit-making organizations of the landlord and the entrepreneur, respectively. The economic units of the tenants and home-industry workers are oriented, both in the imposed division of functions and in the mode of combining work efforts, as in the whole of their economic conduct, primarily to the obligations which the order of the estate or the putting-out relationship dictates to them. Apart from that, they are households. Their acquisitive efforts are not autonomous, but heteronomous efforts oriented to the enterprise of the landlord or the entrepreneur. Depending upon the degree to which this orientation is substantively standardized, the division of functions may approach the purely technical type of division within one and the same enterprise which is typical of the factory.

19. *Social Aspects of the Division of Labor—* (*Continued*)

From a social point of view, the modes of the division of labor may be further classified according to the mode in which the economic advantages, which are regarded as returns for the different functions, are appropriated. Objects of appropriation may be: the opportunities of disposing of, and obtaining a return from, human labor services (*Leistungsverwertungschancen*); the material means of production;[36] and the opportunities for profit from managerial functions.[37] (On the sociological concept of appropriation, see above, chap. I, sec. 10).

When the utilization rights for labor services are appropriated, the services themselves may either, (1) go to an individual recipient (a lord) or to an organization, or (2) they may be sold on the market. In either case one of the following four, radically different, possibilities may apply:

(a) Monopolistic appropriation of the opportunities for disposal of labor services by the individual worker himself: the case of "craft-organized free labor." The appropriated rights may either be hereditary and alienable, in which case type (1) above is illustrated by the Indian village artisan and type (2) by certain medieval non-personal craft rights; or they may be strictly personal and inalienable, as under type (1) all "rights to an office"; or, finally, they may be hereditary, but inalienable, as under types (1) and (2) certain medieval, but above all Indian, craft rights, and medieval "offices" of the most diverse kind. In all these cases appropriation may be unconditional or subject to certain substantive conditions.

(b) The second possibility is that the right of utilization of labor services is appropriated to an "owner" of the worker: the case of "unfree labor." The property rights in the worker may be both hereditary and alienable—the case of slavery proper. Or, though it is hereditary, it may not be freely alienable, but, e.g., only together with the material means of production, particularly the land. This includes serfdom and hereditary dependency.

> The appropriation of the use of labor by a lord may be limited by substantive conditions, as in serfdom. The worker cannot leave his status of his own free will, but neither can it arbitrarily be taken from him.

The appropriated rights of disposal of labor services may be used by the owner for purposes of budgetary administration, as a source of income in kind or in money, or as a source of labor services in his household, as in the case of domestic slaves or serfs. Or it may be used as a means of profit. In that case the dependent may be obligated to deliver goods or to work on raw materials provided by the owner. The owner will then sell the product. This is unfree domestic industry. He may, finally, use his laborer in an organized shop—a slave or serf workshop.

> The person herein designated as the "owner" may be involved in the work process himself in a managerial capacity or even in part as a work-

er, but this need not be true. It may be that his position as owner, *ipso facto,* makes him the managing agent. But this is by no means necessary and is very generally not the case.

The use of slaves and serfs, the latter including various types of dependents, as part of a process of budgetary administration and as source of rent revenue, but not as workers in a profit-making enterprise, was typical of Antiquity and of the early Middle Ages. There are, for instance, cuneiform inscriptions which mention slaves of a Persian prince who were bound out as apprentices, possibly to be used later for labor services in the household, but perhaps to be set to work in substantive freedom for their own customers, making a regular payment to the owner (an early equivalent of the Greek ἀποφορά, the Russian *obrok,* and the German *Hals-* or *Leibzins*). Though by no means without exception, this tended to be the rule for Greek slaves; and in Rome this type of independent economic activity with a *peculium* or *merx peculiaris* and, naturally, payments to the owner, found reflection in various legal institutions. In the Middle Ages, body serfdom (*Leibherrschaft*) frequently involved merely a right to claim payments from otherwise almost independent persons. This was usual in western and southern Germany. In Russia, also, *de facto* limitation to the receipt of these payments (*obrok*) from an otherwise independent serf was, if not universal, at least very common, although the legal status of these persons remained precarious.

The use of unfree labor for "business" purposes has taken the following principal forms, particularly in the domestic industries on seigneurial estates, including various royal estates, among them probably those of the Pharaohs: (1) Unfree obligation to payments in kind—the delivery of goods in kind, the raw material for which was produced by the workers themselves as well as worked on by them. Flax is an example; (2) unfree domestic industry—work on material provided by the lord. The product could be sold at least in part for money by the lord. But in many cases, as in Antiquity, the tendency was to confine market sale to occasional instances. In early modern times, however, particularly in the German-Slavic border regions this was not the case; it was there, though not only there, that domestic industries developed on the estates of landlords. The utilization in a continuous organization could take the form of unfree home-industry labor or of unfree workshop labor. Both forms are common. The latter was one of the various forms of the *ergasterion* of Antiquity. It was found on the estates of the Pharaohs, in temple workshops, and according to the testimony of tomb frescoes, also on the estates of private owners or lords, in the Orient, in Greece (Demosthenes' shops in Athens), in the Roman estate workshops (see the description by Gummerus), in the Carolingian *genitium* (that is, a *gynaikeion*), and in more recent times for example in the Russian serf factories (see Tugan-Baranovski's book on the Russian factory).[38]

(c) The third possibility is the absence of any sort of appropriation: formally "free" labor, in this sense that the services of labor are the subject of a contractual relationship which is formally free on both sides. The contract may, however, be substantively regulated in various ways through a conventional or legal order governing the conditions of labor.

Freely contracted labor may be used in various ways. In the first place, in a budgetary unit, as occasional labor (what Bücher calls *Lohnwerk*), either in the household of the employer (*Stör*) or in that of the worker himself (*Heimwerk* in Bücher's terminology). Or it may be permanent, again performed in the household of the employer, as in the case of domestic service, or in that of the worker, as typical of the colonate. It may, on the other hand, be used for profit, again on an occasional or a permanent basis; and in both cases either in the worker's own home or on premises provided by the employer. The latter is true of workers on an estate or in a workshop, but especially of the factory.

> Where the worker is employed in a budgetary unit, he is directly in the service of a consumer who supervises his labor. Otherwise, he is in the service of a profit-making entrepreneur. Though the form is often legally identical, economically the difference is fundamental. *Coloni* may be in either status; but it is more typical for them to be workers in an *oikos*.

(d) The fourth possibility is that opportunities for disposal of labor services may be appropriated by an organization of workers, either without any appropriation by the individual worker or with important limitations on such appropriation. This may involve absolute or relative closure against outsiders and also prohibition of the dismissal of workers from employment by management without consent of the workers, or at least some kind of limitations on power of dismissal.

> Examples of the type of appropriation involving closure of the group are castes of workers or the type of miners' association found in the Medieval mining industry, the organized groups or retainers sometimes found at courts, or the "thresher tenure" (*Dreschgärtner*) on landed estates in Germany. This type of appropriation is found throughout the social history of all parts of the world in an endless variety of forms. The second type involving limitations on powers of dismissal, which is also very widespread, plays an important part in the modern situation in the "closed shop" of trade unions and especially in the "works councils."

Every form of appropriation of jobs in profit-making enterprises by workers, like the converse case of appropriation of the services of workers by owners, involves limitations on the free recruitment of the labor force. This means that workers cannot be selected solely on grounds of their technical efficiency, and to this extent there is a limitation on the *formal* rationalization of economic activity. Appropriation of jobs also imposes substantive limitations on *technical* rationality, namely: (1) if the exploitation for profit of the products of labor is appropriated by an owner, through the tendency to restrict the work effort, either by tradition, or by convention, or by contract; also through the reduction or complete disappearance (if the worker is fully owned, a slave) of the worker's own interest in optimal effort; (2) if the exploitation for profit of the products is also appropriated by the workers, there may be a conflict of the worker's self-interest, which lies in the maintenance of his traditional mode of life, with the attempts of his employer to get him to produce at the optimum technical level or to use other means of production in place of labor. For employers, there is always the possibility of transforming their exploitation of labor into a mere source of income. Any appropriation of the exploitation of products by the workers thus generally leads under otherwise favorable circumstances to a more or less complete expropriation of the owner from management. But it also regularly tends to place workers in a state of dependence on people with whom they deal who enjoy a more favorable market position. These, such as putting-out entrepreneurs, then tend to assume a managerial position.

1. The very opposite forms of appropriation—that of jobs by workers and that of workers by owners—nevertheless have in practice very similar results. This should not be surprising. In the first place, the two tendencies are very generally formally related. This is true when appropriation of the workers by an owner coincides with appropriation of opportunities for jobs by a closed organization of workers, as has happened in the manor associations. In such cases it is natural that exploitation of labor services should, to a large extent, be stereotyped; hence, that work effort should be restricted and that the workers have little self-interest in the output. The result is generally a successful resistance of workers against any sort of technical innovation. But even where this does not occur, the fact that workers are appropriated by an owner means in practice that he is obliged to make use of this particular labor force. He is not in a position, like the modern factory manager, to select according to technical needs, but must utilize those he has without selection. This is particularly true of slave labor. Any attempt to exact performance from appropriated workers beyond that which has become traditionally established encounters traditional obstacles. These could only be overcome by the most ruthless methods, which are not without their danger from the point of view of the owner's self-interest, since they might undermine the traditionalistic bases of his authority. Hence almost universally the work effort of appropriated workers has shown a tendency to restriction. Even where, as was particularly true of eastern Europe at the beginning of the modern age, this was broken by the power of the lords, the development of higher technical levels of production was impeded by the absence of the selective process and by the absence of any element of self-interest or own risk-taking on the part of the appropriated workers.

When jobs have been formally appropriated by workers, the same result has come about even more rapidly.

2. Appropriation by workers was typical for the development in the early Middle Ages (10th to 13th century). The Carolingian *Beunden*[39] and all other beginnings of large-scale agricultural enterprise declined and disappeared. The rents and dues paid to landlords and lords holding rights over persons became stereotyped at a low level; and an increasing proportion of the products in kind, in agriculture and mining, and of the money proceeds from the handicrafts, went to the workers. In just this form this development was peculiar to the Western world. The principal circumstances which favored it were as follows: (a) The fact that the propertied classes were heavily involved in political and military activity; (b) the absence of a suitable administrative staff. These two circumstances made it impossible for them to utilize these workers in any other way than as a source of rent payments; (c) the fact that the freedom of movement of workers between the potential employers competing for their services could not easily be restricted; (d) the numerous opportunities of opening up new land, new mines, and new local markets; (e) the primitive level of the technical tradition. The more the appropriation of profit opportunities *by* the workers replaced the appropriation *of* workers *by* owners, the more the owners were dispossessed of their rights of control and became mere recipients of rents and dues. Classical examples are the mining industry and the English guilds. Even at this early period the process tended to go further, to the point of redemption or repudiation of the obligation to make payments to a lord altogether, on the principle that "A townsman is a freeman." Almost immediately all this led to a differentiation of the opportunities of making profit by market transactions, arising either from within the group of workers themselves or from without through the development of trade.

20. *Social Aspects of the Division of Labor: The Appropriation of the Material Means of Production*

The material means of production may be appropriated by workers as individuals or as organizations, by owners, or by regulating groups consisting of third parties.

When appropriated by workers, it may be by the individual worker who then becomes the "owner" of the material means of production; or the appropriation may be carried out by a completely or relatively closed group of workers so that, though the individual worker is not the owner, the organization is. Such an organization may carry out its functions as a unitary economy on a "communist" basis, or with appropriation of shares (*genossenschaftlich*). In all these cases, appropriation may be used for the purposes of budgetary administration or for profit making.

Appropriation of the means of production by individual workers may exist in a system of complete market freedom of the small peasants, artisans, boatmen, or carters, or under the aegis of a regulating group. Where it is not the individual but an organization which owns the means of production, there is a wide variety of possibilities, varying particularly with the extent to which the system is of a budgetary or a profit-making character. The household economy, which is in principle not necessarily by origin or in fact communistic (see Part Two, ch. III), may be oriented wholly to provision for its own needs. Or it may, perhaps only occasionally, dispose of surpluses of certain types of raw material accumulated by virtue of a favorable location, or of products derived from some particular technical skill, as a means to better provision. This occasional sale may then develop into a regular system of profit-making exchange. In such cases it is common for "tribal" crafts to develop, with interethnic functional specialization and trade between the tribes, since the chances of finding a market often depend on maintaining a monopoly, which in turn is usually secured by inherited trade secrets. From this may develop ambulatory crafts or possibly pariah[40] crafts or, where these groups are united in a political structure and where there are ritual barriers between the ethnic elements, castes, as in India.

The case where members of the group possess appropriated shares is that of "producers' co-operation."[41] Household economies may, with the development of money accounting, approach this type. Otherwise, it is occasionally found as an organization of workmen. It was of great significance in one important case, that of the mining industry of the early Middle Ages.

Since appropriation by organized groups of workers has already been dealt with, appropriation by "owners" or organized groups of them can only mean the expropriation of the workers from the means of production, not merely as individuals, but as a whole. An owner may in this connection appropriate one or more of the following items: land, including water; subterranean wealth; sources of power; work premises; labor equipment, such as tools, apparatus and machinery; and raw materials. In any given case all these may be concentrated in a single ownership or they may be appropriated by different owners. The owners may employ the means of production they appropriate in a context of budgetary administration, either as means to provide for their own needs or as sources of income by lending them out. In the latter case, the loans may in turn be used by the borrower for budgetary purposes or as means for earning a profit, either in a profit-making establishment without capital accounting or as capital goods (in their own enterprise). Finally, the owner may use them as capital goods in his own enterprise.

The appropriating agency may be an organization engaged in economic activity. In this case, all the alternatives just outlined are open to it.

It is, finally, also possible that the means of production should be appropriated by an organization which only *regulates* economic activity, which does not itself use them as capital goods or as a source of income, but places them at the disposal of its members.

I. When *land* is appropriated by individual economic units, it is usually for the period of actual cultivation until the harvest or, so far as, by virtue of clearing or irrigation, land is itself an artifact, for the period of continuous cultivation. It is only when scarcity of land has become noticeable that it is common for rights of cultivation, pasturage and use of timber to be reserved to the members of a settlement group, and for the extent of their use to be limited.

(1) When that happens, appropriation may be carried out by an organization. This may be of differing sizes, according to the mode of use, to which the land is put—for gardens, meadows, arable land, pastures, or woodland. These have been appropriated by progressively larger groups, from the individual household to the whole tribe. Typical cases are the appropriation of arable land, meadows, and pastures by a kinship group or a neighborhood group, usually a village. Woodland has usually been appropriated by broader territorial groups, differing greatly in character and extent. The individual household has typically appropriated garden land and the area around the house and has had shares in the arable fields and meadows. The system of shares may find expression (i) in the *de facto* egalitarianism of the assignment of newly tilled fields where cultivation is "ambulatory" (as in the so-called field-grass husbandry), or (ii) in rationally systematic redistribution under sedentary cultivation. The latter is usually the consequence of either fiscal claims for which the village members are collectively held responsible, or of political claims of the members for equality. The unit of the production organization has usually been the household (on which see Part Two, ch. III and IV).

(2) Appropriation of the land may also be to a lord or seigneur (*Grundherr*). This seigneurial position, as will be discussed later, may be based primarily on the individual's position of authority in a kinship group or as tribal chieftain with claims to exact labor services (see Part Two, ch. IV), or on fiscal or military authority, or on some form of organization for the systematic exploitation of new land or an irrigation project. Seigneurial domination over land (*Grundherrschaft*) may be made a source of utilities by the employment of the unfree labor of slaves or serfs. This, in turn, may be administered as part of a budgetary unit, through deliveries in kind or labor services, or as a means of profit, as a "plantation." On the other hand, it may be exploited with free labor. Here again it may be treated in budgetary terms, drawing income from the land in the form of payments in kind or from share-cropping by tenants or of money rents from tenants. In both cases the equipment used may be provided by the tenant himself, or by the seigneur (colo-

nate). A lord may also exploit his holdings as a source of profit in the form of a large-scale rational economic enterprise.

Where the land is used as part of a budgetary economy with unfree labor, the lord is apt to be bound traditionally in his exploitation of it, both with respect to his labor personnel, which is not subject to selection, and to their functions. The use of unfree labor in a profit-making establishment, the "plantation," occurred only in a few cases, notably in Antiquity in Carthage and in Rome, and in modern times in the plantations of colonial areas and in the Southern States of North America. The use of land in large-scale profit-making enterprises with free labor has occurred only in the modern Western World. It is the mode of development of the medieval landlordship or seigneurie (*Grundherrschaft*), in particular the way in which it was broken up, which has been most decisive in determining the modern forms of land appropriation. The modern pure type knows only the following categories: the owner of the land, the capitalistic tenant, and the propertyless agricultural laborer. But this pure type is exceptional, found principally in England.

II. Sources of wealth adapted to exploitation by *mining* may be appropriated in the following ways: (a) By the owner of the land, who in the past has usually been a seigneur; (b) by a political overlord (owner of the regal prerogatives or "royalties"); (c) by any person discovering deposits worthy of mining (*Bergbaufreiheit*); (d) by an organization of workers; and (e) by a profit-making enterprise. Seigneurs and owners of "royalties" may administer their holdings themselves, as they did occasionally in the early Middle Ages; or they may use them as a source of income, by leasing them to an organized group of workers or to any discoverer whatever or to anyone who was a member of a given group. This was the case with the "freed mountains" (*gefreite Berge*) of the Middle Ages and was the origin of the institution of "mining freedom" (*Bergbaufreiheit*).[42]

In the Middle Ages, the groups of organized mine workers were typically closed membership groups with shares held by the members, where each member was under obligation, either to the seigneurial owner, or to the other members collectively responsible to him, to work in the mine. This obligation was balanced by a right to a share in the products. There was also a type of a pure "owners" association, each sharing in the proceeds or the contributions required due to losses. The tendency was for the seigneurial owners to be progressively expropriated in favor of the workers; but these, in turn, as their need for investment in installations increased, became more and more dependent on groups with command over capital goods. Thus in the end, the appropriation took the form of a capitalistic *Gewerkschaft*, a limited liability company.

III. Means of production which are *fixed installations,* such as sources of power, particularly water power, "mills" for various different purposes, and workshops, sometimes including the fixed apparatus in them, have in the past, particularly in the Middle Ages, generally been appropriated in one of the following ways: (a) by princes or seigneurs; (b) by towns (either as economically active or merely regulating organizations); (c) by associations of workers, such as guilds (as "regulating" groups), without the development, in any of them, of a unified production organization (*Betrieb*).

In the first two cases, they were usually exploited as a source of income, a charge being made for their use. This has often been combined with interdiction of rival facilities and the compulsory use of those belonging to the lord. Each production unit would make use of the facilities in turn, according to need or, under certain circumstances, it was made the monopoly of a closed, regulative group. Baking ovens, various kinds of grinding mills for grain or oil, fulling mills, polishing installations, slaughter-houses, dye-works, bleaching installations, forges—which were usually, to be sure, leased—, breweries, distilleries, other installations including particularly shipyards in the possession of the Hanseatic towns, and all kinds of market stalls have been appropriated in this pre-capitalistic way, to be exploited by allowing workers to use them in return for a payment; they were thus used as part of the budgetary wealth (*Vermögen*), rather than as capital of the owners (individuals or organizations, including town corporations). This type of production and budgetary exploitation of fixed installations as a source of investment income for the owning individual or group, or possibly production by a producers' co-operative group, has preceded the creation of "fixed capital" of individual business units. Those *using* such installations have tended to treat them in part as means of meeting their own household needs, especially in the case of baking ovens and of brewing and distilling installations, and in part for profit-making operations.

IV. For maritime transport the typical arrangement in the past has been the appropriation of the *ship* by a plurality of owners, who tended to become more and more sharply differentiated from the actual seafarers. The fact that the organization of maritime enterprise then tended to develop into a system of risk-sharing with shippers, in which ship owners, officers, and even the crew, were associated as shippers of freight, did not, however, produce any fundamentally new forms of *appropriation*. It affected only the forms of settling accounts and hence the distribution of profit-making possibilities.

V. Today, it is usual for the installations of all kinds and the tools to be appropriated under *one* controlling agency, as is essential to the modern factory; but in earlier times, this has been exceptional. In particular, the economic character of the Greek and Byzantine *ergasterion* and the corresponding Roman *ergastulum* has been highly ambiguous, a fact which historians have persistently ignored. It was a "workshop" which might, (i) be a part of a budgetary unit in which slaves would carry out production for the owner's own needs, as for the needs of a landed estate, or subsidiary production of goods for sale. But (ii) the workshop might also be used as a source of rent revenue, part of the holdings of a private individual or of an organization, which latter might be a town, as was true of the *ergasteria* of the Piraeus. Such *ergasteria* would then be leased to individuals or to organized closed groups of workers. Thus, when it is stated that an *ergasterion* was exploited, especially a municipal one, it is always necessary to inquire further to whom it belonged and who was the owner of the other means of production necessary for the work process. Did free labor work there? Did they work for their own profit? Or did slaves work there, in which case it is necessary to know who their owners were, and whether they were working on their own account, making ἀποφορά payments to their master, or directly for their master. According to the ways in which these questions are answered, the structure would be radically different from an economic point of view. In the great majority of cases, as late as the Byzantine and Mohammedan types, the *ergasterion* seems to have been primarily a source of rent revenue, and was hence fundamentally different from the modern factory or even its early predecessors. From an economic point of view, this category is, in its economic ambiguity, most closely comparable to the various types of mills found in the Middle Ages.

VI. Even in cases where the workshop and the means of production are appropriated by an individual owner who hires labor, the situation is not, from an economic point of view, necessarily what would usually be called a "factory" today. For this it would be necessary in addition to have the use of mechanical power, of machinery, and of an elaborate internal differentiation and combination of functions. The factory today is a category of the capitalistic economy. Hence in the present discussion the concept "factory" will be confined to a type of establishment which is at least potentially under the control of a profit-making firm with fixed capital, which thus takes the form of an organized workshop with internal differentiation of function, with the appropriation of *all* non-human means of production and with a high degree of mechanization of the work process by the use of mechanical power and machinery. The great workshop of "Jack of Newbury"[43] of the early sixteenth century, which was sung about by balladeers of a later day, did not have any of these features. It is alleged to have contained hundreds of hand looms, which were his property and for the workers of which he bought the raw materials, and also all manner of "welfare" arrangements. But each worker worked independently as if he were at home. Internal differentiation and combination of functions could, to be sure, exist in an Egyptian, Greek, Byzantine or Mohammedan *ergasterion* which a master worked with his unfree laborers. But the Greek texts show clearly that even in such cases is was common for the master to be content with the payment of an ἀποφορά from each worker and perhaps a higher one from the foreman. This alone is sufficient to warn us not to consider such a structure economically equivalent to a factory or even to a workshop like that of "Jack of Newbury." The closest approximation to the factory in the usual sense is found in royal manufactories, like the imperial Chinese porcelain manufactory and the European manufactories of court luxuries, which were modelled on it, and especially those for the production of military equipment. No one can be blamed for calling these "factories." And the Russian workshops operating with serf labor seem at first sight to stand even closer to the modern factory. Here the appropriation of the workers themselves is added to that of the means of production. Nevertheless, for present purposes the concept "factory" will, for the reasons stated, be limited to organized workshops where the material means of production are fully appropriated by an owner, but the workers are not; where there is internal specialization of functions, and where mechanical power and machines which must be "tended" are used. All other types of organized workshops will be designated by that word, with the appropriate adjectives.

2 1. *Social Aspects of the Division of Labor: The Appropriation of Managerial Functions*

(1) In all cases of the management of traditional budgetary (household) units, it is typical for the appropriation of managerial functions to take place either by the titular head himself, such as the head of the family or the kinship group, or by members of an administrative staff appointed for the management of the unit, as in the case of service fiefs of household officials.

(2) In the case of profit-making enterprises, it occurs in the following situations: (a) When management and ordinary labor are entirely or very nearly identical. In this case there is usually also appropriation of the material means of production by the worker. This type of appropriation may be unlimited, that is, hereditary and alienable on the part of the individual, with or without a guaranteed market. It may, on the other hand, be appropriation to an organized group, with appropriation of the function by the individual restricted to personal tenure[44] or subject to substantive regulation, thus limited and dependent on various conditions. Again, a market may or may not be guaranteed. (b) Where management and ordinary work are separated, there may be a monopolistic appropriation of entrepreneurial functions in various possible forms, notably to closed membership groups, such as guilds, or to monopolies granted by the political authority.

(3) In cases where managerial functions are, from a formal point of view, wholly unappropriated, the appropriation of the means of production or of the credit necessary for securing control over them is in practice, in a capitalistic form of organization, identical with appropriation of control of management by the owners of the means of production. Owners can, in such cases, exercise their control by personally managing the business or by appointment of the actual managers. Where there is

a plurality of owners, they will co-operate in the selection. These points are so obvious that there is no need of comment.

Wherever there is appropriation of technically complementary means of production, it generally means, in practice, at least some degree of effective voice in the selection of management and, to a relative extent at least, the expropriation of the workers from management. The expropriation of the individual workers, however, does not necessarily imply the expropriation of workers in general. Though they are formally expropriated, it is possible for an association of workers to be in fact in a position to exact for itself an effective share in management or in the selection of managing personnel.

22. *The Expropriation of Workers from the Means of Production*

The expropriation of the individual worker from ownership of the means of production is determined by purely *technical* factors in the following cases: (a) if the means of production require the services of many workers, at the same time or successively; (b) if sources of power can be rationally exploited only by using them simultaneously for many similar types of work under a unified control; (c) if a technically rational organization of the work process is possible only by combining many complementary processes under continuous common supervision; (d) if special technical training is needed for the management of co-ordinated processes of labor which, in turn, can only be exploited rationally on a large scale; (e) if unified control over the means of production and raw materials creates the possibility of subjecting labor to a stringent discipline and hence of controlling the speed of work and of attaining standardization of effort and of product quality.

These factors, however, do not exclude the possibility of appropriation by an organized group of workers, a producers' co-operative. They necessitate only the separation of the *individual* worker from the means of production.

The expropriation of workers *in general,* including clerical personnel and technically trained persons, from possession of the means of production has its *economic* reasons above all in the following factors: (a) The fact that, other things being equal, it is generally possible to achieve a higher level of economic rationality if the management has extensive control over the selection and the modes of use of workers, as compared with the situation created by the appropriation of jobs or the existence of rights to participate in management. These latter conditions produce technically irrational obstacles as well as economic irrationalities. In particular, considerations appropriate to small-scale budgetary administration and the interests of workers in the maintenance of jobs ("livings") are often in conflict with the rationality of the organization. (b) In a market economy a management which is not hampered by any established rights of the workers, and which enjoys unrestricted control over the goods and equipment which underlie its borrowings, is of superior credit-worthiness. This is particularly true if the management consists of individuals experienced in business affairs and with a good reputation for "safety" derived from their continuous conduct of business. (c) From a historical point of view, the expropriation of labor has arisen since the sixteenth century in an economy characterized by the progressive extensive and intensive expansion of the market system on the one hand, because of the sheer superiority and actual indispensability of a type of management oriented to the particular market situations, and on the other because of the structure of power relationships in the society.

In addition to these general conditions, the effect of the fact that enterprise has been oriented to the exploitation of market advantages has in the following ways favored such expropriation: (a) because it put a premium on capital accounting—which can be effected in the technically most rational manner only with full appropriation of capital goods to the owner—as against any type of economic behavior with less rational accounting procedures; (b) because it put a premium on the purely commercial qualities of the management, as opposed to the technical ones, and on the maintenance of technical and commercial secrets; (c) because it favored a speculative business policy, which again requires expropriation. Further, and in the last analysis quite regardless of the degree of technical rationality, this expropriation is made possible, (d) by the sheer bargaining superiority which in the labor market any kind of property ownership grants vis-à-vis the workers, and which in the commodity markets accrues to any business organization working with capital accounting, owned capital equipment and borrowed funds vis-à-vis any type of competitor operating on a lower level of rationality in methods of calculation or less well situated with respect to capital and credit resources. The fact that the maximum of *formal* rationality in capital accounting is possible only where the workers are subjected to domination by entrepreneurs, is a further specific element of *substantive* irrationality in the modern economic order. Finally, (e), a further economic reason for this expropriation is that free labor and the complete appropriation of the means of production create the most favorable conditions for discipline.

23. *The Expropriation of Workers from the Means of Production—(Continued)*

The expropriation of *all* the workers from the means of production may in practice take the following forms: (1) Management is in the hands of the administrative staff of an organization. This would be true very particularly also of any rationally organized socialist economy, which would retain the expropriation of all workers and merely bring it to completion by the expropriation of the private owners. (2) Managerial functions are, by virtue of their appropriation of the means of production, exercised by the owners or by persons they appoint. The appropriation of control over the persons exercising managerial authority by the interests of ownership may have the following forms: (a) Management by one or more entrepreneurs who are at the same time owners —the immediate appropriation of entrepreneurial functions. This situation, however, does not exclude the possibility that a wide degree of control over the policies of management may rest in hands outside the enterprise, by virtue of their powers over credit or financing—for instance, the bankers or financiers who finance the enterprise; (b) separation of managerial functions from appropriated ownership, especially through limitations of the functions of owners to the appointment of management and through shared free (that is, alienable) appropriation of the enterprise as expressed by shares of the nominal capital (stocks, mining shares). This state, which is related to the purely personal form of appropriation through various types of intermediate forms, is rational in the *formal* sense in that it permits, in contrast to the case of permanent and hereditary appropriation of the management itself of accidentally inherited properties, the selection for managerial posts of the persons best qualified from the point of view of profitability. But in practice it may mean a number of things, such as: That control over the managerial position may come, through appropriation, into the hands of "outside interests" representing the resources of a budgetary unit, or mere wealth (*Vermögen;* see above, ch. II, sec. 10), and seeking above all a high rate of income; or that control over the managerial position comes, through temporary stock acquisitions, into the hands of speculative "outside interests" seeking gains only through the resale of their shares; or that disposition over the managerial position comes into the hands of outside business interests, by virtue of power over markets or over credit, such as banks or "financiers," which may pursue their own business interests, often foreign to those of the organization as such.

We call "outside interests" those which are not primarily oriented to the long-run profitability of the enterprise. This may be true of any kind of budgetary "wealth" interests. It is particularly true, however, of interests which consider their control over the plant and capital goods of the enterprise or of a share in it not as a permanent investment, but as a means of making a purely short-run speculative profit. The types of outside interest which are most readily reconciled with those of the enterprise—that is, its interests in present *and* long-run profitability—are those seeking only income (*rentiers*).

The fact that such "outside" interests can affect the mode of control over managerial positions, even and especially when the highest degree of *formal* rationality in their selection is attained, constitutes a further element of *substantive* irrationality specific to the modern economic order. These might be entirely private "wealth" interests, or business interests which are oriented to ends having no connection whatsoever with the organization, or finally, pure gambling interest. By gaining control of shares, all of these can control the appointment of the managing personnel and, more important, the business policies imposed on this management. The influence exercised by speculative interests outside the producing organizations themselves on the market situation, especially that for capital goods, and thus on the orientation of the production of goods, is *one* of the sources of the phenomena known as the "crises" of the modern market economy. This cannot, however, be further discussed here.

24. *The Concept of Occupation and Types of Occupational Structure*

The term "occupation" (*Beruf*) will be applied to the mode of specialization, specification, and combination of the functions of an individual so far as it constitutes for him the basis of a continuous opportunity for income or earnings. The distribution of occupations may be achieved in the following ways: (1) by means of a heteronomous assignment of functions and of provisions for maintenance within an organization regulating economic activity—unfree differentiation of occupations—or through autonomous orientation to the state of the market for occupational services—free differentiation of occupations; (2) it may rest on the specification or the specialization of functions; (3) it may involve economic exploitation of the services by their bearers on either an autocephalous or a heterocephalous basis.

The structure of occupational differentiation and that of opportunities for business income are closely related. This will be discussed in relation to the problems of "class" and "status" stratification.

On occupation as a basis of status, and on classes in general, see chap. IV, below.[45]

1. Unfree organization of occupations exists in cases where there is compulsory assignment of functions within the organization of a royal estate, a state, a feudal manor, or a commune on the basis of liturgies or of the *oikos* type of structure. The free type of distribution arises from the successful offer of occupational services on the labor market or successful application for free "positions."

2. As was pointed out above in sec. 16, specification of functions was typical of the handicrafts in the Middle Ages; specialization is characteristic of the modern rational business organization. The distribution of occupations in a market economy consists to a large extent of technically irrational specification of functions, rather than of rational specialization of functions, because such an economy is oriented to the market situation and hence to the interests of purchasers and consumers. This orientation determines [the uses to which] the entire bundle of labor services offered by a given productive unit will be put in a manner often different from the specialization of functions [of the given labor force], thus making necessary modes of combination of functions which are technically irrational.

3. Cases of autocephalous occupational specialization are the independent "business" of an artisan, a physician, a lawyer, or an artist. The factory worker and the government official, on the other hand, occupy heterocephalous occupational positions.

The occupational structure of a given social group may vary in the following ways: (a) According to the degree in which well-marked and stable occupations have developed at all. The following circumstances are particularly important in this connection: the development of consumption standards, the development of techniques of production, and the development of large-scale budgetary units in the case of unfree occupational organization, or of market systems in that of free organization; (b) according to the mode and degree of occupational specification or specialization of individual economic units. This will be decisively influenced by the market situation for the services or products of specialized units, which is in turn dependent on adequate purchasing power. It will also be influenced by the mode of distribution of control over capital goods; (c) according to the extent and kind of continuity or change in occupational status. This in turn depends above all on two factors: on the one hand, on the amount of training required for the specialized functions, and on the other hand the degree of stability or instability of opportunities for earnings from them. The latter is in turn dependent on the type and stability of distribution of income and on the state of technology.

Finally, it is always important in studying occupational structure to know the status stratification, with the attendant status-tied types of education and other advantages and opportunities which it creates for certain kinds of skilled occupations.

It is only functions which require a certain minimum of training and for which opportunity of continuous remuneration is available which become the objects of independent and stable occupations. The choice of occupation may rest on tradition, in which case it is usually hereditary; on goal-oriented rational considerations, especially the possibility of returns; on charismatic or on affectual grounds; and finally, in particular, on grounds of prestige with particular reference to status. Originally, the more directly individual "callings" have been dependent primarily on charismatic (magical) elements, while all the rest of the occupational structure, so far as in a differentiated form it existed at all, was traditionally fixed. The requisite charismatic qualities, so far as they were not specifically personal, tended to become the object of a traditional "training" in closed groups, or of hereditary transmission. Individual occupations which were not of a strictly charismatic character first appeared on a liturgical basis in the large-scale households of princes and landed lords, and then in the market economy of the towns. Alongside of this, however, a large role in their development was always played by the literary forms of education with a high status esteem, which arose in close connection with magical, ritual, or priestly ("clerical") professional training.

From what has been said it will be seen that occupational specialization does not necessarily imply continuous rendering of services, either on a liturgical basis for an organization—in a royal household or a workshop—or for a completely free market. Other forms are not only possible but common: (1) Propertyless occupationally specialized workers may be employed on an occasional basis as needed in the service of a relatively stable group of either consumers in household units or employers in profit-making enterprises. In the case of work for *households,* we have the possibility of the expropriation from the worker of at least the raw materials (and hence of the control over the final product); services may be rendered on this basis either on the consumer's premises (*Stör*), whether it be by itinerant workers or by sedentary workers moving around the households of a local clientele, or on the workers' premises: shop or household ("wage work" [in Bücher's terminology][46]). In either case the consumer household provides the raw materials, but it is customary for the worker to own his tools—the mower his scythe, the seamstress her sewing equipment, etc. The cases of *Stör* involve temporary membership in the consumer's household.

The case, contrasting with the above, in which the worker owns *all* means of production, Bücher terms "price work."

Occupationally specialized workers may be employed on an occasional basis by *profit-making enterprises* when at least the raw material, and thus also control over the product, belongs to the employer. In this case there may be migratory labor for a variety of different employers in different units, or occasional or seasonal work for an employer, the work being done in the worker's own household. Migratory harvest labor is an example of the first type. The second type may be illustrated by any type of occasional work at home which supplements the work in the workshop.

Occupational specialization without continuous engagement of the types noted above can also exist if: (2) Economic activity is conducted with appropriated means of production and (i) there is capital accounting and *partial* appropriation—especially, appropriation restricted to the fixed installations—by owners. Examples are workshops and factories transforming raw materials owned by others (*Lohnfabriken*) and, above all, factories producing under contract for an outside entrepreneur who takes charge of sales and other entrepreneurial functions (*verlegte Fabriken*); the former have existed for a long time, while the latter have recently become common. Or, if (ii) there is complete appropriation of the means of production by the workers, with the following possibilities: (a) in small-scale units without capital accounting, either producing for households ("price work" for customers), or producing for commercial enterprises. The latter is a case of domestic industry without expropriation of the means of production. The worker is formally a free craftsman, but is actually bound to a monopolistic group of merchants who are buyers for his product; (b) on a large scale with capital accounting and production for a fixed group of purchasers. This is usually, though not always, the result of market regulation by cartels.

Finally, it must be pointed out that not every case of acquisitive action is necessarily part of an occupational profit-making activity; nor is it necessary that involvement in acquisitive action, however frequent, should imply a continuous specialization with a constant meaningful orientation. With respect to the first observation, we note that "occasional acquisition" is found as a result of the disposal of surpluses produced in a budgetary unit. Corresponding to these is occasional trading of goods by large-scale budgetary units, especially seigneurial estates. From this starting point, it is possible to develop a continuous series of possible "occasional acquisitive acts," such as the occasional speculation of a *rentier,* occasional publication of an article or a poem by a person who is not a professional author, and similar modern phenomena, to the case where such things constitute a "subsidiary occupaiton" (*Nebenberuf*).

As to the second observation, it should be remembered that there are ways of making a living which are continually shifting and fundamentally unstable. A person may shift continually from one type of "occasional" profitable activity to another; or even between normal legitimate earning and begging, stealing, or highway robbery.

The following must be treated in special terms: (a) Support from purely charitable sources; (b) maintenance in an institution on other than a charitable basis, notably a penal institution; (c) regulated acquisition by force; and (d) criminal acquisition; that is, acquisition by force or fraud in violation of the rules of an order. The cases of (b) and (d) are of relatively little interest; (a) has often been of tremendous importance for hierocratic groups, such as mendicant orders; while (c) has been crucial for many political groups in the form of the booty gained from war, and in both cases the economy was profoundly affected. It is characteristic of both these cases that they lie outside the realm of economic activity as such. Hence this is not the place to enter into a more detailed classification. The forms will be treated elsewhere. For reasons which are in part the same, the earnings of civil servants, including military officers, have been mentioned below (sec. 38) only in order to give them a place as a sub-type of the earnings of labor, but without going into the details. To do this, it would be necessary to discuss the structure of relations of domination in the context of which these types of earnings are to be placed.

24a. *The Principal Forms of Appropriation and of Market Relationship*

According to the theoretical schemes which have been developed starting with sec. 15, the classification of the modes of appropriation in their technical, organizational aspects, and of the market relationships, is exceedingly complex. But actually, only a few of the many theoretical possibilities play a really dominant role.

(1) With respect to agricultural land: (a) There is the "ambulatory" cultivation by household units, which changes its location whenever the land has been exhausted. The land is usually appropriated by the tribe while its use is temporarily or permanently appropriated by neighborhood groups, with only temporary appropriation of the use of land to individual households.

The extent of the household group may vary from the individual conjugal family, through various types of extended family groups, to organized kin groups or a widely extended household community. (Agriculture is "ambulatory" as a rule only in relation to arable land, much less commonly and at longer intervals for farmyard sites.)

(b) Sedentary agriculture. The use of arable fields, meadows, pastures, woodland, and water is usually regulated by territorial or village associations for the smaller family household. Gardens and the land immediately surrounding the buildings are normally appropriated by the immediate family; arable fields, usually meadows, and pastures, by the village organization; woodland, by more extensive territorial groups. Redistribution of land is usually possible according to the law, but has generally not been systematically carried through and is hence usually obsolete. Economic activities have generally been regulated by a system of rules applying to the whole village. This is a "primary village economy."

It is only in exceptional cases, such as China, that the extended kinship group has constituted an economic unit. Where this is the case, it has generally taken the form of a rationalized organization, such as a clan association.

(c) Seigneurial rights over land (*Grundherrschaft*) and persons (*Leibherrschaft*) with a central manor of the lord (*Fronhof*) and dependent peasant farms obligated to deliveries in kind and labor services. The land itself and the workers are appropriated by the lord, the *use* of the land and rights to work by the peasants. This is a simple case of *manorial organization based on income in kind*.

(d) Seigneurial or fiscal monopoly of control over the land, with collective responsibility of the peasant community for meeting fiscal obligations. This leads to communal control over and regular systematic redistribution of the land. The land is, as a correlate of the fiscal burden, by decree permanently appropriated to the organized peasant community, not to the individual household; the latter enjoys only rights of use and these are subject to redistribution. Economic activity is regulated by the rules imposed by the manorial or the political lord. This is *manorial* or *fiscal field community* (*Feldgemeinschaft*).

(e) *Unrestricted seigneurial land proprietorship* with exploitation of the dependent peasants as a source of rent income. The land is appropriated by the lord; but *coloni*,[47] sharecroppers, or tenants paying money rent carry out the actual economic activities.

(f) The *plantation*. The land is freely appropriated and worked by purchased slaves. The owner uses both as means of profit-making in a capitalistic enterprise with unfree labor.

(g) The "*estate economy*" (*Gutswirtschaft*). The land is appropriated to owners who either draw rent from it by leasing it to large-scale tenant farmers or farm it themselves for profit. In either case free labor is used, living in their own homesteads or those supplied by the landlord, and—in both cases again—conducting some agricultural production or, in the marginal case, none at all on own account.

(h) Absence of seigneurial ownership (*Grundherrschaft*): a peasant economy with appropriation of the land by the farmer (peasant). In practice this form of appropriation may mean that the land farmed is predominantly inherited land, or, on the other hand, that land lots are freely bought and sold. The former is typical of settlements with scattered farms and large-scale peasant proprietors; the latter, where settlement is in villages and the scale is small.[48]

Where tenants pay a money rent and where peasant proprietors buy and sell land, it is necessary to presuppose an adequate local market for the products of peasant agriculture.

(2) In the field of industry and transport, including mining, and of trade:

(a) *Household industry* carried on primarily as a means of occasional exchange of surpluses, only secondarily as a means of profit. This may involve an *inter-ethnic division of labor,* out of which in turn *caste occupations* have occasionally developed. In both cases appropriation of the sources of raw materials, and hence of the raw material production, is normal; purchase of raw materials and transformation of non-owned raw material ("wage work") are secondary phenomena. In the case of inter-ethnic specialization, *formal* appropriation is often absent. There is, however, generally, and in the case of caste, always, hereditary appropriation of the opportunities for earnings from specified functions by kinship or household groups.

(b) *"Tied" craft production* directly for customers: specification of functions in the service of an organized group of consumers. This may be a dominating group (*oikos* or seigneurial specification), or it may be a closed membership group (demiurgic specification).

There is no market sale. In the first case, we find organization of functions on a budgetary basis, or of labor in a workshop, as in the *ergasterion* of the lord. In the second case, there is hereditary appropriation of the status of the workers which may, however, become alienable, and work is carried out for an appropriated group of customers (consumers). There are the following very limited possibilities of development: (i) Appropriated (*formally* unfree) workers who are carriers of specified functions—of a trade—may be used either as a source of income payments to their owner, in which case they are usually and in spite of their formal servility *substantively* free, working in most cases directly for their own customers (rent slaves); or again, they might be used as unfree domestic craft producers, producing for the owner's profit; or, finally, as workers in the owner's workshop or *ergasterion,* also producing for profit. (ii) This may also develop into a liturgical specification of functions for fiscal purposes, similar to the type of caste occupations.

In the field of mining, there are similar forms, notably the use of unfree labor, slaves or serfs, in productive units controlled by princes or seigneurial owners.

In inland transportation, it is common for transportation installations [roads] to be appropriated by a seigneurial owner as a source of rent revenue. Maintenance services are then compulsorily imposed on specified small peasant holdings. Another possibility is small-scale caravan trade regulated by closed membership groups. The traders would then appropriate the goods themselves.

In the field of maritime transportation: (i) The ownership of ships by an *oikos,* a seigneur or a patrician trading on own account; (ii) co-operative construction and ownership of ships, captain and crew participating in trade on their own account, small travelling merchants constituting the shippers, all parties sharing the risks, and voyages made in strictly regulated "caravans." In all these cases "trade" was still identical with inter-local trade, that is, with transport.

(c) *Free non-agricultural trades.* Free production for consumers in return for a wage, either on the customer's premises or on that of the worker. Usually the raw materials were appropriated by the customer, the tools by the worker, premises and installations, if any were involved, by a lord as a source of income or by organized groups with rights of use in rotation. Another possibility is that both raw materials and tools should be appropriated by the worker who thus managed his own work, whereas premises and stationary equipment belonged to an organized group of workers, such as a guild. In all these cases, it is usual for the regulation of profit-making activity to be carried on by guilds.

In mining, deposits have usually been appropriated by political authorities or by seigneurial owners as sources of rent, while the rights of exploitation have been appropriated by organized groups of workers. Mining operations have been regulated on a guild basis with participation in the work an obligation of the members to the lord, who was interested in the rent, and to the working group (*Berggemeinde*), which was collectively responsible to him and had an interest in the proceeds.

In the field of inland transport, we find boatmen and teamster guilds with fixed rotation of travel assignments among the members and regulation of their opportunities for profit.

In the field of maritime transport, shared ownership of ships, travelling in convoys, and travelling merchants acting as *commenda* partners for businessmen staying at home are typical everywhere.

There are the following stages in the development toward capitalism:

(a) Effective monopolization of money capital by entrepreneurs, used as a means to make advances to labor. Connected with this is the assumption of powers of management over the process of production by virtue of the extension of credit, and of control over the product in spite of the fact that appropriation of the means of production has continued formally in the hands of the workers, as in the handicrafts and in mining; (b) appropriation of the right of marketing products on the basis of previous monopolization both of knowledge of the market and hence of market opportunities and of money capital. This was made possible by the imposition of a monopolistic system of guild regulation or by privileges granted by the political authority in return for periodical payments or for loans; (c) the subjective disciplining of workers who stood in a dependent relationship in the putting-out system, via the supply of raw materials and apparatus by the entrepreneur. A special case is that of the rational monopolistic organization of domestic industries on the basis of privileges granted in the interests of public finances or of the employment of the population. The conditions of work were thereby regulated by imposition from above as part of the concession which made profit-making activity possible; (d) the development of workshops *without* a rational specialization of labor in the process of production, by means of the appropriation by the entrepreneur of all the material means of production. In mining this included the appropriation by individual owners of mineral deposits, galleries, and equipment. In transportation, shipping enterprises fell into the hands of large owners. The universal result was the expropriation of the workers from the means of production; (e) the final step in the transition to capitalistic organization of production was the mechanization of the productive process and of transportation, and its orientation to capital accounting. All material means of production become fixed or working capital; all workers become "hands." As a result of the transformation of enterprises into associations of stock holders, the manager himself becomes expropriated and assumes the formal status of an "official." Even the owner becomes effectively a trustee of the suppliers of credit, the banks.

Of all these various types, the following instances may be noted:

1. In agriculture, type (a), migratory agriculture, is universal. But the sub-type where the effective unit has been the large-scale household or kinship group, is found only occasionally in Europe, quite frequently in East Asia, particularly China. Type (b), sedentary agriculture with land-use-regulating village associations, has been common in Europe and India. Type (c), seigneurial rights over the land with restrictions due to mutual obligations, has been found everywhere and is still common in some parts of the Orient. Type (d), seigneurial or fiscal rights over the land with systematic redistribution of the fields by the peasants, has existed in the more seigneurial type in Russia and in a variant involving the redistribution of land rents in India,[49] and in the more fiscal form in East Asia, the Near East, and Egypt. Type (e), unrestricted seigneurial land ownership drawing rent from small tenants, is typical of Ireland,

but also occurs in Italy, southern France, China, and the eastern parts
of the Hellenistic world in Antiquity. Type (f), the plantation with unfree labor, was characteristic of Carthage and Rome in Antiquity, of
modern colonial areas, and of the Southern States of the United States.
Type (g), the "estate economy" in the form which involves separation
of ownership and exploitation, has been typical of England; in the form
of owner management, of eastern Germany, parts of Austria, Poland,
and western Russia. Finally, type (h), peasant proprietorship, has been
found in France, southern and western Germany, parts of Italy, Scandi-
navia, with certain limitations in south-western Russia, and with modi-
fications particularly in modern China and India.

These wide variations in the forms which the organization of agriculture has finally assumed are only partially explicable in economic terms,
that is, from such factors as the difference between the cultivation of
forest clearings and of areas requiring irrigation. Special historical circumstances played a large role, and especially the forms taken by political
and fiscal obligations and military organization.

2. In the field of industry, the following outline of the distribution
of types may be given. Our knowledge of the situation in transportation
and mining is not sufficiently complete to give such an outline for those
fields.

(a) The first type, tribal crafts, has been found universally; (b) organization on the basis of occupational castes became general only in
India. Elsewhere it has existed only for occupations considered dis-
creditable and sometimes ritually impure; (c) the organization of industry on the basis of the *oikos* is found in all royal households in early
times, but has been most highly developed in Egypt. It has also existed
on seigneurial manors all over the world. Production by demiurgic crafts
was occasionally found everywhere, including the Western World, but
has developed into a pure type only in India. The special case of the use
of control over unfree persons simply as a source of rent was common
in Mediterranean Antiquity. The liturgical specification of functions was
characteristic of Egypt, of the Hellenistic period, of the later Roman
Empire, and has been found at times in China and India; (d) the free
handicraft organization with guild regulations is classically illustrated
in the European Middle Ages and became the predominant form only
there. It has, however, been found all over the world; and guilds, in
particular, have developed very widely, especially in China and the Near
East. It is notable, however, that this type was entirely absent from the
economic organization of the period of Mediterranean "classical" Antiquity. In India, the caste took the place of the guild. Of the stages in
the development toward capitalism, only the second was reached on a

large scale outside the Western World. This difference cannot be explained entirely in purely economic terms.

25. *Conditions Underlying the Calculability of the Productivity of Labor*

1. In the three typical communist forms of organization, non-economic motives play a predominant part (see below, sec. 26). But apart from these cases, there are three primary conditions affecting the optimization of calculable performance by labor engaged in carrying out specifications: (a) The optimum of aptitude for the function; (b) the optimum of skill acquired through practice; (c) the optimum of inclination for the work.

Aptitude, regardless of whether it is the product of hereditary or environmental and educational influences, can only be determined by testing. In business enterprises in a market economy this usually takes the form of a trial period. The Taylor system involves an attempt to work out rational methods of accomplishing this.

Practice, and the resulting skill, can only be perfected by rational and continuous specialization. Today, it is worked out on a basis which is largely empirical, guided by considerations of minimizing costs in the interest of profitability, and limited by these interests. Rational specialization with reference to physiological conditions is only in its beginnings (witness again the Taylor system).

Inclination to work may be oriented to any one of the ways which are open to any other mode of action (see above, ch. I, sec. 2). But in the specific sense of incentive to execute one's own plans or those of persons supervising one's work, it must be determined either by a strong self-interest in the outcome, or by direct or indirect compulsion. The latter is particularly important in relation to work which executes the dispositions of others. This compulsion may consist in the immediate threat of physical force or of other undesirable consequences, or in the probability that unsatisfactory performance will have an adverse effect on earnings.

The second type, which is essential to a market economy, appeals immensely more strongly to the worker's self-interest. It also necessitates freedom of selection according to performance, both qualitatively and quantitatively, though naturally from the point of view of its bearing on profit. In this sense it has a higher degree of formal rationality, from the point of view of technical considerations, than any kind of direct compulsion to work. It presupposes the expropriation of the workers from the means of production by owners is protected by force. As compared with direct compulsion to work, this system involves the transferral, in addition to the responsibility for reproduction (in the family), of part of the worries about selection according to aptitude to the workers themselves. Further, both the need for capital and the capital risks are, as compared with the use of unfree labor, lessened and made more calculable. Finally, through the payment of money wages on a large scale, the market for goods which are objects of mass consumption is broadened.

Other things being equal, positive motives for work are, in the absence of direct compulsion, not obstructed to the same extent as they are for unfree labor. It is true, however, that whenever technical specialization has reached very high levels, the extreme monotony of operations tends to limit incentives to purely material wage considerations. Only when wages are paid in proportion to performance on a piece-rate basis is there an incentive to increasing productivity. In the capitalistic system, the most immediate bases of willingness to work are opportunities for high piece-rate earnings and the danger of dismissal.

The following observations may be made about the situation of free labor separated from the means of production: (a) Other things being equal, the likelihood that people will be willing to work on *affectual* grounds is greater in the case of specification of functions than in that of specialization of functions. This is true because the product of the individual's own work is more clearly evident. In the nature of the case, this is almost equally true wherever the quality of the product is important; (b) *traditional* motivations to work are particularly common in agriculture and in home industries—both cases where also the *general* attitude toward life is traditional. It is characteristic of this that the level of performance is oriented either to products which are stereotyped in quantity and quality or to a traditional level of earnings, or both. Where such an attitude exists, it is difficult to manage labor on a rational basis, and production cannot be increased by such incentives as piece rates. Experience shows, on the other hand, that a traditional patriarchal relationship to a lord or owner is capable of maintaining a high level of affectual incentive to work; (c) motivations based on *absolute values* are usually the result of religious orientations or of the high social esteem in which the particular form of work as such is held. Observation seems to show that all other sources of motivations directed to ultimate values are only transitional.

It goes without saying that the "altruistic" concern of the worker for his own family is a typical element of duty contributing to willingness to work generally.

2. The appropriation of the means of production and personal con-

trol, however formal, over the process of work constitute one of the strongest incentives to unlimited willingness to work. This is the fundamental basis of the extraordinary importance of small units in agriculture, whether in the form of small-scale proprietorship or small tenants who hope to rise to the status of owner. The classical locus of this type of organization is China. The corresponding phenomenon in the functionally specified skilled trades is most marked in India, but it is very important in all parts of Asia and also in Europe in the Middle Ages. In the latter case, the most crucial conflicts have been fought out over the issue of formal autonomy of the individual worker. The existence of the small peasant in a sense depends directly on the absence of capital accounting and on retaining the unity of household and enterprise. His is a specified and not a specialized function, and he tends both to devote more intensive labor to it and to restrict his standard of living in the interest of maintaining his formal independence. In addition, this system of agriculture makes possible the use of all manner of by-products and even "waste" in the household in a way which would not be possible in a larger farm unit. All the information we have available goes to show that capitalistic organization in agriculture is, where management is in the hands of the owner, far more sensitive to cyclical movements than small-scale peasant farming (see the author's figures in the *Verhandlungen des deutschen Juristentags,* vol. xxiv). [49a]

In industry, the corresponding small-scale type has retained its importance right up to the period of mechanization and of the most minute specialization and combination of functions. Even as late as the sixteenth century, as actually happened in England [1555], it was possible simply to forbid the operation of workshops like that of "Jack of Newbury" without catastrophic results for the economic situation of the workers. This was true because the combination in a single shop of looms, appropriated by one owner and operated by workers, could not, under the market conditions of the time, without any far-reaching increase in the specialization and co-ordination of labor functions, lead to an improvement in the prospect of profit for the entrepreneur large enough to compensate with certainty for the increase in risk and the cost of operating the shop. Above all, in industry an enterprise with large investments in fixed capital is not only, as in agriculture, sensitive to cyclical fluctuations, but also in the highest degree to every form of irrationality—that is, lack of calculability—in public administration and the administration of justice, as it existed everywhere outside the modern Western World. It has hence been possible, as in the competition with the Russian "factory" and everywhere else, for decentralized domestic industry to dominate the field. This was true up to the point, which was reached *before* the introduction of mechanical power and machine tools, where, with the broadening of market opportunities, the need for exact cost accounting and standardization of product became marked. In combination with technically rational apparatus, using water power and horse-gins, this led to the development of economic enterprises with internal specialization. Mechanical motors and machines could then be fitted in. Until this point had been reached, it was possible for all the large-scale industrial establishments, which occasionally had appeared all over the world, to be eliminated again without any serious prejudice to the economic situation of all those involved in them and without any serious danger to the interest of consumers. This situation changed only with the appearance of the factory. But willingness to work on the part of factory labor has been primarily determined by a combination of the transfer of responsibility for maintenance to the workers personally and the corresponding powerful indirect compulsion to work, as symbolized in the English workhouse system, and it has permanently remained oriented to the compulsory guarantee of the property system. This is demonstrated by the marked decline in willingness to work at the present time which resulted from the collapse of this coercive power in the [1918] revolution.

26. *Forms of Communism*

Communist arrangements for the communal or associational organization of work which are indifferent to calculation are not based on a consideration of means for obtaining an optimum of provisions, but, rather, on direct feelings of mutual solidarity. They have thus tended historically, up to the present, to develop on the basis of common value attitudes of a primarily non-economic character. There are three main types: (1) The household communism of the family, resting on a traditional and affectual basis; (2) the military communism of comrades in an army; (3) the communism based on love and charity in a religious community.

Cases (2) and (3) rest primarily on a specific emotional or charismatic basis. Always, however, they either (a) stand in direct conflict with the rational or traditional, economically specialized organization of their environment; such communist groups either work themselves or, in direct contrast, are supported purely by contributions from patrons, or both. Or (b) they may constitute a budgetary organization of privileged persons, ruling over other household units which are excluded from their organization, and are supported by voluntary contributions or liturgies of the latter. Or (c) finally, they are consumer household units, distinct from any profit-making enterprises but drawing income from them, and thus in an associative relationship with them.

The first of these modes of support (a) is typical of communities based on religious belief or some *Weltanschauung*—such as monastic communities which renounce the world altogether or carry on communal labor, sectarian groups and utopian socialists.

The second mode (b) is typical of military groups which rest on a wholly or partially communistic basis. Examples are the "men's house" in many primitive societies, the Spartan *syssitia*, the Ligurian pirate groups, the entourage of Calif Omar, the communism, in consumption and partly in requisitioning, of armies in the field in every age. A similar state of affairs is found in authoritarian religious groups—as in the Jesuit state in Paraguay and communities of mendicant monks in India and elsewhere.

The third mode (c) is typical of family households in a market economy.

Willingness to work and consumption without calculation within these communities are a result of the non-economic attitudes characteristic of them. In the military and religious cases, they are to an appreciable extent based on a feeling of separateness from the ordinary everyday world and of conflict with it. Modern communist movements are, so far as they aim for a communist organization of the masses, dependent on "value-rational" appeals to their disciples, and on arguments from expediency (*zweckrational*) in their [external] propaganda. In both cases, thus, they rest their position on specifically *rational* considerations and, in contrast to the military and religious communities, on considerations concerned with the everyday profane world.[50] Their prospects of success under ordinary conditions rest on entirely different subjective conditions than those of groups which are oriented to exceptional activities, to other-worldly values, or to other primarily non-economic considerations.

27. *Capital Goods and Capital Accounting*

The embryonic forms of capital goods are typically found in commodities traded in inter-local [as against local] or inter-tribal exchange, provided that "trade" (see sec. 29) appears as an activity clearly distinct from the mere procurement of goods on a household (budgetary) basis. For the swapping (*Eigenhandel*) of household economies—trading-off of surpluses—cannot be oriented to capital accounting. The inter-tribally sold products of household, clan or tribal crafts are *commodities*, while the means of procurement, as long as they remain one's own output, are only tools or raw materials, but not capital goods. The same goes for the market products and means of procurement of the peasant and the feudal lord as long as economic activity is not oriented to capital accounting, if only in its most primitive forms such as were incipient already in [the manual on estate management of the elder] Cato.

It is obvious that the internal movement of goods within the domain of a feudal lord or of an *oikos,* including occasional exchange and the common forms of internal exchange of products, is the antithesis of trade based on capital accounting. The trade engaged in by an *oikos,* like that of the Pharaohs, even when it is not concerned solely with provision for need and thus does not act as a budgetary unit but as one oriented to profit, is not for present purposes necessarily capitalistic. This would only be the case if it were oriented to capital accounting, particularly to an ex-ante estimate in money of the chances of profit from a transaction. Such estimates were made by the professional travelling merchants, whether they were engaged in selling on *commenda* basis for others, or in disposing of goods co-operatively marketed by an organized group. It is here, in the form of "occasional" enterprise, that the source of capital accounting and of the use of goods as capital is to be found.

Human beings (slaves and serfs) and fixed installations of all types which are used by seigneurial owners as sources of rent are, in the nature of the case, only rent-producing household property and not capital goods, similar to the securities which today yield interest or dividends for a private investor oriented to obtain an income from his wealth and perhaps some speculative gains. Investment of this household type should be clearly distinguished from the temporary investment of business capital by an enterprise. Goods which a lord over land or persons receives from his dependents in payment of the obligations due him by virtue of his seigneurial powers, and then puts up for sale, are not capital goods for the present terminological purposes, but only commodities. In such cases capital accounting—and above all, estimates of cost—are lacking in principle, not merely in practice. On the other hand, where slaves are used in an enterprise as a means of profit, particularly where there is an organized slave market and widespread purchase and sale of slaves, they do constitute capital goods. Where corvée-based production units (*Fronbetriebe*) work with a labor force of (hereditary) dependents who are not freely alienable and transferable, we shall not talk of capitalistic economic establishments, but of profit-making economic establishments with bound labor, regardless of whether we are dealing with agricultural production or unfree household industry. The decisive aspect is whether the tie is mutual—whether the lord is also bound to the worker.

In industry, production for sale by free workers with their own raw materials and tools ("price work") is a case of small-scale capitalistic enterprise. The putting-out industry is capitalistic, but decentralized; whereas every case of an organized workshop under capitalistic control is centralized capitalistic organization. All types of "wage work" of occasional workers, whether in the employer's or in the worker's home, are mere forms of dependent work which are sometimes exploited in the interest of the budgetary economy, sometimes in the interest of the employer's profit.

The decisive point is thus not so much the empirical fact, but rather the theoretical possibility of the use of capital accounting.

28. *The Concept of Trade and Its Principal Forms*

In addition to the various types of specialized and specified functions, which have already been discussed, every market economy (even, normally, one subject to substantive regulation) knows another function: namely mediation in the process of disposing of a producer's own control over goods or acquiring such control from others. This function can be carried out in any one of the following forms: (1) By the members of the administrative staff of an organized economic group, in return for payments in kind or in money which are fixed or vary with the services performed; (2) by an organized group created especially to provide for the selling and purchasing needs of its members; (3) by the members of a specialized occupational group working for their own profit and remunerated by fees or commissions without themselves acquiring control of the goods they handle; they act, that is, as agents, but in terms of a wide variety of legal forms; (4) by a specialized occupational group engaged in trade as a capitalistic profit-making enterprise (trade on own account). Such persons purchase goods with the expectation of being able to resell them at a profit, or sell for future delivery with the expectation of being able to cover their obligations before that date at a profitable figure. This may be done by buying and selling entirely freely in the market or subject to substantive regulation; (5) by a continuous regulated process, under the aegis of an organized political group, of expropriation of goods against compensation and of voluntary or enforced disposal of these goods to customers, again against compensation: compulsory trade; (6) by the professional lending of money or procurement of credit for the purpose of effectuating business payments or for the acquisition of means of production on credit; such transactions may be with business enterprises or with other organized groups, particularly political bodies. The economic function of the credit may be to finance current payments or the acquisition of capital goods.

Cases (4) and (5), and only these, will be called "trade." Case (4) is "free" trade, case (5) "compulsory monopolistic" trade.

Type (1) is illustrated for budgetary units by the *negotiatores* and *actores* who have acted on behalf of princes, landlords, monasteries, etc., and for profit-making enterprises by various types of travelling salesmen; type (2) is illustrated by various kinds of co-operative buying and selling agencies, including consumers' co-operative societies; type (3) includes brokers, commission merchants, forwarding agents, insurance agents, and various other kinds of agents; type (4) is illustrated for the case of free market transactions by modern trade, and for the regulated case by various types of heteronomously imposed or autonomously agreed divisions of the market with an allocation of the transactions with certain customers or of the transactions in certain commodities, or by the substantive regulation of the terms of exchange by the order of a political body or some other type of co-operative group; type (5) is illustrated by the state monopoly of the grain trade.

29. *The Concept of Trade and Its Principal Forms— (Continued)*

Free trade on own account (type 4), which alone will be dealt with for the present, is always a matter of profit-making enterprise, never of budgetary administration. It is hence under all normal conditions, if not always, a matter of earning money profits by contracts of purchase and sale. It may, however, be carried on (a) by an organization subsidiary to a budgetary economy, or (b) it may be an inseparable part of a total function through which goods are brought to a state of local consumability.

Case (a) is illustrated by members of a budgetary unit designated specifically to dispose of surpluses of that unit's production on their own account. If, however, it is a matter simply of "occasional" sale by *different* members at *different* times, it is not even a subsidiary enterprise, but where the members in question devote themselves entirely and on their own financial responsibility to sale or purchase, it is an example of the type (4), though somewhat modified. If, on the other hand, they act for the account of the unit as a whole, it is a case of the type (1).

Case (b) is illustrated by peddlers and other small traders who travel *with* their goods, and who thus primarily perform the function of transporting goods to the place of sale. They have hence been mentioned above in connection with the function of transportation. Travelling *commenda* traders may be a transitional form between types (3) and

(4). Whether the transportation service is primary and the trading profit secondary, or *vice versa,* is generally quite indefinite. In any case, all persons included in these categories are "traders."

Trade on the individual's own account (type 4) is always carried on on the basis of appropriation of the means of procurement, even though his control may be made possible only by borrowing. It is always the trader who bears the capital risk on his own account; and, correspondingly, it is he who, by virtue of his appropriation of the means of procurement, enjoys the opportunity for profit.

Specialization and specification of functions in the field of free trade on own account may take place in a variety of different ways. From an economic point of view, it is for the present most important to distinguish them according to the types of economic unit between which the merchant mediates: (i) Trade between households (budgetary units) with a surplus and other households which consume the surplus; (ii) trade between profit-making enterprises, themselves producers or merchants, and households (budgetary units) which consume the product. The latter include, of course, all types of organizations, in particular, political bodies; (iii) trade between one profit-making enterprise and another.

The first two cases come close to what is usually called "retail trade," which involves sale to consumers without reference to the sources from which the goods were obtained. The third case corresponds to "wholesale trade."

Trade may be oriented to the market or to customers. In the former case it may be a consumers' market, normally with the goods actually present. It may, on the other hand, be a market for business enterprises, in which case the goods may actually be present, as at fairs and expositions (usually though not necessarily, seasonal), or the goods may not be present, as in trade on commodity exchanges (usually, though not necessarily, permanent). If trade is oriented directly to customers, providing for the needs of a relatively fixed group of purchasers, it may be to households (budgetary units), as in retail trade, or to profit-making enterprises. The latter may in turn be producing units or retail enterprises or, finally, other wholesale enterprises. There may be various levels of middlemen in this sense, varying from the one nearest the producers to the one who sells to the retailer.

According to the geographical source of the goods disposed of, trade may be "interlocal" or "local."

The merchant may be in a position in fact to secure purchases on his own terms from the economic units which sell to him—putting-out trade. He may, on the other hand, be in a position to dictate the terms of his sales to the economic units which buy from him—traders' monopoly.

The first type is closely related to the putting-out organization of industry and is generally found combined with it. The second is "substantively regulated" trade, a variety of type (4).

It goes without saying that every market-oriented business enterprise must dispose of its own goods, even if it is primarily a producing enterprise. This type of marketing is not, however, "mediation" in the sense of the above definition so long as no members of the administrative staff are specialized for this and only this purpose (such as travelling salesman). Only then is a specialized "trading" function being performed. There are, of course, all manner of transitional forms.

The calculations underlying trading activity will be called "speculative" to the extent to which they are oriented to possibilities, the realization of which is regarded as fortuitous and is in this sense uncalculable. In this sense the merchant assumes the burden of "uncertainty."[51] The transition from rational calculation to what is in this sense speculative calculation is entirely continuous, since no calculation which attempts to forecast future situations can be completely secured against unexpected "accidental" factors. The distinction thus has reference only to a difference in the *degree* of rationality.

The forms of technical and economic specialization and specification of function in trade do not differ substantially from those in other fields. The department store corresponds to the factory in that it permits the most extensive development of internal specialization of function.

29a. The Concept of Trade and Its Principal Forms— (Concluded)

The term "banks" will be used to designate those types of profit-making "trading" enterprise which make a specialized function of administering or procuring money.

Money may be administered for private households by taking private deposit accounts and caring for the property of private individuals. It may also be administered for political bodies, as when a bank carries the account of a government, and for profit-making enterprise, by carrying business deposits and their current accounts.

Money may be procured for the needs of budgetary units, as in extending private consumption credit to private individuals, or in extending credit to political bodies. It may be procured for profit-making enterprises for the purpose of making payments to third persons, as in the creation of bills of exchange or the provision of checks or drafts for remittances. It may also be used to make advances on future payments due from customers, especially in the form of the discounting of bills of exchange. It may, finally, be used to give credit for the purchase of capital goods.

Formally, it is indifferent whether the bank (I) advances this money from its own funds or promises to make it available on demand, as in the provision for over-drafts of a current account, and whether the loan is or is not accompanied by a pledge or any other form of security provided by the borrower; or, (2) whether the bank, by some type of guarantee or in some other manner, influences others to grant the funds.

In practice, the business policy of banks is normally aimed to make a profit by relending funds which have been lent to them or placed at their disposal.

The funds which a bank lends may be obtained from stocks of bullion or of coin from the existing mints which it holds on credit, or by its own creation of certificates (*banco*-money) or of means of circulation (bank notes), or, finally, from the deposits of private individuals who have placed their money at its disposal.

Whether a bank borrows on its own to obtain the funds it lends out or creates means of circulation, it must, if it is acting rationally, attempt to provide for coverage to maintain its liquidity—that is, it must keep a sufficient stock of cash reserves or arrange the terms of credit granted in such a manner that it can always meet its normal payment obligations.

As a rule, the observance of liquidity ratios by money-creating (i.e., note-issuing) banks is provided for in imposed regulations by organizations (merchant guilds or political bodies). These regulations are at the same time usually designed to protect the chosen monetary system of an area as far as possible against changes in the substantive validity of the money, and thus to protect the (formal) rationality of the economic calculations of budgetary units, above all those of the political body, and of profit-making enterprises against disturbances from (substantive) irrationalities. In particular, the most stable rate of exchange possible for one's own money against the monies of other monetary areas, with which trade or credit relations exist or are desired, is usually striven for. This type of monetary policy, which attempts to control the factors of irrationality in the monetary field, will, following G. F. Knapp, be called "lytric" policy. In the strictly laissez-faire state, this is the most important function in the realm of economic policy which the state would undertake. In its rational form this type of policy is entirely restricted to the modern state.

The policy measures of the Chinese with respect to copper and paper money and the Roman coinage policy will be discussed at the proper point, but they did not constitute a modern lytric monetary policy. Only the *banco*-money policy of the Chinese guilds, which formed the model for the Hamburg *banco* mark, came up to modern standards of rational-ity.[52]

The term "financing" (*Finanzierungsgeschäfte*) will be applied to all business transactions which are oriented to obtaining control, in one of the following ways, of favorable opportunities for profit-making by busi-ness enterprise, regardless of whether they are carried on by banks or by other agencies, including individuals, as an occasional source of profit or as a subsidiary enterprise, or as part of the speculative operations of a "financier": (a) through the transformation of rights to appropriated profit opportunities into securities or other negotiable instruments, and by the acquisition of these securities, either directly or through such subsidiary enterprises as are described below under (c); (b) by the sys-tematic tender (or, occasionally, refusal) of business credit; (c) through compulsory joining, if necessary or desired, of hitherto competing enter-prises, either (i) in the form of monopolistic regulation of enterprises at the same stage of production (cartellization), or (ii) in the form of monopolistic fusion under one management of hitherto competing enter-prises for the purpose of weeding out the least profitable ones (merger), or (iii) in the not necessarily monopolistic form of the fusion of special-ized enterprises at successive stages of a production process (vertical com-bination), or finally (iv) in the form of an attempted domination of many enterprises through operations with their shares (trusts, holding companies) or the creation of new enterprises for the purpose of increas-ing profits or merely to extend personal power (financing as such).

> Of course, financing operations are often carried out by banks and, as a general rule, unavoidably involve their participation. But the main control often lies in the hands of stock brokers, like Harriman, or of individual large-scale entrepreneurs in production, like Carnegie. The formation of cartels is also often the work of large-scale entrepreneurs, like Kirdorf; while that of trusts is more likely to be the work of "finan-ciers," like Gould, Rockefeller, Stinnes, and Rathenau. This will be further discussed below.

30. *The Conditions of Maximum Formal Rationality of Capital Accounting*

The following are the principal conditions necessary for obtaining a maximum of formal rationality of capital accounting in production enter-prises: (1) complete appropriation of all material means of production by owners and the complete absence of all formal appropriation of op-portunities for profit in the market; that is, market freedom; (2) complete autonomy in the selection of management by the owners, thus complete absence of formal appropriation of rights to managerial functions; (3) complete absence of appropriation of jobs and of opportunities for earning by workers and, conversely, the absence of appropriation of workers by owners. This implies free labor, freedom of the labor market, and freedom in the selection of workers; (4) complete absence of substantive regulation of consumption, production, and prices, or of other forms of regulation which limit freedom of contract or specify conditions of exchange. This may be called substantive freedom of contract; (5) complete calculability of the technical conditions of the production process; that is, a mechanically rational technology; (6) complete calculability of the functioning of public administration and the legal order and a reliable purely formal guarantee of all contracts by the political authority. This is a formally rational administration and law; (7) the most complete separation possible of the enterprise and its conditions of success and failure from the household or private budgetary unit and its property interests. It is particularly important that the capital at the disposal of the enterprise should be clearly distinguished from the private wealth of the owners, and should not be subject to division or dispersion through inheritance. For large-scale enterprises, this condition tends to approach an optimum from a formal point of view: in the fields of transport, manufacture, and mining, if they are organized in corporate form with freely transferrable shares and limited liability, and in the field of agriculture, if there are relatively long-term leases for large-scale production units; (8) a monetary system with the highest possible degree of formal rationality.

Only a few points are in need of comment, though even these have already been touched on.

(1) With respect to the freedom of labor and of jobs from appropriation, it is true that certain types of unfree labor, particularly full-fledged slavery, have guaranteed what is formally a more complete power of disposal over the worker than is the case with employment for wages. But there are various reasons why this is less favorable to rationality and efficiency than the employment of free labor: (a) The amount of capital which it was necessary to invest in human resources through the purchase and maintenance of slaves has been much greater than that required by the employment of free labor; (b) the capital risk attendant on slave ownership has not only been greater but specifically irrational in that slave labor has been exposed to all manner of non-economic influences, particularly to political influence in a very high degree; (c) the slave market and correspondingly the prices of slaves have been particularly subject to fluctuation, which has made a balancing of profit and loss on a rational basis exceedingly difficult; (d) for similar reasons,

particularly involving the political situation, there has been a difficult problem of recruitment of slave labor forces; (e) when slaves have been permitted to enjoy family relationships, this has made the use of slave labor more expensive in that the owner has had to bear the cost of maintaining the women and of rearing children. Very often, he has had no way in which he could make rational economic use of these elements as part of his labor force; (f) hence the most complete exploitation of slave labor has been possible only when they were separated from family relationships and subjected to a ruthless discipline. Where this has happened it has greatly accentuated the difficulties of the problem of recruitment; (g) it has in general been impossible to use slave labor in the operation of tools and apparatus, the efficiency of which required a high level of responsibility and of involvement of the operator's self-interest; (h) perhaps most important of all has been the impossibility of selection, of employment only after trying out in the job, and of dismissal in accordance with fluctuations of the business situation or when personal efficiency declined.

Hence the employment of slave labor has only been possible in general under the following conditions: (a) Where it has been possible to maintain slaves very cheaply; (b) where there has been an opportunity for regular recruitment through a well-supplied slave market; (c) in agricultural production on a large scale of the plantation type, or in very simple industrial processes. The most important examples of this type of relatively successful use of slaves are the Carthaginian and Roman plantations, those of colonial areas and of the Southern United States, and the Russian "factories." The drying up of the slave market, which resulted from the pacification of the Empire, led to the decay of the plantations of Antiquity.[53] In North America, the same situation led to a continual search for cheap new land, since it was impossible to meet the costs of slaves and pay a land rent at the same time. In Russia, the serf "factories" were barely able to meet the competition of the *kustar* type of household industry and were totally unable to compete with free factory labor. Even before the emancipation of the serfs, petitions for permission to dismiss workers were common, and the factories decayed with the introduction of shops using free labor.

When workers are employed for wages, the following advantages to industrial profitability and efficiency are conspicuous: (a) Capital risk and the necessary capital investment are smaller; (b) the costs of reproduction and of bringing up children fall entirely on the worker. His wife and children must seek employment on their own account; (c) largely for this reason, the risk of dismissal is an important incentive to the maximization of production; (d) it is possible to select the labor force according to ability and willingness to work.

(2) The following comment may be made on the separation of enterprise and household. The separation in England of the producing farm *enterprise,* leasing the land and operating with capital accounting, from the entailed *ownership* of the land is by no means fortuitous, but

is the outcome of an undisturbed development over centuries which was characterized by the absence of an effective protection of the status of peasants. This in turn was a consequence of the country's insular position. Every joining of the *ownership* of land with the *cultivation* of the land turns the land into a capital good for the economic unit, thus increasing the capital requirements and the capital risks of this unit. It impedes the separation of the household from the economic establishment; the settlements paid out at inheritance, for instance, burden the resources of the enterprise. It reduces the liquidity of the entrepreneur's capital and introduces a number of irrational factors into his capital accounting. Hence the separation of landownership from the organization of agricultural production is, from a formal point of view, a step which promotes the rationality of capital accounting. It goes without saying, however, that any substantive evaluation of this phenomenon is quite another matter, and its conclusions may be quite different depending on the values underlying the judgment.

31. *The Principal Modes of Capitalistic Orientation of Profit-Making*

The "capitalistic" orientation of profit-making activity (in the case of rationality, this means: the orientation to capital accounting) can take a number of qualitatively different forms, each of which represents a definite type:

1. It may be orientation to the profit possibilities in continuous buying and selling on the market ("trade") with free exchange—that is, absence of formal and at least relative absence of substantive compulsion to effect any given exchange; or it may be orientation to the profit possibilities in continuous production of goods in enterprises with capital accounting.

2. It may be orientation to the profit possibilities in trade and speculation in different currencies, in the taking over of payment functions of all sorts and in the creation of means of payment; the same with respect to the professional extension of credit, either for consumption or for profit-making purposes.

3. It may be orientation to opportunities for predatory profit from political organizations or persons connected with politics. This includes the financing of wars or revolutions and the financing of party leaders by loans and supplies.

4. It may be orientation to the profit opportunities in continuous business activity which arise by virtue of domination by force or of a position of power guaranteed by the political authority. There are two

main sub-types: colonial profits, either through the operation of planta-tions with compulsory deliveries or compulsory labor or through monopo-listic and compulsory trade, and fiscal profits, through the farming of taxes and of offices, whether at home or in colonies.

5. It may be orientation to profit opportunities in unusual transac-tions with political bodies.

6. It may be orientation to profit opportunities of the following types: (a) in purely speculative transactions in standardized commodities or in the securities of enterprises; (b) in the execution of the continuous financial operations of political bodies; (c) in the promotional financing of new enterprises in the form of sale of securities to investors; (d) in the speculative financing of capitalistic enterprises and of various other types of economic organization with the purpose of a profitable regula-tion of market situations or of attaining power.

Types (1) and (6) are to a large extent peculiar to the modern West-ern World. The other types have been common all over the world for thousands of years wherever the possibilities of exchange and money economy (for type 2) and money financing (for types 3–5) have been present. In the Western World they have not had such a dominant importance as modes of profit-making as they had in Antiquity, except in restricted areas and for relatively brief periods, particularly in times of war. Where large areas have been pacified for a long period, as in the Chinese and later Roman Empire, these types have tended to decline, leaving only trade, money changing, and lending as forms of capitalistic acquisition. For the capitalistic financing of political activities was every-where the product of the competition of states with one another for power, and of the corresponding competition for capital which moved freely between them. All this ended only with the establishment of the unified empires.

> The point of view here stated has, if the author's memory is accurate, been previously put forward in the clearest form by J. Plenge in his *Von der Diskontpolitik zur Herrschaft über den Geldmarkt* (Berlin 1913). Before that a similar position seems to have been taken only in the author's article, "*Agrarverhältnisse im Altertum,*" 1909 [reprinted in *GAzSW*, 1924; cf. 275ff.]

It is only in the modern Western World that rational capitalistic enterprises with fixed capital, free labor, the rational specialization and combination of functions, and the allocation of productive functions on the basis of capitalistic enterprises, bound together in a market economy, are to be found. In other words, we find the capitalistic type of organization of labor, which in formal terms is purely voluntary, as the typical and dominant mode of providing for the wants of the masses of the population, with expropriation of the workers from the means of production and appropriation of the enterprises by security owners. It is also only here that we find public credit in the form of issues of government securities, the "going public" of business enterprises, the floating of security issues and financing carried on as the specialized function of rational business enterprises, trade in commodities and securities on organized exchanges, money and capital markets, monopolistic organizations as a form of rational business organization of the entrepreneurial *production* of goods, and not only of the trade in them.

This difference calls for an explanation and the explanation cannot be given on economic grounds alone. Types (3) to (5) inclusive will be treated here together as "politically oriented capitalism." The whole of the later discussion will be devoted particularly to the problem of explaining the difference. In general terms, it is possible only to make the following statements:

1. It is clear from the very beginning that the politically oriented events and processes which open up these profit opportunities exploited by political capitalism are irrational from an economic point of view— that is, from the point of view of orientation to market advantages and thus to the consumption needs of budgetary units.

2. It is further clear that purely speculative profit opportunities and pure consumption credit are irrational from the point of view both of want satisfaction and of the production of goods, because they are determined by the fortuitous distribution of ownership and of market advantages. The same may also be true of opportunities for promotion and financing, under certain circumstances; but this is not necessarily always the case.

Apart from the rational capitalistic enterprise, the modern economic order is unique in its monetary system and in the commercialization of ownership shares in enterprises through the various forms of securities. Both these peculiarities must be discussed—first the monetary system.

32. *The Monetary System of the Modern State and the Different Kinds of Money: Currency Money*

1. (a) The modern state has universally assumed the monopoly of regulating the monetary system by statute; and (b) almost without exception, the monopoly of creating money, at least for coined money.

Originally, purely fiscal considerations were decisive in the creation of this monopoly—seigniorage (minting fees) and other profits from coinage. This was the motive for the prohibition of the use of foreign money. But the monopolization of issue of money has not been universal even up into the modern age. Thus, up until the currency reform [of 1871–1873] foreign coins were current in Bremen.

(c) With the increasing importance of its taxation and its own economic enterprises, the state has become both the largest receiver and the largest maker of payments in the society, either through its own pay offices or through those maintained on its behalf. Quite apart from the monopoly of monetary regulation and issue, because of the tremendous importance of the financial transactions of the state the behavior of the state treasurers in their monetary transactions is of crucial significance for the monetary system—above all, what kind of money they *actually* have at hand and hence can pay out, and what kind of money they force on the public as legal tender, and further, what kind of money they *actually* accept and what kind they partially or fully repudiate.

Thus, paper money is partially repudiated if customs duties have to be paid in gold, and was fully repudiated (at least ultimately) in the case of the *assignats* of the French Revolution, the money of the Confederate States of America, and that issued by the Chinese Government during the Tai Ping Rebellion.

In terms of its legal properties, money can be defined as a "legal means of payment" which everyone, including also and especially the public pay offices, is obligated to accept and to pay, either up to a given amount or without limit. In terms of the behavior of the state (*regiminal*) it may be defined as that money which public pay offices accept in payment and for which they in turn enforce acceptance in their payments; legal compulsory money is that money, in particular, which they impose in their payments. The "imposition" may occur by virtue of existing legal authority for reasons of monetary policy, as in the case of the [German silver] Taler and the [French silver] five-franc piece after the discontinuance—as we know, never really put into effect—of the coining of silver [1871 and 1876]; or it may occur because the state is incapable of paying in any other means of payment. In the latter case, an existing legal authority to enforce acceptance may now be employed for the first time, or an *ad hoc* legal authority may be created, as is almost always true in cases of resort to paper money. In this last case, what usually happens is that a means of exchange, which was previously by law or *de facto* redeemable in definitive money, whether its acceptance could be legally imposed or not, will now be *de facto* imposed and by the same token become *de facto* unredeemable.

By passing a suitable law, a state can turn any object into a "legal means of payment" and any chartal object into "money" in the sense of a means of payment. It can establish for them any desired set of "value scales" or, in the case of "market money," "currency relations" [see above, ch. II, sec. 6]. There are, however, certain formal disturbances of the monetary system in these cases which the state can either not suppress at all or only with great difficulties:

(a) In the case of administrative money, the forgery of notes, which is almost always very profitable; and (b) with all forms of metallic money, the non-monetary use of the metal as a raw material, where its products have a high value. This is particularly true when the metal in question is in an undervalued currency relation to others. It is also, in the case of market money, exceedingly difficult to prevent the export of the coins to other countries where that currency metal has a higher value. Finally, it is difficult to compel the offer of a legal monetary metal for coinage where it is undervalued with respect to the currency money (coins or paper).

With paper money the rate of exchange of one currency unit of the metal with its nominal equivalent of paper always becomes too unfavorable for the metal when redeemability of the notes is suspended, and this is what happens when it is no longer possible to make payments in metal money.

The exchange ratios between several kinds of market money may be determined (a) by fixing the relation for each particular case; (b) by establishing rates periodically; and (c) by legal establishment of permanent rates, as in bimetallism.

In cases (a) and (b) it is usual that only one metal is the effective currency (in the Middle Ages it was silver), while the others are used as trading coins with varying rates. The complete separation of the specific modes of use of different types of market money is rare in modern monetary systems, but has at times been common, as in China and in the Middle Ages.

2. The definition of money as a legal means of payment and as the creature of the "lytric" administration of political bodies is, from a sociological point of view, not exhaustive. This definition, to put it in G. F. Knapp's words, starts from "the fact of the existence of debts,"[54] especially of tax debts to the state and of interest debts of the state. What is relevant for the legal discharge of such debts is the continuity of the *nominal* unit of money, even though the monetary material may have changed, or, if the nominal unit should change, the "historical definition" of the new nominal unit. Beyond that, the individual today values the nominal unit of money as a certain proportional part of his nominal money income, and not as a chartal piece of metal or note.

The state can through its legislation—or its administrative staff through the actual behavior of its pay offices—indeed dictate the *formal* validity of the "currency" of the monetary area which it rules.

> Provided, that is, that it employs modern methods of administration. It was not, however, possible at all times, for instance, in China. There in earlier times it has generally not been possible because payments by and to the government were too small in relation to the total field of transactions. Even recently it appears that the Chinese Government has not been able to make silver into a "limited money" currency with a gold reserve because it was not sufficiently powerful to suppress the counterfeiting which would undoubtedly have ensued.

However, it is not merely a matter of dealing with existing debts, but also with exchange in the present and the contraction of new debts to be paid in the future. But in this connection the orientation of the parties is primarily to the status of money as a means of exchange [see above, ch. II, sec. 6], and thus to the probability that it will be at some future time acceptable in exchange for specified or unspecified goods in price relationships which are capable of approximate estimate.

> 1. Under certain circumstance, it is true, the probability that urgent debts can be paid off to the state or private individuals from the proceeds may also be importantly involved. This case may, however, be left out of account here because it only arises in emergency situations.
> 2. In spite of the fact that it is otherwise absolutely correct and brilliantly executed, hence of permanently fundamental importance, it is at this point that the incompleteness of G. F. Knapp's *Staatliche Theorie des Geldes* becomes evident.

Furthermore, the state on its part needs the money which it receives through taxation or from other sources also as a means of exchange, though not only for that purpose, but often in fact to a very large extent for the payment of interest on its debt. But its creditors, in the latter case, will then wish to employ it as a means of exchange; indeed this is the main reason why they desire money. And it is almost always true that the state itself needs money to a large degree, sometimes even entirely, as a means of exchange to cover future purchases of goods and supplies in the market. Hence, however necessary it is to distinguish it analytically, it is not, after all, the fact that money is a means of payment which is decisive.

The exchange possibility of money against other specific goods, which rests on its valuation in relation to marketable goods, will be called its "substantive" validity, as opposed to its formal, legal validity as a means of payment and the frequently existing legal compulsion for its formal use as a means of exchange.

In principle, as an observable fact, a monetary unit has a substantive valuation only in relation to definite types of goods and only for each separate individual as his own valuation on the basis of the marginal utility of money for him, which will vary with his income. This marginal utility is changed for the individual with any increase in the quantity of money at his disposal. Thus the marginal utility of money to the issuing authority falls, not only, but above all, when it creates administrative money and uses it for obtaining goods by exchange or forces it on the public as a means of payment. There is a secondary change in the same direction for those persons who deal with the state and who, because of the higher prices resulting from the lowered marginal utility of money to public bodies, become the possessors of larger money stocks. The "purchasing power" now at their disposal—that is, the lowering of the marginal utility of money for these possessors—can in turn result in an increase in prices paid to those from whom *they* purchase, etc. If, on the other hand, the state were to withdraw from circulation part of the notes it receives—that is, if it should not pay them out again, but destroy them—the result would be that the marginal utility of money of its lessened money stocks would rise, and it would have to curtail its expenditures correspondingly, that is, it would reduce its demand prices appropriately. The results would be the exact opposite of those just outlined. It is hence possible for administrative money, though by no means only this, to have an important effect on the price structure in any given monetary area. (The speed at which this will occur and the different ways in which it affects different goods cannot be discussed here).

3. A cheapening and increase in the supply, or vice versa, a rise in cost and curtailment of the supply in the production of monetary metals could have a similar effect in *all* countries using it for monetary purposes. Monetary and non-monetary uses of metals are closely interdependent, but the only case in which the non-monetary use of the metal has been decisive for its valuation as money has been that of copper in China. Gold will enjoy an equivalent valuation in the nominal unit of gold money less costs of coining as long as it is used as a means of payment between monetary areas and is also the market money in the monetary areas of the leading commercial powers. In the past this was true also of silver and would be today if silver were still in the same position as gold. A metal which is not used as a means of payment between monetary areas, but constitutes market money in some of them, will naturally have a definite value in terms of the nominal monetary unit of those areas. But these in turn will, according to the costs of adding to the supply and according to the quantities in circulation, and, finally, according

to the so-called "balance of payments," have a fluctuating exchange relationship to other currencies. Finally, a precious metal which is universally used for restricted coinage into administrative money, but not as
market money, is primarily valued on the basis of its non-monetary use.
The question is always whether the metal in question can be profitably
produced and at what rate. When it is completely demonetized, this
valuation depends entirely on its money cost of production reckoned in
international means of payment in relation to the non-monetary demand
for it. If, on the other hand, it is used universally as market money and
as an international means of payment, its valuation will depend on costs
in relation primarily to the monetary demand for it. When, finally, it has
a limited use as market or administrative money, its valuation will be
determined in the long run by whichever of the two demands for it, as
expressed in terms of international means of payment, is able to afford
better to pay the costs of production. If its use as market money is
limited to a particular monetary area, it is unlikely in the long run that
its monetary use will be decisive for the valuation, for the exchange rate
of such special-standard areas to other monetary areas will tend to fall,
and it is only when international trade is completely cut off—as in China
and Japan in the past, and in the areas still actually cut off from each
other after the war today—that this will not affect domestic prices. The
same is true for the case of a metal used as regulated [i.e., limited
coinage] administrative money; the strictly limited possibility of the use
of the metal as money could be decisive for its valuation only if it would
be minted in great quantities. The long-run outcome would in this case,
however, be similar to that of a metal used as market money only in a
restricted area.

> Though it was temporarily realized in practice in China, the monop-
> olization of the total production and use of a monetary metal is essen-
> tially a theoretical, limiting case. If several competing monetary areas
> are involved and wage labor is used, it does not alter the situation as
> much as possibly might be expected. For if all payments by government
> agencies were made in terms of this metal, every attempt to limit its
> coinage or to tax it very heavily, which might well yield large profit,
> would have the same result as it did in the case of the very high Chinese
> seigniorage. First, in relation to the metal the money would become
> very highly valued, and if wage labor were used, mining operations
> would to a large extent become unprofitable. As the amount in circula-
> tion declined, there would result a "contra-inflation"; and it is possible,
> as actually happened in China where this led at times to complete
> freedom of coinage, that this would go so far as to induce the use of
> money substitutes and a large extension of the area of natural economy.
> This also happened in China. If a market economy were to be main-

tained, it would be hardly possible for monetary policy in the long run to act otherwise than as if free coinage were legally in force. The only difference is that minting would no longer be left to the initiative of interested parties. With complete socialism, on the other hand, the problem of money would cease to be significant and the precious metals would hardly be produced at all.

4. The fact that the precious metals have normally become the monetary standard and the material from which money is made is historically an outcome of their function as ornaments and hence, specifically, as gifts. But apart from purely technical factors, this use was also determined by the fact that they were goods which were typically dealt with by weight. Their maintenance in this function is not at first sight obvious since today, for all except the smallest payments, everyone normally uses notes, especially bank-notes, and expects to receive them in payment. There are, however, important motives underlying retention of metal standards.

5. In all modern states, not only is the issue of money in the form of notes legally regulated, but it is monopolized by the state. It is either carried out directly by the state itself, or by one or a few issuing agencies enjoying special privileges but subject to the control of the state—the banks of issue.

6. The term "public currency money" (*regiminales Kurantgeld*)[55] will be applied only to money which is actually paid out by public agencies and acceptance of which is enforced. On the other hand, any other money which, though not paid out under compulsory acceptance, is used in transactions between private individuals by virtue of formal legal provisions, will be called "accessory standard money." Money which must legally be accepted in private transactions only up to a given maximum amount, will be called "change" (*Scheidegeld*). (This terminology is based on that of Knapp. This is even more definitely true in what follows.)

"Definitive" currency money means public currency money; whereas any type of money is to be called "provisional" currency money so far as it is in fact effectively exchangeable for or redeemable in terms of definitive currency.

7. In the long run, public currency money must naturally coincide with the effective currency. It cannot be a possibly separate, merely "official" legal tender currency. Effective currency, however, is necessarily one of three things: (a) free market money; (b) unregulated; or (c) regulated administrative money. The public treasury does not make its payments simply by deciding to apply the rules of a monetary system which somehow seems to it ideal, but its acts are determined by its own financial interests and those of important economic groups.

With regard to its chartal form, an effective standard money may be metallic money or note money.[56] Only metallic money can be a free market money, but this is not necessarily the case for all metallic money.

It is free market money when the lytric administration will coin any quantity of the standard metal or will exchange it for chartal coins— "hylodromy."[57] According, then, to the precious metal which is chosen as the standard, there will be an effective gold, silver, or copper standard. Whether the lytric administration is in fact in a position to maintain an actual hylodromic system does not depend simply on its own desires, but on whether individuals are interested in presenting metal for coinage.

It is thus possible for hylodromy to exist "officially" without existing "effectively." Whatever the official position may be, it is not effective (a) when, given hylodromy with several metals, one or more of these is at the official rate *under*valued with respect to the market price of the raw material. In that case, naturally, only the *over*valued metal will be offered to the mint for coinage and to creditors in payments. If the public pay offices do not participate in this trend, the *over*valued coins will pile up in their hands until they, too, have nothing else to offer in their payments. If the price relation is rigidly enough maintained, the *under*valued coins will then be melted down, or they will be exchanged by weight, as commodities, against the coins of the *over*valued metal.

(b) Hylodromy is also not effective if persons making payments, including especially public agencies under stress of necessity, continually and on a large scale make use of their formal right or usurped power to compel acceptance of another means of payment, whether metal or notes, which is not presently provisional [i.e. redeemable] money, but either has been accessory money or, if previously provisional, has ceased to be redeemable because of the insolvency of the issuing agency.

In case (a) hylodromy always ceases, and the same thing happens in case (b) when accessory forms of money or forms which are no longer effectively provisional are forced on the public persistently on a large scale.

The outcome in case (a) is to confine the maintenance of the fixed rate to the overvalued metal, which then becomes the only free market money; the result is thus a new·metallic standard. In case (b) the accessory metal or notes which are no longer effectively provisional become the standard money. In the first case we get a "restricted money" standard; in the second, a paper standard.

It is also possible for hylodromy to be effective without being official in the sense of being legally established.

An example is the competition of the various coining authorities in the Middle Ages, determined by their fiscal interest in seigniorage, to mint as much as possible of the monetary metals. There was no formal establishment of hylodromy at that time, but the actual situation was much as if there had been.

In view of what has just been said, a "monometallic legal standard," which may be gold, silver, or copper, will be said to exist when one metal is by law hylodromic. A "multimetallic legal standard," on the other hand, exists when more than one metal is used (it may be two or three) and they are freely coined in a fixed ratio to each other. A "parallel legal standard" exists when several metals are freely coinable *without* a fixed ratio. A standard metal and a metallic standard will only be spoken of for that metal which is effectively hylodromic, and thus, in practice, constitutes actual market money.

Legally, all countries of the Latin Union were under bimetallism until the suspension of the free coinage of silver, which followed the German currency reform [1871]. But effectively, as a rule, only the metal which was for the time being overvalued was actually a standard metal. The legal stabilization of the exchange ratio, however, worked so well that the change was often scarcely noted and there seemed to be effective bimetallism. But insofar as the ratio shifted, the coins of the undervalued money became accessory money. (This account of the matter coincides closely with that of Knapp). At least where there is competition between several autocephalous and autonomous minting agencies, bimetallism is an effective monetary state only as a transitory phenomenon and is usually only a legal, as opposed to an effective, state of affairs.

The fact that the undervalued metal is not brought to the mint is naturally the result not of administrative action, but of the changed market situation in relation to the persistence of the legal coinage ratio of the metals. It would, of course, be possible for the mint to continue to coin that metal at a loss as administrative money, but since the non-monetary uses of the money are more profitable, it could not be kept in circulation.

33. *Restricted Money*

Any type of metallic money which is not hylodromic will be called "restricted money" (*Sperrgeld*) if it is currency money. Restricted money may circulate as accessory money; that is, having a fixed relationship to some other currency money in the same monetary area. This latter may be another form of restricted money, paper money, or a market money.

Or restricted money may be oriented to an international standard. This is the case when it is the sole currency money in its own area, and provision is made for having international means of payment available for making payments abroad, either in coin or in bullion. This is a "convertible restricted money" standard with a reserve fund of foreign exchange.

(a) Restricted money will be called "particular" when it is the only currency money, but is not oriented to an international standard.

Restricted money may then be valued internationally *ad hoc* each time international means of payment or foreign exchange is bought; or, when this is possible, it may be given a fixed relation to the international standard. Talers and silver five-franc pieces were restricted money with a fixed relation to the currency money of the same country; both were accessory money. The Dutch silver gulden has been oriented to the international gold standard after having been "particular" for a short time after the restriction of coinage, and now the rupee is in the same position. This is also true of the Chinese dollar which, since the coinage regulation of 24 May 1910, is "particular" as long as hylodromy, which is not mentioned in the statute, does also *de facto* not exist. The orientation to the international gold standard, as recommended by the American Commission, was rejected.

In the case of a "restricted" money, free coinage at fixed rates (hylodromy) would be very profitable to the private owners of the precious metals. Nevertheless, and precisely for this reason, restriction is maintained because it is feared that the introduction of hylodromy of the metal of the formerly restricted money would lead to abandonment as unprofitable of the hylodromy of the other metal which was fixed in too low a ratio to it. The monetary stock of this metal, which would now become "obstructed" (see next paragraph), would be put to more profitable non-monetary uses. The reason why a rational lytric administration wishes to avoid this is that the other metal, which would be forced out, is an international means of payment.

(b) Restricted currency money will be called "obstructed" market money when, contrary to the case just cited, free coinage exists legally, but is unprofitable to private business and hence does not take place. This lack of profitability may rest on an unfavorable relation between the market price of the metal and its monetary ratio to the market money, if a metal, or to paper money. Such money must at some time in the past have been market money; but, with multimetallism, changes in the relative market prices of the metals or, with multi- or monometallism, financial catastrophes, must have made the payment of metallic money by the government impossible and must have forced it to adopt paper money and to make it irredeemable. In consequence the private business preconditions of effective hylodromy have ceased to exist. This money will then no longer be used in transactions—at least, insofar as action is rational.

(c) Apart from restricted currency money, which alone has been called "restricted money" here, there may be restricted "change" money —that is, money which must be accepted as means of payment only up to a given amount. Usually, though not necessarily, it is then intentionally coined at a rate which overvalues it in relation to standard coin to protect it from being melted down. Usually, then, it has the status of provisional money in that it is redeemable at certain places. (This case is a phenomenon of everyday experience and has no special importance for present purposes.)

All "change" money and many types of restricted metallic money occupy a place in monetary systems similar to that of note (today: paper) money. They differ from it only in that the monetary metal has a non-monetary use which is of some importance. Restricted metallic money is very nearly a means of circulation when it is provisional money; that is, when there is adequate provision for redemption in market money.

34. *Note Money*

Note money naturally is always administrative money. For the purposes of a sociological theory of money, it is always the specific chartal form of the document including the specific formal meaning printed on it which constitutes "money," and not the claim to something else which it may, though it need not, represent. Indeed, in the case of unredeemable paper money, such a claim is altogether absent.

From a formal legal point of view, note money may consist in (at least officially) redeemable certificates of indebtedness, acknowledged by a private individual, as in the case of the English goldsmiths in the seventeenth century, by a privileged bank, as in the case of bank-notes, or by a political body, as in the case of government notes. If it is effectively redeemable and thus functions only as a circulating medium or provisional money, it may be fully covered—thus constituting a certificate—or it may be covered only sufficiently to meet normal demands for redemption, which makes it a circulating medium. Coverage may be in terms of specified weights of bullion (as in the case of a *banco-currency*) or of metal coin.

It is almost always the case that note money has first been issued as a reedemable form of provisional money. In modern times, it has been typically a medium of circulation, almost always in the form of bank-notes. They have therefore been denominated in terms of units of an existing metallic standard.

1. The first part of the last paragraph, naturally, is not true of cases where one form of note money has been replaced by another; for example, where government notes have been replaced by bank-notes, or vice versa. But this is not a case of a primary issue of money.

2. It is of course true that means of exchange and of payment may exist which do not take a chartal form, i.e., are not coins or notes or other material objects. There is no doubt of this. It is not, however, expedient to speak of these as "money," but to use the term "unit of account" or some other term which, according to the particular case, is appropriate. It is characteristic of money that it is associated with particular quantities of chartal artifacts. This is a property which is very far from being merely external or of secondary importance.

If what has previously been provisional money has its redeemability suspended, it is important to distinguish whether the interested parties regard this as a temporary measure or as definitive for as long as they can predict. In the first case it would be usual, since metallic money or bullion is sought after for all international payments, for the note money to fall to a discount in relation to its nominal metal equivalent. This is not, however, by any means inevitable; and the discount is often moderate. The discount may, however, become large if the need for foreign exchange is very acute. In the second case, after a time a definitive "paper money standard" will develop. Then it is no longer appropriate to speak of a "discount" on the monetary unit, but rather, at least in the usage of the past, of "debasement."

It is not beyond the range of possibilities that the market price of the metal of the former market money, which is now obstructed, and in terms of which the issue is denominated, may for some reason fall radically relative to international means of payment, while the fall in the value of the paper currency is less marked. This must have the result (as it actually did in Austria and Russia) that what was earlier the nominal unit in terms of weight of the metal (of silver in those two cases) could now be purchased with a smaller nominal amount in the notes, which had now become independent of it. That is readily understandable. Thus, even though in the initial stages of a pure paper standard the unit of paper money is probably without exception valued in international exchange at a lower figure than the same nominal amount of metal, because this step always results from inability to pay, the subsequent development depends, as in the cases of Austria and Russia, on the development of the balance of payments which determines the foreign demand for domestic means of payment, on the amount of paper money issued, and on the degree of success with which the issuing authority is able to obtain an adequate supply of international means of payment. These three factors can (and in fact at times did) shape up in such a way that the exchange rate against the international means of payment —in this case: gold—of the paper money is increasingly stabilized or even rises, while at the same time the earlier standard metal falls in price relative to the international standard. In the case of silver, this happened (vis-à-vis gold) because of the increased and cheapened production of the metal and because of its progressive demonetization. A true independent paper standard exists in the case where there is no longer any prospect of effective resumption of redemption in terms of metal at the former rate.

35. *The Formal and Substantive Validity of Money*

It is true that by law and administrative action a state can today insure the *formal* validity of a type of money as the standard in its own area of power, provided it remains itself in a position to make payments in this money.

It will not remain in a position to do this if it has allowed what was previously an accessory or provisional type of money to become free market money (in the case of a metallic money) or autonomous paper money (in the case of note money). This is because these types of money will then accumulate in the hands of the government until it commands no other kind and is hence forced to impose them in its own payments. (Knapp has rightly maintained that this is the normal process in the case of "obstructional" changes in the standard.)

But naturally this formal power implies nothing as to the *substantive* validity of money; that is, the rate at which it will be accepted in exchange for commodities. Nor does it yield any knowledge of whether and to what extent the monetary authorities can influence its substantive validity. Experience shows that it is possible for the political authority to attain, by such measures as the rationing of consumption, the control of production, and the enforcement of maximum or minimum prices, a high degree of control of this substantive validity, at least with respect to goods or services which are present or produced within its own territory. It is equally demonstrable from experience, however, that there are exceedingly important limits to the effectiveness of this kind of control, which will be discussed elsewhere. But in any case, such measures obviously do not belong in the category of monetary administration. The rational type of modern monetary policy has, on the contrary, had quite a different aim. The tendency has been to attempt to influence the substantive valuation of domestic currency in terms of foreign currency, that is, the market price of the home currency expressed in units of foreign currencies, usually to maintain stability or in some cases to attain the highest possible ratio. Among the interests determining such policy are those of prestige and political power. But on the economic side, the decisive ones are financial interest, with particular reference to future foreign loans, and other very powerful business interests, notably of importers and of industries which have to use raw materials from abroad. Finally, the interests as consumers of those elements in the population which purchase imported goods are involved. Today there can be no doubt that "lytric" policy is in fact primarily concerned with regulation of the foreign exchanges.

> Both this and what follows are closely in agreement with Knapp. Both in its form and content, his book is one of the greatest masterpieces of German literary style and scientific acumen. It is unfortunate that most of the specialist critics have concentrated on the problems which he deliberately ignored—a small number indeed (although in some cases not altogether unimportant).

While England probably still came into the gold standard somewhat reluctantly, because silver, which was desired as the official standard, was undervalued by the official ratio, all the other states in the modern world with a modern form of organization have chosen their monetary standard with a view to the most stable possible exchange relation with the English gold standard. They chose either a pure gold standard, a gold standard with restricted accessory silver money, or a restricted silver or regulated note standard with a lytric policy concerned primarily with the maintenance of gold reserves for international payments. The adoption of pure paper standards has always been a result of political catastrophe, wherever this has been the only way to meet the problem of inability to pay in what was previously the standard money. This is happening on a large scale today.[58]

It seems to be true that for the purpose of stabilizing foreign exchange in relation to gold, the free coinage of fixed rates of gold in one's own monetary system is not the only possible means. The parity of exchange between different types of hylodromic chartal gold coinage can in fact become seriously disturbed, although it is true that the possibility of obtaining international means of payment in case of need by means of exporting and recoining gold is always greatly improved by internal hylodromy and can be temporarily negated only through natural obstacles to trade or embargoes on the export of gold as long as this hylodromy exists. But on the other hand it is also true, as experience shows, that under normal peace-time conditions it is quite possible for an area with a well-ordered legal system, favorable conditions of production and a lytric policy which is deliberately oriented to procuring adequate foreign exchange for international payments, to maintain a relatively stable exchange rate. Yet, if other things are equal, this involves markedly higher burdens to state finances and to persons in need of gold. Exactly the same would be true, of course, if silver were the principal means of payment in international transactions and were recognized as such in the principal trading nations of the world.

36. *Methods and Aims of Monetary Policy*

Among the more elementary of the typical methods (specific measures will not in general be dealt with here) of lytric policy in relation to foreign exchange are the following:

(a) In countries with gold hylodromy: (1) The backing of the circulating medium, so far as it is not covered by gold, with commercial paper; that is, claims to payments for goods which have been sold, which are guaranteed by safe persons or, in other words, proved entrepreneurs. The transactions of the note issuing banks on their own account are as far as possible limited to dealing with such bills, to making loans on the security of stocks of goods, to the receipt of deposits, the clearing of check payments, and, finally, acting as financial agent for the state; (2) the "discount policy" of the banks of issue. This consists in raising the rate of interest charged on bills discounted when there is a probability that payments abroad will create a demand for gold sufficient to threaten the internal stock of gold, especially that in the hands of the issuing bank. The purpose is to encourage owners of foreign balances to take advantage of the higher rate of interest and to discourage domestic borrowing.

(b) In areas with a restricted metal standard other than gold or with a paper standard, the following are the principal measures: (1) Discount policy similar to that described under (a:2) in order to check undue expansion of credit; (2) a gold-premium policy. This is a measure which is also common in gold-standard areas with an accessory restricted silver currency; (3) a deliberate policy of gold purchases and deliberate control of the foreign exchange rate by purchase and sale of foreign bills.

This policy is in the first instance oriented purely to lytric considerations, but under certain circumstances it may come to involve substantive regulation of economic activity. The note-issuing banks occupy a position of great power in the system of commercial banks, since the latter are often dependent on the credit extended by the bank of issue.

The bank of issue may influence the other banks to regulate the money market, that is, the conditions on which short-term credit is given, in a uniform way, and from there proceed to a deliberate regulation of business credit, thereby influencing the direction of the production of goods. This is, within the framework of a capitalistic economic order, the closest approach to a planned economy. It is formally merely a matter of voluntary adjustments, but actually involves substantive regulation of economic activity within the territory controlled by the political authority in question.

These measures were all typical before the war. They were used in the interest of a monetary policy which was primarily oriented to the stabilization of a currency or, in case changes were desired, as in countries with restricted or paper money, at most to attempts to bring about a gradual rise in the foreign exchange value of the currency. It was, thus, in the last analysis, oriented to the hylodromic monetary systems of the most important trading nations.

But strong interests exist which desire just the reverse policy. They favor a lytric policy of the following type: (1) Measures which would lead to a fall in the foreign exchange price of their own money in order to improve the position of exporting interests; (2) by increasing the issue of money through free coinage of silver in addition to gold (which would have meant *instead of* it), and even in some cases deliberate issue of paper money, to decrease the value of money in relation to domestic goods and thereby, what is the same thing, to raise the money prices of domestic goods. The object has been to improve prospects for profit in the production of such goods, an increase in the price of which as reckoned in terms of domestic currency was thought to be the first consequence of the increase of the amount of domestic money in circulation and of the attendant fall in its foreign exchange value. The intended process is termed "inflation."

The following points may be noted: (1) though its quantitative importance is still controversial, it is very probable that with any type of hylodromy a very great cheapening in the production of the precious metal or other source of increase in its supply, as through very cheap forced seizures, will lead to a noticeable tendency toward a rise in the prices at least of many products in areas where that metal is the monetary standard, and in differing degrees of all products. (2) It is at the same time an undoubted fact that, in areas with an independent paper standard, situations of severe financial pressure, especially war, lead the monetary authorities to orient their policy overwhelmingly to the financial requirements of the war. It is equally clear that countries with hylodromy or with restricted metallic money have, in similar circumstances, not only suspended redemption of their notes in circulation, but have gone further to establish a definitive and pure paper standard. But in the latter case, the metal money, now become accessory money, could, because its premium in relation to notes is ignored, only be used for non-monetary purposes. It thus disappeared from circulation. Finally, it is a fact that in cases of such shifts to a pure paper standard, occurring along with unlimited issue of paper money, inflation has in fact ensued with all its consequences on a colossal scale.

When all these processes are compared, it will be seen that so long as freely coined market money exists, the possibility of inflation will be narrowly limited. This will be true in the first place for mechanical reasons: though it is somewhat elastic, the quantity of the precious metal in question available for monetary use is ultimately firmly limited. Secondly, there are economic reasons in that here the creation of money takes place on the initiative of private interests, so that the demand for coinage is oriented to the needs of the market system for means of payment. Inflation, then, is only possible if restricted metal money (such as today silver in gold-standard countries) is thrown open to free coinage. However, if the restricted metal can be produced very cheaply and in large quantities, the effect may be very great.

Inflation through an increase in the quantity of "means of circulation" is conceivable only as the result of a very gradual increase in the circulation through a lengthening of credit terms. The limits are elastic, but in the last resort this process is strictly limited by the necessity for maintaining the solvency of the note-issuing bank. There is acute danger of inflation only if there is danger that the bank will become insolvent. Normally this is likely to occur only where there is a paper standard resulting from war needs. (Cases like the gold inflation of Sweden during the war, resulting from the export of war materials, are the result of such special circumstances that they need not be considered here.)

Where an independent paper standard has once been established, there may not be any greater danger of inflation itself (since in time of war almost all countries soon go over to a paper standard), but in general there is a noticeably greater possibility of the development of the consequences of inflation. The pressure of financial difficulties and of the increased wage and salary demands and other costs which are caused by the higher prices will noticeably strengthen the tendency of financial administrations to continue the inflation even if there is no absolute necessity to do so and in spite of the possibility to suppress it if strong sacrifices are incurred. The differences in this respect between paper currency and other currencies is, even if only quantitative, certainly noticeable, as the financial conduct [during and after the War] of the

Allies as a group, of Germany, and of both Austria and Russia finally, can show.

Lytric policy may thus, especially in the case of accessory restricted metal or of paper money, be an inflationary policy. In a country which, like the United States, has had relatively so little interest in the foreign exchange value of her money, this has been true for a time under quite normal conditions without being based on any motives derived from financial needs of the state. In a number of countries which fell into inflationary measures during the War, the pressure of necessity has been such as to lead to the continuance of an inflationary policy afterwards.

This is not the place to develop a theory of inflation. Inflation always means, in the first place, a particular way of increasing the purchasing power of certain interests. We will only note that any lytric policy oriented to the *substantive* rationality of a planned economy, which it would seem to be far easier to develop with administrative and especially paper money, is at the same time far more likely to come to serve interests which, from the point of view of exchange rate stabilization, are irrational. For *formal* rationality (of the market-economy type) of lytric policy, and hence of the monetary system, can, in conformity with the definition of "rationality" consistently held to here, only mean: the exclusion of all such interests which are either not market-oriented, like the financial interests of the state, or are not interested in the maintenance of stable exchange relations with other currencies as an optimum basis for rational calculation, but which, on the contrary, are primarily oriented to the creation of purchasing power for certain interest groups by means of inflation and to its maintenance even if there is no longer any need for the issue of new money from the point of view of public finances. Whether especially this latter process is to be praised or censured is, naturally, not a question capable of solution on empirical grounds. Of its empirical existence there can be no doubt.

It is furthermore true that proponents of a point of view which is oriented to *substantive* social ideals can find a very important opening for criticism in the very fact that the creation of money and currency is, in a pure market economy, made an object of the play of interests oriented only to profitability, and is not considered in terms of the "right" volume or the "right" type of money. They might with reason argue that it is only administrative money which can be "managed," but not market money. Thus the use of administrative money, especially paper money, which can be cheaply produced in any desired form and quantity is, from the point of view of a *substantive* rationality, whatever its goals, the only correct way to handle the monetary question. This argument is conclusive in formal logical terms. Its value, however, is naturally limited in view of the fact that in the future as in the past it will be the "interests" of individuals rather than the "ideas" of an economic administration which will rule the world.[59] Thus, the possibility of conflict between *formal* rationality in the present sense and the *substantive* rationality which could theoretically be constructed for a lytric authority entirely free of any obligation to maintain hylodromy of a metal, has been demonstrated also for this point. That was the sole purpose of this discussion.

It is evident that this whole treatment of money consists only in a kind of discussion with Knapp's magnificent book, *Die Staatliche Theorie des Geldes,* a discussion which is, however, confined to points relevant to the present problems and carried out on a highly schematic basis, entirely neglecting the finer points. Quite at variance with its author's intentions, though perhaps not entirely without fault on his part, the work immediately was utilized in support of value judgments. It was naturally greeted with especial warmth by the Austrian lytric administration, with its partiality to paper money. Events have by no means disproved Knapp's theory in any point, though they have shown, what was known beforehand, that it is incomplete in its treatment of the *substantive* validity of money. It will now be necessary to justify this statement in more detail.

36a. Excursus: *A Critical Note on the "State Theory of Money"*

Knapp victoriously demonstrates that in every case the recent monetary policy both of states themselves and of agencies under the direction of the state have, in their efforts to adopt a gold standard or some other standard approximating this as closely as possible, been primarily concerned with the exchange value of their currency in terms of others, particularly the English. The object has been to maintain a certain exchange parity with the English gold standard, the money of the world's largest trading area which was universally used as a means of payment in international trade. To accomplish this, Germany first demonetized silver; then France, Switzerland, and the other countries of the Latin Union, Holland, and finally India ceased to treat silver as market money and made it into restricted money. Apart from this they undertook indirectly gold-hylodromic measures to provide for foreign payments in gold. Austria and Russia did the same, in that the lytric administration of these countries using unredeemable, independent paper money took indirectly gold-hylodromic measures so as to be in a position to make at

least foreign payments in gold at any time. They were thus concerned
entirely with obtaining the greatest possible stability of their foreign
exchange rates. Knapp concludes from this that stabilization of the
foreign exchange rate is the only factor which makes the particular
monetary material and hylodromy at all significant. He concludes that
this end of foreign exchange rate stability is served just as well by the
indirectly hylodromic measures of the paper currency administrations (as
in Austria and Russia) as by directly hylodromic measures. His claim is
not, to be sure, strictly and literally true under *ceteris paribus* conditions
for areas of full hylodromy in the same metal. For, as long as two areas
which maintain a hylodromic coinage in the same metal refrain from
embargoes on the exportation of the monetary metal, whether they are
both gold-standard or silver-standard countries, the fact of the existence
of the same hylodromy on both sides undoubtedly facilitates the maintenance of exchange parity considerably. Yet, under normal conditions
Knapp's conclusion is to a large extent correct. But this does not prove
that in the choice of a monetary material—above all today in the choice
between a metal, whether gold or silver, and note money—this would
be the only set of considerations which could be important. (The special
circumstances which are involved in bimetallism and restricted money
have already been discussed and can reasonably be left aside here.)

Such a claim would imply that a paper standard and a metallic standard behave in all other respects in the same way. But even from a formal
point of view the difference is significant. Paper money is necessarily a
form of administrative money, which may be true of metallic money,
but is not necessarily so. It is impossible for paper money to be "freely
coined." The difference between depreciated paper money, such as the
assignats, and the type of depreciation of silver which might at some
future time result from its universal demonetization, making it exclusively an industrial raw material, is not negligible; it is true, however,
that Knapp occasionally grants this. Paper has been and is today (1920)
by no means a freely available good, just as the precious metals are not.
But the difference, both in the objective possibility of increased production and in the costs of production in relation to probable demand, is
enormous, since the production of metals is to a relative degree so definitely dependent on the existence of mineral deposits. This difference
justifies the proposition that a lytric administration was, before the war,
in a position to produce paper money, if it so desired, in unlimited
quantities. This is a significant difference even from copper, as used in
China, certainly from silver, and very decidedly from gold. The costs
would be, relatively speaking, negligible. Furthermore, the nominal
value of the notes could be determined arbitrarily and need bear no

particular relation to the amount of paper used. In the case of metallic money, this last has been true only of its use as "change" money; thus not in any comparable degree or sense. It was certainly not true of currency metal. In the latter case, the available quantity was indeed somewhat elastic, but nevertheless immensely more rigidly limited than the produceability of paper. This fact has imposed limits on the arbitrariness of monetary policy. It is of course true that, so far as the lytric administration has been oriented exclusively to the maintenance of the greatest possible stability of foreign exchange rates, it would be subject to very definite normative limitations on its creation of note money, even though not to technical limitations. This is the answer Knapp might well give, and in giving it he would be right, although only from a formal point of view. And how about fully "independent" paper money? The situation is the same, Knapp would say, pointing to Austria and Russia: "only" the purely technical limitations imposed by the scarcity of monetary metals are absent. The question is, whether this absence is an altogether unimportant difference—a question which Knapp ignores. "Against death," he might say, meaning that of a currency, "no potion has yet been found." If the present (1920) absolute and abnormal obstruction of paper production be ignored, there unquestionably have been and still are certain factors tending to unlimited issue of paper money. In the first place, there are the interests of those in political authority who, as Knapp also assumes, bear ultimate responsibility for monetary policy, and there are also certain private interests. Both are not of necessity primarily concerned with the maintenance of stable foreign exchange rates. It is even true, at least temporarily, that their interests might lie in the directly opposite direction. These interests can, either from within the political and monetary administration or by exercising a strong pressure on it, have an important influence on policy which would lead to "inflation" or what Knapp, who strictly avoids the term, could only describe as a case of the issue of paper money which is not "admissible" because it is not oriented to the international rate of exchange.

There are, in the first place, financial temptations to resort to inflation. An average depreciation of the German mark by inflation to 1/20th of its former value in relation to the most important domestic commodities and property objects would—once profits and wages had become adapted to this level of prices—mean, it may here be assumed, that all internal commodities and labor services would nominally be valued 20 times as high as before. This would further mean, for those in this fortunate situation, a reduction of the war debt to 1/20th of its original level. The state, which would receive a proportionate increase in its income from taxation as nominal money incomes rose, would at least enjoy important relief from this source. This is indeed an attractive prospect. It is clear that someone would have to bear the costs, but it would be neither the state nor one of these two categories of private individuals, entrepreneurs and wage earners. The prospect is even more attractive of being able to pay old foreign debts in a monetary unit which can be manufactured at will and at negligible cost. Apart from the possibility of political intervention, there is of course the objection that the use of this policy toward foreign loans would endanger future credit. But the state is often more concerned with the present than with the more or less remote future. Furthermore, there are entrepreneurs who would be only too glad to see the prices of their products increased twenty-fold through inflation if, as is altogether possible, the nominal wages of workers, because of lack of bargaining power or through lack of understanding of the situation or for any other reason, were to increase "only" five- or possibly ten-fold.

It is usual for acute inflation from public finance motives of this kind to be sharply disapproved by experts in economic policy. It is certainly not compatible with Knapp's form of exchange-rate oriented monetary policy. On the other hand, a deliberate but very gradual increase of the volume of means of circulation, of the type which is sometimes undertaken by central banks by facilitating the extension of credit, is often looked upon favorably as a means of stimulating speculative attitudes. By holding out prospect of greater profits, it is held to stimulate the spirit of enterprise and with that an increase in capitalistic production by encouraging the investment of free money in profit-making enterprise, rather than its investment in fixed-interest securities. We have to ask, however, what is the effect of this more conservative policy on the stability of the exchange rate? Its direct effect—that is, the consequences of the stimulation of the spirit of enterprise—may be to create a more favorable balance of payment, or at least to check the fall in the foreign exchange position of the domestic currency. How often this works out and how strong the influence is, is, of course, another question. Also, no attempt will here be made to discuss whether the effects of a moderate increase in the volume of currency caused by state requirements for money would be similar. The costs of such an expansion of the stock of currency money, which would be relatively harmless to the foreign exchange position, would be gradually paid by the same groups which would be subject to "confiscation" in a case of acute inflation. This includes all those whose nominal income remains the same or who have securities with a constant nominal value, above all, the receivers of fixed-interest bond income, and those who earn salaries which are "fixed" in that they can be raised only through a severe struggle. It is thus not possible to interpret Knapp as meaning that it is only the stability of foreign exchange which is significant as a criterion for the management of paper money; indeed, he does not claim this. Nor is it legitimate to believe, as he does, that there is a very high probability that this will empirically be the only criterion. It cannot, however, be denied that it would indeed be the decisive criterion of a lytric policy which is completely rational in Knapp's sense, that is, one which seeks as far as possible to prevent disturbances of the price relations resulting from monetary policies (a definition which Knapp does not himself spell out). But it cannot be admitted, and Knapp does not claim this either, that the practical significance of the kind of monetary policy formulated is limited to the question of the stability of foreign exchange rates.

Inflation has here been spoken of as a source of price revolutions or at least slow price level increases, and it has been pointed out that it may be caused by the desire to bring about such price level changes. Naturally, an inflation so extensive as to create a price revolution will inevitably upset the stability of foreign exchange; though this is by no means necessarily true of gradual increases in the circulating medium. Knapp would admit that. He obviously assumes, and rightly, that there is no place in his theory for a currency policy concerned with commodity prices, whether it be revolutionary, evolutionary, or conservative. Why does he do this? Presumably for the following formal reasons:

The exchange relationship between the standards of two or more countries is expressed daily in a small number of formally unambiguous and uniform market prices of currencies, which can be used as a guide to a rational lytric policy. It is further possible for a lytric authority, especially one concerned with the means of circulation, to make certain estimates (but only *estimates,* based on anterior demand conditions periodically observed in the market) of the probable fluctuations of a given stock of means of payment which will be required, for payment purposes alone, by a given population linked in market relationships over a certain future period, provided conditions in general remain approximately unchanged. But it is not possible to estimate in the same sense, quantitatively, the effect on prices—revolutionary or gradual increase, or perhaps a decrease—of a currency expansion or contraction over a certain future period. To do this, it would, in the case of inflation, to which attention will be confined, be necessary to know the following additional facts: (1) The existing distribution of income; (2) connected with this, the present policy conclusions derived therefrom of the different individuals engaged in economic activity; (3) the channels the inflationary process would follow, that is, who would be the primary and subsequent recipients of newly-issued money. This would involve knowing the sequence in which nominal incomes are raised by the inflation and the extent to which this would take place; (4) the way in which the newly-created demand for goods would be exercised, for consumption, for building up property investments, or for new capital. This would be important quantitatively, but even more so qualitatively; (5) the direction of the consequent changes in prices and of the further income changes resulting in turn, and all the innumerable further attendant phenomena of purchasing power redistribution, and also the volume of the (possible) stimulated increase in goods production. All these are data which would depend entirely on the decisions made by individuals when faced with the new economic situation. And these decisions would in turn react on the expectations as to prices of other individuals; only the consequent struggle of interests can determine the actual future prices. In such a situation there can clearly be no question of forecasting in the form of such predictions as that the issue of an additional billion of currency units would result in increases in the pig-iron price of "X" or in the grain price of "Y." The prospect is made even more difficult by the fact that it is possible temporarily to establish effective price regulation of domestic commodities, even though these can only be maximum and not minimum prices and their effectiveness is definitely limited. But even if this impossible task of calculating specific prices were accomplished, it would be of relatively little use. This would only determine the amount of money required as a means of payment, but in addition to this, and on a much larger scale, money would be required in the form of credit as a means of obtaining capital goods. Here, possible consequences of a proposed inflationary measure are involved which are inaccessible to any kind of accurate forecasting. It is thus understandable that, all things considered, Knapp should have entirely neglected the possibility of inflationary price policies being used in the modern market economy as a deliberate rational policy comparable to that of maintenance of foreign exchange stability.

But historically the existence of such policies is a fact. To be sure, in a crude form and under much more primitive conditions of money economy, inflation and deflation have been repeatedly attempted with the Chinese copper currency, though they have led to serious failures. In America, inflation has been proposed. Knapp, however, since his book operates on the basis only of what he calls demonstrable assumptions, contents himself with giving the advice that the state ought to be careful in the issue of independent paper money. Since he is entirely oriented to the criterion of exchange rate stability, this advice *appears* to be relatively unequivocal; inflationary debasement and depreciation in foreign exchange are usually very closely associated. But they are not identical, and it is far from true that every inflation is primarily caused by the foreign exchange situation. Knapp does not explicitly admit, but neither does he deny, that an inflationary money regime has been urged for reasons of price policy among others by the American silver producers during the free silver campaign and by the farmers who demanded "greenbacks," but not only in these cases. It is probably comforting to him that it has never been successful over a long period.

But the situation is by no means so simple as this. Whether or not they have been *intended* simply to raise the price level, inflations of this sort have in fact often taken place; and even in the Far East, to say nothing of Europe, such catastrophes as met the *assignats* are by no means unknown. This is a fact which a *substantive* theory of money must deal with. Knapp, of all people, certainly would not maintain that there is no difference whatever between the depreciation of silver and the depreciation of the *assignats*. Even formally this is not the case. What has been depreciated is not silver coin, but, on the contrary, the raw silver for industrial purposes. Coined chartal silver, on the contrary, being restricted, has often had the opposite fate. On the other hand, it was not the paper available for industrial purposes which was "depreciated," but only the chartal *assignats*. It is true, as Knapp would rightly point out, that they would fall to zero or to their values to collectors or as museum pieces only when they had finally been repudiated by the state. Thus even this results from a "state" action. This may be granted, but their material value may have fallen to a minute proportion of what it formerly was, before their formal repudiation, in spite of the fact that they were still nominally valid for making payments of public obligations.

But quite apart from such catastrophes, history provides a considerable number of examples of inflation, and, on the other hand, in China, of deflationary movements as a result of non-monetary use of monetary metals. It is necessary to do more than merely to note that under some circumstances certain kinds of money which were not accessory before, have become so, have tended to accumulate in the hands of the state, and have rendered obstructional changes in the standard necessary. A substantive theory of money should at least formulate the question as to how prices and income, and hence the whole economic system, are influenced in such cases, even though it is, for the reasons which have been given, perhaps questionable how far it will be able to achieve a theoretical solution. Similarly, a problem is suggested by the fact that, as a result of relative decline in the prices of either silver or gold in terms of the other, France, which has been formally a country of bimetallism, in fact has operated at times on a gold standard alone, and at others on a silver standard, while the other metal became accessory. In such a case it is not sufficient merely to call attention to the fact that the resulting price changes originate from a *monetary* source. The same is true in other cases where the monetary material has been changed. We also want to know what are the sources of an increase in the supply of a precious metal, whether it has stemmed from booty (as in the case of Cortez and Pizarro), from enrichment through trade (as in China early in the Christian era and since the sixteenth century), or from an increase of production. So far as the latter is the source, has production merely increased, or has it also become cheaper, and why? What is the part which may have been played by changes in the non-monetary uses of the metal? It may be that for a particular economic area, as, for instance, the Mediterranean area in Antiquity, a definitive export has taken place to an entirely distinct area like China or India, as happened in the early centuries of the Christian era. Or the reasons may lie wholly or partly in a change in the monetary demand arising from changes in customs touching the use of money, such as use in small transactions. How all these and various other possibilities tend to affect the situation is a subject which ought to be discussed in a monetary theory.

Finally, it is necessary to discuss the regulation of the "demand" for money in a market economy, and to inquire into the meaning of this concept. One thing is clear, that it is the actual demand for means of payment on the part of the parties to market relationships which determines the creation of free market money under free coinage. Furthermore, it is the effective demand for means of payment and, above all, for credit, on the part of market participants, in combination with care for the solvency of the banks of issue and the norms which have been established with this in view, which determines the policies for means of circulation of modern banks of issue. All this is oriented to the requirements of interested parties, as is in conformity with the general character of the modern economic order.

It is only this which, under the formal legal conditions of our economic system, can correctly be called "demand for money." This concept is thus quite indifferent with respect to substantive criteria, as is the related one of effective demand for goods. In a market economy there is an inherent limit to the creation of money only in the case of metallic money. But it is precisely the existence of this limit, as has already been pointed out, which constitutes the significance of the precious metals for monetary systems. The restriction of standard money to a material which is not capable of unlimited production at will, particularly to one of the precious metals, in combination with the "coverage" of means of circulation by this standard, sets a limit to any sort of creation of money. Even though it does not exclude a certain elasticity and does not make an evolutionary type of credit inflation altogether impossible, it still has a significant degree of rigidity. Where money is made out of a material which is, for practical purposes, capable of unlimited production, like paper, there is no such mechanical limit. In this case, there is no doubt that it is the free decision of the political authorities which is the regulator of the quantity of money, unimpeded by any such mechanical restraints. That, however, means, as has been indicated, determination by their conception of the financial interests of the political authority or even, under certain circumstances, the purely personal interests of the members of the administrative staff, as was true of the use of the printing presses by the Red armies. The significance of metallic standards today lies precisely in the elimination of these interests from influence on the monetary situation, or more precisely, since they may always try to influence the state, urging it to abandon metal in favor of a pure paper standard, in a certain restraint on such interests. In spite of the mechanical character of its operation, a metallic standard nevertheless makes possible a higher degree of formal rationality in a market economy because it permits action to be oriented wholly to market advantages. It is, of course, true, as demonstrated by the experience of Austria and Russia, that the monetary policy of lytric authorities under a pure paper standard is not necessarily oriented either to the purely personal interests of the authority or the administrative staff, or to the financial interests of the state (which would mean the least expensive creation of the greatest possible volume of means of payment, without concern for what happens to the currency as a means of exchange). But the danger that such an orientation should become dominant is, nonetheless, continually present under a paper standard, while in a hylodromic system (free market money) it does not exist in a comparable sense. From the point of view of the formal order of a market economy, the existence of this danger is an "irrational" factor present in any form of monetary system other than a hylodromic standard. This is true in spite of the fact that it may be readily admitted that, on account of its mechanical character, such a monetary system itself possesses only a relative degree of formal rationality. So much Knapp could and should admit.

However incredibly primitive the older forms of the quantity theory of money were, there is no denying that any inflation with the issue of paper money determined by financial needs of the state is in danger of causing "debasement" of the currency. Nobody, not even Knapp, would deny this. But his reasons for dismissing it as unimportant are thoroughly unconvincing. The "amphitropic" position of each individual, meaning that every man is both a debtor and creditor, which Knapp in all seriousness puts forward as proof of the absolute indifference of any currency "debasement,"[60] is, as we now all know from personal experience, a mere phantom. What becomes of this position, not only for the *rentier*, but also for every one on a fixed salary, whose income remains constant in nominal units or, at best, is doubled if state finances and the mood of the bureaucracies permit, while his expenditures may, in nominal units, have increased twenty-fold, as it happens to us nowadays? What becomes of it for any long-term creditor? Such radical alterations in the (substantive) validity of money today produce a chronic tendency toward social revolution, even if many entrepreneurs are in a position to profit from the international exchange situation, and if some (very few) workers are powerful enough to secure increases in their nominal wages. It is, of course, open to anyone to welcome this revolutionary effect and the accompanying tremendous unsettlement of the market economy. Such an opinion cannot be scientifically refuted. Rightly or wrongly, some can hope that this tendency will lead to the transformation of a market economy into socialism. Or some may expect proof for the thesis that only a regulated economy with small-scale production units is capable of substantive rationality, regardless of the sacrifices its establishment would entail. It is impossible for science to decide such questions, but at the same time it is its duty to state the facts about these effects as clearly and objectively as possible. Knapp's assumption that people are both debtors and creditors in the same degree, which in the generalized form he gives the proposition is quite untenable, serves only to obscure the situation. There are particular errors in his work, but the above seems to be the most important element of *incompleteness* in his theory. It is this which has led also some scholars who otherwise would have no reason to be hostile to his work, to attack his theory on grounds of "principle."

37. *The Non-Monetary Significance of Political Bodies for the Economic Order*

The significance for the economic system apart from the monetary order of the fact that autonomous political organizations exist lies above all in the following aspects:

(1) In the fact that, other things being nearly equal, they tend to prefer their own subjects as sources of supply for the utilities they need. The impact of this fact is the greater, the more the economy of these

political bodies has a monopolistic character or that of a system of budgetary satisfaction of needs; hence it is presently on the increase.

(2) In the possibility deliberately to encourage, restrain, or regulate trade transactions across its boundaries on the basis of some substantive criteria—that is, to conduct a foreign trade policy.

(3) In the possibility of various types of formal and substantive regulation of economic activity by political bodies, differing in stringency and in type.

(4) In the important consequences of the very great differences in the structure of authority and of political power and in the closely related structure of administration and of social classes, especially of those which enjoy the highest prestige, and of the attitudes toward earning and profit-making which derive from these.

(5) In the competition among the directing authorities of these political bodies to increase their own power and to provide the members under their authority with means of consumption and acquisition and with the corresponding opportunities for earnings and profits.

(6) In the differences in ways in which these bodies provide for their own needs. On this see the following section.

38. *The Financing of Political Bodies*

The most direct connection between the economic system and primarily non-economic organizations lies in the way in which they secure the means of carrying on their corporate activity as such; that is, the activity of the administrative staff itself and that which is directed by it (see chap. I, sec. 12). This mode of provision may be called "financing" in the broadest sense, which includes the provision of goods in kind.

Financing—that is, the provision of corporate activity with economically scarce means—may, considering only the simplest types, be organized in the following ways:

(1) Intermittently, based either on purely voluntary or on compulsory contributions or services. Voluntary "intermittent" financing may take one of three forms:

(a) That of large gifts or endowments.[61] This is typical in relation to charitable, scientific, and other ends which are primarily neither economic nor political.

(b) That of begging. This is typical of certain kinds of ascetic communities.

In India, however, we also find secular castes of beggars, and elsewhere, particularly in China, organized groups of beggars are found.

Begging may in these cases be extensively monopolized and systematized with territorial assignments. Also, because response is regarded as a duty or as meritorious, begging may lose its intermittent character and in fact tend to become a tax-like source of income.

(c) That of gifts, which are formally voluntary, to persons recognized as politically or socially superior. This includes gifts to chiefs, princes, patrons, feudal lords over land or persons. Because of the fact that they have become conventional, these may in fact be closely approximated to compulsory payments. But usually, they are not worked out on a basis of rational expediency, but are generally made on certain traditional occasions, such as particular anniversaries or on the occasion of events of family or political significance.

Intermittent financing may, on the other hand, be based on compulsory contributions.

The type case for compulsory "intermittent" financing is furnished by such organizations as the *Camorra* in southern Italy and the *Mafia* in Sicily, and similar organized groups elsewhere. In India there have existed ritually separated castes of "thieves" and "robbers," and in China sects and secret societies with a similar method of economic provision. The payments are "intermittent" only on the surface, because they are formally illegal. In practice they often assume the character of periodic "subscriptions," paid in exchange for the rendering of certain services—notably, of a guarantee of security. About twenty years ago, a Neapolitan manufacturer replied to my doubts concerning the effectiveness of the *Camorra* with respect to business enterprises: "Signore, la Camorra mi prende X lire nel mese, ma garantisce la sicurezza,—lo Stato me ne prende 10 · X, e garantisce: niente." [Sir, the *Camorra* takes X lire a month from me, but guarantees me security; the state takes ten times that amount, and guarantees me nothing.] The secret societies typical of Africa—perhaps rudiments of the former "men's house"—operate in a similar way (as secret courts), thus insuring security. Political groups may, like the Ligurian "pirate state," rest primarily on the profits of booty, but this has never been the exclusive source of support over a long period.

(2) Financing may, on the other hand, be organized on a permanent basis.

A.—This may take place without any independent economic production on the part of the organization. It may then consist in contributions of goods, which may be based on a money economy. If so, money contributions are collected and provisions are obtained by the money purchase of the necessary utilities. In this case, all compensation of members of the administrative staff takes the form of money salaries. Contributions of goods may, on the other hand, be organized on the basis of a natural economy. Then, members are assessed with specific contributions in kind. Within this category, there are the following sub-types: the administrative staff may be provided for by benefices in kind and the needs of the group met in the same way. On the other hand, the contributions which were collected in kind may be sold wholly or in part for money and provision made in monetary terms.

Whether in money or in kind, the principal elementary types of contribution are the following:

(a) Taxes; that is, contributions which may be a proportion of all possessions (in the money economy: of wealth), or of all receipts (in the money economy: of incomes), or, finally, only of the means of production or from certain kinds of profit-making enterprises (so-called "yield taxes").

(b) Fees; that is, payments for using or taking advantage of facilities provided by the organization, of its property or of its services.

(c) "Imposts" on such things as specific types of use or consumption of commodities, specific kinds of transactions, above all, the transportation of goods (customs) and the turn-over of goods (excise duties and sales tax).

Contributions may be collected by the organization itself or leased out ("farmed") or lent out or pledged. The leasing of collection for a fixed sum of money ("tax farming") may have a rational effect on the fiscal system since it may be the only possible way to budget accounts. Lending and pledging are usually irrational from the fiscal point of view, normally resulting from financial necessity or usurpation on the part of the administrative staff, a result of the absence of a dependable administrative organization.

A permanent appropriation of the receipts from contributions by creditors of the state, by private guarantors of the army or of tax payments, by unpaid mercenary captains (*condottieri*) and soldiers, and, finally, by holders of rights to official positions, will be called the granting of benefices (*Verpfründung*). This may in turn take the form of individual appropriation or collective appropriation with freedom of replacement from the group which has collectively carried out the appropriation.

Financing without any economic production on the part of the organization itself may also take place by the imposition of obligations to personal services; that is, direct personal services with specification of the work to be done.

B.—Permanent financing may further, contrary to the above cases, be based on the existence of a productive establishment under the direct control of the organization. Such an establishment may be a budgetary unit, as an *oikos* or a feudal domain, or it may be a profit-making enterprise, which, in turn, may compete freely with other profit-making enterprises or be a monopoly.

Once more, exploitation may be directly under the administration of the organization or it may be farmed out, leased, or pledged.

C.—Finally, it is possible for financing to be organized "liturgically" by means of burdens which are associated with privileges. These may involve "positive privileges," as when a group is freed from the burden of making particular contributions, or (possibly identical with the former case) "negative privileges," as when certain burdens are placed on particular groups. The latter are usually either status groups (*Stände*) or property or income classes. Finally, the liturgic type may be organized "correlatively" by associating specific monopolies with the burden of performing certain services or supplying certain goods. This may take the form of organization of "estates," that is, of compulsorily forming the members of the organization into hereditarily closed liturgical classes on the basis of property and occupation, each enjoying status privileges. Or it may be carried out capitalistically, by creating closed guilds or cartels, with monopolistic rights and a corresponding obligation to make money contributions.

This very rough classification applies to all kinds of organizations. Examples, however, will be given only in terms of political bodies.

The system of provision through money contributions without economic production is typical of the modern state. It is, however, quite out of the question to attempt here even a summary analysis of modern systems of taxation. What will first have to be discussed at length is the "sociological location" of taxation—that is, the type of structure of domination that has typically led to the development of certain kinds of contributions (as, e.g., fees, excises, or taxes).

Contributions in kind, even in the case of fees, customs, excises, and sales taxes, were common throughout the Middle Ages. Their commutation into money payments is a relatively modern phenomenon.

Deliveries of goods in kind are typical in the form of tribute or of assessments of products laid upon dependent economic units. The transportation of in-kind contributions is possible only for small political units or under exceptionally favorable transportation conditions, as were provided by the Nile and the Chinese Grand Canal. Otherwise it is necessary for the contributions to be converted into money if the final recipient is to benefit from them. This was common in Antiquity. It is also possible for them to be exchanged, according to the distance they have to be transported, into objects with higher price-to-weight ratios. This is said to have been done in ancient China.

Examples of obligations to personal service are obligations to military service, to serve in courts and on juries, to maintain roads and bridges, to work on a dyke or in a mine, and all sorts of compulsory service for corporate purposes which are found in various types of organizations. The type case is furnished by the "*corvée* state," of which the best example is the New Kingdom of ancient Egypt. Similar conditions were found at some periods in China, to a lesser extent in India and to a still less extent in the late Roman Empire and in many organizations of the early Middle Ages. Support by the granting of benefices is illustrated by the following cases: (1) In China, collectively to the body of successful examinees for official positions; (2) in India, to the private guarantors of military services and tax payments; (3) to unpaid *condottieri* and mercenary soldiers, as in the late Caliphate and under the regime of the Mamelukes; (4) to creditors of the state, as in the sale of offices common everywhere.

Provision from the organization's own productive establishment administered on a budgetary basis is illustrated by the exploitation of domains under direct control for the household of the king, and in the obligation of subjects to compulsory services if used, as in Egypt, to produce goods needed by the court or for political purposes in directly controlled production establishments. Modern examples are factories maintained by the state for the manufacture of munitions or of military clothing.

The use of productive establishments for profit in free competition with private enterprise is rare, but has occurred occasionally, as, for instance, in the case of the [Prussian] *Seehandlung*.[62] On the other hand, the monopolistic type is very common in all periods of history, but reached its highest development in the Western World from the sixteenth to the eighteenth centuries.

Positive privileges on a liturgical basis are illustrated by the exemption of the *literati* in China from feudal obligations. There are similar exemptions of privileged groups from the more menial tasks all over the world. In many countries educated people have been exempt from military service.

Negative privilege is to be found in the extra liturgical burdens placed upon wealth in the democracies of Antiquity. It is also illustrated by the burden placed on the classes who did not enjoy the exemptions in the cases just mentioned.

To take the "correlative" case under (C.) above: the subjection of privileged classes to specified liturgical obligations is the most important form of systematic provision for public needs on a basis other than that of regular taxation. In China, India, and Egypt, the countries with the earliest development of "hydraulic" bureaucracy, liturgical organization was based on obligations to deliveries and services in kind. It was in part taken over from these sources by the Hellenistic states and by the late Roman Empire, though there, to be sure, to an important extent it took the form of liturgical obligations to pay money taxes rather than contributions in kind. This type of provision always involves the organization of the population in terms of occupationally differentiated classes. It is by no means out of the question that it might reappear again in the modern world in this form if public provision by taxation should fall down and the satisfaction of private wants by capitalistic enterprise becomes subject to extensive regulation by the state. Up until now, the financial difficulties of the modern state could be adequately met by the compulsory creation of producer cartels with monopoly rights in exchange against money contributions; an example could be the compulsory control of the gunpowder factories in Spain with monopoly protection against new foundations and a continuous high contribution to the state treasury. The idea is suggestive: one might proceed in the same way in the "socialization" of the capitalistic enterprises of individual branches, by imposing compulsory cartels or combinations with obligations to pay large sums in taxes. Thus they could be made useful for fiscal purposes, while production would continue to be oriented rationally to the price situation.

39. Repercussions of Public Financing on Private Economic Activity

The way in which political and hierocratic bodies provide for their corporate needs has very important repercussions on the structure of private economic activity. A state based exclusively on money contributions, conducting the collection of the taxes (but no other economic activity) through its own staff, and calling on personal service contributions only for political and judicial purposes, provides an optimal environment for a rational market-oriented capitalism. A state which collects money taxes by tax farming is a favorable environment for the development of politically oriented capitalism, but it does not encourage the orientation of profit-making activity to the market. The granting of rights to contributions and their distribution as benefices normally tends to check the development of capitalism by creating vested interests in the maintenance of existing sources of fees and contributions. It thus tends to stereotyping and traditionalizing of the economic system.

A political body based purely on deliveries in kind does not promote the development of capitalism. On the contrary, it hinders it to the extent to which it involves rigid binding of the structure of production in a form which, from a point of view of profit-making enterprise, is irrational.

A system of provision by compulsory services in kind hinders the development of market capitalism above all through the confiscation of the labor force and the consequent impediments to the development of a free labor market. It is unfavorable to politically oriented capitalism because it removes the typical prospective advantages which enable it to develop.

Financing by means of monopolistic profit-making enterprises has in common with the use of contributions in kind which are sold for money and with liturgical obligations on property, the fact that they are all unfavorable to the development of a type of capitalism which is autonomously oriented to the market. On the contrary, they tend to repress it by fiscal measures which, from the point of view of the market, are irrational, such as the establishment of privileges and of opportunities for money making through other channels. They are, on the other hand, under certain conditions favorable to politically oriented capitalism.

What is important for profit-making enterprises with fixed capital and careful capital accounting is, in formal terms, above all, the calculability of the tax load. Substantively, it is important that there shall not be unduly heavy burdens placed on the capitalistic employment of resources, which means, above all, on market turnover. On the other hand, speculative trade capitalism is compatible with any form of organization of public finances which does not, through tying it to liturgical obligations, directly inhibit the trader's exploitation of goods as commodities.

Though important, the form of organization of the obligations imposed by public finance is not sufficient to determine completely the orientation of economic activity. In spite of the apparent absence of all the more important obstacles of this type, no important development of rational capitalism has occurred in large areas and for long periods. On the other hand, there are cases where, in spite of what appear to be very serious obstacles placed in its way by the system of public finances, such a development has taken place. Various factors seem to have played a part. Substantively, state economic policy may be very largely oriented to non-economic ends. The development of the intellectual disciplines due to certain value-attitudes derived from ethical and tion, obstructions due to certain value-attitudes derived from ethical and religious sources have tended to limit the development of an autonomous capitalistic system of the modern type to certain areas. It must, furthermore, not be forgotten that forms of establishment and of the firm must, like technical products, be "invented." In an historical analysis, we can only point out certain circumstances which exert negative influences on the relevant thought processes—that is, influences which impede or even obstruct them—or such which exert a positive, favoring influence. It is not, however, possible to prove a strictly inevitable causal relationship in such cases, any more than it is possible in any other case of strictly individual events.[63]

Apropos of the last statement, it may be noted that the concrete individual events also in the field of the natural sciences can be rigorously reduced to their particular causal components only under very special circumstances. There is thus no difference in principle between the field of action and other fields.[64]

At this point it is possible to give only a few provisional indications of the fundamentally important interrelationships between the form of organization and administration of political bodies and the economic system.

1. Historically, the most important case of obstruction of the development of market capitalism by turning public contributions into privately held benefices is China. The conferring of contributions as fiefs, which often cannot be differentiated from this, had the same effect in the Near East since the time of the Caliphs. Both will be discussed in the proper place. Tax farming is found in India, in the Near East, and in the Western World in Antiquity and the Middle Ages. Particularly, however, in Antiquity, as in the development of the Roman class of tax-farming financiers, the *equites*, it became decisive in determining the mode of orientation of capitalistic acquisition. In India and the Near East, on the other hand, it was more important in determining the development and distribution of wealth, notably of land ownership.

2. The most important case in history of the obstruction of capital-istic development by a liturgical organization of public finance is that of later Antiquity. It was perhaps also important in India after the Buddhist era and at certain periods in China. This also will be discussed later.

3. The most important historical case of the monopolistic diversion of capitalism is, after the Hellenistic, especially the Ptolemaic pre-cursors, the period of royal monopolies and monopolistic concessions in early modern times, which again will be discussed in the proper place. A prelude to this development might be seen in certain measures intro-duced by Emperor Frederick II in Sicily, perhaps following a Byzantine model, and its final struggle in the conflict of the Stuarts with the Long Parliament.[65]

This whole discussion in such an abstract form has been introduced only in order to make an approximately correct formulation of problems possible. But before returning to the stages of development of economic activity and the conditions underlying that development, it is necessary to undertake a strictly sociological analysis of the non-economic compo-nents.

40. *The Influence of Economic Factors on the Formation of Organizations*

Economic considerations have one very general kind of sociological importance for the formation of organizations if, as is almost always true, the directing authority and the administrative staff are remunerated.

If this is the case, an overwhelmingly strong set of economic interests become bound up with the continuation of the organization, even though its primary ideological basis may in the meantime have ceased to exist.

It is an everyday occurrence that organizations of all kinds which, even in the eyes of the participants, have become "meaningless," continue to exist because an executive secretary or some other official makes his "living" in this manner and otherwise would have no means of support.

Every advantage which is appropriated, or even under certain circumstances one which has not been formally appropriated, *may* have the effect of stereotyping existing forms of social action. Among the opportunities for economic profit or earnings in the field of the peaceful provision for everyday wants, it is in general *only* the opportunities open to profit-making enterprise which constitute autonomous forces that are in a rational sense *revolutionary;* but even of them this is not always true.

For example, the interests of bankers in maintaining their commissions long obstructed the recognition of endorsements on bills of exchange. Similar cases of the obstruction of formally rational institutions by vested interests, which may well be interests in capitalistic profits, will frequently be met with below. They are, however, appreciably rarer than obstructions resulting from such factors as appropriation of benefices, status advantages, and various economically irrational forces.

41. *The Mainspring of Economic Activity*

All economic activity in a market economy is undertaken and carried through by individuals acting to provide for their own ideal or material interests. This is naturally just as true when economic activity is oriented to the patterns of order of organizations, whether they themselves are partly engaged in economic activity, are primarily economic in character, or merely regulate economic activity. Strangely enough, this fact is often not taken account of.

In an economic system organized on a socialist basis, there would be no fundamental difference in this respect. The decision-making, of course, would lie in the hands of the central authority, and the functions of the individual engaged in the production of goods would be limited to the performance of "technical" services; that is, to "labor" in the sense of the term employed here. This would be true so long as the individuals were being administered "dictatorially," that is, by autocratic determination from above in which they had no voice. But once any right of "codetermination" were granted to the population, this would immediately make possible, also in a formal sense, the fighting out of interest conflicts centering on the manner of decision-making and, above all, on the question of how much should be saved (i.e., put aside from current production). But this is not the decisive point. What is decisive is that in socialism, too, the individual will under these conditions ask first whether to him, personally, the rations allotted and the work assigned, as compared with other possibilities, appear to conform with his own interests. This is the criterion by which he would orient his behavior, and violent power struggles would be the normal result: struggles over the alteration or maintenance of rations once allotted—as, for instance, over ration supplements for heavy labor; appropriations or expropriations of particular jobs, sought after because of extra remuneration or pleasant working conditions; work cessations, such as in strikes or lock-outs; restrictions of production to enforce changes in the conditions of work in particular branches; boycotts and the forcible dismissal of unpopular supervisors— in short, appropriation processes of all kinds and interest struggles would also then be the normal phenomena of life. The fact that they would for the most part be fought out through organized groups, and that advantages would be enjoyed on the one hand by the workers engaged in the most essential services, on the other hand by those who were physically strongest, would simply reflect the existing situation. But however that might be, it would be the interests of the individual, possibly organized in terms of the similar interests of many individuals as opposed to those of others, which would underlie all action. The *structure* of interests and the relevant situation would be different, and there would be other *means* of pursuing interests, but this fundamental factor would remain just as relevant as before. It is of course true that economic action which is oriented on purely ideological grounds to the interests of others does exist. But it is even more certain that the mass of men do not act in this way, and it is an induction from experience that they cannot do so and never will.

In a completely socialized planned economy there would be scope only for the following: (a) the distribution of real goods on the basis of planned rationed needs; (b) the production of these goods according to a plan of production. "Income" as a category of the money economy would necessarily disappear, but rationed "receipts" would be possible.

In a market economy the striving for *income* is necessarily the ultimate driving force of all economic activity. For every disposition, insofar as it makes a claim on goods or utilities which are not available to the actor in a form fully ready for whatever use he intends, presupposes the acquisition of and disposition over future income, and practically every existing power of control over goods and services presupposes previous income. All business profits of enterprises will at some stage and in some form be turned into the income of economically acting individuals. In a "regulated economy" the principal aim of the regulations is generally to affect in some manner the distribution of income. (In a "natural economy" we find no "income" in the usage of the present terminology; instead there are "receipts" in the form of goods and services which cannot be valued in terms of a unitary means of exchange.)

Income and receipts may, from a sociological point of view, take the following principal forms and be derived from the following principal sources:

A.—Incomes and receipts from personal services derived from specialized or specified functions:

(1) Wages: (a) Freely determined wage incomes or receipts contracted at fixed rates per time period; (b) the same, determined on some established scale (salaries or in-kind remuneration of public officials and civil servants); (c) the labor return of hired workers on contracted piece rates; (d) entirely open labor returns.

(2) Gains: (a) Free exchange profits deriving from the procurement of goods and services on an entrepreneurial basis; (b) the same, but regulated. In cases (a) and (b), "incomes" are calculated as net returns after the deduction of costs. (c) Predatory gains; (d) Gains derived from positions of political authority, fee incomes of an office, bribes, tax farming, etc., obtained by the appropriation of power. In cases (c) and (d), costs will be deducted to calculate "income" only if the activity is conducted as a continuous organized mode of acquisition; otherwise the gross revenue is usually considered "income."

B.—Income and receipts from property, derived from the exploitation of control over important means of production:

(1) Those in which "income" is normally calculated as "net rent" after the deduction of costs. (a) Rent obtained from the ownership of human beings, as in the case of slaves, serfs or freedmen. These may be receipts in money or in kind; they may be fixed in amount or consist in shares of the source's earnings after the deduction of costs of maintenance. (b) Appropriated revenues derived from positions of political authority (after the deduction of the costs of administration). (c) Rental revenues derived from the ownership of land (*métayage* payments or fixed rents per unit of time, either in kind or in money, seigneurial rent revenues—after deduction of land taxes and costs of maintenance). (d) House rents after deduction of expenses. (e) Rent receipts from appropriated monopolies (feudal *banalités,* patent royalties after the deduction of fees).

(2) Property income and receipts normally not requiring deduction

of costs from gross revenues: (a) Investment income (interest paid to households or profit-making enterprises in return for the right to utilize their resources or capital—see above, ch. II, sec. 11). (b) "Interest" from cattle loans (*Viehrenten*).[66] (c) "Interest" from other loans of concrete objects, and contracted "annuities in kind" (*Deputatrenten*). (d) Interest on money loans. (e) Money interest on mortgages. (f) Money returns from securities, which may consist in fixed interest or in dividends varying with profitability. (g) Other shares in profits, such as shares in the proceeds of "occasional" profit-making ventures and in profits from rational speculative operations, and shares in the rational long-run profit-making activities of all sorts of enterprises.

All "gains" and the dividend incomes from shares are either not contracted (as to rate or amount) in advance, or only indirectly contracted incomes (namely, through the agreement on prices or piece rates). Fixed interest and wages, leases of land, and house rents are contracted incomes. Income from the exercise of power, from ownership of human beings, from seigneurial authority over land, and predatory incomes all involve appropriation by force. Income from property may be divorced from any occupation in case the recipient lets others utilize the property. Wages, salaries, labor profits, and entrepreneurial profits are, on the other hand, occupational incomes. Other types of property incomes and gains may be either one or the other. An exhaustive classification is not intended here.

Of all types of incomes, it is particularly those from business profits and the contracted piece rate or free labor incomes which have a dynamic, revolutionary significance for economic life. Next to these stand incomes derived from free exchange and, in quite different ways, under certain circumstances, the "predatory" incomes.

Those having a static, conservative influence on economic activity are above all incomes drawn in accordance with a predetermined scale, namely salaries, wages reckoned per unit of working time, gains from the exploitation of office powers, and normally all kinds of fixed interest and rents.[67]

The *economic* source of "incomes" (in an exchange economy) lies in a great majority of cases in the exchange situation on the market for goods and labor services. Thus, in the last analysis, it is determined by consumers' demand, in connection with the more or less strong natural or statutory monopolistic position of the parties to market relationships.

The economic source of "receipts" (in a natural economy) generally lies in the monopolistic appropriation of opportunities to exploit property or services for a return.

The underpinning of all these incomes is nothing but the *possibility* of violence in the defence of appropriated advantages (see above, ch. II, sec. 1, pt. 4). Predatory incomes and related modes of acquisition are the return on *actual* violence. An exhaustive classification had to be foregone in this very rough first sketch.

In spite of many disagreements on particular points, I consider the sections on "income" in R. Liefmann's works to be among the most valuable of his contributions.[68] The problems of economic theory involved cannot be explored any further here; the interrelations between the economic dynamics and the social order will have to be discussed time and again.

NOTES

Unless otherwise indicated, notes are by Parsons.

1. In the economic sense.

2. Robert Liefmann, *Grundsätze der Volkswirtschaftslehre*, vol. I, 3rd ed. (Stuttgart 1923), p. 74ff. and *passim*. (Wi)

3. See Franz Oppenheimer, *System der Soziologie*, Part III, *Theorie der reinen und politischen Ökonomie*, 5th ed. (Jena 1923), pp. 146–152. (Wi)

4. The German word *Technik* which Weber uses here covers both the meanings of the English word "technique" and of "technology." Since the distinction is not explicitly made in Weber's terminology, it will have to be introduced according to the context in the translation.

5. The term *Verfügungsgewalt*, of which Weber makes a great deal of use, is of legal origin, implying legally sanctioned powers of control and disposal. This, of course, has no place in a purely economic conceptual scheme but is essential to a sociological treatment of economic systems. It is another way of saying that concretely economic action depends on a system of property relations.

6. This is one of the many differences between China and the Western World which Weber related to the difference of orientation to economic activities, growing out of the religious differences of the two civilizations. See his *The Religion of China: Confucianism and Taoism*, transl. H. H. Gerth (Glencoe, Ill. 1951).

7. *Beschaffung*. Weber uses this term, which could be translated variously as "making available," "bringing forth," "providing," etc., throughout this chapter in combinations where today the term "production" has become usual, and we normally translate it in this way. However, the term does cover, beyond production in the narrow sense, also all manner of activities which make available goods, services, money, or anything else useful—that is, transport (as noted here), trade, banking, etc. Wherever it was necessary to indicate this wider meaning clearly, we have translated the term as "procurement." (Wi)

8. It is a striking fact that, particularly in primitive society, a very large proportion of economically significant exchange is formally treated as an exchange of gifts. A return gift of suitable value is definitely obligatory but the specific characteristic of purely economically rational exchange, namely bargaining, is not only absent but is specifically prohibited.

9. The type case Weber has in mind is the relation of the state to the modern system of property and contract. Whether or not private citizens will engage in any given activity is not determined by the law. The latter is restricted

to the enforcement of certain formal rules governing whoever does engage in such activities.

10. This is a term which is not in general use in German economics, but which Weber took over, as he notes below, from G. F. Knapp. There seems to be no suitable English term and its use has hence been retained.

11. *Theorie des Geldes und der Umlaufsmittel* (Munich 1912). English edition: *The Theory of Money and Credit*, trsl. H. E. Batson (London 1934; 2d rev. ed., New Haven 1953). (Wi)

12. English edition: *The State Theory of Money*, abridged ed., trsl. by H. M. Lucas and J. Bonar, publ. for the Royal Economic Society (London 1924). (Wi)

13. Weber, as will become clear further on in this chapter, in common with many of his contemporaries (including the leaders of the Bolshevik revolution in Russia) strongly identified "socialism" and "communism" with the absence of money and monetary categories (money prices, money wages, etc.). In the event, these categories were, of course, used in the Communist countries even in the substantial absence of free markets, although their use was attended by many difficulties, as yet unresolved, in the determination of rational prices. This is true for the internal economy of these countries, but particularly true for the exchange relations *between* the Communist countries (coexisting "communist organizations") which are mentioned here. For the state of the debate in Weber's day, see F. A. Hayek (ed.), *Collectivist Economic Planning* (London 1935); an appreciation of Weber's contribution, p. 32ff. (Wi)

14. The concept *Haushalt,* as distinguished from *Erwerb,* is central to Weber's analysis in this context. He means by it essentially what Aristotle meant by the "management of a household" (Jowett's translation). It is a question of rational allocation of resources in providing for a given set of needs. The concept of budget and budgetary management seems to be the closest English equivalent in common use.

15. Corresponding to the distinction of *Haushalt* and *Erwerb,* Weber distinguishes *Vermögen* and *Kapital*. They are, of course, classes of property distinguished in terms of their function in the management of an economic unit. There is no English equivalent of *Vermögen* in this sense, and it has seemed necessary to employ the more general term "wealth." Where there is danger of confusion, it will be amplified as "budgetary wealth."

16. In common usage the term *Erwerben* would perhaps best be translated as "acquisition." This has not, however, been used, as Weber is here using the term in a technical sense as the antithesis of *Haushalten*. "Profit-Making" brings out this specific meaning much more clearly.

17. Since Weber wrote, there has been an extensive discussion of the problem of whether rational allocation of resources was possible in a completely socialistic economy in which there were no independent, competitively determined prices. The principal weight of technical opinion seems at present to take the opposite position from that which Weber defends here. A discussion of the problem will be found in Oskar Lange and F. M. Taylor, *On the Economic Theory of Socialism,* edited by B. E. Lippincott (Minneapolis 1938). This book includes a bibliography on the subject.

18. For the relevant articles by K. Rodbertus, see *Jahrbücher für Nationalökonomie und Statistik,* vols. IV, V, and VIII (1865–1869); K. Bücher, *Industrial Evolution,* trsl. S. M. Wickett (New York 1901). (Wi)

19. On *banco*-currencies, see *Economic History,* 189f; on the Egyptian "grain deposit banks," *ibid.,* 59. (Wi)

20. Otto Neurath, *Bayerische Sozialisierungserfahrungen,* Vienna 1920; *id.,*

Vollsozialisierung. Von der nächsten u. übernächsten Zukunft (*Deutsche Gemeinwirtschaft*, vol. 15; Jena 1920), and bibliography given there. Neurath, incidentally, had not only written about and agitated for economic socialization, but also briefly worked as director of the Bavarian *Zentralwirtschaftsamt*, the agency in charge of socialization plans, during the *Räterepublik* or "soviet" phase of the Bavarian revolutionary regime in the spring of 1919; when he was brought to trial after the suppression of the revolution, Weber testified in his defense. See A. Mitchell, *Revolution in Bavaria 1918–1919* (Princeton 1965), pp. 293–305; Marianne Weber, *Max Weber* (Tübingen 1926), pp. 673 & 677; Ernst Niekisch, *Gewagtes Leben* (Köln 1958), pp. 53–57. (Wi)

21. J. C. L. Simonde de Sismondi, Essay X ("De la condition des cultivateurs dans la Campagne de Rome") in his *Études sur l'Économie Politique*, vol. II (Paris 1838); W. Sombart, *Die römische Campagna. Eine sozialökonomische Studie* (Leipzig 1888). (Wi)

22. Oppenheimer, who was for part of his life associated with the Henry George movement, saw the ultimate basis of capitalism in the appropriation of land; he was himself the founder of a "free land" movement. (Wi)

23. English translation in F. A. Hayek (ed.), *Collectivist Economic Planning* (London 1935). (Wi)

24. Weber seems to have said in this passage in a somewhat involved way what has come to be generally accepted among the more critical economic theorists and the welfare economists. A simpler way of stating the same point is provided by the doctrine of maximum satisfaction. This states the conditions under which, to use Weber's phrase, formal and substantive rationality would coincide. It is generally conceded that among these conditions is the absence of certain types of inequality of wealth. One of the best statements of the problem is that of Frank H. Knight in his essay "The Ethics of Competition," which is reprinted in the book of that title. The problem of the relations of formal and substantive rationality has for Weber, however, wider ramifications.

25. Proposals for the introduction of a planned economy made in the early summer of 1919 by the first *Reichswirtschaftsminister* of the Weimar Republic, the Social Democrat Rudolf Wissell and his Undersecretary Wichard von Moellendorff. After the rejection of his plans, Wissell resigned in July of that year and was replaced by an opponent of planning. Cf. Arthur Rosenberg, *A History of the German Republic*, trsl. I. F. D. Morrow and M. Sieveking (London 1936), 108ff. The text of the proposals is included in Wissell's justification of his conduct of office: *Praktische Wirtschaftspolitik. Unterlagen zur Beurteilung einer fünfmonatlichen Wirtschaftsführung* (Berlin 1919), and in part also in *Deutsche Gemeinwirtschaft*, vols. 9 and 10 (Jena 1919). (Wi)

26. English ed.: *Industrial Evolution*, transl. (from the 3rd German edition, 1900) by S. Morley Wickoff (New York 1901). (Wi)

27. In a good deal of his discussion, Weber uses the term *Betrieb* in a context where this distinction is not important. To avoid a confusion of terms, it has in general been found most convenient to translate *Betrieb* as "enterprise" (cf. the definition of "enterprise" as continuous rational activity, above, ch. I:15). But wherever the distinction made here is important in the context, the term "establishment" is used. *Unternehmen* has for the same reason been translated as "firm." (Wi)

28. See above note. In most cases it has so far seemed best to translate *Erwerbsbetrieb* with "enterprise."

29. See below, ch. II, sec. 20, point V. (Wi)

30. Weber here sides with Karl Bücher against a theory of developmental

stages propounded mainly by Gustav Schmoller, who defines stages in terms of ruling groups. Cf. Schmoller, "Städtische, territoriale und staatliche Wirtschafts-politik," *Jahrb. f. Gesetzgebung, Verwaltung u. Volkswirtschaft,* VIII (1884), 4ff. and II (1904), 668ff.; Bücher, "The Rise of the National Economy," in his *Industrial Evolution, op. cit.,* 83–149. For the polemic between Schmoller and Bücher, see *Jb. f. G., V. & V.,* XVII and XVIII (1893–1894). See also below, Part Two, ch. XVI:i:4. (Wi)

31. The corresponding German terms are: *Hauswirtschaft, Dorfwirtschaft, grundherrliche* and *patrimonialfürstliche Haushaltswirtschaft, Stadtwirtschaft, Territorialwirtschaft,* and *Volkswirtschaft.*

32. What Weber apparently has in mind is the type of "trust" which controls all stages of the process of production from raw material to the finished product. Thus many of our steel enterprises have not only blast furnaces and rolling mills, but coal mines, coke ovens, railways and ships, and iron ore mines. The most notable example in Germany in Weber's time was the Stinnes combine.

33. The *demiurgoi* were the public craftsmen ("those who work for the people") of ancient Greece. Whether they were really on an annual retainer, rather than being paid for the individual job, is still controversial (cf. M. I. Finley, *The World of Oddyseus* [New York 1959], 51f.); Weber himself usually cites the public artisans of Indian villages as an example (e.g., *Economic History,* 34f., 103f.) (Wi)

34. K. Rodbertus, "Zur Geschichte der römischen Tributsteuern seit Augustus," *Jahrbücher f. Nationalök. u. Statistik,* IV (1865); cf. also *Economic History,* 108. (Wi)

35. Carolingian Imperial regulation prescribing detailed management procedures for the royal estates (*villae*). (Wi)

36. Discussed in sec 20, below. (Wi)

37. Discussed in sec. 21, below. (Wi)

38. On Demosthenes' shops and the Carolingian women's house (*genitium*), see *Economic History,* 104ff.; on Roman estate shops, H. Gummerus, *Der römische Gutsbetrieb als wirtschaftl. Organismus nach den Werken des Cato, Varro und Columella* (Leipzig 1906); on the Russian serf factory, see M. I. Tugan-Baranovskii, *Geschichte der russischen Fabrik,* transl. B. Minzes (Berlin 1900). (Wi)

39. *Beunden* were plots of land exempt from the cultivation regulations (crop rotation, grazing rights, etc.) of the village (*Mark-*) association; in contrast to ordinary arable, they could be fenced. *Herrenbeunden,* or unrestricted seigneurial farms operated by a special official (*Beundehofmann*), are found in early documents. J. & W. Grimm, *Deutsches Wörterbuch,* I (Leipzig 1854). (Wi)

40. The term *Paria* is used by Weber in a technical sense to designate a group occupying the same territorial area as others, but separated from them by ritual barriers which severely limit social intercourse between the groups. It has been common for such groups to have specialized occupations, particularly occupations which are despised in the larger society.

41. What is ordinarily called a "producers' co-operative association" would be included in this type, but Weber conceives the type more broadly. In certain respects, for instance, the medieval village community could be considered an example.

42. On the "freed mountains" and "mining freedom," see *Economic History,* 142f. (Wi)

43. His real name was John Winchcombe. See W. J. Ashley, *An Introduc-*

tion to English Economic History and Theory, II (London 1893), 229f. and 255f., who reprints part of the poem; also *Economic History,* 132. (Wi)

44. That is without rights of inheritance or alienation. See above chap. I, sec. 10.

45. This chapter is, however, a mere fragment which Weber intended to develop on a scale comparable with the others. Hence most of the material to which this note refers was probably never written down.

46. For a discussion of *Stör,* "wage work," and "price work," see Karl Bücher, *Industrial Evolution, op. cit.,* chap. 4. (Wi)

47. On *coloni,* see *Economic History,* 56, 73. (Wi)

48. It seems curious that in this classification Weber failed to mention the type of agricultural organization which has become predominant in the staple agricultural production of much of the United States and Canada. Of the European types this comes closest to large-scale peasant proprietorship, but is much more definitely oriented to the market for a single staple, such as wheat. Indeed, in many respects this type of farm is closely comparable to some kinds of small-scale industrial enterprise.

49. On this peculiar phenomenon, see *Economic History,* 35. (Wi)

49a. Memorandum on the question of a legal provision to protect the homesteads of smallholders against legal execution ("Empfiehlt sich die Einführung eines Heimstättenrechtes, insbesondere zum Schutz des kleinen Grundbesitzes gegen Zwangsvollstreckung?") in *Deutscher Juristentag* XXIV (1897), *Verhandlungen,* II, 15–32. (W)

50. Weber uses the term *Alltag* in a technical sense, which is contrasted with *Charisma.* The antithesis will play a leading role in chap. III. In his use of the terms, however, an ambiguity appears of which he was probably not aware. In some contexts, *Alltag* means routine, as contrasted with things which are exceptional or extraordinary and hence temporary. Thus, the charismatic movement led by a prophet is, in the nature of the case, temporary, and if it is to survive at all must find a routine basis of organization. In other contexts, *Alltag* means the profane, as contrasted with the sacred. The theoretical significance of this ambiguity has been analysed in [Parsons,] *Structure of Social Action,* chap. xvii.

51. There are several different factors involved in the inability to predict future events with complete certainty. Perhaps the best known analysis of these factors is that of F. H. Knight in his *Risk, Uncertainty and Profit.*

52. On the Chinese and Hamburg *banco*-money (deposit certificates), see *Economic History,* 189f. (Wi)

53. In a well-known essay, "The Social Causes of the Decay of Ancient Civilization," (*J. of General Education,* V, 1950, 75–88), Weber attributed to this factor an important role in the economic decline and through this the cultural changes of the Roman Empire.

54. G. F. Knapp, *The State Theory of Money, op. cit.,* 11. (Wi)

55. For the exact definition of "currency money," see Knapp, *The State Theory of Money,* 100ff. (Wi)

56. Note money is discussed in sec. 34, below; metal money in this and the following section. (Wi)

57. Most of the special terminology employed here was coined by Knapp, but never came to be really widely used. "Lytric," from the Greek *lytron* = means of payment, designates specifically the agencies or institutions connected with payments or regulating payment instruments. "Hylodromy," literally the rate of exchange (*Kurs = dromos*) of currency metals (matter = *hyle*), Knapp defines

as a state characterized by "the deliberate fixing of the price of a hylic metal" (Knapp, *The State Theory of Money*, 79). (Wi)

58. It should be borne in mind that this was written in 1919 or 1920. The situation has clearly been radically changed by the developments since that time.

59. This is an application of Weber's general theory of the relations of interests and ideas, which is much further developed in his writings on the Sociology of Religion. The most important point is that he refused to accept the common dilemma that a given act is motivated either by interests or by ideas. The influence of ideas is rather to be found in their function of defining the situations in which interests are pursued. Beside in Weber's own works, this point is developed in [Parsons'] article "The Role of Ideas in Social Action," *American Sociological Review*, October 1938.

60. Knapp, *The State Theory of Money*, 48. (Wi)

61. *Mäzenatisch*. This term is commonly used in German but not in the precise sense which Weber gives it here. There seems to be no equivalent single term in English, so the idea has been conveyed by a phrase.

62. For the complex history of this institution, the later *Preussische Staatsbank*, see W. O. Henderson, *The State and the Industrial Revolution in Prussia, 1740–1870* (Liverpool 1958), 119–147. Founded in 1772 by Frederick II as a primarily government-owned overseas trade agency, the *Seehandlung* eventually turned into a fully government-owned commercial bank used to float state loans and, to some extent, to finance desired industrial development. (Wi)

63. The methodological problems touched here have been further discussed in various of the essays collected in the volume *GAzW*. The most essential point is that Weber held that no scientific analysis in the natural or the social field ever exhausts the concrete individuality of the empirical world. Scientific conceptual schemes and the causal explanations attained through their use are always in important respects abstract.

64. Cf. Weber's essay on "Roscher und Knies und die logischen Probleme der historischen Nationalökonomie," *GAzW*, 2nd ed., 1951, 56, 64ff. (Wi)

65. See *Economic History*, 213 and 256f. (Wi)

66. On cattle loans, see *Economic History*, 56 and 201. (Wi)

67. The distinction here made between those types of economic interest having a dynamic and a static influence on economic activity respectively, is strikingly similar to that made by Pareto between "speculators" and "rentiers;" see *The Mind and Society*, especially secs. 22, 34ff.

68. See Robert Liefmann, *Ertrag und Einkommen auf Grundlage einer rein subjektiven Wertlehre* (Jena 1907); Liefmann, *Grundsätze der Volkswirtschaftslehre* (Stuttgart 1919), vol. II, parts VIII–IX, esp. 636–710. (Wi)

THE TYPES OF LEGITIMATE DOMINATION

i

The Basis of Legitimacy

1. *Domination and Legitimacy*

Domination was defined above (ch. I:16) as the probability that certain specific commands (or all commands) will be obeyed by a given group of persons. It thus does not include every mode of exercising "power" or "influence" over other persons. Domination ("authority")[1] in this sense may be based on the most diverse motives of compliance: all the way from simple habituation to the most purely rational calculation of advantage. Hence every genuine form of domination implies a minimum of voluntary compliance, that is, an *interest* (based on ulterior motives or genuine acceptance) in obedience.

Not every case of domination makes use of economic means; still less does it always have economic objectives. However, normally the rule over a considerable number of persons requires a staff (cf. ch. I:12), that is, a *special* group which can normally be trusted to execute the general policy as well as the specific commands. The members of the administrative staff may be bound to obedience to their superior (or superiors) by custom, by affectual ties, by a purely material complex of

interests, or by ideal (*wertrationale*) motives. The quality of these motives largely determines the type of domination. *Purely* material interests
and calculations of advantages as the basis of solidarity between the chief
and his administrative staff result, in this as in other connexions, in a
relatively unstable situation. Normally other elements, affectual and
ideal, supplement such interests. In certain exceptional cases the former
alone may be decisive. In everyday life these relationships, like others,
are governed by custom and material calculation of advantage. But custom, personal advantage, purely affectual or ideal motives of solidarity,
do not form a sufficiently reliable basis for a given domination. In addition there is normally a further element, the belief in *legitimacy*.

Experience shows that in no instance does domination voluntarily
limit itself to the appeal to material or affectual or ideal motives as a basis
for its continuance. In addition every such system attempts to establish
and to cultivate the belief in its legitimacy. But according to the kind of
legitimacy which is claimed, the type of obedience, the kind of administrative staff developed to guarantee it, and the mode of exercising authority, will all differ fundamentally. Equally fundamental is the variation in
effect. Hence, it is useful to classify the types of domination according
to the kind of claim to legitimacy typically made by each. In doing this,
it is best to start from modern and therefore more familiar examples.

1. The choice of this rather than some other basis of classification
can only be justified by its results. The fact that certain other typical
criteria of variation are thereby neglected for the time being and can
only be introduced at a later stage is not a decisive difficulty. The legitimacy of a system of control has far more than a merely "ideal" significance, if only because it has very definite relations to the legitimacy of
property.

2. Not every claim which is protected by custom or law should
be spoken of as involving a relation of authority. Otherwise the worker,
in his claim for fulfilment of the wage contract, would be exercising authority over his employer because his claim can, on occasion, be enforced
by order of a court. Actually his formal status is that of party to a contractual relationship with his employer, in which he has certain "rights"
to receive payments. At the same time the concept of an authority relationship (*Herrschaftsverhältnis*) naturally does not exclude the possibility that it has originated in a formally free contract. This is true of the
authority of the employer over the worker as manifested in the former's
rules and instructions regarding the work process; and also of the *authority* of a feudal lord over a vassal who has freely entered into the relation
of fealty. That subjection to military discipline is formally "involuntary"
while that to the discipline of the factory is voluntary does not alter the
fact that the latter is also a case of subjection to *authority*. The position
of a bureaucratic official is also entered into by contract and can be

freely resigned, and even the status of "subject" can often be freely entered into and (in certain circumstances) freely repudiated. Only in the limiting case of the slave is formal subjection to authority absolutely involuntary.

On the other hand, we shall not speak of formal domination if a monopolistic position permits a person to exert economic power, that is, to dictate the terms of exchange to contractual partners. Taken by itself, this does not constitute authority any more than any other kind of influence which is derived from some kind of superiority, as by virtue of erotic attractiveness, skill in sport or in discussion. Even if a big bank is in a position to force other banks into a cartel arrangement, this will not alone be sufficient to justify calling it an authority. But if there is an immediate relation of command and obedience such that the management of the first bank can give orders to the others with the claim that they shall, and the probability that they will, be obeyed regardless of particular content, and if their carrying out is supervised, it is another matter. Naturally, here as everywhere the transitions are gradual; there are all sorts of intermediate steps between mere indebtedness and debt slavery. Even the position of a "salon" can come very close to the borderline of authoritarian domination and yet not necessarily constitute "authority." Sharp differentiation in concrete fact is often impossible, but this makes clarity in the analytical distinctions all the more important.

3. Naturally, the legitimacy of a system of domination may be treated sociologically only as the probability that to a relevant degree the appropriate attitudes will exist, and the corresponding practical conduct ensue. It is by no means true that every case of submissiveness to persons in positions of power is primarily (or even at all) oriented to this belief. Loyalty may be hypocritically simulated by individuals or by whole groups on purely opportunistic grounds, or carried out in practice for reasons of material self-interest. Or people may submit from individual weakness and helplessness because there is no acceptable alternative. But these considerations are not decisive for the classification of types of domination. What is important is the fact that in a given case the particular claim to legitimacy is to a significant degree and according to its type treated as "valid"; that this fact confirms the position of the persons claiming authority and that it helps to determine the choice of means of its exercise.

Furthermore, a system of domination may—as often occurs in practice —be so completely protected, on the one hand by the obvious community of interests between the chief and his administrative staff (bodyguards, Pretorians, "red" or "white" guards) as opposed to the subjects, on the other hand by the helplessness of the latter, that it can afford to drop even the pretense of a claim to legitimacy. But even then the mode of legitimation of the relation between chief and his staff may vary widely according to the type of basis of the relation of the authority between them, and, as will be shown, this variation is highly significant for the structure of domination.

4. "Obedience" will be taken to mean that the action of the person obeying follows in essentials such a course that the content of the command may be taken to have become the basis of action for its own sake. Furthermore, the fact that it is so taken is referable only to the formal obligation, without regard to the actor's own attitude to the value or lack of value of the content of the command as such.

5. Subjectively, the causal sequence may vary, especially as between "intuition" and "sympathetic agreement." This distinction is not, however, significant for the present classification of types of authority.

6. The scope of determination of social relationships and cultural phenomena by virtue of domination is considerably broader than appears at first sight. For instance, the authority exercised in the schools has much to do with the determination of the forms of speech and of written language which are regarded as orthodox. Dialects used as the "chancellery language" of autocephalous political units, hence of their rulers, have often become orthodox forms of speech and writing and have even led to the formation of separate "nations" (for instance, the separation of Holland from Germany). The rule by parents and the school, however, extends far beyond the determination of such cultural patterns, which are perhaps only apparently formal, to the formation of the young, and hence of human beings generally.

7. The fact that the chief and his administrative staff often appear formally as servants or agents of those they rule, naturally does nothing whatever to disprove the quality of dominance. There will be occasion later to speak of the substantive features of so-called "democracy." But a certain minimum of assured power to issue commands, thus of domination, must be provided for in nearly every conceivable case.

2. *The Three Pure Types of Authority*

There are three pure types of legitimate domination. The validity of the claims to legitimacy may be based on:

1. Rational grounds—resting on a belief in the legality of enacted rules and the right of those elevated to authority under such rules to issue commands (legal authority).

2. Traditional grounds—resting on an established belief in the sanctity of immemorial traditions and the legitimacy of those exercising authority under them (traditional authority); or finally,

3. Charismatic grounds—resting on devotion to the exceptional sanctity, heroism or exemplary character of an individual person, and of the normative patterns or order revealed or ordained by him (charismatic authority).

In the case of legal authority, obedience is owed to the legally established impersonal order. It extends to the persons exercising the authority of office under it by virtue of the formal legality of their commands and only within the scope of authority of the office. In the case of traditional authority, obedience is owed to the *person* of the chief who occupies the traditionally sanctioned position of authority and who is (within its sphere) bound by tradition. But here the obligation of obedience is a matter of personal loyalty within the area of accustomed obligations. In the case of charismatic authority, it is the charismatically qualified leader as such who is obeyed by virtue of personal trust in his revelation, his heroism or his exemplary qualities so far as they fall within the scope of the individual's belief in his charisma.

1. The usefulness of the above classification can only be judged by its results in promoting systematic analysis. The concept of "charisma" ("the gift of grace") is taken from the vocabulary of early Christianity. For the Christian hierocracy Rudolf Sohm, in his *Kirchenrecht,* was the first to clarify the substance of the concept, even though he did not use the same terminology. Others (for instance, Holl in *Enthusiasmus und Bussgewalt*) have clarified certain important consequences of it. It is thus nothing new.

2. The fact that none of these three ideal types, the elucidation of which will occupy the following pages, is usually to be found in historical cases in "pure" form, is naturally not a valid objection to attempting their conceptual formulation in the sharpest possible form. In this respect the present case is no different from many others. Later on (sec. 11 ff.) the transformation of pure charisma by the process of routinization will be discussed and thereby the relevance of the concept to the understanding of empirical systems of authority considerably increased. But even so it may be said of every historical phenomenon of authority that it is not likely to be "as an open book." Analysis in terms of sociological types has, after all, as compared with purely empirical historical investigation, certain advantages which should not be minimized. That is, it can in the particular case of a concrete form of authority determine what conforms to or approximates such types as "charisma," "hereditary charisma," "the charisma of office," "patriarchy," "bureaucracy," the authority of status groups, and in doing so it can work with relatively unambiguous concepts. But the idea that the whole of concrete historical reality can be exhausted in the conceptual scheme about to be developed is as far from the author's thoughts as anything could be.

Legal Authority With a Bureaucratic Administrative Staff

Note: The specifically modern type of administration has intentionally been taken as a point of departure in order to make it possible later to contrast the others with it.

3. *Legal Authority: The Pure Type*

Legal authority rests on the acceptance of the validity of the following mutually inter-dependent ideas.

1. That any given legal norm may be established by agreement or by imposition, on grounds of expediency or value-rationality or both, with a claim to obedience at least on the part of the members of the organization. This is, however, usually extended to include all persons within the sphere of power in question—which in the case of territorial bodies is the territorial area—who stand in certain social relationships or carry out forms of social action which in the order governing the organization have been declared to be relevant.

2. That every body of law consists essentially in a consistent system of abstract rules which have normally been intentionally established. Furthermore, administration of law is held to consist in the application of these rules to particular cases; the administrative process in the rational pursuit of the interests which are specified in the order governing the organization within the limits laid down by legal precepts and following principles which are capable of generalized formulation and are approved in the order governing the group, or at least not disapproved in it.

3. That thus the typical person in authority, the "superior," is himself subject to an impersonal order by orienting his actions to it in his own dispositions and commands. (This is true not only for persons exercising legal authority who are in the usual sense "officials," but, for instance, for the elected president of a state.)

4. That the person who obeys authority does so, as it is usually stated, only in his capacity as a "member" of the organization and what he obeys is only "the law." (He may in this connection be the member

of an association, of a community, of a church, or a citizen of a state.)

5. In conformity with point 3, it is held that the members of the organization, insofar as they obey a person in authority, do not owe this obedience to him as an individual, but to the impersonal order. Hence, it follows that there is an obligation to obedience only within the sphere of the rationally delimited jurisdiction which, in terms of the order, has been given to him.

The following may thus be said to be the fundamental categories of rational legal authority:

(1) A continuous rule-bound conduct of official business.

(2) A specified sphere of competence (jurisdiction). This involves: (a) A sphere of obligations to perform functions which has been marked off as part of a systematic division of labor. (b) The provision of the incumbent with the necessary powers. (c) That the necessary means of compulsion are clearly defined and their use is subject to definite conditions. A unit exercising authority which is organized in this way will be called an "administrative organ" or "agency" (Behörde).

> There are administrative organs in this sense in large-scale private enterprises, in parties and armies, as well as in the state and the church. An elected president, a cabinet of ministers, or a body of elected "People's Representatives" also in this sense constitute administrative organs. This is not, however, the place to discuss these concepts. Not every administrative organ is provided with compulsory powers. But this distinction is not important for present purposes.

(3) The organization of offices follows the principle of hierarchy; that is, each lower office is under the control and supervision of a higher one. There is a right of appeal and of statement of grievances from the lower to the higher. Hierarchies differ in respect to whether and in what cases complaints can lead to a "correct" ruling from a higher authority itself, or whether the responsibility for such changes is left to the lower office, the conduct of which was the subject of the complaint.

(4) The rules which regulate the conduct of an office may be technical rules or norms.[2] In both cases, if their application is to be fully rational, specialized training is necessary. It is thus normally true that only a person who has demonstrated an adequate technical training is qualified to be a member of the administrative staff of such an organized group, and hence only such persons are eligible for appointment to official positions. The administrative staff of a rational organization thus typically consists of "officials," whether the organization be devoted to political, hierocratic, economic—in particular, capitalistic—or other ends.

(5) In the rational type it is a matter of principle that the members of the administrative staff should be completely separated from owner-

ship of the means of production or administration. Officials, employees, and workers attached to the administrative staff do not themselves own the non-human means of production and administration. These are rather provided for their use, in kind or in money, and the official is obligated to render an accounting of their use. There exists, furthermore, in principle complete separation of the organization's property (respectively, capital), and the personal property (household) of the official. There is a corresponding separation of the place in which official functions are carried out—the "office" in the sense of premises—from the living quarters.

(6) In the rational type case, there is also a complete absence of appropriation of his official position by the incumbent. Where "rights" to an office exist, as in the case of judges, and recently of an increasing proportion of officials and even of workers, they do not normally serve the purpose of appropriation by the official, but of securing the purely objective and independent character of the conduct of the office so that it is oriented only to the relevant norms.

(7) Administrative acts, decisions, and rules are formulated and recorded in writing, even in cases where oral discussion is the rule or is even mandatory. This applies at least to preliminary discussions and proposals, to final decisions, and to all sorts of orders and rules. The combination of written documents and a continuous operation by officials constitutes the "office" (*Bureau*)[3] which is the central focus of all types of modern organized action.

(8) Legal authority can be exercised in a wide variety of different forms which will be distinguished and discussed later. The following ideal-typical analysis will be deliberately confined for the time being to the administrative staff that is most unambiguously a structure of domination: "officialdom" or "bureaucracy."

In the above outline no mention has been made of the kind of head appropriate to a system of legal authority. This is a consequence of certain considerations which can only be made entirely understandable at a later stage in the analysis. There are very important types of rational domination which, with respect to the ultimate source of authority, belong to other categories. This is true of the hereditary charismatic type, as illustrated by hereditary monarchy, and of the pure charismatic type of a president chosen by a plebiscite. Other cases involve rational elements at important points, but are made up of a combination of bureaucratic and charismatic components, as is true of the cabinet form of government. Still others are subject to the authority of the chiefs of other organizations, whether their character be charismatic or bureaucratic; thus the formal head of a government department under a parliamentary regime may be a minister who occupies his position because of his authority in a party. The type of rational, legal administrative staff is capable of application in all kinds of situations and contexts. It is the most important mechanism for the administration of everyday affairs. For in that sphere, the exercise of authority consists precisely in administration.

4. *Legal Authority: The Pure Type* (*Continued*)

The purest type of exercise of legal authority is that which employs a bureaucratic administrative staff. Only the supreme chief of the organization occupies his position of dominance (*Herrenstellung*) by virtue of appropriation, of election, or of having been designated for the succession. But even *his* authority consists in a sphere of legal "competence." The whole administrative staff under the supreme authority then consists, in the purest type, of individual officials (constituting a "monocracy" as opposed to the "collegial" type, which will be discussed below) who are appointed and function according to the following criteria:

(1) They are personally free and subject to authority only with respect to their impersonal official obligations.

(2) They are organized in a clearly defined hierarchy of offices.

(3) Each office has a clearly defined sphere of competence in the legal sense.

(4) The office is filled by a free contractual relationship. Thus, in principle, there is free selection.

(5) Candidates are selected on the basis of technical qualifications. In the most rational case, this is tested by examination or guaranteed by diplomas certifying technical training, or both. They are *appointed,* not elected.

(6) They are remunerated by fixed salaries in money, for the most part with a right to pensions. Only under certain circumstances does the employing authority, especially in private organizations, have a right to terminate the appointment, but the official is always free to resign. The salary scale is graded according to rank in the hierarchy; but in addition to this criterion, the responsibility of the position and the requirements of the incumbent's social status may be taken into account (cf. ch. IV).

(7) The office is treated as the sole, or at least the primary, occupation of the incumbent.

(8) It constitutes a career. There is a system of "promotion" according to seniority or to achievement, or both. Promotion is dependent on the judgment of superiors.

(9) The official works entirely separated from ownership of the means of administration and without appropriation of his position.

(10) He is subject to strict and systematic discipline and control in the conduct of the office.

This type of organization is in principle applicable with equal facility to a wide variety of different fields. It may be applied in profit-making business or in charitable organizations, or in any number of other types of private enterprises serving ideal or material ends. It is equally applicable to political and to hierocratic organizations. With the varying degrees of approximation to a pure type, its historical existence can be demonstrated in all these fields.

1. For example, bureaucracy is found in private clinics, as well as in endowed hospitals or the hospitals maintained by religious orders. Bureaucratic organization is well illustrated by the administrative role of the priesthood (*Kaplanokratie*) in the modern [Catholic] church, which has expropriated almost all of the old church benefices, which were in former days to a large extent subject to private appropriation. It is also illustrated by the notion of a [Papal] universal episcopate, which is thought of as formally constituting a universal legal competence in religious matters. Similarly, the doctrine of Papal infallibility is thought of as in fact involving a universal competence, but only one which functions "ex cathedra" in the sphere of the office, thus implying the typical distinction between the sphere of office and that of the private affairs of the incumbent. The same phenomena are found in the large-scale capitalistic enterprise; and the larger it is, the greater their role. And this is not less true of political parties, which will be discussed separately. Finally, the modern army is essentially a bureaucratic organization administered by that peculiar type of military functionary, the "officer."

2. Bureaucratic authority is carried out in its purest form where it is most clearly dominated by the principle of appointment. There is no such thing as a hierarchical organization of elected officials. In the first place, it is impossible to attain a stringency of discipline even approaching that in the appointed type, since the subordinate official can stand on his own election and since his prospects are not dependent on the superior's judgment. (On elected officials, see below, sec. 14.)

3. Appointment by free contract, which makes free selection possible, is essential to modern bureaucracy. Where there is a hierarchical organization with impersonal spheres of competence, but occupied by unfree officials—like slaves or *ministeriales,* who, however, function in a formally bureaucratic manner—the term "patrimonial bureaucracy" will be used.

4. The role of technical qualifications in bureaucratic organizations is continually increasing. Even an official in a party or a trade-union organization is in need of specialized knowledge, though it is usually developed by experience rather than by formal training. In the modern

state, the only "offices" for which no technical qualifications are required are those of ministers and presidents. This only goes to prove that they are "officials" only in a formal sense, and not substantively, just like the managing director or president of a large business corporation. There is no question but that the "position" of the capitalistic entrepreneur is as definitely appropriated as is that of a monarch. Thus at the top of a bureaucratic organization, there is necessarily an element which is at least not purely bureaucratic. The category of bureaucracy is one applying only to the exercise of control by means of a particular kind of administrative staff.

5. The bureaucratic official normally receives a fixed salary. (By contrast, sources of income which are privately appropriated will be called "benefices" (*Pfründen*)—on this concept, see below, sec. 8.) Bureaucratic salaries are also normally paid in money. Though this is not essential to the concept of bureaucracy, it is the arrangement which best fits the pure type. (Payments in kind are apt to have the character of benefices, and the receipt of a benefice normally implies the appropriation of opportunities for earnings and of positions.) There are, however, gradual transitions in this field with many intermediate types. Appropriation by virtue of leasing or sale of offices or the pledge of income from office are phenomena foreign to the pure type of bureaucracy (cf. *infra*, sec. 7a: iii:3).

6. "Offices" which do not constitute the incumbent's principal occupation, in particular "honorary" offices, belong in other categories, which will be discussed later (sec. 19f.). The typical "bureaucratic" official occupies the office as his principal occupation.

7. With respect to the separation of the official from ownership of the means of administration, the situation is exactly the same in the field of public administration and in private bureaucratic organizations, such as the large-scale capitalistic enterprise.

8. Collegial bodies will be discussed separately below (section 15). At the present time they are rapidly decreasing in importance in favor of types of organization which are in fact, and for the most part formally as well, subject to the authority of a single head. For instance, the collegial "governments" in Prussia have long since given way to the monocratic "district president" (*Regierungspräsident*). The decisive factor in this development has been the need for rapid, clear decisions, free of the necessity of compromise between different opinions and also free of shifting majorities.

9. The modern army officer is a type of appointed official who is clearly marked off by certain status distinctions. This will be discussed elsewhere (ch. IV). In this respect such officers differ radically from elected military leaders, from charismatic *condottieri* (sec. 10), from the type of officers who recruit and lead mercenary armies as a capitalistic enterprise, and, finally, from the incumbents of commissions which have been purchased (sec. 7a). There may be gradual transitions between these types. The patrimonial "retainer," who is separated from the means

of carrying out his function, and the proprietor of a mercenary army for capitalistic purposes have, along with the private capitalistic entrepreneur, been pioneers in the organization of the modern type of bureaucracy. This will be discussed in detail below.

5. *Monocratic Bureaucracy*

Experience tends universally to show that the purely bureaucratic type of administrative organization—that is, the monocratic variety of bureaucracy—is, from a purely technical point of view, capable of attaining the highest degree of efficiency and is in this sense formally the most rational known means of exercising authority over human beings. It is superior to any other form in precision, in stability, in the stringency of its discipline, and in its reliability. It thus makes possible a particularly high degree of calculability of results for the heads of the organization and for those acting in relation to it. It is finally superior both in intensive efficiency and in the scope of its operations, and is formally capable of application to all kinds of administrative tasks.

The development of modern forms of organization in all fields is nothing less than identical with the development and continual spread of bureaucratic administration. This is true of church and state, of armies, political parties, economic enterprises, interest groups, endowments, clubs, and many others. Its development is, to take the most striking case, at the root of the modern Western state. However many forms there may be which do not appear to fit this pattern, such as collegial representative bodies, parliamentary committees, soviets, honorary officers, lay judges, and what not, and however many people may complain about the "red tape," it would be sheer illusion to think for a moment that continuous administrative work can be carried out in any field except by means of officials working in offices. The whole pattern of everyday life is cut to fit this framework. If bureaucratic administration is, other things being equal, always the most rational type from a technical point of view, the needs of mass administration make it today completely indispensable. The choice is only that between bureaucracy and dilettantism in the field of administration.

The primary source of the superiority of bureaucratic administration lies in the role of technical knowledge which, through the development of modern technology and business methods in the production of goods, has become completely indispensable. In this respect, it makes no difference whether the economic system is organized on a capitalistic or a socialistic basis. Indeed, if in the latter case a comparable level of technical efficiency were to be achieved, it would mean a tremendous increase in the importance of professional bureaucrats.

When those subject to bureaucratic control seek to escape the influence of the existing bureaucratic apparatus, this is normally possible only by creating an organization of their own which is equally subject to bureaucratization. Similarly the existing bureaucratic apparatus is driven to continue functioning by the most powerful interests which are material and objective, but also ideal in character. Without it, a society like our own—with its separation of officials, employees, and workers from ownership of the means of administration, and its dependence on discipline and on technical training—could no longer function. The only exception would be those groups, such as the peasantry, who are still in possession of their own means of subsistence. Even in the case of revolution by force or of occupation by an enemy, the bureaucratic machinery will normally continue to function just as it has for the previous legal government.

The question is always who controls the existing bureaucratic machinery. And such control is possible only in a very limited degree to persons who are not technical specialists. Generally speaking, the highest-ranking career official is more likely to get his way in the long run than his nominal superior, the cabinet minister, who is not a specialist.

Though by no means alone, the capitalistic system has undeniably played a major role in the development of bureaucracy. Indeed, without it capitalistic production could not continue and any rational type of socialism would have simply to take it over and increase its importance. Its development, largely under capitalistic auspices, has created an urgent need for stable, strict, intensive, and calculable administration. It is this need which is so fateful to any kind of large-scale administration. Only by reversion in every field—political, religious, economic, etc.—to small-scale organization would it be possible to any considerable extent to escape its influence. On the one hand, capitalism in its modern stages of development requires the bureaucracy, though both have arisen from different historical sources. Conversely, capitalism is the most rational economic basis for bureaucratic administration and enables it to develop in the most rational form, especially because, from a fiscal point of view, it supplies the necessary money resources.

Along with these fiscal conditions of efficient bureaucratic administration, there are certain extremely important conditions in the fields of communication and transportation. The precision of its functioning requires the services of the railway, the telegraph, and the telephone, and becomes increasingly dependent on them. A socialistic form of organization would not alter this fact. It would be a question (cf. ch. II, sec. 12) whether in a socialistic system it would be possible to provide conditions for carrying out as stringent a bureaucratic organization as has been possible in a capitalistic order. For socialism would, in fact, require a still higher degree of formal bureaucratization than capitalism. If this should prove not to be possible, it would demonstrate the existence of another of those fundamental elements of irrationality—a conflict between formal and substantive rationality of the sort which sociology so often encounters.

Bureaucratic administration means fundamentally domination through knowledge. This is the feature of it which makes it specifically rational. This consists on the one hand in technical knowledge which, by itself, is sufficient to ensure it a position of extraordinary power. But in addition to this, bureaucratic organizations, or the holders of power who make use of them, have the tendency to increase their power still further by the knowledge growing out of experience in the service. For they acquire through the conduct of office a special knowledge of facts and have available a store of documentary material peculiar to themselves. While not peculiar to bureaucratic organizations, the concept of "official secrets" is certainly typical of them. It stands in relation to technical knowledge in somewhat the same position as commercial secrets do to technological training. It is a product of the striving for power.

Superior to bureaucracy in the knowledge of techniques and facts is only the capitalist entrepreneur, within his own sphere of interest. He is the only type who has been able to maintain at least relative immunity from subjection to the control of rational bureaucratic knowledge. In large-scale organizations, all others are inevitably subject to bureaucratic control, just as they have fallen under the dominance of precision machinery in the mass production of goods.

In general, bureaucratic domination has the following social consequences:

(1) The tendency to "levelling" in the interest of the broadest possible basis of recruitment in terms of technical competence.

(2) The tendency to plutocracy growing out of the interest in the greatest possible length of technical training. Today this often lasts up to the age of thirty.

(3) The dominance of a spirit of formalistic impersonality: "*Sine ira et studio,*" without hatred or passion, and hence without affection or enthusiasm. The dominant norms are concepts of straightforward duty without regard to personal considerations. Everyone is subject to formal equality of treatment; that is, everyone in the same empirical situation. This is the spirit in which the ideal official conducts his office.

The development of bureaucracy greatly favors the levelling of status, and this can be shown historically to be the normal tendency. Conversely, every process of social levelling creates a favorable situation for the development of bureaucracy by eliminating the office-holder who rules by virtue of status privileges and the appropriation of the means and powers of administration; in the interests of "equality," it also eliminates those who can hold office on an honorary basis or as an avocation by virtue of their wealth. Everywhere bureaucratization foreshadows mass democracy, which will be discussed in another connection.

The "spirit" of rational bureaucracy has normally the following general characteristics:

(1) Formalism, which is promoted by all the interests which are concerned with the security of their own personal situation, whatever this may consist in. Otherwise the door would be open to arbitrariness and hence formalism is the line of least resistance.

(2) There is another tendency, which is apparently, and in part genuinely, in contradiction to the above. It is the tendency of officials to treat their official function from what is substantively a utilitarian point of view in the interest of the welfare of those under their authority. But this utilitarian tendency is generally expressed in the enactment of corresponding regulatory measures which themselves have a formal character and tend to be treated in a formalistic spirit. (This will be further discussed in the Sociology of Law). This tendency to substantive rationality is supported by all those subject to authority who are not included in the group mentioned above as interested in the protection of advantages already secured. The problems which open up at this point belong in the theory of "democracy."

iii

Traditional Authority

6. *The Pure Type*

Authority will be called traditional if legitimacy is claimed for it and believed in by virtue of the sanctity of age-old rules and powers. The masters are designated according to traditional rules and are obeyed because of their traditional status (*Eigenwürde*). This type of organized rule is, in the simplest case, primarily based on personal loyalty which results from common upbringing. The person exercising authority is not a "superior," but a personal master, his administrative staff does not consist mainly of officials but of personal retainers, and the ruled are not "members" of an association but are either his traditional "comrades" (sec. 7a) or his "subjects." Personal loyalty, not the official's impersonal duty, determines the relations of the administrative staff to the master.

Obedience is owed not to enacted rules but to the person who occupies a position of authority by tradition or who has been chosen for it by the traditional master. The commands of such a person are legitimized in one of two ways:

a) partly in terms of traditions which themselves directly determine the content of the command and are believed to be valid within certain limits that cannot be overstepped without endangering the master's traditional status;

b) partly in terms of the master's discretion in that sphere which tradition leaves open to him; this traditional prerogative rests primarily on the fact that the obligations of personal obedience tend to be essentially unlimited.

Thus there is a double sphere:

a) that of action which is bound to specific traditions;
b) that of action which is free of specific rules.

In the latter sphere, the master is free to do good turns on the basis of his personal pleasure and likes, particularly in return for gifts—the historical sources of dues (*Gebühren*). So far as his action follows principles at all, these are governed by considerations of ethical common sense, of equity or of utilitarian expediency. They are not formal principles, as in the case of legal authority. The exercise of power is oriented toward the consideration of how far master and staff can go in view of the subjects' traditional compliance without arousing their resistance. When resistance occurs, it is directed against the master or his servant personally, the accusation being that he failed to observe the traditional limits of his power. Opposition is not directed against the system as such—it is a case of "traditionalist revolution."

In the pure type of traditional authority it is impossible for law or administrative rule to be deliberately created by legislation. Rules which in fact are innovations can be legitimized only by the claim that they have been "valid of yore," but have only now been recognized by means of "Wisdom" [the *Weistum* of ancient Germanic law]. Legal decisions as "finding of the law" (*Rechtsfindung*) can refer only to documents of tradition, namely to precedents and earlier decisions.

7. *The Pure Type* (*Continued*)

The master rules with or without an administrative staff. On the latter case, see sec. 7a:1.

The typical administrative staff is recruited from one or more of the following sources:

(I) From persons who are already related to the chief by traditional ties of loyalty. This will be called patrimonial recruitment. Such persons may be

    a) kinsmen,
    b) slaves,
    c) dependents who are officers of the household, especially *ministeriales,*
    d) clients,
    e) *coloni,*
    f) freedmen;

(II) Recruitment may be extra-patrimonial, including

    a) persons in a relation of purely personal loyalty such as all sorts of "favorites,"
    b) persons standing in a relation of fealty to their lord (vassals), and, finally,
    c) free men who voluntarily enter into a relation of personal loyalty as officials.

On I.a) Under traditionalist domination it is very common for the most important posts to be filled with members of the ruling family or clan.

b) In patrimonial administrations it is common for slaves and freedmen to rise even to the highest positions. It has not been rare for Grand Viziers to have been at one time slaves.

c) The typical household officials have been the following: the seneschal, the marshal, the chamberlain, the carver (*Truchsess*), the majordomo, who was the head of the service personnel and possibly of the vassals. These are to be found everywhere in Europe. In the Orient, in addition, the head eunuch, who was in charge of the harem, was particularly important, and in African kingdoms, the executioner. Furthermore, the ruler's personal physician, the astrologer and similar persons have been common.

d) In China and in Egypt, the principal source of recruitment for patrimonial officials lay in the clientele of the king.

e) Armies of *coloni* have been known throughout the Orient and were typical of the Roman nobility. (Even in modern times, in the Mohammedan world, armies of slaves have existed.)

On II.a) The regime of favorites is characteristic of every patrimonial rule and has often been the occasion for traditionalist revolutions.

b) The vassals will be treated separately.

c) Bureaucracy has first developed in patrimonial states with a body of officials recruited from extra-patrimonial sources; but, as will be shown soon, these officials were at first personal followers of their master.

In the pure type of traditional rule, the following features of a bureaucratic administrative staff are absent:

a) a clearly defined sphere of competence subject to impersonal rules,

b) a rationally established hierarchy,

c) a regular system of appointment on the basis of free contract, and orderly promotion,

d) technical training as a regular requirement,

e) (frequently) fixed salaries, in the type case paid in money.

On a): In place of a well-defined functional jurisdiction, there is a conflicting series of tasks and powers which at first are assigned at the master's discretion. However, they tend to become permanent and are often traditionally stereotyped. These competing functions originate particularly in the competition for sources of income which are at the disposal of the master himself and of his representatives. It is often in the first instance through these interests that definite functional spheres are first marked off and genuine administrative organs come into being.

At first, persons with permanent functions are household officials. Their (extra-patrimonial) functions outside the administration of the household are often in fields of activity which bear a relatively superficial analogy to their household function, or which originated in a discretionary act of the master and later became traditionally stereotyped. In addition to household officials, there have existed primarily only persons with *ad hoc* commissions.

> The absence of distinct spheres of competence is evident from a perusal of the list of the titles of officials in any of the ancient Oriental states. With rare exceptions, it is impossible to associate with these titles a set of rationally delimited functions which have remained stable over a considerable period.
>
> The process of delimiting permanent functions as a result of competition among and compromise between interests seeking favors, income, and other forms of advantage is clearly evident in the Middle Ages. This phenomenon has had very important consequences. The financial interests of the powerful royal courts and of the powerful legal profession in England were largely responsible for vitiating or curbing the influence of Roman and Canon law. In all periods the irrational division of official functions has been stereotyped by the existence of an established set of rights to fees and perquisites.

On b): The question of who shall decide a matter or deal with appeals—whether an agent shall be in charge of this, and which one, or

whether the master reserves decision for himself—is treated either traditionally, at times by considering the provenience of certain legal norms
and precedents taken over from the outside (*Oberhof-System*);[3a] or
entirely on the basis of the master's discretion in such manner that all
agents have to yield to his personal intervention.

Next to the traditionalist system of the [precedent-setting outside]
"superior" court (*Oberhof*) we find the principle of Germanic law, deriving from the ruler's political prerogative, that in his presence the
jurisdiction of any court is suspended. The *ius evocandi* and its modern
derivative, chamber justice (*Kabinettsjustiz*), stem from the same source
and the ruler's discretion. Particularly in the Middle Ages the *Oberhof*
was very often the agency whose writ declared and interpreted the law,
and accordingly the source from which the law of a given locality was
imported.

On c): The household officials and favorites are often recruited in
a purely patrimonial fashion: they are slaves or dependents (*ministeriales*) of the master. If recruitment has been extra-patrimonial, they
have tended to be benefice-holders whom he can freely remove. A fundamental change in this situation is first brought about by the rise of free
vassals and the filling of offices by a contract of fealty. However, since
fiefs are by no means determined by functional considerations, this does
not alter the situation with respect to a) and b) [the lack of definite
spheres of competence and clearly determined hierarchical relationships].
Except under certain circumstances when the administrative staff is organized on a prebendal basis, "promotion" is completely up to the master's
discretion (see sec. 8).

On d): Rational technical training as a basic qualification for office
is scarcely to be found among household officials and favorites. However,
a fundamental change in administrative practice occurs wherever there
is even a beginning of technical training for appointees, regardless of
its content.

For some offices a certain amount of empirical training has been necessary from very early times. This is particularly true of the art of reading and writing which was originally truly a rare "art." This has often,
most strikingly in China, had a decisive influence on the whole development of culture through the mode of life of the literati. It eliminated
the recruiting of officials from intra-patrimonial sources and thus limited
the ruler's power by confronting him with a status group (cf. sec. 7a: III).

On e): Household officials and favorites are usually supported and
equipped in the master's household. Generally, their dissociation from
the lord's own table means the creation of benefices, at first usually
benefices in kind. It is easy for these to become traditionally stereotyped
in amount and kind. In addition, or instead of them, the officials who

live outside the lord's household and the lord himself count on various fees, which are often collected without any regular rate or scale, being agreed upon from case to case with those seeking favors. (On the concept of benefices see sec. 8.)

7a. Gerontocracy, Patriarchalism and Patrimonialism

I. *Gerontocracy* and *primary patriarchalism* are the most elementary types of traditional domination where the master has no personal administrative staff.

The term gerontocracy is applied to a situation where so far as rule over the group is organized at all it is in the hands of elders—which originally was understood literally as the eldest in actual years, who are the most familiar with the sacred traditions. This is common in groups which are not primarily of an economic or kinship character. "Patriarchalism" is the situation where, within a group (household) which is usually organized on both an economic and a kinship basis, a particular individual governs who is designated by a definite rule of inheritance. Gerontocracy and patriarchalism are frequently found side by side. The decisive characteristic of both is the belief of the members that domination, even though it is an inherent traditional right of the master, must definitely be exercized as a joint right in the interest of all members and is thus not freely appropriated by the incumbent. In order that this shall be maintained, it is crucial that in both cases there is a complete absence of a personal (patrimonial) staff. Hence the master is still largely dependent upon the willingness of the members to comply with his orders since he has no machinery to enforce them. Therefore, the members (*Genossen*) are not yet really subjects (*Untertanen*).

Their membership exists by tradition and not by enactment. Obedience is owed to the master, not to any enacted regulation. However, it is owed to the master only by virtue of his traditional status. He is thus on his part strictly bound by tradition.

> The different types of gerontocracy will be discussed later. Elementary patriarchalism is related to it in that the patriarch's authority carries strict obligations to obedience only within his own household. Apart from this, as in the case of the Arabian Sheik, it has only an exemplary effect, in the manner of charismatic authority, or must resort to advice and similar means of exerting influence.

II. *Patrimonialism* and, in the extreme case, *sultanism* tend to arise whenever traditional domination develops an administration and a military force which are purely personal instruments of the master. Only then are the group members treated as subjects. Previously the master's authority appeared as a pre-eminent group right, now it turns into his personal right, which he appropriates in the same way as he would any ordinary object of possession. In principle, he can exploit his right like any economic asset—sell it, pledge it as security, or divide it by inheritance. The primary external support of patrimonial power is provided by slaves (who are often branded), *coloni* and conscripted subjects, but also by mercenary bodyguards and armies (patrimonial troops); the latter practice is designed to maximize the solidarity of interest between master and staff. By controlling these instruments the ruler can broaden the range of his arbitrary power and put himself in a position to grant grace and favors at the expense of the traditional limitations of patriarchal and gerontocratic structures. Where domination is primarily traditional, even though it is exercised by virtue of the ruler's personal autonomy, it will be called *patrimonial authority;* where it indeed operates primarily on the basis of discretion, it will be called *sultanism.* The transition is definitely continuous. Both forms of domination are distinguished from elementary patriarchalism by the presense of a personal staff.

> Sometimes it appears that sultanism is completely unrestrained by tradition, but this is never in fact the case. The non-traditional element is not, however, rationalized in impersonal terms, but consists only in an extreme development of the ruler's discretion. It is this which distinguishes it from every form of rational authority.

III. *Estate-type domination (ständische Herrschaft)*[4] is that form of patrimonial authority under which the administrative staff appropriates particular powers and the corresponding economic assets. As in all similar cases (cf. ch. II, sec. 19), appropriation may take the following forms:

a) Appropriation may be carried out by an organized group or by a category of persons distinguished by particular characteristics, or

b) it may be carried out by individuals, for life, on a hereditary basis, or as free property.

Domination of the estate-type thus involves:

a) always a limitation of the lord's discretion in selecting his administrative staff because positions or seigneurial powers have been appropriated by

    a) an organized group,

    β) a status group (see ch. IV), or

b) often—and this will be considered as typical—appropriation by the individual staff members of

    a) the positions, including in general the economic advantages associated with them,

    β) the material means of administration,

    γ) the governing powers.

Those holding appropriated positions may have originated historically
1) from members of an administrative staff which was not previously an
independent status group, or 2) before the appropriation, they may not
have belonged to the staff.

Where governing powers are appropriated, the costs of administration
are met indiscriminately from the incumbent's own and his appropriated
means. Holders of military powers and seigneurial members of the "feudal" army (*ständisches Heer*) equip themselves and possibly their own
patrimonial or feudal contingents. It is also possible that the provision
of administrative means and of the administrative staff itself is appropriated as the object of a profit-making enterprise, on the basis of fixed
contributions from the ruler's magazines or treasury. This was true in
particular of the mercenary armies in the sixteenth and seventeenth century in Europe—examples of "capitalist armies."

Where appropriation is complete, all the powers of government are
divided between the ruler and the administrative staff members, each
on the basis of his personal rights (*Eigenrecht*); or autonomous powers
are created and regulated by special decrees of the ruler or special compromises with the holders of appropriated rights.

On 1): An example are the holders of court offices which have become appropriated as fiefs. An example for 2) are seigneurs who appropriated powers by virtue of their privileged position or by usurpation,
using the former as a legalization of the latter.

Appropriation by an *individual* may rest on

1. leasing,
2. pledging as security,
3. sale,
4. privileges, which may be personal, hereditary or freely appropriated, unconditional or subject to the performance of certain functions;
such a privilege may be

a) granted in return for services or for the sake of "buying"
compliance, or

b) it may constitute merely the formal recognition of actual
usurpation of powers;

5. appropriation by an organized group or a status group, usually a
consequence of a compromise between the ruler and his administrative
staff or between him and an unorganized status group; this may

α) leave the ruler completely or relatively free in his selection
of individuals, or

β) it may lay down rigid rules for the selection of incumbents;

6. fiefs, a case which we must deal with separately.

1. In the cases of gerontocracy and pure patriarchalism, so far as there are clear ideas on the subject at all, the means of administration are generally appropriated by the group as a whole or by the participating households. The administrative functions are performed on behalf of the group as a whole. Appropriation by the master personally is a phenomenon of patrimonialism. It may vary enormously in degree to the extreme cases of a claim to full proprietorship of the land (*Bodenregal*) and to the status of master over subjects treated as negotiable slaves. Estate-type appropriation generally means the appropriation of at least part of the means of administration by the members of the administrative staff. In the case of pure patrimonialism, there is complete separation of the functionary from the means of carrying out his function. But exactly the opposite is true of the estate-type of patrimonialism. The person exercising governing powers has personal control of the means of administration—if not all, at least of an important part of them. In full possession of these means were the feudal knight, who provided his own equipment, the count, who by virtue of holding his fief took the court fees and other perquisites for himself and met his feudal obligations from his own means (including the appropriated ones), and the Indian *jagirdar*, who provided and equipped a military unit from the proceeds of his tax benefice. On the other hand, a colonel who recruited a mercenary regiment on his own account, but received certain payments from the royal exchequer and covered his deficit either by curtailing the service or from booty or requisitions, was only partly in possession of the means of administration and was subject to certain regulations. By contrast, the Pharaoh, who organized armies of slaves or *coloni,* put his clients in command of them, and clothed, fed and equipped them from his own storehouses, was acting as a patrimonial lord in full personal control of the means of administration. It is not always the formal mode of organization which is decisive. The Mamelukes were formally purchased slaves. In fact, however, they monopolized the powers of government as completely as any group of *ministeriales* has ever monopolized the service fiefs.

There are examples of service land appropriated by a closed group without any individual appropriation. Where this occurs, land may be freely granted to individuals by the lord as long as they are members of the group (case III:a:a) or the grant may be subject to regulations specifying qualifications (case III:a:β). Thus, military or possibly ritual qualifications have been required of the candidates, but once they are given, close blood relations have had priority. The situation is similar in the case of manorial or guild artisans or of peasants whose services have been attached for military or administrative purposes.

2. Appropriation by lease, especially tax farming, by pledging as security, or by sale, have been found in the Occident, but also in the Orient and in India. In Antiquity, it was not uncommon for priesthoods to be sold at auction. In the case of leasing, the aim has been partly a practical financial one to meet stringencies caused especially by the costs of war. It has partly also been a matter of the technique of

financing, to insure a stable money income available for budgetary uses. Pledging as security and sale have generally arisen from the first aim. In the Papal States the purpose was also the creation of rents for nephews (*Nepotenrenten*). Appropriation by pledging played a significant role in France as late as the eighteenth century in filling judicial posts in the *parlements*. The appropriation of officers' commissions by regulated purchase continued in the British army well into the nineteenth century. Privileges, as a sanction of usurpation, as a reward, or as an incentive for political services, were common in the Middle Ages in Europe as well as elsewhere.

8. *Patrimonial Maintenance: Benefices and Fiefs*

The patrimonial retainer may receive his support in any of the following ways:

a) by living from the lord's table,

b) by allowances (usually in kind) from the lord's magazines or treasury,

c) by rights of land use in return for services ("service-land"),

d) by the appropriation of property income, fees or taxes,

e) by fiefs.

We shall speak of *benefices* insofar as the forms of maintenance b) through d) are always newly granted in a traditional fashion which determines amount or locality, and insofar as they can be appropriated by the individual, although not hereditarily. When an administrative staff is, in principle, supported in this form, we shall speak of *prebendalism*. In such a situation there may be a system of promotion on a basis of seniority or of particular objectively determined achievements, and it may also happen that a certain social status and hence a sense of status honor (*Standesehre*) are required as a criterion of eligibility. (On the concept of the status group: *Stand*, see ch. IV.)

Appropriated seigneurial powers will be called a *fief* if they are granted primarily to particular qualified individuals by a contract and if the reciprocal rights and duties involved are primarily oriented to conventional standards of status honor, particularly in a military sense. If an administrative staff is primarily supported by fiefs, we will speak of [Western] *feudalism* (*Lehensfeudalismus*).

The transition between fiefs and military benefices is so gradual that at times they are almost indistinguishable. (This will be further discussed below in ch. IV.)

In cases d) and e), sometimes also in c), the individual who has appropriated governing powers pays the cost of his administration, possibly of military equipment, in the manner indicated above, from the proceeds of his benefice or fief. His own authority may then become patrimonial (hence, hereditary, alienable, and capable of division by inheritance.)

1. The earliest form of support for royal retainers, household officials, priests and other types of patrimonial (for example, manorial) retainers has been their presence at the lord's table or their support by discretionary allowances from his stores. The "men's house," which is the oldest form of professional military organizations—to be dealt with later—, very often adheres to the consumptive household communism of a ruling stratum. Separation from the table of the lord (or of the temple or cathedral) and the substitution of allowances or service-land has by no means always been regarded with approval. It has, however, usually resulted from the establishment of independent families. Allowances in kind granted to such temple priests and officials constituted the original form of support of officials throughout the Near East and also existed in China, India, and often in the Occident. The use of land in return for military service is found throughout the Orient since early Antiquity, and also in medieval Germany, as a means of providing for *ministeriales,* manorial officials and other functionaries. The income sources of the Turkish *spahis,* the Japanese *samurai,* and various similar types of Oriental retainers and knights are, in the present terminology, "benefices" and not "fiefs," as will be pointed out later. In some cases they have been derived from the rents of certain lands; in others, from the tax income of certain districts. In the latter case, they have generally been combined with appropriation of governmental powers in the same district. The concept of the fief can be further developed only in relation to that of the state. Its object may be a manor—a form of patrimonial domination —or it may be any of various kinds of claims to property income and fees.

2. The appropriation of property income and rights to fees and the proceeds of taxes in the form of benefices and fiefs of all sorts is widespread. In India, particularly, it became an independent and highly developed practice. The usual arrangement was the granting of rights to these sources of income in return for the provision of military contingents and the payment of administrative costs.

9. *Estate-Type Domination and Its Division of Powers*

In the pure type, patrimonial domination, especially of the estate-type, regards all governing powers and the corresponding economic rights as privately appropriated economic advantages. This does not mean that these powers are qualitatively undifferentiated. Some important ones are appropriated in a form subject to special regulations. In particular, the appropriation of judicial and military powers tends to be treated as a legal basis for a privileged status position of those appropriating them, as compared to the appropriation of purely economic advantages having to do with the income from domains, from taxes, or perquisites. Within the latter category, again, there tends to be a differentiation of those which are primarily patrimonial from those which are primarily extra-patrimonial or fiscal in the mode of appropriation. For our terminology the decisive fact is that, regardless of content, governing powers and the related emoluments are treated as private rights.

> In his *Der deutsche Staat des Mittelalters,* von Below is quite right in emphasizing that the appropriation of judicial authority was singled out and became a source of privileged status, and that it is impossible to prove that the medieval political organization had either a purely patri-monial or a purely feudal character. Nevertheless, so far as judicial authority and other rights of a purely political origin are treated as private rights, it is for present purposes terminologically correct to speak of patrimonial domination. The concept itself, as is well known, has been most consistently developed by Haller in his *Restauration der Staatswissenschaften.* Historically there has never been a purely patri-monial state.[5]

IV. We shall speak of the *estate-type division of powers (ständische Gewaltenteilung)* when organized groups of persons privileged by ap-propriated seigneurial powers conclude *compromises* with their ruler. As the occasion warrants, the subject of such compromises may be political or administrative regulations, concrete administrative decisions or super-visory measures. At times the members of such groups may participate directly on their own authority and with their own staffs.

> 1. Under certain circumstances, groups, such as peasants, which do not enjoy a privileged social position, may be included. This does not, however, alter the concept. For the decisive point is the fact that the members of the privileged group have independent rights. If socially privileged groups were absent, the case would obviously belong under another type.
> 2. The type case has been fully developed only in the Occident. We must deal separately and in detail with its characteristics and with the reasons for its development.
> 3. As a rule, such a status group did not have an administrative staff of its own, especially not one with independent governing powers.

9a. Traditional Domination and the Economy

The primary effect of traditional domination on economic activities is usually in a very general way to strengthen traditional attitudes. This is most conspicuous under gerontocratic and purely patriarchal domina-tion, which cannot use an administrative machinery against the members of the group and hence is strongly dependent for its own legitimacy upon the safeguarding of tradition in every respect.

I. Beyond this, the typical mode of financing a traditional structure of domination affects the economy (cf. ch. II, sec. 38). In this respect, patrimonialism may use a wide variety of approaches. The following, however, are particularly important:

A. An *oikos* maintained by the ruler where needs are met on a liturgical basis wholly or primarily in kind (in the form of contributions and compulsory services). In this case, economic relationships tend to be strictly tradition-bound. The development of markets is obstructed, the use of money is primarily consumptive, and the development of capitalism is impossible.

B. Provisioning the services of socially privileged groups has very similar effects. Though not necessarily to the same extent, the development of markets is also limited in this case by the fact that the property and the productive capacity of the individual economic units are largely pre-empted for the ruler's needs.

C. Furthermore, patrimonialism can resort to monopolistic want satisfaction, which in part may rely on profit-making enterprises, fee-taking or taxation. In this case, the development of markets is, according to the type of monopolies involved, more or less seriously limited by irrational factors. The important openings for profit are in the hands of the ruler and of his administrative staff. Capitalism is thereby either directly obstructed, if the ruler maintains his own administration, or is diverted into political capitalism, if there is tax farming, leasing or sale of offices, and capitalist provision for armies and administration (see ch. II, sec. 31).

Even where it is carried out in money terms, the financing of patrimonialism and even more of sultanism tends to have irrational consequences for the following reasons:

1) The obligations placed on sources of direct taxation tend both in amount and in kind to remain bound to tradition. At the same time there is complete freedom—and hence arbitrariness—in the determination of a) fees and b) of newly imposed obligations, and c) in the organization of monopolies. This element of arbitrariness is at least claimed as a right. It is historically most effective in case a), because the lord and his staff must be asked for the "favor" of action, far less effective in case b), and of varying effectiveness in case c).

2) Two bases of the rationalization of economic activity are entirely lacking; namely, a basis for the calculability of obligations and of the extent of freedom which will be allowed to private enterprise.

D. In individual cases, however, patrimonial fiscal policy may have a rationalizing effect by systematically cultivating its sources of taxation and by organizing monopolies rationally. This, however, is "accidental" and dependent on specific historical circumstances, some of which existed in the Occident.

If there is estate-type division of powers, fiscal policy tends to be a result of compromise. This makes the burdens relatively predictable and eliminates or at least sharply limits the ruler's powers to impose new burdens and, above all, to create monopolies. Whether the resulting fiscal policy tends to promote or to limit rational economic activity depends largely on the type of ruling group; primarily, it depends on whether it is a *feudal* or a *patrician* stratum. The dominance of the feudal stratum tends, because the structure of feudalized powers of government is normally patrimonial, to set rigid limits to the freedom of acquisitive activity and the development of markets. It may even involve deliberate attempts to suppress them to protect the power of the feudal stratum. The predominance of a patrician [urban] stratum may have the opposite effect.

1. What has been said above must suffice for the present. It will be necessary to return to these questions repeatedly in different connections.

2. Examples for IA): the *oikos* of ancient Egypt and in India; IB): large parts of the Hellenistic world, the late Roman Empire, China, India, to some extent Russia and the Islamic states; IC): Ptolemaic Egypt, to some extent the Byzantine Empire, and in a different way the regime of the Stuarts in England; ID): the Occidental patrimonial states in the period of "enlightened despotism," especially Colbert's policies.

II. It is not only the financial policy of most patrimonial regimes which tends to restrict the development of rational economic activity, but above all the general character of their administrative practices. This is true in the following respects:

a) Traditionalism places serious obstacles in the way of formally rational regulations, which can be depended upon to remain stable and hence are calculable in their economic implications and exploitability.

b) A staff of officials with formal technical training is typically absent.

(The fact that it developed in the patrimonial states of the Occident is, as will be shown, accounted for by unique conditions. This stratum developed for the most part out of sources wholly different from the general structure of patrimonialism.)

c) There is a wide scope for actual arbitrariness and the expression of purely personal whims on the part of the ruler and the members of his administrative staff. The opening for bribery and corruption, which is simply a matter of the disorganization of an unregulated system of fees, would be the least serious effect of this if it remained a constant quantity, because then it would become calculable in practice. But it tends to be a matter which is settled from case to case with every individual official and thus highly variable. If offices are leased, the incumbent is put in a position where it is to his immediate interest to get back the capital he has invested by any available means of extortion, however irrational.

d) Patriarchalism and patrimonialism have an inherent tendency to regulate economic activity in terms of utilitarian, welfare or absolute values. This tendency stems from the character of the claim to legitimacy and the interest in the contentment of the subjects. It breaks down the type of *formal* rationality which is oriented to a technical legal order. This type of influence is decisive in the case of hierocratic patrimonialism. In the case of pure sultanism, on the other hand, it is fiscal arbitrariness which is likely to be most important.

For all these reasons, under the dominance of a patrimonial regime only certain types of capitalism are able to develop:

a) capitalist trading,

b) capitalist tax farming, lease and sale of offices,

c) capitalist provision of supplies for the state and the financing of wars,

d) under certain circumstances, capitalist plantations and other colonial enterprises.

All these forms are indigenous to patrimonial regimes and often reach a very high level of development. This is not, however, true of the type of profit-making enterprise with heavy investments in fixed capital and a rational organization of free labor which is oriented to the market purchases of private consumers. This type of capitalism is altogether too sensitive to all sorts of irrationalities in the administration of law, administration and taxation, for these upset the basis of *calculability*.

The situation is fundamentally different only in cases where a patrimonial ruler, in the interest of his own power and financial provision, develops a rational system of administration with technically specialized officials. For this to happen, it is necessary 1) that technical training should be available; 2) there must be a sufficiently powerful incentive to embark on such a policy—usually the sharp competition between a plurality of patrimonial powers within the same cultural area; 3) a very special factor is necessary, namely, the participation of urban communes as a financial support in the competition of the patrimonial units.

1. The major forerunners of the modern, specifically Western form of capitalism are to be found in the organized urban communes of Eu-

rope with their particular type of relatively rational administration. Its primary development took place from the sixteenth to the eighteenth centuries within the framework of the class structure and political organization (*ständischen politischen Verbände*) of Holland and England, which were distinguished by the unusual power of the bourgeois strata and the preponderance of their economic interests. The fiscal and utilitarian imitations, which were introduced into the purely patrimonial or largely feudal (*feudal-ständisch*) states of the Continent, have in common with the Stuart system of monopolistic industry the fact that they do not stand in the main line of continuity with the later autonomous capitalistic development. This is true in spite of the fact that particular measures of agricultural and industrial policy—so far and because they were oriented to English, Dutch, and later to French, models—played a very important part in creating some of the essential conditions for this later development. All this will be discussed further on.

2. In certain fields the patrimonial states of the Middle Ages developed a type of formally rational administrative staff which consisted especially of persons with legal training both in the civil and the canon law, and which differed fundamentally from the corresponding administrative staffs in political bodies of any other time or place. It will be necessary later to inquire more fully into the sources of this development and into its significance. For the present it is not possible to go beyond the very general observations introduced above.

iv
Charismatic Authority

1 0. *Charismatic Authority and Charismatic Community*

The term "charisma" will be applied to a certain quality of an individual personality by virtue of which he is considered extraordinary and treated as endowed with supernatural, superhuman, or at least specifically exceptional powers or qualities. These are such as are not accessible to the ordinary person, but are regarded as of divine origin or as exemplary, and on the basis of them the individual concerned is treated as a "leader." In primitive circumstances this peculiar kind of quality is thought of as resting on magical powers, whether of prophets, persons with a reputation for therapeutic or legal wisdom, leaders in the hunt, or heroes in war. How the quality in question would be ultimately judged from any ethical, aesthetic, or other such point of view is naturally entirely indifferent for purposes of definition. What is alone important is how the individual is actually regarded by those subject to charismatic authority, by his "followers" or "disciples."

For present purposes it will be necessary to treat a variety of different types as being endowed with charisma in this sense. It includes the state of a "berserk" whose spells of maniac passion have, apparently wrongly, sometimes been attributed to the use of drugs. In medieval Byzantium a group of these men endowed with the charisma of fighting frenzy was maintained as a kind of weapon. It includes the "shaman," the magician who in the pure type has to be subject to epileptoid seizures as a means of falling into trances. Another type is represented by Joseph Smith, the founder of Mormonism, who may have been a very sophisticated swindler (although this cannot be definitely established). Finally it includes the type of *littérateur*, such as Kurt Eisner,[6] who is overwhelmed by his own demagogic success. Value-free sociological analysis will treat all these on the same level as it does the charisma of men who are the "greatest" heroes, prophets, and saviors according to conventional judgements.

I. It is recognition on the part of those subject to authority which is decisive for the validity of charisma. This recognition is freely given and guaranteed by what is held to be a proof, originally always a miracle, and consists in devotion to the corresponding revelation, hero worship, or absolute trust in the leader. But where charisma is genuine, it is not this which is the basis of the claim to legitimacy. This basis lies rather in the conception that it is the duty of those subject to charismatic authority to recognize its genuineness and to act accordingly. Psychologically this recognition is a matter of complete personal devotion to the possessor of the quality, arising out of enthusiasm, or of despair and hope.

No prophet has ever regarded his quality as dependent on the attitudes of the masses toward him. No elective king or military leader has ever treated those who have resisted him or tried to ignore him otherwise than as delinquent in duty. Failure to take part in a military expedition under such leader, even though the recruitment is formally voluntary, has universally met with disdain.

II. If proof and success elude the leader for long, if he appears deserted by his god or his magical or heroic powers, above all, if his leadership fails to benefit his followers, it is likely that his charismatic authority will disappear. This is the genuine meaning of the divine right of kings (*Gottesgnadentum*).

Even the old Germanic kings were sometimes rejected with scorn. Similar phenomena are very common among so-called primitive peoples.

In China the charismatic quality of the monarch, which was transmitted unchanged by heredity, was upheld so rigidly that any misfortune whatever, not only defeats in war, but drought, floods, or astronomical phenomena which were considered unlucky, forced him to do public penance and might even force his abdication. If such things occurred, it was a sign that he did not possess the requisite charismatic virtue and was thus not a legitimate "Son of Heaven."

III. An organized group subject to charismatic authority will be called a charismatic community (*Gemeinde*). It is based on an emotional form of communal relationship (*Vergemeinschaftung*). The administrative staff of a charismatic leader does not consist of "officials"; least of all are its members technically trained. It is not chosen on the basis of social privilege nor from the point of view of domestic or personal dependency. It is rather chosen in terms of the charismatic qualities of its members. The prophet has his disciples; the warlord his bodyguard; the leader, generally, his agents (*Vertrauensmänner*). There is no such thing as appointment or dismissal, no career, no promotion. There is only a call at the instance of the leader on the basis of the charismatic qualification of those he summons. There is no hierarchy; the leader merely intervenes in general or in individual cases when he considers the members of his staff lacking in charismatic qualification for a given task. There is no such thing as a bailiwick or definite sphere of competence, and no appropriation of official powers on the basis of social privileges. There may, however, be territorial or functional limits to charismatic powers and to the individual's mission. There is no such thing as a salary or a benefice.

Disciples or followers tend to live primarily in a communistic relationship with their leader on means which have been provided by voluntary gift. There are no established administrative organs. In their place are agents who have been provided with charismatic authority by their chief or who possess charisma of their own. There is no system of formal rules, of abstract legal principles, and hence no process of rational judicial decision oriented to them. But equally there is no legal wisdom oriented to judicial precedent. Formally concrete judgments are newly created from case to case and are originally regarded as divine judgments and revelations. From a substantive point of view, every charismatic authority would have to subscribe to the proposition, "It is written . . . but I say unto you . . ." The genuine prophet, like the genuine military leader and every true leader in this sense, preaches, creates, or demands *new* obligations—most typically, by virtue of revelation, oracle, inspiration, or of his own will, which are recognized by the members of the religious, military, or party group because they come from such a source. Recognition is a duty. When such an authority comes into conflict with the competing authority of another who also claims charismatic sanction, the only recourse is to some kind of a contest, by magical means or an actual physical battle of the leaders. In principle, only one side can be right in such a conflict; the other must be guilty of a wrong which has to be expiated.

Since it is "extra-ordinary," charismatic authority is sharply opposed to rational, and particularly bureaucratic, authority, and to traditional authority, whether in its patriarchal, patrimonial, or estate variants, all of which are everyday forms of domination; while the charismatic type is the direct antithesis of this. Bureaucratic authority is specifically rational in the sense of being bound to intellectually analysable rules; while charismatic authority is specifically irrational in the sense of being foreign to all rules. Traditional authority is bound to the precedents handed down from the past and to this extent is also oriented to rules. Within the sphere of its claims, charismatic authority repudiates the past, and is in this sense a specifically revolutionary force. It recognizes no appropriation of positions of power by virtue of the possession of property, either on the part of a chief or of socially privileged groups. The only basis of legitimacy for it is personal charisma so long as it is proved; that is, as long as it receives recognition and as long as the followers and disciples prove their usefulness charismatically.

> The above is scarcely in need of further discussion. What has been said applies to purely plebiscitary rulers (Napoleon's "rule of genius" elevated people of humble origin to thrones and high military commands) just as much as it applies to religious prophets or war heroes.

IV. Pure charisma is specifically foreign to economic considerations. Wherever it appears, it constitutes a "call" in the most emphatic sense of the word, a "mission" or a "spiritual duty." In the pure type, it disdains and repudiates economic exploitation of the gifts of grace as a source of income, though, to be sure, this often remains more an ideal than a fact. It is not that charisma always demands a renunciation of property or even of acquisition, as under certain circumstances prophets and their disciples do. The heroic warrior and his followers actively seek booty; the elective ruler or the charismatic party leader requires the material means of power. The former in addition requires a brilliant display of his authority to bolster his prestige. What is despised, so long as the genuinely charismatic type is adhered to, is traditional or rational everyday economizing, the attainment of a regular income by continuous economic activity devoted to this end. Support by gifts, either on a grand scale involving donation, endowment, bribery and honoraria, or by begging, constitute the voluntary type of support. On the other hand, "booty" and extortion, whether by force or by other means, is the typical form of charismatic provision for needs. From the point of view of rational economic activity, charismatic want satisfaction is a typical anti-economic force. It repudiates any sort of involvement in the everyday routine world. It can only tolerate, with an attitude of complete emotional indifference, irregular, unsystematic acquisitive acts. In that it relieves the recipient of economic concerns, dependence on property income can be the economic basis of a charismatic mode of life for some groups; but that is unusual for the normal charismatic "revolutionary."

The fact that incumbency of church office has been forbidden to the Jesuits is a rationalized application of this principle of discipleship. The fact that all the "virtuosi" of asceticism, the mendicant orders, and fighters for a faith belong in this category, is quite clear. Almost all prophets have been supported by voluntary gifts. The well-known saying of St. Paul, "If a man does not work, neither shall he eat," was directed against the parasitic swarm of charismatic missionaries. It obviously has nothing to do with a positive valuation of economic activity for its own sake, but only lays it down as a duty of each individual somehow to provide for his own support. This because he realized that the purely charismatic parable of the lilies of the field was not capable of literal application, but at best "taking no thought for the morrow" could be hoped for. On the other hand, in a case of a primarily artistic type of charismatic discipleship it is conceivable that insulation from economic struggle should mean limitation of those really eligible to the "economically independent"; that is, to persons living on income from property. This has been true of the circle of Stefan George, at least in its primary intentions.

V. In traditionalist periods, charisma is *the* great revolutionary force. The likewise revolutionary force of "reason" works from *without*: by altering the situations of life and hence its problems, finally in this way changing men's attitudes toward them; or it intellectualizes the individual. Charisma, on the other hand, *may* effect a subjective or *internal* reorientation born out of suffering, conflicts, or enthusiasm. It may then result in a radical alteration of the central attitudes and directions of action with a completely new orientation of all attitudes toward the different problems of the "world."[7] In prerationalistic periods, tradition and charisma between them have almost exhausted the whole of the orientation of action.

V

The Routinization of Charisma

11. *The Rise of the Charismatic Community and the Problem of Succession*

In its pure form charismatic authority has a character specifically foreign to everyday routine structures. The social relationships directly involved are strictly personal, based on the validity and practice of charismatic personal qualities. If this is not to remain a purely transitory phenomenon, but to take on the character of a permanent relationship, a "community" of disciples or followers or a party organization or any sort of political or hierocratic organization, it is necessary for the character of charismatic authority to become radically changed. Indeed, in its pure form charismatic authority may be said to exist only *in natu nascendi*. It cannot remain stable, but becomes either traditionalized or rationalized, or a combination of both.

The following are the principal motives underlying this transformation: (a) The ideal and also the material interests of the followers in the continuation and the continual reactivation of the community, (b) the still stronger ideal and also stronger material interests of the members of the administrative staff, the disciples, the party workers, or others in continuing their relationship. Not only this, but they have an interest in continuing it in such a way that both from an ideal and a material point of view, their own position is put on a stable everyday basis. This means, above all, making it possible to participate in normal family relationships or at least to enjoy a secure social position in place of the kind of discipleship which is cut off from ordinary worldly connections, notably in the family and in economic relationships.

These interests generally become conspicuously evident with the disappearance of the personal charismatic leader and with the problem of *succession*. The way in which this problem is met—if it is met at all and the charismatic community continues to exist or now begins to emerge—is of crucial importance for the character of the subsequent social relationships. The following are the principal possible types of solution:—

(a) The *search* for a new charismatic leader on the basis of criteria of the qualities which will fit him for the position of authority.

This is to be found in a relatively pure type in the process of choice of a new Dalai Lama. It consists in the search for a child with characteristics which are interpreted to mean that he is a reincarnation of the Buddha. This is very similar to the choice of the new Bull of Apis.

In this case the legitimacy of the new charismatic leader is bound to certain distinguishing characteristics; thus, to rules with respect to which a tradition arises. The result is a process of traditionalization in favor of which the purely personal character of leadership is reduced.

(b) *Revelation* manifested in oracles, lots, divine judgments, or other techniques of selection. In this case the legitimacy of the new leader is dependent on the legitimacy of the *technique* of his selection. This involves a form of legalization.

It is said that at times the *Shofetim* [Judges] of Israel had this character. Saul is said to have been chosen by the old war oracle.

(c) Designation on the part of the original charismatic leader of his own successor and his recognition on the part of the followers.

This is a very common form. Originally, the Roman magistracies were filled entirely in this way. The system survived most clearly into later times in the appointment of the *dictator* and in the institution of the *interrex*.[8]

In this case legitimacy is *acquired* through the act of designation.

(d) Designation of a successor by the charismatically qualified administrative staff and his recognition by the community. In its typical form this process should quite definitely not be interpreted as "election" or "nomination" or anything of the sort. It is not a matter of free selection, but of one which is strictly bound to objective duty. It is not to be determined merely by majority vote, but is a question of arriving at the correct designation, the designation of the right person who is truly endowed with charisma. It is quite possible that the minority and not the majority should be right in such a case. Unanimity is often required. It is obligatory to acknowledge a mistake and persistence in error is a serious offense. Making a wrong choice is a genuine wrong requiring expiation. Originally it was a magical offence.

Nevertheless, in such a case it is easy for legitimacy to take on the character of an acquired right which is justified by standards of the correctness of the process by which the position was acquired, for the most part, by its having been acquired in accordance with certain formalities such as coronation.

This was the original meaning of the coronation of bishops and kings in the Western world by the clergy or the high nobility with the "consent" of the community. There are numerous analogous phenomena all over the world. The fact that this is the origin of the modern conception of "election" raises problems which will have to be gone into later.[9]

(e) The conception that charisma is a quality transmitted by heredity; thus that it is participated in by the kinsmen of its bearer, particularly by his closest relatives. This is the case of *hereditary charisma*. The order of hereditary succession in such a case need not be the same as that which is in force for appropriated rights, but may differ from it. It is also sometimes necessary to select the proper heir within the kinship group by some of the methods just spoken of.

> Thus in certain African states brothers have had to fight for the succession. In China, succession had to take place in such a way that the relation of the living group to the ancestral spirits was not disturbed. The rule either of seniority or of designation by the followers has been very common in the Orient. Hence, in the House of Osman, it used to be obligatory to kill off all other possible aspirants.

Only in Medieval Europe and in Japan, elsewhere sporadically, has the principle of primogeniture, as governing the inheritance of authority, become clearly established. This has greatly facilitated the consolidation of political groups in that it has eliminated struggle between a plurality of candidates from the same charismatic family.

In the case of hereditary charisma, recognition is no longer paid to the charismatic qualities of the individual, but to the legitimacy of the position he has acquired by hereditary succession. This may lead in the direction either of traditionalization or of legalization. The concept of divine right is fundamentally altered and now comes to mean authority by virtue of a personal right which is not dependent on the recognition of those subject to authority. Personal charisma may be totally absent.

> Hereditary monarchy is a conspicuous illustration. In Asia there have been very numerous hereditary priesthoods; also, frequently, the hereditary charisma of kinship groups has been treated as a criterion of social rank and of eligibility for fiefs and benefices.

(f) The concept that charisma may be transmitted by ritual means from one bearer to another or may be created in a new person. The concept was originally magical. It involves a dissociation of charisma from a particular individual, making it an objective, transferrable entity. In particular, it may become the *charisma of office*. In this case the belief in legitimacy is no longer directed to the individual, but to the acquired qualities and to the effectiveness of the ritual acts.

> The most important example is the transmission of priestly charisma by anointing, consecration, or the laying on of hands; and of royal au-

thority, by anointing and by coronation. The *character indelebilis* thus acquired means that the charismatic qualities and powers of the office are emancipated from the personal qualities of the priest. For precisely this reason, this has, from the Donatist and the Montanist heresies down to the Puritan revolution, been the subject of continual conflicts. The "hireling" of the Quakers is the preacher endowed with the charisma of office.

1 2. *Types of Appropriation by the Charismatic Staff*

Concomitant with the routinization of charisma with a view to insuring adequate succession, go the interests in its routinization on the part of the administrative staff. It is only in the initial stages and so long as the charismatic leader acts in a way which is completely outside everyday social organization, that it is possible for his followers to live communistically in a community of faith and enthusiasm, on gifts, booty, or sporadic acquisition. Only the members of the small group of enthusiastic disciples and followers are prepared to devote their lives purely idealistically to their call. The great majority of disciples and followers will in the long run "make their living" out of their "calling" in a material sense as well. Indeed, this must be the case if the movement is not to disintegrate.

Hence, the routinization of charisma also takes the form of the appropriation of powers and of economic advantages by the followers or disciples, and of regulating recruitment. This process of traditionalization or of legalization, according to whether rational legislation is involved or not, may take any one of a number of typical forms.

1. The original basis of recruitment is personal charisma. However, with routinization, the followers or disciples may set up norms for recruitment, in particular involving training or tests of eligibility. Charisma can only be "awakened" and "tested"; it cannot be "learned" or "taught." All types of magical asceticism, as practiced by magicians and heroes, and all novitiates, belong in this category. These are means of closing the administrative staff. (On the charismatic type of education, see ch. IV below [unfinished].)

Only the proved novice is allowed to exercise authority. A genuine charismatic leader is in a position to oppose this type of prerequisite for membership; his successor is not free to do so, at least if he is chosen by the administrative staff.

This type is illustrated by the magical and warrior asceticism of the "men's house" with initiation ceremonies and age groups. An indi-

vidual who has not successfully gone through the initiation, remains a
"woman"; that is, he is excluded from the charismatic group.

2. It is easy for charismatic norms to be transformed into those defining a traditional social status (on a hereditary charismatic basis). If
the leader is chosen on a hereditary basis, the same is likely to happen
in the selection and deployment of the staff and even the followers.
The term "clan state" (*Geschlechterstaat*) will be applied when a
political body is organized strictly and completely in terms of this principle of hereditary charisma. In such a case, all appropriation of governing powers, of fiefs, benefices, and all sorts of economic advantages follow the same pattern. The result is that all powers and advantages of
all sorts become traditionalized. The heads of families, who are traditional gerontocrats or patriarchs without personal charismatic legitimacy,
regulate the exercise of these powers which cannot be taken away from
their family. It is not the type of position he occupies which determines
the rank of a man or of his family, but rather the hereditary charismatic
rank of his family determines the position he will occupy.

Japan, before the development of bureaucracy, was organized in this
way. The same was undoubtedly true of China as well where, before
the rationalization which took place in the territorial states, authority
was in the hands of the "old families." Other types of examples are furnished by the caste system in India, and by Russia before the *mestnichestvo* was introduced. Indeed, all hereditary social classes with established privileges belong in the same category.

3. The administrative staff may seek and achieve the creation and
appropriation of *individual* positions and the corresponding economic
advantages for its members. In that case, according to whether the
tendency is to traditionalization or legalization, there will develop (a)
benefices, (b) offices, or (c) fiefs. In the first case a prebendal organization will result; in the second, patrimonialism or bureaucracy; in the
third, feudalism. These revenue sources become appropriated and replace
provision from gifts or booty without settled relation to the everyday
economic structure.

Case (a), benefices, may consist in rights to the proceeds of begging,
to payments in kind, or to the proceeds of money taxes, or finally, to the
proceeds of fees. The latter may result from the former through the
regulation of the original provision by free gifts or by "booty" in terms
of a rational organization or finance.

Regularized begging is found in Buddhism; benefices in kind, in the
Chinese and Japanese "rice rents"; support by money taxation has been

the rule in all the rationalized conquest states. The last case is common everywhere, especially on the part of priests and judges and, in India, even the military authorities.

Case (b), the transformation of the charismatic mission into an office, may have more of a patrimonial or more of a bureaucratic character. The former is much the more common; the latter is found principally in Antiquity and in the modern Western world. Elsewhere it is exceptional.

In case (c), only land may be appropriated as a fief, whereas the position as such retains its originally charismatic character, or powers and authority may be fully appropriated as fiefs. It is difficult to distinguish the two cases. However, orientation to the charismatic character of the position was slow to disappear, also in the Middle Ages.

12a. *Status Honor and the Legitimation of Authority*

For charisma to be transformed into an everyday phenomenon, it is necessary that its anti-economic character should be altered. It must be adapted to some form of fiscal organization to provide for the needs of the group and hence to the economic conditions necessary for raising taxes and contributions. When a charismatic movement develops in the direction of prebendal provision, the "laity" becomes differentiated from the "clergy"—derived from κλῆρος, meaning a "share"—, that is, the participating members of the charismatic administrative staff which has now become routinized. These are the priests of the developing "church." Correspondingly, in a developing political body—the "state" in the rational case—vassals, benefice-holders, officials or appointed party officials (instead of voluntary party workers and functionaries) are differentiated from the "tax payers."

> This process is very conspicuous in Buddhism and in the Hindu sects—see the Sociology of Religion below. The same is true in all conquest states which have become rationalized to form permanent structures; also of parties and other originally charismatic structures.

It follows that, in the course of routinization, the charismatically ruled organization is largely transformed into one of the everyday authorities, the patrimonial form, especially in its estate-type or bureaucratic variant. Its original peculiarities are apt to be retained in the charismatic status honor acquired by heredity or office-holding. This applies to all who participate in the appropriation, the chief himself and the members of his staff. It is thus a matter of the type of prestige enjoyed by ruling groups. A hereditary monarch by "divine right" is not a simple patrimonial chief, patriarch, or sheik; a vassal is not a mere household retainer or official. Further details must be deferred to the analysis of status groups.

As a rule, routinization is not free of conflict. In the early stages personal claims on the charisma of the chief are not easily forgotten and the conflict between the charisma of the office or of hereditary status with personal charisma is a typical process in many historical situations.

1. The power of absolution—that is, the power to absolve from mortal sins—was held originally only by personal charismatic martyrs or ascetics, but became transformed into a power of the office of bishop or priest. This process was much slower in the Orient than in the Occident because in the latter is was influenced by the Roman conception of office. Revolutions under a charismatic leader, directed against hereditary charismatic powers or the powers of office, are to be found in all types of organizations, from states to trade unions. (This last is particularly conspicuous at the present time [1918/20].) The more highly developed the interdependence of different economic units in a monetary economy, the greater the pressure of the everyday needs of the followers of the charismatic movement becomes. The effect of this is to strengthen the tendency to routinization, which is everywhere operative, and as a rule has rapidly won out. Charisma is a phenomenon typical of prophetic movements or of expansive political movements in their early stages. But as soon as domination is well established, and above all as soon as control over large masses of people exists, it gives way to the forces of everyday routine.

2. One of the decisive motives underlying all cases of the routinization of charisma is naturally the striving for security. This means legitimization, on the one hand, of positions of authority and social prestige, on the other hand, of the economic advantages enjoyed by the followers and sympathizers of the leader. Another important motive, however, lies in the objective necessity of adapting the order and the staff organization to the normal, everyday needs and conditions of carrying on administration. In this connection, in particular, there are always points at which traditions of administrative practice and of judicial decision can take hold as these are needed by the normal administrative staff and those subject to its authority. It is further necessary that there should be some definite order introduced into the organization of the administrative staff itself. Finally, as will be discussed in detail below, it is necessary for the administrative staff and all its administrative practices to be adapted to everyday economic conditions. It is not possible for the costs of permanent, routine administration to be met by "booty," contributions, gifts, and hospitality, as is typical of the pure type of military and prophetic charisma.

3. The process of routinization is thus not by any means confined to the problem of succession and does not stop when this has been solved. On the contrary, the most fundamental problem is that of making a transition from a charismatic administrative staff, and the corresponding principles of administration, to one which is adapted to everyday conditions. The problem of succession, however, is crucial because through it occurs the routinization of the charismatic focus of the structure. In it, the character of the leader himself and of his claim to legitimacy is altered. This process involves peculiar and characteristic conceptions which are understandable only in this context and do not apply to the problem of transition to traditional or legal patterns of order and types or administrative organization. The most important of the modes of meeting the problem of succession are the charismatic designation of a successor and hereditary charisma.

4. As has already been noted, the most important historical example of designation by the charismatic leader of his own successor is Rome. For the *rex*, this arrangement is attested by tradition; while for the appointment of the *dictator* and of the co-emperor and successor in the Principate, it has existed in historical times. The way in which all the higher magistrates were invested with the *imperium* shows clearly that they also were designated as successors by the military commander, subject to recognition by the citizen army. The fact that candidates were examined by the magistrate in office and that originally they could be excluded on what were obviously arbitrary grounds shows clearly what was the nature of the development.

5. The most important examples of designation of a successor by the charismatic followers of the leader are to be found in the election of bishops, and particularly of the Pope, by the original system of designation by the clergy and recognition by the lay community. The investigations of U. Stutz have made it probable that the election of the German king was modelled on that of the bishops.[10] He was designated by a group of qualified princes and recognized by the "people," that is, those bearing arms. Similar arrangements are very common.

6. The classical case of the development of hereditary charisma is that of caste in India. All occupational qualifications, and in particular all the qualifications for positions of authority and power, have there come to be regarded as strictly bound to the inheritance of charisma. Eligibility for fiefs, involving governing powers, was limited to members of the royal kinship group, the fiefs being granted by the eldest of the group. All types of religious office, including the extraordinarily important and influential position of *guru*, the *directeur de l'âme*, were treated as bound to hereditary charismatic qualities. The same is true of all sorts of relations to traditional customers and of all positions in the village organization, such as priest, barber, laundryman, watchman, etc. The foundation of a sect always meant the development of a hereditary hierarchy, as was true also of Taoism in China. Also in the Japanese

"feudal" state, before the introduction of a patrimonial officialdom on the Chinese model, which then led to prebends and a new feudalization, social organization was based purely on hereditary charisma.

This kind of hereditary charismatic right to positions of authority has been developed in similar ways all over the world. Qualification by virtue of individual achievement has been replaced by qualification by birth. This is everywhere the basis of the development of hereditary aristocracies, in the Roman nobility, in the concept of the *stirps regia,* which Tacitus describes among the Germans, in the rules of eligibility to tournaments and monasteries in the late Middle Ages, and even in the genealogical research conducted on behalf of the *parvenu* aristocracy of the United States. Indeed, this is to be found everywhere where hereditary status groups have become established.

Relationship to the economy: The process of routinization of charisma is in very important respects identical with adaptation to the conditions of the economy, since this is the principal continually operating force in everyday life. Economic conditions in this connection play a leading role and do not constitute merely a dependent variable. To a very large extent the transition to hereditary charisma or the charisma of office serves as a means of legitimizing existing or recently acquired powers of control over economic goods. Along with the ideology of loyalty, which is certainly by no means unimportant, allegiance to hereditary monarchy in particular is very strongly influenced by the consideration that all inherited and legitimately acquired property would be endangered if people stopped believing in the sanctity of hereditary succession to the throne. It is hence by no means fortuitous that hereditary monarchy is more adequate to the propertied strata than to the proletariat.

Beyond this, it is not possible to say anything in general terms, which would at the same time be substantial and valuable, on the relations of the various possible modes of adaptation to the economic order. This must be reserved to the more detailed treatment. The development of a prebendal structure, of feudalism, and the appropriation of all sorts of advantages on a hereditary charismatic basis may in all cases have the same stereotyping effect on the economic order if they develop from charismatic starting points as if they developed from early patrimonial or bureaucratic stages. In economic respects, too, the revolutionary impact of charisma is usually tremendous; at first, it is often destructive, because it means new modes of orientation. But routinization leads to the exact reverse.

The economics of charismatic revolutions will have to be discussed separately; it is a different matter altogether.

vi

Feudalism

12b. Occidental Feudalism and Its Conflict with Patrimonialism

The case noted above, under sec. 12:3c [the fief], requires separate discussion. This is because a structure of domination may develop out of it which is different both from patrimonialism and from genuine or hereditary charisma and which has had a very great historical significance, namely, feudalism. We will distinguish two types: the one based on fiefs (*Lehensfeudalismus*) and the other based on benefices (prebendal feudalism). All other forms in which the use of land is granted in exchange for military service really have a patrimonial character and hence will not be treated here separately. For the different kinds of benefices will be discussed later in detail.

A. A fief involves the following elements:

(1) The appropriation of powers and rights of exercising authority. Appropriation as a fief may apply only to powers relevant within a master's household or it may be extended to include those of a political association. The latter type may be restricted to economic rights—that is, fiscal rights—or it may also include political powers proper. Fiefs are granted in return for specific services. Normally they are primarily of a military character, but they may also include administrative functions. The grant of the fief takes a very specific form. It is carried out

(2) on a purely personal basis for the lifetime of the lord and of the recipient of the fief, his vassal.

(3) The relationship is established by a contract, thus it is supposed that the vassal is a free man.

(4) If feudalism is based on fiefs, the recipient adheres to the style of life of a knightly status group.

(5) The contract of fealty is not an ordinary business contract, but establishes a solidary, fraternal relationship which involves reciprocal obligations of loyalty, to be sure, on a legally unequal basis. These obligations are upheld by

(a) knightly status honor, and (b) are clearly delimited.

The transition pointed out above at the end of section 12 [i.e., from

mere appropriation of land to full appropriation of powers] takes place
a) when fiefs are appropriated hereditarily, subject only to the condition
that each new vassal have the necessary qualifications and will pledge
fealty to his lord, and the existing vassals will do so to a new lord; *β*)
when the feudal administrative staff compels the lord to fill every
vacancy (*Leihezwang*), since all fiefs are considered part of the maintenance fund for the members of the knightly status group.

The first step took place relatively early in the Middle Ages; the
second, later on. The struggle of kings and princes with their vassals
were above all directed, though not usually explicitly, toward the
elimination of this principle, since it prevented the rise of a patrimonial
regime.

B. If an administration is based completely on the granting of fiefs
—and *Lehensfeudalismus* has never been historically realized in the pure
type any more than has pure patrimonialism—, this involves the following features:

(1) The authority of the lord is reduced to the likelihood that the
vassals will remain faithful to their oaths of fealty.

(2) The political association is completely replaced by a system of
relations of purely personal loyalty between the lord and his vassals and
between these in turn and their own sub-vassals (sub-infeudation) and
so on. Only a lord's own vassals are bound to fealty to him; whereas they
in turn can claim the fealty of their own vassals, and so on.

(3) Only in the case of a "felony" does the lord have a right to
deprive his vassal of his fief, and the same in turn applies to the vassal
in his relation to his own vassal. When such a case, however, arises, in
enforcing his rights against a vassal who has broken the oath of fealty,
the lord is dependent on the help of his other vassals or on the passivity
of the sub-vassals of the guilty party. Either source of support can only
be counted on when the relevant group recognizes that a felony has
actually been committed. However, even then the overlord cannot count
on the non-interference of sub-vassals unless he has at least been able to
secure recognition on their part of the principle that a struggle against
an overlord is an exceptional state. Overlords have always attempted to
establish this principle but not always with success.

(4) There is a hierarchy of social rank corresponding to the hierarchy of fiefs through the process of sub-infeudation—the order of the
Heerschilde in the Mirror of Saxon Law (*Sachsenspiegel*). This is not,
however, a judicious and administrative hierarchy. For whether an order
or a decision can be challenged and to what authority appeal can be made
is in principle a matter for the respective court of appeals (*Oberhof*)

and does not depend on the hierarchy of feudal relationships. (It is theoretically possible for the *Oberhof* authority to be granted to a status-equal of the local judicial lord, but in practice this was not the case.)

(5) The elements in the population who do not hold fiefs involving patrimonial or political authority are "subjects" (*Hintersassen*); that is, they are patrimonial dependents. They are dependent on the holders of fiefs to the extent that their traditional status determines or permits it, or so far as the coercive power in the hands of the possessors of military fiefs compels it, since they are to a large extent defenseless. Just as the supreme lord is under obligation to grant land in fief, those who do not hold fiefs are always under the authority of a lord; in both cases the rule is: *nulle terre sans seigneur*. The sole survival of the old immediate political powers of the ruler is the principle, which is almost always recognized, that political authority, particularly judicial authority, is turned over to the ruler whenever he is personally present.

(6) Powers over the household (inluding domains, slaves and serfs), the fiscal rights of the political group to the receipt of taxes and contributions, and specifically political powers of jurisdiction and compulsion to military service—thus powers over free men—all become objects of feudal grants in the same way. However, as a rule the strictly political powers are subject to special regulation.

> In ancient China the granting of economic income in fiefs and of territorial authority were distinguished in name as well as in fact. The distinctions in name are not found in the European Middle Ages, but there were clear distinctions in the holder's status and in numerous other particular points.

It is not usual for political powers to be fully appropriated in the same way as property rights in fiefs. Numerous transitional forms and irregularities remain. One conspicuous difference is the existence of a status distinction between those enjoying only economic or fiscal rights and those with strictly political powers, notably judicial and military authority. Only the latter are *political* vassals.

It goes without saying that whenever *Lehensfeudalismus* is highly developed, the overlord's authority is precarious. This is because it is very dependent on the voluntary obedience and hence the purely personal loyalty of the members of the administrative staff, who, by virtue of the feudal structure, are themselves in possession of the means of administration. Hence, the latent struggle for authority becomes chronic between the lord and his vassal, and the ideal extent of feudal authority has never been effectively carried out in practice or remained effective on a permanent basis.

Rather, the feudal lord may attempt to improve his position in one of the following ways:

(a) He may not rely on the purely personal loyalty of his vassals, but may attempt to secure his position by limiting or forbidding sub-infeudation.

This was common in Western feudalism, but often was initiated by the administrative staff in the interest of their own power. The same was true of the alliance of princes in China in 630 B.C.

He may attempt to establish the principle that the fealty of a sub-vassal to his immediate lord is void in case of war against the higher lord.

Or, if possible, the attempt is made to obligate the sub-vassal to direct fealty to him, the liege lord.

(b) The feudal chief may seek to implement his control of the administration of political powers in a variety of ways. He may grant all the subjects a right of appeal to him or his courts. He may station supervising agents at the courts of his political vassals. He may attempt to enforce a right to collect taxes from the subjects of all his vassals. He may appoint certain officials of the political vassals. Finally, he may attempt to enforce the principle that all political authority is forfeited to him in his personal presence or beyond that to any agent he designates and that he, as the supreme lord, is entitled to try any case in his own court at will.

(c) It is possible for a supreme lord to attain and maintain his power against vassals, as well as against other types of holders of appropriated authority, only if he creates or re-creates an administrative staff under his personal control and organizes it in an appropriate manner. There are three main possibilities.

(1) It may be a patrimonial staff. (This was to a large extent what happened in the European Middle Ages and in Japan in the *Bakufu* of the *Shogun,* who exercised a very effective control over the feudal *Daimyos.*)

(2) It may be an extra-patrimonial staff recruited from a status group with literary education.

The principal examples are clerical officials, whether Christian or Brahman; *kayasths* (Buddhist, Lamaist, or Mohammedan);[10a] or humanists, such as the Confucian scholars in China. On the peculiarities of such groups and their immense importance for cultural development, see ch. IV [unfinished].

(3) Or it may be a group of technically trained officials, particularly legal and military specialists.

This was proposed in China in the eleventh century by Wang An-Shi, but by that time it was directed against the classical scholars and not the feudal magnates. In the Occident, such a bureaucracy was recruited for civil administration from university-trained men. In the Church the primary training was in the Canon Law, in the State, the Roman Law. In England, it was the Common Law, which had, however, been rationalized under the influence of Roman modes of thought. In this development lie some origins of the modern Western state. The development of Western military organization took a somewhat different course. The feudal organization was first replaced by capitalistic military entrepreneurs, the *condottieri*. These structures were in turn appropriated by the territorial princes with the development of a rational administration of royal finance from the seventeenth century on. In England and France, it happened somewhat earlier.

This struggle of the feudal chief with his feudal administrative staff in the Western World, though not in Japan, largely coincided with his struggle against the power of corporately organized privileged groups (*Stände-Korporationen*). In modern times it everywhere issued in the ruler's victory, and that meant in bureaucratic administration. This happened first in the Western World, then in Japan; in India, and perhaps also in China, it happened in the wake of foreign rule. Along with purely historical power constellations, economic conditions have played a very important part in this process in the Western World. Above all, it was influenced by the rise of the bourgeoisie in the towns, which had an organization peculiar to Europe. It was in addition aided by the competition for power by means of rational—that is, bureaucratic—administration among the different states. This led, from fiscal motives, to a crucially important alliance with capitalistic interests, as will be shown later.

12c. Prebendal Feudalism and Other Variants

Not every kind of "feudalism" involves the fief in the Occidental sense. In addition, there is above all:

A. prebendal feudalism, which has a fiscal basis.

This was typical of the Islamic Near East and of India under the Moguls. On the other hand, *ancient* Chinese feudalism before the time of Shi Huang Ti had at least in part a structure of fiefs, though benefices were also involved. Japanese feudalism also involved fiefs, but they were subject in the case of the *Daimyos* to a rather stringent control on the part of the supreme lord (*Bakufu*), and the fiefs of the Samurai and the Buke were really benefices of *ministeriales* (although they often came to be appropriated) which were registered according to their yield in terms of rice rent (*kokudaka*).

Prebendal feudalism exists when (1) benefices which are valued and granted according to the income they yield are appropriated and where (2) appropriation is, in principle, though not always effectively, carried out only on a personal basis in accordance with services, thus involving the possibility of promotion. (This was, at least from the legal point of view, true of the benefices held by the Turkish *sipahi*.)

Finally and above all, (3) it does not involve primarily a free relation of personal fealty arising from a contract of personal loyalty with the lord as the basis of a particular fief. It is rather a matter primarily of fiscal considerations in the context of a system of financing which is otherwise patrimonial, often sultanistic. This is for the most part made evident by the fact that the prebends are assessed according to their tax value.

It is very common for the *Lehensfeudalismus* to originate in a system of want satisfaction of the political group on the basis of a purely natural economy and in terms of personal obligations (personal services and military services). The principal motive is to replace the insufficiently trained popular levy, whose members can no longer equip themselves and are needed in the economy, with a well-trained and equipped army of knights who are bound to their chief by personal honor. Prebendal feudalism, on the other hand, usually originates in the reversion from monetary financing to financing in kind. The following are the principal reasons leading to such a policy:—

(a) The transfer of the risk involved in fluctuating income to an entrepreneur; that is, a sort of tax farming.

a) Rights to such income may be transferred in return for undertaking to supply certain particular army contingents, such as cavalry, sometimes war chariots, armored troops, supply trains, or artillery, for a patrimonial army. (This was common in the Chinese Middle Ages. Quotas for the army in each of the different categories were established for a particular territorial area.)

Either in addition to this or alone, prebendal feudalism may be established as a means of *β*) meeting the costs of civil administration and of *γ*) securing tax payments for the royal treasury. (This was common in India.)

δ) In return for these various services, in the first instance to enable those who undertook them to meet their obligations, an appropriation of governmental power in varying degrees and respects was permitted. Such appropriation has usually been for a limited period and subject to repurchase. But when means to do this have been lacking, it has often in fact been definitive. Those who hold such definitively appropriated powers then become, at the very least, landlords, as opposed to mere land-owners, and often come into the possession of extensive political powers.

This process has been typical above all of India. It is the source of the powers over land of the *Zamindars,* the *Jagirdars,* and the *Tuluk-dars.* It is also found in a large part of the Near East, as C. H. Becker has clearly shown—he was the first to understand the difference from the European fief.[11] The primary basis lies in the leasing of taxes. As a secondary consequence, it developed into a "manorial" system. The Rumanian Boyars—the descendants of the most heterogeneous society the world has ever seen, of Jews, Germans, Greeks, and various others —were also tax farmers who on this basis appropriated governing authority.

(b) Inability to pay the contingents of a patrimonial army may lead to an usurpation of the sources of taxation on their part, which is subsequently legalized. The result is that appropriation of the land and of the subjects is carried out by the officers and members of the army. (This was true of the famous Khans of the empire of the Caliphs. It was the source or the model for all forms of Oriental appropriation, including the Mameluke army, which was formally composed of slaves.)

It is by no means inevitable that this should lead to systematic registration as a basis for the granting of benefices. But this is a readily available course and has often actually been followed out. (We shall not yet discuss how far the "fiefs" of the Turkish *sipahi* were genuine fiefs or whether they were closer to benefices. From a legal point of view, promotion according to achievement was possible.)

It is clear that the two types of feudalism are connected by gradual imperceptible transitions and that it is seldom possible to classify cases with complete definiteness under one category or the other. Furthermore, prebendal feudalism is closely related to a purely prebendal organization, and there are also gradual transitions in this direction.

According to an imprecise terminology, in addition to the fief resting on a free contract with the lord and the feudal benefice, there is:

B. so-called "polis" feudalism, resting on a real or fictitious "synoik-ism" of landlords. These enjoy equal rights in the conduct of a purely military mode of life with high status honor. The economic aspect of the *kleros* is the plot of land which is appropriated by qualified persons on a personal basis and passed on by individual hereditary succession. It is cultivated by the services of unfree persons—assigned as the property of the status group—and forms the basis of provision of military equipment.

This type is found only in Greece, in fully developed form, only in Sparta, and originated out of the "men's house." It has been called "feudalism" because of the set of conventions regulating status honor and of the element of chivalry in the mode of life of a group of landlords. This is hardly legitimate usage. In Rome the term *fundus* corresponds to the Greek *kleros*. There is, however, no information available about the organization of the *curia* (*co-viria* equals the Greek *andreion,* the "men's house). We do not know how far it was similar to the Greek.)

The term "feudal" is often used in a very broad sense to designate all military strata, institutions and conventions which involve any sort of status privileges. This usage will be avoided here as entirely too vague.

C. The second doubtful type is called feudalism for the opposite reason. The fief is present but, on the other hand, is not acquired by a free contract (fraternization either with a lord or with equals), but is bestowed by the order of a patrimonial chief. On the other hand, it may not be administered in the spirit of a knightly mode of life. Finally, both criteria may be absent. Thus there may be service fiefs held by dependent knights; or, conversely, fiefs may be freely acquired but their holders are not subject to a code of chivalry. Finally, fiefs may be granted to clients, coloni, or slaves who are employed as fighting forces. All these cases will be treated here as *benefices*.

The case of dependent knights is illustrated by Occidental and Oriental *ministeriales,* in Japan by the Samurai. Freely recruited soldiers without a chivalrous code are known to the Orient; this was probably the origin of the Ptolemaic military organization. When the hereditary appropriation of service land has led further to the appropriation of the military function as such, the end result is a typical liturgical organization of the state. The third type, the use of unfree military forces, is typical of the so-called warrior caste of ancient Egypt, of the Mamelukes of medieval Egypt, and of various other unfree Oriental and Chinese warriors. These have not always been granted rights in land, but such an arrangement is common.

In such cases, it is imprecise to speak of "feudalism," since it involves military status groups, which, at least from a formal point of view, occupy a negatively privileged position. They will be discussed in Chapter IV.

13. *Combinations of the Different Types of Authority*

The above discussion makes it quite evident that "ruling organizations" which belong only to one or another of these pure types are very exceptional. Furthermore, in relation to legal and traditional authority especially, certain important types, such as the collegial form and some aspects of the feudal, have either not been discussed at all or have been barely suggested. In general, it should be kept clearly in mind that the basis of every authority, and correspondingly of every kind of willingness to obey, is a *belief*, a belief by virtue of which persons exercising authority are lent prestige. The composition of this belief is seldom altogether simple. In the case of "legal authority," it is never purely legal. The belief in legality comes to be established and habitual, and this means it is partly traditional. Violation of the tradition may be fatal to it. Furthermore, it has a charismatic element, at least in the negative sense that persistent and striking lack of success may be sufficient to ruin any government, to undermine its prestige, and to prepare the way for charismatic revolution. For monarchies, hence, it is dangerous to lose wars since that makes it appear that their charisma is no longer genuine. For republics, on the other hand, striking victories may be dangerous in that they put the victorious general in a favorable position for making charismatic claims.

Groups approximating the purely traditional type have certainly existed. But they have never been stable indefinitely and, as is also true of bureaucratic authority, have seldom been without a head who had a personally charismatic status by heredity or office. Under certain circumstances, the charismatic chief can be different from the traditional one. Everyday economic needs have been met under the leadership of traditional authorities; whereas certain exceptional ones, like hunting and the quest of "booty" in war, have had charismatic leadership. The idea of the possibility of "legislation" is also relatively ancient, though for the most part it has been legitimized by oracles. Above all, however, whenever the recruitment of an administrative staff is drawn from extra-patrimonial sources, the result is a type of official which can be differentiated from those of legal bureaucracies only in terms of the ultimate basis of their authority and not in terms of formal status.

Similarly, entirely pure charismatic authority, including the hereditary charismatic type, etc., is rare. It is not impossible, as in the case of Napoleon, for the strictest type of bureaucracy to issue directly from a charismatic movement; or, if not that, all sorts of prebendal and feudal types of organization. Hence, the kind of terminology and classification set forth above has in no sense the aim—indeed, it could not have it—to be exhaustive or to confine the whole of historical reality in a rigid scheme. Its usefulness is derived from the fact that in a given case it is possible to distinguish what aspects of a given organized group can legitimately be identified as falling under or approximating one or another of these categories. For certain purposes this is unquestionably an important advantage.

For all types of authority the fact of the existence and continual functioning of an administrative staff is vital. For the habit of obedience cannot be maintained without organized activity directed to the application and enforcement of the order. It is, indeed, the existence of such activity which is usually meant by the term "organization."[12] For this to exist in turn, it is essential that there should be an adequate degree of the solidarity of interests, both on the ideal and material levels, of the members of the administrative staff with their chief. It is fundamental in understanding the relation of the chief to these members that, so far as this solidarity exists, the chief is stronger than any individual member but is weaker than the members taken together. It is, however, by all means necessary for the members of an administrative staff to enter into a deliberate agreement in order to obstruct or even consciously oppose their chief so successfully that the leadership of the chief becomes impotent. Similarly, any individual who sets out to destroy a rulership must, if he is going to take over the position of power, build up an administrative staff of his own, unless he is in a position to count on the connivance and co-operation of the existing staff against their previous leader.

Solidarity of interest with a chief is maximized at the point where both the legitimacy of the status of the members and the provision for their economic needs is dependent on the chief retaining his position. For any given individual, the possibility of escaping this solidarity varies greatly according to the structure. It is most difficult where there is complete separation from the means of administration, thus in purely traditional patriarchal structures, under pure partimonialism and in bureaucratic organizations resting on formal rules. It is easiest where fiefs or benefices have been appropriated by socially privileged groups.

It is most important, finally, to realize that historical reality involves a continuous, though for the most part latent, conflict beween chiefs and their administrative staffs for appropriation and expropriation in relation to one another. For almost all of cultural development, it has been crucial in what way this struggle has worked out and what has been the character of the stratum of officials dependent upon the chief which has helped him win out in his struggle against the feudal classes or other groups enjoying appropriated powers. In different cases it has been ritually trained literati, the clergy, purely secular clients, household officials, legally trained persons, technically specialized financial officials, or private *honoratiores*, (about whom more will be said later).

One of the reasons why the character of these struggles and of their outcome has been so important, not only to the history of administration as such, but to that of culture generally, is that the type of education has been determined by them and with it the modes of status group formation.

1. Both the extent and the way in which the members of an administrative staff are bound to their chief will vary greatly according to whether they receive salaries, opportunities for profit, allowances, or fiefs. It is, however, a factor common to all of these that anything which endangers the legitimacy of the chief who has granted and who guarantees them, tends at the same time to endanger the legitimacy of these forms of income and the positions of power and prestige which go with membership in the administrative staff. This is one of the reasons why legitimacy, which is often so much neglected in analysing such phenomena, plays a crucially important role.

2. The history of the dissolution of the old system of domination legitimate in Germany up until 1918 is instructive in this connection. The War, on the one hand, went far to break down the authority of tradition; and the German defeat involved a tremendous loss of prestige for the government. These factors combined with systematic habituation to illegal behavior, undermined the amenability to discipline both in the army and in industry and thus prepared the way for the overthrow of the older authority. At the same time, the way in which the old administrative staff continued to function and the way in which its order was simply taken over by the new supreme authorities, is a striking example of the extent to which, under rationalized bureaucratic conditions, the individual member of such a staff is inescapably bound to his technical function. As it has been noted above, this fact is by no means adequately explained by the private economic interests of the members —their concern for their jobs, salaries, and pensions—although it goes without saying that these considerations were not unimportant to the great majority of officials. In addition to this, however, the disinterested ideological factor has been crucial. For the breakdown of administrative organization would, under such conditions, have meant a breakdown of the provision of the whole population, including, of course, the officials themselves, with even the most elementary necessities of life. Hence an appeal was made to the sense of duty of officials, and this was successful. Indeed the objective necessity of this attitude has been recognized even by the previous holders of power and their sympathizers.

3. In the course of the past revolution in Germany, a new administrative staff came into being in the Soviets of workers and soldiers. In the first place it was necessary to develop a technique of organizing these new staffs. Furthermore, their development was closely dependent on the War, notably the possession of weapons by the revolutionary element. Without this factor the revolution would not have been possible at all. (This and its historical analogies will be discussed below.) It was only by the rise of charismatic leaders against the legal authorities and

by the development around them of groups of charismatic followers, that it was possible to take power away from the old authorities. It was furthermore only through the maintenance of the old bureaucratic organization that power once achieved could be retained. Previous to this situation every revolution which has been attempted under modern conditions has failed completely because of the indispensability of trained officials and of the lack of its own organized staff. The conditions under which previous revolutions have succeeded have been altogether different. (See below, the chapter on the theory of revolutions. [Unwritten].)

4. The overthrow of authority on the initiative of the administrative staff has occurred in the past under a wide variety of conditions. Some form of association of the members of the staff has always been a necessary prerequisite. According to the circumstances, it might have more the character of a limited conspiracy or more that of a general solidarity. Both is peculiarly difficult under the conditions to which the modern official is subject; but as the Russian case has shown, it is not altogether impossible. As a general rule, however, such association does not go further than the kind which is open to workers through the ordinary procedure of the strike.

5. The patrimonial character of a body of officials is above all manifested in the fact that admission involves a relation of personal dependency. In the Carolingian system, one became a *puer regis*, under the Angevins, a *familiaris*. Survivals of this have persisted for a very long time.

vii

The Transformation of Charisma in a Democratic Direction

14. *Democratic Legitimacy, Plebiscitary Leadership and Elected Officialdom*[13]

The basically authoritarian principle of charismatic legitimation may be subject to an anti-authoritarian interpretation, for the validity of charismatic authority rests entirely on recognition by the ruled, on "proof" before their eyes. To be sure, this recognition of a charismatically qualified, and hence legitimate, person is treated as a duty. But when the charismatic organization undergoes progressive rationalization, it is readily possible that, instead of recognition being treated as a consequence of legitimacy, it is treated as the basis of legitimacy: *democratic legitimacy*. Then designation of a successor by an administrative staff becomes "preselection," by the predecessor himself "nomination," whereas recognition by the group becomes an "election." The personally legitimated charismatic leader becomes leader by the grace of those who follow him since the latter are formally free to elect and even to depose him— just as the loss of charisma and its efficacy had involved the loss of genuine legitimacy. Now he is the freely elected leader.

Correspondingly, the recognition of charismatic decrees and judicial decisions on the part of the community shifts to the belief that the group has a right to enact, recognize, or appeal laws, according to its own free will, both in general and for an individual case. Under genuinely charismatic authority, on the other hand, conflicts over the correct law may actually be decided by a group vote, but this takes place under the pressure of feeling that there can be only *one* correct decision, and it is a matter of duty to arrive at this. However, in the new interpretation the treatment of law approaches the case of legal authority. The most important transitional type is the legitimation of authority by plebiscite: *plebiscitary leadership*. The most common examples are the modern party leaders. But it is always present in cases where the chief feels himself to be acting on behalf of the masses and is indeed recognized by them. Both the Napoleons are classical examples, in spite of the fact that legitimation by plebiscite took place only after they seized power by force. The second Napoleon also resorted to the plebiscite after a severe loss of prestige. Regardless of how its real value as an expression of the popular will may be regarded, the plebiscite has been the specific means of deriving the legitimacy of authority from the confidence of the ruled, even though the voluntary nature of such confidence is only formal or fictitious.

Once the elective principle has been applied to the chief by a reinterpretation of charisma, it may be extended to the administrative staff. Elective officials whose legitimacy is derived from the confidence of the ruled and who are therefore subject to recall, are typical of certain democracies, for instance, the United States. They are not "bureaucratic" types. Because they have an independent source of legitimacy, they are not strongly integrated into a hierarchical order. To a large extent their "promotion" and assignment is not influenced by their superiors. (There are analogies in other cases where several charismatic structures, which are qualitatively heterogeneous, exist side by side, as in the relations of the Dalai Lama and the Tashi Lama.) Such an administrative structure is greatly inferior as a precision instrument compared to the bureaucratic type with its appointed officials.

1. Plebiscitary democracy—the most important type of *Führer-Demokratie*—is a variant of charismatic authority, which hides behind a legitimacy that is *formally* derived from the will of the governed. The leader (demagogue) rules by virtue of the devotion and trust which his political followers have in him personally. In the first instance his power extends only over those recruited to his following, but if they can hand over the government to him he controls the whole polity. The type is best illustrated by the dictators who emerged in the revolutions of the ancient world and of modern times: the Hellenic *aisymnetai*, tyrants and demagogues; in Rome Gracchus and his successors; in the Italian city states the *capitani del popolo* and mayors; and certain types of political leaders in the German cities such as emerged in the democratic dictatorship of Zürich. In modern states the best examples are the dictatorship of Cromwell, and the leaders of the French Revolution and of the First and Second Empire. Wherever attempts have been made to legitimize this kind of exercise of power, legitimacy has been sought in recognition by the sovereign people through a plebiscite. The leader's personal administrative staff is recruited in a charismatic form usually from able people of humble origin. In Cromwell's case, religious qualifications were taken into account. In that of Robespierre along with personal dependability also certain "ethical" qualities. Napoleon was concerned only with personal ability and adaptability to the needs of his imperial "rule of genius."

At the height of revolutionary dictatorship the position of a member of the administrative staff tends to be that of a person entrusted *ad hoc* with a specific task, subject to recall. This was true of the role of the agents of the "Committee of Public Safety." When a certain kind of municipal "dictators" have been swept into power by the reform movements in American cities the tendency has been to grant them freedom to appoint their own staff. Thus both traditional legitimacy and formal legality tend to be equally ignored by the revolutionary dictator. The tendency of patriarchal authorities, in the administration of justice and in their other functions, has been to act in accordance with substantive ideas of justice, with utilitarian considerations and in terms of reasons of state. These tendencies are paralleled by the revolutionary tribunals and by the substantive postulates of justice of the radical democracy of Antiquity and of modern socialism (of which more will be said in the Soc. of Law, ch. VIII: *vii*). The process of routinization of revolutionary charisma then brings with it changes similar to those brought about by the corresponding process in other respects. Thus the development of a professional army in England goes back to the voluntary army of the faithful in the days of Cromwell. Similarly, the French system of administration by prefects is derived from the charismatic administration of the revolutionary democratic dictatorship.

2. The introduction of elected officials always involves a radical alteration in the position of the charismatic leader. He becomes the "servant" of those under his authority. There is no place for such a type in a technically rational bureaucratic organization. Since he is not ap-

pointed and promoted by his superiors and his position is derived from the votes of the ruled, he is likely to be little interested in the prompt and strict observance of discipline which would be likely to win the favor of superiors. The tendency is rather for electoral positions to become autocephalous spheres of authority. It is in general not possible to attain a high level of technical administrative efficiency with an elected staff of officials. (This is illustrated by a comparison of the elected officials in the individual states in the United States with the appointed officials of the Federal Government. It is similarly shown by comparing the elected municipal officials with the administration of the reform mayors with their own appointed staffs.) It is necessary to distinguish the type of plebiscitary democracy from that which attempts to dispense with leadership altogether. The latter type is characterized by the attempt to minimize the domination of man over man.

It is characteristic of the *Führerdemokratie* that there should in general be a highly emotional type of devotion to and trust in the leader. This accounts for a tendency to favor the type of individual who is most spectacular, who promises the most, or who employs the most effective propaganda measures in the competition for leadership. This is a natural basis for the utopian component which is found in all revolutions. It also dictates the limitations on the level of rationality which, in the modern world, this type of administration can attain. Even in America it has not *always* come up to expectations.

Relationship to the economy: 1. The anti-authoritarian direction of the transformation of charisma normally leads into the path of rationality. If a ruler is dependent on recognition by plebiscite he will usually attempt to support his regime by an organization of officials which functions promptly and efficiently. He will attempt to consolidate the loyalty of those he governs either by winning glory and honor in war or by promoting their material welfare, or under certain circumstances, by attempting to combine both. Success in these will be regarded as proof of the charisma. His first aim will be the destruction of traditional, feudal, patrimonial, and other types of authoritarian powers and privileges. His second aim will have to be to create economic interests which are bound up with his regime as the source of their legitimacy. So far as, in pursuing these policies, he makes use of the formalization and legalization of law he may contribute greatly to the formal rationalization of economic activity.

2. On the other hand, plebiscitary regimes can easily act so as to weaken the formal rationality of economic activity so far as their interests in legitimacy, being dependent on the faith and devotion of the masses, forces them to impose substantive ideas of justice in the economic sphere. This will result in an administration of justice emancipated from formal procedures, as it happens under revolutionary tribunals, war-time ration-

ing and in other cases of limited and controlled production and consumption. This tendency, which is by no means confined to the modern socialist type, will be dominant insofar as the leader is a "social dictator." The causes and consequences of this type cannot yet be discussed.

3. The presence of elective officials is a source of disturbance to formally rational economic life. This is true in the first place because such officials are primarily elected according to party affiliations and not technical competence. Secondly, the risks of recall or failure of re-election make it impossible to pursue a strictly objective course of decision and administration, without regard to such consequences. There is, however, one case where the unfavorable effects for the rationality of economic activity are not evident. This is true where there is a possibility of applying the economic and technical achievements of an old culture to new areas. In this case, the means of production are not yet appropriated and there is a sufficiently wide margin so that the almost inevitable corruption of officials can be taken account of as one of the cost factors, and large-scale profits still be attained [as in the United States].

On 1. The classical example of a favorable effect on economic rationality is to be found in the two Napoleonic regimes. Napoleon I introduced the *Code Napoléon,* compulsory division of estates by inheritance and everywhere destroyed the traditional authorities. It is true that his regime created what almost amounted to fiefs for his deserving followers, and that the soldiers got almost everything, the citizen nothing. But this was compensated for by *la gloire* and, on the whole, the small bourgeois were tolerably well off. Under Napoleon III there was continued adherence to the motto of the era of Louis Philippe: "enrichissez-vous"; grand-scale building; the *Crédit Mobilier,* with its well-known scandal.

On 2. The tendencies of "social dictatorship" are classically illustrated by the Greek democracy of the Periclean age and its aftermath. In Rome the jurors who tried a case were bound by the instructions of the *praetor,* and decisions followed the formal law. But in the Greek *heliaia-*court decisions were made in terms of "substantive" justice—in effect, on the basis of sentimentality, flattery, demagogic invectives and jokes. This can be clearly seen in the court orations of the Athenian rhetors. Analogous phenomena are found in Rome only in the case of political trials, such as Cicero participated in. The consequence was that the development of formal law and formal jurisprudence in the Roman sense became impossible. For the *heliaia* was a "people's court" directly comparable to the revolutionary tribunals of the French Revolution and of the Soviet phase of the revolution in Germany. The jurisdiction of these lay tribunals was by no means confined to politically relevant cases. On the other hand, no revolutionary movement in England has ever interfered with the administration of justice except in cases of major political significance. However, it is true that there was a considerable arbitrary element in the decisions of the justices of the peace, but only insofar as they concerned pure "police" cases *not* involving interests of the propertied.

On 3. The United States of America is the classical example. As late as the early 1900's the author inquired of American workers of English origin why they allowed themselves to be governed by party henchmen who were so often open to corruption. The answer was, in the first place, that in such a big country even though millions of dollars were stolen or embezzled there was still plenty left for everybody, and secondly that these professional politicians were a group which even workers could treat with contempt whereas technical officials of the German type would as a group "lord it over" the workers.

A specialized discussion of relations of economic activity will have to be left for the more detailed treatment below [Part Two].

viii

Collegiality and the Division of Powers

15. Types of Collegiality and of the Division of Powers

On either a traditional or a rational basis authority may be limited and controlled by certain specific means.

The present concern is not with the limitations of authority as such, whether it is determined by tradition or by law. This has already been discussed (secs. 3ff.). Just now it is rather a question of specific social relationships and groups which have the function of limiting authority.

1. Patrimonial and feudal regimes generally have their authority limited by the privileges of status groups. This type of limitation is most highly developed when there is an estate-type division of powers. This situation has already been discussed (sec. 9:IV).

2. A bureaucratic organization may be limited and indeed must be by agencies which act on their own authority alongside the bureaucratic hierarchy. This limitation is inherent in the fully developed legality type so that administrative action can be restricted to what is in conformity with rules. Such limiting agencies have the following principal functions:

(a) supervision of adherence to the rules, if need be, through an inquiry;

(b) a monopoly of creation of the rules which govern the action of officials completely, or at least of those which define the limits of their independent authority;

(c) above all a monopoly of the granting of the means which are necessary for the administrative function. These modes of limitation will be discussed separately below (sec. 16).

3. It is possible for any type of authority to be deprived of its mono-cratic character by the *principle of collegiality*. This may, however, occur in a variety of ways with widely varying significance. The following are the principal types:

(a) It may be that alongside the monocratic holders of governing powers there are other monocratic authorities which, by tradition or legislation, are in a position to delay or to veto acts of the first authority. This is the case of "veto collegiality" (*Kassationskollegialität*).

> The most important examples in Antiquity are the [Roman] tribune and, in its origins, the [Spartan] ephor, in the Middle Ages the *capitano del popolo*, and, in the period after November 9, 1918 until the regular administration was again emancipated from this control, the [German revolutionary] "Councils of Workers and Soldiers" whose delegates (*Vertrauensmänner*) were entitled to "countersign" official acts.

(b) The second type is precisely the opposite of this, namely the arrangement that the acts of an authority which is not monocratic must be carried out only after previous consultation and a vote. That is, their acts are subject to the rule that a plurality of individuals must co-operate for the act to be valid: the case of "functional collegiality." This coopera-tion may follow (α) the principle of unanimity or (β) of decision by majority.

(c) In effect closely related to case (a) is that in which, in order to weaken monocratic power, a plurality of monocratic officials exists, each of whom has equal authority, without specification of function. If a con-flict arises over the same function, there must be a resort either to mechanical means such as lots, rotation, or oracles, or some controlling agency (2a) must intervene. In effect the tendency is for each member of the collegial body to have a power of veto over the others. (The most important example is the collegiality of the Roman magistrates, such as the consuls and the praetors.)

(d) A type which is closely related to case (b) is that in which, although there is an actually monocratic *primus inter pares*, his acts are normally subject to consultation with formally equal members, and dis-agreement in important matters may lead to breaking up of the collegial body by resignation, thus endangering the position of the monocratic chief. This may be called "functional collegiality with a preeminent head."

The most important example is that of the position of the British Prime Minister in relation to his cabinet. This organization has, as is well known, changed greatly in the course of its history. The above formulation, however, is substantially correct for most cases in the period of cabinet government.

Advisory collegial bodies do not necessarily involve a weakening of the power of an autocratic chief but may well lead to a tempering of the exercises of authority in the direction of rationalization. It is, however, also possible that in effect they should gain the upper hand over the chief. This is particularly true if they are representative of well-established status groups. The following are the more important types:

(e) The case noted above under (d) is closely related to that in which a body whose functions are formally only advisory is attached to a monocratic chief. Even though he is not formally bound to follow their advice but only to listen to it, the failure of his policies if this occurs may be attributed to neglect of this advice.

The most important case is that of the Roman Senate as a body advisory to the magistrates. From this there developed an actual dominance over the magistrates, chiefly through the Senate's control of finance. The Senate was probably actually only an advisory body in the early days, but through the actual control of finance and still more through the fact that senators and the formally elected magistrates belonged to the same status group, a situation developed in which the magistrates were in fact bound by the resolutions of the Senate. The formula "*Si eis placeret,*" in which the traditional lack of formal obligation was expressed, came to mean something analogous to "if you please" accompanied by something like a command.

(f) A somewhat different type is found in the case where a collegial body is made up of individuals with specified functions. In such a case the preparation and presentation of a subject is assigned to the individual technical expert who is competent in that field or possibly to several experts, each in a different aspect of the field. Decisions, however, are taken by a vote of the body as a whole.

Most councils of state and similar bodies in the past have more or less closely approximated to this type. This was true of the English Privy Council in the period before the development of cabinet government. Though at times their power has been very great, they have never succeeded in expropriating monarchs. On the contrary, under certain circumstances the monarch has attempted to secure support in his council of state in order to free himself from the control of cabinets which were made up of party leaders. This attempt was made in England, but without success. This type is also an approximately correct description of the ministries or cabinets made up of specialized officials which hereditary monarchs or elective presidents of the American type have appointed for their own support.

(g) A collegial body, the members of which have specified functions, may be a purely advisory body. In this case—as in (e)—it is open to the chief to accept or reject their recommendations, according to his own free decision.

> The only difference is the extreme specialization of functions. This case was approached by the Prussian organization under Frederick William I [1713–40] and is always favorable to consolidating the power of the chief.

(h) The direct antithesis of rationally specialized collegiality is a traditional collegial body consisting of "elders." Their collegial function is primarily to guarantee that the law which is applied is really authentically traditional. Sometimes such bodies have a veto power as a means of upholding the genuine tradition against untraditional legislation. (Examples: *gerousia* [council of elders] in many cases in Antiquity; for veto power, the Areopagus in Athens and the *patres* in Rome, the latter, however, belong primarily in type (l) below.)

(i) One way of weakening domination is by applying the collegial principle to the highest authority whether its supremacy be formal or substantive. Several variations of this type are found, resembling the types d) through g). The powers of individual members of such bodies may be assumed in rotation or may be distributed on a permanent basis. Such bodies are collegial so long as there is a formal requirement that legitimate acts require the participation of all the members.

> One of the most important examples is the Swiss Federal Council, the members of which do not have clearly defined specialized functions, while to some extent the principle of rotation is involved. Another example is found in the revolutionary councils of "People's Commissars" in Russia, Hungary, and for a short time in Germany. In the past such bodies as the "Council of Eleven" in Venice and the colleges of "Ancients" [in other Italian city states] belong in this category.

A great many cases of collegiality in patrimonial or feudal organizations belong in one or another of the following categories:

1) The estate-type division of powers ("estate collegiality").

2) The collegial organization of patrimonial officials which the chief has organized in order to counterbalance the power of organized privileged groups. This is often the position of the councils of state discussed above under (f).

3) Advisory bodies or sometimes bodies with executive authority over which the chief presides or the meetings of which he attends or from

which at least he receives reports. Such bodies are generally made up either of technical experts or of persons of high social prestige or both. In view of the increasingly specialized considerations involved in the functions of government he may hope, through the advice of such bodies, to attain a level of information sufficiently above pure dilettantism so that an intelligent personal decision is possible (case g) above).

In cases of the third type the chief is naturally interested in having heterogeneous and even opposed elements represented, whether this heterogeneity is one of technical opinions or of interest. This is because, on the one hand, he is concerned with the widest possible range of information, and on the other with being in a position to play the opposing interests off against each other.

In the second type, on the contrary, the chief is often, though not always, concerned with uniformity of opinions and attitudes. This is a main source of the "solidary" ministries and cabinets in so-called Constitutional states or others with an effective separation of powers. In the first case the collegial body which represents the appropriated interests will naturally lay stress on uniformity of opinion and solidarity. It is not, however, always possible to attain this, since every kind of appropriation through social privilege creates conflicting interests.

> The first of these types is illustrated by the assemblies of estates and the assemblies of vassals which preceded them frequently not only in Europe but elsewhere—for instance in China. The second type is well illustrated by the administrative, mostly collegial organs which were formed in the early stages of the modern monarchies and which were primarily composed of legal and financial experts. The third type is illustrated by the councils of state of the same monarchies and is also found in other parts of the world. As late as the eighteenth century it was not unknown for an archbishop to have a seat in the English cabinet. Typically, these bodies have been composed of dignitaries such as *Räte von Haus aus*,[14] and typically have had a mixture of *honoratiores* and specialized officials.

(k) Where there is a conflict of interests of status groups it may work out to the advantage of a chief through negotiation and struggle with the various groups. For organizations which are composed of delegated representatives of conflicting interests, whether their basis be in ideal causes, in power, or in economic advantage, may at least in external form be collegial bodies. What goes on within the body is then supposedly a process of adjustment of these conflicts of interest by compromise. (This is the case of "compromise-oriented collegiality," in contrast to office and parliamentary collegiality.)

This type is present in a crude form wherever there is an estate-type division of powers in such a way that decisions can only be arrived at by a compromise between the privileged groups. A more highly rationalized form is built up when the delegated members of the collegial bodies are selected in terms of their permanent status or class position, or in terms of the specific interests they represent. In such a body, unless its character is radically changed, action cannot result from a "vote" in the ordinary sense but is the outcome of a compromise which is either negotiated among the interests themselves or is imposed by the chief after the case for each of the groups involved has been considered.

The peculiar structure of the *Ständestaat* will be discussed more in detail below (ch. XIII). The above formulation applies to such situations as arose through the separation of the bodies representing different social groups. Thus in England the House of Lords was separated from the House of Commons, while the Church did not participate in Parliament at all but had its separate "Convocations." In France, the division came to be that of the nobility, the clergy, and the *tiers état,* while in Germany there were various more complex divisions. These divisions made it necessary to arrive at decisions by a process of compromise, first within one estate and then between estates. The decisions were then generally submitted to the king as recommendations which he was not necessarily bound to follow. Today the theory of representation by occupational groups is very much in vogue. The advocates of this proposal for the most part fail to see that even under these conditions compromises rather than majority decisions would be the only feasible means (see sec. 22 below). Insofar as free workers' councils were the bodies concerned, the tendency would be for questions to be settled in terms of the relative economic power of different groups, and not by majority vote.

(l) A related case is "voting collegiality," where collegial bodies which decide things by vote have been formed out of previously autocephalous and autonomous groups and a (variously gradated) right to a voice in decision-making has been appropriated by the leaders or the delegates of the component groups ("merger collegiality").

Examples are found in the representation of the phylae, the phratries, and the clans in the governing bodies of ancient city-states, in the medieval clans in the time of the *consules,* in the *mercadanza* of the guilds, in the delegates of the crafts (*Fachräte*) to the executive council of a federation of trade unions, in the federal council or senate in federal states, and finally in the distribution of appointments to cabinet posts in coalition ministries. This last case is particularly clear in the case of Switzerland, where posts are distributed in proportion to the number of votes for each party.

(m) A rather special case is the "voting collegiality" of elected parliamentary bodies which is hence in need of separate treatment. Its composition rests on one of two bases. It is either based on leadership, in which case the particular members constitute the following of leaders, or it is composed of collegial party groups without subordination to a specific leader (*führerloser Parlamentarismus*). To understand this it is necessary to discuss the structure of parties (see sec. 18 below).

Except in the case of the monocratic type of "veto collegiality," collegiality almost inevitably involves obstacles to precise, clear, and above all, rapid decision. In certain irrational forms it also places obstacles in the way of technical experts, but in introducing specialized officials monarchs have often found this consequence not altogether unwelcome. With the progressive increase in the necessity for rapid decision and action, however, the importance of this type of collegiality has declined.

Generally speaking, where collegial bodies have had executive authority the tendency has been for the position of the leading member to become substantively and even formally pre-eminent. This is true of the positions of the Bishop and the Pope in the church and of the Prime Minister in cabinets. Any interest in reviving the principle of collegiality in actual executive functions is usually derived from the interest in weakening the power of persons in authority. This, in turn, is derived from mistrust and jealousy of monocratic leadership, not so much on the part of those subject to authority, who are more likely to demand a "leader," as on the part of the members of the administrative staff. This is not only or even primarily true of negatively privileged groups but is, on the contrary, typical of those enjoying positive privileges. Collegiality is in no sense specifically "democratic." Where privileged groups have had to protect their privileges against those who were excluded from them they have always attempted to prevent the rise of monocratic power. Indeed, they have had to do so because such a power could base itself on the support of the underprivileged. Thus, while on the one hand they have tended to enforce strict equality within the privileged group they have tended to set up and maintain collegial bodies to supervise or even to take over power.

> Examples are Sparta, Venice, the Roman Senate before the time of the Gracchi and in Sulla's days, England repeatedly in the eighteenth century, Berne and other Swiss cantons, the medieval patrician towns with their collegial consuls, and the *mercadanza* which comprised the merchant guilds, but not those of the craft workers. The latter very easily became the prey of *nobili* and *signori*.

Collegiality favors greater thoroughness in the weighing of administrative decisions. Apart from the considerations already discussed, where this is more important than precision and rapidity, collegiality tends to be resorted to even to-day. Furthermore, it divides personal responsibility, indeed in the larger bodies this disappears almost entirely, whereas in monocratic organizations it is perfectly clear without question where responsibility lies. Large-scale tasks which require quick and consistent solutions tend in general, for good technical reasons, to fall into the hands of monocratic "dictators," in whom all responsibility is concentrated.

It is impossible for either the internal or the foreign policy of great states to be strongly and consistently carried out on a collegial basis. The dictatorship of the proletariat for the purpose of carrying out the nationalization of industry requires an individual "dictator" with the confidence of the masses. The "masses" as such are not necessarily adverse to this but the people holding power in Parliaments, parties, or, what makes very little difference, in "Soviets," cannot put up with such a dictator. This type has emerged only in Russia through the help of military force and supported by the interests of the peasants in the solidary maintenance of their newly acquired control of the land.

Finally, a few remarks may be made which partly summarize and partly supplement what has already been said. From a historical point of view, collegiality has had two principal kinds of significance:

a) It has involved a plurality of incumbents of the same office, or a number of persons in offices whose spheres of authority were directly competing, each with a mutual power of veto. This is primarily a matter of a technical separation of powers in order to minimize authority. The most conspicuous instance of this type of collegiality is that of the Roman magistrates. Their most important significance lay in the fact that every official act was subject to intercession by a magistrate with equal authority, thus greatly limiting the power of any one magistrate. But the magistracy remained an individual office merely multiplied in several copies.

b) The second main type has been that involving collegial decision. In such cases an administrative act is only legitimate when it has been produced by the cooperation of a plurality of people according to the principle of unanimity or of majority. This is the type of collegiality which is dominant in modern times, though it was also known in Antiquity. It may involve collegiality 1) of governmental leadership, 2) of administrative agencies, 3) of advisory bodies.

1) Collegiality in the supreme authority may be derived from the following considerations:—

(a) Its basis may lie in the fact that the governing authority (*Herrschaftsverband*) has arisen from the *Vergemeinschaftung* or *Vergesellschaftung* of previously autocephalous groups and that each of these demands its share of power. This was true of the "synoikism" of the ancient city states with their councils organized on the basis of clans, phratries, and phylae. It was true of the medieval towns with a council representing the important noble families, and of the medieval guild federations, in the *Mercadanza* with the council of the "*Ancients*" or guild deputies. It is also found in the bodies representing the component states in modern federal states and in the collegial structure of the ministries which have been built up by party coalitions (see again the increasing importance of proportional division in Switzerland). Collegiality in this case is a particular case of the representation of status or territorial groups.

(b) It may, secondly, be based on the absence of a leader. This may in turn result from mutual jealousy among those competing for leadership or from the attempt of the subjects to minimize the authority of any individual. It has appeared in most revolutions from a combination of these factors, in such forms as a council of officers or even soldiers of revolutionary troops or the Committee of Public Safety or the Councils of People's Commissars. In times of peace it has been mostly this last motive, antipathy to the individual "strong man," which has underlain the establishment of collegial bodies. Examples are Switzerland and the new constitution of Baden in 1919. (In the last case it was the socialists who most strongly manifested this antipathy; for fear of an "elected monarch" they sacrificed the strict administrative unification which was an absolutely essential condition of successful nationalization. The most decisive influence in this was the attitude of party officials in trade unions, local communities, and party headquarters, all of whom were suspicious of the powers of leadership.)

(c) The third basis may lie in the independent social position of the status groups primarily available for positions of power and monopolizing these positions. In this case collegiality is the product of an aristocratic regime. Every socially privileged class fears the type of leader who seeks support in the emotional devotion of the masses just as much as the type of democracy without leaders fears the rise of "demagogues." The senatorial regime in Rome, various attempts to rule through closed councils, and the Venetian and similar constitutions all belong in this category.

(d) The fourth basis may lie in the attempt of monarchs to counteract increasing expropriation at the hands of a technically trained bureaucracy. In the modern Western state, modern administrative organization was first introduced at the top with the establishment of collegial bodies. This was similar to what happened to the patrimonial states of the Orient, in China, Persia, the empire of the Caliphs, and in the Ottoman Empire, all of which served as models for Europe. A monarch is not only afraid of the power of particular individuals but hopes above all to be in a position, in the votes and counter-votes of a collegial body, to hold the balance himself. Furthermore, since he tends to become more and more of a dilettante he can also hope in this way to have a better comprehension of the details of administration than if he abdicated in favor of individual officials. (Generally speaking the functions of the highest bodies have been a mixture of advisory and executive elements. It is only in the field of finance, where arbitrariness has particularly irrational consequences, that, as in the case of the [1495–97] reform of Emperor Maximilian, the power of the monarch was immediately clipped by the professional officialdom. In this case there were powerful factors forcing the monarch to give way.)

(e) Another basis lies in the need to reconcile the points of view of different technical specialists and divergent interests, whether material or personal, by collegial discussion, that is, to make compromise possible. This has been particularly true in the organization of municipal affairs, which have on the one hand involved highly technical problems which could be appraised in local terms, and on the other hand have tended to rest heavily on the compromise of material interests. This has been true at least so long as the masses have put up with control by the strata privileged through property and education. The collegiality of ministries rests, from a technical point of view, on a similar basis. In Russia and to a less extent in Imperial Germany, however, it has not been possible to attain effective solidarity between the different parts of the government. The result has been bitter conflict between the different agencies.

The basis in cases (a), (c), and (d) is purely historical. Bureaucratic authority in the modern world has, wherever it has developed in large-scale associations such as states or metropolitan cities, led to a weakening of the role of collegiality in effective control. Collegiality unavoidably obstructs the promptness of decision, the consistency of policy, the clear responsibility of the individual, and ruthlessness to outsiders in combination with the maintenance of discipline within the group. Hence for these and certain other economic and technical reasons in all large states which are involved in world politics, where collegiality has been retained at all, it has been weakened in favor of the prominent position of the political leader, such as the Prime Minister. Incidentally a similar process has taken place in almost all of the large patrimonial organizations, particularly those which have been strictly Sultanistic. There has again and again been the need for a leading personality such as the Grand Vizier in addition to the monarch, unless a regime of favorites has provided a substitute. One person must carry the responsibility, but from a legal point of view the monarch himself could not do this.

2) Collegiality as employed in agencies acting under the direction of higher authorities has been primarily intended to promote objectivity and integrity and to this end to limit the power of individuals. As in respect to the highest authority it has almost everywhere, for the same reasons, given way to the technical superiority of monocratic organizations. This process is illustrated by the fate of the *Regierungen* [provincial "governments"] in Prussia.

3) In purely advisory bodies, collegiality has existed at all times and will probably always continue to exist. It has played a very important part historically. This has been particularly true in cases where the power structure was such that "advice" submitted to a magistrate or a monarch was for practical purposes binding. In the present discussion it is not necessary to carry the analysis further.

The type of collegiality under discussion here is always collegiality in the exercise of authority. It is thus a matter of bodies which either are administrative or which directly influence administrative agencies (through advice). The behavior of assemblies representing status groups and of parliamentary bodies will be taken up later. [See below, sec. *x* of this chapter.]

From a historical point of view it is in terms of collegiality that the concept of an "administrative agency" first came to be fully developed. This is because collegiality has always been linked with a separation of the sphere of office of the members from their private affairs, of public and private staff, and finally of the means of administration from personal property. It is thus by no means fortuitous that the history of modern administration in the Western World begins with the development of collegial bodies composed of technical specialists. Collegial administration has also been the beginning of every permanent organization of patrimonial, feudal, or other types of traditional political structures though in a different way. Only collegial bodies of officials, which were capable of standing together, could gradually expropriate the Occidental monarch, who had become a "dilettante." If officials had been merely individual appointees, the obligation of personal obedience would have made it far more difficult to maintain consistent opposition to irrational decisions of the monarch. When it became evident that a transition to the rule of technical bureaucracy was inevitable, the monarch regularly attempted to extend the system of advisory collegial bodies in the form of councils of state, in order to remain the master in spite of his lack of technical competence by playing off the internal dissensions of these bodies against each other. It was only after rational technical bureaucracy had come to be finally and irrevocably supreme that a need has been felt, particularly in relation to parliaments, for solidarity of the highest collegial bodies under monocratic direction through a prime minister. These bodies were intended to cover the ruler, who in turn protected them. With the latest development the general tendency of monocracy, and hence bureaucracy, in the organization of administration has become definitely victorious.

1. The significance of collegiality in the early stages of the development of modern administration is particularly evident in the struggle which the financial bodies created by Emperor Maximilian to meet the emergencies of the Turkish invasions carried on against his tendency to go over the heads of his officials and to issue orders and pledge securities for loans in accordance with every momentary whim. It was in the sphere of finance that the expropriation of the monarch began, for it was here in the first place that he lacked technical competence. This development occurred first in the Italian city states with their commercially organized system of accounting, then in the Burgundian and French Kingdoms, in the German territorial states, and independently of these in the Norman state of Sicily and in England. In the Near East

the Divans played a similar role, as did the Yamen in China and the Bakufu in Japan. In these cases, however, no rationally trained group of technically competent officials was available, and it was necessary to resort to the empirical knowledge of "experienced" officials. This accounts for the fact that a rationally bureaucratic system did not result. In Rome a somewhat similar role was played by the Senate.

2. The role of collegiality in promoting the separation of the private household from the sphere of office is somewhat similar to that played by the large-scale voluntary trading companies in the separation of the household and the profit-making enterprise on the one hand, of personal property and capital on the other.

16. *The Functionally Specific Division of Powers*

4.[15] It is further possible for authoritative powers to be limited by a functionally specific separation of powers. This means entrusting different individuals with specifically differentiated "functions" and the corresponding powers. In the strictly legal type—as in the constitutional separation of powers—these functions are rationally determined. It follows that in questions which involve two or more authorities it is only by means of a compromise between them that legitimate measures can be taken.

1. Functionally specific separation of powers differs from that based on status groups in that powers are divided in terms of their functionally objective character. This involves some kind of "constitution," which need not, however be formally enacted or written. The setup is such either that different types of measures have to be undertaken by different authorities or that the same type involves the cooperation by informal compromise of a plurality of agencies. It is not merely spheres of competence which are separated in this case but also the ultimate powers.

2. The functionally specific separation of powers is not wholly a modern phenomenon. The division of an independent political authority and an equally independent hierocratic authority instead of either caesaropapism or theocracy belongs in this category. Similarly, there is a certain sense in which the specified spheres of competence of the different Roman magistracies may be thought of as a kind of "separation of powers." The same is true of the specialized charismata of Lamaist Buddhism. In China the Confucian Hanlin Academy and the "censors" had a position which, in relation to the Emperor, was largely independent. In most patrimonial states, but also in the Roman Principate it has been usual for the administration of justice and the civil aspect of finance to be separated from the military establishment, at least in the lower

reaches. But in these cases the concept of separation of powers loses all precision. It is best to restrict its application to the supreme authority itself. If this restriction is accepted then the rational, formally enacted constitutional form of the separation of powers is entirely a modern phenomenon. In a constitutional but non-parliamentary state a budget can be put through only by a process of compromise between the legal authorities, such as the crown, and one or more legislative chambers.

Historically, the separation of powers in Europe developed out of the old system of estates. Its theoretical basis for England was first worked out by Montesquieu and then by Burke. Further back the division of powers began in the process of appropriation of governing powers and of the means of administration by privileged groups. Another important factor lay in the increasing financial needs of the monarchs, both the recurring needs arising from the social and economic development and the exceptional ones of war time. They could not be met without the consent of privileged groups, even though the latter were often the first to insist that they be met. In this situation it was necessary for the estates to reach a compromise, which was the historical origin of compromises over the budget and over legislation. The latter phenomena do not, however, belong in the context of the separation of powers as between estates but to the constitutional type.

3. The constitutional separation of powers is a specifically unstable structure. What determines the actual power structure is the answer to the question what would happen if a constitutionally necessary compromise, such as that over the budget, were not arrived at. An English king who attempted to rule without a budget today would risk his crown, whereas in pre-revolutionary Germany a Prussian king would not, for under the German system the position of the dynasty was dominant.

17. *The Relations of the Political Separation of Powers to the Economy*

1. Collegiality of legal bodies with rationally defined functions may be favorable to objectivity and the absence of personal influences in their administrative actions. Even if such collegiality has a negative influence because it functions imprecisely, the general effect may favor the rationality of economic activity. On the other hand, the big capitalistic interests of the present day, like those of the past, are apt, in political life —in parties and in all other connections that are important to them—to prefer monocracy. For monocracy is, from their point of view, more "discreet." The monocratic chief is more open to personal influence and is more easily swayed, thus making it more readily possible to influence the

administration of justice and other governmental activity in favor of such powerful interests. This is also in accord with German experience.

Conversely, the type of collegiality involving mutual veto powers or that in which collegial bodies have arisen out of the irrational appropriation of power of a traditional administrative staff may have irrational consequences. The type of collegiality of financial bodies, which originated specialized officialdom, has on the whole certainly been favorable to the formal rationalization of economic activity.

> In the United States the monocratic "party boss," rather than the official party organs which are often collegial, was preferred by the big contributors. This accounts for his indispensability. For the same reason, in Germany large sections of so-called "heavy industry" have favored bureaucratic domination rather than parliamentary government with its collegial system.

2. Like every form of appropriation, the separation of powers creates established spheres of authority which, though they may not yet be rational, still introduce an element of calculability into the functioning of the administrative apparatus. Hence, the separation of powers is generally favorable to the formal rationalization of economic activity. Movements which, like the Soviet type, the French Convention, and the Committee of Public Safety, aim to abolish the separation of powers, are definitely concerned with a more or less "just" economic distribution. Accordingly, they work against formal rationalization.

(All details must wait for the extended analyses.)

ix

Parties

1 8. *Definition and Characteristics*[16]

The term "party" will be employed to designate associations, membership in which rests on formally free recruitment. The end to which its activity is devoted is to secure power within an organization for its leaders in order to attain ideal or material advantages for its active members. These advantages may consist in the realization of certain objective policies or the attainment of personal advantages or both. Parties may have an ephemeral character or may be organized with a view to permanent activity. They may appear in all types of organizations and may themselves be organized in any one of a large variety of forms. They may consist of the following of a charismatic leader, of traditional retainers, or of purpose- or value-rational adherents. They may be oriented primarily to personal interests or to objective policies. Officially or merely in fact, they may be solely concerned with the attainment of power for their leaders and with securing positions in the administrative staff for their own members. (Then they are "patronage parties".) They may, on the other hand, predominantly and consciously act in the interests of a status group or a class or of certain objective policies or of abstract principles. (In the latter case they are called "ideological parties.") The attainment of positions in the administrative staff for their members is, however, at the least a secondary aim and objective programs are often merely a means of persuading outsiders to participate.

By definition a party can exist only *within* an organization, in order to influence its policy or gain control of it. Federations of party groups which cut across several corporate bodies are, however, not uncommon.

A party may employ any one of the conceivable means of gaining power. In cases where the government is determined by a formally free ballot and legislation is enacted by vote they are primarily organizations for the attraction of votes. Where voting takes a course in accord with legitimate expectations they are legal parties. The existence of legal parties, because of the fact that their basis is fundamentally one of voluntary adherence, always means that the business of politics is the pursuit of *interests*. (It should, however, be noted that in this context, "interests" is by no means necessarily an economic category. In the first instance, it is a matter of political interests which rest either on an ideological basis or on an interest in power as such.)

In this case the political enterprise is in the hands of:

a) party leaders and their staffs, whereas

b) active party members have for the most part merely the function of acclaiming their leaders. Under certain circumstances, however, they may exercise some forms of control, participate in discussion, voice complaints, or even initiate resolutions within the party;

c) the inactive masses of electors or voters (*Mitläufer*) are merely objects whose votes are sought at election time. Their attitudes are important only for the agitation of the competing parties;

d) contributors to party funds usually remain behind the scenes.

Apart from formally organized legal parties in a polity, there are the following principal types:

a) Charismatic parties arising from disagreement over the charismatic quality of the leader or over the question of who, in charismatic terms, is to be recognized as the correct leader. They create a schism.

b) Traditionalistic parties arising from controversy over the way in which the chief exercises his traditional authority in the sphere of his arbitrary will and grace. They arise in the form of movements to obstruct innovations or in open revolt against them.

c) Parties organized about questions of faith (*Glaubensparteien*). These are usually, though not necessarily, identical with a). They arise out of a disagreement over the content of doctrines or declarations of faith. They take the form of heresies, which are to be found even in rational parties such as the socialist.

d) Appropriation parties [or spoils-oriented parties] arising from conflict with the chief and his administrative staff over the filling of positions in the administrative staff. This type is very often, though by no means necessarily, identical with b).

Structurally, parties may conform to the same types as any other organizations. They may thus be charismatically oriented by devotion to the leader, with the plebiscite as an expression of confidence. They may be traditional with adherence based on the social prestige of the chief or of an eminent neighbor, or they may be rational with adherence to a leader and staff set up by a "constitutional process" of election. These differences may apply both to the basis of obedience of the members, and of the administrative staff. Further elaboration must be reserved to the Sociology of the State. [The *Staatssoziologie* was never written.]

It is of crucial importance for the economic aspect of the distribution of power and for the determination of party policy by what method the party activities are financed. Among the possibilities are small contributions from the masses of members and sympathizers; large contributions from disinterested sympathizers with its cause; direct or indirect sell-out to interested parties; or taxation either of elements under obligation to the party, including its members, or of its defeated opponents. These details, too, belong in the *Staatssoziologie*.

> 1. As has been pointed out, parties can exist by definition only within an organization, whether political or other, and only when there is a struggle for its control. Within a party there may be and very often are sub-parties; for example, as ephemeral structures they are typical in the nomination campaigns of presidential candidates of the American parties. On a permanent basis an example is the "Young Liberals" in Germany. Parties which extend to a number of different polities are illustrated by the Guelphs and Ghibellines in Italy in the thirteenth century and by the modern socialists.

2. The criterion of formally voluntary solicitation and adherence in terms of the rules of the group within which the party exists is treated here as the crucial point. It involves a distinction of major sociological significance from all associations which are prescribed and controlled by the polity. Even where the order of the polity takes notice of the existence of parties, as in the United States and in the German system of proportional representation, the voluntarist component remains. It remains even if an attempt is made to regulate their constitution. But when a party becomes a closed group which is incorporated by law into the administrative staff, as was true of the Guelphs in the Florentine statutes of the thirteenth century, it ceases to be a party and becomes a part of the polity.

3. Under genuinely charismatic domination, parties are necessarily schismatic sects. Their conflict is essentially over questions of faith and, as such, is basically irreconcilable. The situation in a strictly patriarchal body may be somewhat similar. Both these types of parties, at least in the pure form, are radically different from parties in the modern sense. In the usual kind of hereditary monarchy and estate-type organization, it is common for groups of retainers, composed of pretenders to fiefs and offices, to rally around a pretender to the throne. Personal followings are also common in organizations of *honoratiores* such as the aristocratic city states. They are, however, also prominent in some democracies. The modern type of party does not arise except in the legal state with a representative constitution. It will be further analyzed in the Sociology of the State.

4. The classic example of parties in the modern state organized primarily around patronage are the two great American parties of the last generation. Parties primarily oriented to issues and ideology have been the older type of Conservatism and Liberalism, bourgeois Democracy, later the Social Democrats and the [Catholic] Center Party. In all, except the last, there has been a very prominent element of class interest. After the Center attained the principal points of its original program, it became very largely a pure patronage party. In all these types, even those which are most purely an expression of class interests, the (ideal and material) interests of the party leaders and the staff in power, office, and remuneration always play an important part. There is a tendency for the interests of the electorate to be taken into account only so far as their neglect would endanger electoral prospects. This fact is one of the sources of public opposition to political parties as such.

5. The different forms which the internal organization of parties take will be dealt with separately in the proper place. One fact, however, is common to all these forms, namely, that there is a central group of individuals who assume the active direction of party affairs, including the formulation of programs and the selection of candidates. There is, secondly, a group of "members" whose role is notably more passive, and finally, the great mass of citizens whose role is only that of objects of solicitation by the various parties. They merely choose between the

various candidates and programs offered by the different parties. Given the voluntary character of party affiliation this structure is unavoidable. It is this which is meant by the statement that party activity is a matter of "play of interests." (As has already been stated, it is political interests and not economic interests which are involved.) The role of interests in this sense is the second principal point of attack for the opposition to parties as such. In this respect, there is a *formal* similarity between the party system and the system of capitalistic enterprise which rests on the recruitment of formally free labor.

6. The role in party finance of large-scale contributors is by no means confined to the "bourgeois" parties. Thus Paul Singer was a contributor to the Social Democratic party (and, by the way, humanitarian causes) of grand style (and purest motives so far as is known). His whole position as chairman of the party rested on this fact. Furthermore, the parties of the Russian revolution in the Kerensky stage were partly financed by very large Moscow business interests. Other German parties on the "right" have been financed by heavy industry, while the Center party occasionally had large contributions from Catholic millionaires.

For reasons which are readily understandable, the subject of party finances, though one of the most important aspects of the party system, is the most difficult to secure information about. It seems probable that in certain special cases a "machine" has actually been "bought." Apart from the role of individual large contributors, there are two basic alternatives: On the one hand, as in the English system, the electoral candidate may carry the burden of campaign expenses, with the result that the candidates are selected on a plutocratic basis. On the other hand, the costs may be borne by the "machine," in which case the candidates become dependent on the party organization. Parties as permanent organizations have always varied between these two fundamental types, in the thirteenth century in Italy just as much as today. These facts should not be covered up by fine phrases. Of course, there are limits to the power of party finance. It can only exercise an influence insofar as a "market" exists, but as in the case of capitalistic enterprise, the power of the seller as compared with the consumer has been tremendously increased by the suggestive appeal of advertising. This is particularly true of "radical" parties regardless of whether they are on the right or the left.

X

Direct Democracy and Representative Administration [17]

19. *The Conditions of Direct Democracy and of Administration by Notables*

Though a certain minimum of imperative powers in the execution of measures is unavoidable, certain organizations may attempt to reduce it as far as possible. This means that persons in authority are held obligated to act solely in accordance with the will of the members and in their service by virtue of the authority given by them. In small groups where all the members can be assembled at a single place, where they know each other and can be treated socially as equals this can be attained in a high degree. It has, however, been attempted in large groups, notably the corporate cities and city states of the past and certain regional groups.

The following are the principal technical means of attaining this end: (a) Short terms of office, if possible only running between two general meetings of the members; (b) Liability to recall at any time; (c) The principle of rotation or of selection by lot in filling offices so that every member takes a turn at some time. This makes it possible to avoid the position of power of technically trained persons or of those with long experience and command of official secrets; (d) A strictly defined mandate for the conduct of office laid down by the assembly of members. The sphere of competence is thus concretely defined and not of a general character; (e) A strict obligation to render an accounting to the general assembly; (f) The obligation to submit every unusual question which has not been foreseen to the assembly of members or to a committee representing them; (g) The distribution of powers between a large number of offices each with its own particular function; (h) The treatment of office as an avocation and not a full time occupation.

If the administrative staff is chosen by ballot, the process of election takes place in the assembly of members. Administration is primarily oral, with written records only so far as it is necessary to have a clear record of certain rights. All important measures are submitted to the assembly.

This and similar types of administration, as long as the assembly of members is effective, will be called "direct" or "immediate democracy."

1. The North American "township" and the smaller Swiss Cantons such as Glarus, Schwyz, and Appenzell are all, on account of their size alone, on the borderline of applicability of immediate democracy. The Athenian democracy actually overstepped this boundary to an important extent, and the *parlamentum* of the early medieval Italian cities still more radically. Voluntary associations, guilds, scientific, academic, and athletic associations of all sorts often have this form. It is, however, also applicable to the internal organization of aristocratic groups of masters who are unwilling to allow any individual to hold authority over them.

2. In addition to the small scale of the group in numbers or territorial extent, or still better in both, as essential conditions of immediate democracy, is the absence of qualitative functions which can only be adequately handled by professional specialists. Where such a group of professional specialists is present, no matter how strongly the attempt is made to keep them in a dependent position, the seeds of bureaucratization are present. Above all, such persons can neither be appointed nor dismissed according to the procedures appropriate to immediate democracy.

3. Closely related to the rational forms of immediate democracy is the primitive gerontocratic or patriarchal group. This is because those holding authority are expected to administer it in the "service" of the members. However, there are two principal differences: governing powers are normally appropriated and action is strictly bound to tradition. Immediate democracy is either a form of organization of rational groups or may become a rational form. The transitional types will be discussed presently.

20. *Administration by Notables*

Notables (*honoratiores*) are persons (1) whose economic position permits them to hold continuous policy-making and administrative positions in an organization · without (more than nominal) remuneration; (2) who enjoy social prestige of whatever derivation in such a manner that they are likely to hold office by virtue of the member's confidence, which at first is freely given and then traditionally accorded.

Most of all, the notable's position presupposes that the individual is able to live *for* politics without living *from* politics. He must hence be able to count on a certain level of provision from private sources. This condition is most likely to be met by receivers of property income of all sorts, such as landowners, slaveowners, and owners of cattle, real estate, or securities. Along with these, people with a regular occupation are in a favorable position if their occupation is such as to leave them free for political activity as an avocation. This is particularly true of persons whose occupational activity is seasonal, notably agriculture, of lawyers, who have an office staff to depend on, and certain others of the free professions. It is also to a large extent true of patrician merchants whose business is not continuously exacting. The most unfavorably situated are independent industrial entrepreneurs and industrial workers. Every type of immediate democracy has a tendency to shift to a form of government by notables. From an ideal point of view this is because they are held to be especially well-qualified by experience and objectivity. From a material point of view this form of government is especially cheap, indeed, sometimes completely costless. Such a person is partly himself in possession of the means of administration or provides them out of his own private resources, while in part they are put at his disposal by the organization.

　　1. The classification of notables as a status group will be undertaken later [ch. IV]. The primary basis in all primitive societies is wealth, which is often sufficient to make a man a "chief." In addition to this, according to different circumstances, hereditary charisma or economic availability may be more prominent.

　　2. In the American township the tendency has been to favor actual rotation on grounds of natural rights. As opposed to this the immediate democracy of the Swiss Cantons has been characterized by recurrence of the same names and, still more, families among the office holders. The fact that some persons were economically more available than others became also important in the Germanic communes (*Dinggemeinden*), and in the initially, at least in some cases, strictly democratic North-German towns this was one of the sources for the rise of the *meliores,* and hence of the patriciate, who monopolized the city councils.

　　3. Administration by notables is found in all kinds of organizations. It is, for instance, typical of political parties which are not highly bureaucratized. It always means an extensive rather than intensive type of administration. When there are very urgent economic or administrative needs for precise action, though it is free to the group as such, it is hence often very expensive for individual members.

Both immediate democracy and government by notables are technically inadequate, on the one hand in organizations beyond a certain limit of size, constituting more than a few thousand full-fledged members, or on the other hand, where functions are involved which require technical training or continuity of policy. If, in such a case, permanent technical officials are appointed alongside of shifting heads, actual power will normally tend to fall into the hands of the former, who do the real work, while the latter remain essentially dilettantes.

　　A typical example is to be found in the situation of the annually elected head (*Rektor*) of the German university, who administers academic affairs only as a sideline, *vis-á-vis* the syndics, or under certain circumstances even the permanent officials in the university administration (*Kanzlei*). Only an autonomous university president with a long term of office like the American type would, apart from very exceptional cases, be in a position to create a genuinely independent self-government of a university which went beyond phrase-making and expressions of self-importance. In Germany, however, both the vanity of academic faculties and the interests of the state bureaucracy in their own power stand in the way of any such development. Varying according to particular circumstances, similar situations are to be found everywhere.

Immediate democracy and government by notables exist in their genuine forms, free from *Herrschaft*, only so long as parties which contend with each other and attempt to appropriate office do not develop on a permanent basis. If they do, the leader of the contending and victorious party and his staff constitute a structure of domination, regardless of how they attain power and whether they formally retain the previous mode of administration.

(Indeed, this is a relatively common form of destroying the old ways.)

xi

Representation

21. *The Principal Forms and Characteristics*

The primary fact underlying representation is that the action of certain members of an organization, the "representatives," is considered binding on the others or accepted by them as legitimate and obligatory (cf. ch. I, sec. 11). Within the structures of domination, representation takes a variety of typical forms.

1. *Appropriated representation.* In this case the chief or a member of the administrative staff holds appropriated rights of representation. In this form it is very ancient and is found in all kinds of patriarchal and charismatic groups. The power of representation has a traditionally limited scope.

This category covers the sheiks of clans and chiefs of tribes, the headmen of castes in India, hereditary priests of sects, the *patel* of the Indian village, the *Obermärker*, hereditary monarchs, and all sorts of similar patriarchal or patrimonial heads of organizations. Authority to conclude contractual agreements and to agree on binding rules governing their relations with the elders of neighboring tribes exists in what are otherwise exceedingly primitive conditions, as in Australia.

2. Closely related to appropriated representation is *estate-type representation*. This does not constitute representation so far as it is a matter primarily of representing and enforcing appropriated rights or privileges. It may, however, have a representative character and be recognized as such, so far as the effect of the decisions of such bodies as estates extends beyond the personal holders of privileges to the unprivileged groups. This may not be confined to the immediate retainers but may include others who are not in the socially privileged group. These others are regularly bound by the action involved, whether this is merely taken for granted or a representative authority is explicitly claimed.

> This is true of all feudal courts and assemblies of privileged estates, and included the Estates of the late Middle Ages in Germany and of more recent times. In Antiquity and in non-European areas this institution occurs only sporadically and has not been a universal stage of development.

3. The radical antithesis of this is *"instructed" representation*. In this case elected representatives or representatives chosen by rotation or lot or in any other manner exercise powers of representation which are strictly limited by an imperative mandate and a right of recall. This type of "representative" is, in effect, an agent of those he represents.

> The imperative mandate has had for a very long time a place in the most various organizations. For instance, the elected representatives of the communes in France were almost always bound by the *cahiers de doléances*. At the present time this type of representation is particularly prominent in the Soviet type of republican organization where it serves as a substitute for immediate democracy, since the latter is impossible in a mass organization. Instructed mandates are certainly to be found in all sorts of organizations outside the Western World, both in the Middle Ages and in modern times, but nowhere else have they been of great historical significance.

4. *Free representation*. The representative, who is generally elected (and possibly subject to rotation), is not bound by instruction but is in a position to make his own decisions. He is obligated only to express his own genuine conviction, and not to promote the interests of those who have elected him.

Free representation in this sense is not uncommonly an unavoidable consequence of the incompleteness or absence of instructions, but in other cases it is the deliberate object of choice. In so far as this is true, the representative, by virtue of his election, exercises authority over the electors and is not merely their agent. The most prominent example of this type is modern parliamentary representation. It shares with legal authority the general tendency to impersonality, the obligation to conform to abstract norms, political or ethical.

This feature is most pronounced in the case of the parliaments, the representative bodies of the modern political organizations. Their function is not understandable apart from the voluntaristic intervention of the parties. It is the parties which present candidates and programs to the politically passive citizens. They also, by the process of compromise and balloting within the parliament, create the norms which govern the administrative process. They subject the administration to control, support it by their confidence, or overthrow it by withdrawal of confidence whenever, by virtue of commanding a majority of votes, they are in a position to do this.

The party leader and the administrative staff which is appointed by him, consisting of ministers, secretaries of state, and sometimes undersecretaries, constitute the political administration of the state, that is, their position is dependent upon the electoral success of their party, and an electoral defeat forces their resignation. Where party government is fully developed they are imposed on the formal head of the state, the monarch, by the party composition of the parliament. The monarch is expropriated from the actual governing power and his role is limited to two things.

1.) By negotiation with the parties, he selects the effective head and formally legitimizes his position by appointment.

2.) He acts as an agency for legalizing the measures of the party chief who at the time is in power.

The "cabinet" of ministers, a committee of the majority party, may be organized in a monocratic or a more collegial form. The latter is unavoidable in coalition cabinets, whereas the former is more precise in its functioning. The cabinet protects itself from the attacks of its followers who seek office and its opponents by the usual means, by monopolizing official secrets and maintaining solidarity against all outsiders. Unless there is an effective separation of powers, this system involves the complete appropriation of all powers by the party organization in control at the time; not only the top positions but often many of the lower offices become benefices of the party followers. This may be called *parliamentary cabinet government*.

The facts are in many respects best presented in the brilliantly polemical attack on the system by W. Hasbach [*Die parlamentarische Kabinettsregierung, 1919*] which has erroneously been called a "political description." The author in his own essay, *Parlament und Regierung im neugeordneten Deutschland,* has been careful to emphasize that it is a polemical work which has arisen out of the particular situation of the time.

Where the appropriation of power by the party government is not complete but the monarch or a corresponding elected president enjoys independent power especially in appointments to office, including military officers, there is a *constitutional government.* This is likely to be found where there is a formal separation of powers. A special case is an *elective presidency combined with a representative parliament.*

The executive authorities or the chief executive of a parliamentary organization may also be chosen by parliament itself: this is *purely representative government.*

The governing powers of representative bodies may be both limited and legitimized where direct canvassing of the masses of members of the groups is permitted through the *referendum.*

1. It is not representation as such but free representation in conjunction with the presence of parliamentary bodies which is peculiar to the modern Western World. Only relatively small beginnings are to be found in Antiquity and elsewhere in such forms as assemblies of delegates in the confederations of city states. But in principle the members of these bodies were usually bound by instructions.

2. The abolition of imperative mandates has been very strongly influenced by the positions of the monarchs. The French kings regularly demanded that the delegates to the Estates General should be elected on a basis which left them free to vote for the recommendations of the king. If they had been bound by imperative mandates, the king's policy would have been seriously obstructed. In the English Parliament, as will be pointed out below, both the composition and the procedure of the body led to the same result. It is connected with this fact that right up to the Reform Bill of 1867, the members of Parliament regarded themselves as a specially privileged group. This is shown clearly by the rigorous exclusion of publicity. (As late as the middle of the eighteenth century, heavy penalties were laid upon newspapers which reported the transactions of Parliament.) The theory came to be that the parliamentary deputy was a "representative" of the people as a whole and that hence he was not bound by any specific mandates, was not an "agent" but a person in authority (*Herr*). This theory was already well developed in the literature before it received its classical rhetorical form in the French Revolution.

3. It is not yet possible at this point to analyse in detail the process by which the English king and certain others following his example came to be gradually expropriated by the unofficial cabinet system which represented only party groups. This seems at first sight to be a very peculiar development in spite of the universal importance of its consequences. But in view of the fact that bureaucracy was relatively undeveloped in

England, it is by no means so "fortuitous" as has often been claimed. It is also not yet possible to analyse the partly plebiscitarian and partly representative American system of functional separation of powers and the place in it of the referendum (which is essentially an expression of mistrust of corrupt legislative bodies). Also Swiss democracy, and the related forms of purely representative democracy which have recently appeared in some of the German states, will have to be left aside for the present. The purpose of the above discussion was only to outline a few of the most important types.

4. So-called constitutional monarchy, which is above all characterized by appropriation of the power of patronage including the appointment of ministers and of military commanders by the monarch, may come to be very similar to a purely parliamentary regime of the English type. Conversely, the latter by no means necessarily excludes a politically gifted monarch like Edward VII from effective participation in political affairs. He need not be a mere figurehead. Details will be given below.

5. Groups governed by representative bodies are by no means necessarily democratic in the sense that all their members have equal rights. Quite the contrary, it can be shown that the classic soil for the growth of parliamentary government has tended to be an aristocratic or plutocratic society. This was true of England.

Relations to the economic order: These are highly complex and will have to be analyzed separately. For the present primary purposes only the following general remarks will be made:

1. One factor in the development of free representation was the undermining of the economic basis of the older status groups. This made it possible for persons with demagogic gifts to pursue their career regardless of their social position. The source of this undermining process was modern capitalism.

2. Calculability and reliability in the functioning of the legal order and the administrative system is vital to rational capitalism. This need led the bourgeoisie to attempt to impose checks on patrimonial monarchs and the feudal nobility by means of a collegial body in which the bourgeois had a decisive voice, which controlled administration and finance and could exercise an important influence on changes in the legal order.

3. When this transition was taking place, the proletariat had not yet become a political power and did not yet appear dangerous to the bourgeoisie. Furthermore, there was no hesitation in eliminating any threat to the power of the propertied class by means of property qualifications for the franchise.

4. The formal rationalization of the economic order and the state, which was favorable to capitalistic development, could be strongly pro-

moted by parliaments. Furthermore, it seemed relatively easy to secure influence on party organizations.

5. The development of demagogy in the activities of the existing parties was a function of the extension of the franchise. Two main factors have tended to make monarchs and ministers everywhere favorable to universal suffrage, namely, the necessity for the support of the proletariat in foreign conflict and the hope, which has proved to be unjustified, that, as compared to the bourgeoisie, they would be a conservative influence.

6. Parliaments have tended to function smoothly as long as their composition was drawn predominantly from the classes of wealth and culture, that is, as they were composed of *honoratiores*. Established social status rather than class interests as such underlay the party structure. The conflicts tended to be only those between different forms of wealth, but with the rise of class parties to power, especially the proletarian parties, the situation of parliaments has changed radically. Another important factor in the change has been the bureaucratization of party organizations, with its specifically plebiscitary character. The member of parliament thereby ceases to be "master" of the electors and becomes merely a "servant" of the leaders of the party machine. This will have to be discussed more in detail elsewhere.

22. *Representation by the Agents of Interest Groups*

A fifth type of representation is that by the agents of interest groups. This term will be applied to the type of representative body where the selection of members is not a matter of free choice, but where the body consists of persons who are chosen on the basis of their occupations or their social or class membership, each group being represented by persons of its own sort. At the present time the tendency of this type is to representation on an occupational basis.

This kind of representation may, however, have a very different significance, according to certain possible variations within it. In the first place, it will differ widely according to the specific occupations, status groups and classes which are involved, and, secondly, according to whether direct balloting or compromise is the means of settling differences. In the first connection its significance will vary greatly according to the numerical proportions of the different categories. It is possible for such a system to be radically revolutionary or extremely conservative in its character. In every case it is a product of the development of powerful parties representing class interests.

As a rule, this kind of representation is propagated with a view toward disenfranchising certain strata:

(a) either by distributing mandates among the occupations and thus *in fact* disenfranchising the numerically superior masses; or

(b) by *openly and formally* limiting suffrage to the non-propertied and thus by disenfranchising those strata whose power rests on their economic position (the case of a state of Soviets).

It is, at least, the theory that this type of representation weakens the exclusive sway of party interests, though, if experience so far is conclusive, it does not eliminate it. It is also theoretically possible that the role of campaign funds can be lessened, but it is doubtful to what degree this is true. Representative bodies of this type tend toward the absence of effective individual leadership (*Führerlosigkeit*), for the professional representative of an interest group is likely to be the only person who can devote his whole time to his function; among the non-propertied strata this task hence devolves upon the paid secretaries of the organized interest groups.

1. Representation where compromise has provided the means of settling differences is characteristic of all the older historical bodies of "estates." Today it is dominant in the labor-management committees and wherever negotiations between the various separate authorities is the order of the day. It is impossible to assign a numerical value to the "importance" of an occupational group. Above all the interests of the masses of workers on the one hand and of the increasingly smaller number of entrepreneurs, who are likely both to be particularly well informed and to have strong personal interests, somehow have to be taken account of regardless of numbers. These interests are often highly antagonistic, hence majority voting among elements which in status and class affiliation are highly heterogeneous, is exceedingly artificial. The ballot as a basis of final decision is characteristic of settling and expressing the compromise of *parties*. It is not, however, characteristic of the occupational interest groups.

2. The ballot is adequate in social groups where the representation consists of elements of roughly equal social status. Thus the so-called Soviets are made up only of workers. The prototype is the *mercadanza* of the time of the guilds' struggle [for power]. It was composed of delegates of the individual guilds who decided matters by majority vote. It was, however, in fact in danger of secession if certain particularly powerful guilds were out-voted. Even the participation of white-collar workers in Soviets raises problems. It has been usual to put mechanical limits to their share of votes. If representatives of peasants and craftsmen are admitted, the situation becomes still more complicated, and if the so-called "higher" professions and business interests are brought in, it is impossible for questions to be decided by ballot. If a labor-management body is organized in terms of equal representation, the tendency is for

"yellow" unions to support the employers and certain types of employers to support the workers. The result is that the elements which are most lacking in class loyalty (*Klassenwürde*) have the most decisive influence.

But even purely proletarian "Soviets" would in settled times be subject to the development of sharp antagonism between different groups of workers, which would probably paralyze the Soviets in effect. In any case, however, it would open the door for adroit politics in playing the different interests off against each other. This is the reason why the bureaucratic elements have been so friendly to the idea. The same thing would be likely to happen as between representatives of peasants and of industrial workers. Indeed any attempt to organize such representative bodies otherwise than on a strictly revolutionary basis comes down in the last analysis only to another opportunity for electoral manipulation in different forms.

3. The probability of the development of representation on an occupational basis is by no means low. In times of the stabilization of technical and economical development it is particularly high, but in such situations the importance of parties will be reduced at any rate. Unless this situation arises, it is obvious that occupational representative bodies will fail to eliminate parties. On the contrary, as can be clearly seen at the present time, all the way from the "Works Councils" to the Federal Economic Council in Germany, a great mass of new benefices for loyal party henchmen are being created and made use of. Politics is penetrating into the economic order at the same time that economic interests are entering into politics. There are a number of different possible value attitudes toward this situation, but this does not alter the facts.

Genuine parliamentary representation with the voluntaristic play of interests in the political sphere, the resulting plebiscitary party organization with its consequences, and the modern idea of *rational* representation by interest groups, are all peculiar to the Western World. None of these is understandable apart from the peculiar Western development of status groups and classes. Even in the Middle Ages the seeds of these phenomena were present in the Western World, and *only* there. It is only in the Western World that "cities" and "estates" (*rex et regnum*), "bourgeois" and "proletarians" have existed.

NOTES

Unless otherwise indicated, all notes are by Parsons.

1. Weber put *Autorität* in quotation marks and parentheses behind *Herrschaft*, referring to an alternative colloquial term, but the sentence makes it clear that this does not yet specify the basis of compliance. However, the chapter is devoted to a typology of legitimate domination, which will alternatively be translated as authority. The chapter begins with a reformulation of ch. X in Part Two,

and then presents a concise classification of the more descriptive exposition in chs. XI–XVI. (R)

2. Weber does not explain this distinction. By a "technical rule" he probably means a prescribed course of action which is dictated primarily on grounds touching efficiency of the performance of the immediate functions, while by "norms" he probably means rules which limit conduct on grounds other than those of efficiency. Of course, in one sense all rules are norms in that they are prescriptions for conduct, conformity with which is problematical.

3. It has seemed necessary to use the English word "office" in three different meanings, which are distinguished in Weber's discussion by at least two terms. The first is *Amt,* which means "office" in the sense of the institutionally defined status of a person. The second is the "work premises," as in the expression "he spent the afternoon in his office." For this Weber uses *Bureau* as also for the third meaning which he has just defined, the "organized work process of a group." In this last sense an office is a particular type of "enterprise," or *Betrieb* in Weber's sense. This use is established in English in such expressions as "the District Attorney's Office has such and such functions." Which of the three meanings is involved in a given case will generally be clear from the context.

3a. Under the *Oberhof* system, appeal against the local court's decision lay not to the court of the territorial prince but to that of one of the major independent cities with whose legal system the locality had originally been endowed by its ruler. Important "superior courts" (*Oberhöfe*) of this type for large parts of Germany and some areas in the Slavic East were the courts of Freiburg, Lübeck, Magdeburg, and other towns. Cf. H. Mitteis, *Deutsche Rechtsgeschichte* (5th ed., München 1958), 159, 190. (Wi)

4. As Parsons noted, "the term *Stand* with its derivatives is perhaps the most troublesome single term in Weber's text. It refers to a social group the members of which occupy a relatively well-defined common status, particularly with reference to social stratification, though this reference is not always important. In addition to common status, there is the further criterion that the members of a *Stand* have a common mode of life and usually more or less well-defined code of behavior" (Parsons, ed., *Theory,* 347). Parsons chose "decentralized authority" for "estate-type domination" because the members of the administrative staff are independent of their master. However, since the term *ständisch* derives from a specific historical context, even though Weber uses it often in a generic sense, it appeared appropriate to use the English equivalent "estate," which can denote both the medieval Estates and high social rank. *Stand* alone, however, will usually be translated as "status group" or "socially privileged group." (R)

5. Cf. Georg v. Below, *Der deutsche Staat des Mittelalters,* 1914 (sec. ed., 1925); id., *Territorium und Stadt* (sec. ed., 1923), 161ff; id., *Vom Mittelalter bis zur Neuzeit,* 1924; for a critique, see Ernst Kern, *Moderner Staat und Staatsbegriff,* 1949. Karl Ludwig v. Haller, *Restauration der Staatswissenschaft* (sec. ed., vols. 1–4, 1820–22, vol. 5, 1834, vol. 6, 1825). (W)

6. Kurt Eisner, a brilliant Social Democratic (not Communist) intellectual proclaimed the Bavarian Republic in Nov. 1918. He was murdered on Feb. 21, 1919. When the death sentence of the murderer, Count Arco, was commuted to a life sentence in Jan. 1920, Weber announced at the beginning of one of his lectures that he favored Arco's execution on substantive and pragmatic grounds. In the next lecture this resulted in a packed audience and noisy right-wing demonstration, which prevented Weber from lecturing. See now the account of two eyewitnesses in René König and Johannes Winckelmann, eds., *Max Weber*

zum Gedächtnis. Special issue 7 of the *Kölner Zeitschrift für Soziologie,* 1963, 24–29. On this period, cf. also the references in ch. II, n. 20. (R)

7. Weber here uses *Welt* in quotation marks, indicating that it refers to its meaning in what is primarily a religious context. It is the sphere of "worldly" things and interests as distinguished from transcendental religious interests.

8. Cf. Theodor Mommsen, *Abriss des römischen Staatsrechts.* First ed. 1893, sec. ed., 1907, 102ff, 162f. (W)

9. Cf. Fritz Rörig, *Geblütsrecht und freie Wahl in ihrer Auswirkung auf die deutsche Geschichte* (Abhandlungen der Berliner Akademie, 1945/6, Philosophische-Historische Klasse Nr. 6). (W)

10. The works of Ulrich Stutz are listed in Brunner-v. Schwerin, *Grundzüge der deutschen Rechtsgeschichte.* 8th ed. (1930), paragraph 33, 137. (W)

10a. On the *kayasth,* a caste of scribes in Bengal and elsewhere in India, cf. Weber, *Religion of India,* 75f., 298. (Wi)

11. See. C. H. Becker, *Islamstudien* (Leipzig: Quelle und Meyer, 1924), I, ch. 9. (R)

12. For the older definition of "organization," see Part Two, ch. X:3. Weber's definition of *Organisation* refers to the activities of a staff or apparatus, including the sharing of executive powers with the "master" (chief, head). This definition comes close to that of "organized action" (*Verbandshandeln*) in sec. 12, ch. I. The term *Verband,* which I prefer to render as "organization," is more broadly defined, since rules may be enforced by a head alone. Usually, however, a *Verband* has a staff, and Weber almost always uses the term in this sense. Hence, the terminological difference between *Verband* and *Organisation* can be disregarded most of the time. This is an additional reason for rendering *Verband,* which Weber uses much more frequently than *Organisation,* as "organization" in English. (R)

13. Weber titled both headings "The Anti-Authoritarian (*herrschaftsfremde*) Reinterpretation of Charisma," because recognition by the followers may become the *formal* basis of legitimacy, in contrast to the earlier stage in which charisma claims legitimacy and recognition on its own grounds. Since Weber's meaning of "anti-authoritarian" is not obvious without explanation, more descriptive titles were chosen. (R)

14. German territorial princes, since the thirteenth and fourteenth centuries, occasionally called on feudal and ecclesiastic notables for advice. As these counselors were only visiting at court, they were called *Räte von Haus aus,* or *familiares domestici, consiliarii,* etc.; cf. Georg Ludwig von Maurer, *Geschichte der Fronhöfe, der Bauernhöfe und der Hofverfassung in Deutschland* (Erlangen, 1862), II, 237, 240ff, 312f. (GM)

15. This continues the enumeration at the beginning of sec. 15. (R)

16. For the early formulation, see Part Two, ch. IX:6e. (R)

17. For the early formulation, see Part Two, ch. X:2. (R)

CHAPTER **IV**

STATUS GROUPS
AND CLASSES[1]

1. *Class Situation and Class Types*

"Class situation" means the typical probability of
1. procuring goods
2. gaining a position in life and
3. finding inner satisfactions,
a probability which derives from the relative control over goods and skills and from their income-producing uses within a given economic order.

"Class" means all persons in the same class situation.

a) A "*property* class" is primarily determined by property differences,

b) A "*commercial* class" by the marketability of goods and services,

c) A "*social* class" makes up the totality of those class situations within which individual and generational mobility is easy and typical.

Associations of class members—class organizations—may arise on the basis of all three types of classes. However, this does not necessarily happen: "Class situation" and "class" refer only to the same (or similar) interests which an individual shares with others. In principle, the various controls over consumer goods, means of production, assets, resources and skills each constitute a *particular* class situation. A *uniform* class situation prevails only when completely unskilled and propertyless persons are dependent on irregular employment. Mobility among, and stability of, class positions differs greatly; hence, the unity of a social class is highly variable.

[302]

2. *Property Classes*

The primary significance of a positively privileged property class lies in

α) its exclusive acquisition of high-priced consumers goods,

β) its sales monopoly and its ability to pursue systematic policies in this regard,

γ) its monopolization of wealth accumulation out of unconsumed surpluses,

δ) its monopolization of capital formation out of savings, i.e., of the utilization of wealth in the form of loan capital, and its resulting control over executive positions in business,

ε) its monopolization of costly (educational) status privileges.

I. Positively privileged property classes are typically *rentiers*, receiving income from:

    a) men (the case of slave-owners),

    b) land,

    c) mines,

    d) installations (factories and equipment),

    e) ships,

    f) creditors (of livestock, grain or money),

    g) securities.

II. Negatively privileged property classes are typically

    a) the unfree (see under "Status Group"),

    b) the declassed (the *proletarii* of Antiquity),

    c) the "paupers".

In between are the various "middle classes" (*Mittelstandsklassen*), which make a living from their property or their acquired skills. Some of them may be "commercial classes" (entrepreneurs with mainly positive privileges, proletarians with negative ones). However, not all of them fall into the latter category (witness peasants, craftsmen, officials).

The mere differentiation of property classes is not "dynamic," that is, it need not result in class struggles and revolutions. The strongly privileged class of slave owners may coexist with the much less privileged peasants or even the declassed, frequently without any class antagonism and sometimes in solidarity (against the unfree). However, the juxtaposition of property classes *may* lead to revolutionary conflict between

    1. land owners and the declassed or

    2. creditor and debtors (often urban patricians versus rural peasants or small urban craftsmen).

These struggles need not focus on a change of the economic system, but may aim primarily at a redistribution of wealth. In this case we can speak of "property revolutions" (*Besitzklassenrevolutionen*).

A classic example of the lack of class conflict was the relationship of the "poor white trash" to the plantation owners in the Southern States. The "poor white trash" were far more anti-Negro than the plantation owners, who were often imbued with patriarchal sentiments. The major examples for the struggle of the declassed against the propertied date back to Antiquity, as does the antagonism between creditors and debtors and land owners and the declassed.

3. *Commercial Classes*

The primary significance of a positively privileged commercial class lies in

a) the monopolization of entrepreneurial management for the sake of its members and their business interests,

β) the safeguarding of those interests through influence on the economic policy of the political and other organizations.

I. Positively privileged commercial classes are typically *entrepreneurs*:

    a) merchants,

    b) shipowners,

    c) industrial and

    d) agricultural entrepreneurs,

    e) bankers and financiers, *sometimes* also

    f) professionals with sought-after expertise or privileged education (such as lawyers, physicians, artists), or

    g) workers with monopolistic qualifications and skills (natural, or acquired through drill or training).

II. Negatively privileged commercial classes are typically *laborers* with varying qualifications:

    a) skilled

    b) semi-skilled

    c) unskilled.

In between again are "middle classes": the self-employed farmers and craftsmen and frequently:

    a) public and private officials.

    b) the last two groups mentioned in the first category [i.e., the "liberal professions" and the labor groups with exceptional qualifications].

4. *Social Classes*

Social classes are

a) the working class as a whole—the more so, the more automated the work process becomes,

b) the petty bourgeoisie,

c) the propertyless intelligentsia and specialists (technicians, various kinds of white-collar employees, civil servants—possibly with considerable social differences depending on the cost of their training),

d) the classes privileged through property and education.

The unfinished last part of Karl Marx's *Capital* apparently was intended to deal with the issue of class unity in the face of skill differentials. Crucial for this differentiation is the increasing importance of semi-skilled workers, who can be trained on the job in a relatively short time, over the apprenticed and sometimes also the unskilled workers. Semi-skilled qualification too can often become monopolistic (weavers, for example, sometimes achieve their greatest efficiency after five years). It used to be that every worker aspired to be a self-employed small businessman. However, this is less and less feasible. In the generational sequence, the rise of groups a) and b) into c) (technicians, white-collar workers) is relatively the easiest. Within class d) money increasingly buys *everything*, at least in the sequence of generations. In banks and corporations, as well as in the higher ranks of the civil service, class c) members have a chance to move up into class d).

Class-conscious organization succeeds most easily

a) against the immediate economic opponents (workers against entrepreneurs, but *not* against stockholders, who truly draw "unearned" incomes, and also *not* in the case of peasants confronting manorial lords);

b) if large numbers of persons are in the same class situation,

c) if it is technically easy to organize them, especially if they are concentrated at their place of work (as in a "workshop community"),

d) if they are led toward readily understood goals, which are imposed and interpreted by men outside their class (intelligentsia).

5. *Status and Status Group* (Stand)

"Status" (*ständische Lage*) shall mean an effective claim to social esteem in terms of positive or negative privileges; it is typically founded on

a) style of life, hence

b) formal education, which may be

    a) empirical training or

    β) rational instruction, and the corresponding forms of behavior,

c) hereditary or occupational prestige.

In practice, status expresses itself through

    a) connubium,

    β) commensality, possibly

    γ) monopolistic appropriation of privileged modes of acquisition or the abhorrence of certain kinds of acquisition,

    δ) status conventions (traditions) of other kinds.

Status *may* rest on class position of a distinct or an ambiguous kind. However, it is not solely determined by it: Money and an entrepreneurial position are not in themselves status qualifications, although they may lead to them; and the lack of property is not in itself a status disqualification, although this may be a reason for it. Conversely, status may influence, if not completely determine, a class position without being identical with it. The class position of an officer, a civil servant or a student may vary greatly according to their wealth and yet not lead to a different status since upbringing and education create a common style of life.

A "status group" means a plurality of persons who, within a larger group, successfully claim

    a) a special social esteem, and possibly also

    b) status monopolies.

Status groups may come into being:

    a) in the first instance, by virtue of their own style of life, particularly the type of vocation: "self-styled" or occupational status groups,

    b) in the second instance, through hereditary charisma, by virtue of successful claims to higher-ranking descent: hereditary status groups, or

    c) through monopolistic appropriation of political or hierocratic powers: political or hierocratic status groups.

The development of hereditary status groups is generally a form of the (hereditary) appropriation of privileges by an organization or qualified individuals. Every definite appropriation of political powers and the corresponding economic opportunities tends to result in the rise of status groups, and vice-versa.

Commercial classes arise in a market-oriented economy, but status groups arise within the framework of organizations which satisfy their wants through monopolistic liturgies, or in feudal or in *ständisch*-patrimonial fashion. Depending on the prevailing mode of stratification, we shall speak of a "status society" or a "class society." The status group comes closest to the social class and is most unlike the commercial class. Status groups are often created by property classes.

Every status society lives by conventions, which regulate the style of life, and hence creates economically irrational consumption patterns and fetters the free market through monopolistic appropriations and by curbing the individual's earning power. More on that separately.

NOTES

1. For the early formulation of class and status, see Part Two, ch. IX:6. (R)

The Economy and the Arena of

Normative and De Facto Powers

CHAPTER I

THE ECONOMY AND
SOCIAL NORMS

1. Legal Order and Economic Order

A. THE SOCIOLOGICAL CONCEPT OF LAW. When we speak of "law,"
"legal order," or "legal proposition" (*Rechtssatz*), close attention must
be paid to the distinction between the legal and the sociological points
of view. Taking the former, we ask: What is intrinsically valid as law?
That is to say: What significance or, in other words, what *normative*
meaning ought to be attributed in correct logic to a verbal pattern having the form of a legal proposition. But if we take the latter point of
view, we ask: What *actually* happens in a group owing to the *probability*
that persons engaged in social action (*Gemeinschaftshandeln*), especially
those exerting a socially relevant amount of power, subjectively consider
certain norms as valid and practically act according to them, in other
words, orient their own conduct towards these norms? This distinction
also determines, in principle, the relationship between *law* and *economy*.

The juridical point of view, or, more precisely, that of legal dogmatics[1]
aims at the correct meaning of propositions the content of which constitutes an order supposedly determinative for the conduct of a defined
group of persons: in other words, it tries to define the facts to which this
order applies and the way in which it bears upon them. Toward this end,
the jurist, taking for granted the empirical validity of the legal propositions, examines each of them and tries to determine its logically correct
meaning in such a way that all of them can be combined in a system
which is logically coherent, i.e., free from internal contradictions. This
system is the "legal order" in the juridical sense of the word.

Sociological economics (*Sozialökonomie*), on the other hand, con-

[311]

siders actual human activities as they are conditioned by the necessity to take into acount the facts of economic life. We shall apply the term *economic order* to the distribution of the actual control over goods and services, the distribution arising in each case from the particular mode of balancing interests consensually; moreover, the term shall apply to the manner in which goods and services are indeed used by virtue of these powers of disposition, which are based on *de facto* recognition (*Einverständnis*).

It is obvious that these two approaches deal with entirely different problems and that their subjects cannot come directly into contact with one another. The ideal "legal order" of legal theory has nothing directly to do with the world of real economic conduct, since both exist on different levels. One exists in the realm of the "ought," while the other deals with the world of the "is." If it is nevertheless said that the economic and the legal order are intimately related to one another, the latter is understood, not in the legal, but in the sociological sense, i.e., as being *empirically* valid. In this context "legal order" thus assumes a totally different meaning. It refers not to a set of norms of logically demonstrable correctness, but rather to a complex of actual determinants (*Bestimmungsgründe*) of human conduct. This point requires further elaboration.

The fact that some persons act in a certain way because they regard it as prescribed by legal propositions (*Rechtssätze*) is, of course, an essential element in the actual emergence and continued operation of a "legal order." But, as we have seen already in discussing the significance of the "existence" of rational norms,[2] it is by no means necessary that all, or even a majority, of those who engage in such conduct, do so from this motivation. As a matter of fact, such a situation has never occurred. The broad mass of the participants act in a way corresponding to legal norms, not out of obedience regarded as a legal obligation, but either because the environment approves of the conduct and disapproves of its opposite, or merely as a result of unreflective habituation to a regularity of life that has engraved itself as a custom. If the latter attitude were universal, the law would no longer "subjectively" be regarded as such, but would be observed as custom. As long as there is a chance that a coercive appartus will enforce, in a given situation, compliance with those norms, we nevertheless must consider them as "law." Neither is it necessary—according to what was said above—that all those who share a belief in certain norms of behavior, actually live in accordance with that belief at all times. Such a situation, likewise, has never obtained, nor need it obtain, since, according to our general definition, it is the "orientation" of an action toward a norm, rather than the "success" of that norm that is decisive for its validity. "Law," as understood by us, is simply an "order" endowed with certain specific guarantees of the probability of its empirical validity.

The term "guaranteed law" shall be understood to mean that there exists a "coercive apparatus" (in the sense defined earlier),[3] that is, that there are one or more persons whose special task it is to hold themselves ready to apply specially provided means of coercion (legal coercion) for the purpose of norm enforcement. The means of coercion may be physical or psychological, they may be direct or indirect in their operation, and they may be directed, as the case may require, against the participants in the consensual group (*Einverständnisgemeinschaft*) or the association (*Vergesellschaftung*), the organization (*Verband*) or the institution (*Anstalt*), within which the order is (empirically) valid; or they may be aimed at those outside. These means are the "legal regulations" of the group in question.

By no means all norms which are consensually valid in a group—as we shall see later—are "legal norms." Nor are all official functions of the persons constituting the coercive apparatus of a community concerned with legal coercion; we shall rather consider as legal coercion only those actions whose intention is the enforcement of conformity to a norm as such, i.e., because of its being formally accepted as binding. The term will not be applied, however, where conformity of conduct to a norm is sought because of considerations of expediency or other material circumstances. It is obvious that the effectuation of the validity of a norm may in fact be pursued for the most diverse motives. However, we shall designate it as "guaranteed law" only in those cases where these exists the probability that coercion will be applied for the norm's sake. As we shall have opportunity to see, not all law is guaranteed law. We shall speak of law—albeit in the sense of "indirectly guaranteed" or "unguaranteed" law—also in all those cases where the validity of a norm consists in the fact that the mode of orientation of an action toward it has some "legal consequences"; i.e., that there are other norms which associate with the "observance" or "infringement" of the primary norm certain probabilities of consensual action guaranteed, in their turn, by legal coercion. We shall have occasion to illustrate this case which occurs in a large area of legal life. However, in order to avoid further complication, whenever we shall use the term "law" without qualification, we shall mean norms which are directly guaranteed by legal coercion.

Such "guaranteed law" is by no means in all cases guaranteed by "violence" (*Gewalt*) in the sense of the prospect of physical coercion. In our terminology, law, including "guaranteed law" is not characterized by violence or, even less, by that modern technique of effectuating claims of private law through bringing "suit" in a "court," followed by coercive execution of the judgment obtained. The sphere of "public" law, i.e., the norms governing the conduct of the organs of the state and other state-oriented activities, recognizes numerous rights and legal norms, upon the infringement of which a coercive apparatus can be set in motion only through "complaint" or through "remonstance" by members of a limited group of persons, and often without any means of physical coercion. Sociologically, the question of whether or not guaranteed law exists in such a situation depends on the availability of an organized coercive apparatus for the nonviolent exercise of legal coercion. This apparatus must also possess such power that there is in fact a significant probability that the norm will be respected because of the possibility of recourse to such legal coercion.

Today legal coercion by violence is the monopoly of the state. All other groups applying legal coercion by violence are today considered as heteronomous and mostly also as heterocephalous. This is the outcome, however, of certain stages of development. We shall speak of "state" law, i.e., of law guaranteed by the state, only when legal coercion is exercised through the specific, i.e., normally directly *physical,* means of coercion of the political community. Thus, the existence of a "legal norm" in the sense of "state law" means that the following situation obtains: In the case of certain events occurring there is general agreement that certain organs of the community can be expected to go into official action, and the very expectation of such action is apt to induce conformity with the commands derived from the generally accepted interpretation of that legal norm; or, where such conformity has become unattainable, at least to effect reparation or indemnification. The event inducing this consequence, the legal coercion by the state, may consist in certain human acts, for instance, the conclusion or the breach of a contract, or the commission of a tort, But this type of occurrence constitutes only a special instance, since, upon the basis of some empirically valid legal proposition, the coercive instruments of the political powers against persons and things may also be applied where, for example, a river has risen above a certain level. It is in no way inherent, however, in the validity of a legal norm as normally conceived, that those who obey do so, predominantly or in any way, because of the availability of such a coercive apparatus as defined above. The motives for obedience may rather be of many different kinds. In the majority of cases, they are predominantly utilitarian or ethical or subjectively conventional, i.e., consisting of the fear of disapproval by the environment. The nature of these motives is highly relevant in determining the kind and the degree of validity of the law itself. But in so far as the formal sociological concept of guaranteed law, as we intend to use it, is concerned, these psychological facts are irrelevant. In this connection nothing matters except that there be a sufficiently high probability of intervention on the part of a specially designated group of persons, even in those cases where nothing has occurred but the sheer fact of a norm infringement, i.e., on purely formal grounds.

The empirical validity of a norm as a legal norm affects the interests of an individual in many respects. In particular, it may convey to an individual certain calculable chances of having eonomic goods available or of acquiring them under certain conditions in the future. Obviously, the creation or protection of such chances is normally one of the aims of law enactment by those who agree upon a norm or impose it upon others. There are two ways in which such a "chance" may be attributed. The attribution may be a mere by-product of the empirical validity of the norm; in that case the norm is not *meant* to guarantee to an individual the chance which happens to fall to him. It may also be, however, that the norm is specifically meant to provide to the individual such a guaranty, in other words, to grant him a "right." Sociologically, the statement that someone has a right by virtue of the legal order of the state thus normally means the following: He has a chance, factually guaranteed to him by the consensually accepted interpretation of a legal norm, of invoking in favor of his ideal or material interests the aid of a "coercive apparatus" which is in special readiness for this purpose. This aid consists, at least normally, in the readiness of certain persons to come to his support in the event that they are approached in the proper way, and that it is shown that the recourse to such aid is actually guaranteed to him by a "legal norm." Such guaranty is based simply upon the "validity" of the legal proposition, and does not depend upon questions of expediency, discretion, grace, or arbitrary pleasure.

A law, thus, is valid wherever legal help in this sense can be obtained in a relevant measure, even though without recourse to physical or other drastic coercive means. A law can also be said to be valid, viz., in the case of unguaranteed law, if its violation, as, for instance, that of an electoral law, induces, on the ground of some empirically valid norm, legal consequences, for instance, the invalidation of the election, for the execution of which an agency with coercive powers has been established.

For purposes of simplification we shall pass by those "chances" which are produced as mere "by-products." A "right," in the context of the "state," is guaranteed by the coercive power of the political authorities. Wherever the means of coercion which constitute the guaranty of a "right" belong to some authority other than the political, for instance, a hierocracy, we shall speak of "extra-state law."

B. STATE LAW AND EXTRA-STATE LAW. A discussion of the various categories of such extra-state law would be out of place in the present context. All we need to recall is that there exist nonviolent means of coercion which may have the same or, under certain conditions, even greater effectiveness than the violent ones. Frequently, and in fairly large areas even regularly, the threat of such measures as the exclusion from an organization, or a boycott, or the prospect of magically conditioned advantages or disadvantages in this world, or of reward and punishment in the next, are under certain cultural conditions more effective in producing a certain behavior than a political apparatus whose coercive functioning is not always predictable with certainty. Legal forcible coercion exercised by the coercive apparatus of the political community has often come off badly as compared with the coercive power of other, e.g., religious, authorities. In general, the actual scope of its efficiency depends on the circumstances of each concrete case. Within the realm of sociological reality, legal coercion continues to exist, however, as long as some socially *relevant* effects are produced by its power machinery.

The assumption that a state "exists" only if the coercive means of the political community are superior to *all* other communities, is not sociological. "Ecclesiastical law" is still law even where it comes into conflict with "state" law, as it has happened many times and as it is bound to happen again in the case of the relations between the modern state and certain churches, for instance, the Roman-Catholic. In imperial Austria, the Slavic *Zadruga* not only lacked any kind of legal guaranty by the state, but some of its norms were outright contradictory to the official law. Since the consensual action constituting a *Zadruga* has at its disposal its own coercive apparatus for the enforcement of its norms, these norms are to be considered as "law." Only the state, if invoked, would refuse recognition and proceed, through its coercive power, to break it up.

Outside the sphere of the European-Continental legal system, it is no rare occurrence at all that modern state law explicitly treats as "valid" the norms of other organizations and reviews their concrete decisions. American law thus protects labor union labels or regulates the conditions under which a candidate is to be regarded as validly nominated by a party. English judges intervene, on appeal, in the judicial proceedings of a club. Even on the Continent German judges investigate, in defamation cases, the propriety of the rejection of a challenge to a duel, even though duelling is forbidden by law. We shall not enter into a casuistic inquiry of the extent to which such norms thus become "state law." For all the reasons given above and, in particular, for the sake of terminological consistency, we categorically deny that "law" exists only where legal coercion is guaranteed by the political authority. For us, there is no practical reason for such a terminology. A "legal order" shall rather be said to exist wherever coercive means, of a physical or psychological kind, are available; i.e., wherever they are at the disposal of one or more persons who hold themselves ready to use them for this purpose in the case of certain events; in other words, wherever we find a consociation specifically dedicated to the purpose of "legal coercion." The possession of such an apparatus for the exercise of physical coercion has not always been the monopoly of the political community. As far as psychological coercion is concerned, there is no such monopoly even today, as demonstrated by the importance of law guaranteed only by the church.

We have also indicated already that direct guaranty of law and of rights by a coercive apparatus constitutes only one instance of the existence of "law" and of "rights." Even within this limited sphere the coercive apparatus can take on a great variety of forms. In marginal cases, it may consist in the consensually valid chance of coercive intervention by *all* the members of the community in the event of an infringement of a valid norm. However, in that case one cannot properly speak of a "coercive apparatus" unless the conditions under which participation in such coercive intervention is to be obligatory, are firmly fixed. In those cases where the protection of rights is guaranteed by the organs of the political authority, the coercive apparatus may be reinforced by pressure groups: the strict regulations of associations of creditors and landlords, especially their blacklists of unreliable debtors or tenants, often operate more effectively than the prospect of a lawsuit. It goes without saying that this kind of coercion may be extended to claims which the state does not guarantee at all; such claims are nevertheless based on *rights* even though they are guaranteed by authorities other than the state. The law of the state often tries to obstruct the coercive means of other associations; the English Libel Act thus tries to preclude blacklisting by excluding the defense of truth. But the state is not always successful. There are groups stronger than the state in this respect, for instance, those status groups which rely on the "honor code" of the duel as the means of resolving conflicts. With courts of honor and boycott as the coercive means at their disposal, they usually succeed in compelling the fulfillment of obligations as "debts of honor," for instance, gambling debts or the duty to engage in a duel; such debts are intrinsically connected with the specific purposes of the group in question, but, as far as the state is concerned, they are not recognized, or are even proscribed. But the state has been forced, as least partially, to trim its sails.

It would indeed be distorted legal reasoning to demand that such a specific delict as duelling be punished as "attempted murder" or assault and battery. Those crimes are of a quite different character. But it remains a fact that in Germany the readiness to participate in a duel is still a *legal* obligation imposed by the state upon its army officers even though the duel is expressly forbidden by the Criminal Code. The state itself has connected legal consequences with an officer's failure to comply with the honor code. Outside of the status group of army officers the situation is different, however. The typical means of statutory coercion applied by "private" organizations against refractory members is exclusion from the corporate body and its tangible or intangible advantages. In the professional organizations of physicians and lawyers as well as in social or political clubs, it is the *ultima ratio*. The modern political organization has to a large extent usurped the application of these measures of coercion. Thus, recourse to them has been denied to the physicians and lawyers in Germany; in England the state courts have been given jurisdiction to review, on appeal, exclusions from clubs; and in America the courts have power over political parties as well as the right of reviewing, on appeal, the legality of the use of a union label.

This conflict between the means of coercion of various organizations is as old as the law itself. In the past it has not always ended with the triumph of the coercive means of the political body, and even today this has not always been the outcome. A businessman, for instance, who has violated a cartel agreement, has no remedy against a systematic attempt to drive him out of business by underselling. Similarly, there is no protection against being blacklisted for having availed oneself of the plea of illegality of a contract in futures. In the Middle Ages the prohibitions of resorting to the ecclesiastical court contained in the statutes of certain merchants' guilds were clearly invalid from the point of view of canon law, but they persisted nonetheless.[4]

To a considerable extent the state must tolerate the coercive power of organizations even in cases where it is directed not only against members, but also against outsiders on whom the organization tries to impose its own norms. Illustrations are afforded by the efforts of cartels to force outsiders into membership, or by the measures taken by creditors' associations against debtors and tenants.

An important marginal case of coercively guaranteed law, in the sociological sense, is presented by that situation which may be regarded as the very opposite of that which is presented by the modern political communities as well as by those religious communities which apply their own "laws." In the modern communities the law is guaranteed by a "judge" or some other "organ" who is an impartial and disinterested umpire rather than a person who would be characterized by a special relationship with one or the other of the parties. In the situation which we have in mind the means of coercion are provided by those very persons who are linked to the party by close personal relationship, for example, as members of his kinship group. Just as war under modern international law, so under these conditions "vengeance" and "feud" are the only, or at least, the normal, forms of law enforcement. In this case, the "right" of the individual consists, sociologically seen, in the mere probability that the members of his kinship group will respond to their obligation of supporting his feud and blood vengeance (an obligation originally guaranteed by fear of the wrath of supernatural authorities) and that they will possess strength sufficient to support the right claimed by him even though not necessarily to achieve its final triumph.

The term "legal relationship" will be applied to designate that situation in which the content of a right is constituted by a relationship, i.e., the actual or potential actions of concrete persons or of persons to be identified by concrete criteria. The rights contained in a legal relationship may vary in accordance with the actually occurring actions. In this sense a state can be designated as a legal relationship, even in the hypothetical marginal case in which the ruler alone is regarded as endowed with rights (the right to give orders) and where, accordingly, the opportunities of all the other individuals are reduced to reflexes of his regulations.

2. *Law, Convention, and Custom*[5]

A. SIGNIFICANCE OF CUSTOM IN THE FORMATION OF LAW. Law, convention, and custom belong to the same continuum with imperceptible transitions leading from one to the other. We shall define *custom (Sitte)* to mean a typically uniform activity which is kept on the beaten track simply because men are "accustomed" to it and persist in it by unreflective imitation. It is a collective way of acting (*Massenhandeln*), the perpetuation of which by the individual is not "required" in any sense by anyone.

Convention, on the other hand, shall be said to exist wherever a certain conduct is sought to be induced without, however, any coercion, physical or psychological, and, at least under normal circumstances, without any direct reaction other than the expression of approval or disapproval on the part of those persons who constitute the environment of the actor.

"Convention" must be strictly distinguished from *customary law.* We shall abstain here from criticizing this not very useful concept.[6] According to the usual terminology, the validity of a norm as customary law consists in the very likelihood that a coercive apparatus will go into action for its enforcement although it derives from mere consensus rather than from enactment. Convention, on the contrary, is characterized by the very absence of any coercive apparatus, i.e., of any, at least relatively clearly delimited, group of persons who would continuously hold themselves ready for the special task of legal coercion through physical or psychological means.

The existence of a mere custom, even unaccompanied by convention, can be of far-reaching economic signifiance. The level of economic need, which constitutes the basis of all "economic activity," is comprehensively conditioned by mere custom. The individual might free himself of it without arousing the slightest disapproval. In fact, however, he cannot escape from it except with the greatest difficulty, and it does not change except where it comes gradually to give way to the imitation of the different custom of some other social group.

We shall see[7] that the uniformity of mere usages can be of importance in the formation of social groups and in facilitating intermarriage. It may also give a certain, though rather intangible, impetus toward the formation of feelings of "ethnic" identification and, in that way, contribute to the creation of community. At any rate, adherence to what has as such become customary is such a strong component of all conduct and, consequently, of all social action, that legal coercion, where it transforms a custom into a legal obligation (by invocation of the "usual") often adds practically nothing to its effectiveness, and, where it opposes custom, frequently fails in the attempt to influence actual conduct. Convention is equally effective, if not even more. In countless situations the individual depends on his environment for a spontaneous response not guaranteed by any earthly or transcendental authority. The existence of a "convention" may thus be far more determinative of his conduct than the existence of legal enforcement machinery.

Obviously, the borderline between custom and convention is fluid. The further we go back in history, the more we find that conduct, and particularly social action, is determined in an ever more comprehensive sphere exclusively by orientation to what is customary. The more this is so, the more disquieting are the effects of any deviation from the customary. In this situation, any such deviation seems to act on the psyche of the average individual like the disturbance of an organic function. This, in turn, seems to reinforce custom.

Present ethnological literature does not allow us to determine very clearly the point of transition from the stage of mere custom to the, at first vaguely and dimly experienced, "consensual" character of social action, or, in other words, to the conception of the binding nature of certain accustomed modes of conduct. Even less can we trace the changes of the scope of activities with respect to which this transition took place. We shall thus by-pass this problem. It is entirely a question of terminology and convenience at which point of this continuum one shall assume the existence of the subjective conception of a "legal obligation." Objectively the chance of the factual occurrence of a violent reaction against certain types of conduct has always been present among human beings as well as among animals. It would be far-fetched, however, to assume in every such case the existence of a consensually valid norm, or that the action in question would be directed by a clearly conceived conscious purpose. Perhaps, a rudimentary conception of "duty" may be determinative in the behavior of some domestic animals to a greater extent than may be found in aboriginal man, if we may use this highly ambiguous concept in what is in this context a clearly intelligible sense. We have no access, however, to the "subjective" experiences of the first *homo sapiens* and such concepts as the allegedly primordial, or even *a priori,* character of law or convention are of no use whatsoever to empirical sociology. It is not due to the assumed binding force of some rule or norm that the conduct of primitive man manifests certain external factual regularities, especially in his relation to his fellows. On the contrary, those organically conditioned regularities which we have to accept as psychophysical reality, are primary. It is from them that the concept of "natural norms" arises. The inner orientation towards such regularities contains in itself very tangible inhibitions against "innovations," a fact which can be observed even today by everyone in his daily experiences, and it constitutes a strong support for the belief in such binding norms.

B. CHANGE THROUGH INSPIRATION AND EMPATHY. In view of such observation we must ask how anything new can ever arise in this world, oriented as it is toward the regular as the empirically valid. No doubt innovations have been induced from the outside, i.e., by changes in the external conditions of life. But the response evoked by external change may be the extinction of life as well as its reorientation; there is no way of foretelling. Furthermore, external change is by no means a necessary precondition for innovation: in some of the most significant cases, it has not even been a contributing factor in the establishment of a new order. The evidence of ethnology seems rather to show that the most important source of innovation has been the influence of individuals who have experienced certain "abnormal" states (which are frequently, but not always, regarded by present-day psychiatry as pathological) and hence have been capable of exercising a special influence on others. We are not discussing here the origin of these experiences which appear to be "new" as a consequence of their "abnormality," but rather their effects. These influences which overcome the inertia of the customary may originate from a variety of psychological occurrences. To Hellpach[8] we owe the distinction between two categories which, despite the possibility of intermediate forms, nonetheless appear as polar types. The first, inspiration, consists in the sudden awakening, through drastic means, of the awareness that a certain action "ought" to be done by him who has this experience. In the other form, that of empathy or identification, the influencing person's attitude is emphatically experienced by one or more others. The types of action which are produced in these ways may vary greatly. Very often, however, a collective action (*massenhaftes Gemeinschaftshandeln*) is induced which is oriented toward the influencing person and his experience and from which, in turn, certain kinds of consensus with corresponding contents may be developed. If they are "adapted" to the external environment, they will survive. The effects of "empathy" and, even more so, of "inspiration" (usually lumped together under the ambiguous term "suggestion") constitute the major sources for the realization of actual innovations whose establishment as regularities will, in turn, reinforce the sense of "oughtness," by which they may possibly be accompanied. The feeling of oughtness—as soon as it has developed any conceptual meaning—may undoubtedly appear as something primary and original even in the case of innovation. Particularly in the case of "inspiration" it may constitute a psychological component. It is confusing, however, when imitation of new conduct is regarded as the basic and primary element in its diffusion. Undoubtedly, imitation is of extraordinary importance, but as a general rule it is secondary and constitutes only a special case. If the conduct of a dog, man's oldest companion, is "inspired" by man, such conduct, obviously, cannot be described as "imitation of man by dog." In a very large number of cases, the relation between the persons influencing and those influenced is exactly of this kind. In some cases, it may approximate "empathy," in others, "imitation," conditioned either by rational purpose or in the ways of "mass psychology."

In any case, however, the emerging innovation is most likely to produce consensus and ultimately law, when it derives from a strong inspiration or an intensive identification. In such cases a convention will result or, under certain circumstances, even consensual coercive action against deviants. As long as religious faith is strong, convention, the approval or disapproval by the environment, engenders, as historical experience shows, the hope and faith that the supernatural powers too will reward or punish those actions which are approved or disapproved in this world. Convention, under appropriate conditions, may also produce the further belief that not only the actor himself but also those around him may have to suffer from the wrath of those supernatural powers, and that, therefore, reaction is incumbent upon all, acting either individually or through the coercive apparatus of some organization. In consequence of the constant recurrence of a certain pattern of conduct, the idea may arise in the minds of the guarantors of a particular norm, that they are confronted no longer with mere custom or convention, but with a legal obligation requiring enforcement. A norm which has attained such practical validity is called customary law. Eventually, the interests involved may engender a rationally considered desire to secure the convention, or the obligation of customary law, against subversion, and to place it explicitly under the guarantee of an enforcement machinery, i.e., to transform it into enacted law. Particularly in the field of the internal distribution of power among the organs of an institutional order experience reveals a continuous scale of transitions from norms of conduct guaranteed by mere convention to those which are regarded as binding and guaranteed by law. A striking example is presented by the development of the British "constitution."

C. BORDERLINE ZONES BETWEEN CONVENTION, CUSTOM AND LAW. Finally, any rebellion against convention may lead the environment to make use of its coercively guaranteed rights in a manner detrimental to the rebel; for instance, the host uses his right as master of the house against the guest who has merely infringed upon the conventional rules of social amenity; or a war lord uses his legal power of dismissal against the officer who has infringed upon the code of honor. In such cases the conventional rule is, in fact, indirectly supported by coercive means. The situation differs from that of "unguaranteed" law insofar as the initiation of the coercive measures is a factual, but not a legal, consequence of the infringement of the convention, although the legal right to exclude anyone from his house belongs to the master as such. But a directly unguaranteed legal proposition draws its validity from the fact that its violation engenders consequences somehow *via* a guaranteed legal norm. Where, on the other hand, a legal norm refers to "good morals" (*die guten Sitten*),[9] i.e., conventions worthy of approval, the fulfillment of the conventional obligations has also become a legal obligation and we have a case of indirectly guaranteed law.

There are also numerous instances of intermediate types, as, for example, the courts of love of the Troubadours of Provence which had "jurisdiction" in matters of love;[10] or the "judge" in his original role as arbitrator seeking to procure a settlement between feuding antagonists, perhaps also rendering a verdict, but lacking coercive powers of his own; or, finally, modern international courts of arbitration. In such cases, the amorphous approval or disapproval of the environment has crystallized into a set of commands, prohibitions, and permissions authoritatively promulgated, i.e., a concretely organized pattern of psychic coercion. Excepting situations of mere play, as, for instance, the courts of love, such cases may be classified as "law" provided the judgment is normally backed not only by the personal, and therefore irrelevant, opinion of the judge, but by, at least, some boycott as self-help of the kinship group, the state, or some other group of persons whose right has been violated, as in the last two of the illustrations above.

According to our definition, the fact that some type of conduct is "approved" or "disapproved" by ever so many persons is insufficient to constitute it as a "convention"; it is essential that such attitudes are likely to find expression in a specific environment. This latter term is, of course, not meant in any geographical sense. But there must be some test for defining that group of persons which constitutes the environment of the person in question. It does not matter in this context whether the test is constituted by profession, kinship, neighborhood, status group, ethnic group, religion, political allegiance, or anything else. Nor does it matter that the membership is changeable or unstable. For the existence of a convention in our sense it is not required that the environment be constituted by an organization (as we understand that term). The very opposite is frequently the case. But the validity of law, presupposing, as we have seen, the existence of an enforcement machinery, is necessarily a corollary of organizational action. (Of course, this does not mean that only organizational action—or even mere social action—is legally regulated by organization.) In this sense the organization may be said to be the "sustainer" of the law.

On the other hand, we are far from asserting that legal rules, in the sense here used, would offer the only standard of subjective orientation for social, consensual, rationally controlled, organizational or institutional action, which, we must remember, is nothing but a segment of sociologically relevant conduct in general. If the order of an organization is understood to be characteristic of, or indispensable to, the actual course of social action, then this order is only to a small extent the result of an orientation toward legal rules. To the extent that the regularities are consciously oriented towards rules at all and do not merely spring from unreflective habituation, they are of the nature of "custom" and "convention"; often they are predominantly rational maxims of purposeful self-interested action, on the effective operation of which each participant is counting for his own conduct as well as that of all others. This expectation is, indeed, justified objectively, especially since the maxim, though lacking legal guaranties, often constitutes the subject matter of some association or consensus. The chance of legal coercion which, as already mentioned, motivates even "legal" conduct only to a slight extent, is also objectively an ultimate guaranty for no more than a fraction of the actual course of consensually oriented conduct.

It should thus be clear that, from the point of view of sociology, the transitions from mere usage to convention and from it to law are fluid.

3. Excursus *in Response to Rudolf Stammler*

Even from a non-sociological point of view it is wrong to distinguish between law and ethics by asserting that legal norms regulate mere external conduct, while moral norms regulate only matters of conscience. The law, it is true, does not always regard the intention of an action as relevant, and there have been legal propositions and legal systems in which legal consequences, including even punishment, are merely determined by external events. But this situation is not the normal one. Legal consequences attach to *bona* or *mala fides,* or intention, or moral turpitude, and a good many other purely subjective factors. Moral commandments, on the other hand, are aiming at overcoming in external conduct those anti-normative impulses which form part of the "mental attitude."

From the normative point of view we should thus distinguish between the two phenomena not as external and subjective, but as representing different degrees of normativeness.

From the sociological point of view, however, ethical validity is normally identical with validity "on religious grounds" or "by virtue of convention." Only an abstract standard of conduct subjectively conceived as derived from ultimate axioms could be regarded as an exclusively ethical norm, and this only in so far as this conception would acquire practical significance in conduct. Such conceptions have in fact often had real significance. But wherever this has been the case, they have been a relatively late product of philosophical reflection. In the past, as well as in the present, "moral commandments" in contrast to legal commands are, from a sociological point of view, normally either religiously or conventionally conditioned maxims of conduct. They are not distinguished from law by hard and fast criteria. There is no socially important moral commandment which has not been a legal command at one time or another.

Stammler's distinction between convention and legal norm according to whether or not the fulfillment of the norm is dependent upon the free will of the individual[11] is of no use whatsoever. It is incorrect to say that the fulfillment of conventional "obligations," for instance of a rule of social etiquette, is not "imposed" on the individual, and that its non-

fulfillment would simply result in, or coincide with, the free and voluntary separation from a voluntary consociation. It may be admitted that
there are norms of this kind, but they exist not only in the sphere of
convention, but equally in that of law. The *clausula rebus sic stantibus*
in fact often lends itself to such use. At any rate, the distinction between
conventional rule and legal norm in Stammler's own sociology is not
centered on this test. Not only the theoretically constructed anarchical
society, the "theory" and "critique" of which Stammler has elaborated
with the aid of his scholastic concepts, but also a good number of consociations existing in the real world have dispensed with the legal character of their conventional norms. They have done so on the assumption
that the mere fact of the social disapproval of norm infringement with
its, often very real, indirect consequences will suffice as a sanction. From
the sociological point of view, legal order and conventional order do thus
not constitute any basic contrast, since, quite apart from obvious cases
of transition, convention, too, is sustained by psychological as well as
(at least indirectly) physical coercion. It is only with regard to the
sociological *structure* of coercion that they differ: The conventional order
lacks specialized personnel for the implementation of coercive power
(enforcement machinery: priests, judges, police, the military, etc.).

Above all, Stammler confuses the ideal validity of a norm with the
assumed validity of a norm in its actual influence on empirical action.
The former can be deduced systematically by legal theorists and moral
philosophers; the latter, instead, ought to be the subject of empirical
observation. Furthermore, Stammler confuses the normative regulation
of conduct by rules whose "oughtness" is factually accepted by a sizable
number of persons, with the factual regularities of human conduct.
These two concepts are to be strictly separated, however.

It is by way of conventional rules that merely factual regularities of
action, i.e., usages, are frequently transformed into binding norms, guaranteed primarily by psychological coercion. Convention thus makes tradition. The mere fact of the regular recurrence of certain events somehow confers on them the dignity of oughtness. This is true with regard
to natural events as well as to action conditioned organically or by unreflective imitation of, or adaptation to, external conditions of life. It
applies to the accustomed course of the stars as ordained by the divine
powers, as well as to the seasonal floods of the Nile or the accustomed
way of remunerating slave laborers, who by the law are unconditionally
surrendered to the power of their masters.

Whenever the regularities of action have become conventionalized,
i.e., whenever a statistically frequent action (*Massenhandeln*) has become a consensually oriented action (*Einverständnishandeln*)—this is, in

our terminology, the real meaning of this development—we shall speak of "tradition."

It cannot be overstressed that the mere habituation to a mode of action, the inclination to preserve this habituation, and, much more so, tradition, have a formidable influence in favor of a habituated legal order, even where such an order originally derives from legal enactment. This influence is more powerful than any reflection on impending means of coercion or other consequences, considering also the fact that at least some of those who act according to the "norms" are totally unaware of them.

The transition from the merely unreflective formation of a habit to the conscious acceptance of the maxim that action should be in accordance with a norm is always fluid. The mere statistical regularity of an action leads to the emergence of moral and legal convictions with corresponding contents. The threat of physical and psychologial coercion, on the other hand, imposes a certain mode of action and thus produces habituation and thereby regularity of action.

Law and convention are intertwined as cause and effect in the actions of men, with, against, and beside, one another. It is grossly misleading to consider law and convention as the "forms" of conduct in contrast with its "substance" as Stammler does. The belief in the legal or conventional oughtness of a certain action is, from a sociological point of view, merely a superadditum increasing the degree of probability with which an acting person can calculate certain *consequences* of his action. Economic theory therefore properly disregards the character of the norms to some extent. For the economist the fact that someone "possesses" something simply means that he can count on other persons not to interfere with his disposition over the object. This mutual respect of the right of disposition may be based on a variety of considerations. It may derive from deference to conventional or legal norms, or from considerations of self-interest on the part of each participant. Whatever the reason, it is of no primary concern to economic theory. The fact that a person "owes" something to another can be translated, sociologically, into the following terms: a certain commitment (through promise, tort, or other cause) of one person to another; the expectation, based thereon, that in due course the former will yield to the latter his right of disposition over the goods concerned; the existence of a chance that this expectation will be fulfilled. The psychological motives involved are of no primary interest to the economist.

An exchange of goods means: the transfer of an object, according to an agreement, from the factual control of one person to that of another, this transfer being based on the assumption that another object is to be transferred from the factual control of the second to that of the first. Of those who take part in a debtor-creditor relationship or in a barter, each one expects that the other will conform to his own intentions. It is not necessary, however, to assume conceptually any "order" outside or above the two parties to guarantee, command, or enforce compliance by means of coercive machinery or social disapproval. Nor is it necessary to assume the subjetive belief of either or both parties in any "binding" norm. For the partner to an exchange can depend on the other partner's *egoistic interest* in the future continuation of exchange relationships or other similar motives to offset his inclination to break his promise—a fact which appears tangibly in the so-called "silent trade" among primitive peoples as well as in modern business, especially on the stock exchange.

Assuming purely expediential rationality, each participant can and does, in fact, depend on the probability that under normal circumstances the other party will act "as if" he accepted as "binding" the norm that one has to fulfill his promises. Conceptually this is quite sufficient. But it goes without saying that it makes a difference whether the partner's expectation in this respect is supported by one or both of the following guaranties: 1. the factually wide currency, in the environment, of the subjective belief in the objective validity of such a norm (consensus); 2. even more so, the creation of a conventional guaranty through regard for social approval or disapproval, or of a legal guaranty through the existence of enforcement machinery.

Can it be said that a stable private economic system of the modern type would be "unthinkable" without legal guaranties? As a matter of fact we see that in most business transactions it never occurs to anyone even to think of taking legal action. Agreements on the stock exchange, for example, take place between professional traders in such forms as in the vast majority of cases exclude "proof" in cases of bad faith: the contracts are oral, or are recorded by marks and notations in the trader's own notebook. Nevertheless, a dispute practically never occurs. Likewise, there are organizations pursuing purely economic ends the rules of which nonetheless dispense entirely, or almost entirely, with legal protection from the state. Certain types of "cartels" were illustrative of this class of organization. It often happened also that agreements which had been concluded and were valid according to private law were rendered inoperative through the dissolution of the organization, as there was no longer a formally legitimated plaintiff. In these instances, the organization with its own coercive apparatus had a system of "law" which was totally lacking in the power of forcible legal coercion. Such coercion, at any rate, was available only so long as the organization was in existence. As a result of the peculiar subjective attitude of the participants, cartel contracts often had not even any effective conventional guarantee. However, they often functioned nonetheless for a long time and quite efficiently in consequence of the convergent interests of all the participants.

Despite all such facts, it is obvious that forcible legal guarantee, especially where exercised by the state, is not a matter of indifference to such organizations. Today economic exchange is quite overwhelmingly guaranteed by the threat of legal coercion. The normal intention in an act of exchange is to acquire certain subjective "rights," i.e., in sociological terms, the probability of support of one's power of disposition by the coercive apparatus of the state. Economic goods today are normally at the same time *legitimately acquired rights*; they are the very building material for the universe of the economic order. Nonetheless, even today they do not constitute the total range of objects of exchange.

Economic opportunities which are not guaranteed by the legal order, or the guaranty of which is even refused on grounds of policy by the legal order, can and do constitute objects of exchange transactions which are not only not illegitimate but perfectly legitimate. They include, for instance, the transfer, against compensation, of the goodwill of a business. The sale of a goodwill today normally engenders certain private law claims of the purchaser against the seller, namely, that he will refrain from certain actions and will perform certain others, for instance, "introduce" the purchaser to the customers. But the legal order does not enforce the claims against third parties. Yet, there have been and still are cases in which the coercive apparatus of the political authority is available for the exercise of direct coercion in favor of the owner or purchaser of a "market," as for instance in the case of a guild monopoly or some other legally protected monopoly. It is well known that Fichte[12] considered it as the essential characteristic of modern legal development that, in contrast to such cases, the modern state guarantees only claims on concrete usable goods or labor services. Besides, so-called "free competition" finds its legal expression in this very fact. Yet, although such "opportunities" have remained objects of economic exchange even without legal protection against third parties, the absence of legal guaranties has nevertheless far-reaching economic consequences. But from the point of view of economics and sociology it remains a fact that, on general principle, at least, the interference of legal guaranties merely increases the degree of certainty with which an economically relevant action can be calculated in advance.

The legal regulation of a subject matter has never been carried out in all its implications anywhere. This would require the availability of some human agency which in every case of the kind in question would be regarded as being capable of determining, in accordance with some conceived norm, what ought to be done "by law." We shall by-pass here the interaction between consociation and legal order: as we have seen elsewhere, any rational consociation, and therefore, any order of social and consensual action is posterior in this respect. Nor shall we discuss here the proposition that the development of social and consensual action continually creates entirely new situations and raises problems which can be solved by the accepted norms or by the usual logic of jurisprudence only in appearance or by spurious reasoning (cf. in this respect the thesis of the "free-law" movement).

We are concerned here with a more basic problem: It is a fact that the most "fundamental" questions often are left unregulated by law even in legal orders which are otherwise thoroughly rationalized. Let us illustrate two specific types of this phenomenon:

(1) A "constitutional" monarch dismisses his responsible minister and fails to replace him by any new appointee so that there is no one to countersign his acts. What is to be done "by law" in such a situation? This question is not regulated in any constitution anywhere in the world. What is clear is no more than that certain acts of the government cannot be "validly" taken.

(2) Most constitutions equally omit consideration of the following question: What is to be done when those parties whose agreement is necessary for the adoption of the budget are unable to reach an agreement?

The first problem is described by Jellinek as "moot" for all practical purposes.[13] He is right. What is of interest to us is just to know why it is "moot." The second type of "constitutional gap," on the other hand, has become very practical, as is well known.[14] If we understand "constitution," in the sociological sense, as the modus of distribution of power which determines the possibility of regulating social action, we may, indeed, venture the proposition that any community's constitution *in the sociological sense* is determined by the fact of where and how its constitution *in the juridical sense* contains such "gaps," especially with regard to basic questions. At times such gaps of the second type have been left intentionally where a constitution was rationally enacted by consensus or imposition. This was done simply because the interested party or parties who exercised the decisive influence on the drafting of the constitution in question expected that he or they would ultimately have sufficient power to control, in accordance with their own desires, that portion of social action which, while lacking a basis in any enacted norm, yet had to be carried on somehow. Returning to our illustration: they expected to govern without a budget.

Gaps of the first type mentioned above, on the other hand, usually remain open for another reason: Experience seems to teach convincingly that the self-interest of the party or parties concerned (in our example,

of the monarch) will at all times suffice so to condition his way of acting
that the "absurd" though legally possible situation (in our example, the
lack of a responsible minister) will never occur. Despite the "gap," general consensus considers it as the unquestionable "duty" of the monarch
to appoint a minister. As there are legal consequences attached to this
duty, it is to be considered as an "indirectly guaranteed legal obligation."
Such ensuing legal consequences are: the impossibility of executing certain acts in a valid manner, i.e., of attaining the possibility of having them
guaranteed through the coercive apparatus. But for the rest, it is not established, either by law or convention, what is to be done to carry on the
administration of the state in case the ruler should not fulfill this duty;
and since this case has never occurred thus far, there is no custom either
which could become the source for a decision. This situation constitutes
a striking illustration of the fact that law, convention, and custom are
by no means the only forces to be counted on as guarantee for such conduct of another person as is expected of, promised by, or otherwise regarded as due from, him. Beside and above these, there is another force
to be reckoned with: the other person's self-interest in the continuation
of a certain consensual action as such. The certainty with which the
monarch's compliance with an assumedly binding duty can be anticipated
is no doubt greater, but only by a matter of degree, than the certainty—
if we may return now to our previous example—with which a partner
to an exchange counts, and in the case of continued intercourse, may
continue to count, upon the other party's conduct to conform with his
own expectations. This certainty exists even though the transaction in
question may lack any normative regulation or coercive guaranty.

What is relevant here is merely the observation that the legal as well
as the conventional regulation of consensual or rationally regulated action
may be, as a matter of principle, incomplete and, under certain circumstances, will be so quite consciously. While the orientation of social action
to a norm is constitutive of consociation in any and every case, the coercive apparatus does not have this function with regard to the totality
of all stable and institutionally organizational action. If the absurd case
of illustration (1) were to occur, it would certainly set legal speculation to work immediately and then perhaps,.a conventional, or even legal,
regulation would come into existence. But in the meantime the problem
would already have been actually solved by some social or consensual or
rationally regulated action the details of which would depend upon the
nature of the concrete situation. Normative regulation is one important
causal component of consensual action, but it is not, as claimed by
Stammler, its universal "form."

For a discipline such as sociology, which searches for empirical regularities and types, the legal guarantees and their underlying normative conceptions are of interest both as consequences and as causes or concomitant causes of certain regularities of human action which are as such directly relevant to sociology, or of regularities of natural occurrences engendered by human action which as such are indirectly relevant to sociology.

Factual regularities *of* conduct ("customs") can, as we have seen, become the source of rules *for* conduct ("conventions," "law"). The reverse, however, may be equally true. Regularities may be produced by legal norms, acting by themselves or in combination with other factors. This applies not only to those regularities which directly realize the content of the legal norm in question, but equally to regularities of a different kind. The fact that an official, for example, goes to his office regularly every day is a direct consequence of the order contained in a legal norm which is accepted as "valid" in practice. On the other hand, the fact that a traveling salesman of a factory visits the retailers regularly each year for the solicitation of orders is only an indirect effect of legal norms, viz., of those which permit free competition for customers and thus necessitate that they be wooed. The fact that fewer children die when nursing mothers abstain from work as a result of a legal or conventional "norm" is certainly a consequence of the validity of that norm. Where it is an enacted legal norm, this result has certainly been one of the rationally conceived ends of the creators of that norm; but it is obvious that they can decree only the abstention from work and not the lower death rate. Even with regard to directly commanded or prohibited conduct, the practical effectiveness of the validity of a coercive norm is obviously problematic. Observance follows to an "adequate" degree, but never without exceptions. Powerful interests may indeed induce a situation in which a legal norm is violated, without ensuing punishment, not only in isolated instances, but prevalently and permanently, in spite of the coercive apparatus on which the "validity" of the norm is founded. When such a situation has become stabilized and when, accordingly, prevailing practice rather than the pretense of the written law has become normative of conduct in the conviction of the participants, the guaranteeing coercive power will ultimately cease to compel conduct to conform to the latter. In such case, the legal theorist speaks of "derogation through customary law."

"Valid" legal norms, which are guaranteed by the coercive apparatus of the political authority, and conventional rules may also coexist, however, in a state of chronic conflict. We have observed such a situation in the case of the duel, where private revenge has been transformed by convention. And while it is not at all unusual that legal norms are rationally enacted with the purpose of changing existing "customs" and conventions, the normal development is more usually as follows: a legal order is empirically "valid" owing not so much to the availability of coercive guaranties as to its habituation as "usage" and its "routinization." To this should be added the pressure of convention which, in most cases, disapproves any flagrant deviation from conduct corresponding to that order.

For the legal theorist the (ideological) validity of a legal norm is conceptually the *prius*. Conduct which is not directly regulated by law is regarded by him as legally "permitted" and thus equally affected by the legal order, at least ideologically. For the sociologist, on the other hand, the legal, and particularly the rationally enacted, regulation of conduct is empirically only one of the factors motivating social action; moreover, it is a factor which usually appears late in history and whose effectiveness varies greatly. The beginnings of actual regularity and "usage," shrouded in darkness everywhere, are attributed by the sociologist, as we have seen, to the instinctive habituation of a pattern of conduct which was "adapted" to given necessities. At least initially, this pattern of conduct was neither conditioned nor changed by an enacted norm. The increasing intervention of enacted norms is, from our point of view, only one of the components, however characteristic, of that process of rationalization and association whose growing penetration into all spheres of social action we shall have to trace as a most essential dynamic factor in development.

4. *Summary of the Most General Relations Between Law and Economy*

In sum, we can say about the most general relationships between law and economy, which alone concern us here, the following:

(1) Law (in the sociological sense) guarantees by no means only economic interests but rather the most diverse interests ranging from the most elementary one of protection of personal security to such purely ideal goods as personal honor or the honor of the divine powers. Above all, it guarantees political, ecclesiastical, familial, and other positions of authority as well as positions of social preëminence of any kind which may indeed be economically conditioned or economically relevant in the most diverse ways, but which are neither economic in themselves nor sought for preponderantly economic ends.

(2) Under certain conditions a "legal order" can remain unchanged

while economic relations are undergoing a radical transformation. In theory, a socialist system of production could be brought about without the change of even a single paragraph of our laws, simply by the gradual, free contractual acquisition of all the means of production by the political authority. This example is extreme; but, for the purpose of theoretical speculation, extreme examples are most useful. Should such a situation ever come about—which is most unlikely, though theoretically not unthinkable—the legal order would still be bound to apply its coercive machinery in case its aid were invoked for the enforcement of those obligations which are characteristic of a productive system based on private property. Only, this case would never occur in fact.[15]

(3) The legal status of a matter may be basically different according to the point of view of the legal system from which it is considered. But such differences [of legal classification] need not have any relevant economic consequences provided only that on those points which generally are relevant economically, the *practical* effects are the same for the interested parties. This not only is possible, but it actually happens widely, although it must be conceded that any variation of legal classification may engender some economic consequences somewhere. Thus totally different forms of action would have been applicable in Rome depending on whether the "lease" of a mine were to be regarded legally as a lease in the strict sense of the term, or as a purchase. But the practical effects of the difference for economic life would certainly have been very slight.[16]

(4) Obviously, legal guaranties are directly at the service of economic interests to a very large extent. Even where this does not seem to be, or actually is not, the case, economic interests are among the strongest factors influencing the creation of law. For, any authority guaranteeing a legal order depends, in some way, upon the consensual action of the constitutive social groups, and the formation of social groups depends, to a large extent, upon constellations of material interests.

(5) Only a limited measure of success can be attained through the threat of coercion supporting the legal order. This applies especially to the economic sphere, owing to a number of external circumstances as well as to its own peculiar nature. It would be quibbling, however, to assert that law cannot "enforce" any particular economic conduct, on the ground that we would have to say, with regard to all its means of coercion, that *coactus tamen voluit* ("Although coerced, it was still his will.") For this is true, without exception, of all coercion which does not treat the person to be coerced simply as an inanimate object. Even the most drastic means of coercion and punishment are bound to fail where the subjects remain recalcitrant. In many spheres such a situation would always mean that the participants have not been educated to

acquiescence. Such education to acquiescence in the law of the time and place has, as a general rule, increased with growing pacification. Thus it should seem that the chances of enforcing economic conduct would have increased, too. Yet, the power of law over economic conduct has in many respects grown weaker rather than stronger as compared with earlier conditions. The effectiveness of maximum price regulations, for example, has always been precarious, but under present-day conditions they have an even smaller chance of success than ever before.

Thus the measure of possible influence on economic activity is not simply a function of the general level of acquiescence towards legal co-ercion. The limits of the actual success of legal coercion in the economic sphere rather arise from two main sources. One is constituted by the limitations of the economic capacity of the persons affected. There are limits not only to the stock itself of available goods, but also to the way in which that stock can possibly be used. For the patterns of use and of relationship among the various economic units are determined by habit and can be adjusted to heteronomous norms, if at all, only by difficult reorientations of all economic dispositions, and hardly without losses, which means, never without frictions. These difficulties increase with the degree of development and universality of a particular form of consensual action, namely, the interdependence of the individual economic units in the market, and, consequently, the dependence of every one upon the conduct of others. The second source of the limitation of successful legal coercion in the economic sphere lies in the relative proportion of strength of private economic interests on the one hand and interests promoting conformance to the rules of law on the other. The inclination to forego economic opportunity simply in order to act legally is obviously slight, unless circumvention of the formal law is strongly disapproved by a powerful convention, and such a situation is not likely to arise where the interests affected by a legal innovation are widespread. Besides, it is often not difficult to disguise the circumvention of a law in the economic sphere. Quite particularly insensitive to legal influence are, as experience has shown, those effects which derive directly from the ultimate sources of economic action, such as the estimates of economic value and the formation of prices. This applies particularly to those situations where the determinants in production and consumption do not lie within a com-pletely transparent and directly manageable complex of consensual con-duct. It is obvious, besides, that those who continuously operate in the market have a far greater rational knowledge of the market and interest situation than the legislators and enforcement officers whose interest is only formal. In an economy based on all-embracing interdependence on the market the possible and unintended repercussions of a legal measure must to a large extent escape the foresight of the legislator simply because they depend upon private interested parties. It is those private interested parties who are in a position to distort the intended meaning of a legal norm to the point of turning it into its very opposite, as has often happened in the past. In view of these difficulties, the extent of factual impact of the law on economic conduct cannot be determined generally, but must be calculated for each particular case. It belongs thus to the field of case studies in social economics. In general, no more can be asserted than that, from a purely theoretical point of view, the complete monopolization of a market, which entails a far greater perspicuity of the situation, technically facilitates the control by law of that particular sector of the economy. If it, nevertheless, does not always in fact increase the opportunities for such control, this result is usually due either to legal particularism arising from the existence of competing political associations, or to the power of the private interests amenable to the monopolistic control and thus resisting the enforcement of the law.

(6) From the purely theoretical point of view, legal guaranty *by the state* is not indispensable to any basic economic phenomenon. The protection of property, for example, can be provided by the mutual aid system of kinship groups. Creditors' rights have sometimes been protected more efficiently by a religious community's threat of excommunication than by political bodies. "Money," too, has existed in almost all of its forms, without the state's guaranty of its acceptability as a means of payment. Even "chartal" money, i.e., money which derives its character as means of payment from the marking of pieces rather than from their substantive content, is conceivable without the guaranty by the state. Occasionally chartal money of non-state origin appeared even in spite of the existence of an apparatus of legal coercion by the state: the ancient Babylonians, for instance, did not have "coins" in the sense of a means of payment constituting legal tender by proclamation of the political authority, but contracts were apparently in use under which payment was to be made in pieces of a fifth of a shekel designated as such by the stamp of a certain "firm" (as we would say).[17] There was thus lacking any guaranty "proclaimed" by the state; the chosen unit of value was derived, not from the state, but from private contract. Yet the means of payment was "chartal" in character, and the state guaranteed coercively the concrete deal.

Conceptually the "state" thus is not indispensable to any economic activity. But an economic system, especially of the modern type, could certainly not exist without a legal order with very special features which could not develop except in the frame of a public legal order. Present-day economic life rests on opportunities acquired through contracts. It is true, the private interests in the obligations of contract, and the common interest of all property holders in the mutual protection of property are still considerable, and individuals are still markedly influenced by convention and custom even today. Yet, the influence of these factors has declined due to the disintegration of tradition, i.e., of the tradition-determined relationships as well as of the belief in their sacredness. Furthermore, class interests have come to diverge more sharply from one another than ever before. The tempo of modern business communication requires a promptly and predictably functioning legal system, i.e., one which is guaranteed by the strongest coercive power. Finally, modern economic life by its very nature has destroyed those other associations which used to be the bearers of law and thus of legal guaranties. This has been the result of the development of the market. The universal predominance of the market consociation requires on the one hand a legal system the functioning of which is *calculable* in accordance with rational rules. On the other hand, the constant expansion of the market, which we shall get to know as an inherent tendency of the market consociation, has favored the monopolization and regulation of all "legitimate" coercive power by *one* universalist coercive institution through the disintegration of all particularist status-determined and other coercive structures which have been resting mainly on economic monopolies.

NOTES

Unless otherwise indicated, notes are by Rheinstein. For full references of works mentioned, see Sociology of Law, ch. VIII:*i*, n. 1.

1. Legal dogmatics (*dogmatische Rechtswissenschaft*)—the term frequently used in German to mean the legal science of the law itself as distinguished from such ways of looking upon law from the outside as philosophy, history, or sociology of law.

2. See now Part One, ch. I:5, but the reference is presumably to "Some Categories of Interpretive Sociology," *GAzW* 443. (R)

3. See *op. cit.*, 445, 447f., 466. (R)

4. Cf. below, ch. VIII:*v*:8.

5. This is an early formulation of the relationship between usage, custom, interest constellation, law and convention, repeated in Part I, sec. 4–6. (R)

6. Cf. below, ch. VIII:*iii*:1.

7. Cf. Part Two, ch. IV:2. (W)

8. Willy Hellpach (1877–1955), professor of medicine, known by his highly original investigations on the influence of meteorological and geographic phenomena upon the mind. See his "Die geistigen Epidemien," *Die Gesellschaft*, XI, 1906.

9. Cf. German Civil Code, Sec. 138: "A transaction which is contrary to good morals is void"; Sec. 826: "One who causes harm to another intentionally and in a manner which is against good morals, has to compensate the other for such harm."

10. The "courts of love" (*cours d'amour*) belonged to the amusements of polite society at the high period of chivalry and the troubadours (twelfth to thir-

teenth century) They are reported to have consisted of circles of ladies who were organized in the way of courts and rendered judgments and opinions in matters of courtly love and manners. They flourished in southern France, especially Provence, where they came to an end with the collapse of Provençal society in the "crusade" against the Albigensian heretics. In the late Middle Ages, a brilliant court of love is reported to have flourished for some years at the Burgundian court; cf. HUIZINGA, WANING OF THE MIDDLE AGES (1924), c. 8, p. 103. On the courts of love in general, see CAPEFIGUE, LES COURS D'AMOUR (1863); RAJNA, LE CORTI D'AMORE (1890); and the article by F. Bonnardot in 2 LA GRANDE ENCYCLOPÉDIE 805, with further literature.

11. Rudolf Stammler, *Wirtschaft und Recht nach der materialistischen Geschichtsauffassung* (1896), 12.

12. Joh. Gottlieb Fichte, *Der geschlossene Handelsstaat* (1800), Bk. I, c. 7.

13. GESETZ UND VERORDNUNG (1887) 295; VERFASSUNGSÄNDERUNG UND VERFASSUNGSWANDEL (1906) 43.

14. The situation arose in Prussia when the predominantly liberal Diet early in 1860 refused to pass Bismarck's budget because of its disapproval of his policy of armaments (so-called Era of Conflict or *Konfliktsperiode*). In Austria, too, Parliament (*Reichsrat*) repeatedly was unable to reach agreement on a budget during that period of conflict between the several ethnic groups of the Monarchy which preceded the outbreak of World War I.

15. The norms of the legal order existing before the total socialization took place could also be applied after its occurrence, if legal title to the various means of production were to be ascribed not to one single, central public authority but to formally autonomous public institutions or corporations which are to regulate their relationships to each other by contractual transactions, subject to the directions of, and control by, the central planning authority. Such a situation does indeed exist in the Soviet Union. Cf. H. J. BERMAN, JUSTICE IN RUSSIA (1950), and review by Rheinstein (1951) 64 HARV. L. REV. 1387.

16. Cf. in American law the controversy as to the correct legal classification of a mining or oil and gas lease: does the transaction create a profit a prendre, or does it give to the "lessee" the title to the minerals, or does it result in the creation of a leasehold interest in the strict sense of the term? As in Rome, the "proper" classification may be relevant in some practical respect as, for instance, with regard to the question of whether, in the case of the death of the lessee—if he should ever be an individual!—his interest descends as real, or is to be distributed as personal, property. In the former case it would, ordinarily, not be touched for the payment of debts of the deceased until all the personal property has been exhausted; in the latter, the "lease" would be immediately available for the creditors along with the other "personal" assets of the decedent. But, by and large, the economic situation is one and the same whichever of the various legal classifications is applied.

17. No reference to a practice of the kind mentioned could be located except the following passage in B. MAISSNER, BABYLONIEN UND ASSYRIEN (1920) 356: "As one could not generally rely upon the weight and fineness of the silver and thus had to check (*xâtu*), one preferred to receive silver bearing a stamp (*kanku*) by which the weight and fineness would be guaranteed. In contracts from the period of the first Babylonian dynasty we find shekels mentioned 'with a stamp'(?) of Babylon (Vorderasiatische Bibliothek VI, No. 217, 15) or shekels 'from the city of Zahan' or 'from Grossippar' (Brit. Mus. Cuneiform Tablets IV, 47, 19a)."

CHAPTER **11**

THE ECONOMIC
RELATIONSHIPS OF
ORGANIZED GROUPS

1. *Economic Action and Economically Active Groups*

Most social groups engage in economic activities. Contrary to an unsuitable usage, we shall not consider every instrumental (*zweckrationale*) action as economic. Thus, praying for a spiritual good is not an economic act, even though it may have a definite purpose according to some religious doctrine. We also shall not include every economizing activity, neither intellectual economizing in concept formation nor an esthetic "economy of means"; artistic creations are often the highly unprofitable outcome of ever-renewed attempts at simplification. Just as little is the mere adherence to the technical maxim of the "optimum"—the relatively greatest result with the least expenditure of means—an economic act; rather, it is a matter of purpose-rational technique. We shall speak of economic action only if the satisfaction of a need depends, in the actor's judgment, upon relatively *scarce* resources and a *limited* number of possible actions, and if this state of affairs evokes specific reactions. Decisive for such rational action is, of course, the fact that this scarcity is *subjectively* presumed and that action is oriented to it.

We will not deal here with any detailed "casuistry" and terminology. However, we will distinguish two types of economic action: (1) The first is the satisfaction of one's own wants, which may be of any conceivable kind, ranging from food to religious edification, if there is a scarcity of goods and services in relation to demand. It is conventional to think particularly of everyday needs—the so-called material needs—when the

[339]

term "economy" is used. However, prayers and masses too *may* become economic objects if the persons qualified to say them are in short supply and can only be secured for a price, just like the daily bread. Bushmen drawings, to which a high artistic value is often attributed, are not economic objects, not even products of labor in the economic sense, yet artistic products that are rated much lower become economic objects if they are relatively scarce. (2) The second type of economic action concerns profit-making by controlling and disposing of scarce goods.

Social action (*soziales Handeln*) may be related to the economy in diverse ways.[1]

Rationally controlled action (*Gesellschaftshandeln*) may be oriented, in the actor's eyes, to purely economic results—want satisfaction or profit-making. In this case an "*economic group*" comes into being. However, rationally controlled action may use economic operations as a means for achieving different goals. In this case we have a "*group with secondary economic interests*" (*wirtschaftende Gemeinschaft*). Social action may also combine economic and non-economic goals, or none of these cases may occur. The dividing line between groups with primary and secondary economic interests is fluid. Strictly speaking, the first state of affairs prevails only in those groups that strive for profit by taking advantage of scarcity conditions, that is, profit-making enterprises, for all groups oriented merely toward want satisfaction resort to economic action only so far as the relation of supply and demand makes it necessary. In this regard, there is no difference between the economic activities of a family, a charitable endowment, a military administration, or an association for joint forest clearing or hunting. To be sure, there seems to be a difference between social action that comes into being essentially for the sake of satisfying economic demands, as in the case of forest clearing, and action with goals (such as military training) that necessitates economic activities merely because of scarcity conditions. But in reality this distinction is very tenuous and can be clearly drawn only to the extent that social action would remain the same in the absence of any scarcity.

Social action that constitutes a group neither with primary nor secondary economic interests may in various respects be influenced by scarcity factors and to that extent be economically determined. Conversely, such action may also determine the nature and course of economic activities. Most of the time both influences are at work. Social action unrelated to either of the two groups is not unusual. Every joint walk may be an example. Groups that are economically unimportant are quite frequent. However, a special case of economically relevant groups consists of those whose norms regulate the economic behavior of the participants but whose organs do not continuously direct economic activities through immediate participation, concrete instructions or injunctions: These are *"regulatory groups."* They include all kinds of political and many religious groups, and numerous others, among them those associated specifically for the sake of economic regulation (such as cooperatives of fishermen or peasants).

As we have said, groups that are not somehow economically determined are extremely rare. However, the degree of this influence varies widely and, above all, the economic determination of social action is ambiguous—contrary to the assumption of so-called historical materialism. Phenomena that must be treated as constants in economic analysis are very often compatible with significant structural variations—from a sociological viewpoint—among the groups that comprise them or coexist with them, including groups with primary and secondary economic interests. Even the assertion that social structures and the economy are "functionally" related is a biased view, which cannot be justified as an historical generalization, if an unambiguous interdependence is assumed. For the forms of social action follow "laws of their own," as we shall see time and again, and even apart from this fact, they may in a given case always be co-determined by other than economic causes. However, at some point economic conditions tend to become causally important, and often decisive, for almost all social groups, at least those which have major cultural significance; conversely, the economy is usually also influenced by the autonomous structure of social action within which it exists. No significant generalization can be made as to when and how this will occur. However, we can generalize about the degree of elective affinity between concrete structures of social action and concrete forms of economic organization; that means, we can state in general terms whether they further or impede or exclude one another—whether they are "adequate" or "inadequate" in relation to one another. We will have to deal frequently with such relations of adequacy. Moreover, at least some generalization can be advanced about the manner in which economic interests tend to result in social action of a certain type.

2. *Open and Closed Economic Relationships*

One frequent economic determinant is the competition for a livelihood—offices, clients and other remunerative opportunities. When the number of competitors increases in relation to the profit span, the participants become interested in curbing competition. Usually one group of competitors takes some externally identifiable characteristic of another group of (actual or potential) competitors—race, language, religion, local or social origin, descent, residence, etc.—as a pretext for attempting their exlusion. It does not matter which characteristic is chosen in the individual case: whatever suggests itself most easily is seized upon. Such group action may provoke a corresponding reaction on the part of those against whom it is directed.

In spite of their continued competition against one another, the jointly acting competitors now form an "interest group" toward outsiders; there is a growing tendency to set up some kind of association with rational regulations; if the monopolistic interests persist, the time comes when the competitors, or another group whom they can influence (for example, a political community), establish a legal order that limits competition through formal monopolies; from then on, certain persons are available as "organs" to protect the monopolistic practices, if need be, with force. In such a case, the interest group has developed into a "*legally privileged group*" (*Rechtsgemeinschaft*) and the participants have become "*privileged members*" (*Rechtsgenossen*). Such closure, as we want to call it, is an ever-recurring process; it is the source of property in land as well as of all guild and other group monopolies.

The tendency toward the monopolization of specific, usually economic opportunities is always the driving force in such cases as: "cooperative organization," which always means closed monopolistic groups, for example, of fishermen taking their name from a certain fishing area; the establishment of an association of engineering graduates, which seeks to secure a legal, or at least factual, monopoly over certain positions;[2] the exclusion of outsiders from sharing in the fields and commons of a village; "patriotic" associations of shop clerks;[3] the *ministeriales*, knights, university graduates and craftsmen of a given region or locality; ex-soldiers entitled to civil service positions—all these groups first engage in some joint action (*Gemeinschaftshandeln*) and later perhaps an explicit association. This monopolization is directed against competitors who share some positive or negative characteristics; its purpose is always the closure of social and economic opportunities to *outsiders*. Its extent may vary widely, especially so far as the group member shares in the apportionment of monopolistic advantages. These may remain open to all monopoly holders, who can therefore freely compete with one another; witness the holders of occupational patents (graduates entitled to certain positions or master-craftsmen privileged with regard to customers and the employment of apprentices). However, such opportunities may also be "closed" to *insiders*. This can be done in various ways: (a) Positions may be rotated: the short-run appointment of some holders of office benefices had this purpose; (b) Grants may be revocable, such as the individual disposition over fields in a strictly organized rural commune, for example, the Russian *mir*;[4] (c) Grants may be for life, as is the rule for all prebends, offices, monopolies of master-craftsmen, rights in using the commons, and originally also for the apportionment of fields in most village communes; (d) The member and his heirs may get definite grants with the stipulation that they cannot be given to others or only to group members: witness the κλῆρος (the warrior prebend of Antiquity), the service fiefs of the *ministeriales,* and monopolies on hereditary offices and crafts; (e) Finally, only the number of shares may be limited, but the holder may freely dispose of his own without the knowledge or permission of the other group members, as in a stock-holding company. These different stages of internal closure will be called stages in the *appropriation* of the social and economic opportunities that have been monopolized by the group.

If the appropriated monopolistic opportunities are released for exchange outside the group, thus becoming completely "free" property, the old monopolistic association is doomed. Its remnants are the appropriated powers of disposition which appear on the market as "acquired rights" of individuals. For all property in natural resources developed historically out of the gradual appropriation of the monopolistic shares of group members. In contrast to the present, not only concrete goods but also social and economic opportunities of all kinds were the object of appropriation. Of course, manner, degree, and ease of the appropriation vary widely with the technical nature of the object and of the opportunities, which may lend themselves to appropriation in very different degrees. For example, a person subsisting by, or gaining an income from, the cultivation of a given field is bound to a concrete and clearly delimited material object, but this is not the case with customers. Appropriation is not motivated by the fact that the object produces a yield only through amelioration, hence that to some extent it is the product of the user's labor, for this is even more true of an acquired clientele, although in a different manner; rather, customers cannot be "registered" as easily as real estate. It is quite natural that the extent of an appropriation depends upon such differences among objects. Here, however, we want to emphasize that the process is in principle the same in both cases, even though the pace of appropriation may vary: monopolized social and economic opportunities are "closed" even to insiders. Hence, groups differ in varying degrees with regard to external or internal "openness" or "closure."

3. *Group Structures and Economic Interests: Monopolist versus Expansionist Tendencies*

This monopolistic tendency takes on specific forms when groups are formed by persons with shared qualities *acquired* through upbringing, apprenticeship and training. These characteristics may be economic qualifications of some kind, the holding of the same or of similar offices, a knightly or ascetic way of life, etc. If in such a case an association results from social action, it tends toward the *guild*. Full members make a vocation out of monopolizing the disposition of spiritual, intellectual, social and economic goods, duties and positions. Only those are admitted to the unrestricted practice of the vocation who (1) have completed a novitiate in order to aquire the proper training, (2) have proven their qualification, and (3) sometimes have passed through further waiting periods and met additional requirements. This development follows a typical pattern in groups ranging from the juvenile student fraternities, through knightly associations and craft-guilds, to the qualifications required of the modern officials and employees. It is true that the interest in guaranteeing an efficient performance may everywhere have some importance; the participants may desire it for idealistic or materialistic reasons in spite of their possibly continuing competition with one another: local craftsmen may desire it for the sake of their business reputation, *ministeriales* and knights of a given association for the sake of their professional reputation and also their own military security, and ascetic groups for fear that the gods and demons may turn their wrath against all members because of faulty manipulations. (For example, in almost all primitive tribes, persons who sang falsely during a ritual dance were originally slain in expiation of such an offense.)[5] But normally this concern for efficient performance recedes behind the interest in limiting the supply of candidates for the benefices and honors of a given occupation. The novitiates, waiting periods, masterpieces and other demands, particularly the expensive entertainment of group members, are more often economic than professional tests of qualification.

Such monopolistic tendencies and similar economic considerations have often played a significant role in *impeding* the expansion of a group. For example, Attic democracy increasingly sought to limit the number of those who could share in the advantages of citizenship, and thus limited its own political expansion. The Quaker propaganda was brought to a standstill by an ultimately similar constellation of economic interests. The Islamic missionary ardor, originally a religious obligation, found its limits in the conquering warriors' desire to have a non-Islamic, and hence underprivileged, population that could provide for the maintenance of the privileged believers—the type case for many similar phenomena.

On the other hand, it is a typical occurrence that individuals live by representing group interests or, in some other manner, ideologically or economically from the existence of a group. Hence social action may be propagated, perpetuated and transformed into an association in cases in which this might not have happened otherwise. This kind of interest may have the most diverse intellectual roots: In the 19th century the Romantic ideologists and their epigoni awakened numerous declining language groups of "interesting" peoples to the purposive cultivation of their language. German secondary and university teachers helped save small Slavic language groups, about whom they felt the intellectual need to write books.

However, such purely ideological group existence is a less effective lever than economic interest. If a group pays somebody to act as a continuous and deliberate "organ" of their common interests, or if such interest representation pays in other respects, an association comes into being that provides a strong guarantee for the continuance of concerted action under all circumstances. Henceforth, some persons are professionally interested in the retention of the existing, and the recruitment of new, members. It does not matter here whether they are paid to represent (hidden or naked) sexual interests[6] or other "non-material" or, finally, economic interests (trade unions, management associations and similar organizations), whether they are public speakers paid by the piece or salaried secretaries. The pattern of intermittent and irrational action is replaced by a systematic rational "enterprise," which continues to function long after the original enthusiasm of the participants for their ideals has vanished.

In various ways capitalist interests proper may have a stake in the propagation of certain group activities. For example, [in Imperial Germany] the owners of German "Gothic" type fonts want to preserve this "patriotic" kind of lettering [instead of using Latin *Antiqua*]; similarly, innkeepers who permit Social Democratic meetings even though their premises are kept off limits for military personnel have a stake in the size of the party's membership. Everybody can think of many examples of this type for every kind of social action.

Whether we deal with employees or capitalist employers, all these instances of economic interest have one feature in common: The interest in the substance of the shared ideals necessarily recedes behind the interest in the persistence or propaganda of the group, irrespective of the content of its activities. A most impressive example is the complete disappearance of ideological substance in the American parties, but the greatest example, of course, is the age-old connection between capitalist interests and the expansion of political communities. On the one hand, these communities can exert an extraordinary influence on the economy, on the other they can extract tremendous revenues, so that the capitalist interests can profit most from them: directly by rendering paid services or making advances on expected revenues, and indirectly through the exploitation of objects within the realm of the political community. In Antiquity and at the beginning of modern history the focus of capitalist acquisition centered on such politically determined "imperialist" profits, and today again capitalism moves increasingly in this direction. Every expansion of a country's power sphere increases the profit potential of the respective capitalist interests.

These economic interests, which favor the expansion of a group, may not only be counteracted by the monopolistic tendencies discussed above, but also by other economic interests that originate in a group's closure and exclusiveness. We have already stated in general terms that voluntary organizations tend to transcend their rational primary purpose and to create relationships among the participants that may have quite different goals: As a rule, an overarching communal relationship (*übergreifende Vergemeinschaftung*) attaches itself to the association (*Vergesellschaftung*). Of course, this is not always true; it occurs only in cases in which social action presupposes some personal, not merely business, contacts. For example, a person can acquire stocks irrespective of his personal qualities, merely by virtue of an economic transaction, and generally without the knowledge and consent of the other stockholders. A similar orientation prevails in all those associations that make membership dependent upon a purely formal condition or achievement and do not examine the individual himself. This occurs very often in certain purely economic groups and also in some voluntary political organizations; in general, this orientation is everywhere the more likely, the more rational and specialized the group purpose is. However, there are many associations in which admission presupposes, expressly or silently, qualifications and in which those overarching communal relationships arise. This, of course, happens particularly when the members make admission dependent upon an investigation and approval of the candidate's personal qualities. At least as a rule, the candidate is scrutinized not only with regard to his usefulness for the organization but also "existentially," with regard to personal characteristics esteemed by the members.

We cannot classify here the various modes of association according to the degree of their exclusiveness. It suffices to say that such selectness exists in associations of the most diverse kinds. Not only a religious sect, but also a social club, for instance, a veterans' association or even a bowling club, as a rule admit nobody who is personally objectionable to the members. This very fact "legitimizes" the new member toward the outside, far beyond the qualities that are important to the group's purpose. Membership provides him with advantageous connections, again far beyond the specific goals of the organization. Hence, it is very common that persons belong to an organization although they are not really interested in its purpose, merely for the sake of those economically valuable legitimations and connections that accrue from membership. Taken by themselves, these motives may contain a strong incentive for joining and hence enlarging the group, but the opposite effect is created by the members' interest in monopolizing those advantages and in increasing their economic value through restriction to the smallest possible circle. The smaller and the more exclusive such a circle is, the higher will be both the economic value and the social prestige of membership.

Finally, we must briefly deal with another frequent relationship between the economy and group activities: the deliberate offer of economic advantages in the interest of preserving and expanding a primarily non-economic group. This happens particularly when several similar groups compete for membership: witness political parties and religious communities. American sects, for instance, arrange artistic, athletic and other entertainment and lower the conditions for divorced persons remarrying; the unlimited underbidding of marriage regulations was only recently curbed by regular cartelization. In addition to arranging excursions and similar activities, religious and political parties establish youth groups and women chapters and participate eagerly in purely municipal or other basically non-political activities, which enable them to grant economic favors to local private interests. To a very large extent, the invasion of municipal, co-operative or other agencies by such groups has a direct economic motivation: it helps them to maintain their functionaries through office benefices and social status and to shift the operating costs to these other agencies. Suitable for this purpose are jobs in municipalities, producers' and consumers' co-operatives, health insurance funds, trade unions and similar organizations; and on a vast scale, of course, political offices and benefices or other prestigious or remunerative positions that can be secured from the political authorities—professorships included. If a group is sufficiently large in a system of parliamentary government, it can procure such support for its leaders and members, just like the political parties, for which this is essential.

In the present context we want to emphasize only the general fact that non-economic groups also establish economic organizations, especially for propaganda purposes. Many charitable activities of religious groups have such a purpose, and this is even more true of the Christian,

Liberal, Socialist and Patriotic trade unions and mutual benefit funds, of savings and insurance institutes and, on a massive scale, of the consumers' and producers' co-operatives. Some Italian co-operatives, for instance, demanded the certification of confession before hiring a worker. In Germany [before 1918] the Poles organized credit lending, mortgage payments and farm acquisition in an unusually impressive fashion; during the Revolution of 1905/6 the various Russian parties immediately pursued similarly modern policies. Sometimes commercial enterprises are established: banks, hotels (like the socialist *Hôtellerie du Peuple* in Ostende) and even factories (also in Belgium). If this happens, the dominant groups in a political community, particularly the civil service, resort to similar methods in order to stay in power, and organize everything from economically advantageous "patriotic" associations and activities to state-controlled loan associations (such as the *Preussenkasse*). The technical details of such propagandistic methods do not concern us here.

In this section we merely wanted to state in general terms, and to illustrate with some typical examples, the coexistence and opposition of expansionist and monopolist economic interests within diverse groups. We must forego any further details since this would require a special study of the various kinds of associations. Instead, we must deal briefly with the most frequent relationship between group activities and the economy: the fact that an extraordinarily large number of groups have secondary economic interests. Normally, these groups must have developed some kind of rational association; exceptions are those that develop out of the household (see ch. IV:2 below).

4. *Five Types of Want Satisfaction by Economically Active Groups*

Social action that has become rational association will have an established order for want satisfaction if it requires goods and services for its operations. In principle, there are five typical ways of securing these goods and services—as far as possible, the examples will be taken from political groups, since they have the most highly developed arrangements:

(1) The *oikos* type with its collective natural economy. The group members must render fixed personal services, which may be equal for all or specialized (for instance, universal conscription of all able-bodied men or specialized military duties as craftsmen—(*Ökonomiehandwerker*); moreover, they must meet the material needs by fixed payments

in kind (for the royal table or the military administration). Thus, these goods and services are not produced for the market but for the group's collective economy (for instance, a self-sufficient manorial or royal household—the pure type of the *oikos*—or a military administration that is completely dependent upon services and payments in kind, as—approximately—in ancient Egypt).

(2) *Market-oriented assessments* that make it possible for a group to meet its demands by buying equipment and employing workers, officials and mercenaries; these assessments may be compulsory taxes, regular dues, or fees at certain occasions; they may also be tributes from persons who are not otherwise group members, but who (a) benefit from certain advantages and opportunities (such as a Registry Office for real estate or some other agency) or physical facilities (such as roads)—the principle involved is that of a compensation for services rendered: fees in the technical sense; tributes may also be levied on persons who (b) simply happen to be within the group's power sphere (contributions from persons who are merely residents, duties from persons and goods passing through the group's territory).

(3) *Production for the market*: an enterprise sells its products and services and surrenders its profits to the group of which it is a part. The enterprise may not have a formal monopoly (witness the Prussian *Seehandlung* and the *Grande Chartreuse*), or it may be of the monopolist type that has been frequent in the past and the present (such as the post office). Obviously, every kind of combination is possible between these three, logically most consistent types. Money may be substituted for payments in kind, natural products may be sold on the market, capital goods may be secured directly by payments in kind or bought with the help of assessments. As a rule, the components of these types are combined with one another.

(4) The *maecenatic type*: Voluntary contributions are made by persons who can afford them and who have material or ideal interests in the group, whether or not they are members in other respects. (In the case of religious and political groups, the typical forms here are religious endowments, political subsidies by big contributors, but also the mendicant orders and the [not-so-] voluntary "gifts" to princes in early historical times.) There are no fixed rules and obligations and no necessary connections between contributions and other forms of participation: the sponsor may remain completely outside the group.

(5) *Contributions and services linked to positive and negative privileges.* (a) The positive variant occurs primarily when a certain economic or social monopoly is guaranteed or, conversely, when certain

privileged status groups or monopolized groups are completely or partly exempt. Hence contributions and services are not required according to general rules from the various property and income strata or the—at least in principle—freely accessible kinds of property and occupation; rather, they are required according to the specific economic and political powers and monopolies that have been granted to an individual or a group by the larger community. (Examples are manorial estates, tax privileges or special levies for guilds or certain status groups.) The point is that these demands are raised as a correlate of, or compensation for, the guarantee or appropriation of privileges. Thus, the method of want satisfaction creates or stabilizes a monopolistic differentiation of the group by virtue of the closure of the social and economic opportunities granted to its various strata. An important special case are the many diverse forms of feudal or patrimonial administration, with their linkage to appropriated power positions that permit the necessary amount of concerted action. (In the *Ständestaat* the prince must meet the costs of government from his patrimonial possessions, just like the feudal participants in political or patrimonial power and status, the vassals, *ministeriales* etc., must use their own means.) Most of the time, this mode of want satisfaction involves contributions in kind. However, under capitalism analogous phenomena may occur: for example, in one way or another, the political authorities may guarantee a monopoly to a group of entrepreneurs and in return impose contributions directly or through taxation. This method, which was widespread during the mercantilist era, is presently quite important again—witness the liquor tax in Germany.[7]

(b) Want satisfaction through negative privileges is called *liturgy*: We speak of *class liturgy*, if economically costly obligations are tied to a certain size or amount of property that is not privileged by any monopoly; at best, those affected can take turns. Examples are the *trierarchoi* and *choregoi* in Athens and the compulsory tax-farmers in the Hellenistic states. We speak of *status liturgy*, if the obligations are linked to monopolistic groups in such a manner that the members cannot withdraw unilaterally and hence remain collectively liable for satisfying the needs of the larger political unit. Examples are the compulsory guilds of ancient Egypt and late Antiquity; the hereditary attachment of the Russian peasants to the village, which is collectively liable for taxes; the more or less strict immobility of *coloni* and peasants throughout history, with their collective liability for paying taxes and, possibly, for providing recruits; and the Roman *decuriones*, who were collectively responsible for the taxes which they had to levy.

As a rule, the last type (5) of want satisfaction is inherently limited to compulsory associations, especially the political ones.

5. *Effects of Want Satisfaction and Taxation on Capitalism and Mercantilism*

The various modes of want satisfaction, always the result of struggles between different interests, often exert a far-reaching influence beyond their direct purpose. This may lead to a considerable degree of economic regulation: witness in particular the liturgical modes of want satisfaction. Even when this is not directly the case, these modes may strongly affect the development and the direction of the economy. For example, status-liturgy greatly contributed to the "closure" of social and economic opportunities, to the stabilization of status groups, and thus to the elimination of private capital formation. Moreover, if a political community satisfies its wants by public enterprises or by production for the market, private capitalism also tends to be eliminated. Monopolistic want satisfaction, too, affects private capitalism, but it may stimulate as well as impede private capital formation. This depends upon the particular nature of the state-sponsored monopolies. Ancient capitalism was suffocated because the Roman empire resorted increasingly to status-liturgy and partly also to public want satisfaction. Today, capitalist enterprises run by municipalities or the state in part redirect and in part displace private capitalism: the fact that the German exchanges have not quoted rail stocks since the railroads were nationalized is not only important for their position but also for the nature of property formation.[8] Private capitalism is retarded (for example, the growth of private distilleries), if monopolies are protected by the state and stabilized with state subsidies (as in the case of the German liquor tax). Conversely, during the Middle Ages and in early modern times, the trade and colonial monopolies at first facilitated the rise of capitalism, since under the given conditions only monopolies provided a sufficient profit span for capitalist enterprises. But later—in England during the 17th century—these monopolies impeded capitalist profit interests and provoked so much bitter opposition that they collapsed. Thus, the effect of tax-based monopolies is equivocal. However, clearly favorable to capitalist development has been want satisfaction through taxation and the market; in the extreme case, the open market is used as much as possible for administrative needs, including the recruitment and training of troops by private entrepreneurs, and all means are secured through tax monies. This presupposes, of course, a fully developed money economy and also a strictly rational and efficient administration: a bureaucracy.

This precondition is particularly important with regard to the taxation of personal ("mobile") property, a difficult undertaking everywhere, especially in a democracy. We must deal briefly with these difficulties, since they have greatly affected the rise of modern capitalism. Even where the propertyless strata are dominant, the taxation of personal property meets certain limits as long as the propertied can freely leave the community. The degree of mobility depends not only on the relative importance of membership in this particular community for the propertied, but also on the nature of the property. Within compulsory associations, particularly political communities, all property utilization that is largely dependent on real estate is stationary, in contrast to personal property which is either monetary or easily exchangeable. If propertied families leave a community, those staying behind must pay more taxes; in a community dependent on a market economy, and particularly a labor market, the have-nots may find their economic opportunities so much reduced that they will abandon any reckless attempt at taxing the haves or will even deliberately favor them. Whether this will indeed happen, depends upon the economic structure of the community. In democratic Athens such considerations were outweighed by the incentives for taxing the propertied, since the Athenian state lived largely from the tributes of subjects and had an economy in which the labor market (in the modern sense of the term) did not yet determine the class situation of the masses.

Under modern conditions the reverse is usually true. Today communities in which the propertyless have seized power are often very cautious toward the propertied. Municipalities under socialist control, such as the city of Catania, have attracted factories with substantial tax-benefits, because the socialist rank and file were more interested in better job opportunities and in directly ameliorating their class situation, than in "just" property distribution and "equitable" taxation. Likewise, in spite of conflicting interests in a given case, landlords, speculators in building land, retailers and craftsmen tend to think first of their immediate class-determined interests; therefore, all kinds of mercantilism have been a frequent, though highly varied, phenomenon in all types of communities. This is all the more so since those concerned with the relative power position of a community also have an interest in preserving the tax base and great fortunes capable of granting them loans; hence, they are forced to treat personal property cautiously. Thus, even where the have-nots are in control, personal property may either expect mercantilist privileges or at least exemption from liturgies and taxes, *provided* a plurality of communities competes with one another among which the property owners can choose their domicile. One example is the United States, in which the separatism of the individual states led to the failure of all serious attempts at unifying consumer interests; more limited, but still pertinent is the case of the municipalities of a country, and finally there are the independent countries themselves.

For the rest, the method of taxation depends, of course, very much on the relative power position of the various groups in a community, and on the nature of the economic system. Every increase of want satisfaction in kind favors the liturgical method. Thus, in Egypt the liturgical system originated in the Pharaonic period, and the course of the late Roman liturgical state, which was modelled after the Egyptian example, was determined by the largely natural economy of the conquered inland areas and the relative decline of the capitalist strata; in turn, these strata lost their former importance because the political and administrative transformation of the Empire eliminated the tax-farmer and the exploitation of the subjects through usury.

If personal ("mobile") property is dominant, the propertied everywhere unburden themselves of liturgical want satisfaction and shift the tax burden to the masses. In Rome military service used to be liturgically classified according to property and to involve the self-equipment of the propertied citizens; then, however, the knightly strata were freed from military service and replaced by the state-equipped proletarian army, elsewhere the mercenary army, the costs of which were met by mass taxation. Instead of satisfying extraordinary public wants through the property tax or compulsory loans without interest, that is, through the liturgical liability of the propertied, the Middle Ages everywhere resorted to interest-bearing loans, land mortgages, customs and other assessments; thus, the propertied used pressing public needs as a source for profit and rent. Sometimes these practices would almost reduce a city's administration and tax system to an instrument of state creditors, as it happened for a time in Genoa.

Finally, at the beginning of modern history, the various countries engaged in the struggle for power needed ever more capital for political reasons and because of the expanding money economy. This resulted in that memorable alliance between the rising states and the sought-after and privileged capitalist powers that was a major factor in creating modern capitalism and fully justifies the designation "mercantilist" for the policies of that epoch. This usage is justified even though, in Antiquity and modern times, "mercantilism," as the protection of personal ("mobile") property, existed wherever several political communities competed with one another by enlarging their tax base and by promoting capital formation for the sake of obtaining private loans. The fact that "mercantilism" at the beginning of modern history had a specific character and specific effects had two reasons: (1) the political structure of the competing states and of their economy—this will be treated later—, and (2) the novel structure of emergent modern capitalism, especially industrial capitalism, which was unknown to Antiquity and in the long run profited greatly from state protection. At any rate, from that time dates that European competitive struggle between large, approximately equal and purely political structures which has had such a global impact. It is well known that this political competition has remained one of the most important motives of the capitalist protectionism that emerged then and today continues in different forms. Neither the trade nor the monetary policies of the modern states—those policies most closely linked to the central interests of the present economic system—can be understood without this peculiar political competition and "equilibrium" among the European states during the last five hundred years—a phenomenon which Ranke recognized in his first work as the world-historical distinctiveness of this era.[9]

NOTES

1. This sentence appears to be a later insertion. The term *soziales Handeln* does not recur in the chapter; rather, Weber uses the older equivalent *Gemeinschaftshandeln*.

2. As is his wont, Weber uses the name of a given association in a generic sense, but also with an undertone of irony. In this case he refers to the *Verband der Diplomingenieure*, the association of engineering graduates from the Technical Colleges (*Hochschulen*), which ranked lower in prestige than the older universities. Such graduates often took pains to differentiate themselves from the products of engineering schools without university status and protected diplomas.

3. The Patriotic Association of Business Clerks was a union of white-collar employees who emphasized their social distance from the working class by pronounced nationalism. The association remained a prominent right-wing organization in the Weimar Republic.

4. Cf. Weber, *Economic History*, 30f.

5. Weber speaks later (ch. VI:8) of this as a practice among American Indians; Fischoff translates instead "India," but Ralph Linton locates the practice in Polynesia; see *The Tree of Culture* (New York: Knopf, 1955), 192.

6. Weber may refer here to contemporary events: female lecturers advocating free love and the right to illegitimate children, and a Freudian psychiatrist who proclaimed "sexual communism," appeared in Heidelberg and aroused his ire. However, Weber was by no means anti-feminist. When his wife organized a convention of the *Bund deutscher Frauenvereine* in Heidelberg in 1910, a faculty member attacked this meeting in a newspaper article as an assembly of spinsters, widows, Jewesses and sterile women—the last category obviously meant to include Marianne Weber. Weber wrote his wife's public defense, but this led to allegations that he was hiding behind her and refusing to duel in her behalf. The upshot was one of Weber's several involved lawsuits. Weber also helped Else von Richthofen, his first female doctorate candidate, to become the first female factory inspector in the state of Baden in 1900. (Her sister was the wife of D. H. Lawrence.) See Marianne Weber, *Max Weber*, 263f, 411ff and 472ff.

7. The Liquor Tax of 1909 was a major factor in ending the coalition between Liberals and Conservatives in the Reichstag and in precipitating Chancellor Bülow's resignation. At issue was a tax reform which would pay for the mounting military expenditures and at the same time distribute more equitably the tax burden among the various social strata.

8. In 1875, about half of the rapidly growing German railroads were still in private hands. Railshares were a major object of speculation before the great crash of 1873. The Prussian state, which had built railroads since 1847, embarked on large-scale nationalization after 1878. However, the interest in preventing further stock speculations was less important than were military considerations. Cf. Gustav Stolper, *German Economy: 1870–1940.* (New York: Reynal & Hitchcock, 1940), 72f.

9. Leopold von Ranke, *Histories of the Latin and Teuton Nations: 1495–1514* (London, 1909), G. R. Dennis, trans. First published in the summer of 1824. Cf. Theodore von Laue, *Leopold Ranke: The Formative Years* (Princeton: University Press, 1950), 24–32.

HOUSEHOLD, NEIGHBORHOOD AND KIN GROUP[1]

1. *The Household: Familial, Capitalistic and Communistic Solidarity*

An examination of the specific, often highly complex effects of the ways in which social groups satisfy their economic wants does not belong into this general review, and concrete individual instances will be considered merely as examples.

While abandoning any attempt to systematically classify the various kinds of groups according to the structure, content and means of social action—a task which belongs to general sociology—, we turn to a brief elucidation of those types of groups which are of the greatest importance for our exposition. Only the relationship of the economy to "society"—in our case, the general structures of human groups—will be discussed here and not the relationship between the economic sphere and specific areas of culture—literature, art, science, etc. Contents and directions of social action are discussed only insofar as they give rise to specific forms that are also economically relevant. The resulting boundary is no doubt quite fluid. At any rate, we shall be concerned only with certain universal types of groups. What follows is only a general characterization. Concrete historical forms of these groups will be discussed in greater detail in connection with "authority" [ch. X–XV].

The relationships between father, mother and children, established by a stable sexual union, appear to us today as particularly "natural" relationships. However, separated from the household as a unit of economic maintenance, the sexually based relationship between husband and wife, and the physiologically determined relationship between father and children are wholly unstable and tenuous. The father relationship cannot exist without a stable economic household unit of father and mother; even where there is such a unit the father relationship may not always be of great import. Of all the relationships arising from sexual intercourse, only the mother-child relationship is "natural," because it is a biologically based household unit that lasts until the child is able to search for means of subsistence on his own.

Next comes the sibling group, which the Greeks called *homogalaktes* [literally: persons suckled with the same milk]. Here, too, the decisive point is not the fact of the common mother but that of common maintenance. Manifold group relationships emerge, in addition to sexual and physiological relationships, as soon as the family emerges as a specific social institution. Historically, the concept of the family had several meanings, and it is useful only if its particular meaning is always clearly defined. More will be said later on about this.

Although the grouping of mother and children must be regarded as (in the present sense) the most primitive sort of family, it does not mean —indeed, it is unimaginable—that there ever were societies with maternal groupings only. As far as it is known, wherever the maternal grouping prevails as a family type, group relationships, economic and military, exist among men as well, and so do those of men with women (both sexual and economic). The pure maternal grouping as a normal, but obviously secondary, form is often found precisely where men's everyday life is confined to the stable community of a "men's house," at first for military purposes, later on for other reasons. Men's houses [*Männerhäuser*] can be found in various countries as a specific concomitant and a resultant of militaristic development.

One cannot think of marriage as a mere combination of sexual union and socialization agency involving father, mother, and children. The concept of marriage can be defined only with reference to other groups and relationships besides these. Marriage as a social institution comes into existence everywhere only as an antithesis to sexual relationships which are *not* regarded as marriage. The existence of a marriage means that (1) a relationship formed against the will of the wife's or the husband's kin will not be tolerated and may even be avenged by an organization, such as in olden times the kinsmen of the husband or of the wife or both. (2) It means especially that only children born of stable sexual relationships within a more inclusive economic, political, religious, or other community to which one or both parents belong will be treated, by virtue of their descent, as equal members of an organization—house, village, kin, political group, status group, religious group; while descendants who are a product of other sexual relationships will not be treated in such a manner. This and nothing else is the meaning of the distinction between birth in wedlock and out of wedlock. The prerequisites of a legitimate marriage, the classes of persons not allowed to enter into stable relationships with each other, the kinds of permission and kinds of kinship or other connections required for their validity, the usages which must be observed—all these matters are regulated by the "sacred" traditions and the laws of those groups. Thus, it is the regulations of groups other than mere sexual groupings and sibling communities of experience which endow the marriage with its specific quality. We do not intend to expound here the anthropologically very significant development of these regulations, since it is only their most important economic aspects which concern us.

Sexual relationships and the relationships between children based on the fact of their common parent or parents can engender social action only by becoming the normal, though not the only, bases of a specific economic organization: the household.

The household cannot be regarded as simply a primitive institution. Its prerequisite is not a "household" in the present-day sense of the word, but rather a certain degree of organized cultivation of soil.

The household does not seem to have existed in a primitive economy of hunters and nomads. However, even under the conditions of a technically well-advanced agriculture, the household is often secondary with respect to a preceding state which accorded more power to the inclusive kinship and neighborhood group on the one hand, and more freedom to the individual vis-a-vis the parents, children, grandchildren, and siblings on the other hand. The almost complete separation of the husband's and wife's means and belongings, which was very frequent especially where social differentiation was low, seems to point in this direction, as does the occasional custom according to which man and wife were seated back to back during their meals or even took their meals separately, and the fact that within the political group there existed independent organizations of women with female chieftains alongside the men's organizations. However, one should not infer from such facts the existence of an individualistic primitive condition. Rather, conditions that are due to a certain type of military organization, such as the man's absence from the house for his military service, lead to a "manless" household management by the wives and mothers. Such conditions were residually preserved in the family structure of the Spartans, which was based on the man's absence from the home and separation of belongings.

The size and inclusiveness of the household varies. But it is the most widespread economic group and involves continuous and intensive social action. It is the fundamental basis of loyalty and authority, which in turn is the basis of many other groups. This "authority" is of two kinds: (1) the authority derived from superior strength; and (2) the authority derived from practical knowledge and experience. It is, thus, the authority of men as against women and children; of the able-bodied as against those of lesser capability; of the adult as against the child; of the old as against the young. The "loyalty" is one of subjects toward the holders of authority and toward one another. As reverence for ancestors, it finds its way into religion; as a loyalty of the patrimonial official, retainer, or vassal, it becomes a part of the relationships originally having a domestic character.

In terms of economic and personal relationships, the household in its "pure," though not necessarily primitive, form implies solidarity in dealing with the outside and communism of property and consumption of everyday goods within (household communism). The principle of solidarity in facing the outside world was still found in its pure form in the periodically contractually regulated households as entrepreneurial units in the medieval cities of northern and central Italy, especially those most advanced in capitalist economy. All members of the household, including at times even the clerks and apprentices who were members by contract, were jointly responsible to the creditors. This is the historic source of the joint liability of the owners of a private company for the debts incurred by the firm. This concept of joint liability was of great importance in the subsequent development of the legal forms of modern capitalism.[2]

There was nothing corresponding to our law of inheritance in the old household communism. In its place there was, rather, the simple idea that the household is "immortal." If one of its members dies, or is expelled (after committing an inexpiable ill deed), or is permitted to join another household (by adoption), or is dismissed (*emancipatio*), or leaves out of his own accord (where this is permitted), he cannot possibly lay claim to his "share." By leaving the household he has relinquished his share. If a member of the household dies, the joint economy of the survivors simply goes on. The Swiss *Gemeinderschaften* operate in such a way to the present day.[3]

The principle of household communism, according to which everybody contributes what he can and takes what he needs (as far as the supply of goods suffices), constitutes even today the essential feature of our family household, but is limited in the main to household consumption.

Common residence is an essential attribute of the pure type of household. Increase in size brings about a division and creation of separate households. In order to keep the property and the labor force intact, a compromise based on local decentralization without partition can be adopted. Granting some special privileges to the individual household is an inevitable consequence of such a solution. Such a partition can be carried to a complete legal separation and independence in the control of the business, yet at the same time a surprisingly large measure of household communism can still be preserved. It happens in Europe, particularly in the Alpine countries (cf. Swiss hotel-keepers' families), and also in the large family firms of international trade that, while the household and household authority have outwardly completely disappeared, a communism of risk and profit, i.e., sharing of profit and loss of otherwise altogether independent business managements, continues to exist.

I have been told about conditions in international houses with earnings amounting to millions, whose capital belongs for the most part, but not exclusively, to relatives of varying degree and whose management is predominantly, but not solely, in the hands of the members of the family. The individual establishments operate in very diverse lines of business; they possess highly variable amounts of capital and labor force; and they achieve widely variable profits. In spite of this, after the deduction of the usual interest on capital, the annual returns of all the branches are simply thrown into one hopper, divided into equal portions, and allotted according to an amazingly simple formula (often by the number of heads). The household communism on this level is being preserved for the sake of mutual economic support, which guarantees a balancing of capital requirements and capital surplus between the business establishments and spares them from having to solicit credit from outsiders. The "calculative spirit" thus does not extend to the distribution of balance-sheet results, but it dominates all the more within the individual enterprise: even a close relative without capital and working as an employee will not be paid more than any other employee, because calculated costs of operation cannot be arbitrarily altered in favor of one individual without creating dissatisfaction in others. Beyond the balance sheet, those lucky enough to participate enter the "realm of equality and brotherhood."

2. *The Neighborhood: An Unsentimental Economic Brotherhood*

The household meets the everyday demands for goods and labor. In a self-sufficient agrarian economy a good deal of the extraordinary demands at special occasions, during natural calamities and social emergencies are met by social action that transcends the individual household: the assistance of the neighborhood. For us, the neighborhood is not only the "natural" one of the rural settlement but every permanent or ephemeral community of interest that derives from physical proximity; of course, if not specified further, we refer most of the time to the neighborhood of households settled close to one another.

The group of neighbors may take on different forms depending on the type of settlement: scattered farms, a village, a city street or a slum; neighborly social action may have different degrees of intensity and, especially in the modern city, it may be almost non-existent. To be sure, the extent of mutual help and of sacrifices that even today occurs frequently in the apartment houses of the poor may be astonishing to one who discovers it for the first time. However, not only the fleeting "togetherness" in streetcar, railroad or hotel, but also the enduring one in an apartment house is by and large oriented toward maintaining the greatest possible *distance* in spite (or because) of the physical proximity, and some social action is likely only in cases of common danger. We cannot discuss here why this attitude has become so conspicuous under modern conditions as a result of the specific sense of individual dignity created by them. Suffice it to note that the same ambivalence has always occurred in the stable rural neighborhood: the individual peasant does not like any interference with his affairs, no matter how well-meant it may be. Neighborly co-operation is an exception, although it recurs regularly. It is always less intensive and more discontinuous than the social action of the household, and the circle of participants is far more unstable. For in general, the neighborhood group is merely based on the simple fact that people happen to reside close to one another. In the self-sufficient rural economy of early history the typical neighborhood is the village, a group of households bordering upon each other. However, the neighborhood may also be effective beyond the fixed boundaries of other, in particular political, structures. In practice, neighborhood means mutual dependence in case of distress, especially when the transportation technology is undeveloped. The neighbor is the typical helper in need, and hence neighborhood is brotherhood, albeit in an unpathetic, primarily economic sense. If the household is short of means, mutual help may be requested: the loans of implements and goods free of charge, and "free labor for the asking" (*Bittarbeit*) in case of urgent need. This mutual help is guided by the primeval popular ethics which is as unsentimental as it is universal: "Do unto others as you would have them do unto you." (This is also nicely indicated by the Roman term *mutuum* for an interest-free loan.) For everybody may get into a situation in which he needs the help of others. If a compensation is provided, it consists in feasting the helpers, as in the typical case of neighborly help for house construction (still practiced in the German East). If an exchange takes place, the maxim applies: "Brothers do not bargain with one another." This eliminates the rational market principle of price determination.

Neighborliness is not restricted to social equals. Voluntary labor (*Bittarbeit*), which has great practical importance, is not only given to the needy but also to the economic powers-that-be, especially at harvest time, when the big landowner needs it most. In return, the helpers expect that he protect their common interests against other powers, and also that he grant surplus land free of charge or for the usual labor assistance —the *precarium* was land for the asking. The helpers trust that he will give them food during a famine and show charity in other ways, which he indeed does since he too is time and again dependent on them. In time this purely customary labor may become the basis of manorial services and thus give rise to patrimonial domination if the lord's power and the indispensability of his protection increase, and if he succeeds in turning custom into a right.

Even though the neighborhood is the typical locus of brotherhood, neighbors do not necessarily maintain "brotherly" relations. On the contrary: Wherever popularly prescribed behavior is vitiated by personal enmity and conflicting interests, hostility tends to be extreme and lasting, exactly because the opponents are aware of their breach of common ethics and seek to justify themselves, and also because the personal relations had been particularly close and frequent.

The neighborhood may amount to an amorphous social action, with fluctuating participation, hence be "open" and intermittent. Firm boundaries tend to arise only when a closed association emerges, and this occurs as a rule when the neighborhood becomes an economic group proper or an economically regulatory group. This may happen for economic reasons, in the typical fashion familiar to us; for example, when pastures and forests become scarce, their use may be regulated in a "co-operative" (*genossenschaftlich*) manner, that means, monopolistically. However, the neighborhood is not necessarily an economic, or a regulatory, group, and where it is, it is so in greatly varying degrees. The neighborhood may regulate the behavior of its members either through an association of its own: witness the *Flurzwang* [the compulsory regulation of tilling and crop rotation under the open-field system]; or a regulation may be imposed by outsiders (individuals or communities), with whom the neighbors are associated economically or politically (for example, the landlords of tenement houses). But all of this is not essential for neighborly social action. Even in the self-sufficient household economy of early times, there is no necessary identity among neighborhood, the forest regulations of political communities, especially the village, the territorial economic association (for example, the *Markgemeinschaft*) and the polity; they may be related in very diverse ways. The size of the territorial economic associations may vary according to the objects they comprise. Fields, pastures, forests and hunting grounds are often controlled by different groups, which overlap with one another and with the polity. Wherever peaceful activities are the primary means of making a living, the agent of joint work, the household, is likely to have control, and wherever maintenance depends upon land seized by force, the polity, and more so for extensively used land, such as hunting grounds and forests, than for pastures and fields.

Furthermore, the individual types of possessions tend to become scarce at different historical stages and hence subject to regulatory association; forests may still be free objects when pastures and fields are already economic ones and their use has been regulated and appropriated. Hence, diverse territorial associations may appropriate different kinds of land.

The neighborhood is the natural basis of the local community (*Gemeinde*)—a structure which arises only, as we shall see later [cf. ch. XVI, "The City"], by virtue of political action comprising a *multitude* of neighborhoods. Moreover, the neighborhood may itself become the basis of political action, if it controls a territory such as a village; and in the course of organizational rationalization, it may engage in activities of all kinds (from public schools and religious functions to the systematic settling of necessary crafts), or the polity may impose them as an obligation. But the essence of neighborly social action is merely that sombre economic brotherhood practiced in case of need.

3. *The Regulation of Sexual Relations in the Household*

We shall now return to the household, the most "natural" of the externally closed types of social action. Typically, the development from the primeval household communism runs counter to the kind of communism described in the previous example [in sec. 1], when profits and losses were shared in spite of the separation of the households; rather, typical is the internal weakening of household communism, that means, the progress of internal closure in the face of the continued external unity of the household.

The earliest substantial inroads into unmitigated communist house authority proceed not directly from economic motives but apparently from the development of exclusive sexual claims of the male over women subjected to their authority. This may result in a highly casuistic but strictly enforced regulation of sex relations, especially if social action is not much rationalized in other respects. It is true that sexual rights sometimes occur in "communist" form (polyandry), but in all known instances such polyandric rights constitute only a relative communism: a limited number of men (brothers or the members of a men's house) are exclusive co-owners by virtue of the common acquisition of a woman.

Nowhere do we find unregulated, amorphous sexual promiscuity within the house, even if sexual relations between siblings are a recognized institution; at least nowhere on a normative basis. On the contrary, any kind of communist sexual freedom is most thoroughly banished from a house in which there is communist property ownership. The [younger] members of such a household could adjust to this because their sexual attraction to one another was minimized by having grown up together. Subsequent normative elaboration was obviously in the interest of safeguarding solidarity and domestic peace in the face of jealousies. Where the members of the house belong to different sibs because of sib exogamy and hence would be free to engage in sexual relations, they are nevertheless forced to avoid one another because house exogamy is older than sib exogamy and persists next to it. The beginnings of regulated exogamy can perhaps be found in exchange arrangements of households and of sibs, which resulted from their division. At any rate, sexual relations are even disapproved of among close relatives among whom this would be permissible according to the sib code (for example, among very close paternal relatives under rules of matrilineal exogamy). As an institution, the marriage between siblings and relatives is commonly limited to socially prominent families, especially royal houses; its purpose is the preservation of economic resources, probably also the avoidance of struggles among pretenders, and finally the purity of the blood—hence it is a secondary phenomenon.

As a rule, then, a man acquires exclusive sexual rights over a woman when he takes her into his house or enters her house if his means are insufficient. Of course, this exclusiveness, too, has often enough been precarious vis-à-vis the autocratic head of the house. Notorious are the liberties, for example, which the father-in-law of an extended Russian family could take up until modern times. Normally, however, the household differentiates itself into permanent sexual unions with their offspring. In our times, the household consists of the parents and their children, together with the personal servants and at most a spinster relative. However, the household of earlier periods was not always very large; often it was small if finding sustenance required dispersion. However, history has known many households ("extended families") based on parent and child relations but comprising grandchildren, brothers, cousins and outsiders, to a degree which has become very rare in advanced countries. The extended family prevails where a large number of hands are required, hence where agriculture is intensive, and also where property is intended to remain concentrated in the interest of social and economic dominance, hence in aristocratic and plutocratic strata.

Apart from the very early closure of sexual relations within the household, the sexual sphere was further narrowed, especially at otherwise low levels of cultural differentiation, by structures that overlapped with domestic authority. In fact, one can say that these imposed the first decisive limitations on domestic authority. As blood relationships gain importance, incest transcends the house to include other relatives and becomes subject to casuistic regulation by the *kin group* (*Sippe*).

4. *The Kin Group and Its Economic Effects on the Household*

The kin group is not as "natural" a group as the household or the neighborhood. As a rule, its social action is discontinuous and lacks association; in fact, the kin group proves that social action is possible even if the participants do not know one another and action is merely passive (refraining from sexual relations, for example). The kin group presupposes the existence of others within a larger community. It is the natural vehicle of all fealty (*Treue*). Friendship is originally an artificial blood brotherhood. The vassal as well as the modern officer are not only subordinates but also the lord's brothers, "comrades" (that means, "roommates," originally household members). Substantively, the kin group competes with the household in the sphere of sexual relations and in-group solidarity; it is a protective group, which substitutes for our detective force and vice squad; and it is also a group of expectant heirs made up of those former household members who left when it was divided or when they married, and of their descendants. Hence with the kin group begins inheritance outside the household. Since members are committed to blood revenge, the in-group solidarity of the kin group may become more important than loyalty toward partiarchal authority.

We should keep in mind that the kin group is not an extended or decentralized household or a superordinate structure uniting several households: that may be the case, but as a rule it is not. Whether a particular kin group cuts across the households or comprises all members depends upon its structure, which may assign father and children to different groups, as we shall see later. Kin membership may not mean more than that marriage within the group is prohibited (exogamy); in this case the members may have common marks of identification and may believe in common descent from a natural object, most of the time an animal, which the members are usually not allowed to eat (totemism).

Furthermore, the kin members are forbidden to engage in combat with one another; they must practice blood revenge and be collectively liable to it, at least in the case of close relatives. Blood revenge in turn requires the joint declaration of a feud in case of a homicide and establishes the right and the duty of the kin members to receive and to pay a compensation (*Wergild*). The kin group is also open to Divine revenge in case of perjury, since it provides oath-bound witnesses at a trial. In this manner the kin group guarantees the security and legal personality of the individual.

Finally, the neighborhood established by a settlement (a village, a rural commune of villages—*Markgenossenschaft*) may coincide with the kin group; then the household is indeed a unit of the kin group. Even if this is not the case, the kin members often retain very palpable rights in relation to domestic authority: a veto against the sale of property, the right of participating in the selling of daughters into marriage and of receiving part of the bridal price, the rights of providing a legal guardian, etc.

Collective selfhelp is for the kin group the most typical means of reacting to infringements upon its interests. The oldest procedures approximating a trial are compulsory arbitration of conflict *within* the household or the kin group, either by the household head or the kin elder who best knows the customs, and mutually agreed arbitration *between* several households and kin groups. The kin group competes with political groups as an independent, overlapping group deriving from common descent, which may be actual, fictitious or artificially created through blood brotherhood; it is a complex of obligations and loyalties between persons who may belong not only to different households but also to different political and even language groups. The kin group may be completely unorganized, a kind of passive counter-image of the authoritarian household. For its normal functioning it does not require a leader with powers of control; indeed, as a rule, the kin group is merely an amorphous circle of persons who may be identified positively by forming a religious community and negatively by their refraining from the violation or consumption of a joint sacred object (taboo); we shall deal later [ch. VI] with the religious rationale for such behavior. It seems scarcely possible to assume, as Gierke has done, that kin groups with some kind of continuous government are the older form; rather, the reverse is the rule:

kin groups become associations only when it seems desirable to erect economic or social monopolies against outsiders. If the kin group has a head and functions as a political group, it may serve originally extraneous purposes of a political, military or economic nature; in this case it becomes part of a heterogeneous social structure—witness the *gens* as a subdivision of the *curia* or the [Germanic] "sibs" as military units.

Especially in periods in which social action is otherwise scarcely developed, household, kin group, neighborhood and political community typically overlap in such a manner that the members of a household and a village may belong to different kin groups, and the kin members to different political and even language communities. Hence it is possible that neighbors or members of the same political group and even of the same household are expected to practice blood revenge against one another. These drastically conflicting obligations were removed only when the political community gradually monopolized the use of physical force. However, if political action occurs only intermittently, when there is an external threat or booty seekers associate, the kin group's importance and the rationalization of its structure and obligations may approximate scholastic casuistry (as for example in Australia).

The manner in which the kin groups are organized and regulate sexual relations is important because of the repercussions on the composition and the economic structure of the households. Domestic authority over a child derives from matrilineal or patrilineal descent, and this in turn defines the other households in which the child has a property share, in particular access to economic opportunities which these households appropriated within economic, status, or political groups. Hence those other groups are interested in the manner in which household membership is established; in any given case the prevailing order is a resultant of the economic and also the political interests of all groups involved. It should be clearly understood from the beginning that as soon as a household becomes part of other groups that control economic and other opportunities, it cannot freely attribute membership, the less so the more limited these opportunities become. Patrilineal or matrilineal descent and their consequences are determined by the most diverse interests, which cannot be analyzed here in detail. In the case of matrilineal descent the child is protected and disciplined by the mother's brothers, apart from his father, and also receives his inheritance from them (*avunculate*); the mother exercises domestic authority only in rare cases subject to special conditions. In a patrilineal system, the child is subject to the power of his paternal relatives, apart from his father's, and he inherits from them. Today kinship and succession are as a rule cognate, that means, there is no difference between the father's and the mother's side, whereas domestic authority is exercised by the father or, if he is not there, often by a close relative who is appointed as a guardian and supervised by the public authorities; however, in the past patrilineal and matrilineal principles were often mutually exclusive. This did not necessarily mean that only one applied in a given group to all households; one principle might apply in one household, the other in another one. In the simplest case this competition of the two principles originated in property differentiation. Like all children, daughters are considered economic assets of the household into which they are born. The household decides their disposition. The head might offer them to his guests, just like his own wife, or he might permit sexual relations temporarily or permanently in exchange for goods and services. This "prostitution" of female household members accounts for many cases that are subsumed under the imprecise collective name of *matriarchy* (*Mutterrecht*): Husband and wife each remain members of their own household, the children belong to the mother's household, and the father is for them an alien who merely pays "alimony" (in modern terminology) to the household head. Hence husband, wife and children do not form a household of their own.

However, if there is such a household it may have a patrilineal or matrilineal basis. The man who can afford to pay cash for a woman takes her out of her household and kin group into his own. In this case the woman and her children are fully owned by the man's household. However, a man who cannot pay for a woman whom he desires must join her household, if its head permits the union, either temporarily in order to work off her price ("service marriage") or permanently, and then the woman's household retains control over her and the children. Thus the head of a well-to-do household buys women from less prosperous households for himself and his sons (so-called *diga*-marriage) or forces impecunious suitors to join his own household (*bina*-marriage). Hence patrilineal and matrilineal descent and the domestic authority of the father's or the mother's household may exist side by side for different persons within the *same* household. In this simple case patrilineal descent is always linked to control by the father's household, and vice versa. This relationship grows more complex when the husband takes the wife into his household and thus places her under its authority, but when matrilineal attribution remains, that means, when the children belong to the mother's kin group as her exogamous sex group and are subject to the rules of blood revenge and inheritance of her group. As a technical term, *matriarchy* ("mother right") should be restricted to this phenomenon. To be sure, as far as we know, matriarchy does not occur in this form in which the father's relation to the children is extremely restricted because they are legally aliens in spite of his authority. However, there are various intermediate stages: The mother's house may yield her to the father's household and yet retain certain rights in her and her children. Frequently matrilineal rules of kin exogamy apply because superstitious fear of incest persists; moreover, matrilineal rules of succession are often retained in varying degrees. This is likely to give rise to many conflicts between the two kin groups, the outcome of which depends very much on the land holdings, the influence of the village neighborhood and the role of military associations.

NOTES

1. The chapter titles of chs. III and IV and the subheadings were chosen by the English editor in an attempt to make clearer the content of the various sections and to come closer to Weber's original outline, which envisaged a chapter on "Household, Oikos and Enterprise," to be followed by "Neighborhood, Kin Group and Community." However, the text reverses some of the chapter sequence, unless the changes were made by the original editors.

For another discussion of marriage and kinship in relation to economic factors, see Weber's *Economic History,* 37–53, and Marianne Weber's *Ehefrau und Mutter in der Rechtsentwicklung* (1907); for other background literature, see below, Soc. of Law, ch. VIII: *ii,* nn. 18, 70–74.

2. On this point, see Weber's dissertation: *Zur Geschichte der Handelsgesellschaften im Mittelalter* (Stuttgart 1889), reprinted in *GAzSW,* 312–443, esp. ch. III ("Die Familien- und Arbeitsgemeinschaften").

3. Cf. Eugen Huber, *System and Geschichte des Schweizer Privatrechts* (1893), vol. IV, and Max Huber, *Gemeinderschaften der Schweiz* (Breslau 1897).

CHAPTER IV

HOUSEHOLD, ENTERPRISE AND OIKOS

1. The Impact of Economic, Military and Political Groups on Joint Property Law and Succession in the Household

Unfortunately, the relationships between kin group, village, the "commune" of villages (*Markgenossenschaft*) and political association belong to the most obscure and least investigated areas of ethnography and economic history. Not one case has been completely elucidated, neither the primitive stages of civilized peoples nor the so-called primitive tribes (*Naturvölker*), not even the American Indians, in spite of Morgan's research. The neighborhood organization of a village may originate in a given case in the division of the inheritance of a household. When nomadic cultivation is replaced by permanent agriculture, land may be assigned on a kinship basis, since the latter is usually taken into account in military organization; thus the territory of a village (*Dorfgemarkung*) may be considered kin property. This seems to have happened in ancient Germanic times, since the sources speak of *genealogiae* as the owners of village territory even when it appears that the land was not occupied by a noble family with its retainers. However, this was probably not the rule. As far as we know, the military bodies of a hundred or a thousand men, which developed from cadres into territorial units, were not unambiguously linked to the kin groups, and neither were the latter to the "rural communes" (*Markgemeinschaften*).

We can make only three generalizations: (1) Land may be primarily a place to work on. In this case all land and all yield belong to the women's kin groups, as long as cultivation is primarily women's work.

The father does not leave any land to his children, since it is handed down through the mother's house and kin group; the paternal inheritance comprises only military equipment, weapons, horses and tools of male crafts. In pure form this case is rare. (2) Conversely, land may be considered male property won and defended by force; unarmed persons, especially women, cannot have a share in it. Hence, the father's local political association may be interested in retaining his sons as military manpower; since the sons join the father's military group, they inherit the land from him, and only movable property from the mother. (3) The neighborhood composed of a village or a "rural commune" (*Markgenossenschaft*) always controls the land gained through joint deforestation, that means, through men's work, and does not permit its inheritance by children who do not continuously fulfill their obligations toward the association. The clash of these practices, and possibly of even more complex ones, may have very diverse results. However, we cannot make a fourth generalization that might suggest itself in view of these practices: that the primarily military character of a group points unambiguously to the predominance of the father's house and of male ("agnatic") family and property attribution. Rather this depends on the type of military organization. The able-bodied age-groups may permanently live in barracks; typical examples are the "men's house" described by Schurtz or the Spartan *syssitiae*.[1] In this case the men's absence frequently establishes the household as a "maternal grouping" in which children and property are attributed to the maternal household, or the woman achieves at least a relative domestic independence, as it is reported for Sparta. The numerous means that were specifically invented to intimidate and rob women—for example, the periodic predatory exploits of the *duk-duk*—[2] are an attempt by the men who have left the household to strengthen their threatened authority.

However, when the members of a military caste were landowners living dispersed in the countryside, the patriarchal and agnatic structure of household and kin group became usually predominant. As far as our historical knowledge goes, the empire-building peoples of the Far East and India, the Near East, the Mediterranean and the European North developed patrilineal descent and exclusively agnatic attribution of kinship and property; contrary to a frequent assumption, the Egyptians also had patrilineal descent even though they did not have agnatic attribution. The major reason for this phenomenon is that great empires cannot be maintained in the long run by small monopolistic, staff-like groups of warriors who live closely together in the manner of "men's houses"; in a natural economy empire-building requires as a rule the patrimonial and seigneurial control of the land, even if this subjection proceeds from groups of closely settled warriors, as in Antiquity. The manorial administration develops quite naturally out of the patriarchal household that is turned into an apparatus of domination; everywhere the manor originates in patriarchal authority. Hence, there is no serious evidence for the assertion that the predominance of patrilineal descent among those peoples was ever preceded by another order, ever since kinship relations among them had been regulated by any law at all. Particularly worthless is the hypothesis of a once universal prevalence of matriarchal marriage. This construct confuses very heterogeneous phenomena: it blurs the difference between primitive conditions under which parent-child relations are not legally regulated at all, hence the mother is indeed closer to the children whom she feeds and rears, and a *legal* arrangement deserving the name "matriarchy" (*Mutterrecht*). Equally erroneous is the idea that marriage by abduction was a universal intermediate stage between "matriarchy" and "patriarchy." A woman can be legitimately acquired from another household only through exchange or purchase. Abduction results in feud and restitution. It is true that for the hero the abducted woman is a trophy, just like the scalp of the enemy, but we cannot say that actual abduction was a stage in legal history.

Because of the very predominance of patriarchy, property law develops in the great empires in the direction of steadily *weakening* unlimited patriarchal power. Since legal restraints were originally missing, no distinction was made between "legitimate" and "illegitimate" children; in the Germanic law of the Middle Ages the master's right to identify "his" child was a residue of the once unlimited power of the patriarch. This state of affairs was definitely changed only with the intervention of political and economic groups, which made membership dependent upon "legitimate" descent, that means, on permanent relations with women from their own circle. The most important stage in the development of this principle, the very distinction between "legitimate" and "illegitimate" children and the protection of the right of succession for the former, is usually reached when the propertied or status-privileged strata no longer regard women merely as chattel and begin to protect by contract daughters, and their children, against the original discretion of the buyer. From then on his property is supposed to be inherited only by the children from this marriage. Hence the motivating force of this development is not the man's but the woman's interest in "legitimate" children. As status aspirations and the corresponding costs of living rise, the woman, who is now regarded as a luxury possession, receives a dowry; at the same time this represents the compensation for her share in the household—a purpose clearly stipulated in ancient Oriental and Hellenic law—and provides her with the material means of destroying the husband's unlimited discretion, since he must return the dowry if he divorces her. In time, this purpose was achieved, in different degrees and not always through formal law, but often so successfully that only an endowed marriage was considered a marriage proper (ἔγγραφος γάμος in Egypt).

We cannot deal here further with the development of joint property rights. Decisive changes occur wherever the military importance of land declines as a possession taken by force or as the basis of maintaining able-bodied men (capable of equipping themselves); then real estate can be used primarily for economic purposes, especially in the cities, and daughters too can succeed to land. The compromise between the interests of husband and wife and of their kin varies greatly depending on whether the family lives primarily from joint *labor earnings* or from rent-producing *property*.

In the Occidental Middle Ages the institution of joint property prevailed in the former case and that of joint administration (actually the administration and utilization of the wife's property by the husband) in the latter; in addition, since the feudal families did not want to release any land, widows were maintained through a rent attached to family holdings, as it occurred typically in England (dower marriage). For the rest the most diverse determinants may come into play. The social conditions of the Roman and English nobility were similar in some respects, but very different in others. Whereas in ancient Rome the wife became economically and personally emancipated by virtue of the freely dissolvable marriage, yet was completely unprotected as a widow and had no legal control whatsoever over her children, in England the wife remained under coverture which prevented any economic and legal independence and made it almost impossible for her to dissolve the feudal "dower marriage." The difference seems to have been owing to the more developed urban character of the Roman nobility, on the one hand, and the impact of Christian patriarchalism in the English family on the other. Whereas feudal marriage law persisted in England and French marriage law was shaped by petty-bourgeois and militaristic considerations—in the *Code Napoléon* through the personal influence of its creator—, bureaucratic states (such as Austria and Russia) have minimized sex differences in the joint property law; this levelling tends to go furthest where militarism has receded most in the ruling classes. With the advance of the market economy the marital property structure is also strongly influenced by the need to protect creditors. The manifold arrangements deriving from these factors do not belong in the present context.

The "legitimate" marriage that developed out of the wife's interests does not necessarily lead to a speedy adoption of monogamy. The wife whose children are privileged in relation to succession may be distinguished as the "chief wife" in a circle of other wives, as it was the case in the Orient, in Egypt and in most civilized Asian areas. This type of semi-polygamy was of course everywhere a privilege of the propertied strata. The ownership of several wives is lucrative only when women still do most of the agricultural work, at most when their textile production is especially profitable (as is still assumed in the Talmud); for example, the possession of a large number of women is considered a profitable capital investment by the chieftains in Caffraria; this presupposes, of course, that the man has the necessary means to buy women. But polygamy is too costly for all middle-income groups in an economy in which male work predominates, and especially in social strata in which women work only as dilettantes or for luxury needs in jobs considered beneath the dignity of freemen. Monogamy was institutionalized first among the Hellenes (even though the royal families did not consistently adhere to it as late as the period of the Diadochs) and among the Romans; it fitted into the household structure of the emergent urban patriciate. Subsequently Christianity raised monogamy to an absolute norm for ascetic reasons, in contrast to at least the early stages of all other religions. In the main, polygamy persisted in those cases in which the strictly patriarchal structure of political authority helped to preserve the discretion of the household head.

The institution of the dowry affects the development of the household in two ways: (1) As against the children of concubines, the "legitimate" children achieve special legal status as the sole inheritors of the paternal property; (2) the husband's economic position tends to be differentiated according to the wife's dowry, which in turn depends on her family's wealth. It is true that the dowry becomes formally subject to the husband's discretion (especially in Roman law), but in fact it tends to be set aside as a "special account." Thus the calculating spirit enters into the relations between the family members.

However, at this stage other economic motives have usually begun this dissolution of the household. Undifferentiated communism was economically deflected at such an early stage that it existed historically perhaps only in marginal cases. In principle, artifacts such as tools, arms, jewelry and clothes may be used by their producer alone or preferentially, and they are inherited not necessarily by the group but by other qualified individuals. (Examples are riding horse and sword, in the Middle Ages the *Heergewäte,* the *Gerade,* etc.) These incipient forms of the individual right to succession developed very early even under authoritarian house communism; however, their beginnings probably antecede the household itself and are found wherever tools are produced by individuals. In the case of arms, the same development was probably owing to the intervention of military powers interested in equipping the most able-bodied men.

2. *The Disintegration of the Household: The Rise of the Calculative Spirit and of the Modern Capitalist Enterprise*

In the course of cultural development, the internal and external determinants of the weakening of household authority gain ascendancy. Operating from within, and correlated with the quantitative growth of economic means and resources, is the development and differentiation of abilities and wants. With the multiplication of life chances and opportunities, the individual becomes less and less content with being bound to rigid and undifferentiated forms of life prescribed by the group. Increasingly he desires to shape his life as an individual and to enjoy the fruits of his own abilities and labor as he himself wishes.

The disintegration of the household authority is furthered by a number of other groups. One factor is the fiscal interest in a more intensive exploitation of the individual taxpayer. These groups may work contrary to the household's interests in keeping property intact for the sake of military self-equipment. The usual consequence of these disintegrative tendencies is, in the first place, the increasing likelihood of division in case of inheritance or marriage of children. In the early times of relatively primitive agriculture, employment of mass labor was the only means of increasing land yields. As a result, the household grew in size. However, the development of individualized production brought about a decrease in the size of households, which continued until the family of parents and children constitutes the norm today.

The function of the household has changed so radically that it is becoming increasingly inopportune for an individual to join a large communistic household. An individual no longer gets protection from the household and kinship groups but rather from political authority, which exercises compulsory jurisdiction. Furthermore, household and occupation become ecologically separated, and the household is no longer a unit of common production but of common consumption. Moreover, the individual receives his entire education increasingly from outside his home and by means which are supplied by various enterprises: schools, bookstores, theaters, concert halls, clubs, meetings, etc. He can no longer regard the household as the bearer of those cultural values in whose service he places himself.

This decrease in the size of households is not due to a growing "sub-jectivism," understood as a stage of social psychological development, but to the *objective* determinants of its growth. It should not be overlooked that there exist also hindrances to this development, particularly on the highest levels of the economic scale. In agriculture, the possibility of unrestricted splitting up of landed estates is tied in with certain tech-nological conditions. An integrated estate, even a large one, with valuable buildings on it, can be partitioned only at a loss. The division is tech-nically facilitated by mixed holdings and village settlement. Isolated loca-tion makes such a partition difficult. Separate farms and large estates, operated with an intensive expenditure of capital, therefore tend to be inherited by one individual. A small farm, operated with intensive ex-penditure of labor on scattered holdings, has a tendency to continuous splintering. In addition, the separate farm and large estate are much more suitable objects from which to extract payments in favor of movable property [i.e., money lenders] in the form of permanent or long-term mortgages, and they are thus kept intact for the benefit of the creditors.

Large property-holding, being a determinant of position and prestige, is conducive to the desire to keep it intact in the family. A small farm, on the other hand, is merely a place where work is done. There is an ap-positeness between the seigneurial standard of life, with its fixed con-ventions, and the large household. Given the spaciousness of, say, a castle and the almost inevitable "inner distance" even between the closest relatives, these large households do not restrain the freedom that the individual demands to such an extent as does the middle-class house-hold, which may consist of an equally large number of persons but occupies a smaller space and lacks the aristocratic sense of distance, and whose members, moreover, typically have far more differentiated life interests than do those of an estate-seated gentry family. Today, the large household provides an appropriate way of life, aside from the seigneurial one, only for the highly intense ideological community of a sect, whether religious, social-ethical or artistic—corresponding to the monasteries and the cloister-like communities of the past.

Even where the household unit remains outwardly intact, the internal dissolution of household communism by virtue of the growing sense of calculation (*Rechenhaftigkeit*) goes on irresistibly in the course of cul-tural development. Let us look at the consequences of this factor in somewhat greater detail.

As early as in the large capitalistic households of medieval cities—for example, in Florence—every person had his own account. He has pocket money (*danari borsinghi*) at his disposal. Specific limits are set for certain expenditures—for example, if he invites a visitor for a stay. The member must settle his account in the same way as do partners in any modern trading company. He has capital shares "in" the house and [separate "outside"] wealth (*fuori della compagnia*) which the house controls and for which it pays him interest, but which is not regarded as working capital proper and therefore does not share in the profit.[3] Thus, a rational association takes the place of the "natural" participation in the household's social action with its advantages and obligations. The individual is born into the household, but even as a child he is already a potential business partner of the rationally managed enterprise. It is evident that such conduct became possible only within the framework of a money economy, which therefore plays a crucial role in the internal dissolution of the household. The money eonomy makes possible an objective calculation both of the productive performances and of the consumption of the individuals, and for the first time makes it possible for them to satisfy their wants freely, through the indirect exchange medium of money.

The parallelism of money economy and attenuation of household authority is, of course, far from complete. Domestic authority and household are relatively independent of economic conditions, in spite of the latters' great importance, and appear "irrational" from an economic point of view; in fact, they often shape economic relationships because of their own historic structure. For example, the *patria potestas,* which the head of a Roman family retained until the end of his life, had economic and social as well as political and religious roots (the preservation of a patrician household, military affiliation according to kinship and, probably, house, and the father's position as house priest). The *patria potestas* persisted during the most diverse economic stages before it was finally attenuated under the Empire, even toward the children. In China, the same situation was perpetuated by the principle of filial piety, which was carried to an extreme by the code of duties and furthered by the state and the bureaucratic status ethic of Confucianism, in part for reasons of political domestication. This principle led not only to economically untenable consequences (as in the mourning regulations) but also to politically questionable results (for example, large-scale office vacancies, because piety toward the late father—originally, fear of the dead man's envy—forbade the use of his property and the occupation of his office).

Economic factors originally determined to a large extent whether a property was inherited by one person or principal heir or whether it was divided. This practice varies with economic influences, but it cannot be explained solely by economic factors, and especially not by modern economic conditions. This was demonstrated particularly in the recent studies of Sering and others.[4] Under identical conditions and in contiguous areas, there exist often quite disparate systems, affected especially by different ethnic composition, e.g., Poles and Germans. The far-reaching economic consequences of these differing structures were caused by factors that could be regarded as economically "irrational" from the very beginning, or that became irrational as a consequence of changes in economic conditions.

In spite of all, the economic realities intervene in a compelling manner. First, there are characteristic differences depending on whether economic gain is attributed to common work or to common property. If the former situation obtains, the household authority is usually basically unstable, no matter how autocratic it may be. Mere separation from the parental household and the establishment of an independent household is sufficient for a person to be set free from the household authority. This is mostly the case in the large households of primitive agricultural peoples. The *emancipatio legis Saxonicae* of the German law clearly has its economic foundation in the importance of personal labor, which prevailed at the time.

On the other hand, the household authority is typically stable wherever ownership of livestock, and property in general, forms the prime economic basis. This is particularly true when land ceases to be abundant and becomes a scarce commodity. For reasons already alluded to, family and lineage cohesion is generally an attribute of the landed aristocracy. The man without any landed property or with only little of it is also without lineage group.

The same difference is to be found in the capitalistic stage of development. The large households of Florence and other parts of northern Italy practiced the principle of joint responsibility and of maintaining the property intact. In the trading places of the Mediterranean, especially in Sicily and southern Italy, the exact opposite was the case: each adult member of the household could at any time request his share while the legator was still alive. Nor did joint personal liability to the outsiders exist. In the family enterprises of northern Italy, the inherited capital represented the basis of economic power to a greater degree than did the personal business activities of the partners. The opposite was true in southern Italy, where common property was treated as a product of common work. With the increasing importance of capital, the former practice gained ascendancy. In this case, the capitalist economy, a "later" stage in terms of a theory of development starting with undifferentiated social action, determines a theoretically "earlier" structure in which the household members are more tightly bound to the household and subjected to household authority.

However, at the same time a far more significant, and *uniquely Occidental,* transformation of domestic authority and household was under way in these Florentine and other business-oriented medieval houses.

The entire economic arrangements of such large households were periodically regulated by *contract*. Whereas, originally, the personal funds and the business organization were regulated by the same set of rules, the situation gradually changed. Continuous capitalist acquisition became a special vocation performed in an increasingly separate enterprise. An autonomous rational association emerged out of the social action of the household, in such a way that the old identity of household, workshop and office fell apart, which had been taken for granted in the undifferentiated household as well as the ancient *oikos,* to be discussed in the next section. First, the household ceased to exist as a necessary basis of rational business association. Henceforth, the partner was not necessarily—or typically—a house member. Consequently, business assets had to be separated from the private property of the partners. Similarly, a distinction began to be made between the business employees and the domestic servants. Above all, the commercial debts had to be distinguished from the private debts of the partners, and joint responsibility had to be limited to the former, which were identified as such by being contracted under the "firm," the business name.

This whole development is obviously a precise parallel to the separation of the bureaucratic office as a "vocation" from private life, the "bureau" from the private household, the official assets and liabilities from private property, and the official dealings from private dealings; this will be discussed in the analysis of authority [chapter XI]. The capitalist enterprise, created by the household which eventually retreats from it, thus is related from the very beginning to the "bureau" and the now obvious bureaucratization of the private economy.

But the factor of decisive importance in this development is not the spatial differentiation or separation of the household from the work-shop and the store. This is rather typical of the bazaar system of the Islamic cities in the Orient, which rests throughout on the separation of the castle (*kasbah*), bazaar (*suk*), and residences. What is crucial is the separation of household and business for accounting and legal purposes, and the development of a suitable body of laws, such as the commercial register, elimination of dependence of the association and the firm upon the family, separate property of the private firm or limited partnership, and appropriate laws on bankruptcy. This fundamentally important development is the characteristic feature of the Occident, and it is worthy of note that the legal forms of our present commercial law were almost all developed as early as the Middle Ages—whereas they were almost entirely foreign to the law of Antiquity with its capitalism that was quantitatively sometimes much more developed. This is one of the many phenomena characterizing most clearly the qualitative uniqueness of the development of modern capitalism, since both the concentration of the family property for the purpose of mutual economic support and the development of a "firm" from a family name existed, for example, in China as well. There, too, the joint liability of the family stands behind the debts of the individual. The name used by a company in commercial transactions does not provide information about the actual proprietor: there, too, the "firm" is related to the business organization and not to the household. But the laws on private property and bankruptcy as they were developed in Europe seem to be absent in China, where two things are of special relevance: Association and credit, until the modern era, were to a large degree dependent on the kinship group. Likewise, the keeping of the property intact in the well-to-do kinship groups and the mutual granting of credit within the kinship groups served different purposes. They were concerned not with capitalistic profit but with raising money to cover the costs of family members' preparation for the examinations and afterwards for the purchase of an office. The incumbency of the office then offered the relatives an opportunity to recover their expenses with a profit from the legal and illegal revenues that the office afforded. Furthermore, these relatives could benefit from the protection of the office-holder. It was the chances of the politically rather than economically determined gain that were conducive to the "capitalistic" cohesion of the family, especially one that was well-off economically.

The capitalistic type of association which corresponds to our joint-stock company and is completely detached, at least formally, from kinship and personal ties has its antecedents in Antiquity only in the area of politically oriented capitalism, i.e., in companies of tax-farmers. In the Middle Ages, such associations were also organized in part for colonizing ventures—such as the big partnerships of the *maone* in Genoa —and in part for state credit—such as the Genoese group of creditors which for all practical purposes held the municipal finances under sequester. In the realm of private enterprise, a purely commercial and capitalistic type of association initially developed only in the form of *ad hoc* groupings in long-distance trade, such as the *commenda* association which can be found already in Old Babylonian law and later quite universally: A financier entrusts his capital to a travelling merchant for a concrete voyage, with profit or loss distribution on this basis. This is the form typical for the period of "intermittent trade" (*Gelegenheitshandel*). Enterprises in the form of joint-stock corporations which were monopolistically privileged by the political powers, especially colonial undertakings, constituted the transition to the application of such organizational types also in purely private business.

3. *The Alternative Development: The* Oikos

These kinds of undertakings which, as the basis of a capitalist enterprise, constitute its most radical separation from the original identity with the household do not particularly concern us at this point. Rather, we shall turn to a radically different way in which a household may evolve. The disintegration of the household and of domestic authority because of exchange with the outside, and the resulting rise of the capitalist enterprise proceed in juxtaposition to the household's internal evolution into an *oikos,* as Rodbertus called it.[5] This is not simply any large household or one which produces on its own various products, agricultural or industrial; rather, it is the authoritarian household of a prince, manorial lord or patrician. Its dominant motive is not capitalistic acquisition but the lord's organized want satisfaction in kind. For this purpose, he may resort to any means, including large-scale trade. Decisive for him is the utilization of property, not capital investment. The essence of the oikos is organized want satisfaction, even if market-oriented enterprises are attached to it. Of course, there is a scale of imperceptible transitions between the two modes of economic orientation, and often also a more or less rapid transformation from one into the other. In reality, if there is a relatively developed technology, the oikos is rarely a purely collective natural economy; for it can exist purely only if it permanently eliminates all exchange, and practices, or at least aims at, autarky, hence if it is a self-sufficient economy so far as possible. In this case an apparatus of house-dependent labor, which often is highly specialized, produces all the goods and personal services, economic, military and sacral, which the ruler requires. His own land provides the raw materials, his workshops with their personally unfree labor supply all other materials. The remaining services are provided by servants, officials, house priests and warriors. Exchange takes place only if surplus is to be dumped or if goods simply cannot be procured in any other way. This state of affairs was approximated to a considerable extent by the royal economies of the Orient, especially of Egypt, and to a lesser degree by the households of the Homeric aristocrats and princes; those of the Persian and Frankish kings also appear quite similar. In the Roman empire the landed estates moved increasingly in this direction as they grew in size, the slave supply fell off and capitalist acquisition was curbed by bureaucracy and liturgy. But the medieval manor took the opposite course with the increasing importance of trade, the cities and the money economy. However, in all these cases the oikos was never really self-sufficient. The Pharaoh engaged in foreign trade just as did the majority of the early princes and aristocrats of the Mediterranean; their treasuries depended heavily upon trade proceeds. As early as the Frankish kingdom the seigneurs received substantial amounts of money or various tributes which had cash-value. The *capitularia* took for granted that the royal *fisci* were free to sell whatever was not needed by the court and the army. In all better known cases only a part of the unfree work-force of the big owners of land and people was completely tied to their household. Those most strictly attached to the household were the personal servants and the workers who labored in the master's self-sufficient household and were wholly maintained by him: the case of *autarkic utilization of labor*. However, another group of strictly attached workers consists of those who produced for the market; the Carthaginian, Sicilian and Roman plantation owners employed their barrack slaves in this fashion, as did the father of Demosthenes with the slaves in his two *ergasteria* or, in modern times, the Russian landlords with the peasants in their factories: these are cases of the *capitalist utilization of unfree labor*. However, many slaves on the plantations and in the *ergasteria* were bought on the market, hence they were not "produced" in the household. Unfree workers born in the master's household presuppose some kind of unfree "family," and this implies an attenuation of attachment and normally also of the full exploitation of labor power. Therefore, the majority of these hereditarily unfree workers is not employed in centralized enterprises, but surrenders only part of their work capacity to the master, and pays him more or less arbitrary and traditionally fixed taxes in kind or in coin. Whether the master prefers to use his unfree workers as a work-force or as a source of revenue depends above all on what yields most to him in a given situation. Barrack slaves without families can be replaced only if they are very cheap and plentiful; this presupposes continuous slavery wars and low food costs (a Southern climate). Hereditarily attached peasants, moreover, can pay money taxes only if there is a (local) market, and this in turn requires a degree of urban development. Where this was low, and the harvest yield could be fully used only through export, as in the German and European East at the beginning of modern times (in contrast to the West) and in the "Black Earth" regions of Russia in the nineteenth century, the forced labor of the peasants was the only way of making money. In this way large-scale market-oriented enterprise developed within the oikos. The owner of an oikos may become almost indistinguishable, or wholly identical, with a capitalist entrepreneur, if he establishes large industrial undertaking with his own unfree labor, or rented unfree or even free workers; he may use the latter two groups either partly or exclusively, and he may run his own or rented *ergasteria*. A major example for this transformation are the creators of the Silesian *starost* [i.e., village steward] industries.[6]

Ultimately, the oikos is defined only by the rent-producing utilization of property, but in terms of the owner's primary interest this meaning may become practically indistinguishable from, or outright identical with, entrepreneurial capital proper. The manorial origin of the *starost-industry* is visible only because of the particular combination of enterprises: large-scale lumbering with brick-yards, distilleries, sugar refineries, coal mines, that means, of enterprises that are not integrated, along technically or economically suggested, horizontal or vertical lines, like the modern combines and mixed firms. However, a manorial lord who adds a foundry or a steelmill to his coal mines, or a lumbermill and papermill to his lumbering operations may in practice bring about the same result. Only the starting point, not the end product are different. In the ancient *ergasteria,* too, we find incipient combinations based on the possession of raw materials. The father of Demosthenes, who descended from a family of Attic merchants, was an importer of ivory which he sold τῷ βουλομένῳ [i.e., to anyone desiring it, to any comer] and which was used as inlay for knife handles and furniture. He eventually trained slaves to manufacture knives in his own workshop and, in addition, had to take over the *ergasterion,* that means, mostly the slaves, of a bankrupt cabinet-maker. He combined these holdings into both a cutlery and a furniture *ergasterion.* The *ergasterion* developed further during the Hellenistic period, especially in Alexandria, up until early Islamic times. The use of unfree craftsmen as a source of rent was widely known throughout Antiquity, both in the Orient and the Occident, during the early Middle Ages, and in Russia until the emancipation of the serfs. The master may rent his slaves, as Nikias did with masses of unskilled slaves for the mine-owners. He may turn them into skilled craftsmen, a practice found in all Antiquity, from a contract in which [the Persian] crown prince Kambyses [6th century B.C.] is mentioned as the owner of the trainer, up to the [late Roman] pandects, but it is also found in Russia as late as the 18th and 19th century. The master may also leave it to the slaves, after he arranged for their training, to work for their own account in exchange for a rent (Greek: *apophora,* Babylonian: *mandaku,* German: *Halssteuer,* Russian: *obrok*). The master may also provide them with a workshop and capital equipment (*peculium*) as well as working capital (*merx peculiaris*). Historically, we find all imaginable transitions from almost total mobility to complete regimentation in barracks. A more detailed description of the "enterprises" emerging within the oikos and run by either the master or the unfree belongs into a different set of topics. However, the transformation of the oikos into a patrimonial rulership will be discussed in the analysis of the forms of domination.

NOTES

1. Heinrich Schurtz, *Altersklassen und Männerbünde* (1902). (W)—For further literature, see Soc. of Law, ch. VIII:*ii*, n. 13.

2. *Duk-Duk:* secret society of the New Britain Archipelago N.E. of New Guinea. Cf. Graf von Pfeil, "Duk-Duk," 27 *Journal of Anthropol. Institut.*, 181; E. A. Weber, *The Duk-Duk* (1929). (Rh) For a more detailed description of the Duk-Duk, see below, ch. IX:2.

3. Cf. Weber, *Handelsgesellschaften*, ch. V, in GAzSW, 411ff.

4. See, e.g., Max Sering et al., *Die Vererbung des ländlichen Grundbesitzes im Königreich Preussen* (Berlin: Parey, 1908). Cf. also *GAzSW*, 463f.

5. Karl Johann Rodbertus (1805–75), who championed a conservative form of socialism, advanced the theory that all of Antiquity should be classified as falling into the stage of the "*oikos* economy," a concept created by him; cf. Weber, *Agrarverhältnisse*, in GAzSW, 7, and *supra*, Part One, ch. II, n. 34.

6. The term could not be traced, but elsewhere Weber refers to "the typical *starost*-industry of Silesia and Bohemia—thus styled, as is well known, by Engel—which is a form of 'wealth-utilization,' as contrasted to the 'capital-utilization' of bourgeois industry . . ." (*AfS*, Vol. 38 [1914], 544). The reference might be to the famous Prussian statistician Ernst Engel (1821–1896). On this phenomenon and the origin of Silesian and Bohemian linen industry, see also *Economic History*, 104; Arthur Salz, *Geschichte der böhmischen Industrie in der Neuzeit* (Munich: Duncker & Humblot, 1913), 365–383.

CHAPTER V

ETHNIC GROUPS

1. "Race" Membership[1]

A much more problematic source of social action than the sources analyzed above is "race identity": common inherited and inheritable traits that actually derive from common descent. Of course, race creates a "group" only when it is subjectively perceived as a common trait: this happens only when a neighborhood or the mere proximity of racially different persons is the basis of joint (mostly political) action, or conversely, when some common experiences of members of the same race are linked to some antagonism against members of an *obviously* different group. The resulting social action is usually merely negative: those who are obviously different are avoided and despised or, conversely, viewed with superstitious awe. Persons who arc externally different are simply despised irrespective of what they accomplish or what they are, or they are venerated superstitiously if they are too powerful in the long run. In this case antipathy is the primary and normal reaction. However, this antipathy is shared not just by persons with anthropological similarities, and its extent is by no means determined by the degree of anthropological relatedness; furthermore, this antipathy is linked not only to inherited traits but just as much to other visible differences.

If the degree of objective racial difference can be determined, among other things, purely physiologically by establishing whether hybrids reproduce themselves at approximately normal rates, the subjective aspects, the reciprocal racial attraction and repulsion, might be measured by finding out whether sexual relations arè preferred or rare between two groups, and whether they are carried on permanently or temporarily and irregularly. In all groups with a developed "ethnic" consciousness the existence or absence of intermarriage (*connubium*) would then be a normal consequence of racial attraction or segregation. Serious research on the sexual attraction and repulsion between different ethnic groups is only incipient, but there is not the slightest doubt that racial factors, that means, common descent, influence the incidence of sexual relations and of marriage, sometimes decisively. However, the existence of several million mulattoes in the United States speaks clearly against the assumption of a "natural" racial antipathy, even among quite different races. Apart from the laws against biracial marriages in the Southern states, sexual relations between the two races are now abhorred by both sides, but this development began only with the Emancipation and resulted from the Negroes' demand for equal civil rights. Hence this abhorrence on the part of the Whites is socially determined by the previously sketched tendency toward the monopolization of social power and honor, a tendency which in this case happens to be linked to race.

The *connubium* itself, that means, the fact that the offspring from a permanent sexual relationship can share in the activities and advantages of the father's political, economic or status group, depends on many circumstances. Under undiminished patriarchal powers, which we treat elsewhere, the father was free to grant equal rights to his children from slaves. Moreover, the glorification of abduction by the hero made racial mixing a normal event within the ruling strata. However, patriarchal discretion was progressively curtailed with the monopolistic closure, by now familiar to us, of political, status or other groups and with the monopolization of marriage opportunities; these tendencies restricted the *connubium* to the offspring from a permanent sexual union within the given political, religious, economic and status group. This also produced a high incidence of inbreeding. The "endogamy" of a group is probably everywhere a secondary product of such tendencies, if we define it not merely as the fact that a permanent sexual union occurs primarily on the basis of joint membership in some association, but as a process of social action in which only endogamous children are accepted as full members. (The term "sib endogamy" should not be used; there is no such thing unless we want to refer to the levirate marriage and arrangements in which daughters have the right to succession, but these have secondary, religious and political origins.) "Pure" anthropological types are often a secondary consequence of such closure; examples are sects (as in India) as well as pariah peoples, that means, groups that are socially despised yet wanted as neighbors because they have monopolized indispensable skills.

Reasons other than actual racial kinship influence the degree to which blood relationship is taken into account. In the United States the smallest admixture of Negro blood disqualifies a person unconditionally, whereas very considerable admixtures of Indian blood do not. Doubtlessly, it is important that Negroes appear esthetically even more alien than Indians, but it remains very significant that Negroes were slaves and hence disqualified in the status hierarchy. The conventional *connubium* is far less impeded by anthropological differences than by status differences, that means, differences due to socialization and upbringing (*Bildung* in the widest sense of the word). Mere anthropological differences account for little, except in cases of extreme esthetic antipathy.

2. *The Belief in Common Ethnicity: Its Multiple Social Origins and Theoretical Ambiguities*

The question of whether conspicuous "racial" differences are based on biological heredity or on tradition is usually of no importance as far as their effect on mutual attraction or repulsion is concerned. This is true of the development of endogamous conjugal groups, and even more so of attraction and repulsion in other kinds of social intercourse, i.e., whether all sorts of friendly, companionable, or economic relationships between such groups are established easily and on the footing of mutual trust and respect, or whether such relationships are established with difficulty and with precautions that betray mistrust.

The more or less easy emergence of social circles in the broadest sense of the word (*soziale Verkehrsgemeinschaft*) may be linked to the most superficial features of historically accidental habits just as much as to inherited racial characteristics. That the different custom is not understood in its subjective meaning since the cultural key to it is lacking, is almost as decisive as the peculiarity of the custom as such. But, as we shall soon see, not all repulsion is attributable to the absence of a "consensual group." Differences in the styles of beard and hairdo, clothes, food and eating habits, division of labor between the sexes, and all kinds of other visible differences can, in a given case, give rise to repulsion and contempt, but the actual extent of these differences is irrelevant for the emotional impact, as is illustrated by primitive travel descriptions, the Histories of Herodotus or the older prescientific ethnography. Seen from their positive aspect, however, these differences may give rise to consciousness of kind, which may become as easily the bearer of group relationships as groups ranging from the household and neighborhood to political and religious communities are usually the bearers of shared customs. All differences of customs can sustain a specific sense of honor or dignity in their practitioners. The original motives or reasons for the inception of different habits of life are forgotten and the contrasts are then perpetuated as conventions. In this manner, any group can create customs, and it can also effect, in certain circumstances very decisively, the selection of anthropological types. This it can do by providing favorable chances of survival and reproduction for certain hereditary qualities and traits. This holds both for internal assimilation and for external differentiation.

Any cultural trait, no matter how superficial, can serve as a starting point for the familiar tendency to monopolistic closure. However, the universal force of imitation has the general effect of only gradually changing the traditional customs and usages, just as anthropological types are changed only gradually by racial mixing. But if there are sharp boundaries between areas of observable styles of life, they are due to conscious monopolistic closure, which started from small differences that were then cultivated and intensified; or they are due to the peaceful or warlike migrations of groups that previously lived far from each other and had accommodated themselves to their heterogeneous conditions of existence. Similarly, strikingly different racial types, bred in isolation, may live in sharply segregated proximity to one another either because of monopolistic closure or because of migration. We can conclude then that similarity and contrast of physical type and custom, regardless of whether they are biologically inherited or culturally transmitted, are subject to the same conditions of group life, in origin as well as in effectiveness, and identical in their potential for group formation. The difference lies partly in the differential instability of type and custom, partly in the fixed (though often unknown) limit to engendering new hereditary qualities. Compared to this, the scope for assimilation of new customs is incomparably greater, although there are considerable variations in the transmissibility of traditions.

Almost any kind of similarity or contrast of physical type and of habits can induce the belief that affinity or disaffinity exists between groups that attract or repel each other. Not every belief in tribal affinity, however, is founded on the resemblance of customs or of physical type. But in spite of great variations in this area, such a belief can exist and can develop group-forming powers when it is buttressed by a memory of an actual migration, be it colonization or individual migration. The persistent effect of the old ways and of childhood reminiscences continues as a source of native-country sentiment (*Heimatsgefühl*) among emigrants even when they have become so thoroughly adjusted to the new country that return to their homeland would be intolerable (this being the case of most German-Americans, for example).

In colonies, the attachment to the colonists' homeland survives despite considerable mixing with the inhabitants of the colonial land and despite profound changes in tradition and hereditary type as well. In case of political colonization, the decisive factor is the need for political support. In general, the continuation of relationships created by marriage is important, and so are the market relationships, provided that the "customs" remained unchanged. These market relationships between the homeland and the colony may be very close, as long as the consumer standards remain similar, and especially when colonies are in an almost absolutely alien environment and within an alien political territory.

The belief in group affinity, regardless of whether it has any objective foundation, can have important consequences especially for the formation of a political community. We shall call "ethnic groups" those human groups that entertain a subjective belief in their common descent because of similarities of physical type or of customs or both, or because of memories of colonization and migration; this belief must be important for the propagation of group formation; conversely, it does not matter whether or not an objective blood relationship exists. Ethnic membership (*Gemeinsamkeit*) differs from the kinship group precisely by being a presumed identity, not a group with concrete social action, like the latter. In our sense, ethnic membership does not constitute a group; it only facilitates group formation of any kind, particularly in the political sphere. On the other hand, it is primarily the political community, no matter how artificially organized, that inspires the belief in common ethnicity. This belief tends to persist even after the disintegration of the political community, unless drastic differences in the custom, physical type, or, above all, language exist among its members.

This artificial origin of the belief in common ethnicity follows the previously described pattern [cf. chapter II:3] of rational association turning into personal relationships. If rationally regulated action is not widespread, almost any association, even the most rational one, creates an overarching communal consciousness; this takes the form of a brotherhood on the basis of the belief in common ethnicity. As late as the Greek city state, even the most arbitrary division of the polis became for the member an association with at least a common cult and often a common fictitious ancestor. The twelve tribes of Israel were subdivisions of a political community, and they alternated in performing certain functions on a monthly basis. The same holds for the Greek tribes (*phylai*) and their subdivisions; the latter, too, were regarded as units of common ethnic descent. It is true that the original division may have been induced by political or actual ethnic differences, but the effect was the same when such a division was made quite rationally and schematically, after the break-up of old groups and relinquishment of local cohesion, as it was done by Cleisthenes. It does not follow, therefore, that the Greek polis was actually or originally a tribal or lineage state, but that ethnic fictions were a sign of the rather low degree of rationalization of Greek political life. Conversely, it is a symptom of the greater rationalization of Rome that its old schematic subdivisions (*curiae*) took on religious importance, with a pretense to ethnic origin, to only a small degree.

The belief in common ethnicity often delimits "social circles," which in turn are not always identical with endogamous connubial groups, for greatly varying numbers of persons may be encompassed by both. Their similarity rests on the belief in a specific "honor" of their members, not shared by the outsiders, that is, the sense of "ethnic honor" (a phenomenon closely related to status honor, which will be discussed later). These few remarks must suffice at this point. A specialized sociological study of ethnicity would have to make a finer distinction between these concepts than we have done for our limited purposes.

Groups, in turn, can engender sentiments of likeness which will persist even after their demise and will have an "ethnic" connotation. The political community in particular can produce such an effect. But most directly, such an effect is created by the *language group,* which is the bearer of a specific "cultural possession of the masses" (*Massenkulturgut*) and makes mutual understanding (*Verstehen*) possible or easier.

Wherever the memory of the origin of a community by peaceful secession or emigration ("colony," *ver sacrum,* and the like) from a mother community remains for some reason alive, there undoubtedly exists a very specific and often extremely powerful sense of ethnic identity, which is determined by several factors: shared political memories or, even more importantly in early times, persistent ties with the old cult, or the strengthening of kinship and other groups, both in the old and the new community, or other persistent relationships. Where these ties are lacking, or once they cease to exist, the sense of ethnic group membership is absent, regardless of how close the kinship may be.

Apart from the community of language, which may or may not coincide with objective, or subjectively believed, consanguinity, and apart from common religious belief, which is also independent of consanguinity, the ethnic differences that remain are, on the one hand, esthetically conspicuous differences of the physical appearance (as mentioned before) and, on the other hand and of equal weight, the perceptible differences in the *conduct of everyday life.* Of special importance are precisely those items which may otherwise seem to be of small social relevance, since when ethnic differentiation is concerned it is always the conspicuous differences that come into play.

Common language and the ritual regulation of life, as determined by shared religious beliefs, everywhere are conducive to feelings of ethnic affinity, especially since the intelligibility of the behavior of others is the most fundamental presupposition of group formation. But since we shall not consider these two elements in the present context, we ask: what is it that remains? It must be admitted that palpable differences in dialect and differences of religion in themselves do not exclude sentiments of common ethnicity. Next to pronounced differences in the economic way of life, the belief in ethnic affinity has at all times been affected by outward differences in clothes, in the style of housing, food and eating habits, the division of labor between the sexes and between the free and the unfree. That is to say, these things concern one's conception of what is correct and proper and, above all, of what affects the individual's sense of honor and dignity. All those things we shall find later on as objects of specific differences between status groups. The conviction of the excellence of one's own customs and the inferiority of alien ones, a conviction which sustains the sense of ethnic honor, is actually quite analogous to the sense of honor of distinctive status groups.

The sense of ethnic honor is a specific honor of the masses (*Massenehre*), for it is accessible to anybody who belongs to the subjectively believed community of descent. The "poor white trash," i.e., the propertyless and, in the absence of job opportunities, very often destitute white inhabitants of the southern states of the United States of America in the period of slavery, were the actual bearers of racial antipathy, which was quite foreign to the planters. This was so because the social honor of the "poor whites" was dependent upon the social *déclassement* of the Negroes.

And behind all ethnic diversities there is somehow naturally the notion of the "chosen people," which is merely a counterpart of status differentiation translated into the plane of horizontal co-existence. The idea of a chosen people derives its popularity from the fact that it can be claimed to an equal degree by any and every member of the mutually despising groups, in contrast to status differentiation which always rests on subordination. Consequently, ethnic repulsion may take hold of all conceivable differences among the notions of propriety and transform them into "ethnic conventions."

Besides the previously mentioned elements, which were still more or less closely related to the economic order, conventionalization (a term expounded elsewhere) may take hold of such things as a hairdo or style of beard and the like. The differences thereof have an "ethnically" repulsive effect, because they are thought of as symbols of ethnic membership. Of course, the repulsion is not always based merely on the "symbolic" character of the distinguishing traits. The fact that the Scythian women oiled their hair with butter, which then gave off a rancid odor, while Greek women used perfumed oil to achieve the same purpose, thwarted—according to an ancient report—all attempts at social intercourse between the aristocratic ladies of these two groups. The smell of

butter certainly had a more compelling effect than even the most prominent racial differences, or—as far as I could see—the "Negro odor," of
which so many fables are told. In general, racial qualities are effective only
as limiting factors with regard to the belief in common ethnicity, such as
in case of an excessively heterogeneous and esthetically unaccepted
physical type; they are not positively group-forming.

Pronounced differences of custom, which play a role equal to that
of inherited physical type in the creation of feelings of common ethnicity and notions of kinship, are usually caused, in addition to linguistic
and religious differences, by the diverse economic and political conditions
of various social groups. If we ignore cases of clear-cut linguistic boundaries and sharply demarcated political or religious communities as a
basis of differences of custom—and these in fact are lacking in wide areas
of the African and South American continents—then there are only
gradual transitions of custom and no immutable ethnic frontiers, except
those due to gross geographical differences. The sharp demarcations of
areas wherein ethnically relevant customs predominate, which were not
conditioned either by political or economic or religious factors, usually
came into existence by way of migration or expansion, when groups of
people that had previously lived in complete or partial isolation from
each other and became accommodated to heterogeneous conditions of
existence came to live side by side. As a result, the obvious contrast
usually evokes, on both sides, the idea of blood disaffinity (*Blutsfremd-
heit*), regardless of the objective state of affairs.

It is understandably difficult to determine in general—and even in a
concrete individual case—what influence specific ethnic factors (i.e.,
the belief in a blood relationship, or its opposite, which rests on similarities, or differences, of a person's physical appearance and style of life)
have on the formation of a group.

There is no difference between the ethnically relevant customs and
customs in general, as far as their effect is concerned. The belief in
common descent, in combination with a similarity of customs, is likely
to promote the spread of the activities of one part of an ethnic group
among the rest, since the awareness of ethnic identity furthers imitation.
This is especially true of the propaganda of religious groups.

It is not feasible to go beyond these vague generalizations. The content of joint activities that are possible on an ethnic basis remains indefinite. There is a corresponding ambiguity of concepts denoting
ethnically determined action, that means, determined by the belief in
blood relationship. Such concepts are *Völkerschaft, Stamm* (tribe),
Volk (people), each of which is ordinarily used in the sense of an ethnic
subdivision of the following one (although the first two may be used in

reversed order). Using such terms, one usually implies either the existence of a contemporary political community, no matter how loosely
organized, or memories of an extinct political community, such as they
are preserved in epic tales and legends; or the existence of a linguistic
or dialect group; or, finally, of a religious group. In the past, cults in
particular were the typical concomitant of a tribal or *Volk* consciousness.
But in the absence of the political community, contemporary or past, the
external delimitation of the group was usually indistinct. The cult communities of Germanic tribes, as late as the Burgundian period [6th
century A.D.], were probably rudiments of political communities and
therefore pretty well defined. By contrast, the Delphian oracle, the undoubted cultic symbol of Hellenism, also revealed information to the
barbarians and accepted their veneration, and it was an organized cult
only among some Greek segments, excluding the most powerful cities.
The cult as an exponent of ethnic identity is thus generally either a
remnant of a largely political community which once existed but was
destroyed by disunion and colonization, or it is—as in the case of the
Delphian Apollo—a product of a *Kulturgemeinschaft* brought about by
other than purely ethnic conditions, but which in turn gives rise to the
belief in blood relationship. All history shows how easily political action
can give rise to the belief in blood relationship, unless gross differences
of anthropological type impede it.

3. *Tribe and Political Community: The Disutility of the Notion of "Ethnic Group"*

The tribe is clearly delimited when it is a subdivision of a polity,
which, in fact, often establishes it. In this case, the artificial origin is
revealed by the round numbers in which tribes usually appear, for
example, the previously mentioned division of the people of Israel into
twelve tribes, the three Doric *phylai* and the various *phylai* of the other
Hellenes. When a political community was newly established or re-
organized, the population was newly divided. Hence the tribe is here a
political artifact, even though it soon adopts the whole symbolism of
blood-relationship and particularly a tribal cult. Even today it is not rare
that political artifacts develop a sense of affinity akin to that of blood
relationship. Very schematic constructs such as those states of the United
States that were made into squares according to their latitude have a
strong sense of identity; it is also not rare that families travel from New
York to Richmond to make an expected child a "Virginian."

Such artificiality does not preclude the possibility that the Hellenic *phylai*, for example, were at one time independent and that the polis used them schematically when they were merged into a political association. However, tribes that existed before the *polis* were either identical with the corresponding political groups which were subsequently associated into a *polis*, and in this case they were called *ethnos*, not *phyle*; or, as it probably happened many times, the politically unorganized tribe, as a presumed "blood community," lived from the memory that it once engaged in joint political action, typically a single conquest or defense, and then such political memories constituted the tribe. Thus, the fact that tribal consciousness was primarily formed by common political experiences and not by common descent appears to have been a frequent source of the belief in common ethnicity.

Of course, this was not the only source: Common customs may have diverse origins. Ultimately, they derive largely from adaptation to natural conditions and the imitation of neighbors. In practice, however, tribal consciousness usually has a political meaning: in case of military danger or opportunity, it easily provides the basis for joint political action on the part of tribal members or *Volksgenossen* who consider one another as blood relatives. The eruption of a drive to political action is thus one of the major potentialities inherent in the rather ambiguous notions of tribe and people. Such intermittent political action may easily develop into the moral duty of all members of tribe or people (*Volk*) to support one another in case of a military attack, even if there is no corresponding political association; violators of this solidarity may suffer the fate of the [Germanic, pro-Roman] sibs of Segestes and Inguiomer—expulsion from the tribal territory—, even if the tribe has no organized government. If the tribe has reached this stage, it has indeed become a continuous political community, no matter how inactive in peacetime, and hence unstable, it may be. However, even under favorable conditions the transition from the habitual to the customary and therefore obligatory is very fluid. All in all, the notion of "ethnically" determined social action subsumes phenomena that a rigorous sociological analysis—as we do not attempt it here—would have to distinguish carefully: the actual subjective effect of those customs conditioned by heredity and those determined by tradition; the differential impact of the varying content of custom; the influence of common language, religion and political action, past and present, upon the formation of customs; the extent to which such factors create attraction and repulsion, and especially the belief in affinity or disaffinity of blood; the consequences of this belief for social action in general, and specifically for action on the basis of shared custom or blood relationship, for diverse sexual relations, etc.—all of this would have to be studied in detail. It is certain that in this process the collective term "ethnic" would be abandoned, for it is unsuitable for a really rigorous analysis. However, we do not pursue sociology for its own sake and therefore limit ourselves to showing briefly the diverse factors that are hidden behind this seemingly uniform phenomenon.

The concept of the "ethnic" group, which dissolves if we define our terms exactly, corresponds in this regard to one of the most vexing, since emotionally charged concepts: the *nation,* as soon as we attempt a sociological definition.

4. Nationality and Cultural Prestige[2]

The concept of "nationality" shares with that of the "people" (*Volk*) —in the "ethnic" sense—the vague connotation that whatever is felt to be distinctively common must derive from common descent. In reality, of course, persons who consider themselves members of the same nationality are often much less related by common descent than are persons belonging to different and hostile nationalities. Differences of nationality may exist even among groups closely related by common descent, merely because they have different religious persuasions, as in the case of Serbs and Croats. The concrete reasons for the belief in joint nationality and for the resulting social action vary greatly.

Today, in the age of language conflicts, a shared common language is pre-eminently considered the normal basis of nationality. Whatever the "nation" means beyond a mere "language group" can be found in the specific objective of its social action, and this can only be the *autonomous polity.* Indeed, "nation state" has become conceptually identical with "state" based on common language. In reality, however, such modern nation states exist next to many others that comprise several language groups, even though these others usually have one official language. A common language is also insufficient in sustaining a sense of national identity (*Nationalgefühl*)—a concept which we will leave undefined for the present. Aside from the examples of the Serbs and Croats, this is demonstrated by the Irish, the Swiss and the German-speaking Alsatians; these groups do not consider themselves as members, at least not as full members, of the "nation" associated with their language. Conversely, language differences do not necessarily preclude a sense of joint nationality: The German-speaking Alsatians considered themselves—and most of them still do—as part of the French "nation," even though not in the same sense as French-speaking nationals. Hence there are qualitative degrees of the belief in common nationality.

Many German-speaking Alsatians feel a sense of community with the French because they share certain customs and some of their "sensual culture" (*Sinnenkultur*)—as Wittich in particular has pointed out—and also because of common political experiences. This can be understood by any visitor who walks through the museum in Colmar, which is rich in relics such as tricolors, *pompier* and military helmets, edicts by Louis Philippe and especially memorabilia from the French Revolution; these may appear trivial to the outsider, but they have sentimental value for the Alsatians.[3] This sense of community came into being by virtue of common political and, indirectly, social experiences which are highly valued by the masses as symbols of the destruction of feudalism, and the story of these events takes the place of the heroic legends of primitive peoples. *La grande nation* was the liberator from feudal servitude, she was the bearer of civilization (*Kultur*), her language was *the* civilized language; German appeared as a dialect suitable for everyday communication. Hence the attachment to those who speak the language of civilization is an obvious parallel to the sense of community based on common language, but the two phenomena are not identical; rather, we deal here with an attitude that derives from a partial sharing of the same culture and from shared political experiences.

Until a short time ago most Poles in Upper Silesia had no strongly developed sense of Polish nationality that was antagonistic to the Prussian state, which is based essentially on the German language. The Poles were loyal if passive "Prussians," but they were not "Germans" interested in the existence of the *Reich;* the majority did not feel a conscious or a strong need to segregate themselves from German-speaking fellow-citizens. Hence, in this case there was no sense of nationality based on common language, and there was no *Kulturgemeinschaft* in view of the lack of cultural development.

Among the Baltic Germans we find neither much of a sense of nationality amounting to a high valuation of the language bonds with the Germans, nor a desire for political union with the *Reich;* in fact, most of them would abhor such a unification. However, they segregate themselves rigorously from the Slavic environment, and especially from the Russians, primarily because of status considerations and partly because both sides have different customs and cultural values which are mutually unintelligible and disdained. This segregation exists in spite of, and partly because of, the fact that the Baltic Germans are intensely loyal vassals of the Tsar and have been as interested as any "national" Russian (*Nationalrusse*) in the predominance of the Imperial Russian system, which they provide with officials and which in turn maintains their descendants. Hence, here too we do not find any sense of nationality in the modern meaning of the term (oriented toward a common language and culture). The case is similar to that of the purely proletarian Poles: loyalty toward the state is combined with a sense of group identity that is limited to a common language group within this larger community and strongly modified by status factors. Of course, the Baltic Germans are no longer a cohesive status group, even though the differences are not as extreme as within the white population of the American South.

Finally, there are cases for which the term nationality does not seem to be quite fitting; witness the sense of identity shared by the Swiss and the Belgians or the inhabitants of Luxemburg and Liechtenstein. We hesitate to call them "nations," not because of their relative smallness— the Dutch appear to us as a nation—, but because these neutralized states have purposively forsaken power. The Swiss are not a nation if we take as criteria common language or common literature and art. Yet they have a strong sense of community despite some recent disintegrative tendencies. This sense of identity is not only sustained by loyalty toward the body politic but also by what are perceived to be common customs (irrespective of actual differences). These customs are largely shaped by the differences in social structure between Switzerland and Germany, but also all other big and hence militaristic powers. Because of the impact of bigness on the internal power structure, it appears to the Swiss that their customs can be preserved only by a separate political existence.

The loyalty of the French Canadians toward the English polity is today determined above all by the deep antipathy against the economic and social structure, and the way of life, of the neighboring United States; hence membership in the Dominion of Canada appears as a guarantee of their own traditions.

This classification could easily be enlarged, as every rigorous socio- logical investigation would have to do. It turns out that feelings of identity subsumed under the term "national" are not uniform but may derive from diverse sources: Differences in the economic and social structure and in the internal power structure, with its impact on the customs, may play a role, but within the German *Reich* customs are very diverse; shared political memories, religion, language and, finally, racial features may be source of the sense of nationality. Racial factors often have a peculiar impact. From the viewpoint of the Whites in the United States, Negroes and Whites are not united by a common sense of nation- ality, but the Negroes have a sense of American nationality at least by claiming a right to it. On the other hand, the pride of the Swiss in their own distinctiveness, and their willingness to defend it vigorously, is neither qualitatively different nor less widespread than the same attitudes in any "great" and powerful "nation." Time and again we find that the concept "nation" directs us to political power. Hence, the concept seems to refer—if it refers at all to a uniform phenomenon—to a specific kind of pathos which is linked to the idea of a powerful political community of people who share a common language, or religion, or common customs, or political memories; such a state may already exist or it may be desired. The more power is emphasized, the closer appears to be the link between nation and state. This pathetic pride in the power of one's own community, or this longing for it, may be much more widespread in relatively small language groups such as the Hungarians, Czechs or Greeks than in a similar but much larger community such as the Germans 150 years ago, when they were essentially a language group without pretensions to national power.

NOTES

1. On race and civilization, see also Weber's polemical speech against A. Ploetz at the first meeting of the German Sociological Association, Frankfurt, 1910, in *GAzSS*, 456–62. Two years later, at the second meeting of the Association in Berlin, Weber took the floor again after a presentation by Franz Oppenheimer. Among other things, Weber said (*op. cit.,* 489):
"With race theories you can prove and disprove anything you want. It is a scientific crime to attempt the circumvention, by the uncritical use of completely unclarified racial hypotheses, of the sociological study of Antiquity, which of course is much more difficult, but by no means without hope of success; after all, we can no longer find out to what extent the qualities of the Hellenes and Romans rested on inherited dispositions. The problem of such relationships has not yet been solved by the most careful and toilsome investigations of living subjects, even if undertaken in the laboratory and with the means of exact experimentation."
2. Cf. the related section on "The Nation" in ch. IX:5.
3. See Werner Wittich, *Deutsche und französische Kultur im Elsass* (Strassburg: Schlesier und Schweikhardt, 1900), 38ff; for a French transl., see "Le génie national des races française et allemande en Alsace." *Revue internationale de Sociologie,* vol. X, 1902, 777–824 and 857–907, esp. 814ff. Cf. also Weber, *GAzRS,* I, 25, n. 1; *GAzSS,* 484. "Outsiders," in contrast to the pre-1914 custodian who showed Weber his greatest treasures, cherish the Colmar museum for one of the most powerful works of art of the late Middle Ages, Grünewald's "Isenheim Altar."

INDEX

The index covers all three volumes of *Economy and Society* and is divided into three parts: (*i*) An index of contemporary scholars cited by Weber; (*ii*) an index of other names mentioned in the text, mainly historical; and (*iii*) a subject index. The Introduction and the editorial notes have not been indexed. For the orientation of the reader the volume-breakdown of the page numbers is shown at the foot of every page.

i
SCHOLARS

HISTORICAL NAMES

SUBJECT INDEX

Gerontocracy (*cont.*)
  defined, 231
  economy and, 237–38
  immediate democracy and, 290
Geschlechterherrschaft, *see* Patrimonial
    domination
Geschlechterstaat, *see* Clan-state
Gesellschaftshandeln, *see* Rationally
    controlled action
Glarus (Switzerland), 290
Gods, *see* Religion—gods in
Greece
  appropriation of means of production
    in, 134, 135
  charisma in
    education, 1144, 1145
    transformation, 1137, 1138
  the city in
    confraternity, 1242
    economy, 1335
    extra-urban associations, 1245,
      1246
    fortress, 1221, 1222, 1224
  democracy in
    democratization, 986–87, 1311–
      15
    justice, 795
  elections in, 1129
  ethnicity in, 389, 391, 393, 394
  feudal, 262
    defined, 1071
    games, 1105–6
    status honor, 1105
  games in, 1105–6, 1367
  hierocracy in, 1160
    caesaropapism, 1176
    economy, 1183
    social preconditions, 1177, 1178
  law in
    contracts, 676, 682, 717, 723,
      739, 741
    legal norms, 769, 773
    notables, 795, 799
    tort, 650
  lower classes in, 481, 1343, 1344,
    1346, 1347
  military discipline in, 1151, 1154
  mystery religions and
    congregations, 455
    mystagogues, 447

Greece (*cont.*)
  philosophical ethicists, 445, 467
  prophets, 441–43
  nationality in, 398
  oikos and, 383
  patrician city in, 1289, 1291
    family-charisma, 1282
    kingship, 1284, 1285
  patrimonial
    duties, 1046
    trade, 1093, 1104
  philosophy in, 445, 502, 503, 567
  plebiscitary regime in, 270
  religion in, 408–10
    anti-plebeian, 508–9
    destiny, 431
    ethics, 438
    intellectualism, 500
    legal order, 430
    lower classes, 481
    martial heroism, 539
    nobility, 473, 478
    orgies, 554
    universalism, 419
    war, 474
    women, 490
  slavery in, 127
  status in
    status honor, 937
    structure, 1354–56
  tax-farming in, 966
  tyrannis in, 444, 1315, 1316, 1317
  See also specific Greek cities
Groups, *see specific groups. For ex-*
    ample: Ethnic groups; Kinship
    groups; Organized groups; So-
    cial groups
Guilds
  army and Asian, 1262
  city, 1278–79
    craft, 1301, 1342–45, 1347, 1362
    medieval plebeian city, 1301–2,
      1304–7, 1325, 1336
    mutual protection, 1256–57
    patrician city opposed by, 1281–
      82
  collegiality in, 276, 277
  contractual law and, 716
  dispossession and English, 130
  immediate democracy in, 290

Volume One: 1–398; *Volume Two:* 399–940; *Volume Three:* 941–1469.

Volume One: 1–398; *Volume Two:*

Market economy
  appropriation and, 112–13, 144–50
  in the city, 1212–15, 1223–26
  colonials and, 289
  commercial classes and, 306
  competition and, 43
  consequences of, 337
  defined, 67, 82
  delimitations of, 1379–80
  division of labor and, 122–23
  domination by, 943–46
  economic action and, 202
  interdependence in, 335
  interests, and pacification of population, 908–9
  law and
    contracts, 698–99, 730–31
    monopolization, 336
  labor and
    class situation, 927–28, 930, 931
    productivity, 150–53
    unfree labor, 382
  market relations and, 676, 735
  in medieval plebeian city, 1328–31
  open social relationships and, 44–45
  patrimonialism and, 1091
  regulation and, 82–85
  source of crises in modern, 140
  want satisfaction and, 109–10, 349
Marktgemeinschaft (market relations), 676, 735; *see also* Market economy
Marxism, 516, 777, 1091
  natural law and, 872, 874
Massenhandeln, see Collective action
Matriarchy
  defined, 368
  marriage and, 372
  men's houses and
    maternal groupings, 357
    Spartan maternal households, 371
Meaning, 4–5, 7, 57; *see also* Sociology
Mecca (Arabia), 444, 473, 625, 693, 1016, 1241, 1273, 1296
  confraternity in, 1251–52
  as pre-communal patrician city, 1231–34
Medina (Arabia), 444, 624, 625, 820
Men's houses, 1287
  charismatic education and, 1144
  contractual law and, 671

Men's houses (*cont.*)
  Greek and Roman, 262
  maternal groupings and, 357
  military discipline and, 1153
  sexual relationships and, 364
  Spartan, and maternal households, 371
  warriors as basis for, 906–7
Mercenaries
  army of, 596, 1364
  financing of, 198
  in Holland, 1152
  in Italy, 259, 1318–20
  patrimonial use of, 1017–18, 1021, 1046
  in Switzerland, 908
Mestnichestvo, 985, 1066–67
Mexico, 741, 877
Middle classes, *see* Bourgeoisie; Petty-bourgeoisie
Migration, economic systems and, 70
Milan (Italy), 1252, 1302, 1318
Mithraism, 485, 505, 510
  masculine orientation of, 490
  as salvation religion, 475, 476
Modena (Italy), 1318
Mohammedanism, *see* Islam
Monasticism
  begging and, 194
  Buddhist, 456, 461, 551, 629, 1123–24
    supernatural powers, 1165–66
  Byzantine, 588
    art, 609
  Christian, 502, 555, 1201
  communism in, 154
  economy and
    coolies, 586
    crafts, 1184
    land, 1182–83
    stabilization, 1096
  exclusiveness of, 1205
  hierocracy and
    achievements, 1168–70
    ambivalence, 1166–68
    uses of monasticism, 1170–73
    rationalization of, 1168–70
  in India, 453
  intellectualism and, 501
  Islamic, 569, 624
  of monk and warrior, 1153